ECONOMICS
TODAY

THE MACRO VIEW

THE ADDISON-WESLEY SERIES IN ECONOMICS

Abel/Bernanke
Macroeconomics

Allen
Managerial Economics

Berndt
The Practice of Econometrics

Bierman/Fernandez
Game Theory

Binger/Hoffman
Microeconomics with Calculus

Bowles/Edwards
Understanding Capitalism

Branson
Macroeconomic Theory and Policy

Brown/Hogendorn
International Economics

Browning/Zupan
Microeconomic Theory and
Applications

Burgess
The Economics of Regulation and
Antitrust

Byrns/Stone
Economics

Canterbery
The Literate Economist

Carlton/Perloff
Modern Industrial Organization

Caves/Frankel/Jones
World Trade and Payments

Cooter/Ulen
Law and Economics

Ehrenberg/Smith
Modern Labor Economics

Ekelund/Tollison
Economics: Private Markets and
Public Choice

Filer/Hamermesh/Rees
The Economics of Work and Pay

Fusfeld
The Age of the Economist

Gibson
International Finance: Exchange
Rates and Financial Flows

Gordon
Macroeconomics

Gregory
Essentials of Economics

Gregory/Ruffin
Basic Economics

Gregory/Stuart
Soviet and Post Soviet Economic
Structure and Performance

Griffiths/Wall
Intermediate Microeconomics

Gros/Steinherr
Winds of Change: Economic
Transition in Central and Eastern
Europe

Hartwick/Olewiler
The Economics of Natural Resource
Use

Hogendorn
Economic Development

**Hoy/Livernois/McKenna/
Rees/Stengos**
Mathematics For Economics

Hubbard
Money, the Financial System, and the
Economy

Hughes/Cain
American Economic History

Husted/Melvin
International Economics

Invisible Hand
Economics in Action, Interactive
Software

Krugman/Obstfeld
International Economics: Theory and
Policy

Kwoka/White
The Antitrust Revolution

Laidler
The Demand for Money

Lesser/Dodds/Zerbe
Environmental Economics and Policy

Lipsey/Courant
Economics

McCarty
Dollars and Sense

Melvin
International Money and Finance

Miller
Economics Today

Miller/Benjamin/North
The Economics of Public Issues

Miller/Fishe
Microeconomics: Price Theory in
Practice

Miller/Van Hoose
Essentials of Money, Banking, and
Financial Markets

Mills/Hamilton
Urban Economics

Mishkin
The Economics of Money, Banking,
and Financial Markets

Parkin
Economics

Petersen
Business and Government

Phelps
Health Economics

Riddell/Shackelford/Stamos
Economics

Ritter/Silber/Udell
Principles of Money, Banking, and
Financial Markets

Rohlf
Introduction to Economic
Reasoning

Ruffin/Gregory
Principles of Economics

Salvatore
Microeconomics

Sargent
Rational Expectations and Inflation

Scherer
Industry Structure, Strategy, and
Public Policy

Schotter
Microeconomics: A Modern
Approach

Sherman/Kolk
Business Cycles and Forecasting

Smith
Case Studies in Economic
Development

Studenmund
Using Econometrics

Su
Economic Fluctuations and
Forecasting

Tietenberg
Environmental and Natural Resource
Economics

Tietenberg
Environmental Economics
and Policy

Todaro
Economic Development

Zerbe/Dively
Benefit-Cost Analysis

Ninth Edition

ECONOMICS TODAY

THE MACRO VIEW

ROGER LeROY MILLER

INSTITUTE FOR UNIVERSITY STUDIES, ARLINGTON, TEXAS

ADDISON-WESLEY

An imprint of Addison Wesley Longman, Inc.

Reading, Massachusetts • Menlo Park, California • New York • Harlow, England
Dan Mills, Ontario • Sydney • Mexico City • Madrid • Amsterdam

Photo Credits
Page 3, Frank Siteman/Stock, Boston; page 17, Hans Halberstadt/Photo Researchers; page 45, Jeff Greenberg, PhotoEdit; page 73, Jean-Marc Giboux/Gamma-Liaison; page 94, AP/Wide World; page 116, © Martin Rogers/Stock, Boston; page 141, David Young-Wolff/PhotoEdit; page 163, © Mark Antman/The Image Works; page 165, © Frank Siteman, The Picture Cube; page 165, © Bernsau/The Image Works; page 187, Reuters/Bobby Yip/Archive; page 207, Reuter/Bettmann; page 227, G. Merillon/Gamma; page 245, Reuters/Bettmann; page 275, Reuters/Bettmann; page 297, AP/Wide World; page 302, © Topham/The Image Works; page 319, Security First Network Bank; page 339, General Motors Acceptance Corporation; page 364, © Paul Conklin/PhotoEdit; page 388, © Paul Conklin/PhotoEdit; page 733, © Jon Burbank/The Image Works; page 753, © Jeff Greenberg/The Picture Cube; page 761, © Brookins/Richmond Times-Dispatch; page 775, Sanguinetti/Monkmeyer.

Executive Editor: John Greenman
Developmental Editor: Vicki Cohen
Project Editor: Ellen MacElree
Supplements Editor: Julie Zasloff
Design Manager: John Callahan
Cover Designer: Kay Petronio
Text Designer: A Good Thing, Inc.
Cover Photos:
Front cover: Brazil slum: K. McGlynn/The Image Works; seedling: © 1986, George Turner/ Photo Researches; newspapers: PhotoDisk, Inc.; Earth: PhotoDisk, Inc.; satellite dish: Joe Sohm/ The Image Works; heads of State: Reuters/Archive; vote sign: Crandall/The Image Works; soldiers: Photoreporters.
Back cover: Train wreck: Reuters/Bettmann; takeout food window: Spunbarg/Picture Cube; smokestacks: Digital Stock Corp.; ATM machine: PhotoDisk, Inc.; military: Reuters/Bettmann; shopping mall: Nettis/Photo Researchers.
Art Studio: ElectraGraphics, Inc.
Photo Researcher: Mira Schachne
Electronic Production Manager: Su Levine
Desktop Administrator: Laura Leever
Electronic Page Makeup: Laura Leever
Printer and Binder: R. R. Donnelley & Sons Company
Cover Printer: Phoenix Color

Library of Congress Cataloging-in-Publication Data

Miller, Roger LeRoy.
    Economics today: the macro view / Roger LeRoy Miller. — 9th ed.
        p.   cm.—(The Addison-Wesley series in economics)
    Includes index.
    ISBN 0-673-98056-1 (alk. paper)
    1. Macroeconomics.   2. Economics.   I. Title.
    HB172.5.M54   1997
    339—dc20   96-16629
                                                                              CIP

ISBN 0-673-98056-1
2345678910—DOW—   979899

To Lavina:

Thanks for so many years of your faithful and tireless assistance. We'll keep it up well into the twenty-first century.

R.L.M.

CONTENTS IN BRIEF

In this volume, Chapter 18 is followed by Chapter 33.

CONTENTS IN DETAIL

In this volume, Chapter 18 is followed by Chapter 33.

EXAMPLES

DOMESTIC EXAMPLES

Domestic Policy Examples

THINKING CRITICALLY ABOUT THE MEDIA

ISSUES AND APPLICATIONS

TO THE INSTRUCTOR

In a sense, part of our work as educators is being done for us by politicians whose every economic pronouncement, regardless of its accuracy, is duly reported by the media. Our students are constantly bombarded by differing economic views of the world. One of our jobs is to teach these very same students to distinguish truth from fiction and fact from opinion. As professional economists, most of us are quite convinced that an understanding of the economic way of thinking provides a powerful engine of analysis for today's students so that they can in fact separate the "chaff" from the "wheat." One of the key new features in this ninth edition of *Economics Today: The Macro View* explicitly addresses the media.

THINKING CRITICALLY ABOUT THE MEDIA

At least once, and sometimes two or three times, in a chapter there is a set-off feature titled "Thinking Critically About the Media" with an appropriate subheading. Each topic has been selected so as to highlight a newsworthy event and to go beyond the media's coverage of it, often with surprising results. The topics are listed on page xx.

DID YOU KNOW THAT . . . ?

To entice your students further, each chapter begins with a provocative and often significant set of facts, introduced in the form of a question: "Did You Know That . . . ?" Your students cannot fail to be intrigued.

THE CUTTING EDGE—TODAY'S TECHNOLOGY

What's new in telecommunications, computers, digital sound and imaging, and other marvels of the world of electronics is perhaps more familiar to students than to many professors. So it is not by chance that I use cutting-edge high-tech examples throughout the text to illustrate the basic principles of economics. Your students demand a modern look and feel in their study materials—and that is what they get in the ninth edition of *Economics Today: The Macro View.*

A WORLD OF GLOBAL EXAMPLES

High-speed telecommunications coupled with the opening up of the former Soviet Union and Eastern Europe, as well as increased trade with Latin America, Asia, and a booming mainland China, dictate a globalization of the principles of economics text. The ninth edition is truly global in scope. In every chapter, your students are exposed to economic principles demonstrated in set-off features, preceded by a globe, called simply "International Example." There are 34 international examples in this edition. You can see the full list on page xviii.

Examples Closer to Home

Of course, the United States has its share of relevant and exciting examples that can be used to demonstrate economic principles. In this edition, there are 25 new domestic examples. A full list is presented on page xix.

Policy Matters

Many of the economic discussions presented by the media involve important policy issues. In the ninth edition, your students are explicitly exposed to important policy questions both on the domestic and international fronts. There are 8 international and 11 domestic policy examples. A full list appears on pages xviii–xix.

ISSUES AND APPLICATIONS

It has been a tradition in all editions of *Economics Today: The Macro View* to present at the end of each chapter a section titled "Issues and Applications." The 21 "Issues and Applications" are *all new.* Their format is designed to encourage your students to apply economic concepts and to think critically about how they have applied those concepts. To this end, each "Issues and Applications" section has a list of *concepts applied* at the beginning and is followed by two or three critical-thinking questions titled "For Critical Analysis." You will find suggested answers to these critical-thinking questions in the *Instructor's Resource Binder.* The titles of the new "Issues and Applications" features for the ninth edition are found on page xxi.

Critical Thinking Throughout

In addition to the set-off features concerning the media, your students are exposed to further critical-thinking exercises at the end of each example. The questions following each example are headed "For Critical Analysis." They attempt to get your students to take the analysis one step further to develop their critical-thinking skills. Essentially, the students are asked to "think like economists." The answers to all "For Critical Analysis" questions are found in the *Instructor's Manual.*

As stated earlier, two or three additional critical-thinking questions appear at the end of each "Issues and Applications" section.

PEDAGOGY WITH A PURPOSE

You and your students will notice how carefully the pedagogy in each chapter fits together as a whole. My purpose continues to be to guide your students in their study of our science with a positive approach. The result is what I believe to be state-of-the-art motivational, conceptual, and review pedagogy:

- A *chapter-opening issue* that relates directly to the "Issues and Applications" section at the end of that chapter
- A list of *preview points* and completely self-contained answers
- A *chapter outline*
- *Marginal definitions,* with important terms boldfaced when first introduced in the text
- *Concepts in brief* summarized at the end of major sections
- A *point-by-point end-of-chapter summary*
- *Problems,* with answers for every odd-numbered problem at the back of the book
- A session in *computer-aided instruction* for each chapter, available on a free diskette

Interacting with the Internet

The number of Internet users, as well as the number of World Wide Web sites, is growing daily. To help your students use this increasingly valuable resource, I have put together a chapter-ending feature called "Interacting with the Internet." In Chapter 1, your students will get a brief introduction to using the Internet. In appropriate chapters throughout the rest of the text, Internet addresses are provided so that your students can obtain additional information about material covered in the chapter.

The Core of Economics: Theory, Theory, and More Theory

While your students will have their interest piqued by the myriad new examples in this ninth edition, all of those examples serve one basic purpose—to drive home the application of the theory just presented. You will find the latest theoretical concepts in this ninth edition, presented in a logical manner for ease of understanding.

For more specific details on the presentation of theory, see the listing at the end of this preface under the heading "What's New in the Ninth Edition."

Complete Teaching Flexibility

One of the keys to the success of *Economics Today: The Macro View* is that it is suitable for many teaching styles. Instructors who wish to stress theory can do so. Those who wish to stress applications and examples can do that. Furthermore, chapters that are often skipped in shorter courses are placed at the ends of units. The numerous supplements for both instructors and students allow for even further flexibility.

THE REMAINDER OF THE TEACHING AND LEARNING PACKAGE

As you will discover, the ninth edition of *Economics Today: The Macro View* has the most comprehensive, usable, and effective teaching and learning package ever developed for a principles of economics text.

Printed Materials for Students
- *Extended-Coverage Topics*—free booklet
- Reproducible homework assignments—two separate versions
- *Your Economics Life: The Practical Applications of Economics*—free with every new copy
- *Student Learning Guide*

Computer Software for Students
- ET9 Computer-Assisted Instruction
- Graphing Tutorial
- *Economics Tutor*—"games" that teach theory
- Macro Simulation

Multimedia for your Students
Not only are the examples in *Economics Today: The Macro View* on the cutting edge, but so are the supplementary materials for classroom presentation and individual study. They include the following:

Videos
To go with this edition, HarperCollins offers *Economics at Work,* a package of 11 short videos of five to seven minutes each, free to adopters, including such titles as *Cigarettes, Addiction, and Elasticity; Working with Macroeconomics: A Talk with Investment Bankers;* and *Stock Answer: A Guide to the Market.*

Printed Materials for Instructors
- *Test Banks 1, 2,* and *3*—almost 8,000 multiple-choice questions and 500 short-essay questions available on three separate test banks, fully classroom-tested
- *Instructor's Resource Binder*—complete with reproducible supplementary material
- *Instructor's Manual*
- *Instructor's Course Planning Guide and Media Handbook*
- *Economics Today* newsletter

Software for Instructors
- *TestMaster*—in a flexible format
- *QuizMaster-TM*
- Computerized *Instructor's Manual*

Transparencies and Acetates
- LOTS: Lecture Outline and Transparency System
- Full-color acetates and acetate overlays
- Transparency masters

WHAT'S NEW IN THE NINTH EDITION

- *Chapter outline* at the beginning of each chapter
- Chapter opening "Did You Know That . . .?"
- "Thinking Critically About the Media" feature
- "Interacting with the Internet" feature
- 21 new "Issues and Applications" sections
- 25 new domestic examples
- 34 new international examples
- 19 new international and domestic policy examples
- New videos
- A new videodisc
- *Economics Today* CD-ROM

Changes in the Body of the Text
- Marginal definitions all coincide with in-text definitions.
- The link between the preceding theory text and all examples is consistently made clear.

Part 1: Introduction

Chapter 1
- The role of incentives is stressed.

Chapter 2
- Human capital is explicitly mentioned as a separate factor of production.
- Comparative advantage in trade is introduced early.

Chapter 3
- More examples of shifts in supply and demand curves are presented.

Chapter 4
- A discussion of transactions costs and intermediaries is now included.
- An expanded discussion of alternative rationing systems is presented.
- Price supports and minimum wages are now used as examples.

Chapter 5
- There is a complete discussion of correcting for externalities as well as an explicit discussion of property rights.

Chapter 6
- The chapter has been renamed "Economies in Transition" to reflect the worldwide movement toward market systems.

- The role of incentives is further expanded in this chapter, which now includes the four faces of capitalism and a discussion of the transitional phase, called *frontier capitalism,* including the development of the legal system and privatization as well as political opposition to it.
- There is the latest information on Russia and China, as well as where future economic power shifts will lie.

Part 2: Introduction to Macroeconomics and Economic Growth

- The macro section has been reorganized into four parts, with the chapter on economic growth moved forward to reflect increased interest in this important subject.

Chapter 7
- A graphical representation of the determination of unemployment, including job departures and job finders, as well as an expanded presentation of the difference between stocks and flows, is now included.
- There is a new discussion of wage rigidity and wait unemployment.
- There is a full discussion of the problems with the measurement of the Consumer Price Index.
- An explanation of external shocks in the business cycle is new.

Chapter 8
- There is an explanation and analysis of the new *chain-weighted* measure of the growth in real GDP.
- Purchasing power parity has been added here.

Chapter 9
- An expanded discussion of productivity growth and its determinants appears here.
- *New growth theory* is introduced, including growth in technology, R&D, and innovation and knowledge, the importance of human capital, and the effects of an open economy.
- Population and immigration as they affect economic growth are discussed.
- Property rights and entrepreneurship are examined.

Part 3: National Income Determination

Chapter 10
- The graphs have been rationalized and simplified.
- New tables are given on the determinants of aggregate demand and aggregate supply.
- More examples are given of the effects of shifts in the aggregate demand and aggregate supply curves.

Chapter 11
- A better contrast is made between the classical and Keynesian models.
- Open economy analysis is explained with *AD-AS* analysis.

Chapter 12
- The presentation of consumption, income, and the multiplier within the Keynesian framework has been streamlined, as has the presentation of the relationship between aggregate demand and the $C + I + G + X$ curve.

Part 4: Fiscal Policy and Deficit Spending

Chapter 13
- Empirical evidence is given with respect to the Ricardian equivalence theorem.
- A complete discussion of the federal government budget cycle and how a bill becomes law is undertaken.

- A fuller explanation of automatic stabilizers, as well as the long-run "soothing" effect of Keynesian fiscal policy, is provided.

Chapter 14

- The chapter, completely reorganized, now makes clear the difference between deficits and the public debt.
- More information on the twin deficits—budget and trade—is presented.

Part 5: Money, Monetary Policy, and Stabilization

Chapter 15

- Discussion of the degrees of liquidity has been expanded.
- A discussion of e-cash has been added.

Chapter 16

- A new discussion of the origins of fractional reserve banking is provided.
- There is an expanded pictorial demonstration of the money multiplier.
- More information on the federal funds rate is given.
- Risk taking by bank managers and moral hazard are discussed.

Chapter 17

- A thorough discussion of the independence of the Fed is presented.

Chapter 18

- There is more information on the distinction between active and passive policy-making, as well as more coverage of the natural rate of unemployment.
- An explanation of the nonaccelerating inflation rate of unemployment (NAIRU) is provided.
- There is more on menu costs theory and on the efficiency wage model.
- There is a discussion of stabilization policy versus the new growth theorists.

Part 9: Global Economics

Chapter 33

- Exhausting mutual gains from exchange is explained.
- The transmission of ideas is presented as an additional benefit from international trade.
- There is more on the cost of protecting American jobs.
- Graphical explanation of the effects of quotas and of tariffs has been simplified.
- Voluntary quotas, including voluntary restraint agreements (VRAs) and voluntary import expansion (VIEs), are discussed.
- The World Trade Organization is covered.

Chapter 34

- A more complete explanation of the mirror image relationship between the capital account and the current account is provided.

Chapter 35

- The importance to economic development of an open economy and an educated population is emphasized.
- The commission of Type II errors because of protectionism is explained.
- The topic of creative destruction is introduced.
- The relationship between population growth and economic development is explored.
- The consequences of foreign aid are analyzed.

ACKNOWLEDGMENTS

For many years now, I have had the good fortune of receiving numerous comments and criticisms from users of *Economics Today: The Macro View.* All of you who have continued to support my work will see the results of your comments in the ninth edition. Specifically, I would like to thank the following reviewers who went beyond the call of duty to help me improve the manuscript of the ninth edition:

John Adams, Northeastern University

Kari Battaglia, University of North Texas

Michael Bull, DeAnza College

Kevin Carey, University of Miami

Richard J. Cebula, Georgia Institute of Technology

Young Back Choi, St. John's University

Carol Cies, Rose State College

Joy L. Clark, Auburn University at Montgomery

Marsha Clayton, University of Arkansas at Monticello

Eleanor D. Craig, University of Delaware

Andrew J. Dane, Angelo State University

James A. Dyal, Indiana University of Pennsylvania

Ishita Edwards, Oxnard College

Frank Falero, California State University, Bakersfield

Alexander Garvin, Indiana University of Pennsylvania

J. P. Gilbert, Mira Costa College

Richard J. Gosselin, Houston Community College

Gary Greene, Manatee Community College

Mehdi Haririan, Bloomsburg University of Pennsylvania

John M. Hill, Delgado Community College

R. Bradley Hoppes, Southwest Missouri State University

Grover Howard, Rio Hondo College

R. Jack Inch, Oakland Community College

Randall G. Kesselring, Arkansas State University

Philip G. King, San Francisco State University

Janet Koscianski, Shippensburg University

Peter Kressler, Rowan College of New Jersey

Margaret Landman, Bridgewater State College

George Lieu, Tuskegee University

Stephen E. Lile, Western Kentucky University

James J. McLain, University of New Orleans

Mary Lou Madden, Sheldon Jackson College

Dan C. Messerschmidt, Lynchburg College

Margaret D. Moore, Franklin University

George L. Nagy, Hudson Valley Community College

Randall E. Parker, East Carolina University

Raymond A. Pepin, Stonehill College

Reneé Prim, Central Piedmont Community College

Robert W. Pulsinelli, Western Kentucky University

Rod D. Raehsler, Clarion University of Pennsylvania

Sandra Rahman, Newbury College

Gautam Raychaudhuri, Northern Illinois University

Barbara Ross-Pfeiffer, Kapiolani Community College

Phil Smith, DeKalb College

Richard L. Sprinkle, University of Texas at El Paso

Rebecca Summary, Southeast Missouri State University

Gary Theige, City College of San Francisco

Deborah Thorsen, Palm Beach Community College

Lee J. Van Scyoc, University of Wisconsin, Oshkosh

Mark A. Wilkening, Blinn College

Peter R. Wyman, Spokane Falls Community College

Whitney Yamamura, American River College

Alex R. Yguado, Mission College, Los Angeles

Those who reviewed previous editions:

Esmond Adams
John R. Aidem
M. C. Alderfer
Leslie J. Anderson
Fatima W. Antar
Aliakbar Ataiifar
Leonard Atencio
Glen W. Atkinson
Thomas R. Atkinson
James Q. Aylesworth
Charlie Ballard
Maurice B. Ballabon
G. Jeffrey Barbour
Daniel Barszcz
Robin L. Bartlett
Robert Becker
Charles Beem
Glen Beeson
Charles Berry
Scott Bloom

M. L. Bodnar
Mary Bone
Karl Bonnhi
Thomas W. Bonsor
John M. Booth
Wesley F. Booth
Thomas Borcherding
Tom Boston
Barry Boyer
Maryanna Boynton
Ronald Brandolini
Fenton L. Broadhead
Elba Brown
William Brown
Maureen Burton
Ralph T. Byrns
Conrad P. Caligaris
Dancy R. Carr
Doris Cash
Thomas H. Cate

Richard Chapman
Carol Cies
Gary Clayton
Warren L. Coats
Ed Coen
Pat Conroy
James Cox
Stephen R. Cox
Eleanor D. Craig
Joanna Cruse
John P. Cullity
Thomas Curtis
Andrew J. Dane
Mahmoud Davoudi
Edward Dennis
Carol Dimamro
William Dougherty
Barry Duman
Diane Dumont
Floyd Durham

G. B. Duwaji
Robert P. Edwards
Alan E. Ellis
Mike Ellis
Frank Emerson
Zaki Eusufzai
John L. Ewing-Smith
Frank Fato
Grant Ferguson
David Fletcher
James Foley
John Foreman
Ralph G. Fowler
Arthur Friedberg
Peter Frost
E. Gabriel
Steve Gardner
Peter C. Garlick
Joe Garwood
Otis Gilley

Frank Glesber
Jack Goddard
Allen C. Goodman
Nicholas Grunt
William Gunther
Demos Hadjiyanis
Martin D. Haney
Ray Harvey
E. L. Hazlett
Sanford B. Helman
John Hensel
Robert Herman
Gus W. Herring
Charles Hill
Morton Hirsch
Benjamin Hitchner
James Horner
Nancy Howe-Ford
R. Jack Inch
Christopher Inya

Tomotaka Ishimine
E. E. Jarvis
Parvis Jenab
S. D. Jevremovic
J. Paul Jewell
Frederick Johnson
David Jones
Lamar B. Jones
Paul A. Joray
Daniel A. Joseph
Craig Justice
Septimus Kai Kai
Devajyoti Kataky
Timothy R. Keely
Ziad Keilany
Norman F. Keiser
E. D. Key
M. Barbara Killen
Bruce Kimzey
Philip G. King

Terrence Kinal
E. R. Kittrell
David Klingman
Charles Knapp
Jerry Knarr
Michael Kupilik
Larry Landrum
Margaret Landman
Keith Langford
Anthony T. Lee
George Lieu
Stephen E. Lile
Lawrence W. Lovick
Warren T. Matthews
Robert McAuliffe
Howard J. McBride
Bruce McClung
John McDowell
E. S. McKuskey
John L. Madden
Glen Marston
John M. Martin
Paul J. Mascotti

James D. Mason
Paul M. Mason
Tom Mathew
Warren Matthews
G. Hartley Mellish
Mike Melvin
Herbert C. Milikien
Joel C. Millonzi
Glenn Milner
Thomas Molloy
Margaret Moore
William E. Morgan
Stephen Morrell
Irving Morrissett
James W. Moser
Martin F. Murray
Jerome Neadly
James E. Needham
Claron Nelson
Douglas Nettleton
Gerald T. O'Boyle
Lucian T. Orlowski
Diane S. Osborne

Jan Palmer
Gerald Parker
Martin M. Perline
Timothy Perri
Jerry Petr
Maurice Pfannesteil
James Phillips
Raymond J. Phillips
I. James Pickl
Dennis Placone
William L. Polvent
Reneé Prim
Robert W. Pulsinelli
Kambriz Raffiee
John Rapp
Ron Reddall
Mitchell Redlo
Charles Reichhelu
Robert S. Rippey
Ray C. Roberts
Richard Romano
Duane Rosa
Richard Rosenberg

Larry Ross
Philip Rothman
John Roufagalas
Patricia Sanderson
Thomas N. Schaap
William A. Schaeffer
William Schaniel
David Schauer
A. C. Schlenker
Scott J. Schroeder
William Scott
Dan Segebarth
Robert Sexton
Augustus Shackelford
Richard Sherman Jr.
Liang-rong Shiau
David Shorow
Vishwa Shukla
R. J. Sidwell
David E. Sisk
Alden Smith
Howard F. Smith

Lynn A. Smith
Steve Smith
William Doyle Smith
Lee Spector
George Spiva
Herbert F. Steeper
William Stine
Allen D. Stone
Osman Suliman
J. M. Sullivan
Rebecca Summary
Joseph L. Swaffar
Frank D. Taylor
Daniel Teferra
Robert P. Thomas
Richard Trieff
George Troxler
William T. Trulove
William N. Trumbull
Arianne K. Turner
John Vahaly
Jim VanBeek

Lee J. Van Scyoc
Roy Van Til
Robert F. Wallace
Henry C. Wallich
Milledge Weathers
Robert G. Welch
Terence West
Wylie Whalthall
Everett E. White
Michael D. White
Raburn M. Williams
James Willis
George Wilson
Travis Wilson
Ken Woodward
Donald Yankovic
Alex Yguado
Paul Young
Shik Young
Mohammed Zaheer
Ed Zajicek
William J. Zimmer Jr.

As always, a major revision cannot be done by the author alone. The entire staff at Addison-Wesley proved tireless in helping me finish this project. My longtime editor, John Greenman, continued to come up with new ideas and made sure that they were carried out correctly. My developmental editor, Vicki Cohen, made sure that the manuscript was complete and accurate. My project editor, Ellen MacElree, was a hard taskmaster, but I appreciate her getting the book out on time. My copyeditor, Bruce Emmer, smoothed out the manuscript. Dr. Willard W. Radell carefully checked every single graph. Masterful proofing was done by Judy Kiviat, Marie-Christine Loiseau, and Daniel K. Benjamin. Julie Zasloff in wizardly fashion produced all of the printed supplements and made sure they all corresponded to the text and came out on time. Finally, Sue Jasin of K&M Consulting probably retyped more than she thought was possible for a revision. To all of these people I wish to extend my sincere thanks and esteem.

If you or your students have comments, be sure to write to me. I am always eager to find ways to improve this text.

R. L. M.

ECONOMICS TODAY

THE MACRO VIEW

PART 1

INTRODUCTION

CHAPTER 1

THE NATURE OF ECONOMICS

For most people, choosing a spouse has never been an inexpensive or easy activity. Not long ago, some people were arguing that the institution of marriage was dying. Yet recent statistics show that the opposite is true: The percentage of Americans getting married has increased. Spouse selection is clearly an activity that most people eventually choose to engage in. A variety of considerations are involved. For example, the ease or difficulty of obtaining a divorce may have an effect on how spouses are chosen; so may the factor called love. Is there a rational, economic reason why individuals prefer a marriage in which there is mutual love? To answer this question, you need to know about the nature of economics.

PREVIEW QUESTIONS

1. What is the difference between microeconomics and macroeconomics?

2. What role does rational self-interest play in economic analysis?

3. Why is the study of economics a science?

4. What is the difference between positive and normative economics?

3

Did You Know That . . . since 1987, the number of fax machines in U.S. offices and homes has increased by over 10,000 percent? During the same time period, the number of bike messengers in downtown New York City *decreased* by over 65 percent. The world around us is definitely changing. Much of that change is due to the dramatically falling cost of communications and information technology. By the late 1990s the computers inside video games will cost only a few hundred dollars yet have 50 times the processing power that a $10 million IBM mainframe had in 1975. Not surprisingly, since the start of the 1990s, American firms have been spending more on communications equipment and computers than on new construction and heavy machinery.

Cyberspace, the information superhighway—call it what you want, but your next home (if not your current one) will almost certainly have an address on it. The percentage of U.S. households that have at least one telephone is close to 100 percent, and those that have video game players is approaching 50 percent. Over 35 percent of homes have personal computers, and more than half of those machines are set up to receive and access information via phone lines. Your decisions about such things as when and what type of computer to buy, whether to accept a collect call from a friend traveling in Europe, and how much time you should invest in learning to use a new multimedia system involve an untold number of variables: where you live, the work your parents do, what your friends think, and so on. But, as you will see, there are economic underpinnings for nearly all the decisions you make.

THE POWER OF ECONOMIC ANALYSIS

Knowing that an economic problem exists every time you make a decision is not enough. You also have to develop a framework that will allow you to analyze solutions to each economic problem—whether you are trying to decide how much to study, which courses to take, whether to finish school, or whether America should send troops abroad or raise tariffs. The framework that you will learn in this text is based on the *economic way of thinking*.

This framework gives you power—the power to reach informed conclusions about what is happening in the world. You can, of course, live your life without the power of economic analysis as part of your analytical framework. Indeed, most people do. But economists believe that economic analysis can help you make better decisions concerning your career, your education, financing your home, and other important areas. In the business world, the power of economic analysis can help you increase your competitive edge as an employee or as the owner of a business. As a voter, for the rest of your life you will be asked to make judgments about policies that are advocated by a particular political party. Many of these policies will deal with questions related to international economics, such as whether the U.S. government should encourage or discourage immigration, prevent foreigners from investing in domestic TV stations and newspapers, or restrict other countries from selling their goods here. Finally, just as taking an art, music, or literature appreciation class increases the pleasure you receive when you view paintings, listen to concerts, or read novels, taking an economics course will increase your understanding when watching the news on TV or reading the newspaper.

DEFINING ECONOMICS

What is economics exactly? Some cynics have defined *economics* as "common sense made difficult." But common sense, by definition, should be within everyone's grasp. You will encounter in the following pages numerous examples that show that economics is, in fact, pure and simple common sense.

Economics
The study of how people allocate their limited resources to satisfy their unlimited wants.

Economics is part of the social sciences and as such seeks explanations of real events. All social sciences analyze human behavior, as opposed to the physical sciences, which generally analyze the behavior of electrons, atoms, and other nonhuman phenomena.

> **Economics is the study of how people allocate their limited resources in an attempt to satisfy their unlimited wants. As such, economics is the study of how people make choices.**

To understand this definition fully, two other words need explaining: *resources* and *wants*. **Resources** are things that have value and, more specifically, are used to produce things that satisfy people's wants. **Wants** are all of the things that people would consume if they had unlimited income.

Resources
Things used to produce other things to satisfy people's wants.

Wants
What people would buy if their incomes were unlimited.

Whenever an individual, a business, or a nation faces alternatives, a choice must be made, and economics helps us study how those choices are made. For example, you have to choose how to spend your limited income. You also have to choose how to spend your limited time. You may have to choose how much of your company's limited funds to spend on advertising and how much to spend on new-product research. In economics, we examine situations in which individuals choose how to do things, when to do things, and with whom to do them. Ultimately, the purpose of economics is to explain choices.

MICROECONOMICS VERSUS MACROECONOMICS

Economics is typically divided into two types of analysis: **microeconomics** and **macroeconomics.**

Microeconomics
The study of decision making undertaken by individuals (or households) and by firms.

> **Microeconomics is the part of economic analysis that studies decision making undertaken by individuals (or households) and by firms. It is like looking through a microscope to focus on the small parts of our economy.**

> **Macroeconomics is the part of economic analysis that studies the behavior of the economy as a whole. It deals with economywide phenomena such as changes in unemployment, the general price level, and national income.**

Macroeconomics
The study of the behavior of the economy as a whole, including such economywide phenomena as changes in unemployment, the general price level, and national income.

Microeconomic analysis, for example, is concerned with the effects of changes in the price of gasoline relative to that of other energy sources. It examines the effects of new taxes on a specific product or industry. If price controls were reinstituted in the United States, how individual firms and consumers would react to them would be in the realm of microeconomics. The raising of wages by an effective union strike would also be analyzed using the tools of microeconomics.

By contrast, issues such as the rate of inflation, the amount of economywide unemployment, and the yearly growth in the output of goods and services in the nation all fall into the realm of macroeconomic analysis. In other words, macroeconomics deals with aggregates, or totals—such as total output in an economy.

Aggregates
Total amounts or quantities; aggregate demand, for example, is total planned expenditures throughout a nation.

Be aware, however, of the blending of microeconomics and macroeconomics in modern economic theory. Modern economists are increasingly using microeconomic analysis—the study of decision making by individuals and by firms—as the basis of macroeconomic analysis. They do this because even though in macroeconomic analysis aggregates are being examined, those aggregates are made up of individuals and firms.

THE ECONOMIC PERSON: RATIONAL SELF-INTEREST

Economists assume that individuals act *as if* motivated by self-interest and respond predictably to opportunities for gain. This central insight of economics was first clearly articulated by Adam Smith in 1776. Smith wrote in his most famous book, *An Inquiry into the*

Nature and Causes of the Wealth of Nations, that "it is not from the benevolence of the butcher, the brewer, or the baker that we expect our dinner, but from their regard to their own interest." Otherwise stated, the typical person about whom economists make behavioral predictions is assumed to look out for his or her own self-interest in a rational manner. Because monetary benefits and costs of actions are often the most easily measured, economists most often make behavioral predictions about individuals' responses to ways to increase their wealth, measured in money terms. Let's see if we can apply the theory of rational self-interest to explain an anomaly concerning the makeup of the U.S. population.

EXAMPLE
The Increasing Native American Population

Look at Figure 1-1. You see that the proportion of Native Americans increased quite dramatically from 1970 to 1990. Can we use Adam Smith's ideas to understand why so many Native Americans have decided to rejoin their tribes? Perhaps. Consider the benefits of being a member of the Mdewakanton *(bday-WAH-kan-toon),* a tribe of about 100 that runs a casino in which in a recent year gamblers wagered over $500 million. Each member of the tribe received over $400,000. There is now a clear economic reason for Native Americans to return home. Over 200 of the nation's 544 tribes have introduced gambling of some sort, and almost half of those have big-time casinos. Reservations are grossing almost $6 billion a year from gaming. Tribe members sometimes get direct payments and others get the benefits of better health care, subsidized mortgages, and jobs. Self-identified Native Americans increased in number by 137 percent between 1970 and 1990.

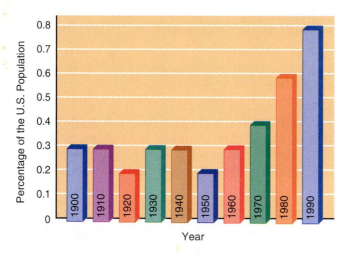

FIGURE 1-1

Native American Population of the United States, 1900–1990
The percentage of the U.S. population identifying itself as Native American has increased substantially in recent decades. Is there an economic explanation for this demographic trend?

FOR CRITICAL ANALYSIS: What nonmonetary reasons are there for Native Americans to rejoin their tribes? ●

The Rationality Assumption

The **rationality assumption** of economics, simply stated, is as follows:

We assume that individuals do not intentionally make decisions that would leave them worse off.

Rationality assumption
The assumption that people do not intentionally make decisions that would leave them worse off.

The distinction here is between what people may think—the realm of psychology and psychiatry and perhaps sociology—and what they do. Economics does *not* involve itself in analyzing individual or group thought processes. Economics looks at what people actually do in life with their limited resources. It does little good to criticize the rationality assumption by stating, "Nobody thinks that way" or "I never think that way" or "How unrealistic! That's as irrational as anyone can get!"

Take the example of driving. When you consider passing another car on a two-lane highway with oncoming traffic, you have to make very quick decisions: You must estimate the speed of the car that you are going to pass, the speed of the oncoming cars, the distance between your car and the oncoming cars, and your car's potential rate of acceleration. If we were to apply a model to your behavior, we would use the laws of calculus. In actual fact, you and most other drivers in such a situation do not actually think of using the laws of calculus, but to predict your behavior, we could make the prediction *as if* you understood the laws of calculus.

In any event, when you observe behavior around you, what may seem irrational often has its basis in the rationality assumption, as you can see by the following example.

EXAMPLE
When It Is Rational *Not* to Learn New Technology

The standard young person's view of older people (particularly one's parents) is that they're reluctant to learn new things. The saying "You can't teach an old dog new tricks" seems to apply. Young people, in contrast, seem eager to learn about new technology—mastering computers and multimedia, playing interactive games, cruising the information superhighway. But there is a rational reason for older people's reduced willingness to learn new technologies. If you are 20 years old and learn a new skill, you will be able to gain returns from your investment in learning over the course of many decades. If you are 60, however, and invest the same amount of time and effort learning the same skill, you will almost certainly not be able to reap those returns for as long a time period. Hence it is perfectly rational for "old dogs" not to want to learn new tricks.

FOR CRITICAL ANALYSIS: Some older people do learn to use new technologies as they emerge. What might explain this behavior? ●

Responding to Incentives

If it can be assumed that individuals never intentionally make decisions that would leave them worse off, then almost by definition they will respond to different incentives. We define **incentives** as the potential rewards available if a particular activity is undertaken. Indeed, much of human behavior can be explained in terms of how individuals respond to changing incentives over time.

Incentives
Rewards for engaging in a particular activity.

Schoolchildren are motivated to do better by a variety of incentive systems, ranging from gold stars and certificates of achievement when they are young to better grades with accompanying promises of a "better life" as they get older. There are, of course, negative incentives that affect our behavior, too. Children who disrupt the class are given after-school detention or sent to the vice principal for other punishment.

Implicitly, people react to changing incentives after they have done some sort of rough comparison of the costs and benefits of various courses of action. In fact, making rational choices invariably involves balancing costs and benefits.

The linked concepts of incentive and costs and benefits can be used to explain seeming anomalies in the world around us.

INTERNATIONAL EXAMPLE
Why Are There So Many Brush Fires in Corsica?

Every summer on Corsica, a French island in the Mediterranean less than half the size of the state of New Jersey, 10,000 to 40,000 acres of brush go up in flames. As many as 37 brush fires have been reported on a single day. One might attribute the prevalence of brush fires to the island's physical differences from other European locations, but that is not the explanation. Rather, the European Union (EU) has provided an incentive for some Corsicans to set brush fires deliberately. When brush is burned, more grazing land becomes available, and most Corsican cattle are left to roam freely on common land. Corsicans who claim that they tend at least 100 head of cattle receive a "suckling cow premium" from the EU, equal to more than $2,000 a month. The large number of brush fires on the island of Corsica is no accident.

FOR CRITICAL ANALYSIS: The average cow in Europe is three years old before she gives birth, whereas in Corsica the average age is a year and a half. Why do you think Corsicans breed their cows faster than other Europeans? ●

Defining Self-Interest

Self-interest does not always mean increasing one's wealth measured in dollars and cents. We assume that individuals seek many goals, not just increased wealth measured in monetary terms. Thus the self-interest part of our economic-person assumption includes goals relating to prestige, friendship, love, power, helping others, creating works of art, and many other matters. We can also think in terms of enlightened self-interest whereby individuals, in the pursuit of what makes them better off, also achieve the betterment of others around them. In brief, individuals are assumed to want the right to further their goals by making decisions about how things around them are used. The head of a charitable organization usually will not turn down an additional contribution, because accepting it lets that person control how that money is used, even if it is always for other people's benefit.

Otherwise stated, charitable acts are not ruled out by self-interest. Giving gifts to relatives can be considered a form of charity that is nonetheless in the self-interest of the giver. But how efficient is such gift giving?

EXAMPLE
The Perceived Value of Gifts

Every holiday season, aunts, uncles, grandparents, mothers, and fathers give gifts to their college-aged loved ones. Joel Waldfogel, an economist at Yale University, surveyed several thousand college students after Christmas to find out the value of holiday gifts. He found that compact discs and outerwear (coats and jackets) had a perceived intrinsic value about equal to their actual cash equivalent. By the time he got down the list to socks, underwear, and cosmetics, the students' valuation was only about 85 percent of the cash value of the gift. He found out that aunts, uncles, and grandparents gave the "worst" gifts and friends, siblings, and parents gave the "best."

FOR CRITICAL ANALYSIS: What argument could you use against the idea of substituting cash or gift certificates for physical gifts? ●

ECONOMICS AS A SCIENCE

Economics is a social science that makes use of the same kinds of methods used in other sciences, such as biology, physics, and chemistry. Similar to these other sciences, economics uses models, or theories. Economic **models, or theories,** are simplified representations of the real world that we use to help us understand, explain, and predict economic phenomena in the real world. There are, of course, differences between sciences. The social sciences—especially economics—make little use of laboratory methods in which changes in variables can be explained under controlled conditions. Rather, social scientists, and especially economists, usually have to examine what has already happened in the real world in order to test their models, or theories.

Models, or theories
Simplified representations of the real world used as the basis for predictions or explanations.

Models and Realism

At the outset it must be emphasized that no model in *any* science, and therefore no economic model, is complete in the sense that it captures *every* detail or interrelationship that exists. Indeed, a model, by definition, is an abstraction from reality. It is conceptually impossible to construct a perfectly complete realistic model. For example, in physics we cannot account for every molecule and its position and certainly not for every atom and subparticle. Not only is such a model impossibly expensive to build, but working with it would be impossibly complex.

The nature of scientific model building is such that the model should capture only the *essential* relationships that are sufficient to analyze the particular problem or answer the particular question with which we are concerned. *An economic model cannot be faulted as unrealistic simply because it does not represent every detail of the real world*. A map of a city that shows only major streets is not necessarily unrealistic if, in fact, all you need to know is how to pass through the city using major streets. As long as a model is realistic in terms of shedding light on the *central* issue at hand or forces at work, it may be useful.

A map is the quintessential model. It is always a simplified representation. It is always unrealistic. But it is also useful in making (refutable) predictions about the world. If the model—the map—predicts that when you take Campus Avenue to the north, you always run into the campus, that is a (refutable) prediction. If our goal is to explain observed behavior, the simplicity or complexity of the model we use is irrelevant. If a simple model can explain observed behavior in repeated settings just as well as a complex one, the simple model has some value and is probably easier to use.

Assumptions

Every model, or theory, must be based on a set of assumptions. Assumptions define the set of circumstances in which our model is most likely to be applicable. When scientists predicted that sailing ships would fall off the edge of the earth, they used the *assumption* that the earth was flat. Columbus did not accept the implications of such a model. He assumed that the world was round. The real-world test of his own model refuted the flat-earth model. Indirectly, then, it was a test of the assumption of the flat-earth model.

EXAMPLE
Getting Directions

Assumptions are a shorthand for reality. Imagine that you have decided to drive from your home in San Diego to downtown San Francisco. Because you have never driven this route, you decide to get directions from the local office of the Automobile Association of America (AAA).

When you ask for directions, the travel planner could give you a set of detailed maps that shows each city through which you will travel—Oceanside, San Clemente, Irvine, Anaheim, Los Angeles, Bakersfield, Modesto, and so on—and then, opening each map, show you exactly how the freeway threads through each of these cities. You would get a nearly complete description of reality because the AAA travel planner will not have used many simplifying assumptions. It is more likely, however, that the travel planner will simply say, "Get on Interstate 5 going north. Stay on it for about 500 miles. Follow the signs for San Francisco. After crossing the toll bridge, take any exit marked 'Downtown.'" By omitting all of the trivial details, the travel planner has told you all that you really need and want to know. The models you will be using in this text are similar to the simplified directions on how to drive from San Diego to San Francisco—they focus on what is relevant to the problem at hand and omit what is not.

FOR CRITICAL ANALYSIS: *In what way do small talk and gossip represent the use of simplifying assumptions?* ●

The *Ceteris Paribus* Assumption: All Other Things Being Equal. Everything in the world seems to relate in some way to everything else in the world. It would be impossible to isolate the effects of changes in one variable on another variable if we always had to worry about the many other variables that might also enter the analysis. As in other sciences, economics uses the **ceteris paribus** assumption. *Ceteris paribus* means "other things constant" or "other things equal."

Consider an example taken from economics. One of the most important determinants of how much of a particular product a family buys is how expensive that product is relative to other products. We know that in addition to relative prices, other factors influence decisions about making purchases. Some of them have to do with income, others with tastes, and yet others with custom and religious beliefs. Whatever these other factors are, we hold them constant when we look at the relationship between changes in prices and changes in how much of a given product people will purchase.

Ceteris paribus [KAY-ter-us PEAR-uh-bus] assumption
The assumption that nothing changes except the factor or factors being studied.

Deciding on the Usefulness of a Model

We generally do not attempt to determine the usefulness, or "goodness," of a model merely by evaluating how realistic its assumptions are. Rather, we consider a model good if it yields usable predictions and implications for the real world. In other words, can we use the model to predict what will happen in the world around us? Does the model provide useful implications of how things happen in our world?

Once we have determined that the model does predict real-world phenomena, the scientific approach to the analysis of the world around us requires that we consider evidence. Evidence is used to test the usefulness of a model. This is why we call economics an **empirical** science, *empirical* meaning that evidence (data) is looked at to see whether we are right. Economists are often engaged in empirically testing their models.

Consider two competing models for the way students act when doing complicated probability problems to choose the best gambles. One model predicts that, based on the assumption of rational self-interest, students who are paid more for better performance will in fact perform better on average during the experiment. A competing model might be that students whose last names start with the letters *A* through *L* will do better than students with last names starting with *M* through *Z,* irrespective of how much they are paid. The model that consistently predicts more accurately is the model that we would normally choose. In this example, the "alphabet" model did not work well: The first letter of the last name of the students who actually did the experiment at UCLA was irrelevant in predicting how well they would perform the mathematical calculations necessary to choose the correct gambles. The model based on rational self-interest predicted well, in contrast.

Empirical
Relying on real-world data in evaluating the usefulness of a model.

Models of Behavior, Not Thought Processes

Take special note of the fact that economists' models do not relate to the way people *think;* they relate to the way people *act,* to what they do in life with their limited resources. Models tend to generalize human behavior. Normally, the economist does not attempt to predict how people will think about a particular topic, such as a higher price of oil products, accelerated inflation, or higher taxes. Rather, the task at hand is to predict how people will act, which may be quite different from what they say they will do (much to the consternation of poll takers and market researchers). The people involved in examining thought processes are psychologists and psychiatrists, not typically economists.

POSITIVE VERSUS NORMATIVE ECONOMICS

Economics uses *positive analysis,* a value-free approach to inquiry. No subjective or moral judgments enter into the analysis. Positive analysis relates to statements such as "If A, then B." For example, "If the price of gasoline goes up relative to all other prices, then the amount of it that people will buy will fall." That is a positive economic statement. It is a statement of *what is*. It is not a statement of anyone's value judgment or subjective feelings. For many problems analyzed in the hard sciences such as physics and chemistry, the analyses are considered to be virtually value-free. After all, how can someone's values enter into a theory of molecular behavior? But economists face a different problem. They deal with the behavior of individuals, not molecules. That makes it more difficult to stick to what we consider to be value-free or **positive economics** without reference to our feelings.

When our values are interjected into the analysis, we enter the realm of **normative economics,** involving *normative analysis*. A positive economic statement is "If the price of

Positive economics
Analysis that is strictly limited to making either purely descriptive statements or scientific predictions; for example, "If A, then B." A statement of *what is.*

Normative economics
Analysis involving value judgments about economic policies; relates to whether things are good or bad. A statement of *what ought to be.*

gas rises, people will buy less." If we add to that analysis the statement "so we should not allow the price to go up," we have entered the realm of normative economics—we have expressed a value judgment. In fact, any time you see the word *should,* you will know that values are entering into the discussion. Just remember that positive statements are concerned with *what is,* whereas normative statements are concerned with *what ought to be.*

Each of us has a desire for different things. That means that we have different values. When we express a value judgment, we are simply saying what we prefer, like, or desire. Because individual values are diverse, we expect—and indeed observe—people expressing widely varying value judgments about how the world ought to be.

A Warning: Recognize Normative Analysis

It is easy to define positive economics. It is quite another matter to catch all unlabeled normative statements in a textbook such as this one (or any other), even though an author goes over the manuscript many times before it is printed. Therefore, do not get the impression that a textbook author will be able to keep all personal values out of the book. They will slip through. In fact, the very choice of which topics to include in an introductory textbook involves normative economics. There is no value-free, or objective, way to decide which topics to use in a textbook. The author's values ultimately make a difference when choices have to be made. But from your own standpoint, you might want to be able to recognize when you are engaging in normative as opposed to positive economic analysis. Reading this text will help equip you for that task.

CONCEPTS IN BRIEF

- A model, or theory, uses assumptions and is by nature a simplification of the real world. The usefulness of a model can be evaluated by bringing empirical evidence to bear on its predictions.

- Models are not necessarily deficient simply because they are unrealistic and use simplifying assumptions, for every model in every science requires simplification compared to the real world.

- Most models use the *ceteris paribus* assumption, that all other things are held constant, or equal.

- Positive economics is value-free and relates to statements that can be refuted, such as "If A, then B." Normative economics involves people's values, and normative statements typically contain the word *should.*

How Relevant Is Love in a Marriage Contract?

Concepts Applied: *Rationality assumption, costs, benefits*

Economist Gary Becker argues that dating can be understood in terms of the rationality assumption. For instance, the better off an individual thinks he or she may be in a marriage, the more that individual is willing to invest in finding the right mate.

Looking for a mate can be analyzed from a sociological, psychological, or anthropological point of view. Here we want to examine this activity in terms of the rationality assumption developed in this chapter. We present an economic analysis based in part on the work of Nobel Prize–winning economist Gary Becker.

Minimizing Costs

According to the rationality assumption, individuals will not knowingly engage in activities that will make them worse off. Consequently, we predict that in choosing a spouse, individuals will naturally want to marry someone with whom they get along. So we predict that likes will attract more often than not: Individuals will tend to marry others with similar values. Dating and "courting" can be viewed as resource-using activities designed to determine with more certainty the values that each potential marriage partner has.

The more benefits one believes can be derived from the marriage contract, the more costs one will incur in searching for a spouse. The longer one searches, the more costs are incurred due to dating and courtship activities. The more durable the marriage contract, the greater the investment people will be willing to make in trying to find the "right" spouse.

Divorce and Wrong Partner Choices

The most durable marriage contract occurs in a legal setting in which divorce is impossible. One benefit is that a spouse cannot later leave because he or she prefers someone else. In many societies, the tendency has been toward fewer restrictions on divorce.

As divorces have become easier (that is to say, less costly), the durability of the marriage contract has seemed to decline. This result follows, at least in part, from economic analysis: As the expected durability of marriage declines, individuals implicitly have less incentive to incur longer searches for the "right" partner. The result: more wrong choices about a partner and hence more frequent divorces.

Why Love Matters

One aspect of love is that the level of happiness of the person loved affects the well-being of the other person. The more one loves another person, the more one is motivated to help that other person. Within a marriage, each spouse is dependent on the other.

When one spouse fails to uphold his or her end of the bargain, this tends to reduce the well-being of the other. Within a marriage, there is no actual iron-clad agreement about who provides what, how, and when. Therefore, it is relatively easy for one spouse not to do what he or she is supposed to do or at least not do it very well. The more love is involved, however, the more each spouse wants to make the other spouse better off. So we predict that marriages work out better the more spouses love each other. Hence individuals generally want to be in a marriage environment in which there is mutual love.

FOR CRITICAL ANALYSIS

1. Is there any difference between what economics predicts about a "good" marriage and what most people believe anyway?
2. If divorce is impossible, how does this affect spouse selection?

CHAPTER SUMMARY

1. Economics as a social science is the study of how individuals make choices to satisfy wants. Wants are defined as what people would buy if their incomes were unlimited.

2. Economics is usually divided into microeconomic analysis, which is the study of individual decision making by households and firms, and macroeconomics, which is the study of nationwide phenomena, such as inflation and unemployment.

3. The rationality assumption is that individuals never intentionally make decisions that would leave them worse off.

4. We use models, or theories, to explain and predict behavior. Models, or theories, are never completely realistic because by definition they are simplifications using assumptions that are not directly testable. The usefulness of a theory, or model, is determined not by the realism of its assumptions but by how well it predicts real-world phenomena.

5. An important simplifying assumption is that all other things are held equal, or constant. This is sometimes known as the *ceteris paribus* assumption.

6. No model in economics relates to individuals' thought processes; all models relate to what people do, not to what they think or say they will do.

7. Much economic analysis involves positive economics; that is, it is value-free. Whenever statements embodying values are made, we enter the realm of normative economics, or how individuals and groups think things ought to be.

DISCUSSION OF PREVIEW QUESTIONS

1. What is the difference between microeconomics and macroeconomics?

Microeconomics is concerned with the choice-making processes of individuals, households, and firms, whereas macroeconomics focuses on the performance of the economy as a whole.

2. What role does rational self-interest play in economic analysis?

Rational self-interest is the assumption that individuals behave in a reasonable (rational) way in making choices to further their interests. In other words, we assume that individuals' actions are motivated primarily by their self-interest, keeping in mind that self-interest can relate to monetary and nonmonetary objectives, such as love, prestige, and helping others.

3. Why is the study of economics a science?

Economics is a science in that it uses models, or theories, that are simplified representations of the real world to analyze and make predictions about the real world. These predictions are then subjected to empirical tests in which real-world data are used to decide whether or not to reject the predictions.

4. What is the difference between positive and normative economics?

Positive economics deals with *what is,* whereas normative economics deals with *what ought to be.* Positive economic statements are of the "if . . . then" variety; they are descriptive and predictive and are not related to what "should" happen. Normative economics, by contrast, is concerned with what ought to be and is intimately tied to value judgments.

PROBLEMS

(Answers to the odd-numbered problems appear at the back of the book.)

1-1. Construct four separate models to predict the probability that a person will die within the next five years. Include only one determining factor in each of your models.

1-2. Does it matter whether all of a model's assumptions are "realistic"? Why or why not?

1-3. Give a refutable implication (one that can be disproved by evidence from the real world) for each of the following models:

   a. The accident rate of drivers is inversely related to their age.
   b. The rate of inflation is directly related to the rate of change in the nation's money supply.
   c. The wages of professional basketball players are directly related to their high school grade point averages.
   d. The rate at which bank employees are promoted is inversely related to their frequency of absenteeism.

1-4. Is gambling an example of rational or irrational behavior? What is the difference between gambling and insurance?

1-5. Over the past 20 years, first-class mail rates have more than tripled, while prices of long-distance phone calls, televisions, and sound systems have decreased. Over a similar period, it has been reported that there has been a steady decline in the ability of high school graduates to communicate effectively in writing. Do you feel that this increase in the relative price of written communi-cation (first-class mail rates) is related to the alleged decline in writing ability? If so, what do you feel is the direction of causation? Which is causing which?

1-6. If there is no way to test a theory with real-world data, can we determine if it is a good theory? Why is empirical evidence used to validate a theory?

1-7. Identify which of the following statements use positive economic analysis and which use normative economic analysis.

   a. The government should not regulate the banking system because recent problems have demonstrated that it does not know what it is doing.
   b. The elimination of barriers to the free movement of individuals across European borders has caused wages to become more equal in many industries.
   c. Paying members of Congress more provides them with less incentive to commit wrongful acts.
   d. We need more restrictions on companies that pollute because air pollution is destroying our way of life.

COMPUTER-ASSISTED INSTRUCTION

Key elements of the scientific way of thinking are illustrated by applying them to everyday situations.

Complete problem and answer appear on disk.

INTERACTING WITH THE INTERNET

The Internet is a web of educational, corporate, and research computer networks around the world. Today, over 40 million people are using it, and more than 60,000 networks are connected to it. Perhaps the most interesting part of the Internet is the World Wide Web, commonly called the Web, which is a vast interlinked network of computer files all over the world. You can use the Internet to find discussion groups, news groups, and electronic publications. The most common use of the Internet is for electronic mail (e-mail).

At many colleges and universities, you can get an e-mail address and a password. Your address is like a mailbox at which you will receive electronic information. Many of the chapters in this ninth edition of *Economics Today* end with Internet addresses and activities that you will find helpful in your study of the principles of economics. In any event, you should get an Internet address now. Pick up a copy of the new user's handbook and start using e-mail.

You can also roam through the user-friendly **gopher** menus. You first open your connection the way you would to send or receive electronic mail. Then you type **gopher** and hit the return (enter) key. (On Windows-based systems, you begin a gopher session by double-clicking on the gopher icon.) You will then be presented with a first-level menu of choices. Choose one by moving the cursor (arrow) up or down to the item you want to open (at the blinking cursor, type in the number of your choice). When you are done playing around, type in **Q.** The largest gopher site is at the University of Minnesota. To reach it, type **gopher** and then type

   tc.umn.edu

If you want to "surf" (browse) economics resources immediately, go directly to Resources for Economists on the Internet by typing in

http://econwpa.wustl.edu/EconFAQ/EconFAQ.html

This site is maintained by Professor William Goffe of the University of Southern Mississippi. This is his "home page," the table of contents for a particular Web site. On this page you will find a catalog of "hypertext" pointers, which are highlighted words or phrases that you can click on to connect to places around the Web.

To get in the last laugh, you might want to look up some economist jokes at

http://www.etla.fi/pkm/joke.html

Happy surfing!

CHAPTER 2

SCARCITY AND THE WORLD OF TRADE-OFFS

Is anything more precious than life itself? Most people would say no, though few of us actually act as if life was our most treasured gift. We routinely act in ways that decrease our expected life, include smoking, having an improper diet, not exercising, exceeding the speed limit, not buckling our seat belts, and passing carelessly on two-lane roads. Government policymakers pass laws to protect human life, but they cannot eliminate every risk that exists. They can, however, force society to spend resources to reduce risk to human life. When they do, a trade-off is involved because risk reduction involves the use of things that are scarce.

PREVIEW QUESTIONS

1. Do affluent people face the problem of scarcity?

2. Fresh air may be consumed at no charge, but is it free of cost to society?

3. Why does the scarcity problem force individuals to consider opportunity costs?

4. Can a "free" college education ever be truly free?

Did You Know That . . . Chris Van Horn, president of CVK Group in Washington, D.C., grosses over $200,000 a year for having people wait in line? Adam Goldin loves working as a "line waiter" because he gets paid for "doing nothing." His job is to arrive early in the morning on Capitol Hill to hold places for lobbyists who must attend congressional hearings. Van Horn charges his more than 100 lobbyists and law firm clients $27 an hour and pays his part-time line waiters like Mr. Goldin $10 an hour. The lawyers and lobbyists who pay professional line waiters are able to use the time they save more productively and earn well above the $27 an hour they have to pay the line waiters. They do not miss the opportunity to be making more income this way. After all, such lobbyists and lawyers do not have an unlimited amount of time. Time is scarce to them.

SCARCITY

Whenever individuals or communities cannot obtain everything they desire simultaneously, choices occur. Choices occur because of *scarcity*. **Scarcity** is the most basic concept in all of economics. Scarcity means that we do not and cannot have enough income or wealth to satisfy our *every* desire. Scarcity exists because human wants always exceed what can be produced with the limited resources and time that nature makes available.

What Scarcity Is Not

Scarcity is not a shortage. After a hurricane hits and cuts off supplies to a community, TV newscasts often show people standing in line to get minimum amounts of cooking fuel and food. A news commentator might say that the line is caused by the "scarcity" of these products. But cooking fuel and food are always scarce—we cannot obtain all that we want at a zero price. Therefore, do not confuse the concept of scarcity, which is general and all-encompassing, with the concept of shortages as evidenced by people waiting in line to obtain a particular product.

Scarcity is not the same thing as poverty. Scarcity occurs among the poor and among the rich. Even the richest person on earth faces scarcity because available time is limited. Low income levels do not create more scarcity. High income levels do not create less scarcity.

Scarcity is a fact of life, like gravity. And just as physicists did not invent gravity, economists did not invent scarcity—it existed well before the first economist ever lived. It exists even when we are not using all of our resources.

Scarcity
A situation in which the ingredients for producing the things that people desire are insufficient to satisfy all wants.

Scarcity and Resources

The scarcity concept arises from the fact that resources are insufficient to satisfy our every desire. Resources are the inputs used in the production of the things that we want. **Production** can be defined as virtually any activity that results in the conversion of resources into products that can be used in consumption. Production includes delivering things from one part of the country to another. It includes taking ice from an ice tray to put it in your soft-drink glass. The resources used in production are called *factors of production*, and some economists use the terms *resources* and *factors of production* interchangeably. The total quantity of all resources that an economy has at any one time determines what that economy can produce.

Factors of production can be classified in many ways. Here is one such classification:

1. **Land. Land** encompasses all the nonhuman gifts of nature, including timber, water, fish, minerals, and the original fertility of land. It is often called the *natural resource*.

Production
Any activity that results in the conversion of resources into products that can be used in consumption.

Land
The natural resources that are available from nature. Land as a resource includes location, original fertility and mineral deposits, topography, climate, water, and vegetation.

Labor
Productive contributions of humans who work, involving both mental and physical activities.

Physical capital
All manufactured resources, including buildings, equipment, machines, and improvements to land that is used for production.

Human capital
The accumulated training and education of workers.

Entrepreneurship
The factor of production involving human resources that perform the functions of raising capital, organizing, managing, assembling other factors of production, and making basic business policy decisions. The entrepreneur is a risk taker.

2. **Labor. Labor** is the human resource, which includes all productive contributions made by individuals who work, such as steelworkers, ballet dancers, and professional baseball players.

3. **Physical capital. Physical capital** consists of the factories and equipment used in production. It also includes improvements to natural resources, such as irrigation ditches.

4. **Human capital. Human capital** is the economic characterization of the education and training of workers. How much the nation produces depends not only on how many hours people work but also on how productive they are, and that, in turn, depends in part on education and training. To become more educated, individuals have to devote time and resources, just as a business has to devote resources if it wants to increase its physical capital. Whenever a worker's skills increase, human capital has been improved.

5. **Entrepreneurship.** The factor of production known as **entrepreneurship** (actually a subdivision of labor) involves human resources that perform the functions of organizing, managing, and assembling the other factors of production to make business ventures. Entrepreneurship also encompasses taking risks that involve the possibility of losing large sums of wealth on new ventures. It includes new methods of doing common things and generally experimenting with any type of new thinking that could lead to making more money income. Without entrepreneurship, virtually no business organization could operate.

Goods Versus Economic Goods

Goods
All things from which individuals derive satisfaction or happiness.

Economic goods
Goods that are scarce.

Goods are defined as all things from which individuals derive satisfaction or happiness. Goods therefore include air to breathe and the beauty of a sunset as well as food, cars, and CD players.

Economic goods are a subset of all goods—they are goods derived from scarce resources about which we must constantly make decisions regarding their best use. By definition, the desired quantity of an economic good exceeds the amount that is directly available from nature at a zero price. Virtually every example we use in economics concerns economic goods—cars, CD players, computers, socks, baseball bats, and corn. Weeds are a good example of *bads*—goods for which the desired quantity is much *less* than what nature provides at a zero price.

Services
Mental or physical labor or help purchased by consumers. Examples are the assistance of doctors, lawyers, dentists, repair personnel, housecleaners, educators, retailers, and wholesalers; things purchased or used by consumers that do not have physical characteristics.

Sometimes you will see references to "goods and services." **Services** are tasks that are performed for someone else, such as laundry, cleaning, hospital care, restaurant meal preparation, car polishing, psychological counseling, and teaching. One way of looking at services is thinking of them as *intangible goods*.

WANTS AND NEEDS

Wants are not the same as needs. Indeed, from the economist's point of view, the term *needs* is objectively undefinable. When someone says, "I need some new clothes," there is no way to know whether that person is stating a vague wish, a want, or a life-saving necessity. If the individual making the statement were dying of exposure in a northern country during the winter, we might argue that indeed the person does need clothes—perhaps not new ones, but at least some articles of warm clothing. Typically, however, the term *need* is used very casually in most conversations. What people mean, usually, is that they want something that they do not currently have.

Humans have unlimited wants. Just imagine if every single material want that you might have were satisfied. You can have all of the clothes, cars, houses, CDs, tickets to concerts, and other things that you want. Does that mean that nothing else could add to your total level of happiness? Probably not, because you might think of new goods and services that you could obtain, particularly as they came to market. You would also still be lacking in fulfilling all of your wants for compassion, friendship, love, affection, prestige, musical abilities, sports abilities, and so on.

In reality, every individual has competing wants but cannot satisfy all of them, given limited resources. This is the reality of scarcity. Each person must therefore make choices. Whenever a choice is made to do or buy something, something else that is also desired is not done or not purchased. In other words, in a world of scarcity, every want that ends up being satisfied causes one or more other wants to remain unsatisfied or to be forfeited.

CONCEPTS IN BRIEF

- Scarcity exists because human wants always exceed what can be produced with the limited resources and time that nature makes available.

- We use scarce resources, such as land, labor, physical and human capital, and entrepreneurship, to produce economic goods—goods that are desired but are not directly obtainable from nature to the extent demanded or desired at a zero price.

- Wants are unlimited; they include all material desires and all nonmaterial desires, such as love, affection, power, and prestige.

- The concept of need is difficult to define objectively for every person; consequently, we simply consider that every person's wants are unlimited. In a world of scarcity, satisfaction of one want necessarily means nonsatisfaction of one or more other wants.

SCARCITY, CHOICE, AND OPPORTUNITY COST

The natural fact of scarcity implies that we must make choices. One of the most important results of this fact is that every choice made (or not made, for that matter) means that some opportunity had to be sacrificed. Every choice involves giving up another opportunity to do or use something else.

Consider a practical example. Every choice you make to study one more hour of economics requires that you give up the opportunity to do any of the following activities: study more of another subject, listen to music, sleep, browse at a local store, read a novel, or work out at the gym. Many more opportunities are forgone also if you choose to study economics an additional hour.

Because there were so many alternatives from which to choose, how could you determine the value of what you gave up to engage in that extra hour of studying economics? First of all, no one else can tell you the answer because only you can *subjectively* put a value on the alternatives forgone. Only you know what is the value of another hour of sleep or of an hour looking for the latest CDs. That means that only you can determine the highest-valued, next-best alternative that you had to sacrifice in order to study economics one more hour. It is you who come up with the *subjective* estimate of the expected value of the next-best alternative.

The value of the next-best alternative is called **opportunity cost.** The opportunity cost of any action is the value of what is given up—the next-highest-ranked alternative—

Opportunity cost
The highest-valued, next-best alternative that must be sacrificed to attain something or to satisfy a want.

because a choice was made. When you study one more hour, there may be many alternatives available for the use of that hour, but assume that you can do only one thing in that hour—your next-highest-ranked alternative. What is important is the choice that you would have made if you hadn't studied one more hour. Your opportunity cost is the *next-highest-ranked* alternative, not *all* alternatives.

In economics, cost is always a forgone opportunity.

One way to think about opportunity cost is to understand that when you choose to do something, you lose. What you lose is being able to engage in your next-highest-valued alternative. The cost of your choice is what you lose, which is by definition your next-highest-valued alternative. This is your opportunity cost.

Let's consider the opportunity cost of forcing young men to serve time in the military service.

INTERNATIONAL EXAMPLE
The True Cost of the Military Draft in France

In 1996, the president of France, Jacques Chirac, announced that the government would end the military draft over the following six years. Ultimately, France will end up with 150,000 fewer soldiers. Chirac warned that the change would not result in any budget savings because the smaller professional army would cost the same as the then-current draft system. Each year, a professional military person "costs" 15 times more than a conscript. The annual salary of a professional military person is about 185,000 francs (about $38,000), whereas a conscript is only paid 12,500 francs (about $2,575).

But what is the true cost of a conscript in France? Remember that cost is always a forgone opportunity. If a conscript was making 100,000 francs a year (about $20,000) before being drafted, that is his opportunity cost. In other words, that is the opportunity cost to the nation whether or not that individual is paid the 100,000 francs a year by the French army. Resources are not saved by a nation engaging in conscription. Rather, the true cost to the military is simply hidden from the people.

FOR CRITICAL ANALYSIS: What are some other costs to the nation associated with a military draft? ●

THE WORLD OF TRADE-OFFS

Whenever you engage in any activity using any resource, even time, you are *trading off* the use of that resource for one or more alternative uses. The value of the trade-off is represented by the opportunity cost. The opportunity cost of studying economics has already been mentioned—it is the value of the next-best alternative. When you think of any alternative, you are thinking of trade-offs.

Let's consider a hypothetical example of a one-for-one trade-off between the results of spending time studying economics and accounting. For the sake of this argument, we will assume that additional time studying either economics or accounting will lead to a higher grade in the subject studied more. One of the best ways to examine this trade-off is with a graph. (If you would like a refresher on graphical techniques, study Appendix A at the end of this chapter before going on.)

Graphical Analysis

In Figure 2-1, the expected grade in accounting is measured on the vertical axis of the graph, and the expected grade in economics is measured on the horizontal axis. We simplify the world and assume that you have a maximum of 10 hours per week to spend studying these two subjects and that if you spend all 10 hours on economics, you will get an A in the course. You will, however, fail accounting. Conversely, if you spend all of your 10 hours studying accounting, you will get an A in that subject, but you will flunk economics. Here the trade-off is a special case: one-to-one. A one-to-one trade-off means that the opportunity cost of receiving one grade higher in economics (for example, improving from a C to a B) is one grade lower in accounting (falling from a C to a D).

The Production Possibilities Curve (PPC)

The graph in Figure 2-1 illustrates the relationship between the possible results that can be produced in each of two activities, depending on how much time you choose to devote to each activity. This graph shows a representation of a **production possibilities curve (PPC).**

Consider that you are producing a grade in economics when you study economics and a grade in accounting when you study accounting. Then the graph in Figure 2-1 can be related to the production possibilities you face. The line that goes from A on one axis to A on the other axis therefore becomes a production possibilities curve. It is defined as the maximum quantity of one good or service that can be produced, given that a specific quantity of another is produced. It is a curve that shows the possibilities available for increasing the output of one good or service by reducing the amount of another. In the example in Figure 2-1, your time for studying was limited to 10 hours per week. The two possible outputs were grades in accounting and grades in economics. The particular production possibilities curve presented in Figure 2-1 is a graphical representation of the opportunity cost of studying one more hour in one subject. It is a *straight-line production possibilities curve,* which is a special case. (The more general case will be discussed next.) If you decide to be at point *x* in Figure 2-1, 5 hours of study time will be spent on accounting and 5 hours will be spent on economics. The expected grade in each course will be a C. If you are more interested in getting a B in economics, you will go to point *y* on the production possibilities curve, spending only 2.5 hours on accounting but 7.5 hours on economics. Your expected grade in accounting will then drop from a C to a D.

Production possibilities curve (PPC)

A curve representing all possible combinations of total output that could be produced assuming (1) a fixed amount of productive resources of a given quality and (2) the efficient use of those resources.

FIGURE 2-1

Production Possibilities Curve for Grades in Accounting and Economics (Trade-offs)

We assume that only 10 hours can be spent per week on studying. If the student is at point *x*, equal time (5 hours a week) is spent on both courses and equal grades of C will be received. If a higher grade in economics is desired, the student may go to point *y*, thereby receiving a B in economics but a D in accounting. At point *y*, 2.5 hours are spent on accounting and 7.5 hours on economics.

Note that these trade-offs between expected grades in accounting and economics are the result of *holding constant* total study time as well as all other factors that might influence a student's ability to learn, such as computerized study aids. Quite clearly, if you wished to spend more total time studying, it would be possible to have higher grades in both economics and accounting. In that case, however, we would no longer be on the specific production possibilities curve illustrated in Figure 2-1. We would have to draw a new curve, farther to the right, to show the greater total study time and a different set of possible trade-offs.

CONCEPTS IN BRIEF

- Scarcity requires us to choose. When we choose, we lose the next-highest-valued alternative.
- Cost is always a forgone opportunity.
- Another way to look at opportunity cost is the trade-off that occurs when one activity is undertaken rather than the next-best alternative activity.
- A production possibilities curve (PPC) graphically shows the trade-off that occurs when more of one output is obtained at the sacrifice of another. The PPC is a graphical representation of, among other things, opportunity cost.

THE CHOICES SOCIETY FACES

The straight-line production possibilities curve presented in Figure 2-1 can be generalized to demonstrate the related concepts of scarcity, choice, and trade-offs that our entire nation faces. As you will see, the production possibilities curve is a simple but powerful economic model because it can demonstrate these related concepts. The example we will use is the choice between the production of M-16 semiautomatic rifles and CD-ROM players. We assume for the moment that these are the only two goods that can be produced in the nation. Panel (a) of Figure 2-2 on page 24 gives the various combinations of M-16s and CD-ROM players that are possible. If all resources are devoted to M-16 production, 10 billion per year can be produced. If all resources are devoted to CD-ROM player production, 12 billion per year can be produced. In between are various possible combinations. These combinations are plotted as points *A, B, C, D, E, F,* and *G* in panel (b) of Figure 2-2. If these points are connected with a smooth curve, the nation's production possibilities curve is shown, demonstrating the trade-off between the production of M-16 semiautomatic rifles and CD-ROM players. These trade-offs occur *on* the production possibilities curve.

Notice the major difference in the shape of the production possibilities curves in Figures 2-1 and 2-2. In Figure 2-1, there is a one-to-one trade-off between grades in economics and in accounting. In Figure 2-2, the trade-off between CD-ROM production and M-16 production is not constant, and therefore the production possibilities curve is a *bowed* line. To understand why the production possibilities curve for a society is typically bowed outward, you must understand the assumptions underlying the PPC.

Assumptions Underlying the Production Possibilities Curve

When we draw the curve that is shown in Figure 2-2, we make the following assumptions:
1. That resources are fully employed
2. That we are looking at production over a specific time period—for example, one year

	Panel (a)	
Combination	M-16 Rifles (billions of units per year)	CD-ROM Players (billions of units per year)
A	10.0	0
B	9.6	2
C	9.0	4
D	8.0	6
E	6.6	8
F	4.5	10
G	0	12

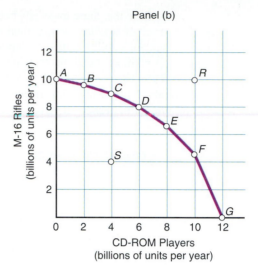

Panel (b)

FIGURE 2-2

Society's Trade-off Between M-16 Rifles and CD-ROM Players
Both the production of M-16 semiautomatic rifles and the production of CD-ROM players are measured in billions of units per year. The various combinations are given in panel (a) and plotted in panel (b). Connecting the points *A–G* with a relatively smooth line gives the society's production possibilities curve for M-16 rifles and CD-ROM players. Point *R* lies outside the production possibilities curve and is therefore unattainable at the point in time for which the graph is drawn. Point *S* lies inside the production possibilities curve and therefore represents an inefficient use of available resources.

3. That the resource inputs, in both quantity and quality, used to produce M-16 rifles or CD-ROM players are fixed over this time period
4. That technology does not change over this time period

Technology is defined as society's pool of applied knowledge concerning how goods and services can be produced by managers, workers, engineers, scientists, and craftspeople, using land and capital. You can think of technology as the formula (or recipe) used to combine factors of production. (When better formulas are developed, more production can be obtained from the same amount of resources.) The level of technology sets the limit on the amount and types of goods and services that we can derive from any given amount of resources. The production possibilities curve is drawn under the assumption that we use the best technology that we currently have available and that this technology doesn't change over the time period under study.

Technology
Society's pool of applied knowledge concerning how goods and services can be produced.

Being off the Production Possibilities Curve

Look again at panel (b) of Figure 2-2. Point *R* lies *outside* the production possibilities curve and is *impossible* to achieve during the time period assumed. By definition, the production possibilities curve indicates the *maximum* quantity of one good given some quantity of the other.

It is possible, however, to be at point *S* in Figure 2-2. That point lies beneath the production possibilities curve. If the nation is at point *S*, it means that its resources are not being fully utilized. This occurs, for example, during periods of unemployment. Point *S* and all such points within the production possibilities curve are always attainable but usually not desirable.

Efficiency

The production possibilities curve can be used to define the notion of efficiency. Whenever the economy is operating on the PPC, at points such as *A, B, C,* or *D,* we say that its production is efficient. Points such as *S* in Figure 2-2, which lie beneath the production possibilities curve, are said to represent production situations that are not efficient.

Efficiency

The case in which a given level of inputs is used to produce the maximum output possible. Alternatively, the situation in which a given output is produced at minimum cost.

Efficiency can mean many things to many people. Even within economics, there are different types of efficiency. Here we are discussing efficiency in production, or productive efficiency. An economy is productively efficient whenever it is producing the maximum output with given technology and resources.

A simple commonsense definition of efficiency is getting the most out of what we have as an economy. Clearly, we are not getting the most that we have if we are at point *S* in panel (b) of Figure 2-2. We can move from point *S* to, say, point *C,* thereby increasing the total quantity of M-16s produced without any decrease in the total quantity of CD-ROM players produced. We can move from point *S* to point *E,* for example, and have both more M-16s and more CD-ROM players. Point *S* is called an **inefficient point,** which is defined as any point below the production possibilities curve.

Inefficient point

Any point below the production possibilities curve at which resources are being used inefficiently.

The concept of economic efficiency relates to how goods are distributed among different individuals and entities. An efficient economy is one in which people who value specific goods relatively the most end up with those goods. If you own a vintage electric Fender guitar, but I value it more than you, I can buy it from you. Such trading benefits you and me mutually. In the process, the economy becomes more efficient. The maximum efficiency an economy can reach is when all such mutual benefits through trade have been exhausted.

The Law of Increasing Relative Cost

In the example in Figure 2-1, the trade-off between a grade in accounting and a grade in economics is one-to-one. The trade-off ratio was fixed. That is to say, the production possibilities curve was a straight line. The curve in Figure 2-2 is a more general case. We have re-created the curve in Figure 2-2 as Figure 2-3. Each combination, *A* through *G,* of M-16s and CD-ROM players is represented on the production possibilities curve. Starting with the production of zero CD-ROM players, the nation can produce 10 billion units of M-16s with its available resources and technology. When we increase production of CD-ROM players from zero to 2 billion units per year, the nation has to give up in M-16s that first vertical arrow, *Aa.* From panel (a) of Figure 2-2 you can see that this is .4 billion M-16s a

FIGURE 2-3

The Law of Increasing Relative Cost
Consider equal increments of CD-ROM player production, as measured on the horizontal axis. All of the horizontal arrows—*aB, bC,* and so on—are of equal length (2 billion units). The opportunity cost of going from 10 billion CD-ROM players per year to 12 billion *(Ff)* is much greater than going from zero units to 2 billion units *(Aa).* The opportunity cost of each additional equal increase in CD-ROM production rises.

year (10.0 billion − 9.6 billion). Again, if we increase production of CD-ROM players by 2 billion units per year, we go from *B* to *C*. In order to do so, the nation has to give up the vertical distance *Bb,* or .6 billion M-16s a year. By the time we go from 10 billion to 12 billion CD-ROM players, to obtain that 2 billion unit increase, we have to forgo the vertical distance *Ff,* or 4.5 billion M-16s. In other words, we see an increase in the opportunity cost of the last 2 billion units of CD-ROM players—4.5 billion M-16s—compared to an equivalent increase in CD-ROM players when we started with none being produced at all—.4 billion M-16s.

What we are observing is called the **law of increasing relative cost.** When society takes more resources and applies them to the production of any specific good, the opportunity cost increases for each additional unit produced. The reason that, as a nation, we face the law of increasing relative cost (which causes the production possibilities curve to bow outward) is that certain resources are better suited for producing some goods than they are for other goods. Resources are generally not *perfectly* adaptable for alternative uses. When increasing the output of a particular good, producers must use less efficient resources than those already used in order to produce the additional output. Hence the cost of producing the additional units increases. With respect to our hypothetical example here, at first the electronic technicians in the armed services would shift over to producing CD-ROM players. After a while, though, janitors and army cooks would be asked to help. Clearly, they would be less effective in making CD-ROM players.

As a rule of thumb, *the more specialized the resources, the more bowed the production possibilities curve.* At the other extreme, if all resources are equally suitable for CD-ROM player production or M-16 production, the curves in Figures 2-2 and 2-3 would approach the straight line shown in our first example in Figure 2-1.

Law of increasing relative cost

The observation that the opportunity cost of additional units of a good generally increases as society attempts to produce more of that good. This accounts for the bowed-out shape of the production possibilities curve.

CONCEPTS IN BRIEF

- Trade-offs are represented graphically by a production possibilities curve showing the maximum quantity of one good or service that can be produced, given a specific quantity of another, from a given set of resources over a specified period of time—for example, one year.

- A PPC is drawn holding the quantity and quality of all resources fixed over the time period under study.

- Points outside the production possibilities curve are unattainable; points inside are attainable but represent an inefficient use or underuse of available resources.

- Because many resources are better suited for certain productive tasks than for others, society's production possibilities curve is bowed outward, following the law of increasing relative cost.

ECONOMIC GROWTH AND THE PRODUCTION POSSIBILITIES CURVE

Over any particular time period, a society cannot be outside the production possibilities curve. Over time, however, it is possible to have more of everything. This occurs through economic growth (why economic growth occurs will be discussed in a later chapter). Figure 2-4 shows the production possibilities curve for M-16 rifles and CD-ROM players shifting outward. The two additional curves shown represent new choices open to an economy that has experienced economic growth. Such economic growth occurs because of

FIGURE 2-4

Economic Growth Allows for More of Everything

If the nation experiences economic growth, the production possibilities curve between M-16 rifles and CD-ROM players will move out, as is shown. This takes time, however, and it does not occur automatically. This means, therefore, that we can have more M-16s and more CD-ROM players only after a period of time during which we have experienced economic growth.

many things, including increases in the number of workers and productive investment in equipment.

Scarcity still exists, however, no matter how much economic growth there is. At any point in time, we will always be on some production possibilities curve; thus we will always face trade-offs. The more we want of one thing, the less we can have of others.

If a nation experiences economic growth, the production possibilities curve between M-16 rifles and CD-ROM players will move outward, as is shown in Figure 2-4. This takes time and does not occur automatically. One reason it will occur involves the choice about how much to consume today.

THE TRADE-OFF BETWEEN THE PRESENT AND THE FUTURE

Consumption
The use of goods and services for personal satisfaction.

The production possibilities curve and economic growth can be used to examine the trade-off between present **consumption** and future consumption. When we consume today, we are using up what we call consumption or consumer goods—food and clothes, for example. And we have already defined physical capital as the manufactured goods, such as machines and factories, used to make other goods and services.

Why We Make Capital Goods

Why would we be willing to use productive resources to make things—capital goods—that we cannot consume directly? For one thing, capital goods enable us to produce larger quantities of consumer goods or to produce them less expensively than we otherwise could. Before fish are "produced" for the market, equipment such as fishing boats, nets, and poles are produced first. Imagine how expensive it would be to obtain fish for market without using these capital goods. Catching fish with one's hands is not an easy task. The price per fish would be very high if capital goods weren't used.

Forgoing Current Consumption

Whenever we use productive resources to make capital goods, we are implicitly forgoing current consumption. We are waiting for some time in the future to consume the fruits that will be reaped from the use of capital goods. In effect, when we forgo current consumption to invest in capital goods, we are engaging in an economic activity that is forward-looking—we do not get instant utility or satisfaction from our activity. Indeed, if we were to produce only consumer goods now and no capital goods, our capacity to produce consumer goods in the future would suffer. Here we see a trade-off situation.

The Trade-off Between Consumption Goods and Capital Goods

To have more consumer goods in the future, we must accept fewer consumer goods today. In other words, an opportunity cost is involved here. Every time we make a choice for more goods today, we incur an opportunity cost of fewer goods tomorrow, and every time we make a choice of more goods in the future, we incur an opportunity cost of fewer goods today. With the resources that we don't use to produce consumer goods for today, we invest in capital goods that will produce more consumer goods for us later. The trade-off is shown in Figure 2-5. On the left in panel (a), you can see this trade-off depicted as a production possibilities curve between capital goods and consumption goods.

Assume that we are willing to give up $1 trillion worth of consumption today. We will be at point A in the left-hand diagram of panel (a). This will allow the economy to grow. We will have more future consumption because we invested in more capital goods today. In the right-hand diagram of panel (a), we see two goods represented, food and recreation. The production possibilities curve will move outward if we collectively decide to restrict consumption each year and invest in capital goods.

In panel (b), we show the results of our willingness to forgo more current consumption. We move to point C, where we have many fewer consumer goods today but produce a lot

Panel (a)

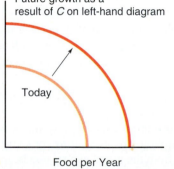

Future growth as a result of A on left-hand diagram

Today

Food per Year

Panel (b)

Future growth as a result of C on left-hand diagram

Today

Food per Year

FIGURE 2-5

Capital Goods and Growth
In panel (a), the nation chooses not to consume $1 trillion, so it invests that amount in capital goods. In panel (b), it chooses even more capital goods. The PPC moves even more to the right on the right-hand diagram in panel (b) as a result.

more capital goods. This leads to more future growth in this simplified model, and thus the production possibilities curve in the right-hand side of panel (b) shifts outward more than it did in the right-hand side of panel (a).

In other words, the more we give up today, the more we can have tomorrow, provided, of course, that the capital goods are productive in future periods and that society desires the consumer goods produced by this additional capital.

INTERNATIONAL EXAMPLE
Consumption Versus Capital Goods in the United States and Japan

The trade-off represented in Figure 2-5 on the production possibilities curve of capital versus consumption goods can be observed in real life when we compare different countries. The Japanese, for example, have chosen to devote more than twice the amount of resources each year to the production of capital goods than we have in the United States. Not surprisingly, the Japanese have until recently experienced economic growth at a much higher rate than the United States has. In effect, then, Japan is represented by panel (b) in Figure 2-5—choosing more capital goods—and America by panel (a)—choosing fewer capital goods.

FOR CRITICAL ANALYSIS: Does this analysis apply to the trade-off between consumption and human capital for you as an individual? If so, how? ●

CONCEPTS IN BRIEF

- The use of capital requires using productive resources to produce capital goods that will later be used to produce consumer goods.
- A trade-off is involved between current consumption and capital goods or, alternatively, between current consumption and future consumption because the more we invest in capital goods today, the greater the amount of consumer goods we can produce in the future and the smaller the amount of consumer goods we can produce today.

SPECIALIZATION AND GREATER PRODUCTIVITY

Specialization
The division of productive activities among persons and regions so that no one individual or one area is totally self-sufficient. An individual may specialize, for example, in law or medicine. A nation may specialize in the production of coffee, computers, or cameras.

Specialization involves working at a relatively well-defined, limited endeavor, such as accounting or teaching. It involves a division of labor among different individuals and regions. Most individuals, in fact, do specialize. For example, you could change the oil in your car if you wanted to. Typically, though, you take your car to a garage and let the mechanic change the oil. You benefit by letting the garage mechanic specialize in changing the oil and in doing other repairs on your car. The specialist will get the job finished sooner than you could and has the proper equipment to make the job go more smoothly. Specialization usually leads to greater productivity, not only for each individual but also for the nation.

Absolute Advantage

Absolute advantage
The ability to produce a good or service at an "absolutely" lower cost, usually measured in units of labor or resource input required to produce one unit of the good or service.

Specialization occurs because different individuals and different nations have different skills. Sometimes it seems that some individuals are better at doing everything than anyone else. A president of a large company might be able to type better than any of the typists, file better than any of the file clerks, and wash windows better than any of the window washers. The president has an **absolute advantage** in all of these endeavors—he uses fewer labor hours for each task than anyone else in the company. The president does not, however, spend his time doing those other activities. Why not? Because he is being paid the most for undertaking the president's managerial duties. The president specializes in one particular task in spite of having an absolute advantage in all tasks. Indeed, absolute advantage is irrelevant in predicting how he uses his time; only *comparative advantage* matters.

Comparative Advantage

Comparative advantage is the ability to perform an activity at the lowest opportunity cost. You have a comparative advantage in one activity whenever you have the lowest opportunity cost of performing that activity. Comparative advantage is always a *relative* concept. You may be able to change the oil in your car; you might even be able to change it faster than the local mechanic. But if the opportunity cost you face by changing the oil exceeds the mechanic's opportunity cost, the mechanic has a comparative advantage in changing the oil. The mechanic faces a lower opportunity cost for that activity.

You may be convinced that everybody can do everything better than you. In this extreme situation, do you still have a comparative advantage? The answer is yes. What you need to do to discover your comparative advantage is to find a job in which your *disadvantage* relative to others is the smallest. You do not have to be a mathematical genius to figure this out. The market tells you very clearly by offering you the highest income for the job for which you have the smallest disadvantage compared to others. Stated differently, to find your comparative advantage no matter how much better everybody else can do the jobs that you want to do, you simply find which job maximizes your income.

The coaches of sports teams are constantly faced with determining each player's comparative advantage. Babe Ruth was originally one of the best pitchers in professional baseball when he played for the Boston Red Sox. After he was traded to the New York Yankees, the owner and the coach decided to make him an outfielder, even though he was a better pitcher than anyone else on the team roster. They wanted "The Babe" to concentrate on his hitting. Good pitchers do not bring in as many fans as home-run kings. Babe Ruth's comparative advantage was clearly in hitting homers rather than practicing and developing his pitching game.

Scarcity, Self-Interest, and Specialization

In Chapter 1, you learned about the assumption of rational self-interest. To repeat, for the purposes of our analyses we assume that individuals are rational in that they will do what is in their own self-interest. They will not consciously carry out actions that will make them worse off. In this chapter, you learned that scarcity requires people to make choices. We assume that they make choices based on their self-interest. When they make these choices, they attempt to maximize benefits net of opportunity cost. In so doing, individuals choose their comparative advantage and end up specializing. Ultimately, when people specialize, they increase the money income they make and therefore become richer. When all individuals and businesses specialize simultaneously, the gains are seen in greater material well-being. With any given set of resources, specialization will result in higher output.

Comparative advantage
The ability to produce a good or service at a lower opportunity cost compared to other producers.

INTERNATIONAL EXAMPLE
Why Foreign Graduate Students Specialize When Studying in the United States

Specialization is evident in the fields of endeavor that foreign students choose when they come to the United States for graduate studies. Consider the following statistics: More than

60 percent of U.S. doctorates in engineering and 55 percent of those in mathematics, computer science, and the physical sciences are earned by foreign-born students. Yet foreign nationals are awarded relatively few advanced degrees in business, law, or medicine. The reason has nothing to do with intelligence or giftedness; it is simply that many more of the best American students choose schools in these professional fields rather than ones offering science and engineering programs.

Why does this specialization occur? For American students, the greatest returns for about the same effort come from business, law, and medicine. In contrast, foreign-born graduate students face fewer language and cultural obstacles (and hence better job prospects) if they choose technical subjects.

When students from foreign countries come to American graduate schools to obtain their Ph.D. degrees, more than 70 percent of them remain in the United States after graduation, thereby augmenting America's supply of engineers and scientists. Such specialization has helped the United States maintain its leadership in both the technoscientific and sociocultural areas.

FOR CRITICAL ANALYSIS: What type of capital do foreign-born students bring with them to the United States? ●

THE DIVISION OF LABOR

Division of labor
The segregation of a resource into different specific tasks; for example, one automobile worker puts on bumpers, another doors, and so on.

In any firm that includes specialized human and nonhuman resources, there is a **division of labor** among those resources. The best-known example of all time comes from one of the earliest and perhaps most famous economists, Adam Smith, who in *The Wealth of Nations* (1776) illustrated the benefits of a division of labor in the making of pins, as depicted in the following example:

> One man draws out the wire, another straightens it, a third cuts it, a fourth points it, a fifth grinds it at the top for receiving the head; to make the head requires two or three distinct operations; to put it on is a peculiar business, to whiten the pins is another; it is even a trade by itself to put them into the paper.

Making pins this way allowed 10 workers without very much skill to make almost 48,000 pins "of a middling size" in a day. One worker, toiling alone, could have made perhaps 20 pins a day; therefore, 10 workers could have produced 200. Division of labor allowed for an increase in the daily output of the pin factory from 200 to 48,000! (Smith did not attribute all of the gain to the division of labor according to talent but credited also the use of machinery and the fact that less time was spent shifting from task to task.)

What we are discussing here involves a division of the resource called labor into different kinds of labor. The different kinds of labor are organized in such a way as to increase the amount of output possible from the fixed resources available. We can therefore talk about an organized division of labor within a firm leading to increased output.

COMPARATIVE ADVANTAGE AND TRADE AMONG NATIONS

Though most of our analysis of absolute advantage, comparative advantage, and specialization has dealt with individuals, it is equally applicable to nations. First consider the United States. The Plains states have a comparative advantage in the production of grains and other agricultural goods. The states to the north and east tend to specialize in industrialized production, such as automobiles. Not surprisingly, grains are shipped from the

Plains states to the northern states, and automobiles are shipped in the reverse direction. Such specialization and trade allow for higher incomes and standards of living. If both the Plains states and the northern states were politically defined as separate nations, the same analysis would still hold, but we would call it international trade. Indeed, Europe is comparable to the United States in area and population, but instead of one nation, Europe has 15. What in America we call *interstate* trade, in Europe they call *international* trade. There is no difference, however, in the economic results—both yield greater economic efficiency and higher average incomes.

Political problems that do not normally arise within a particular nation often do between nations. For example, if California avocado growers develop a cheaper method than growers in southern Florida to produce a tastier avocado, the Florida growers will lose out. They cannot do much about the situation except try to lower their own costs of production or improve their product. If avocado growers in Mexico, however, develop a cheaper method to produce better-tasting avocados, both California and Florida growers can (and likely will) try to raise political barriers that will prevent Mexican avocado growers from freely selling their product in America. U.S. avocado growers will use such arguments as "unfair" competition and loss of American jobs. In so doing, they are only partly right: Avocado-growing jobs may decline in America, but jobs will not necessarily decline overall. If the argument of U.S. avocado growers had any validity, every time a region in the United States developed a better way to produce a product manufactured somewhere else in the country, employment in America would decline. That has never happened and never will.

When nations specialize where they have a comparative advantage and then trade with the rest of the world, the average standard of living in the world rises. In effect, international trade allows the world to move from inside the global production possibilities curve toward the curve itself, thereby improving worldwide economic efficiency.

THINKING CRITICALLY ABOUT THE MEDIA

International Trade

If you watch enough news on TV or frequently read the popular press, you get a distinct impression that international trade is somehow different from trade within our borders. At any given time, the United States is either at economic war with Japan or other countries in Asia or we are fighting with the European Union over whether American films should be allowed to dominate cinema offerings there. International economics is just like any other type of economics; trade is just another economic activity. Indeed, one can think of international trade as a production process that transforms goods that we sell to other countries (exports) into what we buy from other countries (imports). International trade is a mutually beneficial exchange that occurs across political borders. If you imagine a world that was just one country, trade would still exist worldwide, but it would not be called international trade.

CONCEPTS IN BRIEF

- With a given set of resources, specialization results in higher output; in other words, there are gains to specialization in terms of greater material well-being.
- Individuals and nations specialize in their areas of comparative advantage in order to reap the gains of specialization.
- Comparative advantages are found by determining which activities have the lowest opportunity cost—that is, which activities yield the highest return for the time and resources used.
- A division of labor occurs when different workers are assigned different tasks. Together, the workers produce a desired product.

Risk Reduction and the Value of a Human Life

Concepts Applied: Scarcity, opportunity costs, trade-offs

Are some lives worth more than others? The U.S. Department of Transportation values a human life at $2.6 million. Researchers examine the wage premiums that must be paid to the workers in dangerous jobs, such as certain construction work, to determine the value of a life.

How much is a human life worth? That is the question that researchers both in and out of government have had to grapple with ever since government began setting safety standards. None of us act as if life is priceless, yet we could virtually eliminate death in automobile accidents by implementing and enforcing a 5-mile-an-hour speed limit. Most people are willing to trade off some probability of injury or death in an automobile accident against the opportunity to travel faster and hence use less time in transit (in other words, to lower the opportunity cost of travel). As in almost everything else, there is an opportunity cost to preventing accidental death.

How to Value a Life

To make decisions about the net benefits of accident-avoiding government regulation, we need to estimate the value of a human life. One way to do so is simply to look at the lost earnings potential of someone who might die. This method is often used in courtroom battles between the survivors of accident victims and insurance companies.

Most people would, in contrast, be ready (if not able) to pay more than their lost future earnings to avoid death or injury. This willingness-to-pay methodology has been used to estimate the value of human lives in different countries. Researchers examine, for example, how much

of a premium workers in dangerous jobs (construction workers on high steel beams, for example) have to be paid to compensate them for the increased probability of death or injury. The U.S. Department of Transportation examined 50 such studies and came up with a value of human life ranging from $1 million to $4 million. It settled on the figure of $2.6 million. Using similar research methods, other countries have come up with similar numbers, as you can see in Table 2-1.

Opportunity Cost

Looking at Table 2-1, it seems as though some lives are worth more than others. Philosophically, this is obviously absurd; but from an economic point of view, most of the differences are a function of the differences in average annual income per person. In richer countries, individuals can obviously pay more to improve safety because they earn more.

When Prevention Is Not Worth the Cost

Given that we live in a world of scarcity, the use of resources for the prevention of injury or death necessarily

TABLE 2-1

The Value of a Human Life

Country	Value (in U.S. dollars)
United States	2,600,000
Sweden	1,236,000
New Zealand	1,150,000
Britain	1,100,000
Germany	928,000
Belgium	400,000
France	350,000
Netherlands	130,000

Source: R. Willike and S. Beyhoff, "Economic Cost of Road Accidents," as derived from national transportation departments in various countries, cited in "The Price of Life," *The Economist*, December 4, 1993, p. 74.

involves an opportunity cost. The Harvard School of Public Health's Center for Risk Analysis undertook a "lifesaving study" that examined whether we are spending too much on certain types of death and injury prevention. The median cost of a year of life saved by various techniques is represented in Table 2-2. Be aware that the table does not show the cost per life saved but rather the cost *per year* of life saved. This means that radiation control does save lives, but at the cost of about $27 million *per year of life saved.*

The Actual Trade-offs Involved

So trade-offs are clearly involved here. According to the risk analysis study, if the $21.3 billion a year spent on 185 major lifesaving programs were reallocated so that more went to the most beneficial measures, 60,000 deaths a year could be averted.

Consider one possibility. The Environmental Protection Agency proposed rules in 1995 that would increase the cost of paper production but save the lives of some workers engaged in that industry. The estimated cost: $1.9 million per life saved. In contrast, cervical cancer screenings every four years would cost only $10,000 per life saved.

Real Risk Is Falling

Crime and automobile and airplane accidents are in the news daily, but does this mean that the United States is becoming a more dangerous place in which to live? Not according to the National Safety Council, which estimated that the accidental death rate per 100,000 people in the United States fell from about 95 in 1910 to around 30

TABLE 2-2
The Cost of Saving a Year of Life

Preventive Measure	Cost per Year of Life Saved (in U.S. dollars)
Childhood immunization	negligible
Flu shot	600
Water chlorination	4,000
Breast cancer screening	17,000
Home radon control	141,000
Asbestos control	1,900,000
Radiation control	27,400,000

Source: Harvard University, School of Public Health.

today. Though this does not mean that all is well in America, the nation is not as unsafe as people normally think. Although a larger percentage of the population is subject to death or injury due to crime today than in the past, a smaller percentage of the population dies in automobile and air transportation accidents. Moreover, a much smaller percentage of the population suffers fatal injuries on the job than ever before.

FOR CRITICAL ANALYSIS
1. Why is opportunity cost such an important concept in analyzing government programs to save lives?
2. What activities do you engage in to reduce the chances of your premature death? What activities do you engage in that increase such chances?

CHAPTER SUMMARY

1. All societies at all times face the universal problem of scarcity because we cannot obtain everything we want from nature without sacrifice. Thus scarcity and poverty are not synonymous. Even the richest persons face scarcity because they also have to make choices among alternatives.

2. The resources we use to produce desired goods and services can be classified into land, labor, physical and human capital, and entrepreneurship.

3. Goods are all things from which individuals derive satisfaction. Economic goods are those for which the desired quantity exceeds the amount that is directly available from nature at a zero price. The goods that we want are not necessarily those that we need. The term *need* is undefinable in economics, whereas humans have unlimited *wants,* which are defined as the goods and services on which we place a positive value.

4. We measure the cost of anything by what has to be given up in order to have it. This cost is called opportunity cost.

5. The trade-offs we face as individuals and those we face as a society can be represented graphically by a production possibilities curve (PPC). This curve shows the maximum quantity of one good or service that can be produced, given a specific quantity of another, from a given set of resources over a specified period of time, usually one year.

6. Because resources are specialized, production possibilities curves bow outward. This means that each additional increment of one good can be obtained only by giving up more and more of the other goods. This is called the law of increasing relative cost.

7. It is impossible to be outside the production possibilities curve, but we can be inside it. When we are, we are in a situation of unemployment, inefficiently organized resources, or some combination of the two.

8. There is a trade-off between consumption goods and capital goods. The more resources we devote to capital goods, the more consumption goods we can normally have in the future (and less currently). This is because more capital goods allow the economy to grow, thereby moving the production possibilities curve outward.

9. One finds one's comparative advantage by looking at the activity that has the lowest opportunity cost. That is, one's comparative advantage lies in the activity that generates the highest income. By specializing in one's comparative advantage, one is assured of reaping the gains of specialization.

10. Division of labor occurs when workers are assigned different tasks.

DISCUSSION OF PREVIEW QUESTIONS

1. Do affluent people face the problem of scarcity?
Scarcity is a relative concept and exists because wants are great relative to the means of satisfying those wants (wealth or income). Even though affluent people have relatively and absolutely high levels of income or wealth, they nevertheless typically want more than they can have (in luxury goods, power, prestige, and so on).

2. Fresh air may be consumed at no charge, but is it free of cost to society?
Individuals are not charged a price for the use of air. Yet truly fresh air is not free to society. If a good were free to society, every person would be able to use all that he or she wanted to use; no one would have to sacrifice anything in order to use that good, and people would not have to compete for it. In the United States, different groups compete for air; for example, environmentalists and concerned citizens compete with automobile drivers and factories for clean air.

3. Why does the scarcity problem force people to consider opportunity costs?
Individuals have limited incomes; as a consequence, an expenditure on an automobile necessarily precludes expenditures on other goods and services. The same is true for society, which also faces the scarcity problem; if society allocates specific resources to the production of a steel mill, those same resources cannot be allocated elsewhere. Because resources are limited, society is forced to decide how to allocate its available resources; scarcity means that the cost of allocating resources to produce specific goods is ultimately assessed in terms of other goods that are necessarily sacrificed. Because there are millions of ways in which the resources allocated to a steel mill might otherwise be allocated, one is forced to consider the *highest-valued* alternative. We define the opportunity cost of a good as its highest-valued alternative; the opportunity cost of the steel mill to society is the highest-valued output that those same resources could otherwise have produced.

4. Can a "free" college education ever be truly free?
Suppose that you were given a college education without having to pay any fees whatsoever. You could say that you were receiving a free education. But someone is paying for your education because you are using scarce resources—buildings, professors' time, electricity for lighting, etc. The opportunity

cost of your education is certainly not zero, so in that sense it is not free. Furthermore, by going to college, you are giving up the ability to earn income during that time period. Therefore, there is an opportunity cost to your attending classes and studying. You can approximate that opportunity cost by estimating what your current after-tax income would be if you were working instead of going to school.

PROBLEMS

(Answers to the odd-numbered problems appear at the back of the book.)

2-1. The following sets of numbers represent hypothetical production possibilities for a nation in 1998. Plot these points on graph paper.

Butter	Guns
4	0
3	1.6
2	2.4
1	2.8
0	3.0

Does the law of increasing relative cost seem to hold? Why? On the same graph, plot and draw the production possibilities curve that will represent 10 percent economic growth.

2-2. There are 150,000 conscripts (draftees) in the French army, each paid $2,000 a year. The average salary of each conscript prior to military service was $18,500 per year. What does it cost for conscripts in France each year?

2-3. Answer the questions using the following information.

Employee	Daily Work Effort	Production
Ann Jones	4 hours	8 jackets
	4 hours	12 ties
Ned Lopez	4 hours	8 jackets
	4 hours	12 ties
Total daily output		16 jackets
		24 ties

a. Who has an absolute advantage in jacket production?
b. Who has a comparative advantage in tie production?
c. Will Jones and Lopez specialize?
d. If they specialize, what will total output equal?

2-4. Two countries, Workland and Playland, have similar populations and identical production possibilities curves but different preferences. The production possibilities combinations are as follows:

Point	Capital Goods	Consumption Goods
A	0	20
B	1	19 — play
C	2	17
D	3	14
E	4	10 — work
F	5	5

Playland is located at point *B* on the PPC, and Workland is located at point *E*. Assume that this situation continues into the future and that all other things remain the same.

a. What is Workland's opportunity cost of capital goods in terms of consumption goods?
b. What is Playland's opportunity cost of capital goods in terms of consumption goods?
c. How would the PPCs of Workland and Playland be expected to compare to each other 50 years in the future?

2-5. Which of the following are part of the opportunity cost of going to a football game in town instead of watching it on TV at home? Explain why.

a. The expense of lunch in a restaurant prior to the football game.

b. The value of one hour of sleep lost because of a traffic jam after the game.

c. The expense of a babysitter for your children if they are too young to go to a football game.

2-6. Assume that your economics and English exams are scheduled for the same day. How would you determine how much time you should spend study-ing for each exam? Does the grade you are cur-rently receiving in each course affect your deci-sion? Why or why not?

2-7. Some people argue that air is not an economic good. If you agree with this statement, explain why. If you disagree, explain why. (Hint: Is all air the same?)

COMPUTER-ASSISTED INSTRUCTION

If you are given a production possibilities table, can you calculate the opportunity cost of successive units of one good in terms of forgone units of the other? By requiring specific calculations, the concept of opportunity cost is revealed.

Complete problem and answer appear on disk.

READING AND WORKING WITH GRAPHS

A graph is a visual representation of the relationship between variables. In this appendix, we'll stick to just two variables: an **independent variable,** which can change in value freely, and a **dependent variable,** which changes only as a result of changes in the value of the independent variable. For example, if nothing else is changing in your life, your weight depends on the amount of food you eat. Food is the independent variable and weight the dependent variable.

A table is a list of numerical values showing the relationship between two (or more) variables. Any table can be converted into a graph, which is a visual representation of that list. Once you understand how a table can be converted to a graph, you will understand what graphs are and how to construct and use them.

Consider a practical example. A conservationist may try to convince you that driving at lower highway speeds will help you conserve gas. Table A-1 shows the relationship between speed—the independent variable—and the distance you can go on a gallon of gas at that speed—the dependent variable. This table does show a pattern of sorts. As the data in the first column get larger in value, the data in the second column get smaller.

Now let's take a look at the different ways in which variables can be related.

DIRECT AND INVERSE RELATIONSHIPS

Two variables can be related in different ways, some simple, others more complex. For example, a person's weight and height are often related. If we measured the height and weight of thousands of people, we would surely find that taller people tend to weigh more than shorter people. That is, we would discover that there is a **direct relationship** between height and weight. By this we simply mean that an *increase* in one variable is usually associated with an *increase* in the related variable. This can easily be seen in panel (a) of Figure A-1.

Let's look at another simple way in which two variables can be related. Much evidence indicates that as the price of a specific commodity rises, the amount purchased decreases—there is an **inverse relationship** between the variable's price per unit and quantity purchased. A table listing the data for this relationship would indicate that for higher and higher prices, smaller and smaller quantities would be purchased. We see this relationship in panel (b) of Figure A-1.

Independent variable
A variable whose value is determined independently of, or outside, the equation under study.

Dependent variable
A variable whose value changes according to changes in the value of one or more independent variables.

TABLE A-1
Gas Mileage as a Function of Driving Speed

Miles per Hour	Miles per Gallon
45	25
50	24
55	23
60	21
65	19
70	16
75	13

Direct relationship
A relationship between two variables that is positive, meaning that an increase in one variable is associated with an increase in the other and a decrease in one variable is associated with a decrease in the other.

Inverse relationship
A relationship between two variables that is negative, meaning that an increase in one variable is associated with a decrease in the other and a decrease in one variable is associated with an increase in the other.

FIGURE A-1
Relationships

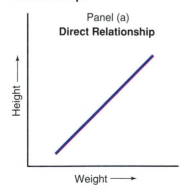

Panel (a)
Direct Relationship

Height — Weight —

Panel (b)
Inverse Relationship

Price — Quantity Purchased —

CONSTRUCTING A GRAPH

Let us now examine how to construct a graph to illustrate a relationship between two variables.

A Number Line

Number line
A line that can be divided into segments of equal length, each associated with a number.

The first step is to become familiar with what is called a **number line.** One is shown in Figure A-2. There are two things that you should know about it.

1. The points on the line divide the line into equal segments.
2. The numbers associated with the points on the line increase in value from left to right; saying it the other way around, the numbers decrease in value from right to left. However you say it, what we're describing is formally called an *ordered set of points*.

On the number line, we have shown the line segments—that is, the distance from 0 to 10 or the distance between 30 and 40. They all appear to be equal and, indeed, are equal to $\frac{1}{2}$ inch. When we use a distance to represent a quantity, such as barrels of oil, graphically, we are *scaling* the number line. In the example shown, the distance between 0 and 10 might represent 10 barrels of oil, or the distance from 0 to 40 might represent 40 barrels. Of course, the scale may differ on different number lines. For example, a distance of 1 inch could represent 10 units on one number line but 5,000 units on another. Notice that on our number line, points to the left of 0 correspond to negative numbers and points to the right of 0 correspond to positive numbers.

Of course, we can also construct a vertical number line. Consider the one in Figure A-3. As we move up this vertical number line, the numbers increase in value; conversely, as we descend, they decrease in value. Below 0 the numbers are negative, and above 0 the numbers are positive. And as on the horizontal number line, all the line segments are equal. This line is divided into segments such that the distance between -2 and -1 is the same as the distance between 0 and 1.

Combining Vertical and Horizontal Number Lines

By drawing the horizontal and vertical lines on the same sheet of paper, we are able to express the relationships between variables graphically. We do this in Figure A-4.

FIGURE A-3
Vertical Number Line

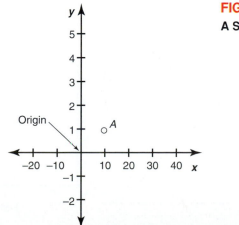

FIGURE A-4
A Set of Coordinate Axes

We draw them (1) so that they intersect at each other's 0 point and (2) so that they are perpendicular to each other. The result is a set of coordinate axes, where each line is called an *axis*. When we have two axes, they span a plane.

For one number line, you need only one number to specify any point on the line; equivalently, when you see a point on the line, you know that it represents one number or one value. With a coordinate value system, you need two numbers to specify a single point in the plane; when you see a single point on a graph, you know that it represents two numbers or two values.

The basic things that you should know about a coordinate number system are that the vertical number line is referred to as the **y axis,** the horizontal number line is referred to as the **x axis,** and the point of intersection of the two lines is referred to as the **origin.**

Any point such as *A* in Figure A-4 represents two numbers—a value of *x* and a value of *y*. But we know more than that; we also know that point *A* represents a positive value of *y* because it is above the *x* axis, and we know that it represents a positive value of *x* because it is to the right of the *y* axis.

Point *A* represents a "paired observation" of the variables *x* and *y;* in particular, in Figure A-4, *A* represents an observation of the pair of values $x = 10$ and $y = 1$. Every point in the coordinate system corresponds to a paired observation of *x* and *y*, which can be simply written (x, y)—the *x* value is always specified first, then the *y* value. When we give the values associated with the position of point *A* in the coordinate number system, we are in effect giving the coordinates of that point. *A*'s coordinates are $x = 10$, $y = 1$, or $(10, 1)$.

GRAPHING NUMBERS IN A TABLE

Consider Table A-2. Column 1 shows different prices for T-shirts, and column 2 gives the number of T-shirts purchased per week at these prices. Notice the pattern of these numbers. As the price of T-shirts falls, the number of T-shirts purchased per week increases. Therefore, an inverse relationship exists between these two variables, and as soon as we represent it on a graph, you will be able to see the relationship. We can graph this relationship using a coordinate number system—a vertical and horizontal number line for each of these two variables. Such a graph is shown in panel (b) of Figure A-5.

y axis
The vertical axis in a graph.

x axis
The horizontal axis in a graph.

Origin
The intersection of the *y* axis and the *x* axis in a graph.

TABLE A-2

T-Shirts Purchased

(1) Price of T-Shirts	(2) Number of T-Shirts Purchased per Week
$10	20
9	30
8	40
7	50
6	60
5	70

FIGURE A-5

Graphing the Relationship Between T-Shirts Purchased and Price

Panel (a)

Price per T-Shirt	T-Shirts Purchased per Week	Point on Graph
$10	20	*I* (20, 10)
9	30	*J* (30, 9)
8	40	*K* (40, 8)
7	50	*L* (50, 7)
6	60	*M* (60, 6)
5	70	*N* (70, 5)

Panel (b)

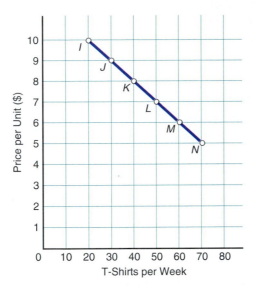

FIGURE A-6

Connecting the Observation Points

In economics, it is conventional to put dollar values on the *y* axis. We therefore construct a vertical number line for price and a horizontal number line, the *x* axis, for quantity of T-shirts purchased per week. The resulting coordinate system allows the plotting of each of the paired observation points; in panel (a), we repeat Table A-2, with a column added expressing these points in paired-data (*x, y*) form. For example, point *J* is the paired observation (30, 9). It indicates that when the price of a T-shirt is $9, 30 will be purchased per week.

If it were possible to sell parts of a T-shirt ($\frac{1}{2}$ or $\frac{1}{20}$ of a shirt), we would have observations at every possible price. That is, we would be able to connect our paired observations, represented as lettered points. Let's assume that we can make T-shirts perfectly divisible. We would then have a line that connects these points, as shown in the graph in Figure A-6.

In short, we have now represented the data from the table in the form of a graph. Note that an inverse relationship between two variables shows up on a graph as a line or curve that slopes *downward* from left to right. (You might as well get used to the idea that economists call a straight line a "curve" even though it may not curve at all. Much of economists' data turn out to be curves, so they refer to everything represented graphically, even straight lines, as curves.)

THE SLOPE OF A LINE (A LINEAR CURVE)

An important property of a curve represented on a graph is its *slope*. Consider Figure A-7 on page 42, which represents the quantities of shoes per week that a seller is willing to offer at different prices. Note that in panel (a) of Figure A-7, as in Figure A-5, we have expressed the coordinates of the points in parentheses in paired-data form.

Slope

The change in the *y* value divided by the corresponding change in the *x* value of a curve; the "incline" of the curve.

The **slope** of a line is defined as the change in the *y* values divided by the corresponding change in the *x* values as we move along the line. Let's move from point *E* to point *D* in panel (b) of Figure A-7. As we move, we note that the change in the *y* values, which is the change in price, is +$20, because we have moved from a price of $20 to a price of $40 per pair. As we move from *E* to *D*, the change in the *x* values is +80; the number of pairs of shoes willingly offered per week rises from 80 to 160 pairs. The slope calculated as a change in the *y* values divided by the change in the *x* values is therefore

$$\frac{20}{80} = \frac{1}{4}$$

FIGURE A-7

A Positively Sloped Curve

Panel (a)

Price per Pair	Pairs of Shoes Offered per Week	Point on Graph
$100	400	A (400, 100)
80	320	B (320, 80)
60	240	C (240, 60)
40	160	D (160, 40)
20	80	E (80, 20)

Panel (b)

It may be helpful for you to think of slope as a "rise" (movement in the vertical direction) over a "run" (movement in the horizontal direction). We show this abstractly in Figure A-8. The slope is measured by the amount of rise divided by the amount of run. In the example in Figure A-8, and of course in Figure A-7, the amount of rise is positive and so is the amount of run. That's because it's a direct relationship. We show an inverse relationship in Figure A-9. The slope is still equal to the rise divided by the run, but in this case the rise and the run have opposite signs because the curve slopes downward. That means that the slope will have to be negative and that we are dealing with an inverse relationship.

Now let's calculate the slope for a different part of the curve in panel (b) of Figure A-7. We will find the slope as we move from point B to point A. Again, we note that the slope, or rise over run, from B to A equals

$$\frac{20}{80} = \frac{1}{4}$$

A specific property of a straight line is that its slope is the same between any two points; in other words, the slope is constant at all points on a straight line in a graph.

We conclude that for our example in Figure A-7, the relationship between the price of a pair of shoes and the number of pairs of shoes willingly offered per week is *linear,* which simply means "in a straight line," and our calculations indicate a constant slope. Moreover, we calculate a direct relationship between these two variables, which turns out to be an

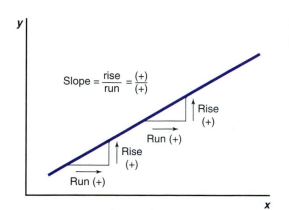

FIGURE A-8

Figuring Positive Slope

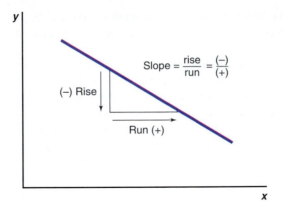

upward-sloping (from left to right) curve. Upward-sloping curves have positive slopes—in this case, it is $+\frac{1}{4}$.

We know that an inverse relationship between two variables shows up as a downward-sloping curve—rise over run will be a negative slope because the rise and run have opposite signs as shown in Figure A-9. When we see a negative slope, we know that increases in one variable are associated with decreases in the other. Therefore, we say that downward-sloping curves have negative slopes. Can you verify that the slope of the graph representing the relationship between T-shirt prices and the quantity of T-shirts purchased per week in Figure A-6 is $-\frac{1}{10}$?

Slopes of Nonlinear Curves

The graph presented in Figure A-10 indicates a *nonlinear* relationship between two variables, total profits and output per unit of time. Inspection of this graph indicates that at first, increases in output lead to increases in total profits; that is, total profits rise as output increases. But beyond some output level, further increases in output cause decreases in total profits.

Can you see how this curve rises at first, reaches a peak at point C, and then falls? This curve relating total profits to output levels appears mountain-shaped.

Considering that this curve is nonlinear (it is obviously not a straight line), should we expect a constant slope when we compute changes in y divided by corresponding changes in x in moving from one point to another? A quick inspection, even without specific numbers, should lead us to conclude that the slopes of lines joining different points in this curve, such as between A and B, B and C, or C and D, will *not* be the same. The curve slopes upward (in a positive direction) for some values and downward (in a negative direction) for

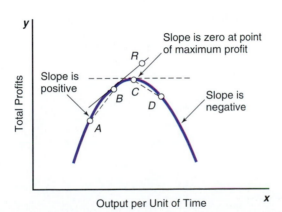

other values. In fact, the slope of the line between any two points on this curve will be different from the slope of the line between any two other points. Each slope will be different as we move along the curve.

Instead of using a line between two points to discuss slope, mathematicians and economists prefer to discuss the slope *at a particular point*. The slope at a point on the curve, such as point B in the graph in Figure A-10, is the slope of a line *tangent* to that point. A tangent line is a straight line that touches a curve at only one point. For example, it might be helpful to think of the tangent at B as the straight line that just "kisses" the curve at point B.

To calculate the slope of a tangent line, you need to have some additional information besides the two values of the point of tangency. For example, in Figure A-10, if we knew that the point R also lay on the tangent line and we knew the two values of that point, we could calculate the slope of the tangent line. We could calculate rise over run between points B and R, and the result would be the slope of the line tangent to the one point B on the curve.

APPENDIX SUMMARY

1. Direct relationships involve a dependent variable changing in the same direction as the change in the independent variable.
2. Inverse relationships involve the dependent variable changing in the opposite direction of the change in the independent variable.
3. When we draw a graph showing the relationship between two economic variables, we are holding all other things constant (the Latin term for which is *ceteris paribus*).
4. We obtain a set of coordinates by putting vertical and horizontal number lines together. The vertical line is called the y axis; the horizontal line, the x axis.

5. The slope of any linear (straight-line) curve is the change in the y values divided by the corresponding change in the x values as we move along the line. Otherwise stated, the slope is calculated as the amount of rise over the amount of run, where rise is movement in the vertical direction and run is movement in the horizontal direction.
6. The slope of a nonlinear curve changes; it is positive when the curve is rising and negative when the curve is falling. At a maximum or minimum point, the slope of the nonlinear curve is zero.

PROBLEMS

(The answer to Problem A-1 appears at the back of the book.)

A-1. Complete the schedule and plot the following function:

$y = 3x$

y	x
	4
	3
	2
	1
	0
	−1
	−2
	−3
	−4

A-2. Complete the schedule and plot the following function:

$y = x^2$

y	x
	4
	3
	2
	1
	0
	−1
	−2
	−3
	−4

CHAPTER 3

DEMAND AND SUPPLY

During the 1974–1975 academic year, foreign students comprised 1.5 percent of all college students. Today, foreign students represent over 3 percent of all college students—an increase of more than 100 percent in their relative proportions. During the same time period, average grades have risen dramatically, particularly at our nation's best-known private universities. Finally, some private universities are actually starting to give discounts on tuition. To understand how these seemingly unrelated phenomena are actually closely related, you will need the tools of supply and demand analysis.

PREVIEW QUESTIONS

1. Why are relative prices important in understanding the law of demand?

2. How can we distinguish between a change in *demand* and a change in *quantity demanded?*

3. Why is there normally a direct relationship between price and quantity supplied (other things being equal)?

4. Why will the market clearing price occur at the intersection of the supply and demand curves rather than at a higher or lower price?

Did You Know That . . . more than 22 million people currently own portable cellular phones? This is a huge jump from the mere 200,000 who owned them in 1985. Since 1992, two out of every three new telephone numbers have been assigned to cellular phones. There are several reasons for the growth of cellular phones, not the least being the dramatic reduction in both price and size due to improved and cheaper computer chips that go into making them. There is something else at work, though. It has to do with crime. In a recent survey, 46 percent of new cellular phone users said that personal safety was the main reason they bought a portable phone. In Florida, for example, most cellular phone companies allow users simply to dial *FHP to reach the Florida Highway Patrol. The rush to cellular phones is worldwide. Over the past decade, sales have grown by nearly 50 percent every year outside the United States.

We could attempt to explain the phenomenon by saying that more people like to use portable phones. But that explanation is neither satisfying nor entirely accurate. If we use the economist's primary set of tools, *demand and supply,* we will have a better understanding of the cellular phone explosion, as well as many other phenomena in our world. Demand and supply are two ways of categorizing the influences on the price of goods that you buy and the quantities available. As such, demand and supply form the basis of virtually all economic analysis of the world around us.

As you will see throughout this text, the operation of the forces of demand and supply take place in *markets.* A **market** is an abstract concept referring to all the arrangements individuals have for exchanging with one another. Goods and services are sold in markets, such as the automobile market, the health market, and the compact disc market. Workers offer their services in the labor market. Companies, or firms, buy workers' labor services in the labor market. Firms also buy other inputs in order to produce the goods and services that you buy as a consumer. Firms purchase machines, buildings, and land. These markets are in operation at all times. One of the most important activities in these markets is the setting of the prices of all of the inputs and outputs that are bought and sold in our complicated economy. To understand the determination of prices, you first need to look at the law of demand.

Market
All of the arrangements that individuals have for exchanging with one another. Thus we can speak of the labor market, the automobile market, and the credit market.

THE LAW OF DEMAND

Demand has a special meaning in economics. It refers to the quantities of specific goods or services that individuals, taken singly or as a group, will purchase at various possible prices, other things being constant. We can therefore talk about the demand for microprocessor chips, French fries, compact disc players, children, and criminal activities.

Associated with the concept of demand is the **law of demand,** which can be stated as follows:

> When the price of a good goes up, people buy less of it, other things being equal. When the price of a good goes down, people buy more of it, other things being equal.

The law of demand tells us that the quantity demanded of any commodity is inversely related to its price, other things being equal. In an inverse relationship, one variable moves up in value when the other moves down. The law of demand states that a change in price causes a change in the quantity demanded in the *opposite* direction.

Notice that we tacked onto the end of the law of demand the statement "other things being equal." We referred to this in Chapter 1 as the *ceteris paribus* assumption. It means, for example, that when we predict that people will buy fewer CD-ROM players if their

Demand
A schedule of how much of a good or service people will purchase at any price during a specified time period, other things being constant.

Law of demand
The observation that there is a negative, or inverse, relationship between the price of any good or service and the quantity demanded, holding other factors constant.

price goes up, we are holding constant the price of all other goods in the economy as well as people's incomes. Implicitly, therefore, if we are assuming that no other prices change when we examine the price behavior of CD-ROM players, we are looking at the *relative* price of CD-ROM players.

The law of demand is supported by millions of observations of people's behavior in the marketplace. Theoretically, it can be derived from an economic model based on rational behavior, as was discussed in Chapter 1. Basically, if nothing else changes and the price of a good falls, the lower price induces us to buy more over a certain period of time because we can enjoy additional net gains that were unavailable at the higher price. For the most part, if you examine your own behavior, you will see that it generally follows the law of demand.

Relative Prices Versus Money Prices

Relative price
The price of a commodity expressed in terms of another commodity.

Money price
The price that we observe today, expressed in today's dollars. Also called the *absolute, nominal,* or *current price.*

The **relative price** of any commodity is its price in terms of another commodity. The price that you pay in dollars and cents for any good or service at any point in time is called its **money price.** Consider an example that you might hear quite often around parents and grandparents. "When I bought my first new car, it cost only fifteen hundred dollars." The implication, of course, is that the price of cars today is outrageously high because the average new car might cost $19,000. But that is not an accurate comparison. What was the price of the average house during that same year? Perhaps it was only $12,000. By comparison, then, given that houses today average about $140,000, the price of a new car today doesn't sound so far out of line, does it?

The point is that money prices during different time periods don't tell you much. You have to find out relative prices. Consider an example of the price of CDs versus cassettes from last year and this year. In Table 3-1, we show the money price of CDs and cassettes for two years during which they have both gone up. That means that we have to pay out in today's dollars and cents more for CDs and more for cassettes. If we look, though, at the relative prices of CDs and cassettes, we find that last year, CDs were twice as expensive as cassettes, whereas this year they are only $1\frac{3}{4}$ times as expensive. Conversely, if we compare cassettes to CDs, last year they cost only half as much as CDs, but today they cost about 57 percent as much. In the one-year period, while both prices have gone up in money terms, the relative price of CDs has fallen (and, equivalently, the relative price of cassettes has risen).

TABLE 3-1
Money Price Versus Relative Price
The money price of both compact discs (CDs) and cassettes has risen. But the relative price of CDs has fallen (or conversely, the relative price of cassettes has risen).

	Money Price		Relative Price	
	Price Last Year	Price This Year	Price Last Year	Price This Year
CDs	$12	$14	$\frac{\$12}{\$6} = 2.0$	$\frac{\$14}{\$8} = 1.75$
Cassettes	$ 6	$ 8	$\frac{\$6}{\$12} = 0.5$	$\frac{\$8}{\$14} = 0.57$

INTERNATIONAL EXAMPLE
Cross-Border Shopping in Europe

The increase in cross-border shopping is a good example of how individuals respond to relative prices rather than absolute, or money, prices. Several times a week, bargain-conscious Basques from Bilbao, Spain, cross the French border (which is without customs or immigration control because it is part of the European Union) to shop for food. At current exchange rates, similar-quality food costs about 40 percent less on the French side of the border. For cost-conscious consumers in Switzerland who live along the border with France, such trips are frequent. Professor Stephen Stearns, of Basel, Switzerland, claims that shopping in France saves a typical family more than 30 percent on its weekly food bill. At current exchange rates, pork and beef cost only half as much in France, and cheese is 40 percent less expensive. Germans and Belgians who live on the border with Luxembourg and the Netherlands often travel to those countries to buy food and consumer products, such as shampoo. The British frequently make a relatively long trip by ferry to France to buy alcoholic beverages, which cost 50 percent less than in Britain. All this border crossing bears out the fact that relative prices, not absolute (money) prices, determine people's shopping habits.

FOR CRITICAL ANALYSIS: How would we calculate the net benefit to cross-border shopping for the people who engage in it? (Hint: What are some of the costs of such shopping?) ●

THINKING CRITICALLY ABOUT THE MEDIA

The Real Price of Stamps

The press is fond of pointing out the rise in the price of a particular good, such as a stamp for first-class mail. In the 1940s, a first-class stamp cost only 3 cents, but by the mid-1990s, it had climbed to 32 cents. That is the absolute price of postage, however. What about the relative price, the price relative to the average of all other prices? The relative price of postage is actually lower today than when it reached its peak in 1975. Many other relative prices have fallen over the years, ranging from gasoline prices to the president's salary. Indeed, relatively speaking, the president's current $200,000-a-year salary is peanuts compared to what President Truman earned in 1947. In relative terms (dollars in 1947), the current president only earns about $30,000, even though in absolute terms, the current president makes more. Remember, everything is relative.

CONCEPTS IN BRIEF

- The law of demand posits an inverse relationship between the quantity demanded of a good and its price, other things being equal.
- The law of demand applies when other things, such as income and the prices of all other goods and services, are held constant.

THE DEMAND SCHEDULE

Let's take a hypothetical demand situation to see how the inverse relationship between the price and the quantity demanded looks (holding other things equal). We will consider the quantity of diskettes demanded *per year*. Without stating the *time dimension,* we could not make sense out of this demand relationship because the numbers would be different if we were talking about the quantity demanded per month or the quantity demanded per decade.

In addition to implicitly or explicitly stating a time dimension for a demand relationship, we are also implicitly referring to *constant-quality* units of the good or service in question. Prices are always expressed in constant-quality units in order to avoid the problem of comparing commodities that are in fact not truly comparable.

In panel (a) of Figure 3-1, we see that if the price were $1 per diskette, 50 of them would be bought each year by our representative individual, but if the price were $5 per diskette,

FIGURE 3-1

The Individual Demand Schedule and the Individual Demand Curve

In panel (a), we show combinations *A* through *E* of the quantities of diskettes demanded, measured in constant-quality units at prices ranging from $5 down to $1 per disk. In panel (b), we plot combinations *A* through *E* on a grid. The result is the individual demand curve for diskettes.

Panel (a)

Combination	Price per Constant-Quality Diskette	Quantity of Constant-Quality Diskettes per Year
A	$5	10
B	4	20
C	3	30
D	2	40
E	1	50

Panel (b)

only 10 diskettes would be bought each year. This reflects the law of demand. Panel (a) is also called simply demand, or a *demand schedule,* because it gives a schedule of alternative quantities demanded per year at different possible prices.

The Demand Curve

Tables expressing relationships between two variables can be represented in graphical terms. To do this, we need only construct a graph that has the price per constant-quality diskette on the vertical axis and the quantity measured in constant-quality diskettes per year on the horizontal axis. All we have to do is take combinations *A* through *E* from panel (a) of Figure 3-1 and plot those points in panel (b). Now we connect the points with a smooth line, and *voilà,* we have a **demand curve.**[1] It is downward-sloping (from left to right) to indicate the inverse relationship between the price of diskettes and the quantity demanded per year. Our presentation of demand schedules and curves applies equally well to all commodities, including toothpicks, hamburgers, textbooks, credit, and labor services. Remember, the demand curve is simply a graphical representation of the law of demand.

Demand curve
A graphical representation of the demand schedule; a negatively sloped line showing the inverse relationship between the price and the quantity demanded (other things being equal).

Individual Versus Market Demand Curves

The demand schedule shown in panel (a) of Figure 3-1 and the resulting demand curve shown in panel (b) are both given for an individual. As we shall see, the determination of price in the marketplace depends on, among other things, the **market demand** for a particular commodity. The way in which we measure a market demand schedule and derive a

Market demand
The demand of all consumers in the marketplace for a particular good or service. The summing at each price of the quantity demanded by each individual.

[1]Even though we call them "curves," for the purposes of exposition we often draw straight lines. In many real-world situations, demand and supply curves will in fact be lines that do curve. To connect the points in panel (b) with a line, we assume that for all prices in between the ones shown, the quantities demanded will be found along that line.

market demand curve for diskettes or any other commodity is by summing (at each price) the individual demand for all those in the market. Suppose that the market demand for diskettes consists of only two buyers: buyer 1, for whom we've already shown the demand schedule, and buyer 2, whose demand schedule is displayed in column 3 of panel (a) of Figure 3-2. Column 1 shows the price, and column 2 shows the quantity demanded by buyer 1 at each price. These data are taken directly from Figure 3-1. In column 3, we show the quantity demanded by buyer 2. Column 4 shows the total quantity demanded at each price, which is obtained by simply adding columns 2 and 3. Graphically, in panel (d) of Figure 3-2, we add the demand curves of buyer 1 [panel (b)] and buyer 2 [panel (c)] to derive the market demand curve.

There are, of course, literally tens of millions of potential consumers of diskettes. We'll simply assume that the summation of all of the consumers in the market results in a demand schedule, given in panel (a) of Figure 3-3, and a demand curve, given in panel (b). The quantity demanded is now measured in billions of units per year. Remember, panel (b) in Figure 3-3 shows the market demand curve for the millions of users of diskettes. The "market" demand curve that we derived in Figure 3-2 was undertaken assuming that there were only two buyers in the entire market. That's why the "market" demand curve for two

.FIGURE 3-2

The Horizontal Summation of Two Demand Schedules

Panel (a) shows how to sum the demand schedule for one buyer with that of another buyer. In column 2 is the quantity demanded by buyer 1, taken from panel (a) of Figure 3-1. Column 4 is the sum of columns 2 and 3. We plot the demand curve for buyer 1 in panel (b) and the demand curve for buyer 2 in panel (c). When we add those two demand curves horizontally, we get the market demand curve for two buyers, shown in panel (d).

Panel (a)

(1) Price per Diskette	(2) Buyer 1 Quantity Demanded	(3) Buyer 2 Quantity Demanded	(4) = (2) + (3) Combined Quantity Demanded per Year
$5	10	10	20
4	20	20	40
3	30	40	70
2	40	50	90
1	50	60	110

Panel (b)
Buyer 1

+

Panel (c)
Buyer 2

=

Panel (d)
Market Demand for Two Buyers

FIGURE 3-3

The Market Demand Schedule for Diskettes

In panel (a), we add up the millions of existing demand schedules for diskettes. In panel (b), we plot the quantities from panel (a) on a grid; connecting them produces the market demand curve for diskettes.

Panel (a)

Price per Constant-Quality Diskette	Total Quantity Demanded of Constant-Quality Diskettes per Year (billions)
$5	2
4	4
3	6
2	8
1	10

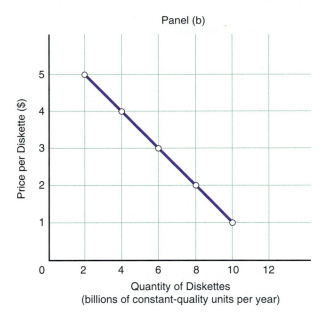

Panel (b)

buyers in panel (d) of Figure 3-2 is not a smooth line, whereas the true market demand curve in panel (b) of Figure 3-3 is a smooth line with no kinks.

Now consider some special aspects of the market demand curve for compact discs.

EXAMPLE
Garth Brooks, Used CDs, and the Law of Demand

A few years ago, country singer Garth Brooks tried to prevent his latest album from being sold to any chain or store that also sells used CDs. His argument was that the used-CD market deprived labels and artists of earnings. His announcement came after Wherehouse Entertainment, Inc., a 339-store retailer based in Torrance, California, started selling used CDs side by side with new releases, at half the price. Brooks, along with the distribution arms of Sony, Warner Music, Capitol-EMI, and MCA, was trying to quash the used-CD market. By so doing, it appears that none of these parties understands the law of demand.

Let's say the price of a new CD is $15. The existence of a secondary used-CD market means that to people who choose to resell their CDs for $5, the cost of a new CD is in fact only $10. Because we know that quantity demanded is inversely related to price, we know that more of a new CD will be sold at a price of $10 than of the same CD at a price of $15. Eliminating the used-CD market would in effect reduce the sales of new CDs.

One reason why CDs command a higher price than vinyl records or cassettes is that they are more durable. This increases their value in the secondary market. Eliminating the used-CD market would cause the real net price of new CDs to rise, leading to fewer purchases of new CDs, more taping off the radio or from friends, and an increase in radio listening.

FOR CRITICAL ANALYSIS: *Can you apply this argument to the used-book market, in which both authors and publishers have long argued that used books are "killing them"?* ●

CONCEPTS IN BRIEF

- We measure the demand schedule both in terms of a time dimension and in constant-quality units.

- The market demand curve is derived by summing the quantity demanded by individuals at each price. Graphically, we add the individual demand curves horizontally to derive the total, or market, demand curve.

SHIFTS IN DEMAND

Assume that the federal government gives every student registered in a college, university, or technical school in the United States a personal computer that uses diskettes. The demand curve presented in panel (b) of Figure 3-3 would no longer be an accurate representation of total market demand for diskettes. What we have to do is shift the curve outward, or to the right, to represent the rise in demand. There will now be an increase in the number of diskettes demanded *at each and every possible price.* The demand curve shown in Figure 3-4 will shift from D_1 to D_2. Take any price, say, $3 per diskette. Originally, before the federal government giveaway of personal computers, the amount demanded at $3 was 6 billion diskettes per year. After the government giveaway, however, the new amount demanded at $3 is 10 billion diskettes per year. What we have seen is a shift in the demand for diskettes.

The shift can also go in the opposite direction. What if colleges uniformly outlawed the use of personal computers by any of their students? Such a regulation would cause a shift inward—to the left—of the demand curve for diskettes. In Figure 3-4, the demand curve would shift to D_3; the amount demanded would now be less at each and every possible price.

The Other Determinants of Demand

The demand curve in panel (b) of Figure 3-3 is drawn with other things held constant, specifically all of the other factors that determine how much will be bought. There are many such determinants. The major other determinants are income; tastes and preferences; the prices of related goods; expectations regarding future prices, future incomes, and future product availability; and population (market size). Let's examine each determinant more closely.

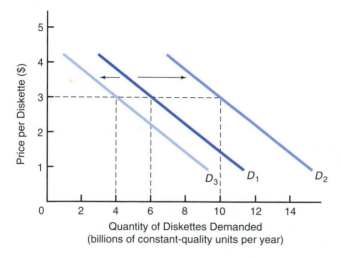

Quantity of Diskettes Demanded
(billions of constant-quality units per year)

FIGURE 3-4

A Shift in the Demand Curve

If some factor other than price changes, the only way we can show its effect is by moving the entire demand curve, say, from D_1 to D_2. We have assumed in our example that the move was precipitated by the government's giving a free personal computer to every registered college student in America. That meant that at *all* prices, a larger number of diskettes would be demanded than before. Curve D_3 represents reduced demand compared to curve D_1, caused by a law prohibiting computers on campus.

Income. For most goods, an increase in income will lead to an increase in demand. The phrase *increase in demand* always refers to a comparison between two different demand curves. Thus for most goods, an increase in income will lead to a rightward shift in the position of the demand curve from, say, D_1 to D_2 in Figure 3-4. You can avoid confusion about shifts in curves by always relating a rise in demand to a rightward shift in the demand curve and a fall in demand to a leftward shift in the demand curve. Goods for which the demand rises when income rises are called **normal goods.** Most goods, such as shoes, computers, and CDs, are "normal goods." For some goods, however, demand *falls* as income rises. These are called **inferior goods.** Beans might be an example. As households get richer, they tend to spend less and less on beans and more and more on meat. (The terms *normal* and *inferior* are merely part of the economist's terminology; no value judgments are associated with them.)

Remember, a shift to the left in the demand curve represents a fall in demand, and a shift to the right represents a rise, or increase, in demand.

Tastes and Preferences. A change in consumer tastes in favor of a good can shift its demand curve outward to the right. When Frisbees® became the rage, the demand curve for them shifted outward to the right; when the rage died out, the demand curve shifted inward to the left. Fashions depend to a large extent on people's tastes and preferences. Economists have little to say about the determination of tastes; that is, they don't have any "good" theories of taste determination or why people buy one brand of product rather than others. Advertisers, however, have various theories that they use to try to make consumers prefer their products over those of competitors.

INTERNATIONAL EXAMPLE
The Slump in Worldwide Sales of Cigars

Cigar manufacturers worldwide are finding out what happens to the demand for their product when there is a shift in tastes. Although the Belgians are the heaviest cigar smokers in the world, they are stubbing out more and more of their cigars. Health scares and increased public pressure in Europe not to pollute indoor spaces are the cause. Between 1988 and 1996, the sales of cigars dropped by over 15 percent worldwide. ERC Statistics International predicts that by the end of the twentieth century, annual cigar smoking will drop at least another 10 percent. Some European manufacturers are looking to Eastern Europe to fill the void in sales. Others are trying to encroach on the cigarette market by launching cigarillos that look like cigarettes.

FOR CRITICAL ANALYSIS: Many countries (including the United States) now ban the advertising of cigars and cigarettes. What do you think this has done to the demand curve for cigars? ●

Prices of Related Goods: Substitutes and Complements. Demand schedules are always drawn with the prices of all other commodities held constant. That is to say, when deriving a given demand curve, we assume that only the price of the good under study changes. For example, when we draw the demand curve for butter, we assume that the price of margarine is held constant. When we draw the demand curve for stereo speakers, we assume that the price of stereo amplifiers is held constant. When we refer to *related goods,* we are talking about goods for which demand is interdependent. If a change in the price of one good shifts the demand for another good, those two goods are related. There

---

Normal goods
Goods for which demand rises as income rises. Most goods are considered normal.

Inferior goods
Goods for which demand falls as income rises.

are two types of related goods: *substitutes* and *complements.* We can define and distinguish between substitutes and complements in terms of how the change in price of one commodity affects the demand for its related commodity.

Butter and margarine are **substitutes.** Let's assume that each originally cost $2 per pound. If the price of butter remains the same and the price of margarine falls from $2 per pound to $1 per pound, people will buy more margarine and less butter. The demand curve for butter will shift inward to the left. If, conversely, the price of margarine rises from $2 per pound to $3 per pound, people will buy more butter and less margarine. The demand curve for butter will shift outward to the right. In other words, an increase in the price of margarine will lead to an increase in the demand for butter, and an increase in the price of butter will lead to an increase in the demand for margarine. For substitutes, a price change in the substitute will cause a change in demand *in the same direction.*

For **complements,** the situation is reversed. Consider stereo speakers and stereo amplifiers. We draw the demand curve for speakers with the price of amplifiers held constant. If the price per constant-quality unit of stereo amplifiers decreases from, say, $500 to $200, that will encourage more people to purchase component stereo systems. They will now buy more speakers, at any given speaker price, than before. The demand curve for speakers will shift outward to the right. If, by contrast, the price of amplifiers increases from $200 to $500, fewer people will purchase component stereo systems. The demand curve for speakers will shift inward to the left. To summarize, a decrease in the price of amplifiers leads to an increase in the demand for speakers. An increase in the price of amplifiers leads to a decrease in the demand for speakers. Thus for complements, a price change in a product will cause a change in demand *in the opposite direction.*

Are new learning technologies complements or substitutes for college instructors? Read on.

Substitutes
Two goods are substitutes when either one can be used for consumption to satisfy a similar want—for example, coffee and tea. The more you buy of one, the less you buy of the other. For substitutes, the change in the price of one causes a shift in demand for the other in the same direction as the price change.

Complements
Two goods are complements if both are used together for consumption or enjoyment—for example, coffee and cream. The more you buy of one, the more you buy of the other. For complements, a change in the price of one causes an opposite shift in the demand for the other.

EXAMPLE
The Future of College Teaching

In this class and in others, you have probably been exposed to some of the new (and old) instructional technologies, some of which include films and videos, interactive computer software, and interactive CD-ROM learning systems. Your professors have used these new technologies as a complement to their teaching, but in the future they may in fact become a substitute for what your professors do in the classroom.

The University of North Dakota, North Dakota State University, and North Dakota State College of Science together offer enough TV courses that a student can earn a college degree in business administration, nursing, or education without ever attending a class. Televised lectures allow a given number of professors to teach a greater number of students. Now consider interactive CD-ROM learning systems. In principle, virtually every college course could be put on CD-ROM, thereby eliminating the need for instructors entirely. Going one step further, institutions of higher learning are now using the Internet to provide instruction. "Distance learning" is already being used by the University of Michigan in conjunction with companies in Hong Kong, South Korea, and Europe. Michigan offers a global M.B.A. through a combination of interactive video classroom instruction, high-speed Internet connections, e-mail, and shared application computing. A professor teaches a course "live" via video and uses the software program Lotus Notes, which allows course information to be sent via the Internet. Students submit their homework assignments the same way.

FOR CRITICAL ANALYSIS: *What do you predict will happen to the demand curve for college professors in the future?* ●

Expectations. Consumers' expectations regarding future prices, future incomes, and future availability may prompt them to buy more or less of a particular good without a change in its current money price. For example, consumers getting wind of a scheduled 100 percent price increase in diskettes next month may buy more of them today at today's prices. Today's demand curve for diskettes will shift from D_1 to D_2 in Figure 3-4 on page 52. The opposite would occur if a decrease in the price of diskettes were scheduled for next month.

Expectations of a rise in income may cause consumers to want to purchase more of everything today at today's prices. Again, such a change in expectations of higher future income will cause a shift in the demand curve from D_1 to D_2 in Figure 3-4.

Finally, expectations that goods will not be available at any price will induce consumers to stock up now, increasing current demand.

Population. An increase in the population in an economy (holding per capita income constant) often shifts the market demand outward for most products. This is because an increase in population leads to an increase in the number of buyers in the market. Conversely, a reduction in the population will shift most market demand curves inward because of the reduction in the number of buyers in the market.

Changes in Demand Versus Changes in Quantity Demanded

We have made repeated references to demand and to quantity demanded. It is important to realize that there is a difference between a *change in demand* and a *change in quantity demanded*.

Demand refers to a schedule of planned rates of purchase and depends on a great many nonprice determinants. Whenever there is a change in a nonprice determinant, there will be a change in demand—a shift in the entire demand curve to the right or to the left.

A quantity demanded is a specific quantity at a specific price, represented by a single point on a demand curve. When price changes, quantity demanded changes according to the law of demand, and there will be a movement from one point to another along the same demand curve. Look at Figure 3-5 on page 56. At a price of $3 per diskette, 6 billion diskettes per year are demanded. If the price falls to $1, quantity demanded increases to 10 billion per year. This movement occurs because the current market price for the product changes. In Figure 3-5, you can see the arrow pointing down the given demand curve D.

When you think of demand, think of the entire curve itself. Quantity demanded, in contrast, is represented by a single point on the demand curve.

A change or shift in demand causes the *entire* curve to move. The *only* thing that can cause the entire curve to move is a change in a determinant *other than its own price.*

In economic analysis, we cannot emphasize too much the following distinction that must constantly be made:

A change in a good's own price leads to a change in quantity demanded, for any given demand curve, other things held constant. This is a movement *on* the curve.

A change in any other determinant of demand leads to a change in demand. This causes a movement *of* the curve.

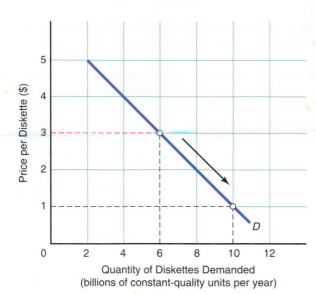

FIGURE 3-5

Movement Along a Given Demand Curve
A change in price changes the quantity of a good demanded. This can be represented as movement along a given demand schedule. If, in our example, the price of diskettes falls from $3 to $1 apiece, the quantity demanded will increase from 6 billion to 10 billion units per year.

CONCEPTS IN BRIEF

• Demand curves are drawn with determinants other than the price of the good held constant. These other determinants are (1) income; (2) tastes and preferences; (3) prices of related goods; (4) expectations about future prices, future incomes, and future availability of goods; and (5) population (number of buyers in the market). If any one of these determinants changes, the demand schedule will shift to the right or to the left.

• A change in demand comes about only because of a change in the other determinants of demand. This change in demand shifts the demand curve to the left or to the right.

• A change in the quantity demanded comes about when there is a change in the price of the good (other things held constant). Such a change in quantity demanded involves a movement along a given demand curve.

THE LAW OF SUPPLY

The other side of the basic model in economics involves the quantities of goods and services that firms are prepared to *supply* to the market. The **supply** of any good or service is the amount that firms are prepared to sell under certain conditions during a specified time period. The relationship between price and quantity supplied, called the **law of supply,** can be summarized as follows:

Supply
A schedule showing the relationship between price and quantity supplied for a specified period of time, other things being equal.

At higher prices, a larger quantity will generally be supplied than at lower prices, all other things held constant. At lower prices, a smaller quantity will generally be supplied than at higher prices, all other things held constant.

There is generally a direct relationship between quantity supplied and price. For supply, as the price rises, the quantity supplied rises; as price falls, the quantity supplied also falls. Producers are normally willing to produce and sell more of their product at a higher price than at a lower price, other things being constant. At $5 per diskette, 3M, Sony, Maxell, Fuji, and other manufacturers would almost certainly be willing to supply a larger quantity than at $1 per unit, assuming, of course, that no other prices in the economy had changed.

Law of supply
The observation that the higher the price of a good, the more of that good sellers will make available over a specified time period, other things being equal.

As with the law of demand, millions of instances in the real world have given us confidence in the law of supply. On a theoretical level, the law of supply is based on a model in which producers and sellers seek to make the most gain possible from their activities. For example, as a diskette manufacturer attempts to produce more and more diskettes over the same time period, it will eventually have to hire more workers, pay overtime wages (which are higher), and overutilize its machines. Only if offered a higher price per diskette will the diskette manufacturer be willing to incur these higher costs. That is why the law of supply implies a direct relationship between price and quantity supplied.

THE SUPPLY SCHEDULE

Just as we were able to construct a demand schedule, we can construct a *supply schedule*, which is a table relating prices to the quantity supplied at each price. A supply schedule can also be referred to simply as *supply*. It is a set of planned production rates that depends on the price of the product. We show the individual supply schedule for a hypothetical producer in panel (a) of Figure 3-6. At $1 per diskette, for example, this producer will supply 20 million diskettes per year; at $5, this producer will supply 55 million diskettes per year.

The Supply Curve

Supply curve
The graphical representation of the supply schedule; a line (curve) showing the supply schedule, which generally slopes upward (has a positive slope), other things being equal.

We can convert the supply schedule in panel (a) of Figure 3-6 into a **supply curve,** just as we earlier created a demand curve in Figure 3-1. All we do is take the price-quantity combinations from panel (a) of Figure 3-6 and plot them in panel (b). We have labeled these combinations *F* through *J*. Connecting these points, we obtain an upward-sloping curve that shows the typically direct relationship between price and quantity supplied. Again, we have to remember that we are talking about quantity supplied *per year*, measured in constant-quality units.

FIGURE 3-6

The Individual Producer's Supply Schedule and Supply Curve for Diskettes
Panel (a) shows that at higher prices, a hypothetical supplier will be willing to provide a greater quantity of diskettes. We plot the various price-quantity combinations in panel (a) on the grid in panel (b). When we connect these points, we find the individual supply curve for diskettes. It is positively sloped.

Panel (a)

Combination	Price per Constant-Quality Diskette	Quantity of Diskettes Supplied (millions of constant-quality units per year)
F	$5	55
G	4	40
H	3	35
I	2	25
J	1	20

Panel (b)

The Market Supply Curve

Just as we had to sum the individual demand curves to get the market demand curve, we need to sum the individual producers' supply curves to get the market supply curve. Look at Figure 3-7, in which we horizontally sum two typical diskette manufacturers' supply curves. Supplier 1's data are taken from Figure 3-6; supplier 2 is added. The numbers are presented in panel (a). The graphical representation of supplier 1 is in panel (b), of supplier 2 in panel (c), and of the summation in panel (d). The result, then, is the supply curve for diskettes for suppliers 1 and 2. There are many more suppliers of diskettes, however. The total market supply schedule and total market demand curve for diskettes are represented in Figure 3-8, with the curve in panel (b) obtained by adding all of the supply curves such as those shown in panels (b) and (c) of Figure 3-7. Notice the difference between the

Panel (a)

(1) Price per Diskette	(2) Supplier 1 Quantity Supplied (millions)	(3) Supplier 2 Quantity Supplied (millions)	(4) = (2) + (3) Combined Quantity Supplied per Year (millions)
$5	55	35	90
4	40	30	70
3	35	20	55
2	25	15	40
1	20	10	30

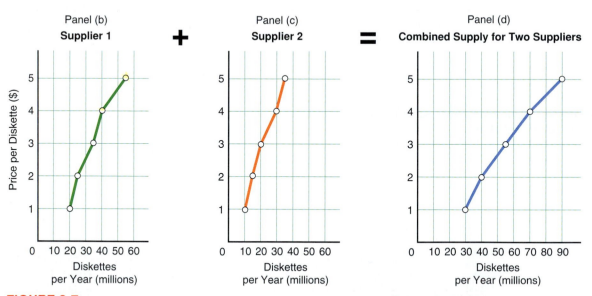

FIGURE 3-7

Horizontal Summation of Supply Curves

In panel (a), we show the data for two individual suppliers of diskettes. Adding how much each is willing to supply at different prices, we come up with the combined quantities supplied in column 4. When we plot the values in columns 2 and 3 on grids in panels (b) and (c) and add them horizontally, we obtain the combined supply curve for the two suppliers in question, shown in panel (d).

FIGURE 3-8

**The Market Supply Schedule and the
Market Supply Curve for Diskettes**
In panel (a), we show the summation of all the individual producers' supply schedules; in panel (b), we graph the resulting
supply curve. It represents the market supply curve for
diskettes and is upward-sloping.

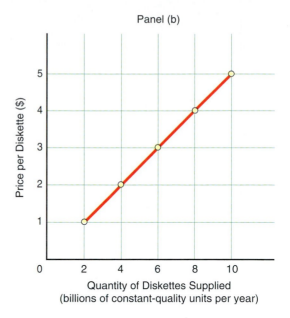
Panel (b)

Panel (a)

Price per Constant-Quality Diskette	Quantity of Diskettes Supplied (billions of constant-quality units per year)
$5	10
4	8
3	6
2	4
1	2

market supply curve with only two suppliers in Figure 3-7 and the one with a large number of suppliers—the entire true market—in panel (b) of Figure 3-8. There are no kinks in the true total market supply curve because there are so many suppliers.

Notice what happens at the market level when price changes. If the price is $3, the quantity supplied is 6 billion diskettes. If the price goes up to $4, the quantity supplied increases to 8 billion per year. If the price falls to $2, the quantity supplied decreases to 4 billion diskettes per year. Changes in quantity supplied are represented by movements along the supply curve in panel (b) of Figure 3-8.

CONCEPTS IN BRIEF

• There is normally a direct, or positive, relationship between price and quantity of a good supplied, other things held constant.

• The supply curve normally shows a direct relationship between price and quantity supplied. The market supply curve is obtained by horizontally adding individual supply curves in the market.

SHIFTS IN SUPPLY

When we looked at demand, we found out that any change in anything relevant besides the price of the good or service caused the demand curve to shift inward or outward. The same is true for the supply curve. If something relevant changes besides the price of the product or service being supplied, we will see the entire supply curve shift.

Consider an example. A new method of putting magnetic material on diskettes has been invented. It reduces the cost of producing a diskette by 50 percent. In this situation, diskette producers will supply more product at *all* prices because their cost of so doing has fallen dramatically. Competition among diskette manufacturers to produce more at each and

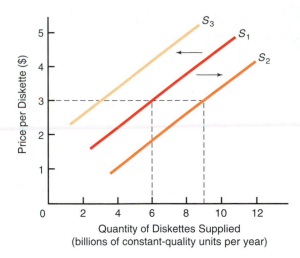

FIGURE 3-9

A Shift in the Supply Schedule
If the cost of producing diskettes were to fall dramatically, the supply schedule would shift rightward from S_1 to S_2 such that at all prices, a larger quantity would be forthcoming from suppliers. Conversely, if the cost of production rose, the supply curve would shift leftward to S_3.

every price will shift the supply schedule of diskettes outward to the right from S_1 to S_2 in Figure 3-9. At a price of $3, the quantity supplied was originally 6 billion diskettes per year, but now the quantity supplied (after the reduction in the costs of production) at $3 a diskette will be 9 billion diskettes a year. (This is similar to what has happened to the supply curve of personal computers and fax machines in recent years as computer memory chip prices have fallen.)

Consider the opposite case. If the cost of the magnetic material needed for making diskettes doubles, the supply curve in Figure 3-9 will shift from S_1 to S_3. At each and every price, the number of diskettes supplied will fall due to the increase in the price of raw materials.

The Other Determinants of Supply

When supply curves are drawn, only the price of the good in question changes, and it is assumed that other things remain constant. The other things assumed constant are the costs of resources (inputs) used to produce the product, technology and productivity, taxes and subsidies, producers' price expectations, and the number of firms in the industry. These are the major nonprice determinants of supply. If *any* of them changes, there will be a shift in the supply curve.

Cost of Inputs Used to Produce the Product. If one or more input prices fall, the supply curve will shift outward to the right; that is, more will be supplied at each and every price. The opposite will be true if one or more inputs become more expensive. For example, when we draw the supply curve of new cars, we are holding the cost of steel (and other inputs) constant. When we draw the supply curve of blue jeans, we are holding the cost of cotton fixed.

Technology and Productivity. Supply curves are drawn by assuming a given technology, or "state of the art." When the available production techniques change, the supply curve will shift. For example, when a better production technique for diskettes becomes available, the supply curve will shift to the right. A larger quantity will be forthcoming at each and every price because the cost of production is lower.

INTERNATIONAL EXAMPLE
Changing Technology and the Supply of Salmon

One example of how changes in technology can shift the supply curve out to the right involves salmon. In 1980, the total worldwide catch of salmon (wild and farmed) was just over 10,000 metric tons. Since 1980, new technology has been developed in what is called aquaculture, or the farm-raising of fish and related products. Aquaculture currently generates over $30 billion in worldwide revenues and is one of the world's fastest-growing industries. Farmed salmon from Chile, Scotland, Canada, Norway, and Iceland now exceeds 240,000 metric tons a year. Thus it is not surprising that despite a depletion of many wild salmon fishing grounds and a worldwide increase in the consumer demand for salmon, the retail price of salmon today (corrected for inflation) is about 50 percent of what it was in 1980.

FOR CRITICAL ANALYSIS: What might slow down the growth in salmon farming throughout the world? ●

Subsidy
A negative tax; a payment to a producer from the government, usually in the form of a cash grant.

Taxes and Subsidies. Certain taxes, such as a per-unit tax, are effectively an addition to production costs and therefore reduce the supply. If the supply curve were S_1 in Figure 3-9, a per-unit tax increase would shift it to S_3. A **subsidy** would do the opposite; it would shift the curve to S_2. Every producer would get a "gift" from the government of a few cents for each unit produced.

Price Expectations. A change in the expectation of a future relative price of a product can affect a producer's current willingness to supply, just as price expectations affect a consumer's current willingness to purchase. For example, diskette suppliers may withhold from the market part of their current supply if they anticipate higher prices in the future. The current amount supplied at each and every price will decrease.

Number of Firms in the Industry. In the short run, when firms can only change the number of employees they use, we hold the number of firms in the industry constant. In the long run, the number of firms (or the size of some existing firms) may change. If the number of firms increases, the supply curve will shift outward to the right. If the number of firms decreases, it will shift inward to the left.

Changes in Supply Versus Changes in Quantity Supplied

We cannot overstress the importance of distinguishing between a movement along the supply curve—which occurs only when the price changes for a given supply curve—and a shift in the supply curve—which occurs only with changes in other nonprice factors. A change in price always brings about a change in quantity supplied along a given supply curve. We move to a different coordinate on the existing supply curve. This is specifically called a *change in quantity supplied.* When price changes, quantity supplied changes, and there will be a movement from one point to another along the same supply curve.

When you think of *supply,* think of the entire curve itself. Quantity supplied is represented by a single point on the supply curve.

A change or shift in supply causes the entire curve to move. The *only* thing that can cause the entire curve to move is a change in a determinant *other than price*.

Consequently,

> **A change in the price leads to a change in the quantity supplied, other things being constant. This is a movement *on* the curve.**
>
> **A change in any other determinant of supply leads to a change in supply. This causes a movement *of* the curve.**

CONCEPTS IN BRIEF

- If the price changes, we *move along* a curve—there is a change in quantity demanded or supplied. If some other determinant changes, we *shift* a curve—there is a change in demand or supply.
- The supply curve is drawn with other things held constant. If other determinants of supply change, the supply curve will shift. The other major determinants are (1) input costs, (2) technology and productivity, (3) taxes and subsidies, (4) expectations of future relative prices, and (5) the number of firms in the industry.

PUTTING DEMAND AND SUPPLY TOGETHER

In the sections on supply and demand, we tried to confine each discussion to supply or demand only. But you have probably already realized that we can't view the world just from the supply side or just from the demand side. There is an interaction between the two. In this section, we will discuss how they interact and how that interaction determines the prices that prevail in our economy. Understanding how demand and supply interact is essential to understanding how prices are determined in our economy and other economies in which the forces of supply and demand are allowed to work.

Let's first combine the demand and supply schedules and then combine the curves.

Demand and Supply Schedules Combined

Let's place panel (a) from Figure 3-3 (the market demand schedule) and panel (a) from Figure 3-8 (the market supply schedule) together in panel (a) of Figure 3-10. Column 1 shows the price; column 2, the quantity supplied per year at any given price; and column 3, the quantity demanded. Column 4 is merely the difference between columns 2 and 3, or the difference between the quantity supplied and the quantity demanded. In column 5, we label those differences as either excess quantity supplied (a surplus) or excess quantity demanded (a shortage). For example, at a price of $1, only 2 billion diskettes would be supplied, but the quantity demanded would be 10 billion. The difference would be −8 billion, which we label excess quantity demanded (a shortage). At the other end of the scale, a price of $5 per diskette would elicit 10 billion in quantity supplied, but quantity demanded would drop to 2 billion, leaving a difference of +8 billion units, which we call excess quantity supplied (a surplus).

Panel (a)

(1) Price per Constant-Quality Diskette	(2) Quantity Supplied (diskettes per year)	(3) Quantity Demanded (diskettes per year)	(4) Difference (2) − (3) (diskettes per year)	(5) Condition
$5	10 billion	2 billion	8 billion	Excess quantity supplied (surplus)
4	8 billion	4 billion	4 billion	Excess quantity supplied (surplus)
3	6 billion	6 billion	0	Market clearing price—equilibrium (no surplus, no shortage)
2	4 billion	8 billion	− 4 billion	Excess quantity demanded (shortage)
1	2 billion	10 billion	− 8 billion	Excess quantity demanded (shortage)

Panel (b)

FIGURE 3-10

Putting Demand and Supply Together

In panel (a), we see that at the price of $3, the quantity supplied and the quantity demanded are equal, resulting in neither an excess in the quantity demanded nor an excess in the quantity supplied. We call this price the equilibrium, or market clearing, price. In panel (b), the intersection of the supply and demand curves is at *E*, at a price of $3 per constant-quality diskette and a quantity of 6 billion per year. At point *E*, there is neither an excess in the quantity demanded nor an excess in the quantity supplied. At a price of $1, the quantity supplied will be only 2 billion disks per year, but the quantity demanded will be 10 billion. The difference is excess quantity demanded at a price of $1. The price will rise, so we will move from point *A* up the supply curve and point *B* up the demand curve to point *E*. At the other extreme, $5 elicits a quantity supplied of 10 billion but a quantity demanded of only 2 billion. The difference is excess quantity supplied at a price of $5. The price will fall, so we will move down the demand curve and the supply curve to the equilibrium price, $3 per diskette.

Now, do you notice something special about the price of $3? At that price, both the quantity supplied and the quantity demanded per year are 6 billion diskettes. The difference then is zero. There is neither excess quantity demanded (shortage) nor excess quantity supplied (surplus). Hence the price of $3 is very special. It is called the **market clearing price**—it clears the market of all excess supply or excess demand. There are no willing consumers who want to pay $3 per diskette but are turned away by sellers, and there are no willing suppliers who want to sell diskettes at $3 who cannot sell all they want at that price. Another term for the market clearing price is the **equilibrium price,** the price at which there is no tendency for change. Consumers are able to get all they want at that price, and suppliers are able to sell the amount that they want at that price.

Market clearing, or **equilibrium, price**
The price that clears the market, at which quantity demanded equals quantity supplied; the price where the demand curve intersects the supply curve.

Equilibrium

We can define **equilibrium** in general as a point from which there tends to be no movement unless demand or supply changes. Any movement away from this point will set into motion certain forces that will cause movement back to it. Therefore, equilibrium is a stable point. Any point that is not at equilibrium is unstable and cannot be maintained.

Equilibrium
The situation when quantity supplied equals quantity demanded at a particular price.

The equilibrium point occurs where the supply and demand curves intersect. The equilibrium price is given on the vertical axis directly to the left of where the supply and demand curves cross. The equilibrium quantity demanded and supplied is given on the horizontal axis directly underneath the intersection of the demand and supply curves. Equilibrium can change whenever there is a *shock*.

A shock to the supply-and-demand system can be represented by a shift in the supply curve, a shift in the demand curve, or a shift in both curves. Any shock to the system will result in a new set of supply-and-demand relationships and a new equilibrium; forces will come into play to move the system from the old price-quantity equilibrium (now a disequilibrium situation) to the new equilibrium, where the new demand and supply curves intersect.

Panel (b) in Figure 3-3 and panel (b) in Figure 3-8 are combined as panel (b) in Figure 3-10 on page 63. The only difference now is that the horizontal axis measures both the quantity supplied and the quantity demanded per year. Everything else is the same. The demand curve is labeled *D*, the supply curve *S*. We have labeled the intersection of the supply curve with the demand curve as point *E*, for equilibrium. That corresponds to a market clearing price of $3, at which both the quantity supplied and the quantity demanded are 6 billion units per year. There is neither excess quantity supplied nor excess quantity demanded. Point *E*, the equilibrium point, always occurs at the intersection of the supply and demand curves. This is the price toward which the market price will automatically tend to gravitate.

EXAMPLE
Dinosaurs and the Price of Amber

When there is a shift in either supply or demand, there is a movement toward equilibrium that usually involves a change in the equilibrium quantity and the equilibrium price. A good example is found in the market for amber, a semiprecious stone that often preserves fossil plants and animals from millions of years ago. In Figure 3-11, you see the original supply and demand curves for amber, labeled S and D_1. The equilibrium price is P_1, and the equilibrium quantity is Q_1. Then along came a book, and later a movie, called *Jurassic Park,* written by Michael Crichton. In the story, million-year-old mosquitoes that had feasted on dinosaurs were trapped in amber. Scientists were able to clone

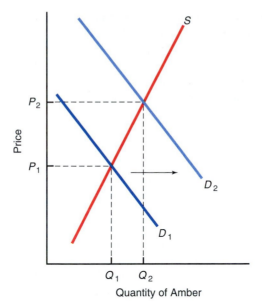

FIGURE 3-11

The Changing Price of Amber
With stable supply, a shift in the demand curve for amber from D_1 to D_2 will cause the equilibrium price of amber to rise from P_1 to P_2 and the equilibrium quantity to increase from Q_1 to Q_2.

various dinosaurs by removing the DNA from the dinosaur blood inside the mosquitoes. (The technique remains in the realm of science fiction.) The success of the book and the movie in the early 1990s made amber suddenly popular; in economic terms, the demand curve for amber shifted outward to D_2. Very quickly, the price rose to P_2 and the equilibrium quantity increased to Q_2.

FOR CRITICAL ANALYSIS: It has been a few years since the dinosaur craze peaked in the United States. How would you represent what is now occurring in the market in amber using supply and demand curves? ●

Shortages

The demand and supply curves depicted in Figure 3-10 represent a situation of equilibrium. But a non-market-clearing, or disequilibrium, price will put into play forces that cause the price to change toward the market clearing price at which equilibrium will again be sustained. Look again at panel (b) in Figure 3-10 on page 63. Suppose that instead of being at the market clearing price of $3 per diskette, for some reason the market price is $1 per diskette. At this price, the quantity demanded exceeds the quantity supplied, the former being 10 billion diskettes per year and the latter, 2 billion per year. We have a situation of excess quantity demanded at the price of $1. This is usually called a **shortage.** Consumers of diskettes would find that they could not buy all that they wished at $1 apiece. But forces will cause the price to rise: Competing consumers will bid up the price, and suppliers will raise the price and increase output, whether explicitly or implicitly. (Remember, some buyers would pay $5 or more rather than do without diskettes. They do not want to be left out.) We would move from points A and B toward point E. The process would stop when the price again reached $3 per diskette.

At this point, it is important to recall a distinction made in Chapter 2:

Shortages and scarcity are not the same thing.

Shortage
A situation in which quantity demanded is greater than quantity supplied at a price below the market clearing price.

A shortage is a situation in which the quantity demanded exceeds the quantity supplied at a price *below* the market clearing price. Our definition of scarcity was much more general and all-encompassing: a situation in which the resources available for producing output are insufficient to satisfy all wants. Any choice necessarily costs an opportunity, and the opportunity is lost. Hence we will always live in a world of scarcity because we must constantly make choices, but we do not necessarily have to live in a world of shortages.

Surpluses

Now let's repeat the experiment with the market price at $5 per diskette rather than at the market clearing price of $3. Clearly, the quantity supplied will exceed the quantity demanded at that price. The result will be an excess quantity supplied at $5 per unit. This excess quantity supplied is often called a **surplus.** Given the curves in panel (b) in Figure 3-10, however, there will be forces pushing the price back down toward $3 per diskette: Competing suppliers will attempt to reduce their inventories by cutting prices and reducing output, and consumers will offer to purchase more at lower prices. Suppliers will want to reduce inventories, which will be above their optimal level; that is, there will be an excess over what each seller believes to be the most profitable stock of diskettes. After all, inventories are costly to hold. But consumers may find out about such excess inventories and see the possibility of obtaining increased quantities of diskettes at a decreased price. It behooves consumers to attempt to obtain a good at a lower price, and they will therefore try to do so. If the two forces of supply and demand are unrestricted, they will bring the price back to $3 per diskette.

Surplus
A situation in which quantity supplied is greater than quantity demanded at a price above the market clearing price.

Shortages and surpluses are resolved in unfettered markets—markets in which price changes are free to occur. The forces that resolve them are those of competition: In the case of shortages, consumers competing for a limited quantity supplied drive up the price; in the case of surpluses, sellers compete for the limited quantity demanded, thus driving prices down to equilibrium. The equilibrium price is the only stable price, and all (unrestricted) market prices tend to gravitate toward it.

What happens when the price is set below the equilibrium price? Here come the scalpers.

POLICY EXAMPLE
Should Shortages in the Ticket Market Be Solved by Scalpers?

If you have ever tried to get tickets to a playoff game in sports, a popular Broadway play, or a superstar's rock concert, you know about "shortages." The standard ticket situation for a Super Bowl is shown in Figure 3-12. At the face-value price of Super Bowl tickets (P_1), the quantity demanded (Q_2) greatly exceeds the quantity supplied (Q_1). Because shortages last only so long as prices and quantities do not change, markets tend to exhibit a movement out of this disequilibrium toward equilibrium. Obviously, the quantity of Super Bowl tickets cannot change, but the price can go as high as P_2.

Enter the scalper. This colorful term is used because when you purchase a ticket that is being resold at a price that is higher than face value, the seller is skimming an extra profit off the top. Every time an event sells out, ticket prices by definition have been lower than

FIGURE 3-12

Shortages of Super Bowl Tickets

The quantity of tickets for any one Super Bowl is fixed at Q_1. At the price per ticket of P_1, the quantity demanded is Q_2, which is greater than Q_1. Consequently, there is an excess quantity demanded at the below–market clearing price. Prices can go as high as P_2 in the scalpers' market.

market clearing prices. Sellouts indicate that the event is very popular and that there may be people without tickets willing to buy high-priced tickets because they place a greater value on the entertainment event than the actual face value of the ticket. Without scalpers, those individuals would not be able to attend the event. In the case of the Super Bowl, various forms of scalping occur nationwide. Tickets for a seat on the 50-yard line have been sold for more than $2,000 a piece. In front of every Super Bowl arena, you can find ticket scalpers hawking their wares.

In most states, scalping is illegal. In Pennsylvania, convicted scalpers are either fined $5,000 or sentenced to two years behind bars. For an economist, such legislation seems strange. As one New York ticket broker said, "I look at scalping like working as a stockbroker, buying low and selling high. If people are willing to pay me the money, what kind of problem is that?"

FOR CRITICAL ANALYSIS: What happens to ticket scalpers who are still holding tickets after an event has started? ●

CONCEPTS IN BRIEF

• The market clearing price occurs at the intersection of the market demand curve and the market supply curve. It is also called the equilibrium price, the price from which there is no tendency to change unless there is a change in demand or supply.

• Whenever the price is greater than the equilibrium price, there is an excess quantity supplied (a surplus).

• Whenever the price is less than the equilibrium price, there is an excess quantity demanded (a shortage).

How Higher Education Has Responded to Changes in Supply and Demand

Concepts Applied: Demand and supply, shifts in demand and supply, relative prices

Dwindling numbers of high school graduates forced colleges to aggressively recruit international students to make up for falling revenues in the past two decades. International students are even more desirable because there is a smaller percentage of them who qualify for financial aid, allowing schools to bring in more revenues.

During the decades after World War II, the pool of high school graduates rose virtually every year until the beginning of the 1980s. In other words, the potential supply of college students only stopped growing about a decade and a half ago. Not surprisingly, during this time period and until just recently, average tuitions at four-year colleges were rising faster than the rate of inflation. But today things are different. High schools now graduate 2.5 million students per year, down from 3.1 million a decade ago. In addition, the Bureau of Labor Statistics says that of the 18 million college graduates expected to enter the labor force between 1992 and 2005, only about 14 million will get jobs that require college training.

Figure 3-13 shows the demand curve for higher education shifting inward from D_1 to D_2. Clearly, at current prices, P_1, there is an excess quantity of higher education supplied. Something has to give.

Increasing Enrollment of Foreign College Students

Figure 3-14 shows the gradual increase in the number of foreign students enrolling in American colleges and universities. There are two reasons why American colleges have been "beating the global bushes" for new students.

The first, of course, is that they constitute an additional supply of potential students to make up for the dwindling supply of U.S. high school graduates. Second, and perhaps more important for many private universities, a much higher percentage of foreign students than American students pay full tuition. Now there are even firms that specialize in organizing foreign recruiting tours for American university admissions officials.

The Effect of Grade Inflation

The cost of attending college obviously includes tuition and textbooks. How much a student has to work to get a good grade is also a part of the cost of going to college. Not surprisingly, as the demand curve has shifted inward starting in the 1980s, colleges and universities throughout the nation have allowed grades to inflate. When Stanford University abolished Ds and Fs, it saw 93 percent of all grades awarded rise to As and Bs. At Harvard University, less than

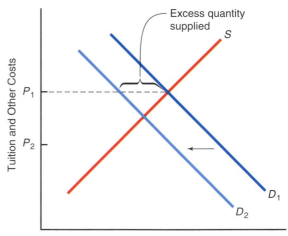

FIGURE 3-13

The "Soft" Market for College Applicants

For a variety of reasons, the demand for higher education has shifted from D_1 to D_2. With a stable supply curve, S, there exists an excess quantity of higher education supplied. Colleges and universities have therefore recruited more foreign students and started discounting tuition.

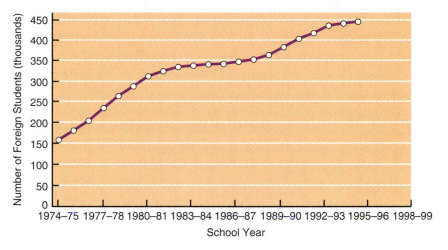

FIGURE 3-14

Foreign College Students in the United States

This graph shows the number of foreign students enrolled in all universities and colleges by school year in the United States.

Source: Institute of International Education.

20 percent of the student body has below a B average, and at Smith College, almost 90 percent of the students get As and Bs.

The Art of Discounting

Private universities are in competition with state universities. A New York resident who attends the University of Rochester and pays full tuition, including room and board, pays $2\frac{1}{2}$ times what the same student would pay to attend a campus of the State University of New York. In order to attract students, private universities have had to offer financial aid. At the University of Rochester, 70 percent of the students receive financial aid that averages $11,000 a year. So when private universities raise tuition, they have to offer even higher scholarships to attract qualified students. They consequently manage to keep only as little as 10 percent of the funds generated by a tuition increase.

What universities have started to do is give discounts on tuition. They may not call them that, but that is what they are. Continuing with the University of Rochester,

starting in the 1995–1996 school year, it cut fees for about half of its incoming freshman class by about 20 percent. George Washington University has been doing the same since 1988. Some colleges are going one step further by offering a type of money-back guarantee. For example, St. John Fisher College in Rochester, New York, offers students up to $5,000 cash if they do not find a job within six months after graduation.

Universities have discovered that the law of demand applies to them, too.

FOR CRITICAL ANALYSIS

1. Investigative reporters from the *Wall Street Journal* recently discovered that some colleges and universities have routinely falsified the SAT data of their incoming students in order to boost their reputations. Would you have expected as many U.S. colleges and universities to have acted this way prior to the 1980s? Why or why not?
2. Assume that a university gave only As to its students. How might this grading policy hurt its graduates?

CHAPTER SUMMARY

1. The law of demand says that at higher prices, individuals will purchase less of a commodity and at lower prices, they will purchase more, other things being equal.
2. Relative prices must be distinguished from absolute, or money, prices. During periods of rising prices, almost all prices go up, but some rise faster than others.

3. All references to the laws of supply and demand refer to constant-quality units of a commodity. A time period for the analysis must also be specified.
4. The demand schedule shows the relationship between various possible prices and their respective quantities purchased per unit time period. Graphically, the demand schedule is a demand curve and is downward-sloping.

5. The determinants of demand other than price are (a) income, (b) tastes and preferences, (c) the prices of related goods, (d) expectations, and (e) population, or market, size. Whenever any of these determinants of demand changes, the demand curve shifts.

6. The supply curve is generally upward-sloping such that at higher prices, more will be forthcoming than at lower prices. At higher prices, suppliers are willing to incur the increasing costs of higher rates of production.

7. The determinants of supply other than price are (a) input costs, (b) technology and productivity, (c) taxes and subsidies, (d) price expectations, and (e) entry and exit of firms.

8. A movement along a demand or supply curve is not the same thing as a shift in the curve. A change in price causes movement along the curve. A change in any other determinant of supply or demand shifts the entire curve.

9. The demand and supply curves intersect at the equilibrium point, marking the market clearing price, where quantity demanded just equals quantity supplied. At that point, the plans of buyers and sellers mesh exactly.

10. When the price of a good is greater than its market clearing price, an excess quantity is supplied at that price; it is called a surplus. When the price is below the market clearing price, an excess quantity is demanded at that price; it is called a shortage.

DISCUSSION OF PREVIEW QUESTIONS

1. Why are relative prices important in understanding the law of demand?

People respond to changes in relative prices rather than absolute prices. If the price of CDs rises by 50 percent next year, while at the same time the prices of everything else, including your wages, also increase by 50 percent, the relative price of CDs has not changed. If nothing else has changed in your life, your normal quantity demanded of CDs will remain about the same. In a world of generally rising prices (inflation), you have to compare the price of one good with the average of all other goods in order to decide whether the relative price of that one good has gone up, gone down, or stayed the same.

An Increase in
Demand

2. How can we distinguish between a change in *demand* and a change in *quantity demanded*?

Use the accompanying graphs to aid you. Because demand is a curve, a change in demand is equivalent to a *shift* in the demand curve. Changes in demand result from changes in the other determinants of demand, such as income, tastes and preferences, expectations, prices of related goods, and population. A change in quantity demanded, given demand, is a movement along a demand curve and results only from a change in the price of the commodity in question.

A Change in
Quantity Demanded

3. Why is there generally a direct relationship between price and quantity supplied (other things being equal)?

In general, businesses experience increasing *extra* costs as they expand output in the short run. This means that additional units of output, which may be quite similar in physical attributes to initial units of output, actually cost the firm more to produce. Consequently, firms often require a higher and higher price (as an incentive) in order to produce more in the short run; this "incentive" effect implies that higher prices, other things being constant, lead to increases in quantity supplied.

4. Why will the market clearing price occur at the intersection of the supply and demand curves rather than at a higher or lower price?

Consider the accompanying graph. To demonstrate that the equilibrium price will be at P_e, we can eliminate all other prices as possibilities. Consider a price above P_e, $8 per unit. By inspection of the graph, we can see that at that price, the quantity supplied exceeds the quantity demanded for this product ($B > A$). Clearly, sellers cannot sell all they wish at $8, and they therefore find it profitable to lower price and decrease output. In fact, this surplus situation exists at *all* prices above P_e. Sellers, competing for sales, will reduce prices if a surplus exists.

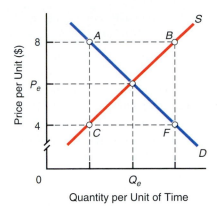

Consider a price of $4 per unit, where the quantity demanded exceeds the quantity supplied ($F > C$); a shortage of this commodity exists at a price of $4 per unit. Buyers will not be able to get all they want at that relatively low price. Because buyers are competing for this good, buyers who are willing to give up more of other goods in order to get this one will offer higher and higher prices. By doing so, they eliminate buyers who are not willing to give up more of other goods. An increase in price encourages sellers to produce and sell more. A shortage exists at *any* price below P_e, and therefore price will rise if it is below P_e.

At P_e, the quantity supplied equals the quantity demanded, Q_e, and both buyers and sellers are able to realize their intentions. Because neither group has an incentive to change its behavior, equilibrium exists at P_e.

PROBLEMS

(Answers to the odd-numbered problems appear at the back of the book.)

3-1. Construct a demand curve and a supply curve for skateboards, based on the data provided in the following tables.

Price per Skateboard	Quantity Demanded per Year
$75	3 million
50	6 million
35	9 million
25	12 million
15	15 million
10	18 million

Price per Skateboard	Quantity Supplied per Year
$75	18 million
50	15 million
35	12 million
25	9 million
15	6 million
10	3 million

What is the equilibrium price? What is the equilibrium quantity at that price?

3-2. "Drugs are obviously complementary to physicians' services." Is this statement always correct?

3-3. Five factors, other than price, that affect the demand for a good were discussed in this chapter. Place each of the following events in its proper category, and state how it would shift the demand curve in parentheses.

  a. New information is disclosed that large doses of vitamin C prevent common colds. (Demand for vitamin C)
  b. A drop in the price of educational interactive CD-ROMs occurs. (Demand for teachers)
  c. A fall in the price of pretzels occurs. (Demand for beer)

3-4. Examine the following table, and then answer the questions.

	Price per Unit Last Year	Price per Unit Today
Heating oil	$1.00	$2.00
Natural gas	.80	3.20

What has happened to the absolute price of heating oil? Of natural gas? What has happened to the price of heating oil relative to the price of natural gas? What has happened to the relative price of heating oil? Will consumers, through time, change their relative purchases? If so, how?

3-5. Suppose that the demand for oranges remains constant but a frost occurs in Florida that could potentially destroy one-third of the orange crop. What will happen to the equilibrium price and quantity for Florida oranges?

3-6. "The demand has increased so much in response to our offering of a $75 rebate that our inventory of portable laptop computers is now running very low." What is wrong with this assertion?

3-7. Analyze the following statement: "Federal farm price supports can never achieve their goals because the above-equilibrium price floors that are established by Congress and the Department of Agriculture invariably create surpluses (quantities supplied in excess of quantities demanded), which in turn drive the price right back down toward equilibrium."

3-8. Suppose that an island economy exists in which there is no money. Suppose further that every Sunday morning, at a certain location, hog farmers and cattle ranchers gather to exchange live pigs for cows. Is this a market, and if so, what do the supply and demand diagrams use as a price? Can you imagine any problems arising at the price at which cows and pigs are exchanged?

3-9. Here is a supply and demand schedule for rain in an Amazon jungle settlement where cloud seeding or other scientific techniques can be used to coax rainfall from the skies.

Price (cruzeiros per yearly centimeter of rain)	Quantity Supplied (centimeters of rain per year)	Quantity Demanded (centimeters of rain per year)
0	200	150
10	225	125
20	250	100
30	275	75
40	300	50
50	325	25
60	350	0
70	375	0
80	400	0

What are the equilibrium price and the equilibrium quantity? Explain.

COMPUTER-ASSISTED INSTRUCTION

By examining the consequence of a specific price change, we examine the roles of the substitution effect and the income effect in producing the law of demand.

Complete problem and answer appear on disk.

CHAPTER 4

EXTENSIONS OF DEMAND AND SUPPLY ANALYSIS

It was billed as the battle of grunge against greed. Eddie Vedder and the other members of Seattle grunge band Pearl Jam decided that the service charges required by Ticketmaster, the biggest distributor of tickets nationwide, were too high. Pearl Jam took the case to Congress, claiming that Ticketmaster was extracting its "pound of flesh" from poor fans nationwide by exploiting its unique position as a middleman in the live rock concert business. As soon as the word *middleman* was uttered, members of Congress started nodding their heads in agreement. To understand about middlemen is to understand about markets and exchange and how the forces of supply and demand can be altered by government actions, all topics discussed in this chapter.

PREVIEW QUESTIONS

1. Does an increase in demand always lead to a rise in price?

2. Can there ever be shortages in a market with no restrictions?

3. How are goods rationed?

4. When would you expect to encounter black markets?

Did **You Know That...** millions of pounds of chemicals called chlorofluoro-carbons (such as Freon) are being illegally imported into the United States every year? Why does a thriving black market in these chemicals exist? Legislation intended to protect the earth's ozone layer has effectively eliminated or taxed heavily the sale of Freon in the United States. Yet because Americans own hundreds of millions of air-conditioned vehicles, home refrigerators, and air conditioners, all of which require Freon, demand for the chemical remains high. When an air conditioner needs fixing, it is often cheaper to pay for illegally imported Freon than to have the unit modified to use a replacement product. Illegal markets such as the one for Freon can be analyzed using the supply and demand analysis you learned in Chapter 3. Similarly, you can use this analysis to examine purport-ed shortages of apartments in Berkeley, Santa Monica, and New York City; the "surplus" of Ph.D.s in engineering and science; and many other similar phenomena. All of these exam-ples are part of our economy, which we can characterize as a price system.

THE PRICE SYSTEM

A **price system,** otherwise known as a *market system,* is one in which relative prices are constantly changing to reflect changes in supply and demand for different commodities. The prices of those commodities are the signals to everyone within the system as to what is relatively scarce and what is relatively abundant. Indeed, it is the *signaling* aspect of the price system that provides the information to buyers and sellers about what should be bought and what should be produced. In a price system, there is a clear-cut chain of events in which any changes in demand and supply cause changes in prices that in turn affect the opportunities that businesses and individuals have for profit and personal gain. Such changes influence our use of resources.

Price system
An economic system in which relative prices are constantly changing to reflect changes in supply and demand for different commodities. The prices of those commodities are signals to everyone within the system as to what is relatively scarce and what is relatively abundant.

EXCHANGE AND MARKETS

The price system features **voluntary exchange,** acts of trading between individuals that make both parties to the trade subjectively better off. The **terms of exchange**—the prices we pay for the desired items—are determined by the interaction of the forces underlying supply and demand. In our economy, the majority of exchanges take place voluntarily in markets. A market encompasses the exchange arrangements of both buyers and sellers that underlie the forces of supply and demand. Indeed, one definition of a market is a low-cost institution for facilitating exchange. A market in essence increases incomes by helping resources move to their highest-valued uses by means of prices. Prices are the providers of information.

Voluntary exchange
An act of trading, done on a voluntary basis, in which both parties to the trade are subjectively better off after the exchange.

Terms of exchange
The terms under which trading takes place. Usually the terms of exchange are equal to the price at which a good is traded.

Transaction Costs

Individuals turn to markets because markets reduce the cost of exchanges. These costs are sometimes referred to as **transaction costs,** which are broadly defined as the costs associated with finding out exactly what is being transacted as well as the cost of enforcing con-tracts. If you were Robinson Crusoe and lived alone on an island, you would never incur a transaction cost. For everyone else, transaction costs are just as real as the costs of produc-

Transaction costs
All of the costs associated with exchanging, including the infor-mational costs of finding out price and quality, service record, and durability of a product, plus the cost of contracting and enforcing that contract.

tion. High-speed large-scale computers have allowed us to reduce transaction costs by increasing our ability to process information and keep records.

Consider some simple examples of transaction costs. The supermarket reduces transaction costs relative to your having to go to numerous specialty stores to obtain the items you desire. Organized stock exchanges, such as the New York Stock Exchange, have reduced transaction costs of buying and selling stocks and bonds. In general, the more organized the market, the lower the transaction costs. One group of individuals who constantly attempt to lower transaction costs are the much maligned middlemen.

The Role of Middlemen

As long as there are costs to bringing together buyers and sellers, there will be an incentive for intermediaries, normally called middlemen, to lower those costs. This means that middlemen specialize in lowering transaction costs. Whenever producers do not sell their products directly to the final consumer, there are, by definition, one or more middlemen involved. Farmers typically sell their output to distributors, who are usually called wholesalers, who then sell those products to supermarkets.

Recently, technology has reduced the need, and hence the job prospects, for middlemen.

EXAMPLE
Technology and the Death of Middlemen

For decades, most airline travelers did not buy tickets directly from the airlines. Instead, they relied on travel agents, who at one time numbered over 30,000. In 1995, the big airline carriers cut commissions paid to these middlemen, usually by capping them at $50 per ticket rather than the normal 10 percent of ticket purchase price. Basically, the airlines have realized that there are high-tech alternatives to travel agents for the distribution of their tickets. On-line computer services, such as CompuServe, allow subscribers to consult airline timetables and to reserve airline tickets from their home personal computers. As people become more and more familiar with how to use computers, modems, and on-line services, the trend toward cutting out the middlemen, at least in airline travel, will continue.

FOR CRITICAL ANALYSIS: How can travel agents more effectively compete with on-line computer services that offer airplane reservations? •

CHANGES IN DEMAND AND SUPPLY

It is in markets that we see the results of changes in demand and supply. In certain situations, it is possible to predict what will happen to equilibrium price and equilibrium quantity when a change occurs in demand or supply. Specifically, whenever one curve is stable while the other curve shifts, we can tell what will happen to price and quantity. Consider the four possibilities in Figure 4-1 on page 76. In panel (a), the supply curve remains stable but demand increases from D_1 to D_2. Note that the result is both an increase in the market clearing price from P_1 to P_2 and an increase in the equilibrium quantity from Q_1 to Q_2.

In panel (b), there is a decrease in demand from D_1 to D_3. This results in a decrease in both the relative price of the good and the equilibrium quantity. Panels (c) and (d) show the

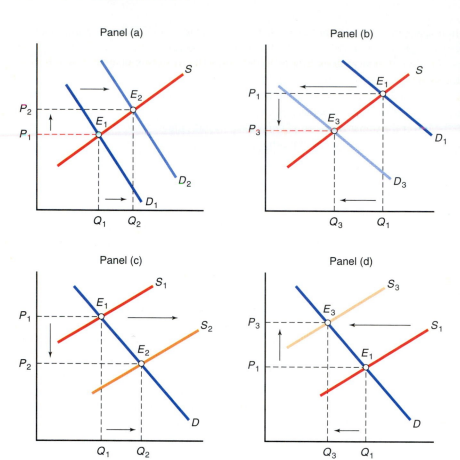

Panel (a)

Panel (b)

Panel (c)

Panel (d)

FIGURE 4-1

Shifts in Demand and in Supply: Determinate Results
In panel (a), the supply curve is stable at S. The demand curve shifts outward from D_1 to D_2. The equilibrium price and quantity rise from P_1, Q_1 to P_2, Q_2, respectively. In panel (b), again the supply curve remains stable at S. The demand curve, however, shifts inward to the left, showing a decrease in demand from D_1 to D_3. Both equilibrium price and equilibrium quantity fall. In panel (c), the demand curve now remains stable at D. The supply curve shifts from S_1 to S_2. The equilibrium price falls from P_1 to P_2. The equilibrium quantity increases, however, from Q_1 to Q_2. In panel (d), the demand curve is stable at D. Supply decreases as shown by a leftward shift of the supply curve from S_1 to S_3. The market clearing price increases from P_1 to P_3. The equilibrium quantity falls from Q_1 to Q_3.

effects of a shift in the supply curve while the demand curve is stable. In panel (c), the supply curve has shifted rightward. The relative price of the product falls; the equilibrium quantity increases. In panel (d), supply has shifted leftward—there has been a supply decrease. The product's relative price increases; the equilibrium quantity decreases.

When Both Demand and Supply Shift

The examples given in Figure 4-1 each showed a theoretically determinate outcome of a shift in either the demand curve holding the supply curve constant or the supply curve holding the demand curve constant. When both supply and demand curves change, the outcome is indeterminate for either equilibrium price or equilibrium quantity.

When both demand and supply increase, all we can be certain of is that equilibrium quantity will increase. We do not know what will happen to equilibrium price until we determine whether demand increased relative to supply (equilibrium price will rise) or supply increased relative to demand (equilibrium price will fall). The same analysis applies to decreases in both demand and supply, except that in this case equilibrium quantity falls.

We can be certain that when demand decreases and supply increases, the equilibrium price will fall, but we do not know what will happen to the equilibrium quantity unless we actually draw the new curves. If supply decreases and demand increases, we can be sure that equilibrium price will rise, but again we do not know what happens to equilibrium quantity without drawing the curves. In every situation in which both supply and demand change, you should always draw graphs to determine the resulting change in equilibrium price and quantity.

PRICE FLEXIBILITY AND ADJUSTMENT SPEED

We have used as an illustration for our analysis a market in which prices are quite flexible. Some markets are indeed like that. In others, however, price flexibility may take the form of indirect adjustments such as hidden payments or quality changes. For example, although the published price of bouquets of flowers may stay the same, the freshness of the flowers may change, meaning that the price per constant-quality unit changes. The published price of French bread might stay the same, but the quality could go up or down, thereby changing the price per constant-quality unit. There are many ways to change prices without actually changing the published price for a *nominal* unit of a product or service.

We must also consider the fact that markets do not return to equilibrium immediately. There must be an adjustment time. A shock to the economy in the form of an oil embargo, a drought, or a long strike will not be absorbed overnight. This means that even in unfettered market situations, in which there are no restrictions on changes in prices and quantities, temporary excess quantities supplied and excess quantities demanded may appear. Our analysis simply indicates what the market clearing price ultimately will be, given a demand curve and a supply curve. Nowhere in the analysis is there any indication of the speed with which a market will get to a new equilibrium if there has been a shock. The price may overshoot the equilibrium level. Remember this warning when we examine changes in demand and in supply due to changes in their nonprice determinants.

Now consider how long it takes the labor market to adjust to changes in supply and demand.

EXAMPLE
Ph.D.s Need Not Apply

During the late 1980s, news articles, TV shows, and radio commentaries proclaimed that the nation was facing a shortage of scientists. The growth in high-tech industries was going to create demands for scientists and engineers that would not be met. The government even suggested that this shortage would endanger national security. The result was an increase in the number of students seeking postgraduate education, especially doctoral degrees in engineering, the sciences, mathematics, and computer science. For example, in 1981–1982, a total of 2,621 Ph.D.s were granted in engineering; by 1991–1992, the number had more than doubled, to 5,488. Similar, though less dramatic, increases were seen in the number of doctorates awarded in the sciences and mathematics.

Yet halfway through the 1990s, joblessness among chemists was at a 20-year high. There were 3 percent fewer jobs for engineers than there had been a decade earlier, and more than 12 percent of 1995 recipients of doctorates in math could not find a job after graduation. What we were seeing was a classic case of adjustment taking time after market forces change. During the 1990s, defense industries downsized, forcing thousands of scientists and engineers out of work. When the particle accelerator being built in Texas was terminated, 1,000 physicists and engineers were "released." Pharmaceutical and biotech firms contracted and merged in the early 1990s. Academia experienced downsizing, too, drying up even more of the demand for Ph.D.s.

FIGURE 4-2

Falling Wages for Recent Ph.D.s

In the 1980s, the supply and demand for Ph.D.s yielded an equilibrium wage rate of W_1. Since then, the supply has shifted outward to S_2, while the demand has decreased to D_2. Wages have fallen somewhat, say, to W_T, but not yet to their equilibrium level of W_2. In the meantime, there is an "oversupply" of Ph.D.s at W_T.

You can see what happened using the supply and demand curves in Figure 4-2. The supply curve shifted from S_1 to S_2 during the period after 1987, reflecting the increase in the number of Ph.D.s being awarded. The demand curve shifted inward from D_1 to D_2, reflecting the decrease in the number of available positions. At the initial equilibrium E_1, the wage rate was W_1, and the equilibrium quantity of Ph.Ds in science, math, and engineering was Q_1. When the supply curve shifted to S_2 and the demand curve to D_2, there was an excess quantity supplied at wage rate W_1. While the wage rate has probably fallen somewhat below that, say, to W_T, it has not yet reached its new equilibrium at W_2. Until it gets to that point, there will be an excess quantity supplied of engineers, scientists, and computer specialists with Ph.D.s.

FOR CRITICAL ANALYSIS: *"The longer the time needed to learn a specialty, the more risk is involved." Analyze this quotation.* •

CONCEPTS IN BRIEF

- The terms of exchange in a voluntary exchange are determined by the interaction of the forces underlying demand and supply. These forces take place in markets, which tend to minimize transaction costs.

- When the demand curve shifts outward or inward with a stable supply curve, equilibrium price and quantity increase or decrease, respectively. When the supply curve shifts outward or inward given a stable demand curve, equilibrium price moves in the direction opposite of equilibrium quantity.

- When there is a shift in demand or supply, the new equilibrium price is not obtained instantaneously. Adjustment takes time.

THE RATIONING FUNCTION OF PRICES

A shortage creates a situation that forces price to rise toward a market clearing, or equilibrium, level. A surplus brings into play forces that cause price to fall toward its market

Water "Rationing"

More and more these days, we hear about the lack of water in some city, state, or country. For seven successive years in the 1980s and 1990s, California suffered droughts and was "forced" to "ration" water. Puerto Rico suffered a drought when rainfall dropped to 35 percent below normal; residents of San Juan were subjected to water cutoffs every other day. These stories about "running out of water" always focus on the supply of water, never on the demand. The demand curve for water slopes downward, just like that for any other good or service. When the supply of strawberries increases in the summer, their prices go down; when the supply decreases, their prices go up. When the supply of water falls because of a drought, one way to ration a smaller supply is to increase the price. For some reason, politicians and media announcers reject this possibility, implying that water is different. Beware when you see the word *rationing* in the media; it typically means that the price of a good or service has not been allowed to reach equilibrium.

clearing level. The synchronization of decisions by buyers and sellers that creates a situation of equilibrium is called the *rationing function of prices*. Prices are indicators of relative scarcity. An equilibrium price clears the market. The plans of buyers and sellers, given the price, are not frustrated.[1] It is the free interaction of buyers and sellers that sets the price that eventually clears the market. Price, in effect, rations a commodity to demanders who are willing and able to pay the highest price. Whenever the rationing function of prices is frustrated by government-enforced price ceilings that set prices below the market clearing level, a prolonged shortage situation is not allowed to be corrected by the upward adjustment of the price.

There are other ways to ration goods. *First come, first served* is one method. *Political power* is another. *Physical force* is yet another. Cultural, religious, and physical differences have been and are used as rationing devices throughout the world.

Consider first come, first served as a rationing device. In countries that do not allow prices to reflect true relative scarcity, first come, first served has become a way of life. We call this *rationing by queues*, where *queue* means "line," as in Britain. Whoever is willing to wait in line the longest obtains meat that is being sold at less than the market clearing price. All who wait in line are paying a higher *total* price than the money price paid for the meat. Personal time has an opportunity cost. To calculate the total price of the meat, we must add up the money price plus the opportunity cost of the time spent waiting.

Lotteries are another way to ration goods. You may have been involved in a rationing-by-lottery scheme during your first year in college when you were assigned a university-provided housing unit. Sometimes for popular classes, rationing by lottery is used to fill the available number of slots.

Rationing by *coupons* has also been used, particularly during wartime. In the United States during World War II, families were allotted coupons that allowed them to purchase specified quantities of rationed goods, such as meat and gasoline. To purchase such goods, you had to pay a specified price *and* give up a coupon.

Rationing by waiting may occur in situations in which entrepreneurs are free to change prices to equate quantity demanded with quantity supplied but choose not to do so. This results in queues of potential buyers. The most obvious conclusion seems to be that the price in the market is being held below equilibrium by some noncompetitive force. That is not true, however.

The reason is that queuing may also arise when the demand characteristics of a market are subject to large or unpredictable fluctuations, and the additional costs to firms (and ultimately to consumers) of constantly changing prices or of holding sufficient inventories or providing sufficient excess capacity to cover these peak demands are greater than the costs to consumers of waiting for the good. This is the usual case of waiting in line to purchase a fast-food lunch or to purchase a movie ticket a few minutes before the next show.

---

[1] There is a difference between frustration and unhappiness. You may be unhappy because you can't buy a Rolls Royce, but if you had sufficient income, you would not be frustrated in your attempt to purchase one at the current market price. By contrast, you would be frustrated if you went to your local supermarket and could get only two cans of your favorite soft drink when you had wanted to purchase a dozen and had the necessary income.

The Essential Role of Rationing

In a world of scarcity, there is, by definition, competition for what is scarce. After all, any resources that are not scarce can be had by everyone at a zero price in as large a quantity as everyone wants, such as air to burn in internal combustion engines. Once scarcity arises, there has to be some method to ration the available resources, goods, and services. The price system is one form of rationing; the others that we mentioned are alternatives. Economists cannot say which system of rationing is best. They can, however, say that rationing via the price system leads to the most efficient use of available resources. This means that generally in a price system, further trades could not occur without making somebody worse off. In other words, in a freely functioning price system, all of the gains from mutually beneficial trade will be exhausted.

CONCEPTS IN BRIEF

- Prices in a market economy perform a rationing function because they reflect relative scarcity, allowing the market to clear. Other ways to ration goods include first come, first served; political power; physical force; lotteries; and coupons.

- Even when businesspeople can change prices, some rationing by waiting will occur. Such queuing arises when there are large unexpected changes in demand coupled with high costs of satisfying those changes immediately.

THE POLICY OF GOVERNMENT-IMPOSED PRICE CONTROLS

The rationing function of prices is often not allowed to operate when governments impose price controls. **Price controls** typically involve setting a **price ceiling**—the maximum price that may be allowed in an exchange. The world has had a long history of price ceilings applied to some goods, wages, rents, and interest rates, among other things. Occasionally a government will set a **price floor**—a minimum price below which a good or service may not be sold. These have most often been applied to wages and agricultural products. Let's consider price controls in terms of price ceilings.

Price Ceilings and Black Markets

As long as a price ceiling is below the market clearing price, imposing a price ceiling creates a shortage, as can be seen in Figure 4-3. At any price below the market clearing, or equilibrium, price of P_e, there will always be a larger quantity demanded than quantity supplied, that is, a shortage. This was discussed initially in Chapter 3. Normally, whenever a shortage exists, there is a tendency for price and output to rise to equilibrium levels. This is exactly what we pointed out when discussing shortages in the labor market. But with a price ceiling, this tendency cannot be fully realized because everyone is forbidden to trade at the equilibrium price.

Price controls
Government-mandated minimum or maximum prices that may be charged for goods and services.

Price ceiling
A legal maximum price that may be charged for a particular good or service.

Price floor
A legal minimum price below which a good or service may not be sold. Legal minimum wages are an example.

FIGURE 4-3

Black Markets

The demand curve is D. The supply curve is S. The equilibrium price is P_e. The government, however, steps in and imposes a maximum price of P_1. At that lower price, the quantity demanded will be Q_d, but the quantity supplied will only be Q_s. There is a shortage, and black markets develop. The implicit price (including nonprice costs) rises to P_2.

Nonprice rationing devices

All methods used to ration scarce goods that are price-controlled. Whenever the price system is not allowed to work, nonprice rationing devices will evolve to ration the affected goods and services.

Black market

A market in which goods are traded at prices above their legal maximum prices or in which illegal goods are sold.

The result is fewer exchanges and **nonprice rationing devices.** In Figure 4-3, at an equilibrium price of P_e, the equilibrium quantity demanded and supplied (or traded) is Q_e. But at the price ceiling of P_1, the equilibrium quantity offered is only Q_s. What happens if there is a shortage? The most obvious nonprice rationing device to help clear the market is queuing, or long lines, which we have already discussed.

Typically, an effective price ceiling leads to a **black market.** A black market is a market in which the price-controlled good is sold at an illegally high price through various methods. For example, if the price of gasoline is controlled at lower than the market clearing price, a gas station attendant may take a cash payment on the side in order to fill up a driver's car (as happened in the 1970s in the United States during price controls on gasoline). If the price of beef is controlled at below its market clearing price, the butcher may give special service to a customer who offers the butcher great seats at an upcoming football game. Indeed, the number of ways in which the true implicit price of a price-controlled good or service can be increased is infinite, limited only by the imagination. (Black markets also occur when goods are made illegal.)

Whenever a nation attempts to freeze all prices, a variety of problems arise. Many of them occurred a few years ago in Mexico.

INTERNATIONAL EXAMPLE
Mexico's Price Freeze and the Shopping Cops

The mid-1990s marked a low point for the Mexican economy when its currency, the peso, plunged in value relative to the dollar and other international currencies. In anticipation of rapidly rising domestic prices, the Mexican government imposed a temporary freeze on all prices. Almost immediately, shoppers began complaining about supermarkets, department stores, car dealerships, and mom and pop stores that were illegally raising their prices. In response, the Mexican Consumer Attorney General's Office sent out a small army of "shopping cops" to impose fines as necessary and temporarily closed hundreds of stores. During one national sample of commercial establishments, the Mexican Consumer Attorney General's Office reported that 70 percent were found to be cheating on the price freeze.

One way merchants got around government price controls was to place "sold" stickers on merchandise. Consumers then had to agree to pay a higher price in order to obtain the goods. Many automobile dealerships refused to deliver cars bought prior to the dramatic reduction in the value of the Mexican peso. Indeed, the number of ways to evade price controls were limited only by the imagination of buyers and sellers.

FOR CRITICAL ANALYSIS: How would you graphically illustrate the situation in Mexico using a supply and demand diagram? •

CONCEPTS IN BRIEF

- Government policy can impose price controls in the form of price ceilings and price floors.

- An effective price ceiling is one that sets the legal price below the market clearing price and is enforced. Effective price ceilings lead to nonprice rationing devices and black markets.

THE POLICY OF CONTROLLING RENTS

Over 200 American cities and towns, including Santa Monica, Berkeley, and New York City, operate under some kind of rent control. **Rent control** is a system under which the local government tells building owners how much they can charge their tenants in rent. In the United States, rent controls date back to at least World War II. The objective of rent control is to keep rents below levels that would be observed in a freely competitive market.

Rent control
The placement of price ceilings on rents in particular cities.

The Functions of Rental Prices

In any housing market, rental prices serve three functions: (1) to promote the efficient maintenance of existing housing and stimulate the construction of new housing, (2) to allocate existing scarce housing among competing claimants, and (3) to ration the use of existing housing by current demanders.

Rent Controls and Construction. Rent controls have discouraged the construction of new rental units. Rents are the most important long-term determinant of profitability, and rent controls have artificially depressed them. Consider some examples. In a recent year in Dallas, Texas, with a 16 percent rental vacancy rate but no rent control laws, 11,000 new rental housing units were built. In the same year in San Francisco, California, only 2,000 units were built. The major difference? San Francisco has only a 1.6 percent vacancy rate but stringent rent control laws. In New York City, except for government-subsidized construction, the only rental units being built are luxury units, which are exempt from controls. In Santa Monica, California, new apartments were not being constructed at all until 1996 when that city's rent control law was softened by the state legislature. New office rental space and commercial developments have always been exempt from rent controls.

Effects on the Existing Supply of Housing. When rental rates are held below equilibrium levels, property owners cannot recover the cost of maintenance, repairs, and capital improvements through higher rents. Hence they curtail these activities. In the extreme situation, taxes, utilities, and the expenses of basic repairs exceed rental receipts. The result is abandoned buildings. Numerous buildings have been abandoned in New York City. Some owners have resorted to arson, hoping to collect the insurance on their empty buildings before the city claims them for back taxes.

In Santa Monica, the result is bizarre contrasts: Run-down rental units sit next to homes costing more than $500,000, and abandoned apartment buildings share the block with luxury car dealerships. With the new law, such an anomaly should gradually disappear.

Rationing the Current Use of Housing. Rent controls also affect the current use of housing because they restrict tenant mobility. Consider the family whose children have gone off to college. That family might want to live in a smaller apartment. But in a rent-controlled environment, there can be a substantial cost to giving up a rent-controlled unit. In New York City, for example, rents can be adjusted only when a tenant leaves. That means that a move from a long-occupied rent-controlled apartment to a smaller apartment can involve a hefty rent hike. This artificial preservation of the status quo has become known in New York as "housing gridlock."

Attempts at Evading Rent Controls

The distortions produced by rent controls lead to efforts by both landlords and tenants to evade the rules. This leads to the growth of expensive government bureaucracies whose job it is to make sure that rent controls aren't evaded. In New York City, landlords have an incentive to make life unpleasant for tenants or to evict them on the slightest pretense. This may be the only way the landlord can raise the rent. The city has responded by making evictions extremely costly for landlords. Eviction requires a tedious and expensive judicial proceeding. Tenants, for their part, routinely try to sublet all or part of their rent-controlled apartments at fees substantially above the rent they pay to the owner. Both the city and the landlords try to prohibit subletting and typically end up in the city's housing courts—an entire judicial system developed to deal with disputes involving rent-controlled apartments. The overflow and appeals from the city's housing courts is now clogging the rest of New York's judicial system. Santa Monica has a similar rent control board. Its budget grew 500 percent in less than a decade. The landlords pay for it through a special annual assessment of more than $150 per rental unit per year.

Who Gains and Who Loses from Rent Controls?

The big losers from rent controls are clearly landlords. But there is another group of losers—low-income individuals, especially single mothers, trying to find their first apartment. Some observers now believe that rent controls have worsened the problem of homeless people in such cities as New York.

Typically, landlords of rent-controlled apartments often charge "key money" before a new tenant is allowed to move in. This is a large up-front cash payment, usually illegal but demanded nonetheless—just one aspect of the black market in rent-controlled apartments. Poor individuals cannot afford a hefty key money payment, nor can they assure the landlord that their rent will be on time or even paid each month. Because controlled rents are usually below market clearing levels, there is little incentive for apartment owners to take any risk on low-income-earning individuals as tenants. This is particularly true when a prospective tenant's chief source of income is a welfare check. Indeed, a large number of the litigants in the New York housing courts are welfare mothers who have missed their rent payments due to emergency expenses or delayed welfare checks. Often their appeals end in evictions and a new home in a temporary public shelter—or on the streets.

Who benefits from rent control? Ample evidence indicates that upper-income professionals benefit the most. These are the people who can use their mastery of the bureaucracy and their large network of friends and connections to exploit the rent control system. Consider that in New York, actresses Mia Farrow and Cicely Tyson live in rent-controlled

apartments, paying well below market rates. So do State Senate Democratic leader Man-
fred Ohrenstein, the director of the Metropolitan Museum of Art, the chairman of Pathmark
Stores, and writer Alistair Cooke.

The average subsidy from rent regulation in New York City has been about $345 a
month for tenant households with annual incomes above $75,000 but only $176 a month
for households with incomes between $10,000 and $20,000. The results of a study by the
Pacific Legal Foundation concerning rent controls in Santa Monica and Berkeley are
instructive. Since the institution of rent controls in those two communities, they have
become more exclusive in terms of median income and average education level compared
to surrounding communities. In other words, both Santa Monica and Berkeley have experienced significant declines in the populations that the legislation was intended to protect.

INTERNATIONAL EXAMPLE
Rent Controls in Bombay

In the mid-1990s, the most expensive capital in the world with respect to
rents was Bombay, India. The annual rent per square foot for *available* unleased space was
estimated at about $177, compared to $45 in midtown Manhattan. In addition, most landlords insist on receiving a year's rent in advance plus an additional security deposit equal
to two years' rent. For major businesses, this can add up to millions of dollars, which are
usually returned, but in three to five years and without payment of any interest.

One reason why Bombay rents are so high is the existence of rent controls and other
laws intended to protect tenants. These controls and restrictions have kept out real estate
developers and even scared owners of rentable property from renting that property, be it
commercial or residential. One rent control law makes it almost impossible for a landlord
to evict a tenant or to raise rents. Tenants can obtain what is called *statutory tenancy,* which
allows them and their descendents to remain without a lease in any property they currently
rent. There are situations in Bombay in which renters from 50 years ago still live in the
same apartment, paying approximately the same rent as they originally did. Not surprisingly, unleased rental space is hard to find and hence quite expensive.

FOR CRITICAL ANALYSIS: *What effect do you think Bombay's high rents might have
on foreign firms' desire to operate in that city?* •

CONCEPTS IN BRIEF

- Rental prices perform three functions: (1) allocating existing scarce housing among competing claimants, (2) promoting efficient maintenance of existing houses and stimulating new housing construction, and (3) rationing the use of existing houses by current demanders.

- Effective rent controls reduce or alter the three functions of rental prices. Construction of new rental units is discouraged. Rent controls decrease spending on maintenance of existing ones and also lead to "housing gridlock."

- There are numerous ways to evade rent controls; key money is one.

PRICE FLOORS IN AGRICULTURE

Another way that government can affect markets is by imposing price floors or price supports.
In the United States, price supports are most often associated with agricultural products.

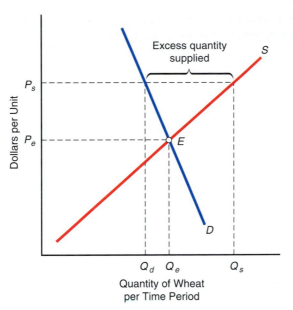

FIGURE 4-4

Agricultural Price Supports
Free market equilibrium occurs at *E*, with an equilibrium price of P_e and an equilibrium quantity of Q_e. When the government set a support price at P_s, the quantity demanded was Q_d, and the quantity supplied was Q_s. The difference was the surplus, which the government bought. Note that farmers' total income was from consumers ($P_s \times Q_d$) plus taxpayers [($Q_s - Q_d) \times P_s$].

Price Supports

During the Great Depression, the federal government swung into action to help farmers. In 1933, it established a system of price supports for many agricultural products. Until recently there were price supports for wheat, feed grains, cotton, rice, soybeans, sorghum, and dairy products. The nature of the supports was quite simple: The government simply chose a *support price* for an agricultural product and then acted to ensure that the price of the product never fell below the support level. Figure 4-4 shows the market demand and supply of wheat. Without a price support program, competitive forces would yield an equilibrium price of P_e and an equilibrium quantity of Q_e. Clearly, if the government sets the support price at P_e or below, nothing will happen, because farmers can sell all they want at the market clearing price of P_e.

Until 1996, however, the government set the support price *above* P_e, at P_s. At a support price of P_s, the quantity demanded is only Q_d, but the quantity supplied is Q_s. The difference between them is called the *excess quantity supplied*, or *surplus*. As simple as this program seems, two questions arise: (1) How did the government decide on the level of the support price P_s? (2) How did it prevent market forces from pushing the actual price down to P_e?

If production exceeded the amount consumers wanted to buy at the support price, what happened to the surplus? Quite simply, the government had to buy the surplus—the difference between Q_s and Q_d—if the price support program was to work. As a practical matter, the government acquired the quantity $Q_s - Q_d$ indirectly through a government agency. The government either stored the surplus or sold it to foreign countries at a greatly reduced price (or gave it away free of charge) under the Food for Peace program.

Who Benefited from Agricultural Price Supports?

Traditionally advocated as a way to guarantee a decent wage for low-income farmers, most of the benefits of agricultural price supports were skewed toward owners of very large farms. Price supports were made on a per-bushel basis, not on a per-farm basis. Thus traditionally, the larger the farm, the bigger the benefit from agricultural price supports. In addition, *all* of the benefits from price supports ultimately accrued to *landowners* on whose land price-supported crops could grow. Except for peanuts, tobacco, and sugar, the price-support program was eliminated in 1996.

PRICE FLOORS IN THE LABOR MARKET

The **minimum wage** is the lowest hourly wage rate that firms may legally pay their workers. Proponents want higher minimum wages to ensure low-income workers a "decent" standard of living. Opponents claim that higher minimum wages cause increased unemployment, particularly among unskilled minority teenagers.

Minimum wage
A wage floor, legislated by government, setting the lowest hourly rate that firms may legally pay workers.

The federal minimum wage started in 1938 at 25 cents an hour, about 40 percent of the average manufacturing wage at the time. Typically, its level has stayed at about 40 to 50 percent of average manufacturing wages. It was increased to $4.25 in 1991 and may be higher by the time you read this. Many states and cities have their own minimum wage laws that sometimes exceed the federal minimum.

What happens when the government passes a floor on wages? The effects can be seen in Figure 4-5. We start off in equilibrium with the equilibrium wage rate of W_e and the equilibrium quantity of labor demanded and supplied equal to Q_e. A minimum wage, W_m, higher than W_e, is imposed. At W_m, the quantity demanded for labor is reduced to Q_d, and some workers now become unemployed. Note that the reduction in employment from Q_e to Q_d, or the distance from B to A, is less than the excess quantity of labor supplied at wage rate W_m. This excess quantity supplied is the distance between A and C, or the distance between Q_d and Q_s. The reason the reduction in employment is smaller than the excess supply of labor at the minimum wage is that the latter also includes a second component that consists of the additional workers who would like to work more hours at the new, higher minimum wage. Some workers may become unemployed as a result of the minimum wage, but others will move to sectors where minimum wage laws do not apply; wages will be pushed down in these uncovered sectors.

In the long run (a time period that is long enough to allow for adjustment by workers and firms), some of the reduction in labor demanded will result from a reduction in the number of firms, and some will result from changes in the number of workers employed by each firm. Economists estimate that a 10 percent increase in the real minimum wage decreases total employment of those affected by 1 to 2 percent.[2]

QUANTITY RESTRICTIONS

Governments can impose quantity restrictions on a market. The most obvious restriction is an outright ban on the ownership or trading of a good. It is presently illegal to buy and sell human organs. It is also currently illegal to buy and sell certain psychoactive drugs such as cocaine, heroin, and marijuana. In some states, it is illegal to start a new hospital without obtaining a license for a particular number of beds to be offered to patients. This licensing requirement effectively limits the quantity of hospital beds in some states. From 1933 to

---

[2]Because we are referring to a long-run analysis here, the reduction in labor demanded would be demonstrated by an eventual shift inward to the left of the short-run demand curve, *D,* in Figure 4-5.

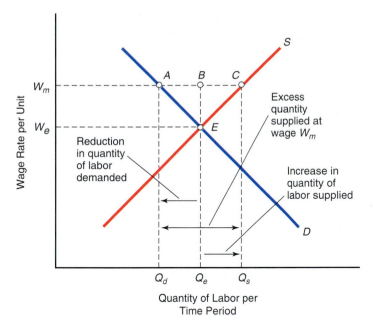

FIGURE 4-5

The Effect of Minimum Wages

The market clearing wage rate is W_e. The market clearing quantity of employment is Q_e, determined by the intersection of supply and demand at point E. A minimum wage equal to W_m is established. The quantity of labor demanded is reduced to Q_d; the reduction in employment from Q_e to Q_d is equal to the distance between B and A. That distance is smaller than the excess quantity of labor supplied at wage rate W_m. The distance between B and C is the increase in the quantity of labor supplied that results from the higher minimum wage rate.

1973, it was illegal for U.S. citizens to own gold except for manufacturing, medicinal, or jewelry purposes.

Some of the most common quantity restrictions exist in the area of international trade. The U.S. government, as well as many foreign governments, imposes import quotas on a variety of goods. An **import quota** is a supply restriction that prohibits the importation of more than a specified quantity of a particular good in a one-year period. The United States has had import quotas on tobacco, sugar, and immigrant labor. For many years, there were import quotas on oil coming into the United States. There are also "voluntary" import quotas on certain goods. Japanese automakers have agreed since 1981 "voluntarily" to restrict the amount of Japanese cars they send to the United States.

Import quota

A physical supply restriction on imports of a particular good, such as sugar. Foreign exporters are unable to sell in the United States more than the quantity specified in the import quota.

POLICY EXAMPLE

Should the Legal Quantity of Cigarettes Supplied Be Set at Zero?

Nicotine has been used as a psychoactive drug by the native people of the Americas for approximately 8,000 years. Five hundred years ago, Christopher Columbus introduced tobacco to the Europeans, who discovered that once they overcame the nausea and dizziness produced by chewing, snorting, or smoking the tobacco, they simply could not get along without it. Nicotine quickly joined alcohol and caffeine as one of the world's principal psychoactive drugs of choice.

In the century after Columbus returned from the Americas with tobacco, the use of and addiction to nicotine spread quickly around the world. There followed numerous efforts to quash what had become known as the "evil weed." In 1603, the Japanese prohibited the use of tobacco and repeatedly increased the penalties for violating the ban, which wasn't lifted until 1625. By the middle of the seventeenth century, similar bans on tobacco were in place in Bavaria, Saxony, Zurich, Turkey, and Russia, with punishments ranging from confiscation of property to execution. Even in the early twentieth century, several state governments in the United States attempted to ban the use of tobacco.

A proposed quantity restriction—outright prohibition—was in the news again a few years ago when the head of the Food and Drug Administration announced that his agency had finally determined that nicotine is addictive. He even argued that it should be classified with marijuana, heroin, and cocaine.

What can we predict if tobacco were ever completely prohibited today? Because tobacco is legal, the supply of illegal tobacco is zero. If the use of tobacco were restricted, the supply of illegal tobacco would not remain zero for long. Even if U.S. tobacco growers were forced out of business, the production of tobacco in other countries would increase to meet the demand. Consequently, the supply curve of illegal tobacco products would shift outward to the right as more foreign sources determined they wanted to enter the illegal U.S. tobacco market. The demand curve for illegal tobacco products would emerge almost immediately after the quantity restriction. The price people pay to satisfy their nicotine addiction would go up.

FOR CRITICAL ANALYSIS: *What other goods or services follow the same analysis as the one presented here?* •

CONCEPTS IN BRIEF

- With a price support system, the government sets a minimum price at which, say, qualifying farm products can be sold. Any farmers who cannot sell at that price can "sell" their surplus to the government. The only way a price support system can survive is for the government or some other entity to buy up the excess quantity supplied at the support price.

- When a floor is placed on wages at a rate that is above market equilibrium, the result is an excess quantity of labor supplied at that minimum wage.

- Quantity restrictions may take the form of import quotas, which are limits on the quantity of specific foreign goods that can be brought into the United States for resale purposes.

Grunge Meets Greed

Concepts Applied: *Markets, exchange, price system, middlemen, rationing, supply and demand*

Pearl Jam's Eddie Vedder refused to sell tickets for the '95–'96 tour through Ticketmaster because the distributor adds on a hefty fee to tickets. Are Ticketmaster's services of convenient ticket purchasing worth the price they charge? Pearl Jam didn't think so.

Arguably, the Seattle grunge band Pearl Jam is one of the most successful rock bands of our time. Not only is it one of the most popular bands in America, but it is also the most revolutionary. Pearl Jam refused to make videos for MTV and VH-1 for its second successful album, *Vs.*, and didn't release any singles from that album in the United States. When the band finally decided to tour after an intentionally long hiatus, it demanded a $20 ceiling on ticket prices, including a top service charge of 10 percent from the nation's leading ticket distributor, Ticketmaster.

Ticketmaster's Position as the Middleman

Ticketmaster distributes tickets nationwide for major entertainment events using a highly sophisticated computer system. When asked about Pearl Jam's claims that Ticketmaster was "gouging" fans, the head of the company, Fred Rosen, said that Ticketmaster's investment in that computer system makes it easier for performers to sell large numbers of tickets. Each year, Ticketmaster sells between 50 and 60 million tickets. Rosen believes that Ticketmaster has the right to be paid for such services and notes that "if Pearl Jam wants to play for free, we will be happy to distribute their tickets for free." Ticketmaster currently charges a fee of $4 to $18 per ticket.

Competition Among Middlemen

In most markets, there is competition among middlemen, and that competition lowers the price of their services. Prior to 1991, Ticketmaster's main competitor was Ticketron. In the 1980s, Ticketron began losing millions of dollars a year and eventually sold out to Ticketmaster in 1991. Apparently Ticketron was not operating as efficiently as Ticketmaster.

The Value That Ticketmaster Adds

Goods have little or no value if consumers cannot obtain them. The value of a good therefore depends on its availability. Middlemen add value to goods without physically changing them by simply making it easier for consumers to purchase them. As a middleman, this is what Ticketmaster does. Major entertainment events, such as a Pearl Jam concert, are most profitable and add value to more consumers when they are performed in large venues, such as football stadiums. It would be virtually impossible to service all of the fans desiring to attend a Pearl Jam concert if tickets were sold only at the box office of the venue where the concert was being held. A computerized nationwide system allows popular bands to sell tickets efficiently for concerts at large-capacity venues.

Pearl Jam's Failed Alternative Distribution System

Pearl Jam originally decided to give concerts without the use of Ticketmaster by distributing tickets through a lottery. Some 175,000 people sent in postcards for the two concerts that were to be held at Constitution Hall in Philadelphia, which seats 3,700 people. Of course, many people who saw those concerts paid extravagant prices by using the services of scalpers. One of the things that Pearl Jam cannot control is the value that fans place on seeing and hearing the band perform live. As long as different fans have different valuations of an activity, there will be some who will willingly give up their tickets at a high enough price, which others will gladly pay.

Neither the lottery nor any other alternatives that Pearl Jam tried to get around the intermediary services of Ticketmaster worked. The band canceled its 1995–1996 tour. Its spokespersons claimed that "touring without Ticketmaster was too complicated." About the same time, the congressional investigation into Ticketmaster for allegedly keeping ticket prices too high quietly closed without any action taken.

Competition for Ticketmaster may be on the horizon, with Massachusetts-based NEXT Ticketing selling tickets via a high-tech phone system and the Internet.

FOR CRITICAL ANALYSIS
1. Assume that Ticketmaster distributes 100 percent of all tickets to live entertainment events in the United States. Why wouldn't Ticketmaster charge an even higher service charge per ticket, say, $50?
2. If Congress passed a law restricting Ticketmaster to a $2 charge per ticket, what might happen as a result?

CHAPTER SUMMARY

1. A price system, otherwise called a market system, allows prices to respond to changes in supply and demand for different commodities. Consumers and business managers' decisions on resource use depend on what happens to prices.
2. Exchanges take place in markets. The terms of exchange—prices—are registered in markets that tend to minimize transaction costs.
3. With a stable supply curve, a rise in demand leads to an increase in equilibrium price and quantity; a decrease in demand leads to a reduction in equilibrium price and quantity. With a stable demand curve, a rise in supply leads to a decrease in equilibrium price and an increase in equilibrium quantity; a fall in supply leads to an increase in equilibrium price and a decrease in equilibrium quantity.
4. When both demand and supply shift at the same time, indeterminate results occur. We must know the direction and degree of each shift in order to predict the change in equilibrium price and quantity.
5. When there is a shift in demand or supply, it takes time for markets to adjust to the new equilibrium. During that time, there will be temporary shortages or surpluses.
6. In a market system, prices perform a rationing function—they ration scarce goods and services. Other ways of rationing include first come, first

served; political power; physical force; lotteries; and coupons.
7. Government-imposed price controls can take the form of price ceilings and price floors. Effective price ceilings—ones that are set below the market clearing price and enforced—lead to nonprice rationing devices and black markets.
8. Rent controls interfere with many of the functions of rental prices. For example, effective rent controls discourage the construction of new rental units. They also encourage "housing gridlock." Landlords lose during effective rent controls. Other losers are typically low-income individuals, especially single mothers, trying to find their first apartments.
9. A price floor can take the form of a government-imposed price support for agricultural products. This creates an excess quantity supplied at the supported price. To maintain that price, the government must buy up the surplus agricultural products. A price floor can apply to wages. When the government-imposed minimum wage exceeds the equilibrium wage rate, an excess quantity of labor is supplied. The result is higher unemployment for the affected group of workers.
10. Quantity restrictions can take the form of import quotas, under which there is a limit to the quantity of the affected good that can be brought into the United States and sold.

DISCUSSION OF PREVIEW QUESTIONS

1. Does an increase in demand always lead to a rise in price?

Yes, provided that the supply curve doesn't shift also. If the supply is stable, every rise in demand will cause a shift outward to the right in the demand curve. The new equilibrium price will be higher than the old equilibrium price. If, however, the supply curve shifts at the same time, you have to know in which direction and by how much. If the supply curve shifts outward, indicating a rise in supply, the equilibrium price can rise if the shift is not as great as in demand. If the increase in supply is greater than in demand, the price can actually fall. We can be sure, though, that if demand increases and supply decreases, the equilibrium price will rise. This can be seen in the accompanying graph.

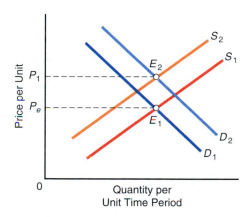

2. Can there ever be shortages in a market with no restrictions?

Yes, there can, because adjustment is never instantaneous. It takes time for the forces of supply and demand to work. In all our graphs, we draw new equilibrium points where a new supply curve meets a new demand curve. That doesn't mean that in the marketplace buyers and sellers will react immediately to a change in supply or demand. Information is not perfect. Moreover, people are often slow to adapt to higher or lower prices. Suppliers may require months or years to respond to an increase in the demand for their product. Consumers take time to respond to new information about changing relative prices.

3. How are goods rationed?

In a pure price system, prices ration goods. Prices are the indicators of relative scarcity. Prices change so that quantity demanded equals quantity supplied. In the absence of a price system, an alternative way to ration goods is first come, first served. In many systems, political power is another method. In certain cultures, physical force is a way to ration goods. Cultural, religious, and physical differences among individuals can be used as rationing devices. The fact is that given a world of scarcity, there has to be some method to ration goods. The price system is only one alternative.

4. When would you expect to encounter black markets?

Black markets occur in two situations. The first occurs whenever a good or service is made illegal by legislation. There are black markets in the United States for prostitution, gambling, and drugs. Second, there are black markets whenever a price ceiling (one type of price control) is imposed on any good or service. The price ceiling has to be below the market clearing price and enforced for a black market to exist, however. Price ceilings on rents in cities in the United States have created black markets for rental units.

PROBLEMS

(Answers to the odd-numbered problems appear at the back of the book.)

4-1. This is a graph of the supply and demand for oranges.

Explain the effect on this graph of each of the following events.

a. It is discovered that oranges can cure acne.
b. A new machine is developed that will automatically pick oranges.
c. The government declares a price floor of 25 cents.
d. The government declares a price floor of 75 cents.
e. The price of grapefruits increases.
f. Income decreases.

4-2. What might be the long-run results of price controls that maintained a good's money price below its equilibrium price? Above its equilibrium price?

4-3. Here is a demand schedule and a supply schedule for scientific hand calculators.

Price	Quantity Demanded	Quantity Supplied
$10	100,000	0
20	60,000	0
30	20,000	0
40	0	0
50	0	100,000
60	0	300,000
70	0	500,000

What are the equilibrium price and the equilibrium quantity? Explain.

4-4. This is a graph of the supply and demand for raisins.

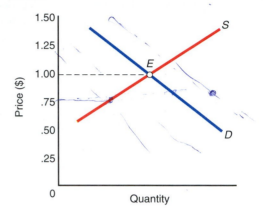

The following series of events occurs. Explain the result of the occurrence of each event.

a. An advertising campaign for California raisins is successful.
b. A fungus wipes out half the grape crop (used to make raisins) in California.
c. The price of bran flakes (a complement) increases.
d. The price of dried cranberries (a substitute) increases.
e. The government declares a price floor of 75 cents.
f. The government imposes and enforces a price ceiling of 75 cents.
g. Income increases (assume that raisins are an inferior good).

4-5. Below is a demand schedule and a supply schedule for lettuce.

Price per Crate	Quantity Demanded (crates per year)	Quantity Supplied (crates per year)
$1	100 million	0 million
2	90 million	10 million
3	70 million	30 million
4	50 million	50 million
5	20 million	80 million

What are the equilibrium price and the equilibrium quantity? At a price of $2 per crate, what is the quantity demanded? The quantity supplied? What is this disequilibrium situation called? What is the magnitude of the disequilibrium, expressed in terms of quantities? Now answer the same questions for a price of $5 per crate.

4-6. What is wrong with the following assertion? "The demand has increased so much in response to our offering of a $500 rebate that our inventory of cars is now running very low."

4-7. Rent control is a price ceiling. There are also legislated price floors. Assume that the equilibrium price for oranges is 10 cents each. Draw the supply and demand diagram to show the effect of a government-imposed price floor, or minimum price, of 15 cents per orange. Be sure to label any shortages or surpluses that result. Then show the effect of a price floor of 5 cents per orange.

COMPUTER-ASSISTED INSTRUCTION

A set of price ceiling and price floor situations is presented. You are asked to predict different outcomes for each situation in both the short and the long run.

Complete problem and answer appear on disk.

CHAPTER 5

THE PUBLIC SECTOR

In the United States over the course of a year, hundreds of thousands of tax attorneys and accountants labor alone or with clients to help those clients reduce their tax liabilities and fill out their tax returns. American taxpayers are each estimated to spend approximately 32 hours a year preparing their taxes. The opportunity cost exceeds $100 billion a year. And that is not the end of the story—many individuals spend a lot of valuable time figuring out ways to change their behavior so as to reduce the taxes they owe. Although there is never any way to avoid the cost of a tax system completely, there are ways to reduce compliance costs to society. One way is to switch to a more simplified tax system. To understand this issue, you need to know more about government and the public sector.

PREVIEW QUESTIONS

1. What problems will you encounter if you refuse to pay a portion of your income tax because you oppose national defense spending?

2. Will you benefit from many so-called tax loopholes when you first start working?

3. In what ways do regressive, proportional, and progressive tax structures differ?

4. Who pays the corporate income tax?

Did You Know That . . . the average American works from January 1 through May
7 each year to pay for all local, state, and federal taxes? The average New York resident works approximately three weeks longer to pay for all of the taxes owed each year.
Looked at another way, the average American in a typical eight-hour day works about 2
hours and 42 minutes to pay for government at all levels. Every citizen, including children,
averages about $8,000 a year in taxes of all kinds. The total amount paid exceeds $2 trillion. What is a trillion dollars? It is a million times a million. Thus it would take more than
2 million millionaires to have as much money as is spent each year by government. So we
cannot ignore the presence of government in our society. Government exists, at a minimum, to take care of what the price system does not do well.

WHAT A PRICE SYSTEM CAN AND CANNOT DO

Throughout the book so far, we have alluded to the benefits of a price system. High on the
list is economic efficiency. In its most ideal form, a price system allows resources to move
from lower-valued uses to higher-valued uses through voluntary exchange. The supreme
point of economic efficiency occurs when all mutually advantageous trades have taken
place. In a price system, consumers are sovereign; that is to say, they have the individual
freedom to decide what they wish to purchase. Politicians and even business managers do
not ultimately decide what is produced; consumers decide. Some proponents of the price
system argue that this is its most important characteristic. A market organization of economic activity generally prevents one person from interfering with another in respect to
most of his or her activities. Competition among sellers protects consumers from coercion
by one seller, and sellers are protected from coercion by one consumer because other consumers are available.

Sometimes the price system does not generate these results, with too few or too many
resources going to specific economic activities. Such situations are called **market failures.**
Market failures prevent the price system from attaining economic efficiency and individual
freedom, as well as other social goals. Market failures offer one of the strongest arguments
in favor of certain economic functions of government, which we now examine.

CORRECTING FOR EXTERNALITIES

In a pure market system, competition generates economic efficiency only when individuals
know the true opportunity cost of their actions. In some circumstances, the price that someone actually pays for a resource, good, or service is higher or lower than the opportunity
cost that all of society pays for that same resource, good, or service.

Consider a hypothetical world in which there is no government regulation against pollution. You are living in a town that until now has had clean air. A steel mill moves into town.
It produces steel and has paid for the inputs—land, labor, capital, and entrepreneurship. The
price it charges for the steel reflects, in this example, only the costs that the steel mill
incurred. In the course of production, however, the mill gets one input—clean air—by simply taking it. This is indeed an input because in the making of steel, the furnaces emit smoke.
The steel mill doesn't have to pay the cost of using the clean air; rather, it is the people in the
community who pay that cost in the form of dirtier clothes, dirtier cars and houses, and more
respiratory illnesses. The effect is similar to what would happen if the steel mill could take
coal or oil or workers' services free. There has been an **externality,** an external cost. Some
of the costs associated with the production of the steel have "spilled over" to affect **third
parties,** parties other than the buyer and the seller of the steel.

Market failure
A situation in which an unrestrained market economy leads
to too few or too many
resources going to a specific
economic activity.

Externality
A consequence of an economic
activity that spills over to affect
third parties. Pollution is an
externality.

Third parties
Parties who are not directly
involved in a given activity or
transaction.

External Costs in Graphical Form

Look at panel (a) in Figure 5-1. Here we show the demand curve for steel to be D. The supply curve is S_1. The supply curve includes only the costs that the firms have to pay. The equilibrium, or market clearing, situation will occur at quantity Q_1. Let us take into account the fact that there are externalities—the external costs that you and your neighbors pay in the form of dirtier clothes, cars, and houses and increased respiratory disease due to the air pollution emitted from the steel mill; we also assume that all other suppliers of steel use clean air without having to pay for it. Let's include these external costs in our graph to find out what the full cost of steel production really is. This is equivalent to saying that the price of an input used in steel production increased. Recall from Chapter 3 that an increase in input prices shifts the supply curve inward to the left. Thus in panel (a) of the figure, the supply curve shifts from S_1 to S_2. If the external costs were somehow taken into account, the equilibrium quantity would fall to Q_2 and the price would rise to P_2. Otherwise, that price is implicitly being paid for, but by two different groups of people. The lower price, P_1, is being explicitly paid for by the purchasers of steel and steel products. The difference between P_2 and P_1 represents the cost that third parties are bearing in the form of dirtier clothes, houses, and cars and increased respiratory illnesses.

External Benefits in Graphical Form

Externalities can also be positive. To demonstrate external benefits in graphical form, we will use the example of inoculations against communicable disease. In panel (b) of Figure

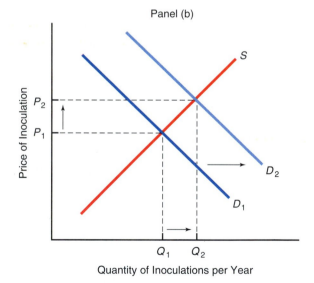

FIGURE 5-1

External Costs and Benefits

In panel (a), we show a situation in which the production of steel generates external costs. If the steel mills ignore pollution, at equilibrium the quantity of steel will be Q_1. If the mills had to pay for the additional cost borne by nearby residents that is caused by the steel mill's production, the supply curve would shift inward to the left to S_2. If consumers were forced to pay a price that reflected the spillover costs, the quantity demanded would fall to Q_2. In panel (b), we show the situation in which inoculations against communicable diseases generate external benefits to those individuals who may not be inoculated but who will benefit because epidemics will not occur. If each individual ignores the external benefit of inoculations, the market clearing quantity will be Q_1. If external benefits are taken into account by purchasers of inoculations, however, the demand curve would shift rightward to D_2. The new equilibrium quantity would be Q_2 and the price would be higher, P_2.

5-1, we show the demand curve as D_1 (without taking account of any external benefits) and the supply curve as S. The equilibrium price is P_1, and the equilibrium quantity is Q_1. We assume, however, that inoculations against communicable diseases generate external benefits to individuals who may not be inoculated but will benefit nevertheless because epidemics will not break out. If such external benefits were taken into account, the demand curve would shift outward from D_1 to D_2. The new equilibrium quantity would be Q_2, and the new equilibrium price would be P_2. With no corrective action, this society is not devoting enough resources to inoculations against communicable diseases.

When there are external costs, the market will tend to *overallocate* resources to the production of the good or service in question, for those goods or services will be deceptively low-priced. With the example of steel, too much will be produced because the steel mill owners and managers are not required to take account of the external cost that steel production is imposing on the rest of society. In essence, the full cost of production is unknown to the owners and managers, so the price they charge the public for steel is lower than it would be otherwise. And of course, the lower price means that buyers are willing and able to buy more. More steel is produced and consumed than is socially optimal.

When there are external benefits, the market *underallocates* resources to the production of that good or service because the good or service is relatively too expensive (because the demand is relatively too low). In a market system, too many of the goods that generate external costs are produced and too few of the goods that generate external benefits are produced.

How the Government Corrects Negative Externalities

The government can in theory correct externality situations in a variety of ways in all cases that warrant such action. In the case of negative externalities, at least two avenues are open to the government: special taxes and legislative regulation or prohibition.

Special Taxes. In our example of the steel mill, the externality problem originates from the fact that the air as a waste disposal place is costless to the firm but not to society. The government could make the steel mill pay a tax for dumping its pollutants into the air. The government could attempt to tax the steel mill commensurate with the cost to third parties from smoke in the air. This, in effect, would be a pollution tax or an **effluent fee.** The ultimate effect would be to reduce the supply of steel and raise the price to consumers, ideally making the price equal to the full cost of production to society.

Effluent fee
A charge to a polluter that gives the right to discharge into the air or water a certain amount of pollution. Also called a *pollution tax.*

Regulation. To correct a negative externality arising from steel production, the government could specify a maximum allowable rate of pollution. This action would require that the steel mill install pollution abatement equipment within its facilities, that it reduce its rate of output, or some combination of the two. Note that the government's job would not be that simple, for it still would have to determine the level of pollution and then actually measure its output from steel production in order to enforce such regulation.

How the Government Corrects Positive Externalities

What can the government do when the production of one good spills *benefits* over to third parties? It has several policy options: financing the production of the good or producing the good itself, subsidies (negative taxes), and regulation.

Government Financing and Production. If the positive externalities seem extremely large, the government has the option of financing the desired additional production facilities so that the "right" amount of the good will be produced. Again consider inoculations against communicable diseases. The government could—and often does—finance campaigns to inoculate the population. It could (and does) even produce and operate centers for inoculation in which such inoculations would be free.

Subsidies. A subsidy is a negative tax; it is a payment made either to a business or to a consumer when the business produces or the consumer buys a good or a service. In the case of inoculations against communicable diseases, the government could subsidize everyone who obtains an inoculation by directly reimbursing those inoculated or by making payments to private firms that provide inoculations. If you are attending a state university, taxpayers are helping to pay the cost of providing your education; you are being subsidized by as much as 80 percent of the total cost. Subsidies reduce the net price to consumers, thereby causing a larger quantity to be demanded.

Regulation. In some cases involving positive externalities, the government can require by law that a certain action be undertaken by individuals in the society. For example, regulations require that all school-age children be inoculated before entering public and private schools. Some people believe that a basic school education itself generates positive externalities. Perhaps as a result of this belief, we have regulations—laws—that require all school-age children to be enrolled in a public or private school.

> **CONCEPTS IN BRIEF**
>
> • External costs lead to an overallocation of resources to the specific economic activity. Two possible ways of correcting these spillovers are taxation and regulation.
>
> • External benefits result in an underallocation of resources to the specific activity. Three possible government corrections are financing the production of the activity, subsidizing private firms or consumers to engage in the activity, and regulation.

THE OTHER ECONOMIC FUNCTIONS OF GOVERNMENT

Besides compensating for externalities, the government performs many other functions that affect the way in which exchange is carried out in the economy. In contrast, the political functions of government have to do with deciding how income should be redistributed among households and selecting which goods and services have special merits and should therefore be treated differently. The economic and political functions of government can and do overlap.

Let's look at four more economic functions of government.

Providing a Legal System

The courts and the police may not at first seem like economic functions of government (although judges and police personnel must be paid). Their activities nonetheless have important consequences on economic activities in any country. You and I enter into contracts constantly, whether they be oral or written, expressed or implied. When we believe that we have been wronged, we seek redress of our grievances within our legal institutions. Moreover, consider the legal system that is necessary for the smooth functioning of our system. Our system has defined quite explicitly the legal status of businesses, the rights of private ownership, and a method for the enforcement of contracts. All relationships among consumers and businesses are governed by the legal rules of the game. We might consider the government in its judicial function, then, as the referee when there are disputes in the economic arena.

Much of our legal system is involved with defining and protecting *property rights*. **Property rights** are the rights of an owner to use and to exchange his or her property. One might say that property rights are really the rules of our economic game. When property rights are well defined, owners of property have an incentive to use that property efficiently. Any mistakes in their decision about the use of property have negative consequences that the owners suffer. Furthermore, when property rights are well defined, owners of property have an incentive to maintain that property so that if those owners ever desire to sell it, it will fetch a better price.

Establishing and maintaining a well-functioning legal system is not a costless activity, as you can see in the following example.

Property rights
The rights of an owner to use and to exchange property.

INTERNATIONAL POLICY EXAMPLE
Who Should Pay the High Cost of a Legal System?

When a huge multinational gets into a lengthy and expensive "shouting match" with its detractors, the public ends up footing part of the legal bill. McDonald's operates worldwide with annual sales of about $40 billion. It has property rights in the goodwill associated with its name. When two unemployed British social activists published a pamphlet with such chapter headings as "McDollar, McGreedy, McCancer, McMurder, McRipoff, McTorture, and McGarbage," McDonald's was not pleased. The pamphlet accused the American company of torturing animals, corrupting children, and exploiting the Third World. So McDonald's went to court in London. When the case began, there were 26 preliminary hearings spread over a four-year time period, and when it went to trial, 180 witnesses were called. McDonald's itself will end up spending many millions of dollars, but British taxpayers will foot the entire bill for the use of the court system. According to the Lord Chancellor's Department, British taxpayers will pay at least £2.5 million (well over $4 million).

Should taxpayers continue to pay for all of the court system? No, according to policymakers in Britain. They have a plan to make litigants pay the full cost of court services, specifically judges' salaries. Once the plan was announced, Scotland increased its courtroom fees, in some cases by 1,000 percent. Such a system that forces litigants to pay for the full opportunity cost of the legal system has yet to be instituted in the United States or elsewhere.

FOR CRITICAL ANALYSIS: *What other costs, besides judges' salaries, do citizens implicitly pay for in their legal system?* ●

Promoting Competition

Many people believe that the only way to attain economic efficiency is through competition. One of the roles of government is to serve as the protector of a competitive economic system. Congress and the various state governments have passed **antitrust legislation.** Such legislation makes illegal certain (but not all) economic activities that might, in legal terms, restrain trade—that is, prevent free competition among actual and potential rival firms in the marketplace. The avowed aim of antitrust legislation is to reduce the power of **monopolies**—firms that have great control over the price of the goods they sell. A large number of antitrust laws have been passed that prohibit specific anticompetitive business behavior. Both the Antitrust Division of the Department of Justice and the Federal Trade Commission attempt to enforce these antitrust laws. Various state judicial agencies also expend efforts at maintaining competition.

Antitrust legislation
Laws that restrict the formation of monopolies and regulate certain anticompetitive business practices.

Monopoly
A firm that has great control over the price of a good. In the extreme case, a monopoly is the only seller of a good or service.

Providing Public Goods

The goods used in our examples up to this point have been **private goods.** When I eat a cheeseburger, you cannot eat the same one. So you and I are rivals for that cheeseburger, just as much as rivals for the title of world champion are. When I use a CD-ROM player, you cannot use the same player. When I use the services of an auto mechanic, that person cannot work at the same time for you. That is the distinguishing feature of private goods— their use is exclusive to the people who purchase or rent them. The **principle of rival consumption** applies to all private goods by definition. Rival consumption is easy to understand. With private goods, either you use them or I use them.

There is an entire class of goods that are not private goods. These are called **public goods.** The principle of rival consumption does not apply to them. That is, they can be consumed *jointly* by many individuals simultaneously. National defense, police protection, and the legal system, for example, are public goods. If you partake of them, you do not necessarily take away from anyone else's share of those goods.

Characteristics of Public Goods. Several distinguishing characteristics of public goods set them apart from all other goods.[1]

1. **Public goods are often indivisible.** You can't buy or sell $5 worth of our ability to annihilate the world with bombs. Public goods cannot usually be produced or sold very easily in small units.
2. **Public goods can be used by more and more people at no additional cost.** Once money has been spent on national defense, the defense protection you receive does not reduce the amount of protection bestowed on anyone else. The opportunity cost of your receiving national defense once it is in place is zero.
3. **Additional users of public goods do not deprive others of any of the services of the goods.** If you turn on your television set, your neighbors don't get weaker reception because of your action.
4. **It is difficult to design a collection system for a public good on the basis of how much individuals use it.** It is nearly impossible to determine how much any person uses or values national defense. No one can be denied the benefits of national defense for failing to pay for that public good. This is often called the **exclusion principle.**

One of the problems of public goods is that the private sector has a difficult, if not impossible, time in providing them. There is little or no incentive for individuals in the private sector to offer public goods because it is so difficult to make a profit in so doing. Consequently, a true public good must necessarily be provided by government.

INTERNATIONAL EXAMPLE
Are Lighthouses a Public Good?

One of the most common examples of a public good is a lighthouse. Arguably, it satisfies all the criteria listed in points 1 through 4. In one instance, however, a lighthouse was not a public good in that a collection system was devised and enforced on the basis of how much individuals used it. In the thirteenth century, the city of Aigues-Mortes, a French southern port, erected a tower, called the King's Tower, designed to assert

---

Private goods
Goods that can be consumed by only one individual at a time. Private goods are subject to the principle of rival consumption.

Principle of rival consumption
The recognition that individuals are rivals in consuming private goods because one person's consumption reduces the amount available for others to consume.

Public goods
Goods to which the principle of rival consumption does not apply; they can be jointly consumed by many individuals simultaneously at no additional cost and with no reduction in quality or quantity.

Exclusion principle
The principle that no one can be excluded from the benefits of a public good, even if that person hasn't paid for it.

---

[1]Sometimes the distinction is made between pure public goods, which have all the characteristics we have described here, and quasi- or near-public goods, which do not. The major feature of near-public goods is that they are jointly consumed, even though nonpaying customers can be, and often are, excluded—for example, movies, football games, and concerts.

the will and power of Louis IX (Saint Louis). The 105-foot tower served as a lighthouse for ships. More important, it served as a lookout so that ships sailing on the open sea, but in its view, did not escape paying for use of the lighthouse. Those payments were then used for the construction of the city walls.

FOR CRITICAL ANALYSIS: *Explain how a lighthouse satisfies the characteristics of public goods described in points 1, 2, and 3.* ●

Free Riders. The nature of public goods leads to the **free-rider problem,** a situation in which some individuals take advantage of the fact that others will take on the burden of paying for public goods such as national defense. Free riders will argue that they receive no value from such government services as national defense and therefore really should not pay for it. Suppose that citizens were taxed directly in proportion to how much they tell an interviewer that they value national defense. Some people will probably tell interviewers that they are unwilling to pay for national defense because they don't want any of it—it is of no value to them. Many of us may end up being free riders when we assume that others will pay for the desired public good. We may all want to be free riders if we believe that someone else will provide the commodity in question that we actually value.

The free-rider problem is a definite problem among nations with respect to the international burden of defense and how it should be shared. A country may choose to belong to a multilateral defense organization, such as the North American Treaty Organization (NATO), but then consistently attempt not to contribute funds to the organization. The nation knows it would be defended by others in NATO if it were attacked but would rather not pay for such defense. In short, it seeks a "free ride."

Free-rider problem
A problem that arises when individuals presume that others will pay for public goods so that, individually, they can escape paying for their portion without causing a reduction in production.

Ensuring Economywide Stability

The government attempts to stabilize the economy by smoothing out the ups and downs in overall business activity. Our economy sometimes faces the problems of unemployment and rising prices. The government, especially the federal government, has made an attempt to solve these problems by trying to stabilize the economy. The notion that the federal government should undertake actions to stabilize business activity is a relatively new idea in the United States, encouraged by high unemployment rates during the Great Depression of the 1930s and subsequent theories about possible ways by which government could reduce unemployment. In 1946, the government passed the Employment Act, a landmark law concerning government responsibility for economic performance. It established three goals for government accountability: full employment, price stability, and economic growth. These goals have provided the justification for many government economic programs during the post–World War II period.

CONCEPTS IN BRIEF

- The economic activities of government include (1) correcting for externalities, (2) providing a judicial system, (3) promoting competition, (4) producing public goods, and (5) ensuring economywide stability.

- Public goods can be consumed jointly. The principle of rival consumption does not apply as it does with private goods.

- Public goods have the following characteristics: (1) They are indivisible; (2) once they are produced, there is no opportunity cost when additional consumers use them; (3) your use of a public good does not deprive others of its simultaneous use; and (4) consumers cannot conveniently be charged on the basis of use.

THE POLITICAL FUNCTIONS OF GOVERNMENT

At least two areas of government are in the realm of political, or normative, functions rather than that of the economic ones discussed in the first part of this chapter. These two areas are (1) the regulation and/or provision of merit and demerit goods and (2) income redistribution.

Merit and Demerit Goods

Certain goods are considered to have special merit. A **merit good** is defined as any good that the political process has deemed socially desirable. (Note that nothing inherent in any particular good makes it a merit good. It is a matter of who chooses.) Some examples of merit goods in our society are museums, ballets, plays, and concerts. In these areas, the government's role is the provision of merit goods to the people in society who would not otherwise purchase them at market clearing prices or who would not purchase an amount of them judged to be sufficient. This provision may take the form of government production and distribution of merit goods. It can also take the form of reimbursement for payment on merit goods or subsidies to producers or consumers for part of the cost of merit goods. Governments do indeed subsidize such merit goods as concerts, ballets, museums, and plays. In most cases, such merit goods would rarely be so numerous without subsidization.

Demerit goods are the opposite of merit goods. They are goods that, through the political process, are deemed socially undesirable. Heroin, cigarettes, gambling, and cocaine are examples. The government exercises its role in the area of demerit goods by taxing, regulating, or prohibiting their manufacture, sale, and use. Governments justify the relatively high taxes on alcohol and tobacco by declaring them demerit goods. The best-known example of governmental exercise of power in this area is the stance against certain psychoactive drugs. Most psychoactives (except nicotine, caffeine, and alcohol) are either expressly prohibited, as is the case for heroin, cocaine, and opium, or heavily regulated, as in the case of prescription psychoactives.

Income Redistribution

Another relatively recent political function of government has been the explicit redistribution of income. This redistribution uses two systems: the progressive income tax (described later in this chapter) and *transfer payments*. **Transfer payments** are payments made to individuals for which in return no services or goods are concurrently rendered. The three key money transfer payments in our system are welfare, Social Security, and unemployment insurance benefits. Income redistribution also includes a large amount of income **transfers in kind,** as opposed to money transfers. Some income transfers in kind are food stamps, Medicare and Medicaid, government health care services, and low-cost public housing.

The government has also engaged in other activities as a form of redistribution of income. For example, the provision of public education is at least in part an attempt to redistribute income by making sure that the very poor have access to education.

Merit good
A good that has been deemed socially desirable through the political process. Museums are an example.

Demerit good
A good that has been deemed socially undesirable through the political process. Heroin is an example.

Transfer payments
Money payments made by governments to individuals for which in return no services or goods are concurrently rendered. Examples are welfare, Social Security, and unemployment insurance benefits.

Transfers in kind
Payments that are in the form of actual goods and services, such as food stamps, low-cost public housing, and medical care, and for which in return no goods or services are rendered concurrently.

CONCEPTS IN BRIEF

- Political, or normative, activities of the government include the provision and regulation of merit and demerit goods and income redistribution.
- Merit and demerit goods do not have any inherent characteristics that qualify them as such; rather, collectively, through the political process, we make judgments about which goods and services are "good" for society and which are "bad."

- Income redistribution can be carried out by a system of progressive taxation, coupled with transfer payments, which can be made in money or in kind, such as food stamps and Medicare.

PAYING FOR THE PUBLIC SECTOR

Jean-Baptiste Colbert, the seventeenth-century French finance minister, said the art of taxation was in "plucking the goose so as to obtain the largest amount of feathers with the least possible amount of hissing." In the United States, governments have designed a variety of methods of plucking the private-sector goose. To analyze any tax system, we must first understand the distinction between marginal tax rates and average tax rates.

Marginal and Average Tax Rates

If somebody says, "I pay 28 percent in taxes," you cannot really tell what that person means unless you know if he or she is referring to average taxes paid or the tax rate on the last dollars earned. The latter concept has to do with the **marginal tax rate.**[2]

The marginal tax rate is expressed as follows:

$$\text{Marginal tax rate} = \frac{\text{change in taxes due}}{\text{change in taxable income}}$$

It is important to understand that the marginal tax rate applies only to the income in the highest **tax bracket** reached, where a tax bracket is defined as a specified level of taxable income to which a specific and unique marginal tax rate is applied.

The marginal tax rate is not the same thing as the **average tax rate,** which is defined as follows:

$$\text{Average tax rate} = \frac{\text{total taxes due}}{\text{total taxable income}}$$

Taxation Systems

No matter how governments raise revenues—from income taxes, sales taxes, or other taxes—all of those taxes can fit into one of three types of taxation systems—proportional, progressive, and regressive, expressing a relationship between the percentage tax, or tax rate, paid and income. To determine whether a tax system is proportional, progressive, or regressive, we simply ask the question, What is the relationship between the average tax rate and the marginal tax rate?

Proportional Taxation. **Proportional taxation** means that regardless of an individual's income, his or her taxes comprise exactly the same proportion. In terms of marginal versus average tax rates, in a proportional taxation system, the marginal tax rate is always equal to the average tax rate. If every dollar is taxed at 20 percent, then the average tax rate is 20 percent, as is the marginal tax rate.

A proportional tax system is also called a *flat-rate tax.* Taxpayers at all income levels end up paying the same *percentage* of their income in taxes. If the proportional tax rate were 20 percent, an individual with an income of $10,000 would pay $2,000 in taxes, while an individual making $100,000 would pay $20,000, the identical 20 percent rate being levied on both.

---

[2]The word *marginal* means "incremental" (or "decremental") here.

Marginal tax rate
The change in the tax payment divided by the change in income, or the percentage of additional dollars that must be paid in taxes. The marginal tax rate is applied to the highest tax bracket of taxable income reached.

Tax bracket
A specified interval of income to which a specific and unique marginal tax rate is applied.

Average tax rate
The total tax payment divided by total income. It is the proportion of total income paid in taxes.

Proportional taxation
A tax system in which regardless of an individual's income, the tax bill comprises exactly the same proportion. Also called a *flat-rate tax.*

Progressive Taxation. Under **progressive taxation,** as a person's taxable income increases, the percentage of income paid in taxes increases. In terms of marginal versus average tax rates, in a progressive system, the marginal tax rate is above the average tax rate. If you are taxed 5 percent on the first $10,000 you make, 10 percent on the next $10,000 you make, and 30 percent on the last $10,000 you make, you face a progressive income tax system. Your marginal tax rate is always above your average tax rate.

Progressive taxation
A tax system in which as income increases, a higher percentage of the additional income is taxed. The marginal tax rate exceeds the average tax rate as income rises.

EXAMPLE
The Most Progressive Tax System of All: College Financial Aid

Strangely enough, it is not a government agency that imposes the most progressive tax system in the United States but rather colleges and universities. Through their financial aid programs, they severely punish parents who earn progressively more income during the years that their children are attending college and receiving financial aid. Starting at very low annual parents' income, most college financial aid departments begin reducing financial aid as parents' incomes rise. This constitutes an implicit additional marginal income tax. In Figure 5-2, you see that federal marginal tax rates start at zero, rise to 19 percent, and then rise again to 32 percent at about $60,000. When one adds the effective impact of the reduction in financial aid for parents in these different tax brackets, the actual marginal tax rate reaches as high as 79 percent. This is because the effective marginal tax rate of losing financial aid as income rises is between 22 and 47 percent, all added on top of local, state, and federal income taxes.

FOR CRITICAL ANALYSIS: *What effect do you think this system of college financial aid has on parents' incentive to earn more income while their children are in college?* ●

FIGURE 5-2

College Financial Aid and High Implicit Marginal Income Tax Rates for Parents
Because most college and university financial aid officers decrease aid to students whose families earn more, parents of college-enrolled children face relatively high implicit marginal income tax rates. At an income of $60,000 the actual rate faced is almost 80 percent.
Source: Data from *Forbes,* January 17, 1994, p. 74.

Regressive taxation
A tax system in which as more dollars are earned, the percentage of tax paid on them falls. The marginal tax rate is less than the average tax rate as income rises.

Regressive Taxation. With **regressive taxation,** a smaller percentage of taxable income is taken in taxes as taxable income increases. The marginal rate is *below* the average rate. As income increases, the marginal tax rate falls, and so does the average tax rate. The U.S. Social Security tax is regressive. Once the legislative maximum taxable wage base is reached, no further Social Security taxes are paid. Consider a simplified hypothetical example: Every dollar up to $50,000 is taxed at 10 percent. After $50,000 there is no Social Security tax. Someone making $100,000 still pays only $5,000 in Social Security taxes. That person's average Social Security tax is 5 percent. The person making $50,000, by contrast, effectively pays 10 percent. The person making $1 million faces an average Social Security tax rate of only .5 percent in our simplified example.

CONCEPTS IN BRIEF

- Marginal tax rates are applied to marginal tax brackets, defined as spreads of income over which the tax rate is constant.
- Tax systems can be proportional, progressive, or regressive, depending on whether the marginal tax rate is the same as, greater than, or less than the average tax rate as income rises.

THE MOST IMPORTANT FEDERAL TAXES

The federal government imposes income taxes on both individuals and corporations and collects Social Security taxes and a variety of other taxes.

The Federal Personal Income Tax

The most important tax in the U.S. economy is the federal personal income tax, which accounts for about 41 percent of all federal revenues. All American citizens, resident aliens, and most others who earn income in the United States are required to pay federal income taxes on all taxable income. The rates that are paid rise up to a specified amount, depending on marital status, and then fall, as can be seen in Table 5-1. Marginal income tax rates at the federal level have varied from as low as 1 percent after the passage of the Sixteenth Amendment to as high as 94 percent (reached in 1944). There were 14 separate tax brackets prior to the Tax Reform Act of 1986, which reduced the number to three. Advocates of a more progressive income tax system in the United States argue that such a system redistributes income from the rich to the poor, taxes people according to their ability to pay, and

TABLE 5-1
Federal Marginal Income Tax Rates
These rates became effective in 1996. The highest rate includes a 10 percent surcharge on taxable income above $263,750.

Single Persons		Married Couples	
Marginal Tax Bracket	Marginal Tax Rate	Marginal Tax Bracket	Marginal Tax Rate
$0–$24,000	15%	$0–$40,100	15%
$24,001–$58,150	28%	$40,101–$96,900	28%
$58,151–$121,300	31%	$96,901–$147,700	31%
$121,301–$263,750	36%	$147,701–$263,750	36%
$263,751 and up	39.6%	$263,751 and up	39.6%

Source: U.S. Department of the Treasury.

taxes people according to the benefits they receive from government. Although there is much controversy over the redistributional nature of our progressive tax system, there is no strong evidence that in fact the tax system has never done much income redistribution in this country. Currently, about 85 percent of all Americans, rich or poor, pay roughly the same proportion of their income in federal income taxes.

The Treatment of Capital Gains

The difference between the buying and selling price of an asset, such as a share of stock or a plot of land, is called a **capital gain** if it is a profit and a **capital loss** if it is not. As of the middle of 1996, short-term capital gains were taxed at ordinary income marginal tax rates.

> **Capital gain**
> The positive difference between the purchase price and the sale price of an asset. If a share of stock is bought for $5 and then sold for $15, the capital gain is $10.

Capital gains are not always real. If you pay $100,000 for a house in one year and sell it for 50 percent more 10 years later, your nominal capital gain is $50,000. But what if, during those 10 years, there had been inflation such that average prices had also gone up by 50 percent? Your *real* capital gain would be zero. But you still have to pay taxes on that $50,000. To counter this problem, many economists have argued that capital gains should be indexed to the rate of inflation. This is exactly what is done with the marginal tax brackets in the federal income tax code. Tax brackets for the purposes of calculating marginal tax rates each year are expanded at the rate of inflation, or the rate at which the average of all prices is rising. So if the rate of inflation is 10 percent, each tax bracket is moved up by 10 percent. The same concept could be applied to capital gains. Thus far, Congress has refused to enact such a measure.

> **Capital loss**
> The negative difference between the purchase price and the sale price of an asset.

The Corporate Income Tax

Corporate income taxes account for about 12 percent of all federal taxes collected and almost 8 percent of all state and local taxes collected. Corporations are generally taxed on the difference between their total revenues (or receipts) and their expenses. The federal corporate income tax structure is given in Table 5-2.

Double Taxation. Because individual stockholders must pay taxes on the dividends they receive, paid out of *after-tax* profits by the corporation, corporate profits are taxed twice. If you receive $1,000 in dividends, you have to declare them as income, and you must pay taxes at your marginal tax rate. Before the corporation was able to pay you those dividends, it had to pay taxes on all its profits, including any that it put back into the company or did not distribute in the form of dividends. Eventually the new investment made possible by those **retained earnings**—profits not given out to stockholders—along with borrowed funds will be reflected in the increased value of the stock in that company. When you sell your stock in that company, you will have to pay taxes on the difference between

> **Retained earnings**
> Earnings that a corporation saves, or retains, for investment in other productive activities; earnings that are not distributed to stockholders.

Corporate Taxable Income	Corporate Tax Rate
$0–$50,000	15%
$50,001–$75,000	25%
$75,001–$10,000,000	34%
$10,000,000 and up	35%

Source: Internal Revenue Service.

TABLE 5-2

Federal Corporate Income Tax Schedule
The rates were in effect through 1997.

what you paid for the stock and what you sold it for. In both cases, dividends and retained earnings (corporate profits) are taxed twice.

Who Really Pays the Corporate Income Tax? Corporations can exist only as long as consumers buy their products, employees make their goods, stockholders (owners) buy their shares, and bondholders buy their bonds. Corporations per se do not do anything. We must ask, then, who really pays the tax on corporate income. This is a question of **tax incidence.** (The question of tax incidence applies to all taxes, including sales taxes and Social Security taxes.) There remains considerable debate about the incidence of corporate taxation. Some economists say that corporations pass their tax burdens on to consumers by charging higher prices. Other economists believe that it is the stockholders who bear most of the tax. Still others believe that employees pay at least part of the tax by receiving lower wages than they would otherwise. Because the debate is not yet settled, we will not hazard a guess here as to what the correct conclusion should be. Suffice it to say that you should be cautious when you advocate increasing corporation income taxes. You may be the one who ultimately ends up paying the increase, at least in part, if you own shares in a corporation, buy its products, or work for it.

Tax incidence

The distribution of tax burdens among various groups in society.

CONCEPTS IN BRIEF

- Because corporations must first pay an income tax on most earnings, the personal income tax shareholders pay on dividends received (or realized capital gains) constitutes double taxation.

- The corporate income tax is paid by one or more of the following groups: stockholder-owners, consumers of corporate-produced products, and employees in corporations.

Social Security and Unemployment Taxes

An increasing percentage of federal tax receipts is accounted for each year by taxes (other than income taxes) levied on payrolls. These taxes are for Social Security, retirement, survivors' disability, and old-age medical benefits (Medicare). As of 1996, the Social Security tax was imposed on earnings up to $62,700 at a rate of 6.2 percent on employers and 6.2 percent on employees. That is, the employer matches your "contribution" to Social Security. (The employer's contribution is really paid, at least in part, in the form of a reduced wage rate paid to employees.) A Medicare tax is imposed on all wage earnings at a combined rate of 2.9 percent. These taxes and the base on which they are levied will rise in the next decade. Social Security taxes came into existence when the Federal Insurance Contributions Act (FICA) was passed in 1935.

There is also a federal unemployment tax, which obviously has something to do with unemployment insurance. This tax rate is 0.8 percent on the first $7,000 of annual wages of each employee who earns more than $1,500. Only the employer makes the tax payment. This tax covers the costs of the unemployment insurance system and the costs of employment services. In addition to this federal tax, some states with an unemployment system impose an additional tax of up to about 3 percent, depending on the past record of the particular employer. An employer who frequently lays off workers will have a slightly higher state unemployment tax rate than an employer who never lays off workers.

It has been argued that Social Security is a system in which current workers subsidize already retired workers. It is also argued that the system is not an insurance system because Social Security benefits are legislated by Congress; they are not part of the original Federal Insurance Contributions Act. Therefore, future generations may decide that they do not want to give large Social Security benefits to retired workers. Even if workers had paid large amounts into Social Security, they could conceivably be denied the benefits of a Social Security retirement income.

INTERNATIONAL EXAMPLE
Chile's Privatized Social Security System

Since 1981, Chile has gradually transformed its government-sponsored social security system into a private pension plan. Entrants into the labor force have been required to contribute 10 percent of their gross monthly earnings to private pension fund accounts that they own outright. During this time period, and even today, virtually anyone still in the public social security system can decide to leave it. Those who choose to leave the public system are given a type of bond that is deposited in their new private pension account to be redeemed at retirement. Fully 94 percent of Chile's labor force is enrolled in 20 competing private pension plans.

FOR CRITICAL ANALYSIS: *Under what circumstances might American workers choose to "opt out" of the current federal Social Security system if they were offered the same options as Chilean workers?* ●

SPENDING, GOVERNMENT SIZE, AND TAX RECEIPTS

The size of the public sector can be measured in many different ways. One way is to count the number of public employees. Another is to look at total government outlays. Government outlays include all of its expenditures on employees, rent, electricity, and the like. In addition, total government outlays include transfer payments, such as welfare and Social Security. In Figure 5-3, you see that government outlays prior to

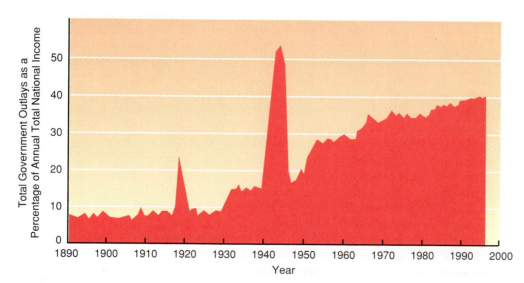

FIGURE 5-3

Total Government Outlays over Time
Here you see that total government outlays (federal, state, and local combined) remained small until the 1930s, except during World War I. Since World War II, government outlays have not fallen back to their historical average.

Sources: Facts and Figures on Government Finance and *Economic Indicators,* various issues.

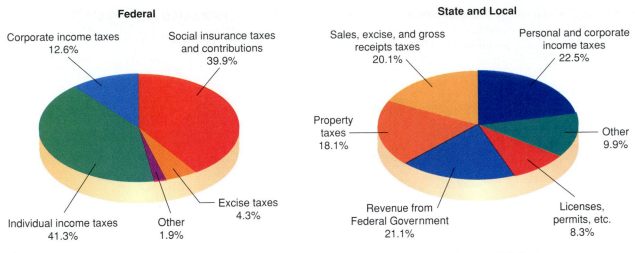

Federal

State and Local

Fiscal Year 1996 Estimate

Fiscal Year 1995 Estimate

FIGURE 5-4

Sources of Government Tax Receipts

Over 80 percent of federal revenues come from income and Social Security taxes, whereas state government revenues are spread more evenly across sources, with less emphasis on taxes based on individual income.

Source: U.S. Department of Commerce, Bureau of Economic Analysis.

World War I did not exceed 10 percent of annual national income. There was a spike during World War I, a general increase during the Great Depression, and then a huge spike during World War II. Contrary to previous postwar periods, since World War II government outlays as a percentage of total national income have not gradually fallen but rather have risen fairly regularly.

Government Receipts

The main revenue raiser for all levels of government is taxes. We show in the two pie diagrams in Figure 5-4 the percentage of receipts from various taxes obtained by the federal government and by state and local governments.

The Federal Government. The largest source of receipts for the federal government is the individual income tax. It accounts for 41.3 percent of all federal revenues. After that come social insurance taxes and contributions (Social Security), which account for 36.9 percent of total revenues. Next come corporate income taxes and then a number of other items, such as taxes on imported goods and excise taxes on such things as gasoline and alcoholic beverages.

State and Local Governments. As can be seen in Figure 5-4, there is quite a bit of difference between the origin of receipts for state and local governments and for the federal government. Personal and corporate income taxes account for only 22.5 percent of total state and local revenues. There are even a number of states that collect no personal income tax. The largest source of state and local receipts is from property taxes (used by local government), sales taxes (used mainly by state governments), and corporate income taxes.

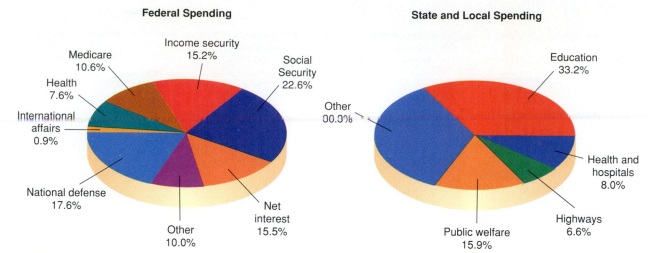

Federal Spending

Medicare 10.6%
Income security 15.2%
Social Security 22.6%
Health 7.6%
International affairs 0.9%
National defense 17.6%
Other 10.0%
Net interest 15.5%

State and Local Spending

Education 33.2%
Other 00.0%
Health and hospitals 8.0%
Public welfare 15.9%
Highways 6.6%

FIGURE 5-5

Federal Government Spending Compared to State and Local Spending

The federal government's spending habits are quite different from those of the states and cities. On the left you can see that the categories of most importance in the federal budget are defense, income security, and Social Security, which make up 55.4 percent. The most important category at the state and local level is education, which makes up 33.2 percent.

Sources: Budget of the United States Government; Government Finances.

Comparing Federal with State and Local Spending. A typical federal government budget is given in Figure 5-5. The largest three categories are defense, income security, and Social Security, which together constitute 55.4 percent of the total federal budget.

The makeup of state and local expenditures is quite different. Education is the biggest category, accounting for 33.2 percent of all expenditures.

CONCEPTS IN BRIEF

- Total government outlays including transfers have continued to grow since World War II and now account for about 40 percent of yearly total national output.

- Government spending at the federal level is different from that at the state and local levels. At the federal level, defense, income security, and Social Security account for about 55 percent of the federal budget. At the state and local levels, education comprises 33 percent of all expenditures.

Should We Switch to a Flat Tax?

Concepts Applied: Average versus marginal tax rates, opportunity cost, progressive income tax system

Each year, American taxpayers spend numerous hours preparing their taxes or hire accountants to do so for them. Switching to a national sales tax, one alternative to our current system, would eliminate the Internal Revenue Service and all of the expenses associated with that organization.

Since the enactment of the federal income tax, Americans have faced a progressive system. The top marginal tax rate soared to 94 percent in 1944, dropped to 92 percent in 1952, dropped again to 91 percent in 1954, and settled in at 50 percent starting in 1982. The Tax Reform Act of 1986 and other acts lowered it to 28 percent in 1988; today it stands at about 40 percent. The idea behind a progressive tax system is that the "rich" should pay more. In actuality, what happens is quite a different story. In Figure 5-6 on page 112, you see that regardless of what the top tax rate is, the federal government obtains around 20 percent of a nation's annual income as tax revenues.

Why? Because people respond to incentives. At high marginal tax rates, the following occurs: (1) Rich people hire more tax lawyers and accountants to help them figure out loopholes in the tax system to avoid high marginal tax rates; (2) some people change their investments to take advantage of loopholes that allow them to pay lower marginal tax rates; (3) some people drop out of the labor force, particularly secondary income earners, such as lower-paid working women; and (4) more people engage in off-the-books "underground" activities for cash on which no income taxes are paid.

An Alternative: The Flat Tax

For decades, many economists have argued in favor of scrapping our progressive income tax system and replacing it with a so-called flat tax. Several members of Congress and presidential candidates praised the approach as well. The idea behind a flat tax is simple. To calculate what you owe, simply subtract the appropriate exemption from your income and multiply the rest by the flat tax, say, 20 percent. For example, a family of four might be able to earn as much as $25,000 or $35,000 a year before it paid any income tax. The major benefits of such a system, according to its advocates, would be the following: (1) fewer resources devoted to figuring out one's taxes, (2) fewer tax attorneys and accountants, who could then be engaged in more productive activities; (3) higher saving and investment; and (4) more economic growth. According to Professor Dale Jorgenson of Harvard University, switching from our current progressive tax system to a flat tax would add about $2.5 trillion to today's current annual national income. Opponents of a flat tax argue that (1) federal revenues will fall and the federal budget deficit will rise; (2) homeowners will no longer get the benefit of deducting their mortgage interest payments from income before taxes are calculated; and (3) the rich will pay few taxes.

Another Alternative: A National Sales Tax

Alternatively, we could apply some form of a national sales tax in place of the current income tax. Such a national sales tax could be in the form of a *value-added tax (VAT)*, which is common throughout Europe. A value-added tax is assessed on the value added by a firm at each stage of production. It is a tax on the value of products that firms sell minus the value of the materials that it bought and used to produce the products. Such a tax is collected by all businesses and remitted directly to the federal government. One of the major benefits of a national sales tax is that it would greatly reduce the Internal Revenue Service and the expenses associated with that organization. A national sales tax or a value-added tax of, say, 15 to 20 percent in lieu of a federal income tax would be quite similar to a consumption tax.

A Consumption Tax

With a *consumption tax,* taxpayers pay taxes only on what they consume (spend) out of income, not what they

111

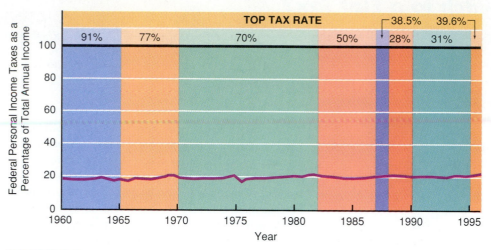

FIGURE 5-6

Changing Maximum Marginal Income Tax Rates and Revenues Collected
At the top of the diagram, you can see listed the top marginal tax rates from 1960 to the present. On the side is the percentage of total annual income collected by the federal government from the income tax system. No matter how high the marginal income tax rate has been, the government has collected about the same percentage of national income in taxes.
Source: Internal Revenue Service.

earn. One way to determine such consumption in any year is simply to subtract what is saved from what is earned. The difference is consumption, and that is the base to which a consumption tax would apply. (A consumption tax is actually equivalent to a national sales tax on all goods and services purchased.) In essence, a consumption tax provides an unlimited deduction for saving. As such, it encourages more saving. As you learned in Chapter 2, the less people choose to consume today, the faster the production possibilities curve will shift outward to the right, leading to more economic growth. Professor Lawrence J. Kitlikoff of Boston University estimated that a switch to a national sales tax or a consumption tax would generate a 27 percent greater capital stock over the 20 years following the introduction of such a system.

What About Fairness?

Every time a new tax system is discussed, the issue of fairness arises. Is it fair, as with a flat federal income tax, that everybody pay the same marginal tax rate, no matter how much he or she earns? Stephen Entin of the Institute for Research on the Economics of Taxation thinks it is:

"It is hard to find a definition of 'fairness' more compelling than the idea that every citizen is treated equally." What about a national sales tax, which might be regressive because the poor spend a larger portion of their income than the rich? Is that a "fair" system? For most economists, these are difficult questions, because they are in the realm of the normative, the value-laden. We can point out that an examination of the evidence shows what reality is. Simply stated, when marginal income tax rates are high, the rich do not, in fact, pay a higher average tax rate than when marginal tax rates are lower. It behooves the rich to find methods to reduce tax liabilities and to expend resources to influence members of Congress to insert an increasing number of loopholes in the Internal Revenue Code in order to reduce effective marginal tax rates on those who earn a lot.

FOR CRITICAL ANALYSIS

1. Do you think employees in the Internal Revenue Service would be for or against the flat-tax system? Explain your choice.
2. Why is a flat-tax system more efficient than a progressive income tax system?

CHAPTER SUMMARY

1. Government can correct external costs through taxation, legislation, and prohibition. It can correct external benefits through financing or production of a good or service, subsidies, and regulation.

2. Government provides a legal system in which the rights of private ownership, the enforcement of contracts, and the legal status of businesses are provided. In other words, government sets the legal rules of the game and enforces them.

3. Public goods, once produced, can be consumed jointly by additional individuals at zero opportunity cost.

4. If users of public goods know that they will be taxed on the basis of their expressed valuation of those public goods, their expressed valuation will be low. They expect to get a free ride.

5. Merit goods (chosen as such, collectively, through the political process) may not be purchased at all or not in sufficient quantities at market clearing prices. Therefore, government subsidizes or provides such

merit goods at a subsidized or zero price to specified classes of consumers.

6. When it is collectively decided that something is a demerit good, government taxes, regulates, or prohibits the manufacture, sale, and use of that good.

7. Marginal tax rates are those paid on the last dollars of income, whereas average taxes rates are determined by the proportion of income paid in income taxes.

8. With a proportional income tax system, marginal rates are constant. With a regressive system, they go down as income rises, and with a progressive system, they go up as income rises.

9. Total government outlays including transfers have continued to grow since World War II and now account for about 40 percent of yearly total national output.

10. Government spending at the federal level is different from that at the state and local levels. Defense, income security, and Social Security account for about 55 percent of the federal budget.

DISCUSSION OF PREVIEW QUESTIONS

1. **What problems will you encounter if you refuse to pay a portion of your income tax because you oppose national defense spending?**

   You must share in national defense collectively with the rest of the country. Unlike private goods, national defense is a public good and must be consumed collectively. You receive national defense benefits whether you choose to or not; the exclusion principle does not work for public goods, such as national defense. The government could make the exclusion principle work better by deporting you to foreign shores if you don't wish to pay for national defense. This is typically not done. If you were allowed to forgo taxes allocated to national defense, the IRS would be swamped with similar requests. Everyone would have an incentive to claim no benefits from national defense (whether true or not) because it must be consumed collectively. So, if you refuse, you may go to jail.

2. **Will you benefit from many so-called tax loopholes when you first start working?**

   Probably not, for you will not be making enough income to put you into the highest marginal income tax bracket. Tax loopholes are more beneficial the more they save you in taxes. At low incomes, your marginal tax rate is low, so each dollar in tax saved because of your use of a tax loophole yields you very little additional after-tax income. If you're in the 15 percent marginal tax bracket, you only benefit by 15 cents for every dollar in tax loopholes you find. Compare this to the benefit for someone in the 39.6 percent marginal tax bracket.

3. **In what ways do regressive, proportional, and progressive tax structures differ?**

   Under a regressive tax structure, the average tax rate (the percentage of income paid in taxes) falls as income rises. The marginal tax rate is below the average tax rate. Proportional tax structures are those in which the average tax rate remains constant as income rises; the marginal tax rate equals the average tax rate. Under a progressive tax structure, the average tax rate rises as income rises; the marginal tax rate is above the average tax rate. Our federal personal income tax system is an example of a progressive system.

4. Who pays the corporate income tax?
Ultimately, only people can be taxed. As a consequence, corporate taxes are ultimately paid by people: corporate owners (in the form of reduced dividends and less stock appreciation for stockholders), consumers of corporate products (in the form of higher prices for goods), and/or employees working for corporations (in the form of lower wages).

PROBLEMS

(Answers to the odd-numbered problems appear at the back of the book.)

5-1. Consider the following system of taxation, which has been labeled *degressive*. The first $5,000 of income is not taxed. After that, all income is assessed at 20 percent (a proportional system). What is the marginal tax rate on $3,000 of taxable income? $10,000? $100,000? What is the average tax rate on $3,000? $10,000? $100,000? What is the maximum average tax rate?

5-2. You are offered two possible bonds to buy as part of your investing program. One is a corporate bond yielding 9 percent. The other is a tax-exempt municipal bond yielding only 6 percent. Assuming that you are certain you will be paid your interest and principal on these two bonds, what marginal tax bracket must you be in to decide in favor of the tax-exempt bond?

5-3. Consider the following tax structure:

Income Bracket	Marginal Tax Rate
$0–$1,500	0%
$1,501–$2,000	14%
$2,001–$3,000	20%

Mr. Smith has an income of $2,500 per annum. Calculate his tax bill for the year. What is his average tax rate? His highest marginal tax rate?

5-4. Assume that Social Security tax payments on wages are 7.65 percent of wages, on wages up to $51,300. No *further* Social Security payments are made on earnings above this figure. Calculate the *average* Social Security tax rate for annual wages of (a) $4,000, (b) $51,300, (c) $56,000, (d) $100,000. Is this Social Security system a progressive, proportional, or regressive tax structure?

5-5. Briefly, what factors could be included as part of the requirements for a "good" tax structure?

5-6. What is meant by the expression "market failure"?

5-7. Is local police protection a public good? Explain.

5-8. TV signals have characteristics of public goods, yet TV stations and commercial networks are private businesses. Analyze this situation.

5-9. Assume that you live in a relatively small suburban neighborhood called Parkwood. The Parkwood Homeowners' Association collects money from homeowners to pay for upkeep of the surrounding stone wall, lighting at the entrances to Parkwood, and mowing the lawn around the perimeter of the area. Each year you are asked to donate $50. No one forces you to do it. There are 100 homeowners in Parkwood.

   a. What percentage of the total yearly revenue of the homeowners' association will you account for?

b. At what level of participation will the absence of your $50 contribution make a difference?

c. If you do not contribute your $50, are you really receiving a totally free ride?

5-10. Assume that the only textile firm that exists has created a negative externality by polluting a nearby stream with the wastes associated with production. Assume further that the government can measure the external costs to the community with accuracy and charges the firm for its pollution, based on the social cost of pollution per unit of textile output. Show how such a charge will lead to a higher selling price for textiles and a reduction in the equilibrium quantity of textiles.

5-11. Label two columns on your paper "Private Goods" and "Public Goods." List each of the following under the heading that describes it better.

a. Sandwich *pr*
b. Public television *pu*
c. Cable television
d. National defense
e. Shirt
f. Elementary education
g. College education
h. Health clinic flu shots
i. Opera
j. Museum
k. Automobile

COMPUTER-ASSISTED INSTRUCTION

The decisions made by people in the government (bureaucrats) and people in the private sector often differ because of the different constraints they face. We show the impact of this on innovation in the ethical drug industry.

Complete problem and answer appear on disk.

INTERACTING WITH THE INTERNET

For both detailed and summary information on the U.S. federal budget, see
   gopher://sunny.stat-usa.gov/11/BudgetFY96
(Future budgets should have a similar name.) It also includes extensive historical and projected future information. Of particular interest is "A Citizen's Guide to the Federal Budget." At
   http://www.ssa.gov/
you can find material on the Social Security System; it is oriented toward both recipients and people interested in how the system works. The Justice Department can be accessed at
   http://www.usdoj.gov/
and the Federal Trade Commission (FTC) at
   http://www.ftc.gov/

CHAPTER 6

ECONOMIES IN TRANSITION

If you visit one of the thousands upon thousands of hilly fields in Peru, you will likely meet a peasant family. That family probably has been tilling the soil in the same spot for decades. Most of these families eke out an existence. Very few of them could, if they wanted to, sell the land they have been tilling for so many years to pursue an alternative line of work. To understand why this is so in Peru requires a grasp of the changes that are occurring in the world's economies in transition.

PREVIEW QUESTION:

1. Why does the scarcit problem force all societi to answer the questions *what, how,* and *for whom?*

2. How can economies classified?

3. Why do we say that economies are mixed economies?

4. What are the "three *P*s" of pure capitalism?

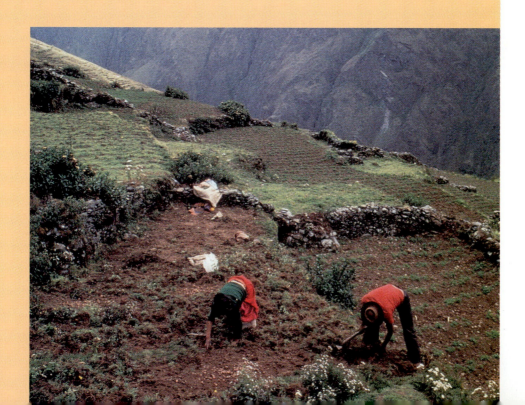

Economic system
The institutional means through which resources are used to satisfy human wants.

Resource allocation
The assignment of resources to specific uses by determining what will be produced, how it will be produced, and for whom it will be produced.

Did You Know That . . . there used to be a country called the Soviet Union whose chief of state in 1960 took off his shoe at the United Nations and pounded it on the desk while shouting, "We will bury you"? That person was Nikita Khrushchev; he died in 1971. It took quite a few more years for his country to die, but die it did. The Soviet Union is no more. The 74-year experiment in trying to run an economy without using the price, or market, system will go down in history as one of the greatest social and economic failures of all time. Just because the Soviet Union dissolved itself at the end of 1991 does not mean that the entire world economy automatically became like that of the United States. In particular, the 15 republics of the former Soviet Union, the Soviet "satellite" countries of Eastern Europe, and other nations, including China, are what we call *economies in transition*.

At any point in time, every nation has its own **economic system, which can be defined as the institutional means through which resources are used to satisfy human wants.** No matter what institutional means—marketplace or government—a nation chooses to use, three basic economic questions must always be answered.

THE THREE BASIC ECONOMIC QUESTIONS

In every nation, no matter what the form of government, what the type of economic system, who is running the government, or how poor or rich it is, three basic economic questions must be answered. They concern the problem of **resource allocation, which is simply how resources are to be allocated.** As such, resource allocation answers the three basic economic questions of *what, how,* and *for whom* goods and services will be produced.

1. *What and how much will be produced?* Literally billions of different things could be produced with society's scarce resources. Some mechanism must exist that causes some things to be produced and others to remain as either inventors' pipe dreams or individuals' unfulfilled desires.

2. *How will it be produced?* There are many ways to produce a desired item. It is possible to use more labor and less capital or vice versa. It is possible to use more unskilled labor and fewer units of skilled labor. Somehow, in some way, a decision must be made as to the particular mix of inputs, the way they should be organized, and how they are brought together at a particular place.

3. *For whom will it be produced?* Once a commodity is produced, who should get it? In a market economy, individuals and businesses purchase commodities with money income. The question then is what mechanism there is to distribute income, which then determines how commodities are distributed throughout the economy.

THE PRICE SYSTEM AND HOW IT ANSWERS THE THREE ECONOMIC QUESTIONS

As explained in Chapter 4, a price (or market) system is an economic system in which (relative) prices are constantly changing to reflect changes in supply and demand for different commodities. In addition, the prices of those commodities are the signals to everyone within the system as to what is relatively scarce and what is relatively abundant. Indeed, it is the *signaling* aspect of the price system that provides the information to buyers and sellers about what should be bought and what should be produced. The price system, which is characteristic of a market economy, is only one possible way to organize society.

What and How Much Will Be Produced?

In a price system, the interaction of demand and supply for each good determines what and how much to produce. Note, however, that if the highest price that consumers are willing to pay is less than the lowest cost at which a good can be produced, output will be zero. That doesn't mean that the price system has failed. Today consumers do not purchase their own private space shuttles. The demand is not high enough in relation to the supply to create a market. But it may be someday.

How Will It Be Produced?

The question of how output will be produced in a price system relates to the efficient use of scarce inputs. Consider the possibility of using only two types of resources, capital and labor. A firm may have the options given in Table 6-1. It can use various combinations of labor and capital to produce the same amount of output. Two hypothetical combinations are given in the table. How, then, is it decided which combination should be used? In the price system, the **least-cost combination** (technique B in our example) will in fact be chosen because it maximizes profits. We assume that the owners of business firms act as if they are maximizing profits. Recall from Chapter 1 that we assume that individuals act *as if* they are rational.

Least-cost combination
The level of input use that produces a given level of output at minimum cost.

In a price system, competition *forces* firms to use least-cost production techniques. Any firm that fails to employ the least costly technique will find that other firms can undercut its price. In other words, other firms that choose the least-cost production technique will be able to offer the product at a lower price and still make a profit. This lower price will induce consumers to shift purchases from the higher-priced firm to the lower-priced firm. Inefficient firms will be forced out of business.

For Whom Will It Be Produced?

This last question that every economic system must answer involves who gets what. In a market system, the choice about what is purchased is made by individuals, but that choice is determined by the ability to pay. Who gets what is determined by the distribution of money income.

Determination of Money Income. In a price system, a consumer's ability to pay for consumer products is based on the size of that consumer's money income. That in turn depends on the quantities, qualities, and types of the various human and nonhuman resources that the individual owns and supplies to the marketplace. It also depends on the prices, or payments, for those resources. When you are selling your human resources as labor

TABLE 6-1

Production Costs for 100 Units of Product X
Technique A or B can be used to produce the same output. Obviously, B will be used because its total cost is less than A's. Using production technique B will generate a $2 savings for every 100 units produced.

Inputs	Input Unit Price	Production Technique A (input units)	Cost	Production Technique B (input units)	Cost
		A		B	
Labor	$10	5	$50	4	$40
Capital	8	4	32	5	40
Total cost of 100 units			82		80

services, your money income is based on the wages you can earn in the labor market. If you own nonhuman resources—physical capital and land, for example—the level of interest and rents that you are paid for your physical capital and land will clearly influence the size of your money income and thus your ability to buy consumer products.

Which Consumers Get What? In a price system, the distribution of finished products to consumers is based on consumers' ability and willingness to pay the market price for the product. If the market price of compact discs is $9, consumers who are able and willing to pay that price will get those CDs. All others won't.

Here we are talking about the *rationing* function of market prices in a price system. Rather than have a central political figure or agency decide which consumers will get which goods, those consumers who are willing and able to pay the market price obtain the goods. That is to say, relative prices ration the available resources, goods, and services at any point in time among those who place the highest value on those items. If scarcity didn't exist, we would not need any system to ration available resources, goods, and services. All of us could have all of everything that we wanted without taking away from what anyone else obtained.

CONCEPTS IN BRIEF

- Any economic system must answer three questions: (1) *What* will be produced? (2) *How* will it be produced? (3) *For whom* will it be produced?

- In a price system, supply and demand determine the prices at which exchanges take place.

- In a price system, firms choose the least-cost combination use of inputs to produce any given output. Competition forces firms to do so.

- In a price system, who gets what is determined by consumers' money income and choices about how to use that money income.

TODAY'S INCREASINGLY ALL-CAPITALIST WORLD

Not long ago, textbooks presented a range of economic systems, usually capitalism, socialism, and communism. **Communism** was intended as a system in which the state disappeared and individuals contributed to the economy according to their productivity and received income according to their needs. Under **socialism,** the state owned a major share of productive resources except labor. **Capitalism** has been defined as a system under which individuals hold government-protected private property rights to all goods, including those used in production, and their own labor.

Pure Capitalism in Theory

In its purest theoretical form, market capitalism, or pure capitalism, has the following attributes:

1. Private property rights exist and are upheld by the judicial system.
2. Prices are allowed to seek their own level as determined by the forces of supply and demand. In this sense, pure capitalism is a price system.
3. Resources, including human labor, are free to move in and out of industries and geographic locations. The movement of resources follows the lure of profits—higher expected profits create an incentive for more resources to go where those profits might occur.

Communism
In its purest form, an economic system in which the state has disappeared and individuals contribute to the economy according to their productivity and are given income according to their needs.

Socialism
An economic system in which the state owns the major share of productive resources except labor. Socialism also usually involves the redistribution of income.

Capitalism
An economic system in which individuals own productive resources; these individuals can use the resources in whatever manner they choose, subject to common protective legal restrictions.

4. Risk takers are rewarded by higher profits, but those whose risks turn out to be bad business decisions suffer the consequences directly in terms of reduced wealth.

5. Decisions about what and how much should be produced, how it should be produced, and for whom it should be produced are left to the market. In a pure market capitalist system, all decisions are decentralized and made by individuals in a process of *spontaneous coordination* throughout the economy.

One way to remember the attributes of pure capitalism is by thinking of the three *P*s: prices, profits, and private property.

The role of government is limited to provision of certain public goods, such as defense, police protection, and a legal framework within which property rights and contracts are enforced.

Pure capitalism has also been called a **laissez-faire** system. The French term means "leave [it] alone" or "let [it] be." A pure capitalist system is one in which the government lets the economic actors in the economy make their own decisions without government constraints.

Laissez-faire
French for "leave [it] alone"; applied to an economic system in which the government minimizes its interference with the economy.

The Importance of Incentives

Though it is doubtful that full-blown communism ever really existed or could survive in a whole economy, various forms of socialism, in which the state owned important parts of the economy, have existed. Indeed, one can argue that the most important distinguishing feature between capitalist countries and everywhere else is the lack of private property rights. Economics predicts that, for example, when an apartment building is owned by no one (that is, owned by the "state"), there is less incentive for anyone to take care of it. This analysis has predicted well with respect to public housing in the United States. Just imagine an entire country for which all housing is public housing. That is what the former Soviet Union was like. (Note that we are not passing judgment on a system that has few private property rights. Rather, we are simply pointing out the predictions that economists can make with respect to how individuals treat such property.)

We pointed out in Chapter 4 that in a world of scarcity, resources must always be rationed. In economic systems in which prices were not allowed to be the rationing device, other methods had to be used. In the former Soviet Union, rationing by queuing (waiting) was one of the most prevalent. Some economists estimated that the average Russian spent as many hours a week waiting in lines as the average American spends watching television.

Today one might say that the collapse of communism has left the world with one system only, the **mixed economy,** in which decisions about how resources are used are made partly by the private sector and partly by the public sector—capitalism with government. Figure 6-1 represents the size of government relative to annual national output. You can see that even among the traditional capitalist countries of the world, there are great variations. These can be regarded as the different faces of capitalism.

Mixed economy
An economic system in which decisions about how resources should be used are made partly by the private sector and partly by the government, or the public sector.

CONCEPTS IN BRIEF

- Communism is an economic system in which, in theory, individuals would produce according to their abilities and consume according to their needs. Under socialism, the state owns most major capital goods and attempts to redistribute income.

- Pure capitalism allows for the spontaneous coordination of millions of individuals by allowing the free play of the three *P*s—prices, profits, and property rights. Often, pure capitalism is called a laissez-faire system.

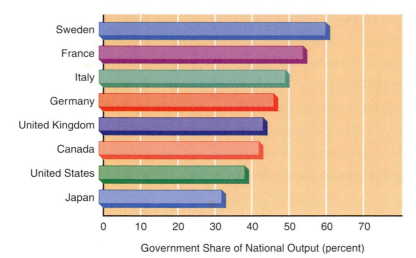

FIGURE 6-1

Percentage of National Yearly Output Accounted for by Government in Various Countries
Even among countries that have embraced capitalism for a long time, government plays an important, but widely different, role. It constitutes over 60 percent of the economy in Sweden, but less than 40 percent in the United States.

Government Share of National Output (percent)

- Incentives matter in any economic system; therefore, in countries that have had few or unenforced property rights, individuals lacked the incentives to take care of most property that wasn't theirs.

- Most economies today can be viewed as mixed in that they combine private decisions and government controls.

THE DIFFERENT FACES OF CAPITALISM

The world is left with a single economic system that, thanks to the diversity of human cultures, has a variety of faces. Table 6-2 presents one way to categorize today's economic systems.

TABLE 6-2

Four Faces of Capitalism

Type of Capitalism	Examples	Characteristics	Problem Areas
Consumer	Canada, United States, New Zealand, Australia, United Kingdom	Borders are relatively open; focus is on profit maximization and laissez-faire.	Low saving and investment rates; income inequality
Producer	Japan, France, Germany	Production is emphasized over consumption; employment is a major policy issue; state controls a relatively large part of the economy.	Consumer dissatisfaction; potential slow future growth rates; inertia within the economy
Family	Indonesia, Malaysia, Thailand, Taiwan	Extended clans dominate business and capital flows.	Lack of modern corporate organizations; lack of money markets
Frontier	Russia, China, Ukraine, Romania, Albania	Many government enterprises pursue for-profit activities; new entrepreneurs emerge every day.	Difficulty of crossing borders; rising criminal activity

Source: Based on, in part, "21st Century Capitalism," *Business Week*, February 23, 1995, p. 19.

THE TRANSITIONAL PHASE: FRONTIER CAPITALISM

Frontier capitalism describes economies in transition from state ownership and control of most of the factors of production to a system of private property rights in which the price system is used to answer the basic economic questions. Table 6-3 presents theoretical stages in the development of frontier capitalism. Two aspects appear to be the most important: developing the legal system and selling off state-owned businesses.

Development of the Legal System

In the United States and many other countries, we take a well-established legal system as a given. That does not imply the total absence of a legal system in countries where we are now seeing frontier capitalism. To be sure, the former Soviet Union had a legal system, but virtually none of it had to do with economic transactions, which were carried out by state dictates. Individuals could not own the factors of production, and therefore, by definition, there were no legal disputes over property rights involving them. Consequently, the legal system in the former Soviet Union and its Eastern European satellites consisted of many volumes of criminal codes—laws against robbery, murder, rape, and theft as well as so-called economic crimes.

Enter the new world of private property rights and unfettered exchange of those rights among buyers and sellers. Now what happens when a buyer claims that a seller breached a particular agreement? In the United States, lawyers, courts, and the Uniform Commercial Code can be used to settle the dispute. Yet until recently in the frontier economies of the former Soviet Union, there was nothing even vaguely comparable. The rule of law in the United States and Great Britain has developed over hundreds of years; we cannot expect that in countries in transition toward full capitalism, an entire body of law and procedure can be developed overnight.

Privatization

The transition toward capitalism requires that the government lessen its role in the economy. This transition involves what has become known as *privatization*. **Privatization** is the transfer of ownership or responsibility for businesses run by the government, so-called *state enterprises,* to individuals and companies in the private sector. Even in capitalist countries, the government has owned and run various parts of the economy. During and after World War II, it became fashionable for many European governments to "nationalize" different industries. This was particularly prevalent in the United Kingdom, where the steel industry was nationalized, for example. In the early 1980s, France nationalized the banking industry. The opposite of nationalization is privatization.

In the early 1980s, Turkey and Chile were the first capitalist countries to start carrying out mass privatization of government-owned businesses. Under Margaret Thatcher, the United Kingdom pioneered the mass privatization of state industry, including the huge road haulage company (NFC), a health care group (Amersham International), British Telecom, British Petroleum, and British Aerospace.

A country must employ some method to put government-owned businesses into the hands of the private sector; government-owned businesses are not simply given away to the first party who asks. Imagine if the U.S. government said that it wanted to sell the United States Postal Service. How would it do so? One way is to sell it outright, but there might not be any buyers who would be willing to pay to take over such a giant money-losing corporation. An alternative would involve selling shares of stock to anyone who wanted to buy

Privatization
The sale or transfer of state-owned property and businesses to the private sector, in part or in whole. Also refers to *contracting out*—letting private business take over government-provided services such as trash collection.

TABLE 6-3
How Frontier Capitalism
Develops

Stage	Characteristics
I	The central government, as the controller of all economic activities, collapses and starts to disappear. The black market, typically involving government enterprises still owned by the state, expands enormously. Many former state factory managers and other bosses become involved in criminal activities using the state's resources. Government corruption flourishes more than before.
II	Small businesses start to flourish. Families pool funds in order to become entrepreneurs. The rules of commerce are not well understood because there is not yet a well-established commercial law system, nor are property rights well defined or protected by the state.
III	The economy is growing, but much of its growth is not measured by government statisticians. Small financial markets, such as stock markets, begin to develop. Foreigners cautiously invest in the new stock markets. The government attempts to develop a clear set of commercial laws.
IV	Foreign corporations are more willing to invest directly in new factories and stores. The state gets serious about selling all businesses that it owns. More resources are devoted to suppressing criminal activity. Commercial law becomes better established and better understood.

them at the stated price. This latter technique is indeed the way in which most privatizations have been carried out in established capitalist countries throughout the world over the past 15 or 20 years.

In the former Soviet Union and in Eastern Europe, alternative systems have been devised. For example, citizens, at various times, have been given vouchers granting them the right to purchase a specified number of shares in particular government-owned companies that were being sold off.

The trend in privatization versus nationalization can be seen in panel (a) of Figure 6-2 on page 124. The cumulative worldwide sales of state-owned enterprises can be seen in panel (b). In Europe, privatization will probably continue at the rate of over $50 billion a year into the next century. Privatization in Latin America will continue much longer. Finally, because privatization in the former Soviet Union and Eastern Europe has in a sense just begun, such wholesale privatization may take a long time indeed.

Political Opposition to Privatization

There is often strong political pressure to slow down or even prevent privatization of state-owned businesses. The political pressure to prevent privatization is derived from simple economics: Managers of state-owned businesses typically have had lifetime job security, better working conditions than they could obtain elsewhere, and little threat of competition. In other words, life for a manager is typically better in a state-owned firm than in that same firm once it has been privatized.

Workers in state-run firms also believe, often rightly, that their lot in life will not be quite so good if the state-owned firm is sold to the private sector. State-owned firms tend to pay their workers higher wages and give them better fringe benefits, including much better pension plans, than similar firms that are privately owned. For example, an examination of state-owned phone companies in France and Germany shows that they have two to three

Panel (a)

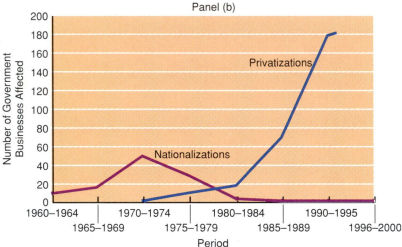

Panel (b)

FIGURE 6-2

The Trend Toward Privatization
Privatization worldwide has been on the upswing since 1985, as shown in panel (a). Nationalizations (the opposite of privatizations) reached their peak in about 1970 as is shown in panel (b).

Source: OECD and *The Economist*, August 21, 1993, p. 19.

times as many workers per telephone customer as the private telephone companies in the United States. This comparative overuse of labor in state-owned firms is even more obvious in the republics of the former Soviet Union and in Eastern Europe.

Economists cannot say whether privatization of state-owned firms is good or bad. Rather, economists can simply state that the rigors of a competitive market will generally cause resources to be used more efficiently after privatization occurs. In the process, however, some managers and workers may be made worse off.

Is There a Right Way to Go About the Transition?

Ever since the fall of the Berlin Wall in 1989, economists have debated whether there is a "right" way for former socialist and communist countries to move toward capitalist systems. The once-communist nations have, indeed, embarked on a social experiment in how to move toward a market economy. Basically, they have chosen two methods—a slow one and a fast one. Romania, Russia, and Ukraine have only gradually privatized their economies, whereas the Czech Republic and, to a lesser extent, Poland and Estonia opted for a "shock treatment."

The rapid move toward a market economy, though not free of problems, has seemed to work better than the go-slow approach. The slower the transition occurs, the more the former entrenched bureaucrats in the state-owned businesses have been able to maintain their power over the use of resources. In the meantime, the state-owned businesses continue to use valuable resources inefficiently in these developing countries.

In contrast, a country like the Czech Republic used a voucher system to privatize over 2,000 state-owned enterprises. All citizens were given vouchers—legal rights evidenced on printed certificates—which could be used to purchase shares of stock in state-owned businesses. A stock market quickly developed in which shares of hundreds of companies are now traded every day. After an initial period of transition to a market economy, the Czech Republic has now achieved one of the lowest unemployment rates in Europe.

We will next examine the current situation of two of the largest countries in the world that are in the throes of frontier capitalism. Both are grappling with the problems of the transition from communism to capitalism.

CONCEPTS IN BRIEF

- Today there are four types of capitalism: consumer, producer, family, and frontier. The last begins when a centralized economy starts collapsing and black markets thrive. Eventually small businesses flourish, and then financial markets develop. Finally, foreign investment is attracted, and state-owned businesses are privatized.

- The development of a well-functioning legal system is one of the most difficult problems for an economy in the frontier capitalism stage. Such economies do not have the laws or courts to handle the new system of property right transfers.

- Privatization, or the turning over to the private sector of state-owned and state-run businesses, is occurring all over the world in all types of economies. There is much political opposition, however, whenever managers in soon-to-be privatized businesses realize that they may face harder times in a private setting.

RUSSIA AND ITS FORMER SATELLITES, YESTERDAY AND TODAY

Russia was the largest republic in the former Soviet Union. The economic system in place was at times called communism and at other times called command socialism. There is no question that it was a command economy in which there was centralized economic leadership and planning. All economies involve planning, of course; the difference is that in capitalist societies, most of the planning is done by private businesses rather than the government. Leaders in the former Soviet Union somehow believed that its economic planners in Moscow could micromanage an economy spanning 11 time zones, involving millions and millions of consumers and producers, and affecting vast quantities of goods and services.

Imagine trying to run a single business that big! No one can. Perhaps more important, state ownership in such a large country resulted in perverse incentives throughout the economy. For example, when the government issued production quotas for glass based on the number of panes, they ended up being almost paper thin and shattering easily. When the government then changed its quotas to weight, the glass panes were so thick that they were useless. In short, former Soviet citizens responded appropriately every time central planners figured out a new way to set production quotas. In the process, untold resources were inefficiently used or completely wasted.

By the time the Soviet Union collapsed in 1991, it consisted of a society in which perhaps 1 or 2 percent of the population (the communists, privileged bureaucrats, athletes, and artists) enjoyed a nice lifestyle and the rest of the citizens were forced to scrape by. The same was true perhaps to an even greater degree in the former East Germany, Romania, Poland, Hungary, Czechoslovakia (now the Czech Republic and Slovakia), and Albania. The standard of living of the average citizen prior to the Soviet Union's breakup was at best a quarter but more realistically one-tenth of that in the United States.

Privatization During Transition

That a former state-owned business in Russia is now privatized does not mean that shareholders control it the way they do in, say, the United States. In the United States, shareholders elect a board of directors, which then chooses upper management. Shareholders can force out directors who have acted improperly and can also show their disapproval by selling their shares of stock and purchasing shares in another company. It will be some time before the same system of control operates on all recently privatized Russian businesses. Many such businesses are actually controlled by their managers and workers and not by shareholders. One can use the analogy of a divorced couple still sharing the same house and the children.

In some former Soviet satellite countries, one arm of government sells a state-owned firm and another reappears as its owner. This has happened a lot in Poland, for example, where the government's Industrial Development Agency is managing one of the 15 funds that were set up to take over 440 formerly state-owned enterprises.

In the businesses that are being run by worker cooperatives, there is little incentive to fire the least efficient workers or to seek more highly qualified workers. Manager-owners do not often do much better. Manager-owners of recently privatized firms in Russia clearly do not want to surrender control.

The Persistence of Old Ways

The more an economy tends toward pure market capitalism, the less place there is for a government elite that is able to usurp economic power and, more important, economic privileges. In Russia today, some of the old Communist Party bases of economic power are being redeveloped. Although newspapers and television stations are now privately owned, their owners are increasingly afraid of angering powerful government interests.

Just a few years ago, President Boris Yeltsin created a new political party named "Our House—Russia." The party was and continues to be backed by wealthy banking and business interests. It consists almost entirely of state bureaucrats and provincial governors and administrators, most of whom are former communists. Prior to the downfall of communism, the political elite were able to use special clinics and hospitals. Today the same persons have the same privileges, although the names of the hospitals have changed. Even a new special food store was built for officials with parliamentary identification cards. Under communism, special food stores served to provide Communist Party elite with low-cost, high-quality food without their having to wait on lines. Why, in Russia's now more capitalistic system, such a special food store has cropped up again remains something of a mystery.

THINKING CRITICALLY ABOUT THE MEDIA

Taking Russia's Pulse

When economists and journalists discuss the transition from the centralized Soviet economy to its current market orientation, they lament the tremendous reduction in national output. Official estimates for the period 1989 to 1995, for example, claim that national output dropped by over 50 percent. True though it may be that output dropped during this time, it is not clear what the actual value of that output was to the population. Much of the reduction was in military hardware, such as missiles. How much did the average citizen lose when that output shrank? Also, fewer television sets and radios were produced during this time period—but the ones produced earlier either never worked properly or tended to explode. Steel mills have been shut down in Russia but they had been using technology that was 45 years old. Further, the official Russian state agency that measures the economy, Goskomstat, has none of the sophistication that the U.S. Department of Commerce and the Bureau of Labor Statistics have for measuring a nation's output. Even if Goskomstat had better computers and more refined techniques, it would still miss a vast off-the-books economy that won't be counted by government statisticians for years to come. All in all, Russia's 150 million people earn more and live better than what Goskomstat statistics say.

The Inevitable Crime Wave

The shift to a market economy in Russia has brought with it a major increase in crime, particularly organized crime. Currently, virtually every small business pays protection money to some gang. Moscow boasts at least a million unregistered firearms, and the country as a whole has over 30 million of them. According to former *Toronto Star* Moscow reporter Stephen Handelman, "The second Russian revolution of this century is awash in corruption, opportunism, and crime." One can compare Russia today with America's Wild West.

One needs to examine the crime statistics more carefully, though, to get a real feeling for what is happening in this nation in transition. Street crime is certainly greater than it used to be under the Soviet regime. But Moscow is still probably safer than New York. With respect to "breaking the law," the legal system is in such a state of flux that probably everyone is breaking the law at one time or another. Because the legal system is in its infancy for facilitating private enterprise, businesspeople have had to resort to extralegal methods to collect debts and enforce contracts. Unfortunately, some of these methods involve firearms and violence.

One can make an analogy with the violence associated with the illegal production and sale of alcoholic beverages during America's experiment with Prohibition (1920–1933) and what is happening in Russia today. The violence associated with the business of illegal booze disappeared with the repeal of Prohibition. It will not disappear so quickly in Russia, but it certainly will eventually fade out as property rights become better established, the legal system increasingly facilitates trade, and the court system gains enough experience to handle legal problems in the business world.

Also, one must look at what used to exist under the old system. Because everything belonged to "the people," there was little in the way of communications, credit, banking, and computerization. Money meant less than did connections and rank in the Communist Party. People who were adept at thriving in such an environment—the Communist Party elite— have had a comparative advantage in the initial stages of transition to a market economy. They maintain the connections with state bureaucrats who controlled resources. It is not surprising that many of those in power today are the same communists who were in power a decade ago.

All of this is simply a transition. The incidence of certain crimes in Russia has actually fallen, as can be seen in Figure 6-3.

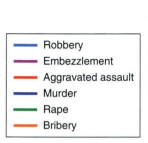

- Robbery
- Embezzlement
- Aggravated assault
- Murder
- Rape
- Bribery

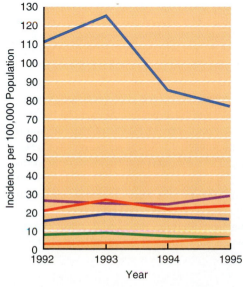

FIGURE 6-3

Crime in Russia

While crime increased after the fall of communism in Russia, its rate has recently stabilized or fallen.

Source: Interior Ministry of Russia.

INTERNATIONAL EXAMPLE
A Booming Business in Facelifts by Russian Plastic Surgeons

One of the beneficiaries of Russia's economic system in transition is the facelift industry. There is as yet no legal procedure in Russia for imposing liability on physicians for malpractice. Consequently, a patient who desires a facelift or other cosmetic surgery has no consent forms to sign, and the physician has no malpractice (liability) insurance to purchase. The result is relatively inexpensive plastic surgery that Germans, Italians, and Americans are taking advantage of. According to one of Russia's best-known plastic surgeons, Igor A. Volf, "Surgeons in the West work in a very rigid frame. They are afraid of being sued by their patients—they fear complications. I do the big, bold operations Western doctors are afraid to do." As word of mouth travels, the demand curve for Russian plastic surgeons is shifting outward to the right.

FOR CRITICAL ANALYSIS: What are the costs that an American contemplating a facelift in Moscow would have to include in making a rational decision about going there? ●

CONCEPTS IN BRIEF

- Russia and its former satellite states in Eastern Europe operated under a system of command socialism with much centralized economic planning. The end result was a declining economy in which a small percentage of the population lived extremely well and the rest very poorly.

- Russia and Eastern Europe are privatizing at varying speeds, depending on the level of political opposition.

- Russia has experienced a crime wave during its transition to capitalism. One can compare this period to America's Wild West and to our period of Prohibition. As property rights and the legal system become more efficient, much of the crime associated with illegal economic activities will probably disappear.

THE PEOPLE'S REPUBLIC OF CHINA

The People's Republic of China remains the largest nation on earth and hence the largest with some form of command socialism. However, a decreasing share of the nation's activity is being guided by government. In fact, China started introducing market reforms in various sectors of the economy well before Russia did.

In 1978, the commune system that had been implemented in the 1950s was replaced by what was known as the *household responsibility system*. Each peasant household became responsible for its own plot of land. Whatever was produced in excess of the minimum obligation to the state remained the property of the household. So the incentives for peasant farmers were quite different from those prior to 1978. Peasants were also encouraged to enrich themselves further by engaging in a variety of economic activities. The results were impressive. Between 1979 and 1984, virtually millions of jobs were created in the urban and rural private sector, and farm productivity increased dramatically.

In the 1980s, the highly centralized planning from Beijing, the capital, was relaxed. Decision-making powers were given to state-owned enterprises at the local level. Indeed,

China had embarked on a gradual sell-off of state-owned enterprises so that the size of the state-run sector, which accounted for 70 percent of industrial production in the mid-1980s, dropped to an estimated 40 percent in 1996. The result was an increase in output. The problem with state-run factories was the **incentive structure.** Managers of those factories never had much incentive to maximize the equivalent of profits. Rather, managers of state-run factories attempted to maximize incomes and benefits for their workers because workers constituted a political constituency that was more important than the politicians at the national level.

Incentive structure
The motivational rewards and costs that individuals face in any given situation. Each economic system has its own incentive structure. The incentive structure is different under a system of private property than under a system of government-owned property, for example.

Two Decades of Economic Reform

Another major economic reform in China began in 1979, when the central government created a special economic zone in Guangdong province, bordering the nation of Hong Kong. In that special zone, the three *P*s of pure capitalism—prices, profits, and private property—have now prevailed for nearly two decades. The result has been economic growth rates that have exceeded those in virtually any other part of the world. Within an area housing less than 1.5 percent of the population, Guangdong province now accounts for about 7 percent of the entire country's industrial output.

Transition Problems in Farming

THINKING CRITICALLY ABOUT THE MEDIA

268 Million Chinese Unemployed?

"China Sees 268 Million Unemployed in 2000." This was the headline a few years ago, reportedly based on statements by mainland Chinese officials in the Labor Ministry. Imagine that—the number of unemployed in China equaling the entire population of men, women, and children in the United States! A frightening prospect, no doubt, but also pure nonsense. Such a large number of unemployed presupposes that there is no way for them to find jobs of any sort. As China shifts toward a market economy, however, many of the unemployed will be able to find jobs in businesses that the current Chinese leadership cannot even conceive of today. That is what happens in a country in transition toward market capitalism. Of course, during the transition, there will be social and human costs associated with higher-than-normal unemployment rates, but that is statistically a temporary blip, not a long-term trend.

Even though the Chinese central government was able to increase agricultural production dramatically when it gave peasants the household responsibility system, the agricultural sector has been lagging well behind the industrial sector in recent years. In effect, China has been undergoing an industrial revolution but not an agricultural one. One of the major problems is that peasants do not have legal title to their land. In other words, farmers cannot obtain legal property rights. As a result, the techniques used by agribusiness companies elsewhere in the world cannot be used by most of China's farmers. Peasants, in effect, have their land on loan from the state. The average size of a peasant farm is less than an acre for a family of six. It takes this family about 60 workdays to cultivate this amount of land, whereas a single American farmer can cultivate the same amount of land in about two hours.

Further, there is every incentive for peasant farmers to leave their rural lands and move to the city, where they can earn approximately four times as much income.

A Major Problem: The Rule of Law

As with virtually all countries experiencing frontier capitalism, China faces the perennial issue of how to establish the rule of law. When no specific property rights exist because resources are owned by "the people," the inevitable result is corruption. As with Russia, there is a sense of the Wild West in China, an atmosphere of lawlessness and unpredictability for anyone doing business. Both the government and the army continue to seek bribes and other favors because those two institutions still control many of the resources and influence the way business is conducted in China.

Only very slowly is China becoming a nation of laws, rather than of men and women. Otherwise stated, only gradually is the institution of a strong legal system being built up in China. The notion of property rights is slow to take in a nation where the communist dogma has denied their legitimacy. A good example is the state-supported bootleg compact disc factories that were first shut down because of international pressure and then reopened a few years ago. That American singers and musicians are being denied royalties seems not to bother some mainland Chinese government officials.

INTERNATIONAL EXAMPLE
A Tale of Two Countries

Approximately 6 million Chinese, most directly from or descended from those on mainland China, live in the state of Hong Kong, a colony leased to the British and scheduled to revert to mainland ownership in mid-1997. A comparison of these two political entities is instructive. During its 99 years as a British colony covering a mere 405 square miles, Hong Kong became the world's eighth-largest trading nation with a higher per capita income than the United Kingdom or France. Total annual output from its 6 million residents exceeded 20 percent of the output of 1.2 billion mainland Chinese. Hong Kong has been the perennial favorite example of economists who wish to show the efficiency of a system following the three Ps—prices, profits, and private property.

Perhaps more important, Hong Kong demonstrates the benefits of a strong legal system. A *Fortune* magazine survey of 500 corporate executives in 32 countries rated Hong Kong above London and New York as the best city for doing business. Commentators have argued that mainland China does not need Hong Kong's money but rather its rule of law. For decades, these laws have provided businesses with predictable rules governing civil and criminal disputes. Hong Kong has had an independent judicial system, contrary to the one almost completely dominated by the Communist Party on the mainland. Whether the mainland's takeover of Hong Kong results in China's learning from Hong Kong remains to be seen.

FOR CRITICAL ANALYSIS: *Reread the discussion of comparative versus absolute advantage in Chapter 2. Hong Kong is basically a barren land with no natural resources. What does this say about absolute versus comparative advantage?* ●

The Slow Pace of Privatization

Virtually all state-run companies in China have provided cradle-to-grave social welfare benefits to their workers. The process of privatization, which started gradually years ago, first requires that these companies slowly eliminate many of these social welfare programs. Such programs are one of the reasons why over 50 percent of state-run enterprises are losing money every year. You can see from Figure 6-4 which state-run industrial enterprises are most prevalent. It clearly will be many years before the Chinese government is completely (if ever) out of the petroleum and tobacco businesses. But as Figure 6-5 shows, a growing percentage of firms are escaping from state control.

FIGURE 6-4

Relative Importance of Government in China's Industry
The government in China owns most of the oil, tobacco, and power industries, but is shedding itself of other industries.

The trend toward privatization in China is inevitably leading to labor dislocations. As state-run enterprises become privatized, new technology will be introduced that will require fewer labor hours per unit of output. Workers have been and will continue to be laid off in recently privatized firms. Laid-off workers will have to seek employment elsewhere, and in the process unemployment rates will rise, at least temporarily.

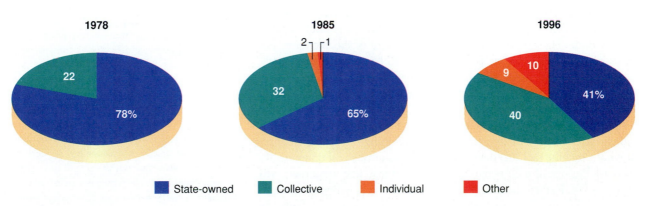

FIGURE 6-5

The Changing Face of China's Business Ownership
State ownership of all industries in China has fallen from 78 percent in 1978 to only 41 percent in 1996.

INTERNATIONAL EXAMPLE
China Eliminates Saturday Work

In 1995, the Chinese government granted its 450 million urban laborers and students Saturdays off. That adds up to about 1.4 billion extra hours of leisure time every week (laborers and students had been putting in a four-hour Saturday workday). The major beneficiaries of this government edict, besides urban laborers and students, seem to be travel agents. They counted the change in work rules as a windfall.

FOR CRITICAL ANALYSIS: What happened to the demand curve for leisure travel after the five-day workweek was instituted? ●

CONCEPTS IN BRIEF

- China started instituting market reforms in 1979 when it created special economic zones in which the three *P*s of capitalism were allowed to work. Problems remain in agriculture because peasant farmers cannot obtain property rights in land.

- The rule of law as capitalist countries know it is coming slowly to China. Government officials sometimes break contract agreements with foreign investors.

- The process of privatization started years ago but is proceeding slowly. The state still owns most of the businesses in oil, tobacco, power, and iron and steel.

FUTURE ECONOMIC POWER SHIFTS

The fact that there are so many economies in transition today is not just a momentary curiosity. It has implications for the future with respect to which nations will become economic powerhouses. Look at the three panels of Figure 6-6. You see in panel (a) that in the mid-1990s, the United States was clearly the world's largest economy. Japan and China were not even half its size. Now look at panel (b), which shows the World Bank's prediction of the largest economies in the year 2020. The leading economic powerhouse then is predicted to be China, with the United States a distant second. (These numbers reflect the total size of the economy, not how rich the average citizen is.) Japan will still be among the top three, but India and Indonesia will have expanded dramatically relative to 1995. Indeed, Asia, including India, will be a major economic power in the year 2020. These developments are reflected in panel (c) of Figure 6-6, where we show the projected shares of world output of today's industrial countries relative to today's developing countries. Realize, however, that the fact that developing Asian countries will dramatically increase the size of their economies does not mean that westerners will be worse off. Rather, the incomes of most westerners will also increase, but not as rapidly. Given that per-person incomes are generally higher in the West than in Asia, westerners will still remain rich by historical standards. The rest of the world is simply catching up with us.

THINKING CRITICALLY ABOUT THE MEDIA

Rich Industrial Nations—Really?

Virtually all news commentators and research organizations continue to classify countries such as the United States, the United Kingdom, and France as the industrial economies. Such an appellation today is a misnomer. In the industrial economies of today, less than one-third of the output is from "industry." Two-thirds of the jobs in so-called industrial economies are from services—doctors, lawyers, computer programmers, and Internet facilitators. Indeed, it might be more appropriate to call the richer countries *knowledge economies* because that is where the primary source of growth will lie—the storage, processing, and distribution of knowledge.

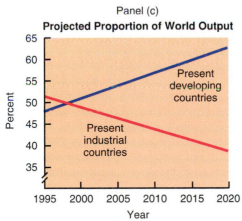

FIGURE 6-6

World Economic Powerhouses, 1995–2020

While the United States is the largest economy today, by 2020, China may be the world's greatest economic power. In any event, the share of world output from developing countries will increase steadily during that same time period.

Source: World Bank, *Global Economic Prospects.*

The Peruvian Transition from No Ownership to Clear Title

Concepts Applied: *Property rights, incentives, markets, economies in transition*

Formal markets do not easily develop where private ownership does not exist. This is the case in Peru, where farmers till family land for generations without a clear title for that land.

By at least one estimate, over three-quarters of the population of Peru is involved in the "informal society." This term was coined by Peruvian economist Hernando de Soto to emphasize the fact that Peru's official economy is quite small. It turns out that only 20 percent of Peru's land is legally owned. On the remaining 80 percent, which has no true legal ownership, peasant families till the land as they have done for generations.

Constructing *Pueblos Jovenes*

Cities are actually constructed on the unowned land. They are called *pueblos jovenes,* which means "young cities." Sometimes people who have been living there for a long time or who have tilled the land surrounding them try to register the land in their name. The process can take anywhere from six months to two years, though, and costs thousands of dollars in fees, much more than any peasant family is normally able to pay.

No Ownership, No Market, No Incentive

It is difficult, if not impossible, to create markets when ownership is nonexistent. Informal markets do evolve, and that is what has happened throughout Peru. But without specifically defined property rights, individuals cannot exchange land, for example. Consequently, in Peru, for generations, no large-scale farming has occurred, nor have peasant families experienced much incentive to

improve the value of the property on which they farm. It is also not surprising that in the *pueblos jovenes,* construction has been of the flimsiest nature, even by families who have inherited substantial sums of money. If a peasant family doesn't know if it can keep its land, the incentive to invest in it is understandably low.

"Suitcase" Farming

The lack of property rights has created a culture of so-called suitcase farmers in the Upper Huallaga and Rio Apurimac valleys. What the farmers produce, though, is not for normal consumption. It is coca bushes, which provide the raw ingredients for cocaine. Peruvian suitcase farmers plant these bushes, cultivate them, quickly sell them to Colombian buyers, and move off the land.

Enter a New System

Since the beginning of the 1990s, Peru's parliament has passed a spate of new property laws. Today, for a nominal cost, it is possible to register ownership of property in a month or so. So far, at least 150,000 families have obtained title to their land for $11 to $15 per parcel.

For a family to establish title to land, the local leaders in the "informal" neighborhoods have to attest that a family has indeed been using the parcel for generations. If no other family contests ownership of that property, it becomes possible for the family to register ownership.

One group objects to providing well-defined property rights to land: the drug dealers who buy coca plants. They are worried that establishing private property rights to land will discourage the suitcase farmers, leading to a smaller supply of the raw ingredient for cocaine. Not surprisingly, the main office of the Institute for Liberty and Democracy, a group that is helping peasants register their land, has been bombed several times.

FOR CRITICAL ANALYSIS

1. What alternatives would suitcase farmers have if they were given clear ownership rights to the land that they farm?
2. Is it possible to have wealth without legal property rights?

CHAPTER SUMMARY

1. The price system answers the resource allocation and distribution questions relating to what and how much will be produced, how it will be produced, and for whom it will be produced. The question of what to produce is answered by the value people place on a good—the highest price they are willing to pay for it. How goods are produced is determined by competition, which inevitably results in least-cost production techniques. Finally, goods and services are distributed to the individuals who are willing and able to pay for them. This answers the question about for whom goods are produced.

2. Pure capitalism can be defined by the three *P*s: prices, profits, and private property.

3. Communism is an economic system in which, theoretically, individuals would produce according to their abilities and consume according to their needs. Under socialism, the state owns most major capital goods and attempts to redistribute income. Most economies today can be viewed as mixed in that they rely on a combination of private decisions and government controls.

4. Incentives matter in any economic system; consequently, in countries that have had few or unenforced property rights, individuals lacked the incentives to take care of property that wasn't theirs.

5. Today there are four types of capitalism: consumer, producer, family, and frontier. The last emerges when a centralized economy starts collapsing and black markets thrive. Eventually, small businesses flourish and financial markets develop. Finally, foreign investment is attracted, and state-owned businesses are privatized.

6. The development of a well-functioning legal system is one of the most difficult problems for an economy in the frontier capitalism stage. Such economies do not have the laws or courts to handle property right protection and transfers.

7. Privatization, or turning over state-owned or state-run businesses to the private sector is occurring all over the world in all types of economies. There is much political opposition, however, whenever managers in soon-to-be-privatized businesses realize that they may face harder times in a private setting.

8. Russia and its former satellite states in Eastern Europe operated under a system of command socialism with much centralized economic planning. The end result was a declining economy in which a small percentage of the population lived extremely well and the rest very poorly.

9. Russia has experienced a crime wave during its transition to capitalism. One can compare this period to America's Wild West and to our period of Prohibition. As property rights and the legal system become more efficient, much of the crime associated with illegal economic activities probably will disappear.

10. China started instituting true market reforms in 1979, when it created special economic zones in which the three *P*s of capitalism—prices, profits, and private property—were allowed to work. Problems remain in agriculture because peasant farmers cannot obtain property rights to land.

11. The process of privatization in China started years ago but is proceeding slowly. The state still owns most of the businesses in oil, tobacco, power, and iron and steel.

12. The United States and Japan will remain economic powerhouses, but China could take the lead over the next 25 years. Other Asian countries, including Indonesia, India, Taiwan, South Korea, and Thailand, will become economically much stronger than they are today.

DISCUSSION OF PREVIEW QUESTIONS

1. Why does the scarcity problem force all societies to answer the questions *what, how,* and *for whom?* Scarcity exists for a society because people want more than their resources will allow them to have.

Society must decide *what* to produce because of scarcity. But if wants are severely restricted and resources are relatively superabundant, the question of *what* to produce is trivial—society simply produces *everything* that everyone wants. Superabundant resources relative to restricted wants also make the question of *how* to produce trivial. If scarcity doesn't exist, superabundant resources can be combined in *any* manner; waste and efficiency have no meaning without scarcity. Similarly, without scarcity, *for whom* is meaningless; *all* people can consume *all* they want.

2. How can economies be classified?

All societies must resolve the three fundamental economic problems: what, how, and for whom? One way to classify economies is according to the manner in which they answer these questions. In particular, we can classify them according to the degree to which *individuals* privately are allowed to make these decisions. Under pure command socialism, practically all economic decisions are made by a central authority; under pure capitalism, practically all economic decisions are made by private individuals pursuing their own economic self-interest.

3. Why do we say that *all* economies are mixed economies?

No economy in the real world is purely capitalistic. Resource allocation decisions in all economies are made by some combination of private individuals and governments. Even under an idealized capitalistic economy, important roles are played by the government; it is generally agreed that government is required for some income redistribution, national defense, protection of property rights, and so on.

4. What are the "three *P*s" of pure capitalism?

They are prices, profits, and property rights. In a pure capitalist economic system, prices are allowed to change when supply or demand changes. Prices are the signals to all about the relative scarcity of different resources. Profits are not constrained. When profits are relatively great in an industry, more resources flow to it. The converse is also true. Finally, property rights exist and are supported by the legal system.

PROBLEMS

(Answers to the odd-numbered problems appear at the back of the book.)

6-1. Suppose that you are an economic planner and you have been told by your country's political leaders that they want to increase automobile production by 10 percent over last year. What other industries will be affected by this decision?

6-2. Some argue that prices and profits automatically follow from well-established property rights. Explain how this might occur.

6-3. A business has found that it makes the most profits when it produces $172 worth of output of a particular product. It can choose from three possible techniques, A, B, and C, to produce the desired level of output. The table gives the amount of inputs these techniques use along with each input price.

a. Which technique will the firm choose, and why?

b. What would the firm's maximum profit be?

c. If the price of labor increases to $4 per unit, which technique will be chosen, and why? What will happen to profits?

Input	Input Unit Price	Production Technique		
		A (units)	B (units)	C (units)
Land	$10	7	4	1
Labor	2	6	7	18
Capital	15	2	6	3
Entrepreneurship	8	1	3	2

6-4. Answer the questions on the basis of the accompanying graph.

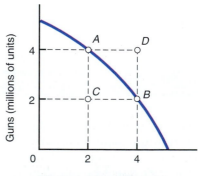

a. A switch to a decentralized, more market-oriented economy might do what to the production possibilities curve, and why?

b. What point on the graph represents an economy with unemployment?

6-5. The table gives the production techniques and input prices for 100 units of product X.

Input	Input Unit Price	Production Technique		
		A (units)	B (units)	C (units)
Labor	$10	6	5	4
Capital	8	5	6	7

a. In a market system, which techniques will be used to produce 100 units of product X?

b. If the market price of a unit of X is $1, which technique will lead to the greatest profit?

c. The output of X is still $1, but the price of labor and capital changes so that labor is $8 and capital is $10. Which production technique will be used?

d. Using the information in (c), what is the potential profit of producing 100 units of X?

6-6. The table gives the production techniques and input prices for one unit of product Y.

Input	Input Unit Price	Production Technique		
		A (units)	B (units)	C (units)
Labor	$10	1	3	2
Capital	5	2	2	4
Land	4	3	1	1

a. If the market price of a unit of product Y is $50, which technique generates the greatest potential profit?

b. If input unit prices change so that labor is $10, capital is $10, and land is $10, which technique will be chosen?

c. Assuming that the unit cost of each input is $10 and the price of a unit of Y is $50, which technique generates the greatest profit?

COMPUTER-ASSISTED INSTRUCTION

The role of prices in communicating information and allocating goods and services are illustrated by examining the ongoing transformation of the economies of Russia and China.

Complete problem and answer appear on disk.

INTERACTING WITH THE INTERNET

Extensive information on Eastern European economic conditions, with an emphasis on financial matters, can be found (for a fee) at

http://www.securities.com/

An excellent source for general information on these and other countries is the CIA's *World Factbook,*

http://www.odci.gov/cia/publications/96fact/index.html

and information on different countries' economic and trade policies can be found at

gopher://gopher.umsl.edu/11/library/govdocs/crpt

A very nice guide with extensive links to trade, economic, and business information for Eastern Europe and the former Soviet Union can be obtained from "REESweb: Russian and East European Studies," sponsored by the University Center for Russian and East European Studies of the University of Pittsburgh. It is located at

http://www.pitt.edu/~cjp/rsecon.html

This is just one section of the university's material on this part of the world.

PART 2

INTRODUCTION TO MACROECONOMICS AND ECONOMIC GROWTH

Chapter 7

The Macroeconomy: Unemployment and Inflation

Chapter 8

Measuring the Economy's Performance

Chapter 9

Economic Growth: Technology, Research and Development, and Knowledge

THE MACROECONOMY: UNEMPLOYMENT AND INFLATION

As a consumer, you certainly worry about changes in the prices of the things you buy. You might even get angry when the prices of your favorite products go up. Government statisticians try to measure what happens to the average of all prices each month by estimating various indexes of price levels. Recently, there have been complaints that government statisticians are not measuring price changes correctly. If the way they measure price level changes ends up reducing the official rate of inflation, how will that affect the economy? To understand this issue, you need to know more about inflation and how it is measured. You will learn more about these topics, as well as unemployment, in this chapter.

PREVIEW QUESTIONS

1. Why is frictional unemployment not necessarily harmful?

2. Does it matter whether inflation is anticipated or not?

3. Who is hurt by inflation?

4. How do we describe the phases of national business fluctuations?

Did You Know That... although the United States is considered a highly advanced industrialized nation, less and less of its employment is involved in manufacturing? The same is true of Japan, Germany, France, Italy, and the United Kingdom, where the number of manufacturing workers has been dropping steadily since 1970, despite significant increases in total adult population. Yet the result has *not* been workers permanently out of jobs. Even so, work is a major policy issue facing many countries today. At the core of macroeconomics—the study of the performance and structure of the national economy—are the issues of employment and, more important, unemployment.

UNEMPLOYMENT

Unemployment is normally defined as adults actively looking for work, but without a job. Unemployment creates a cost to the entire economy in terms of loss of output. One researcher estimated that at the beginning of the 1990s when unemployment was about 7 percent and factories were running at 80 percent of their capacity, the amount of output that the economy lost due to idle resources was almost 4 percent of the total production throughout the United States. (In other words, we were somewhere inside the production possibilities curve that we talked about in Chapter 2.) That was the equivalent of almost $275 billion of schools, houses, restaurant meals, cars, and movies that *could have been* produced. It is no wonder that policymakers closely watch the unemployment figures published by the Department of Labor's Bureau of Labor Statistics.

On a more personal level, the state of being unemployed often results in hardship and failed opportunities as well as a lack of self-respect. Psychological researchers believe that being fired creates at least as much stress as the death of a close friend. The numbers that we present about unemployment can never fully convey its true cost to this or any other nation.

Unemployment
The total number of adults (aged 16 years or older) who are willing and able to work and who are actively looking for work but have not found a job.

Historical Unemployment Rates

The unemployment rate, defined as a proportion of the measured **labor force** that is unemployed, reached a low of 1.2 percent of the labor force at the end of World War II after having exceeded 25 percent during the Great Depression in the 1930s. You can see in Figure 7-1 what happened to unemployment in the United States over the past century. The highest level ever was reached in the Great Depression, but unemployment was also very high during the Panic of 1893.

Labor force
Individuals aged 16 years or older who either have jobs or are looking and available for jobs; the number of employed plus the number of unemployed.

INTERNATIONAL EXAMPLE
Rising Joblessness Worldwide

Several studies have recently predicted increasing worldwide joblessness until at least the beginning of the twenty-first century. It is instructive to place the United States in the worldwide context with respect to unemployment. Table 7-1 shows that the current U.S. unemployment rate is not as low as in Japan or Switzerland but is lower than anywhere else in Europe. In the year 2000, the United States's relative position will have remained the same, but much of Europe on average will see higher rates of unemployment.

FOR CRITICAL ANALYSIS: Does the relative *unemployment rate in the United States have anything to do with the well-being of American workers?* ●

FIGURE 7-1

A Century of Unemployment

Unemployment reached lows during World Wars I and II of less than 2 percent and highs during the Great Depression of more than 25 percent.

Source: U.S. Department of Labor, Bureau of Labor Statistics.

TABLE 7-1
Unemployment Rates Around the World

Country	Projected Unemployment Rate (%)	
	1996	2000
Australia	9.5	11.7
Belgium	12.7	11.8
Canada	10.2	11.5
France	12.2	14.0
Germany	10.0	8.2
Italy	11.9	13.2
Japan	2.8	2.8
Netherlands	9.5	6.8
Spain	24.4	23.7
Sweden	7.8	8.3
Switzerland	3.8	1.3
United Kingdom	8.2	9.4
United States	5.8	5.8

Source: International Labor Organization.

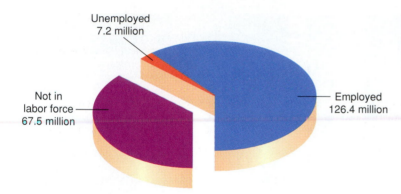

FIGURE 7-2
Adult Population
The population aged 16 and older can be broken down into three groups: people who are employed, those who are unemployed, and those not in the labor force.
Source: U.S. Department of Labor, Bureau of Labor Statistics.

Employment, Unemployment, and the Labor Force

Figure 7-2 presents the population of individuals 16 years of age or older broken into three segments: (1) employed, (2) unemployed, and (3) not in the labor force (a category that includes homemakers, full-time students, and retired persons). Those who are employed and those who are unemployed, added together, make up the labor force. In 1996, the labor force amounted to 126.4 million + 7.2 million = 133.6 million Americans. To calculate the unemployment rate, we simply divide the number of unemployed by the number of people in the labor force and multiply by 100: 7.2 million/133.6 million × 100 = 5.4 percent.

The Arithmetic Determination of Unemployment

Because there is a transition between employment and unemployment at any point in time—people are leaving jobs and others are finding jobs—there is a simple relationship between the employed and the unemployed, as can be seen in Figure 7-3. People departing jobs are shown at the top of the diagram, and people taking new jobs are shown at the bottom. If job leavers and job finders are equal, the unemployment rate stays the same. If departures exceed new hires, the unemployment rate rises.

The number of unemployed is some number at any point in time. It is a **stock** of individuals who do not have a job but are actively looking for one. The same is true for the number of employed. The number of people departing jobs, whether voluntarily or

Stock
The quantity of something, measured at a given point in time—for example, an inventory of goods or a bank account. Stocks are defined independently of time, although they are assessed at a point in time.

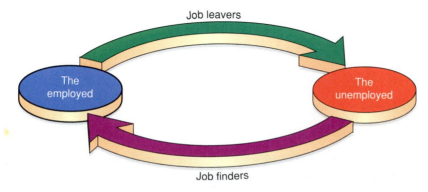

FIGURE 7-3
The Logic of the Unemployment Rate
Job leavers are individuals who are no longer employed and add to the unemployed (except for those who permanently leave the labor force such as new retirees.) When the unemployed find a job, they add to the employed. When both flows are equal, the unemployment rate is stable. If more people leave jobs than find them, the unemployment rate increases, and vice versa.

FIGURE 7-4
Visualizing Stocks and Flows
Unemployment at any point in time is some number that represents a stock, such as the amount of water in a bathtub. People who lose their job constitute a new flow into the bathtub. Those who find a job can be thought of as the water that flows out by the drain.

Flow
A quantity measured per unit of time; something that occurs over time, such as the income you make per week or per year or the number of individuals who are fired every month.

Job loser
An individual in the labor force who was employed and whose employment was involuntarily terminated or who was laid off.

Reentrant
An individual who used to work full time but left the labor force and has now reentered it looking for a job.

Job leaver
An individual in the labor force who quits voluntarily.

New entrant
An individual who has never held a full-time job lasting two weeks or longer but is now in the labor force.

involuntarily, is a **flow,** as is the number of people finding jobs. Picturing a bathtub, as illustrated in Figure 7-4, is a good way of remembering how stocks and flows work.

Unemployment Categories. According to the Bureau of Labor Statistics, an unemployed individual may fall into any of four categories:

1. A **job loser,** whose employment was involuntarily terminated or who was laid off (varies between 40 and 60 percent of the unemployed)
2. A **reentrant,** having worked a full-time job before but having been out of the labor force (varies from 20 to 30 percent of the unemployed)
3. A **job leaver,** who voluntarily ended employment (varies between less than 10 to around 15 percent of the unemployed)
4. A **new entrant,** who has never worked a full-time job for two weeks or longer (varies from 10 to 13 percent of the unemployed)

Duration of Unemployment. If you are out of a job for a week, your situation is typically much less serious than if you are out of a job for 14 weeks. An increase in the duration of unemployment can increase the unemployment rate because workers stay unemployed longer, thereby creating a greater number of them at any given time. The most recent information on duration of unemployment paints the following picture: 37.1 percent of those who become unemployed find a new job by the end of one month, an additional 31.8 percent find a job by the end of two months, and only 16.3 percent are still unemployed after six months. The average duration of unemployment for all unemployed has been 15.2 weeks over the past decade.

When overall business activity goes into a downturn, the duration of unemployment tends to rise, thereby causing much of the increase in the estimated unemployment rate. In a sense, then, it is the increase in the duration of unemployment during a downturn in national economic activity that generates the bad news that concerns policymakers in Washington, D.C. Furthermore, the 16.3 percent who stay unemployed longer than six months are the ones who create the pressure on Congress to "do something." What Congress does typically is extend and supplement unemployment benefits.

The Discouraged Worker Phenomenon. Critics of the published unemployment rate calculated by the federal government believe that there exist numerous **discouraged workers** and "hidden unemployed." Though there is no exact definition or way to measure discouraged workers, the Department of Labor defines them as people who have dropped out of the labor force and are no longer looking for a job because they believe that the job market has little to offer them. To what extent do we want to include in the measured labor force individuals who voluntarily choose not to look for work or those who take but only two minutes a day to scan the want ads and then decide that there are no jobs?

Some economists argue that people who work part time but are willing to work full time should be classified as "semihidden" unemployed. Estimates range as high as 6 million workers at any one time. Offsetting this factor, though, is *overemployment*. An individual working 50 or 60 hours a week is still counted as only one full-time worker.

Labor Force Participation. The way in which we define unemployment and membership in the labor force will affect what is known as the **labor force participation rate.** It is defined as the proportion of working-age individuals who are employed or seeking employment. (If there are discouraged, or hidden, unemployed within any particular group, the labor force participation rate for that particular group will drop.)

Figure 7-5 illustrates the labor force participation rates since 1950. The major change has been the increase in female labor force participation. If we take into account only married women aged 25 to 34, this increase is even more striking because it occurred over a shorter period of time. In 1960, about 29 percent of such women participated in the labor force outside of the home, compared with over 70 percent today. Is there an economic explanation for this increase?

THINKING CRITICALLY ABOUT THE MEDIA

Declining Job Security?

The decade of the 1990s has been labeled by the media as the one during which Americans by the millions lost job security. We have been told that corporate downsizing and global competition have resulted in American workers having to accept job changes as a regular part of their lives. Princeton economist Henry Farber looked at the actual numbers and came up with an entirely different picture. In 1973, some 54 percent of men aged 45 to 54 had been in their jobs for more than ten years, compared with 52 percent today. For workers with less than a high school degree, job tenure has definitely eroded, but for women, job tenure has been steadily rising because more women have career jobs than in the past. Indeed, the latest data show that workers in America stay with the same employer for an average of 5.1 years, longer than at almost any time since 1951.

Discouraged workers
Individuals who have stopped looking for a job because they are convinced that they will not find a suitable one. Typically, they become convinced after unsuccessfully searching for a job.

Labor force participation rate
The percentage of noninstitutionalized working-age individuals who are employed or seeking employment.

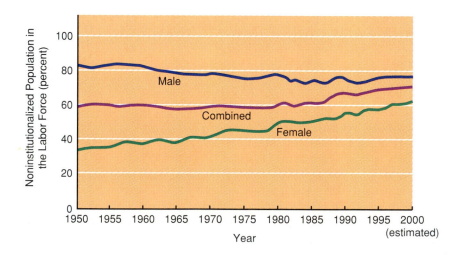

FIGURE 7-5

Labor Force Participation Rates by Sex
The combined labor force participation rate has increased in recent years. However, over the same period, the male participation rate has fallen, and the female rate has risen markedly.

Source: U.S. Department of Labor, Bureau of Labor Statistics.

Overworked Americans

Data show that the average American spends more time today working for pay than in the past. Since 1976, household surveys report that the average number of hours worked per week increased from 42.5 to 46.5 for working husbands and from 39 to 41.5 for working wives. Does this mean that Americans are overworked? Not necessarily. One has to include the total amount of work that American family members perform, such as cooking, doing laundry, and handling other household tasks. Since 1976, the number of hours that couples spend doing work in the home has fallen by almost exactly the same number of hours that working couples have increased work for pay. Thus, American couples are not forgoing additional leisure hours in order to work for more pay. Rather, Americans are simply substituting work for pay for work in the home without pay. This substitution has been possible because of increased labor-saving appliances and smaller families.

EXAMPLE
No-Fault Divorce and Increased Female Labor Force Participation

It is possible to explain the increased female labor participation rate by simply stating that there has been a change in attitudes. But there may be an economic reason behind the dramatic increase in the labor force participation rate of married females. In most states prior to the 1970s, both parties in a marriage had to consent to a divorce, which would normally be granted for a specific legally recognized cause, such as adultery. Specifically, one party or the other had to be found at fault. In most states, wives who did not want a divorce could remain married. Changes in the law in the 1970s saw the advent of no-fault divorce in which only one party had to want the divorce. The other party could not successfully oppose it. The result was less of a guarantee to married women that their financial support would remain intact. As a consequence, a larger percentage of young married women have chosen to enter and remain in the labor market, even while raising a family. For these women, no-fault divorce has created too high a risk if they choose to specialize in at-home work only.

FOR CRITICAL ANALYSIS: Has anything in particular made it more convenient for married women to work outside the home? ●

CONCEPTS IN BRIEF

- Unemployed persons are adults who are willing and able to work and are actively looking for a job but have not found one. The unemployment rate is computed by dividing the number of unemployed by the total labor force, which is equal to those who are employed plus those who are unemployed.

- The unemployed are job losers, reentrants, job leavers, and new entrants to the labor force. The flow of people leaving jobs and people finding jobs determines the stock of unemployed as well as the stock of employed.

- The duration of unemployment affects the unemployment rate. The number of unemployed workers can remain the same, but if the duration of unemployment increases, the measured unemployment rate will go up.

- Whereas overall labor force participation has risen only a bit since World War II, there has been a major increase in female labor force participation, particularly among married women between the ages of 25 and 34.

The Major Types of Unemployment

Unemployment has been categorized into four basic types: frictional, seasonal, structural, and cyclical.

Frictional Unemployment. Of the more than 130 million Americans in the labor force, more than 12 million will have either changed jobs or taken new jobs during the year;

every single month about 1 in 20 workers will have quit, been laid off (told that they will be rehired later), or been permanently fired; another 6 percent will have gone to new jobs or returned to old ones. In the process, more than 20 million persons will have reported themselves unemployed at one time or another. What we call **frictional unemployment** is the continuous flow of individuals from job to job and in and out of employment. There will always be some frictional unemployment as resources are redirected in the market because transaction costs are never zero. To eliminate frictional unemployment, we would have to prevent workers from leaving their present jobs until they had already lined up other jobs at which they would start working immediately and we would have to guarantee first-time job seekers a job *before* they started looking.

Frictional unemployment
Unemployment due to the fact that workers must search for appropriate job offers. This takes time, and so they remain temporarily ("frictionally") unemployed.

Seasonal Unemployment. **Seasonal unemployment** comes and goes with seasons of the year in which the demand for particular jobs rises and falls. In northern states, construction workers can often work only during the warmer months; they are seasonally unemployed during the winter. Summer resort workers can usually get jobs in resorts only during the summer season. They, too, become seasonally unemployed during the winter; the opposite is true for ski resort workers.

Seasonal unemployment
Unemployment resulting from the seasonal pattern of work in specific industries. It is usually due to seasonal fluctuations in demand or to changing weather conditions, rendering work difficult, if not impossible, as in the agriculture, construction, and tourist industries.

Structural Unemployment. Structural changes in our economy cause some workers to become unemployed permanently or for very long periods of time because they cannot find jobs that use their particular skills. This is called **structural unemployment.** Structural unemployment is not caused by general business fluctuations, although business fluctuations may affect it. And unlike frictional unemployment, structural unemployment is not related to the movement of workers from low-paying to high-paying jobs. Structural unemployment results when the consuming public no longer wants to buy an individual's services in that location.

Structural unemployment
Unemployment resulting from fundamental changes in the structure of the economy. It occurs, for example, when the demand for a product falls drastically so that workers specializing in the production of that product find themselves out of work. .

Cyclical Unemployment. **Cyclical unemployment** is related to business fluctuations. It is defined as unemployment associated with changes in business conditions—primarily recessions and depressions. The way to lessen cyclical unemployment would be to reduce the intensity, duration, and frequency of ups and downs of business activity. Economic policymakers attempt, through their policies, to reduce cyclical unemployment by keeping business activity on an even keel.

Cyclical unemployment
Unemployment resulting from business recessions that occur when aggregate (total) demand is insufficient to create full employment.

Full Employment

Does full employment mean that everybody has a job? Certainly not, for not everyone is looking for a job—full-time students and full-time homemakers, for example, are not. Is it possible for everyone who is looking for a job always to find one? No, because transaction costs in the labor market are not zero. Transaction costs include any activity whose goal is to enter into, carry out, or terminate contracts. In the labor market, these costs involve time spent looking for a job, being interviewed, negotiating the pay, and so on.

We will always have some frictional unemployment as individuals move in and out of the labor force, seek higher-paying jobs, and move to different parts of the country. **Full employment** is therefore a vague concept implying some sort of balance or equilibrium in an ever-shifting labor market. Of course, this general notion of full employment must somehow be put into numbers so that economists and others can determine whether the economy has reached the full-employment point. In 1986, the President's Council of Economic Advisers, which generates the *Economic Report of the President* each year (published in February), estimated that full employment in 1986 was at 6.5 percent unemployed. Using this definition, the economy was running at more than full employment from 1987 through the first few months of 1991 and from 1994 until today!

Full employment
As presented by the Council of Economic Advisers, an arbitrary level of unemployment that corresponds to "normal" friction in the labor market. In 1986, the council declared that 6.5 percent unemployment was full employment. Today, it is around 5.5 percent.

Full Employment, Wage Rigidity, and Wait Unemployment

Although the official definition of full employment has changed over the years, there is no question that it occurs at a higher rate of unemployment than it did, say, 40 years ago. Put another way, the apparently unavoidable amount of unemployment in the U.S. economy is growing. In the 1960s it was about 4.5 percent, whereas today it is at least 5.2 percent.

There are many explanations for this increase in the full-employment rate of unemployment. One relates to female labor force participation, which has risen dramatically, bringing with it the possibility of additional frictional unemployment due to the fact that women tend more than men to leave and reenter the labor force in connection with family responsibilities.

Nonetheless, the rise in the full-employment rate of unemployment seems at odds with the standard supply and demand analysis presented in Chapters 3 and 4. There we showed that if prices are allowed to adjust, there will be neither surpluses nor shortages. A certain portion of unemployment can be defined as a surplus of workers at a particular wage rate that is clearly above equilibrium. It must be, then, that there are wage rigidities (because wages are the price of labor) in the labor market. These result in a situation in which workers are waiting. Workers are unemployed because, at the going wage rate, the quantity of labor supplied exceeds the quantity demanded. This is called **wait unemployment,** and it is due to firms' inability to reduce wages in the face of an excess quantity supplied of labor—by wage rigidities. You already examined one cause of wait unemployment in Chapter 4—minimum wage laws. There are others, including the setting of minimum wages for a firm or an industry because of union power, and a variety of other reasons, some of which you will examine in other chapters in this macroeconomic part of your text.

Wait unemployment
Unemployment that is caused by wage rigidities resulting from minimum wages, unions, and other factors.

CONCEPTS IN BRIEF

- Frictional unemployment occurs because of transaction costs in the labor market. For example, workers do not have all the information necessary about vacancies. Structural unemployment occurs when the demand for a commodity permanently decreases so that workers find that the jobs that they are used to doing are no longer available.

- The level of frictional unemployment is used in part to determine our (somewhat arbitrary) definition of full employment.

- When wage rigidities exist because of minimum wage laws, union contracts, and other reasons, wait unemployment may result.

INFLATION

During World War II, you could buy bread for 8 to 10 cents a loaf and have milk delivered fresh to your door for about 25 cents a half gallon. The average price of a new car was less than $700, and the average house cost less than $3,000. Today bread, milk, cars, and houses all cost more—a lot more. Prices in the late 1990s are more than 10 times what they were in 1940. Clearly, this country has experienced quite a bit of *inflation* since then. We define **inflation** as an upward movement in the average level of prices. The opposite of inflation is **deflation,** defined as a downward movement in the average level of prices. Notice that these definitions depend on the *average* level of prices. This means that even during a period of inflation, some prices can be falling if other prices are rising at a faster rate. The price of computers and computer-related equipment has dropped dramatically since the 1960s even though there has been general inflation.

Inflation
The situation in which the average of all prices of goods and services in an economy is rising.

Deflation
The situation in which the average of all prices of goods and services in an economy is falling.

To discuss what has happened to inflation in this and other countries, we have to know how to measure it.

Inflation and the Purchasing Power of Money

A rose may be a rose may be a rose, but a dollar is not always a dollar. The value of a dollar does not stay constant when there is inflation. The value of money is usually talked about in terms of the **purchasing power** of money. A dollar's purchasing power is the real goods and services that it can buy. Consequently, another way of defining inflation is as a decline in the purchasing power of money. The faster the rate of inflation, the greater the drop in the purchasing power of money.

One way to think about inflation and the purchasing power of money is to discuss dollar values in terms of *nominal* versus *real* values. The nominal value of anything is simply its price expressed in today's dollars. In contrast, the real value of anything is its value expressed in purchasing power, which varies with the rate of inflation. Let's say that you received a $100 bill from your grandparents this year. One year from now, the nominal value of that bill will still be $100. The real value will depend on what the purchasing power of money is after one year's worth of inflation. Obviously, if there has been a lot of inflation in one year, the real value of that $100 bill will have dropped.

Purchasing power
The value of money for buying goods and services. If your money income stays the same but the price of one good that you are buying goes up, your effective purchasing power falls, and vice versa.

Measuring the Rate of Inflation

How do we come up with a measure of the rate of inflation? This is indeed a thorny problem for government statisticians. It is easy to determine how much the price of an individual commodity has risen: If last year a light bulb cost 50 cents and this year it costs 75 cents, there has been a 50 percent rise in the price of that light bulb over a one-year period. We can express the change in the individual light bulb price in one of several ways: The price has gone up 25 cents; the price is one and a half (1.5) times as high; the price has risen by 50 percent. An *index number* of this price rise is simply the second way (1.5) multiplied by 100, meaning that the index number would be 150. We multiply by 100 to eliminate decimals because it is easier to think in terms of percentage changes using integers. This is the standard convention adopted for convenience in dealing with index numbers or price levels.

> ### THINKING CRITICALLY ABOUT THE MEDIA
>
> #### Super Bowl Advertising
>
> Each year, the popular press makes sure that everyone knows how much it costs to advertise a 30-second spot during the Super Bowl. A favorite comparison is what it cost for the same 30-second spot during the first Super Bowl in 1967. Back then it cost $50,000, whereas today it costs $1.25 million, or 25 times more. Two problems arise with such a comparison (and all others like it): (1) The price level has increased more than fourfold since 1967, thereby reducing the real (inflation-corrected) increase in Super Bowl advertising prices to only eight times what they were in 1967, and (2) the number of TV game viewers has more than doubled since 1967, further reducing the real advertising cost per viewer to less than four times what it was in 1967.

Computing a Price Index. The measurement problem becomes more complicated when it involves a large number of goods, some of whose prices have risen faster than others and some that have even fallen. What we have to do is pick a representative bundle, a so-called market basket, of goods and compare the cost of that market basket of goods over time. When we do this, we obtain a **price index,** which is defined as the cost of a market basket of goods today, expressed as a percentage of the cost of that identical market basket of goods in some starting year, known as the **base year.**

Price index
The cost of today's market basket of goods expressed as a percentage of the cost of the same market basket during a base year.

Base year
The year that is chosen as the point of reference for comparison of prices in other years.

$$\text{Price index} = \frac{\text{cost today of market basket}}{\text{cost of market basket in base year}} \times 100$$

In the base year the price index will always be 100, because the year in the numerator and in the denominator of the above fraction is the same; therefore, the fraction equals 1, and when we multiply it by 100, we get 100. A simple numerical example is given in Table

TABLE 7-2

Calculating a Price Index for a Two-Good Market Basket

In this simplified example, there are only two goods—corn and micro-computers. The quantities and base-year prices are given in columns 2 and 3. The cost of the 1986 market basket, calculated in column 4, comes to $1,400. The 1998 prices are given in column 5. The cost of the market basket in 1998, calculated in column 6, is $1,700. The price index for 1998 compared with 1986 is 121.43.

(1) Commodity	(2) Market Basket Quantity	(3) 1986 Price per Unit	(4) Cost of Market Basket in 1986	(5) 1998 Price per Unit	(6) Cost of Market Basket at 1998 Prices
Corn	100 bushels	$ 4	$ 400	$ 8	$ 800
Microcomputers	2	500	1,000	450	900
Totals			$1,400		$1,700

$$\text{Price index} = \frac{\text{cost of market basket in 1998}}{\text{cost of market basket in base year 1986}} \times 100 = \frac{\$1,700}{\$1,400} \times 100 = 121.43$$

7-2. In the table there are only two goods in the market basket—corn and microcomputers. The *quantities* in the basket remain the same between the base year, 1986, and the current year, 1998; only the *prices* change. Such a *fixed-quantity* price index is the easiest to compute because the statistician need only look at prices of goods and services sold every year rather than actually observing how much of these goods and services consumers actually purchase each year.

Real-World Price Indexes. Government statisticians calculate a number of price indexes. The most often quoted are the **Consumer Price Index (CPI), the Producer Price Index (PPI), and the GDP deflator.** The CPI attempts to measure changes only in the level of prices of goods and services purchased by wage earners. The PPI attempts to show what has happened to the price level for commodities that firms purchase from other firms. The GDP deflator attempts to show changes in the level of prices of all new goods and services produced in the economy. The most general indicator of inflation is the GDP deflator because it measures the changes in the prices of everything produced in the economy.

The CPI. The Bureau of Labor Statistics (BLS) has the task of identifying a market basket of goods and services of the typical consumer. It uses a survey from 1982–1984 to come up with its estimates. For example, during this base period, out of every consumer dollar spent, almost 17 cents was spent on food and almost 4 cents on transportation. Entertainment got a little more than 10 cents and clothing 6 cents. The largest item was housing, taking about 16 cents of every consumer dollar.

Economists have known for years that the way the BLS measures changes in the Consumer Price Index is flawed. Specifically, the BLS has been unable to account for the way consumers substitute less expensive items for higher-priced items. The reason is that the CPI is a fixed-quantity price index, meaning that each month the BLS samples only prices, rather than relative quantities purchased by consumers. In addition, the BLS has been unable to take account of quality changes as they occur. Even if the BLS captures the dramatically falling price of personal computers, it has been unable to reflect the dramatic improvement in personal computers. Finally, the CPI ignores the introduction of new products.

Consumer Price Index (CPI)
A statistical measure of a weighted average of prices of a specified set of goods and services purchased by wage earners in urban areas.

Producer Price Index (PPI)
A statistical measure of a weighted average of prices of commodities that firms purchase from other firms.

GDP deflator
A price index measuring the changes in prices of all new goods and services produced in the economy.

EXAMPLE
The CPI, New Products, and Breakfast Cereals

By definition, a new product that is successful makes the people who buy it better off. The value that consumers place on a new product is greater than the money price. Hence successful new products should reduce the cost of maintaining a given standard of living and therefore reduce the CPI. Economist Jerry Hausman of MIT did a study of Apple-Cinnamon Cheerios, introduced by General Mills in 1989. Within three years, that cereal had attained a market share of 1.6 percent, thus implying a higher value received by 1.6 percent of breakfast cereal consumers. According to Hausman's calculations, Apple-Cinnamon Cheerios implied a 1.7 percent *reduction* in the average price of cereal (per-constant-quality unit). Using the same methodology, Hausman estimated that the CPI over-estimates the price of cereals by 20 percent. This so-called new-goods bias in the overall CPI has been estimated by other researchers to be as high as .5 percent a year.

FOR CRITICAL ANALYSIS: Why do successful products make consumers better off? ●

The PPI.   There are a number of Producer Price Indexes, including one for food materials, another for intermediate goods (goods used in the production of other goods), and one for finished goods. Most of the producer prices included are in mining, manufacturing, and agriculture. The PPIs can be considered general-purpose indexes for nonretail markets.

Although in the long run the various PPIs and the CPI generally show the same rate of inflation, such is not the case in the short run. Most often the PPIs increase before the CPI because it takes time for producer price increases to show up in the prices that consumers pay for final products. Often changes in the PPIs are watched closely as a hint that inflation is going to increase or decrease.

The GDP Deflator.   The broadest price index reported in the United States is the GDP deflator, where GDP stands for gross domestic product, or annual total national income. Unlike the CPI and the PPIs, the GDP deflator is not based on a fixed market basket of goods and services. The basket is allowed to change with people's consumption and investment patterns. In this sense, the changes in the GDP deflator reflect both price changes and the public's market responses to those price changes. Why? Because new expenditure patterns are allowed to show up in the GDP deflator as people respond to changing prices.

Historical Changes in the CPI.   The Consumer Price Index has shown a fairly dramatic trend upward since about World War II. Figure 7-6 shows the annual rate of change in the Consumer Price Index since 1860. Prior to World War II, there were numerous periods of deflation along with periods of inflation. Persistent year-in and year-out inflation seems to be a post–World War II phenomenon, at least in this country. As far back as before the American Revolution, prices used to rise during war periods but then would fall back to more normal levels afterward. This occurred after the Revolutionary War, the War of 1812, the Civil War, and World War I. Consequently, the overall price level in 1940 wasn't much different from 150 years earlier.

INTERNATIONAL EXAMPLE
Hyperinflation

Referring to Figure 7-6, look at the highest rates of inflation that the United States has experienced. In one year during the Civil War, the estimated inflation rate was over 27 percent. Since then, only during and immediately after wartimes have we had inflation rates greater than 12 percent. Consider, in contrast, the rest of the world. Many countries have experienced and continue to experience **hyperinflation,** an extreme form of inflation during which average prices rise very rapidly. In 1989, Argentina had an inflation rate of 4,923 percent; the following year, in Peru, the rate was 7,481 percent. Russia's 1995 inflation of 340 percent seems almost modest in comparison. The most extreme hyperinflation ever to occur was in Germany in 1923, when prices increased by *700 billion* percent!

Hyperinflation
Extremely rapid rise of the average of all prices in an economy.

FOR CRITICAL ANALYSIS: *As a consumer, how would your behavior change during a period of hyperinflation?* ●

CONCEPTS IN BRIEF

- Once we pick a market basket of goods, we can construct a price index that compares the cost of that market basket today with the cost of the same market basket in a base year.

- The Consumer Price Index (CPI) is the most often used price index in the United States. The Producer Price Index (PPI) is the second most mentioned.

- The GDP deflator measures what is happening to the average price level of *all* new, domestically produced final goods and services in our economy.

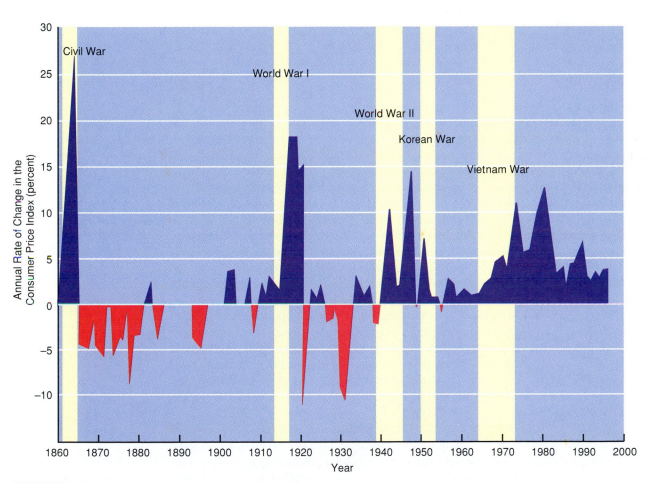

FIGURE 7-6

Inflationary Periods in U.S. History

Since the Civil War, there have been numerous periods of inflation in the United States. Here we show them as reflected by changes in the Consumer Price Index. Since World War II, the periods of inflation have not been followed by periods of deflation; that is, even during peacetime, the price index has continued to rise. The yellow areas represent wartime.

Source: U.S. Department of Labor, Bureau of Labor Statistics.

Anticipated Versus Unanticipated Inflation

Before examining who is hurt by inflation and what the effects of inflation are in general, we have to distinguish between anticipated and unanticipated inflation. We will see that the effects on individuals and the economy are vastly different, depending on which type of inflation exists.

Anticipated inflation is the rate of inflation that the majority of individuals believe will occur. If the rate of inflation this year turns out to be 10 percent, and that's about what most people thought it was going to be, we are in a situation of fully anticipated inflation.

Unanticipated inflation is inflation that comes as a surprise to individuals in the economy. For example, if the inflation rate in a particular year turns out to be 10 percent when on average people thought it was going to be 5 percent, there will have been unanticipated inflation—inflation greater than anticipated.

Some of the problems caused by inflation arise when it is unanticipated, for when it is anticipated, many people are able to protect themselves from its ravages. With the distinction in mind between anticipated and unanticipated inflation, we can easily see the relationship between inflation and interest rates.

> **Anticipated inflation**
> The inflation rate that we believe will occur; when it does, we are in a situation of fully anticipated inflation.
>
> **Unanticipated inflation**
> Inflation at a rate that comes as a surprise, either higher or lower than the rate anticipated.

Inflation and Interest Rates

Let's start in a hypothetical world in which there is no inflation and anticipated inflation is zero. In that world, you may be able to borrow money—to buy a computer or a car, for example—at a **nominal rate of interest** of, say, 10 percent. If you borrow the money to purchase a computer or a car and your anticipation of inflation turns out to be accurate, neither you nor the lender will have been fooled. The dollars you pay back in the years to come will be just as valuable in terms of purchasing power as the dollars that you borrowed.

What you ordinarily need to know when you borrow money is the *real rate of interest* that you will have to pay. The **real rate of interest** is defined as the nominal rate of interest minus the anticipated rate of inflation. If you are able to borrow money at 10 percent and you anticipated an inflation rate of 10 percent, your real rate of interest would be zero—lucky you, particularly if the actual rate of inflation turned out to be 10 percent. In effect, we can say that the nominal rate of interest is equal to the real rate of interest plus an *inflationary premium* to take account of anticipated inflation. That inflationary premium covers depreciation in the purchasing power of the dollars repaid by borrowers.[1] Consider the purchase of a home. In 1982, mortgage rates for the purchase of new homes were around 15 percent. By 1996, they had fallen to around 7 percent. Why would anyone have paid 15 percent in 1982 to borrow money to buy a home? Well, home prices in much of the country had been rising for several years at 25 percent per year, so at 15 percent, mortgage rates seemed like a good deal. By the mid- to late-1990s, home prices in most places were holding steady.

There is fairly strong evidence that inflation rates and nominal interest rates move in parallel fashion. Periods of rapid inflation create periods of high interest rates. In the early 1970s, when the inflation rate was between 4 and 5 percent, average interest rates were around 8 to 10 percent. At the beginning of the 1980s, when the inflation rate was near 9 percent, interest rates had risen to between 12 and 14 percent. By the early 1990s, when the inflation rate was about 3 percent, nominal interest rates had again fallen to between 4 and 8 percent.

> **Nominal rate of interest**
> The market rate of interest expressed in today's dollars.
>
> **Real rate of interest**
> The nominal rate of interest minus the anticipated rate of inflation.

---

[1] Whenever there are relatively high rates of anticipated inflation, we must add an additional factor to the inflationary premium—the product of the real rate of interest times the anticipated rate of inflation. Usually this last term is omitted because the anticipated rate of inflation is not high enough to make much of a difference.

INTERNATIONAL EXAMPLE
Deflation and Real Interest Rates in Japan

Wholesale prices in Japan have been falling for several years. In the past few years, consumer prices also have been falling, which means that Japan has been experiencing *deflation*. What does this have to do with real interest rates in Japan? Real interest rates are roughly equivalent to nominal, or market, rates minus the expected rate of inflation. Market interest rates are rarely negative. If the nominal interest rate a Japanese person has to pay for a mortgage is 4 percent and the expected rate of *deflation* is 3 percent, then the expected real rate of interest is 7 percent, which is extremely high by historical standards. (In the United States, for example, real interest rates have hovered around 3 percent for most of its history.) The point is that in the United States, where we have learned to expect some inflation, we subtract that anticipated inflation from nominal interest rates to obtain real interest rates. In Japan, with expectations of deflation, the Japanese end up *adding* the expected deflationary rate to the nominal rate of interest to get real rates of interest.

FOR CRITICAL ANALYSIS: *Why can't nominal interest rates be negative?* ●

Does Inflation Necessarily Hurt Everyone?

Most people think that inflation is bad. After all, inflation means higher prices, and when we have to pay higher prices, are we not necessarily worse off? The truth is that inflation affects different people differently. Its effects also depend on whether it is anticipated or unanticipated.

Unanticipated Positive Inflation: Creditor Loses, Debtor Gains. Creditors lose and debtors gain with unanticipated positive inflation. In most situations, unanticipated inflation benefits borrowers because they are not charged a nominal interest rate that fully covers the rate of inflation that actually occurred. Why? Because the lender did not anticipate inflation correctly. Whenever inflation rates are underestimated for the life of a loan, creditors lose and debtors gain. The past several decades have known periods of considerable unanticipated (higher than anticipated) inflation—the late 1960s, the early 1970s, and the late 1970s. During those years, creditors lost and debtors gained.

Protecting Against Inflation. Banks attempt to protect themselves against inflation by raising nominal interest rates to reflect anticipated inflation. Adjustable-rate mortgages in fact do just that: The interest rate varies according to what happens to interest rates in the economy. Workers can protect themselves by **cost-of-living adjustments (COLAs),** which are automatic increases in wage rates to take account of increases in the price level.

To the extent that you hold non-interest-bearing cash, you will lose because of inflation. If you have put $100 in a mattress and the inflation rate is 10 percent for the year, you will have lost 10 percent of the purchasing power of that $100. If you have your funds in a non-interest-bearing checking account, you will suffer the same fate. Individuals attempt to reduce the cost of holding cash by putting it into interest-bearing accounts, a wide variety of which often pay nominal rates of interest that reflect anticipated inflation.

The Resource Cost of Inflation. Some economists believe that the main cost of unanticipated inflation is the opportunity cost of resources used to protect against inflation and the distortions introduced as firms attempt to plan for the long run. Individuals have to spend time and resources to figure out ways to cover themselves in case inflation is different from what it has been in the past. That may mean spending a longer time working out

Cost-of-living adjustments (COLAs)

Clauses in contracts that allow for increases in specified nominal values to take account of changes in the cost of living.

more complicated contracts for employment, for purchases of goods in the future, and for purchases of raw materials.

Inflation requires that price lists be changed. This is called the **repricing, or menu, cost of inflation.** The higher the rate of inflation, the higher the repricing cost of inflation. Imagine the repricing cost of inflation in Argentina in 1989 with its rapid inflation compared to that in the United States, where the average inflation rate has rarely reached double digits.

Another major problem with inflation is that usually it does not proceed perfectly evenly. Consequently, the rate of inflation is not exactly what people anticipate. When this is so, the purchasing power of money changes in unanticipated ways. Because money is what we use as the measuring rod of the value of transactions we undertake, we have a more difficult time figuring out what we have really paid for things. As a result, resources tend to be misallocated in such situations because people have not really valued them accurately.

Think of any period during which you have to pay a higher price for something that was cheaper before. You are annoyed. But every time you pay a higher price, that represents the receipt of higher income for someone else. Therefore, it is impossible for all of us to be worse off because of rising prices. There are numerous costs to inflation, but they aren't the ones commonly associated with inflation. One way to think of inflation is that it is simply a *change in the accounting system*. One year the price of fast-food hamburgers averages $1; 10 years later the price of fast-food hamburgers averages $2. Clearly, $1 doesn't mean the same thing 10 years later. If we changed the name of our unit of accounting each year so that one year we paid $1 for fast-food hamburgers and 10 years later we paid, say, 1 peso, this lesson would be driven home.

Repricing, or **menu, cost of inflation**
The cost associated with recalculating prices and printing new price lists when there is inflation.

CONCEPTS IN BRIEF

- Whenever inflation is greater than anticipated, creditors lose and debtors gain. Whenever the rate of inflation is less than anticipated, creditors gain and debtors lose.

- Holders of cash lose during periods of inflation because the purchasing power of their cash depreciates at the rate of inflation.

- Households and businesses spend resources in attempting to protect themselves against unanticipated inflation, thus imposing a resource cost on the economy whenever there is unanticipated inflation.

CHANGING INFLATION AND UNEMPLOYMENT: BUSINESS FLUCTUATIONS

Some years unemployment goes up, some years it goes down. Some years there is a lot of inflation, other years there isn't. We have fluctuations in all aspects of our macroeconomy. The ups and downs in economywide economic activity are sometimes called **business fluctuations.** When business fluctuations are positive, they are called **expansions**—speedups in the pace of national economic activity. The opposite of an expansion is a **contraction,** which is a slowdown in the pace of national economic activity. The top of an expansion is usually called its *peak,* and the bottom of a contraction is usually called its *trough.* Business fluctuations used to be called *business cycles,* but that term no longer seems appropriate because *cycle* implies predetermined or automatic recurrence, and we certainly haven't had automatic recurrent fluctuations in general business and economic activity. What we have had are contractions and expansions that vary greatly in length. For example, nine post–World War II expansions averaged 48 months, but three of those exceeded 55 months, and two lasted less than 25 months.

Business fluctuations
The ups and downs in overall business activity, as evidenced by changes in national income, employment, and the price level.

Expansion
A business fluctuation in which overall business activity is rising at a more rapid rate than previously or at a more rapid rate than the overall historical trend for the nation.

Contraction
A business fluctuation during which the pace of national economic activity is slowing down.

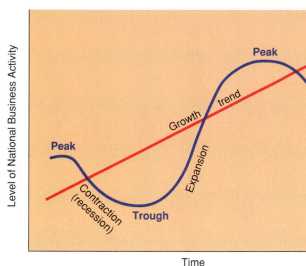

FIGURE 7-7

The Typical Course of Business Fluctuations
An idealized business cycle would go from peak to trough and back again in a regular cycle.

Recession

A period of time during which the rate of growth of business activity is consistently less than its long-term trend or is negative.

Depression

An extremely severe recession.

If the contractionary phase of business fluctuations becomes severe enough, we call it a **recession.** An extremely severe recession is called a **depression.** Typically, at the beginning of a recession, interest rates rise, and as the recession gets worse, they fall. At the same time, people's income starts to fall and the duration of unemployment increases, so that the unemployment rate increases. In times of expansion, the opposite occurs.

In Figure 7-7, you see that typical business fluctuations occur around a growth trend in overall national business activity shown as a straight upward-sloping line. Starting out at a peak, the economy goes into a contraction (recession). Then an expansion starts that moves up to its peak, higher than the last one, and the sequence starts over again.

The official dating of business recessions is done by the National Bureau of Economic Research in New York City; Cambridge, Massachusetts; and Palo Alto, California.

A Historical Picture of Business Activity in the United States

Figure 7-8 on page 158 traces U.S. business activity from 1880 to the present. Note that the long-term trend line is shown as horizontal, so all changes in business activity focus around that trend line. Major changes in business activity in the United States occurred during the Great Depression and World War II. Note that none of the business fluctuations that you see in Figure 7-8 exactly mirror the idealized typical course of a business fluctuation shown in Figure 7-7.

Explaining Business Fluctuations: External Shocks

As you might imagine, because changes in national business activity affect everyone, economists for decades have attempted to understand and explain business fluctuations. For years, one of the most obvious explanations has been external events that tend to disrupt the economy. In many of the graphs in this chapter, you have seen that World War II was a critical point in this nation's economic history. A war is certainly an external shock—something that originates outside of our economy.

Other examples of external shocks, particularly for an agrarian nation, have to do with abrupt changes in the weather. Long-term drought tended to create downturns in national business activity when the majority of Americans worked on farms. Today, major droughts or floods usually affect specific regions of the U.S. economy. Even a hurricane or an earthquake that dramatically affects one area rarely causes a national economic downturn.

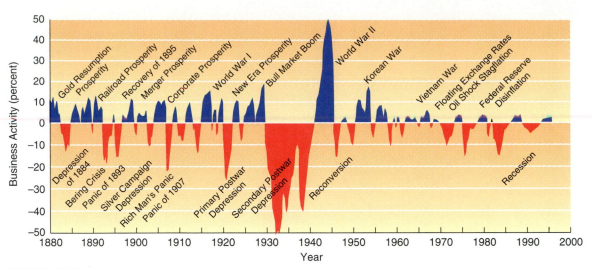

FIGURE 7-8

National Business Activity, 1880 to the Present
Variations around the trend of U.S. business activity have been frequent since 1880.

Source: American Business Activity from 1790 to Today, 67th ed., AmeriTrust Co., January 1996.

In the 1970s, due to actions on the part of certain countries in the Middle East, the United States received an "oil shock." The price of oil increased dramatically then, and some economists argue that this had a major effect on national economic activity.

It is not enough for us to say simply that business downturns are caused by external shocks. In the first place, if that were the only determinant of recessions, there would be little reason to study macroeconomics. Second, we know that historically we have had business recessions in the absence of any external shocks. We therefore need a theory of why national economic activity changes. The remainder of the macro chapters in this book develop a series of models that will help you understand the ups and downs of our business fluctuations.

CONCEPTS IN BRIEF

- The ups and downs in economywide business activity are called business fluctuations, which consist of expansions and contractions in overall business activity.

- The lowest point of a contraction is called the trough; the highest point of an expansion is called the peak.

- A recession is a downturn in business activity for some length of time.

- One possible explanation for business fluctuations relates to external shocks, such as wars, dramatic increases in the price of oil, earthquakes, floods, and droughts.

The Policy Effects of Changes in Measuring the CPI

Concepts Applied: CPI, cost-of-living adjustments (COLAs)

Social Security benefits increase yearly using the CPI to adjust for inflation. Changes in the CPI's definition would have a real effect on the amount recipients receive in their monthly checks.

In the past, it seemed as if only economists and government statisticians were worried about whether the government measured the Consumer Price Index (CPI) accurately. There have always been theoretical arguments about the inability of the Bureau of Labor Statistics to take account of product quality changes as well as the changing mix of products and services purchased by the average American family. If, in response to these and other arguments, changes are made in the way the CPI is measured, it is likely that the CPI will show inflation to be somewhat less than would otherwise have been shown. Is this just a theoretical issue? The answer is a resounding no.

What Is Based on the CPI?

Union and other contracts that relate to wages are often tied to changes in the CPI. Therefore, if the measured rate of inflation—the annual change in the CPI—turns out to be lower because of the new measurement techniques, such cost-of-living clauses will mean lower wage increases for union employees covered by them.

Social Security Payments and the Tax Code

Social Security payments would also be affected by changes in the measured CPI. Because Social Security benefits are tied to changes in the CPI, a smaller increase in the CPI would reduce automatic increases in Social Security benefits. In addition, food stamps and pensions for federal workers are automatically linked to the CPI. They, too, would not increase so much.

Our federal tax system is also in some small way a function of changes in the CPI. The tax brackets that you learned about in Chapter 5 increase along with changes in the CPI, as do personal exemptions. On both counts, a lower rate of growth in the CPI would lead to fewer federal tax revenues.

In the End, What Would It Mean?

If the average increase in the CPI were reduced by just .5 percent a year, the average Social Security recipient would receive about $3,000 less over the next 10 years. When all Social Security recipients are factored in, this would amount to a savings to the federal government of almost $100 billion over that same time period. Similar calculations for other federal benefits tied to the CPI would yield an additional savings of $100 billion. A bipartisan congressional group estimated in 1995 that removing the bias from the CPI would lead to a total reduction in federal outlays by $634 billion over 10 years.

Obviously, small changes in the CPI can have big results.

FOR CRITICAL ANALYSIS
1. What groups would be in favor of not "improving" the measurement of the CPI?
2. Who would benefit from an improvement in the measurement of the CPI?

CHAPTER SUMMARY

1. The labor force consists of all persons who are employed plus those who are unemployed. Those over age 16 who are not in the labor force are full-time students, homemakers, and retired persons. The rate of unemployment is obtained by dividing the number of unemployed by the size of the labor force. If the duration of unemployment increases, the rate of unemployment also increases. Labor force participation rates have increased dramatically for women since World War II.

2. There are four types of unemployment in the United States: frictional, seasonal, structural, and cyclical. There is also wait unemployment, which is caused by wage rigidities, such as minimum wage laws and union contracts.

3. Frictional unemployment is caused by the temporary inability of workers to match their skills and talents with available jobs.

4. Structural unemployment occurs when the demand for a particular skill falls off abruptly.

5. Inflation occurs when the average of all prices of goods and services is rising; deflation occurs when the average of all prices is falling. During periods of inflation, the purchasing power of money falls (by definition).

6. The most commonly used measures of changes in general prices are the Consumer Price Index (CPI), the Producer Price Index (PPI), and the GDP deflator.

7. The nominal rate of interest includes the anticipated rate of inflation. Therefore, when anticipated inflation increases, nominal rates of interest will rise.

8. Whenever the actual rate of inflation turns out to exceed the anticipated rate of inflation, creditors lose and debtors gain because the latter are able to repay debts in cheaper dollars. Of course, if everybody anticipates rising prices, nominal interest rates will rise to take account of this future expected reduction in the purchasing power of the dollar.

9. Workers can protect themselves against inflation by having cost-of-living adjustment (COLA) clauses in their employment contracts.

10. Business fluctuations consist of expansions and contractions. Long contractions are called recessions, and a severe recession is called a depression. One explanation for changes in national economic activity relates to external shocks, such as earthquakes, droughts, floods, wars, and dramatic increases in the price of oil.

DISCUSSION OF PREVIEW QUESTIONS

1. Why is frictional unemployment not necessarily harmful?

Because imperfect information exists in the real world, at any given time some people seeking jobs won't be matched with job vacancies. Given imperfect information, frictional unemployment indicates that the economy is reacting to changes in relative demands and supplies in different sectors. Moreover, frictional unemployment occurs when people climb up the occupational ladder. Thus frictional unemployment is not necessarily harmful to society (or to the individuals involved), and hence the overall unemployment percentage may be a misleading statistic.

2. Does it matter whether inflation is anticipated or not?

Whether inflation is anticipated or not is important to households and firms. When everyone fully and correctly anticipates the rate of future inflation, all contracts will take account of the declining purchasing power of the dollar. Debtors will not be able to gain at the expense of creditors, and employers will not be able to fool employees into agreeing to accept wage increases that do not have an inflationary factor built in. Only when inflation is not anticipated can it have unexpected negative effects on households and firms.

3. Who is hurt by inflation?

In periods of inflation, fixed-income groups are obviously hurt; however, because most retired people collect Social Security payments (which have increased more rapidly than the price level for the past quarter century), this point is easily overstressed. In periods of unanticipated inflation (or when the rate of inflation is more than that anticipated), creditors are hurt at the expense of borrowers, who gain. Also, people locked into long-term contracts to receive fixed nominal-money amounts (bondholders and other moneylenders, and some pensioners) are hurt if the rate of inflation is greater than they had anticipated. People who hold cash are also hurt by inflation; as prices rise, a given amount of cash buys less.

4. How do we describe the phases of national business fluctuations?

When business fluctuations are positive, they are called expansions, and when they are negative, they

are called contractions. The top of the expansion is the peak, and the bottom is the trough. A long-lasting trough is called a recession. If a recession gets very serious, it is called a depression. Recessions are officially dated by the National Bureau of Economic Research.

PROBLEMS

(Answers to the odd-numbered problems appear at the back of the book.)

7-1. Assume that your taxable income is $30,000 per year. Assume further that you are in the 15 percent tax bracket applied to all income from $0 to $30,000. If your taxable income increases to $30,001 per year, you will move into the 28 percent marginal tax bracket. Your boss gives you a raise equal to 4 percent. How much better off are you?

7-2. Assume that you are receiving unemployment benefits of $100 a week. You are offered a job that will pay you $150 a week before taxes. Assume further that you would have to pay 7 percent Social Security taxes plus federal income taxes equal to 15 percent of your salary. What is the opportunity cost of remaining unemployed—that is, how much will it cost you to refuse the job offer?

7-3. Assume that the labor force consists of 100 people and that every month five people become unemployed and five others who were unemployed find jobs.

a. What is the frictional unemployment rate?

b. What is the average duration of unemployment?

Now assume that the only type of unemployment in this economy is frictional.

c. What is the unemployment rate?

Suppose that a system of unemployment compensation is instituted, and the average duration of unemployment rises to two months.

d. What will the unemployment rate for this economy be now?

e. Does a higher unemployment rate necessarily mean that the economy is sicker or that laborers are worse off?

7-4. Suppose that a country has a labor force of 100 people. In January, Miller, Pulsinelli, and Hooper are unemployed; in February, those three find jobs but Stevenson, Conn, and Romano become unemployed. Suppose further that every month the previous three that were unemployed find jobs and three different people become unemployed.

a. What is this country's unemployment rate?

b. What is its frictional unemployment rate?

c. What is the average duration of unemployment?

7-5. a. Suppose that the nominal interest rate is currently 12 percent. If the anticipated inflation rate is zero, what is the real interest rate?

b. The anticipated inflation rate rises to 13 percent while the nominal interest rate remains at 12 percent. Does it make sense to lend money under these circumstances?

7-6. An economic slump occurs and two things happen:

a. Many people stop looking for jobs because they know that the probability of finding a job is low.

b. Many people who become laid off start doing such work at home as growing food and painting and repairing their houses and autos.

Which of these events implies that the official unemployment rate overstates unemployment, and which implies the opposite?

7-7. Columns 1 and 3 in the table show employment and the price level in the economy.

(1) Employment (millions of workers)	(2) Unemployment Rate (%)	(3) Price Level	(4) Rate of Inflation (%)
90	_____	1.00	N.A.
91	_____	1.08	_____
92	_____	1.17	_____
93	_____	1.28	_____
94	_____	1.42	_____
95	_____	1.59	_____
96	_____	1.81	_____
97	_____	2.10	_____

a. Assume that the labor force in the economy is 100 million. Compute and enter in column 2 the unemployment rate at each level of employment. (Hint: Divide the number of workers unemployed by the labor force.)

b. For each row (except the first), compute and enter in column 4 the rate of inflation.

COMPUTER-ASSISTED INSTRUCTION

In this problem, a consumer spends all of her income on pizza, jeans, and wine. Over time, the price of each of these goods changes, and the consumer changes the quantities that she buys. The problem requires step-by-step calculations to derive a Consumer Price Index for specific price-quantity values in specific years.

Complete problem and answer appear on disk.

INTERACTING WITH THE INTERNET

It can be confusing to access U.S. macroeconomic data because they are published and placed on the Internet by several different agencies. However, many of them place each other's data on the Internet, so you can often run across summary and press releases by chance. One major site is the Bureau of Labor Statistics,

http://stats.bls.gov/

Its "Economy at a Glance" section,

http://stats.bls.gov/eag.table.html

and "Most Requested Series,"

http://stats.bls.gov/top20.html

are likely to be of most interest. The BLS covers employment and price data.

The Commerce Department's Electronic Bulletin Board (part of its STAT-USA program) provides a large amount of macroeconomic data as well. It is available in two places: at the Commerce Department itself,

http://www.stat-usa.gov

and at the University of Michigan,

gopher://una.hh.lib.umich.edu:70/11/ebb

under the name "Department of Commerce Economic Data (UMICH)." The former is a fee-based service (with significant free guest access), while the information in the latter is freely available (this odd arrangement occurs because U.S. government data are not copyrighted). The Michigan site has almost all of the data from the Commerce Department.

CHAPTER 8

MEASURING THE ECONOMY'S PERFORMANCE

It is referred to as "underground," "gray," "subterranean," "informal," "off-the-books," or "unofficial." Whatever it is called, the underground economy exists in a big way in the United States and in an even bigger way in Latin America, Europe, and elsewhere. Have you ever bought a cheap umbrella or a pair of earrings from a street vendor? If so, both you and the vendor were partaking in the off-the-books underground economy. If you have ever done odd jobs and been paid in cash or paid someone else in cash to do odd jobs for you, you have participated in the underground economy. How big is this part of the nation's total economic activity? How distorted are official statistics that measure our nation's performance? To understand and answer these questions, you need to know about how the government officially measures the economy's performance each year.

PREVIEW QUESTIONS

1. What is gross domestic product (GDP), and what does it measure?

2. Why are only *final* goods and services evaluated in deriving GDP?

3. Why must depreciation and indirect taxes be added to national income at factor cost in order to derive GDP via the income approach?

4. How does correcting GDP for changes in the price level and population improve the usefulness of GDP estimates?

163

Did **You Know That...** whenever a single person who is currently paying a housekeeper marries that housekeeper, government statistics show that the economy's performance has declined? The reason for this seeming anomaly is that government statisticians do not yet consider unpaid housework as contributing to the total annual national income of the country (even though the same services would have to be purchased if not provided free of charge). In spite of such measurement problems, the statistics about the nation's economic performance are watched closely throughout the year by investors, bankers, businesspeople, and macroeconomic policymakers. After all, most people like to know where they stand financially at the end of each month or year. Why shouldn't we have similar information about the economy as a whole? The way we do this is by using what has become known as **national income accounting,** the main focus of this chapter.

But first we need to look at the flow of income within an economy, for it is the flow of goods and services from businesses to consumers and payments from consumers to businesses that constitutes economic activity.

THE SIMPLE CIRCULAR FLOW

The concept of a circular flow of income (ignoring taxes) involves two principles:

1. **In every economic exchange, the seller receives exactly the same amount that the buyer spends.**
2. **Goods and services flow in one direction and money payments flow in the other.**

In the simple economy shown in Figure 8-1, there are only businesses and households. It is assumed that businesses sell their *entire* output *immediately* to households and that households spend their *entire* income *immediately* on consumer products. Households receive their income by selling the use of whatever factors of production they own, such as labor services.

Profits Explained

We have indicated in Figure 8-1 that profit is a cost of production. You might be under the impression that profits are not part of the cost of producing goods and services; but profits are indeed a part of this cost because entrepreneurs must be rewarded for providing their services or they won't provide them. Their reward, if any, is profit. The reward—the profit—is included in the cost of the factors of production. If there were no expectations of profit, entrepreneurs would not incur the risk associated with the organization of productive activities. That is why we consider profits a cost of doing business.

Total Income or Total Output

The arrow that goes from businesses to households at the bottom of Figure 8-1 is labeled "Total income." What would be a good definition of **total income?** If you answered "the total of all individuals' income," you would be right. But all income is actually a payment for something, whether it be wages paid for labor services, rent paid for the use of land, interest paid for the use of capital, or profits paid to entrepreneurs. It is the amount paid to the resource suppliers. Therefore, total income is also defined as the annual *cost* of producing the entire output of **final goods and services.**

The arrow going from households to businesses at the top of the figure represents the dollar value of output in the economy. This is equal to the total monetary value of all final goods

National income accounting
A measurement system used to estimate national income and its components; one approach to measuring an economy's aggregate performance.

Total income
The yearly amount earned by the nation's resources (factors of production). Total income therefore includes wages, rent, interest payments, and profits that are received, respectively, by workers, landowners, capital owners, and entrepreneurs.

Final goods and services
Goods and services that are at their final stage of production and will not be transformed into yet other goods or services. For example, wheat is normally not a final good because usually it is used to make bread, which is a final good.

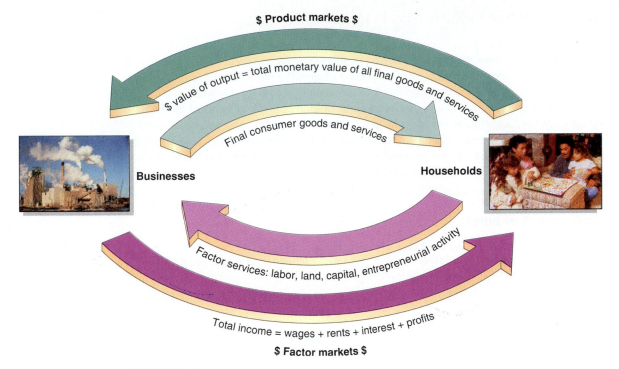

$ Product markets $

$ value of output = total monetary value of all final goods and services

Final consumer goods and services

Businesses   **Households**

Factor services: labor, land, capital, entrepreneurial activity

Total income = wages + rents + interest + profits

$ Factor markets $

FIGURE 8-1

The Circular Flow of Income and Product

Businesses provide final goods and services to households (upper clockwise loop), who in turn pay for them with money (upper counterclockwise loop). Money flows in a counterclockwise direction and can be thought of as a circular flow. The dollar value of output is identical to total income because profits are defined as being equal to total business receipts minus business outlays for wages, rents, and interest.

and services for this simple economy. In essence, it represents the total business receipts from the sale of all final goods and services produced by businesses and consumed by households. Business receipts are the opposite side of household expenditures. When households purchase goods and services with money, that money becomes a *business receipt*. Every transaction, therefore, simultaneously involves an expenditure as well as a receipt.

Product Markets. Transactions in which households buy goods take place in the product markets—that's where households are the buyers and businesses are the sellers of consumer goods. *Product market* transactions are represented in the upper loops in Figure 8-1. Note that consumer goods and services flow to household demanders, while money flows in the opposite direction to business suppliers.

Factor Markets. *Factor market* transactions are represented by the lower loops in Figure 8-1. In the factor market, households are the sellers; they sell resources such as labor, land, capital, and entrepreneurial ability. Businesses are the buyers in factor markets; business expenditures represent receipts or, more simply, income for households. Also, in the lower loops of Figure 8-1, factor services flow from households to businesses, while the money paid for these services flows in the opposite direction from businesses to households. Observe also the circular flow of money (counterclockwise) from households to businesses and back again from businesses to households; it is an endless circular flow.

Why the Dollar Value of Total Output Must Equal Total Income

Total income represents the income received by households in payment for the production of goods and services. Why must total income be identical to the dollar value of total output? First, as Figure 8-1 shows, spending by one group is income to another. Second, it is a matter of simple accounting and the economic definition of profit as a cost of production. Profit is defined as what is *left over* from total business receipts after all other costs—wages, rents, interest—have been paid. If the dollar value of total output is $1,000 and the total of wages, rent, and interest for producing that output is $900, profit is $100. Profit is always the *residual* item that makes total income equal to the dollar value of total output.

CONCEPTS IN BRIEF

- In the circular flow model of income and output, households sell factor services to businesses that pay for those factor services. The receipt of payments is total income. Businesses sell goods and services to households that pay for them.

- The dollar value of total output is equal to the total monetary value of all final goods and services produced.

- The dollar value of final output must always equal total income.

NATIONAL INCOME ACCOUNTING

We have already mentioned that policymakers need information about the state of the national economy. Historical statistical records on the performance of the national economy aid economists in testing their theories about how the economy really works. National income accounting is therefore important. Let's start with the most commonly presented statistic on the national economy.

Gross Domestic Product

Gross domestic product (GDP) represents the total market value of the nation's annual final product, or output, produced per year by factors of production located within national borders. We therefore formally define GDP as the total market value of all final goods and services produced in an economy during a year. We are referring here to a *flow of production*. A nation produces at a certain rate, just as you receive income at a certain rate. Your income flow might be at a rate of $5,000 per year or $50,000 per year. Suppose you are told that someone earns $500. Would you consider this a good salary? There is no way to answer that question unless you know whether the person is earning $500 per month or per week or per day. Thus you have to specify a time period for all flows. Income received is a flow. You must contrast this with, for example, your total accumulated savings, which are a stock measured at a point in time, not across time. Implicit in just about everything we deal with in this chapter is a time period—usually one year. All the measures of domestic product and income are specified as rates measured in dollars per year.

Gross domestic product (GDP)
The total market value of all final goods and services produced by factors of production located within a nation's borders.

Stress on Final Output

GDP does not count **intermediate goods** (goods used up entirely in the production of final goods) because to do so would be to count them twice. For example, even though grain that

Intermediate goods
Goods used up entirely in the production of final goods.

a farmer produces may be that farmer's final product, it is not the final product for the nation. It is sold to make bread. Bread is the final product.

We can use a numerical example to clarify this point further. Our example will involve determining the value added at each stage of production. **Value added** is the amount of dollar value contributed to a product at each stage of its production. In Table 8-1 we see the difference between total value of all sales and value added in the production of a donut. We also see that the sum of the values added is equal to the sale price to the final consumer. It is the 15 cents that is used to measure GDP, not the 32 cents. If we used the 32 cents, we would be double-counting from stages 2 through 5, for each intermediate good would be counted at least twice—once when it was produced and again when the good it was used in making was sold. Such double counting would grossly exaggerate GDP.

Value added
The dollar value of an industry's sales minus the value of intermediate goods (for example, raw materials and parts) used in production.

Exclusion of Financial Transactions, Transfer Payments, and Secondhand Goods

Remember that GDP is the measure of the value of all final goods and services produced in one year. Many more transactions occur that have nothing to do with final goods and services produced. There are financial transactions, transfers of the ownership of preexisting goods, and other transactions that should not and do not get included in our measure of GDP.

TABLE 8-1

Sales Value and Value Added at Each Stage of Donut Production

(1) Stage of Production	(2) Dollar Value of Sales	(3) Value Added
Stage 1: Fertilizer and seed	$.01	$.01
Stage 2: Growing	.02	.01
Stage 3: Milling	.04	.02
Stage 4: Baking	.10	.06
Stage 5: Retailing	.15	.05
Total dollar value of all sales	$.32	Total value added $.15

Stage 1: A farmer purchases a penny's worth of fertilizer and seed, which are used as factors of production in growing wheat.

Stage 2: The farmer grows the wheat, harvests it, and sells it to a miller for 2 cents. Thus we see that the farmer has added 1 cent's worth of value. That 1 cent represents income paid to the farmer.

Stage 3: The miller purchases the wheat for 2 cents and adds 2 cents as the value added; that is, there is 2 cents for the miller as income. The miller sells the ground wheat flour to a donut-baking company.

Stage 4: The donut-baking company buys the flour for 4 cents and adds 6 cents as the value added. It then sells the donut to the final retailer.

Stage 5: The donut retailer sells fresh hot donuts at 15 cents apiece, thus creating an additional value of 5 cents.

We see that the total value of sales resulting from the production of one donut was 32 cents, but the total value added was 15 cents, which is exactly equal to the retail price. The total value added is equal to the sum of all income payments.

Financial Transactions. There are three general categories of purely financial transactions: (1) the buying and selling of securities, (2) government transfer payments, and (3) private transfer payments.

1. **Securities.** When you purchase a share of existing stock in Microsoft Corporation, someone else has sold it to you. In essence, there was merely a *transfer* of ownership rights. You paid $100 to obtain the stock certificate. Someone else received the $100 and gave up the stock certificate. No producing activity was consummated at that time. Hence the $100 transaction is not included when we measure gross domestic product.

2. **Government transfer payments.** Transfer payments are payments for which no productive services are concurrently provided in exchange. The most obvious government transfer payments are Social Security benefits, veterans' payments, and unemployment compensation. The recipients make no contribution to current production in return for such transfer payments (although they may have made contributions in the past to receive them). Government transfer payments are not included in GDP.

3. **Private transfer payments.** Are you receiving money from your parents in order to live at school? Has a wealthy relative ever given you a gift of money? If so, you have been the recipient of a private transfer payment. This is merely a transfer of funds from one individual to another. As such, it does not constitute productive activity and is not included in gross domestic product.

Transfer of Secondhand Goods. If I sell you my two-year-old stereo, no current production is involved. I transfer to you the ownership of a sound system that was produced years ago; in exchange, you transfer to me $550. The original purchase price of the stereo was included in GDP in the year I purchased it. To include it again when I sell it to you would be counting the value of the stereo a second time.

Other Excluded Transactions. Many other transactions are not included in GDP for practical reasons:

1. Household production—home cleaning, child care, and other tasks performed by people within their *own* households and for which they are not paid through the marketplace
2. Otherwise legal underground transactions—those that are legal but not reported and hence not taxed, such as paying housekeepers in cash that is not declared as income
3. Illegal underground activities—these include prostitution, illegal gambling, and the sale of illicit drugs

You will learn more about the size of the underground economy in this and other countries in the Issues and Applications section at the end of this chapter. Right now, let's consider some suggestions for measuring unpaid household production.

INTERNATIONAL POLICY EXAMPLE
Measuring Household Production in France and Norway

In the 1980s, the Decade for Women World Conference passed a resolution calling for all nations to include the unpaid contributions of women in GDP calculations. At least two countries, France and Norway, have started to release "satellite" GDP figures that incorporate estimates of unpaid household production. Australia, Canada, and Germany are studying a similar procedure. Of course, any estimate of unremunerated household work has serious problems. Does one add up the market cost of each activity that an unpaid homemaker provides to the family? If so, the figure turns out to be quite large, in excess of $30,000 a year. Another problem concerns the quality of household work. Some homemakers serve fabulous gourmet meals while others warm up canned and frozen foods. Should they be valued equally? Yet another problem lies in knowing where to *stop* counting: A person can hire a valet to help him or her get dressed in the morning. Should we therefore count the time spent getting dressed as part of unpaid household work? Both men and women perform services around the house every day of the year. Should all of these unremunerated services be included in a new measure of GDP?

FOR CRITICAL ANALYSIS: *In general, which countries would have the smallest amount of unpaid household production? (Hint: Think about labor force participation rates.)* ●

CONCEPTS IN BRIEF

- GDP is the total market value of final goods and services produced in an economy during a one-year period by factors of production within the nation's borders. It represents the flow of production over a one-year period.

- To avoid double counting, we look only at final goods and services produced or, alternatively, at value added.

- In measuring GDP, we must exclude (1) purely financial transactions, such as the buying and selling of securities; (2) government transfer payments and private transfer payments; and (3) the transfer of secondhand goods.

- Many other transactions are excluded from GDP, among them household services rendered by homemakers, underground economy transactions, and illegal economic activities.

TWO MAIN METHODS OF MEASURING GDP

If the definition of GDP is the total value of all final goods and services produced during a year, then to measure GDP we could add up the prices times the quantities of every individual commodity produced. But this would involve a monumental, if not impossible, task for government statisticians.

The circular flow diagram presented in Figure 8-1 gives us a shortcut method for calculating GDP. We can look at the *flow of expenditures,* which consists of consumption, investment, government purchases of goods and services, and net expenditures in the foreign sector (net exports). This is called the **expenditure approach** to measuring GDP, in which we add the dollar value of all final goods and services. We could also use the *flow of income,* looking at the income received by everybody producing goods and services. This is called the **income approach,** in which we add the income received by all factors of production.

Deriving GDP by the Expenditure Approach

Expenditure approach
A way of computing national income by adding up the dollar value at current market prices of all final goods and services.

Income approach
A way of measuring national income by adding up all components of national income, including wages, interest, rent, and profits.

To derive GDP using the expenditure approach, we must look at each of the separate components of expenditures and then add them together. These components are consumption expenditures, investment, government expenditures, and net exports.

Consumption Expenditures. How do we spend our income? As households or as individuals, we spend our income through consumption expenditure (C), which falls into three categories: **durable consumer goods, nondurable consumer goods,** and **services.** Durable goods are *arbitrarily* defined as items that last more than three years; they include automobiles, furniture, and household appliances. Nondurable goods are all the rest, such as food and gasoline. Services are intangible commodities: medical care, education, and so on.

Housing expenditures constitute a major proportion of anybody's annual expenditures. Rental payments on apartments are automatically included in consumption expenditure estimates. People who own their homes, however, do not make rental payments. Consequently, government statisticians estimate what is called the *implicit rental value* of owner-occupied homes. It is equal to the amount of rent you would have to pay if you did not own the home but were renting it from someone else.

Gross Private Domestic Investment. We now turn our attention to **gross private domestic investment** (*I*) undertaken by businesses. When economists refer to investment, they are referring to additions to productive capacity. **Investment** may be thought of as an activity that uses resources today in such a way that they allow for greater production in the future and hence greater consumption in the future. When a business buys new equipment or puts up a new factory, it is investing; it is increasing its capacity to produce in the future.

The layperson's notion of investment often relates to the purchase of stocks and bonds. For our purposes, such transactions simply represent the *transfer of ownership* of assets called stocks and bonds. Thus you must keep in mind the fact that in economics, investment refers *only* to additions to productive capacity, not to transfers of assets.

In our analysis, we will consider the basic components of investment. We have already mentioned the first one, which involves a firm's buying equipment or putting up a new factory. These are called **producer durables,** or **capital goods.** A producer durable, or a capital good, is simply a good that is purchased not to be consumed in its current form but to be used to make other goods and services. The purchase of equipment and factories—capital goods—is called **fixed investment.**

The other type of investment has to do with the change in inventories of raw materials and finished goods. Firms do not immediately sell off all their products to consumers. Some of this final product is usually held in inventory waiting to be sold. Firms hold inventories to meet future expected orders for their products. When a firm increases its inventories of finished products, it is engaging in **inventory investment.** Inventories consist of all finished goods on hand, goods in process, and raw materials.

The reason that we can think of a change in inventories as being a type of investment is that an increase in such inventories provides for future increased consumption possibilities. When inventory investment is zero, the firm is neither adding to nor subtracting from the total stock of goods or raw materials on hand. Thus if the firm keeps the same amount of inventories throughout the year, inventory *investment* has been zero.

In estimating gross private domestic investment, government statisticians also add consumer expenditures on *new* residential structures because new housing represents an addition to our future productive capacity in the sense that a new house can generate housing services in the future.

Government Expenditures. In addition to personal consumption expenditures, there are government purchases of goods and services (*G*). The government buys goods and services from private firms and pays wages and salaries to government employees. Generally, we value goods and services at the prices at which they are sold. But many government goods and services are not sold in the market. Therefore, we cannot use their market value when computing GDP. The value of these goods is considered equal to their *cost*. For

Durable consumer goods
Consumer goods that have a life span of more than three years.

Nondurable consumer goods
Consumer goods that are used up within three years.

Services
Mental or physical labor or help purchased by consumers. Examples are the assistance of doctors, lawyers, dentists, repair personnel, housecleaners, educators, retailers, and wholesalers; things purchased or used by consumers that do not have physical characteristics.

Gross private domestic investment
The creation of capital goods, such as factories and machines, that can yield production and hence consumption in the future. Also included in this definition are changes in business inventories and repairs made to machines or buildings.

Investment
Any use of today's resources to expand tomorrow's production or consumption.

Producer durables, or **capital goods**
Durable goods having an expected service life of more than three years that are used by businesses to produce other goods and services.

Fixed investment
Purchases by businesses of newly produced producer durables, or capital goods, such as production machinery and office equipment.

Inventory investment
Changes in the stocks of finished goods and goods in process, as well as changes in the raw materials that businesses keep on hand. Whenever inventories are decreasing, inventory investment is negative; whenever they are increasing, inventory investment is positive.

example, the value of a newly built road is considered equal to its construction cost and is included in the GDP for the year it was built.

Net Exports (Foreign Expenditures). To get an accurate representation of gross domestic product, we must include the foreign sector. As Americans, we purchase foreign goods called *imports*. The goods that foreigners purchase from us are our *exports*. To get an idea of the *net* expenditures from the foreign sector, we subtract the value of imports from the value of exports to get net exports (*X*) for a year:

$$\text{Net exports } (X) = \text{total exports} - \text{total imports}$$

To understand why we subtract imports rather than ignoring them altogether, consider that we are using the expenditures approach. If we want to estimate *domestic* output, we have to subtract U.S. expenditures on the goods of other nations.

Mathematical Representation Using the Expenditure Approach

We have just defined the components of GDP using the expenditure approach. When we add them all together, we get a definition for GDP, which is as follows:

$$GDP = C + I + G + X$$

where

C = consumption expenditures
I = investment expenditures
G = government expenditures
X = net exports

The Historical Picture. To get an idea of the relationship among *C*, *I*, *G*, and *X*, look at Figure 8-2 on page 172, which shows gross domestic product, personal consumption expenditures, government purchases, and gross private domestic investment plus net exports from 1929 to 1996. When we add up the expenditures of the household, business, government, and foreign sectors, we get GDP.

Depreciation and Net Domestic Product. We have used the terms *gross domestic product* and *gross private domestic investment* without really indicating what *gross* means. The dictionary defines it as "without deductions," as opposed to *net*. Deductions for what? you might ask. The deductions are for something we call **depreciation.** In the course of a year, machines and structures wear out or are used up in the production of domestic product. For example, houses deteriorate as they are occupied, and machines need repairs or they will fall apart and stop working. Most capital, or durable, goods depreciate. An estimate of this is subtracted from gross domestic product to arrive at a figure called **net domestic product (NDP),** which we define as follows:

$$NDP = GDP - \text{depreciation}$$

Depreciation is also called **capital consumption allowance** because it is the amount of the capital stock that has been consumed over a one-year period. In essence, it equals the amount a business would have to put aside to repair and replace deteriorating machines. Because we know that

$$GDP = C + I + G + X$$

THINKING CRITICALLY ABOUT THE MEDIA

Avoiding GDP Mania

Every quarter, the federal government publishes its estimates of the rate of growth of real GDP for the previous quarter on an annualized basis. If, for example, GDP corrected for inflation was estimated to increase by one-half of 1 percent, the government would announce a first-quarter growth rate of 2 percent per year. Once these statistics are announced, journalists have a field day analyzing whether the economy is growing, not growing, slowing down, heading for a soft landing, overheating, and so on. The problem with these initial quarterly statistics is that they are often wrong. On occasion, quarterly annualized GDP growth rates have been corrected a month later by as much as 75 percent! Consequently, it is a good idea to wait a few months and to examine only revised GDP statistics from the U.S. Commerce Department.

Depreciation
Reduction in the value of capital goods over a one-year period due to physical wear and tear and also to obsolescence; also called *capital consumption allowance.*

Net domestic product (NDP)
GDP minus depreciation.

Capital consumption allowance
Another name for depreciation, the amount that businesses would have to save in order to take care of the deterioration of machines and other equipment.

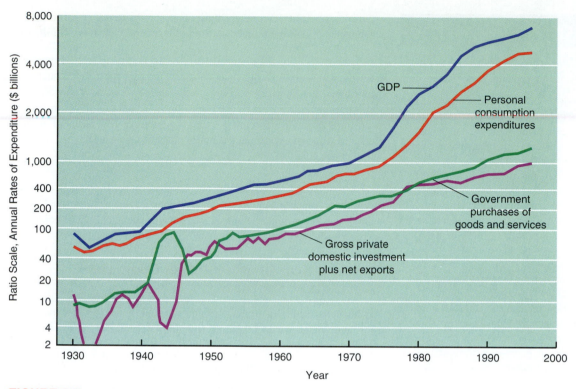

FIGURE 8-2

GDP and Its Components

Here we see a display of gross domestic product, personal consumption expenditures, government purchases, and gross private domestic investment plus net exports for the years 1929–1996. Actually, during the Great Depression of the 1930s, gross private domestic investment *plus* net exports was negative because we were investing very little at that time.

we know that the formula for NDP is

$$NDP = C + I + G + X - \text{depreciation}$$

Alternatively, because net $I = I - \text{depreciation}$,

$$NDP = C + \text{net } I + G + X$$

   Net investment measures *changes* in our capital stock over time and is positive nearly every year. Because depreciation does not vary greatly from year to year as a percentage of GDP, we get a similar picture of what is happening to our national economy by looking at either NDP or GDP data.

Net investment
Gross private domestic investment minus an estimate of the wear and tear on the existing capital stock. Net investment therefore measures the change in capital stock over a one-year period.

CONCEPTS IN BRIEF

• The expenditure approach to measuring GDP requires that we add up consumption expenditures, gross private investment, government purchases, and net exports. Consumption expenditures include consumer durables, consumer nondurables, and services.

- Gross private domestic investment *excludes* transfers of asset ownership. It includes only additions to the productive capacity of a nation, repairs on existing capital goods, and changes in business inventories.
- We value government expenditures at their cost because we do not usually have market prices at which to value government goods and services.
- To obtain net domestic product (NDP), we subtract from GDP the year's depreciation of the existing capital stock.

Deriving GDP by the Income Approach

If you go back to the circular flow diagram in Figure 8-1, you see that product markets are at the top of the diagram and factor markets are at the bottom. We can calculate the value of the circular flow of income and product by looking at expenditures—which we just did—or by looking at total factor payments. Factor payments are called income. We calculate **gross domestic income (GDI),** which we will see is identical to gross domestic product (GDP). Using the income approach, we have four categories of payments to individuals: wages, interest, rent, and profits.

Gross domestic income (GDI)
The sum of all income—wages, interest, rent, and profits—paid to the four factors of production.

1. *Wages.* The most important category is, of course, wages, including salaries and other forms of labor income, such as income in kind and incentive payments. We also count Social Security taxes (both the employees' and the employers' contributions).
2. *Interest.* Here interest payments do not equal the sum of all payments for the use of funds in a year. Instead, interest is expressed in *net* rather than in gross terms. The interest component of total income is only net interest received by households plus net interest paid to us by foreigners. Net interest received by households is the difference between the interest they receive (from savings accounts, certificates of deposit, and the like) and the interest they pay (to banks for mortgages, credit cards, and other loans).
3. *Rent.* Rent is all income earned by individuals for the use of their real (nonmonetary) assets, such as farms, houses, and stores. As stated previously, we have to include here the implicit rental value of owner-occupied houses. Also included in this category are royalties received from copyrights, patents, and assets such as oil wells.
4. *Profits.* Our last category includes total gross corporate profits plus *proprietors' income.* Proprietors' income is income earned from the operation of unincorporated businesses, which include sole proprietorships, partnerships, and producers' cooperatives. It is unincorporated business profit.

All of the payments listed are *actual* factor payments made to owners of the factors of production. When we add them together, though, we do not yet have gross domestic income. We have to take account of two other components: **indirect business taxes,** such as sales and business property taxes, and depreciation, which we have already discussed.

Indirect business taxes
All business taxes except the tax on corporate profits. Indirect business taxes include sales and business property taxes.

Indirect Business Taxes. Indirect taxes are the (nonincome) taxes paid by consumers when they buy goods and services. When you buy a book, you pay the price of the book plus any state and local sales tax. The business is actually acting as the government's agent in collecting the sales tax, which it in turn passes on to the government. Such taxes therefore represent a business expense and are included in gross domestic income.

Depreciation. Just as we had to deduct depreciation to get from GDP to NDP, so we must *add* depreciation to go from net domestic income to gross domestic income. Depreci-

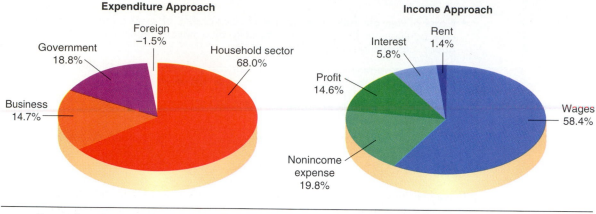

Expenditure Point of View—Product Flow		Income Point of View—Cost Flow	
Expenditures by Different Sectors:		Domestic Income (at Factor Cost):	
Household sector		*Wages*	
Personal consumption expenses	$5,145.0	All wages, salaries, and supplemental employee compensation	$4,419.9
Government sector		*Rent*	
Purchase of goods and services	1,420.0	All rental income of individuals plus implicit rent on owner-occupied dwellings	104.7
Business sector		*Interest*	
Gross private domestic investment (including depreciation)	1,115.5	Net interest paid by business	442.7
Foreign sector		*Profit*	
Net exports of goods and services	−113.6	Proprietorial income	502.3
		Corporate profits before taxes deducted	604.2
		Nonincome expense items	
		Indirect business taxes and other adjustments	674.3
		Depreciation	891.8
		Statistical discrepancy	−73.0
Gross domestic product	$7,566.9	Gross domestic income	$7,566.9

FIGURE 8-3

Gross Domestic Product and Gross Domestic Income, 1996 (in billions of 1996 dollars per year)

By using the two different methods of computing the output of the economy, we come up with gross domestic product and gross domestic income, which are by definition equal. One approach focuses on expenditures, or the flow of product; the other approach concentrates on income, or the flow of costs.

Source: U.S. Department of Commerce. First quarter preliminary data annualized.

ation can be thought of as the portion of the current year's GDP that is used to replace physical capital consumed in the process of production. Because somebody has paid for the replacement, depreciation must be added as a component of gross domestic income.

The last two components of GDP—indirect business taxes and depreciation—are called **nonincome expense items.**

Figure 8-3 shows a comparison between gross domestic product and gross domestic income for 1996. Whether you decide to use the expenditure approach or the income approach, you will come out with the same number. There are sometimes statistical discrepancies, but they are usually relatively small.

Nonincome expense items
The total of indirect business taxes and depreciation.

OTHER COMPONENTS OF NATIONAL INCOME ACCOUNTING

Gross domestic income or product does not really tell how much income people have access to for spending purposes. To get to those kinds of data, we must make some adjustments, which we now do.

National Income (NI)

We know that net domestic product (NDP) represents the total market value of goods and services available for both consumption, used in a broader sense here to mean "resource exhaustion," and net additions to the economy's stock of capital. NDP does not, however, represent the income available to individuals within that economy because it includes indirect business taxes, such as sales taxes. We therefore deduct these indirect business taxes from NDP to arrive at the figure for all factor income of resource owners. The result is what we define as **national income (NI)**—income *earned* by the factors of production.

National income (NI)
The total of all factor payments to resource owners. It can be obtained by subtracting indirect business taxes from NDP.

Personal Income (PI)

National income does not actually represent what is available to individuals to spend because some people obtain income for which they have provided no concurrent good or service and others earn income but do not receive it. In the former category are mainly recipients of transfer payments from the government, such as Social Security, welfare, and food stamps. These payments represent shifts of funds within the economy by way of the government, where no good or service is concurrently rendered in exchange. For the other category, income earned but not received, the most obvious examples are corporate retained earnings that are plowed back into business, contributions to social insurance, and corporate income taxes. When transfer payments are added and when income earned but not received is subtracted, we end up with **personal income (PI)**—income *received* by the factors of production prior to the payment of personal income taxes.

Personal income (PI)
The amount of income that households actually receive before they pay personal income taxes.

Disposable Personal Income (DPI)

Everybody knows that you do not get to take home all your salary. To get **disposable personal income (DPI),** we subtract all personal income taxes from personal income. This is the income that individuals have left for consumption and saving.

Disposable personal income (DPI)
Personal income after personal income taxes have been paid.

Deriving the Components of GDP

Table 8-2 takes you through the steps necessary to derive the various components of GDP. It shows how you go from gross domestic product to net domestic product to national

	Billions of Dollars
Gross domestic product (GDP)	7,566.9
Minus depreciation	−891.8
Net domestic product (NDP)	6,675.1
Minus indirect business taxes and other adjustments	−674.3
National income (NI)	6,000.8
Minus corporate taxes, Social Security contributions, corporate retained earnings	−1,032.5
Plus government and business transfer payments	+1,311.1
Personal income (PI)	6,279.4
Minus personal income tax and nontax payments	−798.7
Disposable personal income (DPI)	5,480.7

TABLE 8-2

Going from GDP to Disposable Income, 1996

Source: U.S. Department of Commerce.

income to personal income and then to disposable personal income. On the endpapers of your book, you can see the historical record for GDP, NDP, NI, PI, and DPI for selected years since 1929.

We have completed our rundown of the different ways that GDP can be computed and of the different variants of national income and product. What we have not yet touched on is the difference between national income measured in this year's dollars and national income representing real goods and services.

CONCEPTS IN BRIEF

- To obtain national income, we subtract indirect business taxes from net domestic product. National income gives us a measure of all factor payments to resource owners.

- To obtain personal income, we must add government transfer payments, such as Social Security benefits and food stamps. We must subtract income earned but not received by factor owners, such as corporate retained earnings, Social Security contributions, and corporate income taxes.

- To obtain disposable personal income, we subtract all personal income taxes from personal income. Disposable personal income is income that individuals actually have for consumption or saving.

DISTINGUISHING BETWEEN NOMINAL AND REAL VALUES

So far we have shown how to measure *nominal* income and product. When we say "nominal," we are referring to income and product expressed in the current "face value" of today's dollar. Given the existence of inflation or deflation in the economy, we must also be able to distinguish between the **nominal values** that we will be looking at and the **real values** underlying them. Nominal values are expressed in current dollars. Real income involves

Nominal values
The values of variables such as GDP and investment expressed in current dollars, also called *money values;* measurement in terms of the actual market prices at which goods are sold.

Real values
Measurement of economic values after adjustments have been made for changes in the average of prices between years.

our command over goods and services—purchasing power—and therefore depends on money income and a set of prices. Thus real income refers to nominal income corrected for changes in the weighted average of all prices. In other words, we must make an adjustment for changes in the price level. Consider an example. Nominal income *per person* in 1960 was only about $2,800 per year. In 1996, nominal income per person was close to $28,000. Were people really that bad off in 1960? No, for nominal income in 1960 is expressed in 1960 prices, not in the prices of today. In today's dollars, the per-person income of 1960 would be closer to $10,000, or almost 40 percent of today's income per person. This is a meaningful comparison between income in 1960 and income today. (The uncorrected 1960 data show per-person income to be only 10 percent of today's income.) Next we will show how we can translate nominal measures of income into real measures by using an appropriate price index, such as the CPI or the GDP deflator discussed in Chapter 7.

Correcting GDP for Price Changes

If a compact disc (CD) costs $15 this year, 10 CDs will have a market value of $150. If next year they cost $20 each, the same 10 CDs will have a market value of $200. In this case, there is no increase in the total quantity of CDs, but the market value will have increased by one-third. Apply this to every single good and service produced and sold in the United States and you realize that changes in GDP, measured in *current* dollars, may not be a very useful indication of economic activity. If we are really interested in variations in the *real* output of the economy, we must correct GDP (and just about everything else we look at) for changes in the average of overall prices from year to year. Basically, we need to generate an index that approximates the changes in average prices and then divide that estimate into the value of output in current dollars to adjust the value of output to what is called **constant dollars,** or dollars corrected for general price level changes. This price-corrected GDP is called *real GDP*.

Constant dollars
Dollars expressed in terms of real purchasing power using a particular year as the base or standard of comparison, in contrast to current dollars.

EXAMPLE
Correcting GDP for Price Level Changes, 1985–1995

Let's take a numerical example to see how we can adjust GDP for changes in prices. We must pick an appropriate price index in order to adjust for these price level changes. We mentioned the Consumer Price Index, the Producer Price Index, and the GDP deflator in Chapter 7. Let's use the GDP deflator to adjust our figures. Table 8-3 gives 11 years of GDP figures. Nominal GDP figures are shown in column 2. The price level index (GDP deflator) is in column 3, with base year of 1992 when the GDP deflator equals 100. Column 4 shows real (inflation-adjusted) GDP in 1992 dollars.

The formula for real GDP is

$$\text{Real GDP} = \frac{\text{nominal GDP}}{\text{price level}} \times 100$$

The step-by-step derivation of real (constant-dollar) GDP is as follows: The base year is 1992, so the price index must equal 100. In 1992, nominal GDP was $6,020.2 billion, and so too was real GDP expressed in 1992 dollars. In 1993, the price level increased to 102.2. Thus to correct 1993's nominal GDP for inflation, we divide the price index, 102.2, into the nominal GDP figure of $6,343.3 billion and then multiply it by 100. The result is $6,206.8 billion, which is 1993 GDP expressed in terms of the purchasing power of dollars in 1992. What about a situation when the price level is lower than in 1992? Look at 1985. Here the price index shown in column 3 is only 78.1. That means that in 1985, the average of all prices was

(1) Year	(2) Nominal GDP (billions of dollars per year)	(3) Price Level Index (base year 1992 = 100)	(4) = [(2) ÷ (3)] × 100 Real GDP (billions of dollars per year in constant 1992 dollars)
1985	4,038.7	78.1	5,171.2
1986	4,268.6	80.1	5,329.1
1987	4,539.9	82.7	5,489.6
1988	4,900.4	85.9	5,704.8
1989	5,250.8	89.7	5,853.7
1990	5,546.1	93.7	5,919.0
1991	5,724.8	97.3	5,883.6
1992	6,020.2	100.0	6,020.2
1993	6,343.3	102.2	6,206.8
1994	6,738.4	104.3	6,460.6
1995	7,007.9	106.3	6,592.6

Source: U.S. Department of Commerce, Bureau of Economic Analysis.

TABLE 8-3

Correcting GDP for Price Changes
To correct GDP for price changes, we first have to pick a price level index (the GDP deflator) with a specific year as its base. In our example, the base level is 1992 prices; the price level index for that year is 100% = 1.00. To obtain 1992 constant-dollar GDP, we divide the price level index into nominal GDP. In other words, we divide column 3 into column 2 (and multiply by 100). This gives us column 4, which is a measure of real GDP expressed in 1992 purchasing power.

about 78 percent of prices in 1992. To obtain 1985 GDP expressed in terms of 1992 purchasing power, we divide nominal GDP, $4,038.7 billion, by 78.1 and then multiply by 100. The result is a larger number—$5,171.2 billion. Column 4 in Table 8-3 is a better measure of how the economy has performed than column 2, which shows nominal GDP changes.

FOR CRITICAL ANALYSIS: *A few years ago, the base year for the GDP deflator was 1982. What does a change in the base year for the price level index affect?* ●

Plotting Nominal and Real GDP

Nominal GDP and real GDP from 1970 to 1996 are plotted in Figure 8-4. Notice that there is quite a big gap between the two GDP figures, reflecting the amount of inflation that has occurred. Note, further, that the choice of a base year is arbitrary. We have chosen 1992 as the base year in our example. This happens to be the base year that will be used by the government.

Per Capita GDP

Looking at changes in real gross domestic product may be deceiving, particularly if the population size has changed significantly. If real GDP over a 10-year period went up 100 percent, you might jump to the conclusion that the material well-being of the economy had increased by that amount. But what if during the same period population increased by 200 percent? Then what would you say? Certainly, the amount of real GDP per person, or *per capita real GDP,* would have fallen, even though total deflated (or real) GDP had risen. What we must do to account not only for price changes but also for population changes is first deflate GDP and then divide by the total population, doing this for each year. If we

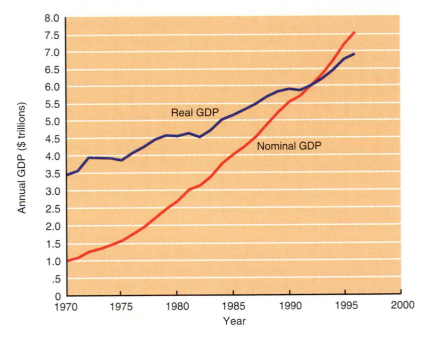

FIGURE 8-4

Nominal and Real GDP

Here we plot both nominal and real GDP. Real GDP is expressed in the purchasing power of 1992 dollars. The gap between the two represents price level changes.

Source: U.S. Department of Commerce.

were to look at certain less developed countries, we would find that in many cases, even though real GDP has risen over the past several decades, per capita real GDP has remained constant or fallen because the population has grown just as rapidly or more quickly.

The difficulties of using GDP as an indicator of social well-being do not end here. In fact, there has been a running battle over the use of GDP statistics because, according to its critics, such numbers do not capture the true overall well-being of a nation. How do we take account of changes in leisure time? How do our national income accounts recognize increased traffic congestion, air pollution in our cities, crime in the streets, and so on? And housework, which constitutes a major amount of the labor performed in the United States, isn't even counted in GDP.

A New Chain-Weighted Measure of the Growth in Real GDP

In December 1995, the Commerce Department's Bureau of Economic Analysis (BEA) made a fundamental change in the way it computes real gross domestic product. Remember that real GDP consists of consumer spending, business investment, government expenditures on goods and services, and net foreign trade. To calculate real GDP, the BEA has used a weighted sum of 1,100 components of these four categories. Until 1996, these 1,100 components were fixed in weight, and their relative importance changed only periodically. For example, the last revision was made in 1987. Otherwise stated, the BEA has been using a *fixed-weight* measure of changes in real GDP.

Now the BEA will change the weights of the different components of real GDP depending on how their relative prices have changed and how their relative shares in the overall economy's output change. The new measure is called *chain-weighted real GDP*. Rather than a specific number, an index is used. Thus to calculate a year's *change* in real GDP, it is necessary to compare one year's index with the previous year's index. For a while, the BEA plans to publish both the chain-weighted real GDP index and its dollar equivalent. You can find chain-weighted real GDP statistics on the front endpapers of this book, which show our national income accounts.

CONCEPTS IN BRIEF

- To correct nominal GDP for price changes, we first use a base year for our price index and assign it the number 100 percent (or 1.00). Then we construct an index based on how a weighted average of the price level has changed relative to that base year. For example, if in the next year a weighted average of the price level indicates that prices have increased by 10 percent, we would assign it the number 110 (or 1.10). We then divide each year's price index, so constructed, into its respective nominal GDP figure (and multiply by 100).

- We can divide the population into real GDP to obtain per capita real GDP.

COMPARING GDP THROUGHOUT THE WORLD

It is relatively easy to compare the standard of living of a family in Los Angeles with that of one living in Boston. Both families get paid in dollars and can buy the same goods and services at Kmart, McDonald's, and Price Costco. It is not so easy, however, to make a similar comparison between a family living in the United States and one in, say, India. The first problem concerns money. Indians get paid in rupees, their national currency, and buy goods and services with those rupees. That means that just as we can compare families in Los Angeles and Boston, we can compare the living standards of a family in Delhi with one in Bombay. But how do we compare the average standard of living in India with that in the United States?

Foreign Exchange Rates

In earlier chapters, you have encountered international examples that involved local currencies, but the dollar equivalent always has been given. The dollar equivalent is calculated by looking up the **foreign exchange rate** that is published daily in major newspapers throughout the world. If you know that you can exchange $1 for 5 francs, the exchange rate is 5 to 1 (or otherwise stated, a franc is worth 20 cents). So if French incomes per capita are, say, 100,000 francs, that translates at an exchange rate of 5 francs to $1, to $20,000. For years, statisticians calculated relative GDP by simply adding up each country's GDP in its local currency and dividing by each respective dollar exchange rate.

Foreign exchange rate
The price of one currency in terms of another.

True Purchasing Power

The problem with simply using foreign exchange rates to convert other countries' GDP and per capita GDP into dollars is that not all goods and services are bought and sold in a world market. Restaurant food, housecleaning services, and home repairs do not get exchanged across countries. In countries that have very low wages, those kinds of services are much cheaper than foreign exchange rate computations would imply. Government statistics claiming that per capita income in some poor country is only $300 a year seems shocking. But such a statistic does not tell you the true standard of living of people in that country. Only by looking at what is called **purchasing power parity** can you determine other countries' true standards of living compared to ours.

Purchasing power parity
Adjustment in exchange rate conversions that takes into account differences in the true cost of living across countries.

TABLE 8-4

Comparing GDP Internationally

Country	Annual GDP Based on Purchasing Power Parity (billions of U.S. dollars)	Per Capita GDP Based on Purchasing Power Parity (U.S. dollars)	Per Capita GDP Based on Foreign Exchange Rates (U.S. dollars)
United States	6,897.2	26,528	26,528
Japan	2,493.8	19,399	26,424
China	2,490.1	1,692	375
Germany	2,007.4	19,870	24,421
France	1,421.6	18,450	23,489
Russia	1,101.8	6,903	2,640
India	1,100.4	1,155	379
Italy	1,099.0	17,050	17,990
United Kingdom	1,088.0	16,352	16,804
Brazil	980.4	5,251	2,794

Sources: International Monetary Fund; World Bank; Organization for Economic Cooperation and Development.

INTERNATIONAL EXAMPLE
Purchasing Power Parity Comparisons of World Incomes

A few years ago, the International Monetary Fund accepted the purchasing power parity approach as the correct one. It started presenting international statistics on each country's GDP relative to every other's based on purchasing power parity. The results were surprising. As you can see from Table 8-4, China has a higher per capita GDP compared to what was measured at market foreign exchange rates.

FOR CRITICAL ANALYSIS: What percentage increase is there in per capita GDP in China when one switches from foreign exchange rates to purchasing power parity? ●

CONCEPTS IN BRIEF

• The foreign exchange rate is the price of one currency in terms of another.

• Statisticians often calculate relative GDP by adding up each country's GDP in its local currency and dividing by the dollar exchange rate.

• Because not all goods and services are bought and sold in the world market, we must correct exchange rate conversions of other countries' GDP figures in order to take into account differences in the true cost of living across countries.

The Worldwide Underground Economy

Concepts Applied: GDP, unemployment rate, incentives, marginal tax rate

GDP statistics do not include "informal" market activities that occur in countries because it is impossible to track these activities. While the United States has a large undergound economy, it is much larger in Spain and other European countries. Here in Spain, street vendors entice shoppers with their goods.

Beyond the difficulties of obtaining accurate measurements of GDP and NP and the like, government statisticians have to face the reality that a certain amount of economic activity can never be captured by official statistics. Why? Because each year, a variety of economic transactions take place completely outside the system. Ordinarily, when one thinks about unofficial or underground activities, one's thoughts immediately turn to drug trafficking, illegal gambling, and prostitution. To be sure, these underground activities are significant. But tens of millions of otherwise law-abiding citizens participate frequently in the "informal" economy. Anybody who buys, sells, or works for cash or an equivalent payment for which no record is kept and on which no taxes are paid is participating in the underground economy.

Incentives Lead the Way

At the heart of the underground economy are the incentives for individuals and businesses. With respect to criminal activity, the incentives are clear: Fines and jail time are enough of an incentive to cause criminals to make sure that none of their activities are reported. For people engaged in noncriminal off-the-books activities, there is one major incentive: to reduce or avoid income and sales taxes. The greater the marginal income tax rate, the greater the incentive to be paid in cash without declaring it. Hence

the underground economy was presumably much smaller in the United States prior to 1913, when the Sixteenth Amendment was passed, allowing Congress to collect federal income taxes. With respect to sales taxes, one would surmise that the amount of unreported retail sales is lower in states such as Oregon and New Hampshire, which have no sales taxes, than in states such as New York and California, which have relatively high sales taxes.

Unemployment and Welfare Benefits Count, Too

An additional incentive for some individuals to work in the underground economy is to avoid losing unemployment benefits or welfare benefits. Consequently, measured unemployment rates are typically biased upward because a certain percentage of the people receiving unemployment benefits are actually working off the books. In some countries, such as Spain, at least 35 percent of the recipients of unemployment benefits now have jobs.

How Big Is the Underground Economy?

By definition, the underground economy is not measured. Therefore, its size is even harder to assess than the size of the "aboveground" economy. Nonetheless, we do have estimates. Table 8-5 presents estimates of the percentage

TABLE 8-5

Estimated Percentage of Services Supplied by the Underground Economy in the United States

Lawn maintenance	90
Domestic help	83
Child care	49
Home improvements/repairs	34
Sewing and laundry services	25
Appliance repairs	17
Car repairs	13

Sources: U.S. Department of Labor; University of Michigan Institute for Social Research.

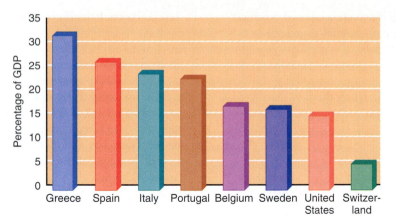

FIGURE 8-5

The Underground Economy in Selected Countries
Source: Organization for Economic Cooperation and Development.

of services supplied by the underground economy, showing both lawn maintenance and domestic help at more than 80 percent. With respect to all underground activity, University of Wisconsin economist Edgar L. Feige estimated that a few years ago it was about $800 billion in the United States. Today, it would be closer to $1 trillion, or about 15 percent of measured GDP.

The Global Underground Economy

The underground economy may seem large in the United States, but it is much larger in Spain and Greece, as can be seen in Figure 8-5. We can conclude on the basis of this figure that official GDP statistics for Greece, Spain, Italy, and Portugal significantly underestimate actual GDP in those countries.

FOR CRITICAL ANALYSIS

1. The Internal Revenue Service periodically makes estimates of tax revenues lost because of the underground economy. It simply multiplies current tax rates times estimated off-the-books income to come up with the figures. Why is the IRS overestimating tax revenues lost due to the underground economy?
2. What change in government policy would reduce the size of the underground economy in the United States?

CHAPTER SUMMARY

1. Households provide labor services, land, capital, and entrepreneurship, for which they are paid wages, rent, interest, and profits. Profits are considered a factor cost—they are the reward for entrepreneurship or risk taking. Profits are a residual payment.
2. In the simplest representation of our economy, there are only households and businesses. The circular flow goes from households to factor markets to businesses and from businesses to product markets to households.
3. National income accounting is the method by which economists attempt to measure statistically the variables with which they are concerned in their study of macroeconomics.
4. One of the concepts most often used in national income accounting is gross domestic product, which is defined as the total market value of all *final* goods and services produced annually by domestic factors of production. The stress on *final* is important to avoid the double counting of intermediate goods used in the production of other goods.
5. We can compute GDP using the expenditure approach or the income approach. In the former, we merely add up the dollar value of all final goods and services; in the latter, we add up the payments generated in producing all those goods and services, or wages, interest, rent, and profits, plus indirect business taxes and depreciation.

6. It is difficult to measure the market value of government expenditures because generally government-provided goods are not sold at a market clearing price. We therefore value government expenditures at their cost for inclusion in our measure of GDP.

7. Investment does not occur when there is merely a transfer of assets among individuals; rather, it occurs only when new productive capacity, such as a machine tool, is built.

8. Part of our capital stock is worn out or becomes obsolete every year. To take account of the expenditures made merely to replace such capital equipment, we subtract depreciation from GDP to yield net domestic product.

9. To correct for price changes, we deflate GDP with a price index to come up with real GDP. To take account of rising population, we divide by population to come up with per capita real GDP.

10. To compare GDP across countries, we must first apply the foreign exchange rate to GDP expressed in the local currency and then adjust the exchange rate to take account of the purchasing power of that income. This is called the purchasing power parity approach.

DISCUSSION OF PREVIEW QUESTIONS

1. What is gross domestic product (GDP), and what does it measure?

Gross domestic product is defined as the market value of all final goods and services produced during one year by domestic factors of production. Because GDP is measured per unit of time, it is a flow concept. Economists try to estimate GDP in order to evaluate the productive performance of an economy during the year; economists also use GDP estimates to aid them in judging overall economic well-being.

2. Why are only *final* goods and services evaluated in deriving GDP?

Because GDP estimates are an attempt to evaluate an economy's performance and to generalize about group well-being, we must be careful to evaluate only final goods and services; otherwise GDP would be exaggerated. For example, because an automobile uses plastic, steel, coke, rubber, coal, and other products in its manufacture, to count each of these *and* the value of the automobile would be double counting. Thus to count steel *and* the automobile when it is sold is to count steel twice and hence to exaggerate the economy's performance and the group's economic well-being. Steel in this instance would not be a final good; it would be an intermediate good.

3. Why must depreciation and indirect business taxes be added to national income at factor cost in order to derive GDP via the income approach?

The expenditure approach to GDP counts expenditures on all final goods and services; in particular, expenditures on *all* investment goods amount to gross investment. The income approach to GDP estimation, by contrast, sums the wages, interest, rent, and profit receipts of income earners. Because depreciation is not a wage, rent, interest, or profit, the expenditure approach would yield a higher number. In order to compare correctly, we must add depreciation to national income at factor cost to calculate GDP via the income approach. Similarly, indirect business taxes (excise, sales, and property taxes) are automatically reflected in the expenditure approach, whereas indirect business taxes are not wages, interest, rent, or profit receipts to factors of production.

4. How does correcting GDP for changes in the price level and population improve the usefulness of GDP estimates?

When the price level is rising (during periods of inflation), GDP estimates would overstate true productive activity and group economic well-being. Similarly, when the general price level is falling (during periods of deflation), GDP estimates would understate productive activity and group economic well-being. If population is rising more rapidly than real output, real GDP estimates would rise, but living standards might well be falling. Dividing by population corrects for such cases. Per capita real GDP is a better clue to productive activity and overall economic well-being than nominal GDP.

PROBLEMS

(Answers to the odd-numbered problems appear at the back of the book.)

8-1. The following are a year's data for a hypothetical economy.

	Billions of Dollars
Consumption	400
Government spending	350
Gross private domestic investment	150
Exports	150
Imports	100
Depreciation	50
Indirect business taxes	25

a. Based on the data, what is the value of GDP? NDP? NI?

b. Suppose that in the next year exports increase to $175 billion, imports increase to $200 billion, and consumption falls to $350 billion. What will GDP be in that year?

c. If the value of depreciation (capital consumption allowance) should ever exceed that of gross private domestic investment, how would this affect the future productivity of the nation?

8-2. Look back at Table 8-3, which explains how to correct GDP for price level changes. Column 4 of that table gives real GDP in terms of 1992 constant dollars. Change the base year to 1987. Recalculate the price level index and then recalculate real GDP—that is, express column 4 in terms of 1987 dollars instead of 1992 dollars.

8-3. Study the following table; then answer the questions.

Stage of Production	Sales Receipts	Intermediate Costs	Value Added
Coal	$2	$0	$2
Steel	5	2	3
Manufactured autos	8	5	3
Sold autos	9	8	1

a. What is the intermediate good for steel production? How much did it cost?

b. What is the value added resulting from auto manufacturing?

c. If automobiles are the only final goods produced in this economy, what would GDP via the expenditures approach be equal to?

d. If automobiles are the only final goods produced in this economy, what would GDP via the income approach be equal to?

8-4. At the top of a piece of paper, write the headings "Production Activity" and "Nonproduction Activity." List each of the following under one of these headings by determining which would go into our measure of GDP.

a. Mr. X sells his used car to Mr. Y.

b. Joe's used car lot sells a car to Mr. Z and receives a $50 profit for doing so.

c. Merrill Lynch receives a brokerage commission for selling stocks.

d. Mr. Arianas buys 100 shares of AT&T stock.

e. Mrs. Romano cooks and keeps house for her family.

f. Mr. Gonzalez mows his own lawn.

g. Mr. Gonzalez mows lawns for a living.

h. Mr. Smith receives a welfare payment.

i. Mr. Johnson sends his daughter $500 for a semester of studies at College U.

8-5. What happens to the official measure of GDP in each of the following situations?

a. A man marries his housekeeper, who then quits working for wages.

b. A drug addict marries her supplier.

c. Homemakers perform the same jobs but switch houses and charge each other for their services.

8-6. Construct a value-added table for various stages in the production and sale of bread.

8-7. Consider the following table for an economy that produces only four goods.

Good	1992 Price	1992 Quantity	1997 Price	1997 Quantity
Pizza	$ 4	10	$ 8	12
Cola	12	20	36	15
T-shirts	6	5	10	15
Business equipment	25	10	30	12

Assuming a 1992 base year:

a. What is nominal GDP for 1992 and 1997?

b. What is real GDP for 1992? For 1997?

8-8. Examine the following figures for a hypothetical year; then calculate GDP, NDP, NI, PI, and DPI.

	Billions of Dollars
Consumption	400
Net exports	−20
Transfer payments	20
Gross investment	100
Social Security contributions	10
Government purchases	120
Net investment	50
Dividends	20
Indirect business taxes	10
Corporate income taxes	30
Personal income taxes	60
Undistributed corporate profits	20

COMPUTER-ASSISTED INSTRUCTION

Complete problem and answer appear on disk.

Coal is transformed into steel, steel is turned into a manufactured auto, and a manufactured auto is sold to a final buyer. You are required to calculate value added at various stages; in the process, it is revealed that the expenditure approach and the income approach to national income accounting yield identical estimates of GDP.

INTERACTING WITH THE INTERNET

Current GDP press releases and other related material, such as historical data, can be found at

gopher://una.hh.lib.umich.edu/11/ebb/nipa

The Bureau of Economic Analysis's Survey of Current Business, which publishes these data, is available at

http://www.stat-usa.gov/BEN/Services/beastat.html

However, you must be a subscriber to access it.

CHAPTER 9

ECONOMIC GROWTH: TECHNOLOGY, RESEARCH AND DEVELOPMENT, AND KNOWLEDGE

The "American way of life" involves a political system that can be loosely defined as representative democracy. Americans for the most part are certain that democracy is good and that our foreign policy should therefore be to foster democracy throughout the world. Political freedom exists in various degrees in the 200 or so nations of the world, yet many of those nations have become democratic only in this decade. Do we have evidence to demonstrate that increased political freedom and more democracy lead to higher standards of living? To answer this question, you need to know how we define economic growth and what its determinants are.

PREVIEW QUESTIONS

1. What is economic growth?

2. What does economic growth measure?

3. What are some of the ways in which you can experience economic growth for yourself or for your family?

4. What are the determinants of economic growth?

Did You Know That... at the turn of the twentieth century, Argentina had the sixth highest per capita income in the world, whereas it is now around fortieth, somewhat below Iran? Consider also that 100 years ago, Hong Kong was basically a barren rock, whereas today its per capita income exceeds that of France and the United Kingdom. How can we explain such dramatic changes in relative living standards? From an arithmetic point of view, the answer is simple: Argentina experienced little and in some cases negative economic growth over the past century, whereas Hong Kong had significant economic growth. That answer, though, does not tell us why economic growth rates differed in these two countries. That is the task of this chapter. Should you care about the rate of economic growth in the United States? The answer is yes, if you care about your future standard of living and that of your children and grandchildren. You have already demonstrated that you care about your future standard of living; otherwise, you would not be bothering to obtain a higher education. Obviously, you want to make sure that you experience economic growth as an individual. Now it is time to consider the nation as a whole.

HOW DO WE DEFINE ECONOMIC GROWTH?

Remember from Chapter 2 that we can show economic growth graphically as an outward shift of a production possibilities curve, as is seen in Figure 9-1. If there is economic growth between 1998 and 2025, the production possibilities curve will shift outward toward the red line. The distance that it shifts represents the amount of economic growth, defined as the increase in the productive capacity of a nation. Although it is possible to come up with a measure of a nation's increased productive capacity, it would not be easy. Therefore, we turn to a more readily obtainable definition of economic growth.

Most people have a general idea of what economic growth means. When a nation grows economically, its citizens must be better off in at least some ways, usually in terms of their material well-being. Typically, though, we do not measure the well-being of any nation solely in terms of its total output of real goods and services or in terms of real GDP without making some adjustments. After all, India has a GDP about three times as large as that in Switzerland. The population in India, though, is about 125 times greater than that in Switzerland. Consequently, we view India as a relatively poor country and Switzerland as a relatively rich country. That means that to measure how much a country is growing in terms of annual increases in real GDP, we have to adjust for population growth. Our formal definition becomes this: **Economic growth** occurs when there are increases in per capita real GDP; it is measured by the rate of change in per capita real GDP per year.

Economic growth
Increases in per capita real GDP measured by its rate of change per year.

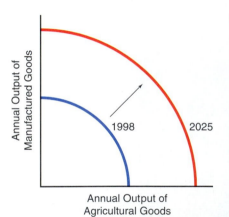

FIGURE 9-1
Economic Growth
If there is growth between 1998 and 2025, the production possibilities curve for the entire economy will shift outward from the blue line labeled 1998 to the red line labeled 2025. The distance that it shifts represents an increase in the productive capacity of the nation.

FIGURE 9-2

The Historical Record of U.S. Economic Growth

The graph traces per capita real GDP in the United States since 1900. Data are given in 1992 dollars.

Source: U.S. Department of Commerce.

Figure 9-2 presents the historical record of real GDP per person in the United States.

INTERNATIONAL EXAMPLE
Growth Rates Around the World

Table 9-1 shows the annual average rate of growth of income per person in selected countries. Notice that the United States during the time period under study is positioned about midway in the pack. In other words, even though we are one of the world's richest countries, our recent rate of economic growth is not particularly high.

TABLE 9-1

Per Capita Growth Rates in Various Countries

Country	Average Annual Rate of Growth of Income Per Capita, 1970–1995 (%)	Country	Average Annual Rate of Growth of Income Per Capita, 1970–1995 (%)
Switzerland	1.8	Italy	2.8
Sweden	1.9	Canada	3.0
Netherlands	2.2	Spain	3.1
United Kingdom	2.3	Japan	4.8
Germany	2.4	Turkey	5.3
France	2.7	China	6.1
United States	2.8		

Sources: World Bank; International Monetary Fund.

FOR CRITICAL ANALYSIS: "*The largest change is from zero to one.*" *Does this statement have anything to do with relative growth rates in poorer versus richer countries?* •

Problems in Definition

Our definition of economic growth says nothing about the *distribution* of output and income. A nation might grow very rapidly in terms of increases in per capita real output, while at the same time its poor people remain poor or become even poorer. Therefore, in assessing the economic growth record of any nation, we must be careful to pinpoint which income groups have benefited the most from such growth.

Real standards of living can go up without any positive economic growth. This can occur if individuals are, on average, enjoying more leisure by working fewer hours but producing as much as they did before. For example, if per capita real GDP in the United States remained at $20,000 a year for a decade, we could not automatically jump to the conclusion that Americans were, on average, no better off. What if, during that same 10-year period, average hours worked fell from 37 per week to 33 per week? That would mean that during the 10 years under study, individuals in the labor force were "earning" four hours more leisure a week. Actually, nothing so extreme has occurred in this country, but something similar has. Average hours worked per week fell steadily until the 1960s, at which time they leveled off. That means that during much of the history of this country, the increase in per capita real GDP *understated* the actual economic growth that we were experiencing because we were enjoying more and more leisure as things progressed.

Is Economic Growth Bad?

Some commentators on our current economic situation believe that the definition of economic growth ignores its negative effects. Some psychologists even contend that we are made worse off because of economic growth. They say that the more we grow, the more "needs" are created so that we feel worse off as we become richer. Our expectations are rising faster than reality, so we presumably always suffer from a sense of disappointment. Clearly, the measurement of economic growth cannot take into account the spiritual and cultural aspects of the good life. As with all activities, there are costs and benefits. You can see some of those listed in Table 9-2.

In any event, any measure of economic growth that we use will be imperfect. Nonetheless, the measures that we do have allow us to make comparisons across countries and over time and, if used judiciously, can enable us to gain important insights. Per-capita real GDP, used so often, is not always an accurate measure of economic well-being, but it is a serviceable measure of productive activity.

Benefits	Costs
Reduction in illiteracy	Environmental pollution
Reduction in poverty	Breakdown of the family
Improved health	Isolation and alienation
Longer lives	Urban congestion
Political stability	

TABLE 9-2

Costs and Benefits of Economic Growth

The Importance of Growth Rates

Notice back in Table 9-1 that the growth rates in real per capita income for most countries differ by very little—generally, only a few percentage points. You might want to know why such small differences in growth rates are important. What would it matter if we grew at 3 percent rather than at 4 percent per year?

It matters a lot—not for next year or the year after but for the more distant future. The power of compound interest is impressive. Let's see what happens with three different annual rates of growth: 3 percent, 4 percent, and 5 percent. We start with $1 trillion per year, which is approximately equal to the gross domestic product of the United States in 1971. We then compound this $1 trillion, or allow it to grow, into the future at these three different growth rates. The difference is huge. In 50 years, $1 trillion per year becomes $4.38 trillion per year if compounded at 3 percent per year. Just one percentage point more in the growth rate, 4 percent, results in a real GDP of $7.11 trillion per year in 50 years, almost double the previous amount. Two percentage points difference in the growth rate— 5 percent per year—results in a real GDP of $11.5 trillion per year in 50 years, or nearly three times as much. Obviously, there is a great difference in the results of economic growth for very small differences in annual growth rates. That is why nations are concerned if the growth rate falls even a little in absolute percentage terms.

Compound Interest. When we talk about growth rates, we are basically talking about compound interest. In Table 9-3, we show how $1 compounded annually grows at different interest rates. We see in the 3 percent column that $1 in 50 years grows to $4.38. We merely multiplied $1 trillion times 4.38 to get the growth figure in our earlier example. In the 5 percent column, $1 grows to $11.50 after 50 years. Again, we multiplied $1 trillion times 11.50 to get the growth figure for 5 percent in the preceding example.

TABLE 9-3

One Dollar Compounded Annually at Different Interest Rates
Here we show the value of a dollar at the end of a specified period during which it has been compounded annually at a specified interest rate. For example, if you took $1 today and invested it at 5 percent per year, it would yield $1.05 at the end of one year. At the end of 10 years, it would equal $1.63, and at the end of 50 years, it would equal $11.50.

Number of Years	3%	4%	5%	6%	8%	10%	20%
1	1.03	1.04	1.05	1.06	1.08	1.10	1.20
2	1.06	1.08	1.10	1.12	1.17	1.21	1.44
3	1.09	1.12	1.16	1.19	1.26	1.33	1.73
4	1.13	1.17	1.22	1.26	1.36	1.46	2.07
5	1.16	1.22	1.28	1.34	1.47	1.61	2.49
6	1.19	1.27	1.34	1.41	1.59	1.77	2.99
7	1.23	1.32	1.41	1.50	1.71	1.94	3.58
8	1.27	1.37	1.48	1.59	1.85	2.14	4.30
9	1.30	1.42	1.55	1.68	2.00	2.35	5.16
10	1.34	1.48	1.63	1.79	2.16	2.59	6.19
20	1.81	2.19	2.65	3.20	4.66	6.72	38.30
30	2.43	3.24	4.32	5.74	10.00	17.40	237.00
40	3.26	4.80	7.04	10.30	21.70	45.30	1,470.00
50	4.38	7.11	11.50	18.40	46.90	117.00	9,100.00

Interest Rate column header spans 3% through 20%.

EXAMPLE
What If the United States Had Grown a Little Bit Less or More Each Year?

In 1870, the per-person real GDP expressed in 1996 dollars was $3,276. That figure had grown to $26,718 by the beginning of 1996. The average economic growth rate was therefore about 1.75 percent per year. What if the U.S. growth rate over the same century and a quarter had been simply 1 percent less—only .75 percent per year? Per capita real GDP in 1996 would have been only 30 percent of what it actually was. The United States would have ranked somewhere around thirty-fifth on the scale of per capita income throughout the world. We would be poorer than Greece or Portugal.

Consider a rosier scenario: What if the U.S. economic rate of growth had been one point higher, or 2.75 percent per year? Today's per capita real GDP would be more than three times its actual value, or about $90,000!

FOR CRITICAL ANALYSIS: Can you relate this example to anything in your own life? (Hint: Use the compound interest rates in Table 9-3 to make various predictions about your future standard of living.) ●

CONCEPTS IN BRIEF

- Economic growth can be defined as the increase in real per capita output measured by its rate of change per year.

- The benefits of economic growth are reductions in illiteracy, poverty, and illness and increases in life spans and political stability. The costs of economic growth may include environmental pollution, alienation, and urban congestion.

- Small percentage-point differences in growth rates lead to large differences in real GDP over time. These differences can be seen by examining a compound interest table such as the one in Table 9-3.

PRODUCTIVITY INCREASES: THE HEART OF ECONOMIC GROWTH

Let's say that you are required to type 10 term papers and homework assignments a year. You have a word processor to do so, but you do not know how to touch-type. You end up spending an average of two hours per typing job. The next summer, you buy a touch-typing tutorial to use on your word processor and spend a few minutes a day improving your typing speed. The following term, you spend only one hour per typing assignment, thereby saving 10 hours a semester. You have become more productive. This concept of productivity relates to your ability (and everyone else's) to produce the same output with fewer labor hours. Thus **labor productivity** is normally measured by dividing the total real domestic output (real GDP) by the number of workers or the number of labor hours. Labor productivity increases whenever average output produced per worker during a specified time period increases. Clearly, there is a relationship between economic growth and increases in labor productivity. If you divide all resources into just capital and labor, economic growth can be defined simply as follows:

Labor productivity
Total real domestic output (real GDP) divided by the number of workers (output per worker).

$$\text{Economic growth} = \text{rate of growth of capital} + \text{rate of growth of labor} +$$
$$\text{rate of growth in the productivity of capital and of labor}$$

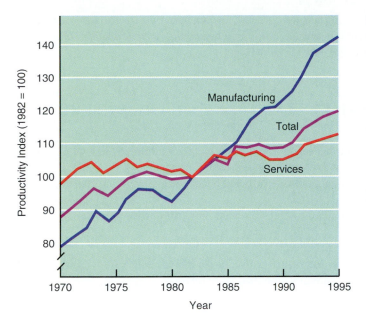

FIGURE 9-3

Nonfarm U.S. Productivity Growth

Whereas productivity growth in the services sector started increasing only in the early 1980s, productivity in the manufacturing sector has been increasing almost consistently since 1970.

Sources: U.S. Department of Commerce; U.S. Department of Labor, Bureau of Labor Statistics.

If everything else remains constant, improvements in labor productivity ultimately lead to economic growth and higher living standards.

Although productivity growth seemed to lag in the United States from the mid-1970s through the mid-1980s, there is quite a bit of evidence that it has been on the rise since then. Figure 9-3 traces productivity growth in the manufacturing and service sectors of the economy as well as total productivity growth.

Productivity as a Prerequisite for International Competitiveness

The recurring major story about the American economy relates to the rate of growth of productivity—or more generally, the lack thereof. The claim in the media is that if the United States fails to sustain high productivity, it will lose out in the competitive race among nations. The fallacy in such media stories is that the benefit of high productivity is somehow related to allowing the United States to compete with other countries. The reality is that with the benefit of high productivity, *any* country can produce more with the same amount of resources. That means that all its residents can consume more, which in turn means a higher standard of living because of higher productivity. As a nation, we would want higher productivity even if no other country in the world existed!

INTERNATIONAL EXAMPLE
How Does U.S. Productivity Stack Up?

Productivity is important because increases in productivity determine the standard of living of a country. For years, statisticians attempted to show that the growth in labor productivity in the United States was less than in Germany, Japan, and the United Kingdom. Indeed, from 1950 to the early 1990s, U.S. labor productivity growth was below that of many other countries. A recent study by the McKenzie Global Institute, however, shows a different result.

The McKenzie consultants examined productivity in various manufacturing industries. In five of the nine industries—automobiles, automobile parts, consumer electronics, metalworking, and steel—Japanese workers are more productive than American workers. In contrast, American workers are more productive than the Japanese in food and beer, computers, and soap and detergents. Because these latter industries are more important overall in terms of percentage of total national output, Japanese workers are only 83 percent as productive as American workers. In steel and metalworking, German workers are as productive as American workers, but in all other sectors, they are less productive. On average, German workers are 79 percent as productive as American workers.

FOR CRITICAL ANALYSIS: *Should we care how productive American workers are in relation to those in the rest of the world? (Be careful—see the accompanying Thinking Critically About the Media box on page 193).* ●

ONE FUNDAMENTAL DETERMINANT OF THE RATE OF ECONOMIC GROWTH: THE RATE OF SAVING

Economic growth does not occur in a vacuum. It is not some predetermined fate of a nation. Rather, economic growth depends on certain fundamental factors. One of the most important factors that affect the rate of economic growth and hence long-term living standards is the rate of saving.

A basic proposition in economics is that if you want more tomorrow, you have to take less today.

To have more consumption in the future, you have to consume less today and save the difference between your consumption and your income.

On a national basis, this implies that higher saving rates eventually mean higher living standards in the long run, all other things held constant. Concern has been growing in America that we are not saving enough, which means that our rate of saving may be too low. Saving is important for economic growth because without saving, we cannot have investment. If all income is consumed each year, there is nothing left over for saving, which could be used by business for investment. If there is no investment in our capital stock, there could be little hope of much economic growth.

The relationship between the rate of savings and per capita real GDP is shown in Figure 9-4. A nation with one of the highest rates of saving is Japan. Why?

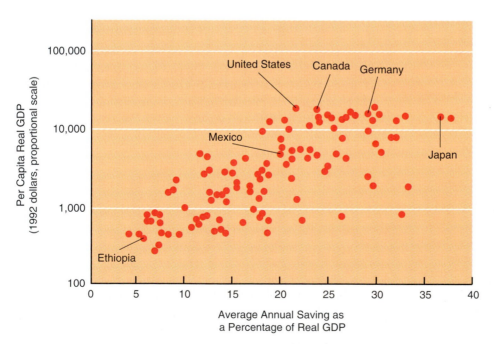

FIGURE 9-4

Relationship Between Rate of Saving and Per Capita Real GDP

This diagram shows the combination of per capita real GDP and the rate of saving expressed as the average percentage of annual real GDP for many nations since 1960. Centrally planned economies and major oil-producing countries are not shown.

Source: After Robert Summers and Alan Heston, "A New Set of International Comparisons of Real Product and Price Level," *Review of Income and Wealth,* March 1988.

INTERNATIONAL EXAMPLE
Why Do the Japanese Save So Much?

The rate of saving in Japan is roughly twice what it has been in the United States, expressed as a percentage of income. One possible reason is because the Japanese have been unable to borrow as freely as their American counterparts. The typical down payment for a Japanese family wishing to buy a house is 40 percent, as opposed to only 10 percent in the United States. The average housing price in Japan is more than twice what it is in the United States. Consequently, to purchase a house, a typical Japanese family has to save more than a typical American family. In addition, the Japanese have for many years been rewarded more for saving than in the United States because their tax system has taxed the rate of return to saving relatively less than in the United States.

FOR CRITICAL ANALYSIS: "The Japanese save more because they are different from Americans." Is this a valid alternative explanation of the relatively high Japanese saving rate? Explain your answer. ●

CONCEPTS IN BRIEF

- Economic growth is numerically equal to the rate of growth of capital plus the rate of growth of labor plus the rate of growth in the productivity of capital and of labor. Improvements in labor productivity, all other things being equal, lead to greater economic growth and higher living standards.

- One fundamental determinant of the rate of growth is the rate of saving. To have more consumption in the future, we have to save rather than consume. In general, countries that have had higher rates of saving have had higher rates of growth in real GDP.

NEW GROWTH THEORY AND WHAT DETERMINES GROWTH

A simple arithmetic definition of economic growth has already been given. Growth rates of capital and labor plus the growth rate in their productivity are simply defined as the components of economic growth. Economists have had good data on the growth of the physical capital stock in the United States as well as on the labor force. But when you add those two growth rates together, you still do not get the total economic growth rate in the United States. The difference has to be due to improvements in productivity. Economists typically labeled this "improvements in technology," and that was that. More recently, proponents of what is now called the **new growth theory** argue that technology cannot simply be looked at as an outside factor without explanation. Technology must be examined from what drives it. What are the forces that make productivity grow in America and elsewhere?

New growth theory
A relatively modern theory of economic growth that examines the factors that determine why technology, research, innovation, and the like are undertaken and how they interact.

Growth in Technology

Consider some startling statistics about the growth in technology. Look at Figure 9-5 on page 196 to learn what may happen to computers in the future. Microprocessor speeds may increase from 350 megahertz to 800 megahertz by the year 2011. By that same year, the size of the thinnest circuit line within a transistor will decrease by 77 percent. The typical

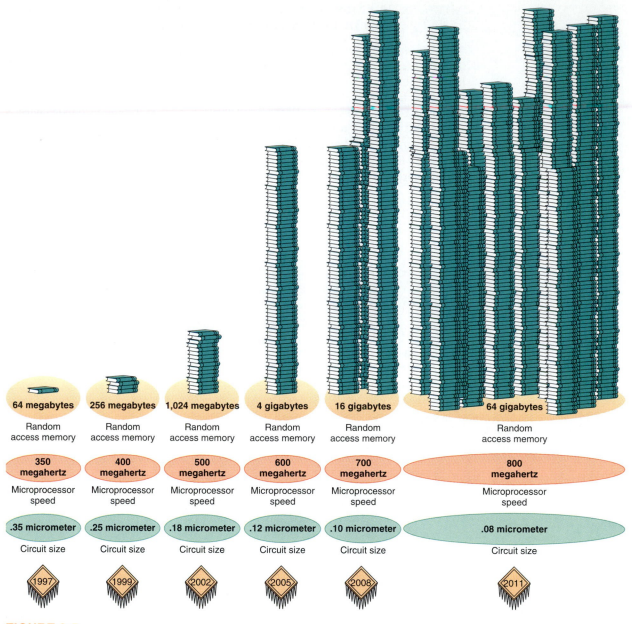

64 megabytes **256 megabytes** **1,024 megabytes** **4 gigabytes** **16 gigabytes** **64 gigabytes**

Random access memory (for each)

| 350 megahertz | 400 megahertz | 500 megahertz | 600 megahertz | 700 megahertz | 800 megahertz |

Microprocessor speed

| .35 micrometer | .25 micrometer | .18 micrometer | .12 micrometer | .10 micrometer | .08 micrometer |

Circuit size

1997 1999 2002 2005 2008 2011

FIGURE 9-5

Growth in Computer Capacity

In 1997, the typical computer may have 64 megabytes of dynamic random access memory. By the year 2002, that will increase to over 1,000 megabytes, or a gigabyte. By 2011, it will be 64 gigabytes. Similarly dramatic increases in microprocessor speed and reductions in transistor circuit thinness will also occur.

Source: Semiconductor Industry Association.

Do New Technologies Signal the End of Work?

Throughout the world, the media as well as numerous "experts" have painted a gloomy picture for the average working person. They point out that the newest technologies have led to a reduction in the percentage of workers who devote their time to manufacturing. Efficient production lines certainly do require fewer workers, and sophisticated telecommunications have reduced the need for physical offices. During one recent talk show in England, the commentator stated that "the rich no longer need the poor. More and more goods can be produced with fewer and fewer workers. Therefore, permanent unemployment will grow." Such commentaries have been popular since the weaving machine with a single operator replaced the work that 10 people did previously. The idea is that the other nine workers were unemployed forever. Both theory and data render such media analyses basically meaningless. In the United States, in spite of dramatic increases in technology, the number of new jobs created has averaged 2.5 million per year since 1975. In the same time period, the population increased over 40 million, but the number of unemployed remained relatively stable at around 8 million. And theoretically, there is no limit to employment. Labor employment is a function of the supply and demand for labor. Demand is not a fixed constant somehow based on a mechanical relationship between the number of widgets produced and the number of workers needed to produce them. Workers released from industries that are more productive because of new technologies must—and do—find employment elsewhere, often in other industries that are expanding. (After all, wants *are* unlimited.)

Patent

A government protection that gives an inventor the exclusive right to make, use, or sell an invention for a limited period of time (currently, 17 years).

memory capacity of computers will jump from 64 megabytes, or about the equivalent text in the *Encyclopaedia Britannica,* to 64 gigabytes—a thousandfold increase.

By 2005, new microchip plants will produce 1,000 transistors a week for every person on earth. Predictions are that computers may become as powerful as the human brain by 2020.

EXAMPLE
Technology and Light

For an even more impressive example of how technology has worked, consider what it has done to the true price of light. Yale University economist William Nordhaus examined the price of 1,000 lumen-hours of light from 1880 to today. Even without correcting for inflation, the price has fallen from 40 cents to about $\frac{1}{10}$ cent. After Nordhaus took account of true changes in other prices, he came up with a startling conclusion: The price of light in 1880 was about 1,000 times more expensive than it is today. Now that's progress.

FOR CRITICAL ANALYSIS: Why do we relate the falling price of artificial light to technological progress? ●

Technology: A Separate Factor of Production

We now recognize that technology must be viewed as a separate factor of production that is sensitive to rewards. Otherwise stated, one of the major foundations of new growth theory is this:

The greater the rewards, the more technological advances we will get.

Let's consider several aspects of technology here, the first one being research and development.

Research and Development

A certain amount of technological advance results from research and development (R&D) activities that have as their goal the development of specific new materials, new products, and new machines. How much spending a nation devotes to R&D can have an impact on its long-term economic growth. Part of how much a nation spends depends on what businesses decide is worth spending. That, in turn, depends on their expected rewards from successful R&D. If your company develops a new way to produce computer memory chips, how much will it be rewarded? The answer depends on whether others can freely copy the new technique.

Patents. To protect new techniques developed through R&D, we have a system of **patents,** protections whereby the federal government gives the patent holder the exclusive right to make, use, and sell an invention for a period of 17 years. One can argue that this special position given owners of patents increases expenditures on R&D and therefore adds to long-term economic growth.

Positive Externalities and R&D. As we discussed in Chapter 5, positive externalities are benefits from an activity that do not spill over to the instigator of the activity. In the case of R&D spending, a certain amount of the benefits go to other companies that do not have to pay for them. In particular, according to economists David Coe of the International Monetary Fund and Elhanan Helpman of Tel Aviv University, about a quarter of the global benefits of R&D investment in the top seven industrialized countries goes to foreigners. For every 1 percent rise in the stock of research and development in America alone, for example, productivity in the rest of the world increases by about .04 percent. One country's R&D expenditures benefit foreigners because foreigners are able to import goods from technologically advanced countries and then use them as inputs in making their own industries more efficient. In addition, countries that import high-tech goods are able to imitate the technology.

The Open Economy and Economic Growth

People who study economic growth today tend to emphasize the importance of the openness of the economy. Free trade encourages a more rapid spread of technology and industrial ideas. Moreover, open economies may experience higher rates of economic growth because their own industries have access to a bigger market. When trade barriers are erected in the form of tariffs and the like, domestic industries become isolated from global technological progress. This occurred for many years in former communist countries and in many developing countries in Latin America and elsewhere. Figure 9-6 shows the relationship between economic growth and the openness as measured by the level of protectionism of a given economy.

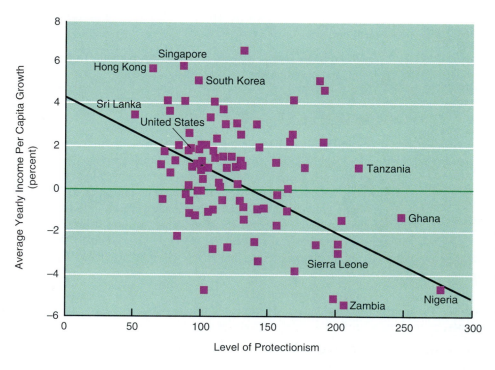

FIGURE 9-6

The Relationship Between Protectionism and Economic Growth
Closed economies are ones in which the government prevents imports from entering the country and sometimes exports from leaving the country. Such protectionism closes off the economy to new technologies. Here you see the relationship between the level of protectionism and economic growth rates measured on a per capita basis. The data seem to indicate that the more closed an economy, the lower its rate of growth, all other things held constant.
Source: Economic Review, Fourth Quarter 1993, p. 3.

Innovation and Knowledge

Innovation
Transforming an invention into something that is useful to humans.

We tend to think of technological progress as, say, the invention of the transistor. But invention means nothing by itself; **innovation** is required. Innovation involves the transformation of something new, such as an invention, into something that benefits the economy either by lowering production costs or providing new goods and services. Indeed, the new growth theorists believe that real wealth creation comes from innovation and that invention is but a facet of innovation.

Historically, technologies have moved relatively slowly from invention to innovation to widespread use, and the dispersion of new technology remains for the most part slow and uncertain. The inventor of the transistor thought it might be used to make better hearing aids. At the time it was invented, the *New York Times*'s sole reference to it was in a small weekly column called "News of Radio." When the laser was invented, no one really knew what it could be used for. It was initially used to help in navigation, measurement, and chemical research. Today, it is used in the reproduction of music, printing, surgery, and telecommunications. Tomorrow, who knows?

Much innovation involves small improvements in the use of an existing technology. Such improvements develop from experimentation and discovery, which has been fostered in the Japanese automobile market, for example.

INTERNATIONAL EXAMPLE
Innovation in the Japanese Auto Industry

The automobile has been around for a century. By the 1950s, U.S. automobile manufacturers were fairly well convinced that they had developed the best and most efficient assembly-line operation in the world. They did so through what were called time-and-motion studies. A "final" set of directions were given to each worker on the assembly line, and that worker adhered to those directions. The Japanese decided to improve on this through a process of experimentation and discovery. In Japanese automobile plants, workers were encouraged to experiment with small changes in how they assembled a car—should the door molding go on before or after the door is put on the car? Gradually, Japanese automobile workers became more efficient than their American counterparts. The process came about through small innovative changes, not one great invention.

FOR CRITICAL ANALYSIS: *How many ways are there to put together a car?* •

The Importance of Ideas and Knowledge

Economist Paul Romer has added at least one important factor that determines the rate of economic growth. He contends that production and manufacturing knowledge is just as important as the other determinants and perhaps even more so. He considers knowledge a factor of production that, like capital, has to be paid for by forgoing current consumption. Economies must therefore invest in knowledge just as they invest in machines. Because past investment in capital may make it more profitable to acquire more knowledge, there exists the possibility of an investment-knowledge cycle in which investment spurs knowledge and knowledge spurs investment. A once-and-for-all increase in a country's rate of investment may permanently raise that country's growth rate. (According to traditional theory, a once-and-for-all increase in the rate of saving and therefore in the rate of investment simply leads to a new steady-state standard of living but not one that continues to increase.)

Another way of looking at knowledge is that it is a store of ideas. According to Romer, ideas are what drive economic growth. We have become, in fact, an idea economy. Consider

Microsoft Corporation. A relatively small percentage of that company's labor force is involved in actually producing diskettes. Rather, a majority of Microsoft workers are attempting to discover new ideas that can be translated to computer code that can then be placed on diskettes. The major conclusion that Romer and other new growth theorists draw is this:

Economic growth can continue as long as we keep coming up with new ideas.

The Importance of Human Capital

Knowledge, ideas, and productivity are all tied together. One of the threads is the quality of the labor force. Increases in the productivity of the labor force are a function of increases in human capital, the fourth factor of production discussed in Chapter 2. Recall that human capital is the knowledge and skills that people in the workforce acquire through education, on-the-job training, and self-teaching. To increase your own human capital, you have to invest by forgoing income-earning activities while you attend school. Society also has to invest in the form of libraries and teachers. According to the new growth theorists, human capital is at least as important as physical capital, particularly when trying to explain international differences in living standards.

As you will see in Chapter 35, one of the most effective ways that developing countries can become developed is by investing in secondary schooling.

One can argue that policy changes that increase human capital will lead to more technological improvements. One of the reasons why concerned citizens, policymakers, and politicians are looking for a change in America's schooling system is that our educational system seems to be falling behind that of other countries. This lag is greatest in science and mathematics—precisely the areas that are required for developing better technology.

CONCEPTS IN BRIEF

- New growth theory argues that the greater the rewards, the more rapid the pace of technology. And greater rewards spur research and development.

- The openness of an economy seems to correlate with its economic rate of growth.

- Invention and innovation are not the same thing. Inventions are useless until innovation transforms them into things that people find valuable.

- According to the new growth economists, economic growth can continue as long as we keep coming up with new ideas.

- Increases in human capital can lead to greater rates of economic growth. These come about by increased education, on-the-job training, and self-teaching.

POPULATION AND IMMIGRATION AS THEY AFFECT ECONOMIC GROWTH

There are several ways to view population growth as it affects economic growth. On the one hand, population growth means an increase in the amount of labor, which, as we have previously learned, is one component of economic growth. On the other hand, population growth can be seen as a drain on the economy because for any given amount of GDP, more population means lower per capita GDP. According to Massachusetts Institute of Technology economist Michael Kremer, the first view is historically correct. His conclusion is that population growth drives technological progress, which then increases economic growth. The theory is simple: If there are 50 percent more people in the United States, there will be 50 percent more geniuses. And with 50 percent more people, the rewards for creativity are commensurately greater. Otherwise stated, the larger the potential market, the greater the incentive to become ingenious.

Does the same argument apply to immigration? Yes, according to economist Julian Simon, whose research points out that "every time our system allows in one more immigrant, on average, the economic welfare of American citizens goes up. . . . Additional immigrants, both the legal and the illegal, raise the standard of living of U.S. natives and have little or no negative impact on any occupational or income class." He further argues that immigrants do not displace natives from jobs but rather create jobs through their purchases and by starting new businesses. Immigrants' earning and spending simply expand the economy.

Not all researchers agree with Simon, and few studies exist to back up the theories advanced here. The area is currently the focus of much research.

PROPERTY RIGHTS AND ENTREPRENEURSHIP

If you were in a country where bank accounts and businesses were periodically expropriated by the government, how willing would you be to leave your money in a savings account or to invest in a business? Certainly you would be less willing than if such things never occurred. In general, the more certain private property rights are, the more capital accumulation there will be. People will be willing to invest their savings in endeavors that will increase their wealth in future years. They have property rights in their wealth that are sanctioned and enforced by the government. In fact, some economic historians have attempted to show that it was the development of well-defined private property rights that allowed Western Europe to increase its growth rate after many centuries of stagnation. The ability and certainty with which they can reap the gains from investing also determine the extent to which business owners in other countries will invest capital in developing countries. The threat of nationalization that hangs over some developing nations probably prevents the massive amount of foreign investment that might be necessary to allow these nations to develop more rapidly.

The property rights, or legal structure, in a nation are closely tied to the degree with which individuals use their own entrepreneurial skills. In Chapter 2, we identified entrepreneurship as the fifth factor of production. Entrepreneurs are the risk takers who seek out new ways to do things and create new products. To the extent that entrepreneurs are allowed to capture the rewards from their entrepreneurial activities, they will seek to engage in those activities. In countries where such rewards cannot be captured because of a lack of property rights, there will be less entrepreneurship. Typically, this results in fewer investments and a lower rate of growth.

CONCEPTS IN BRIEF

- While some economists argue that population growth stifles economic growth, others contend that empirically the opposite is true. The latter economists consequently believe that immigration should be encouraged rather than discouraged.

- Well-defined and protected property rights are important for fostering entrepreneurship. In the absence of well-defined property rights, individuals have less incentive to take risks, and economic growth rates usually suffer.

Democracy and Prosperity: Cause or Effect?

Concepts Applied: *Economic growth, per capita real GDP*

Nondemocratic countries that achieve high standards of living through steady economic growth tend to become more democratic over time. Taiwan had its first full democratic election in 1996. Here, election workers count ballots at a polling station in Taipei.

Most Americans believe that they have the best political system on earth. They support this belief by pointing out the disastrous economic results of the alternative political system called communism that existed in the former Soviet Union and throughout Eastern Europe prior to the 1990s. Does this therefore mean that democracy is good for economic growth? Consistent economic growth in this country seems to imply that the answer is yes (except for the Great Depression, of course). The real question, though, is whether democracy causes economic growth or whether economic growth causes democracy.

Benefits of Democracy

Democracy has the great benefit of reining in government power. In principle and in theory, it provides a check on the ability of public officials to carry out too many unpopular projects. Further, it normally prevents public officials from stealing from state coffers on a grand scale.

Costs of Democracy

Political freedom in the form of democracy carries with it the ability of special-interest groups to gain personally at the expense of society as a whole. Through the democratic process, special-interest groups can prevent lower-priced goods (and labor) from entering the country, quash new businesses that would compete with existing businesses, and impose other inefficient policies.

What Does the Real World Show?

What does the real world tell us about the relationship between democracy and economic growth rates? Economist Robert Barro of Harvard University studied more than 100 countries over the past three decades. After adjusting for differences in other factors, he concluded that "the overall effect of more democracy on the growth rate is moderately negative." The evidence shows that once a moderate amount of political freedom has been attained, democracy either doesn't help economic growth or renders it slightly less than it would have been otherwise.

Could High Economic Growth Cause Democracy?

According to Barro's research, the link between democracy and economic growth is probably reversed. That is to say, when nondemocratic countries have achieved high standards of living through consistent economic growth, they tend to become more democratic over time. There are a number of important examples today, among them Chile, Portugal, South Korea, Spain, and Taiwan. Using this model, Barro predicted that Algeria, Indonesia, Iran, Iraq, Mexico, Peru, Singapore, Sudan, and Syria will all become more democratic by the year 2000.

FOR CRITICAL ANALYSIS

1. Assume that more democracy (increased political freedom) leads to a lower economic rate of growth in some countries. Are there still reasons to encourage more democracy in those countries? If so, what are these reasons?
2. "Political freedoms tend to erode over time if they are out of line with a country's standard of living." Analyze this statement.

CHAPTER SUMMARY

1. Economic growth is defined as the rate of increase in per capita real GDP. It can be shown graphically as an outward shift in the production possibilities curve. Small changes in rates of growth lead to large differences in GDP over time because of compounding.

2. Economic growth can be defined as numerically equal to the rate of growth of capital plus the rate of growth of labor plus the rate of growth in the productivity of capital and of labor.

3. To consume more in the future, you have to not consume—save—today. The rate of saving is a key determinant of a nation's rate of economic growth.

4. The new growth theorists argue that advances in technology are a function of the rewards to those advances. In particular, research and development will increase the more it is rewarded.

5. The more open an economy, the faster its rate of economic growth.

6. Although inventions are important, they have no value until they are made useful by innovation. Innovations may be slow to occur and may involve small improvements in the use of existing technologies. Economic growth can continue as long as we keep coming up with new ideas.

7. Increases in human capital can occur because of schooling and on-the-job training. Schooling requires a personal investment by the student—giving up consumption that would otherwise be available through for-pay work—as well as investment by society in teachers and libraries. Differences in standards of living across countries can, to some extent, be explained by differences in the level of human capital investment.

8. Empirically, increased population size has been associated with higher rates of economic growth. Consequently, immigration can be viewed as good rather than bad.

9. Well-defined property rights and resulting entrepreneurship may explain differences in rates of economic growth. Increased certainty about property rights may lead to more capital accumulation and higher rates of economic growth in nations in which property rights have been uncertain in the past.

DISCUSSION OF PREVIEW QUESTIONS

1. **What is economic growth?**
   By economic growth, economists are referring to the rate of increase in an economy's real level of output over time. It is generally agreed that the rate of changes in per capita (corrected for population change) real (corrected for price level changes) GDP is a good measure of an economy's economic growth. The very long-run economic growth rate for the United States is approximately 1.75 percent per year—with much deviation around this trend line, of course.

2. **What does economic growth measure?**
   Many people try to make inferences about changes in economic well-being from a nation's economic growth rate; presumably, higher growth rates imply more rapid increases in living standards. Others have argued that increased income inequality may accompany rapid economic growth, as a relatively small percentage of the population may benefit from economic growth while the majority experiences little economic improvement. Critics also point out that rapid economic growth is not necessarily consistent with increases in the spiritual, cultural, and environmental quality of life. However, because per capita increases in real GDP do not measure the increased leisure that usually accompanies economic growth, this measure may *understate* economic well-being. Economic growth is therefore a rather crude measure of changes in a nation's well-being and is perhaps a better indicator of its productive activity.

3. **What are some of the ways in which you can experience economic growth for yourself or for your family?**
   You can experience economic growth only if you are willing to sacrifice something. When you continue to go to school, you are sacrificing your current ability to earn and consume income. But in exchange for that sacrifice, you are developing skills and talents that will allow you to have a higher income in the future. You are investing in yourself (human capital) by sacrificing current consumption now.

If you wish to accumulate much wealth during your lifetime, you must be willing to sacrifice current consumption. You do this by not consuming all of your income—that is, by saving part of it. The more you save, the more you can accumulate. In particular, if you invest your accumulated savings in wise savings outlets, you will be rewarded by a compounded rate of growth so that in the future you will have accumulated larger amounts of wealth.

4. **What are the determinants of economic growth?**
One obvious determinant of economic growth is the quantity and quality of a nation's natural resources—

although this determinant can easily be exaggerated. Hence many slowly developing nations have bountiful natural resources, and some rapidly developing areas have very few. The quality and quantity of labor and capital are also important determinants of economic growth, as is a nation's rate of technological progress. A decidedly underrated determinant of economic growth is the industriousness and willingness of people to be productive—which is surely related to personal incentives related to property rights. The certainty of property rights may also affect a nation's growth rate.

PROBLEMS

(Answers to the odd-numbered problems appear at the back of the book.)

9-1. The graph shows the production possibilities frontier for an economy. Which of the labeled points would be associated with the highest feasible growth rate for this economy?

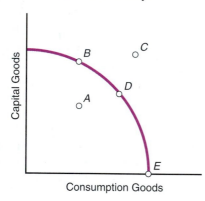

Consumption Goods

9-2. Why might an economy be operating inside its production possibilities curve?

9-3. Consider the following table, which describes growth rate data for four countries between 1989 and 1998.

a. Which country has the largest rate of output growth per capita?
b. Which country has the smallest rate of output growth per capita?

Country	Annual Growth Rate (%)			
	J	K	L	M
Nominal GDP	20	15	10	5
Price level	5	3	6	2
Population	5	8	2	1

9-4. Use Table 9-3 (page 191) to answer the following questions.

a. Country A has a growth rate of 3 percent, and country B has a growth rate of 4 percent. Assume that they both start off with equal incomes. How much richer will country A be after 10 years? After 50 years?
b. Assume that country A has twice the income per capita of country B. Country A is growing at 3 percent, and country B is growing at 4 percent. Will country B ever catch up? If so, when?

COMPUTER-ASSISTED INSTRUCTION

The links among global integration, markets, and economic growth are explored.

Complete problem and answer appear on disk.

MICRO FOUNDATIONS: AGGREGATE DEMAND AND AGGREGATE SUPPLY

In a matter of minutes on January 17, 1995, fifty-story office buildings, steel and concrete freeways, and tens of thousands of houses collapsed in the Japanese city of Kobe. The earthquake measured 7.2 on the Richter scale. Thousands of people were killed and hundreds of thousands left homeless. The estimated cost of rebuilding: $110 billion. To understand what effect this terrible tragedy had on the economy of Japan, you need to understand how aggregate demand and aggregate supply work together to create the equilibrium level of real GDP.

PREVIEW QUESTIONS

1. Why does the aggregate demand curve slope downward?

2. Why does the short-run aggregate supply curve slope upward?

3. Why is the long-run aggregate supply curve vertical?

4. How can we show improvements in technology using aggregate demand and aggregate supply analysis?

Did You Know That . . . the U.S. Department of Commerce provides a monthly publication of over 100 pages of statistics on the economy called *Survey of Current Business,* but prior to the 1970s, the same publication was called *Business Cycle Digest?* Purportedly, the Department of Commerce changed the name of this publication because government economists in the 1960s thought that the "business cycle" was dead because the American economy had experienced a relatively long period of expansion. Today, no one believes that national business fluctuations are obsolete. Since the time the Department of Commerce changed the name of its statistical publication, the economy has experienced five recessions. So we still need to understand why national business activity fluctuates. In this chapter you will learn about one way to explain changes in output, unemployment, and the price level in our economy.

SPENDING AND TOTAL EXPENDITURES

As explained in Chapters 7 and 8, GDP is the dollar value of total expenditures on domestically produced final goods and services. Because all expenditures are made by individuals, firms, or governments, the total value of these expenditures must be what each of these market participants decides it shall be. The decisions of individuals, managers of firms, and government officials determine the annual dollar value of total expenditures. You can certainly see this in your role as an individual. You decide what the total value of your expenditures will be in a year. You decide how much you want to spend and how much you want to save. Thus if we want to know what determines the total value of GDP, the answer would be clear: the spending decisions of individuals like you; firms; and local, state, and national governments. In an open economy, we must also include foreign individuals, firms, and governments (foreigners, for short) that decide to spend their money income in the United States.

Simply stating that the dollar value of total expenditures in this country depends on what individuals, firms, governments, and foreigners decide to do really doesn't tell us much, though. Two important issues remain:

1. What determines the total amount that individuals, firms, governments, and foreigners want to spend?
2. What determines whether this spending will result in a higher output of goods and services (quantities) or higher prices (inflation)?

The way we will answer these questions in this chapter is by developing the concepts of *aggregate demand* and *aggregate supply.* **Aggregate demand** is the total of all planned expenditures in the economy. **Aggregate supply** is the total of all planned production in the economy. Given these definitions, we can now proceed to construct an aggregate demand curve and an aggregate supply curve.

Aggregate demand
The total of all planned expenditures for the entire economy.

Aggregate supply
The total of all planned production for the entire economy.

THE AGGREGATE DEMAND CURVE

The **aggregate demand curve,** *AD,* gives the various quantities of all final commodities demanded at various price levels, all other things held constant. Recall the components of GDP that you studied in Chapter 8: consumption spending, investment expenditures, government purchases, and net foreign demand for domestic production. They are all components of aggregate demand. Throughout this chapter and the next, whenever you see the aggregate demand curve, realize that it is a shorthand way of talking about the components

Aggregate demand curve
A curve showing planned purchase rates for all goods and services in the economy at various price levels, all other things held constant.

of GDP that are measured by government statisticians when they calculate total economic activity each year. In Chapter 12 you will look more closely at the relationship between these components and in particular how consumption spending depends on income.

Aggregate Demand Curve

The aggregate demand curve gives the total amount of *real* domestic income that will be purchased at each price level. Real domestic income consists of the output of final goods and services in the economy—everything produced for final use by either businesses or households. This includes stereos, socks, shoes, medical and legal services, computers, and millions of other goods and services that people buy each year. A graphic representation of the aggregate demand curve is seen in Figure 10-1. On the horizontal axis is measured real gross domestic output, or real GDP. For our measure of the price level, we use the GDP price deflator on the vertical axis. The aggregate demand curve is labeled *AD*. If the GDP deflator is 100, aggregate quantity demanded is $8 trillion per year (point *A*). At price level 120 it is $7 trillion per year (point *B*). At price level 140 it is $6 trillion per year (point *C*). The higher the price level, the lower will be the total real output demanded by the economy, everything else remaining constant, as shown by the arrow along *AD* in Figure 10-1. Conversely, the lower the price level, the higher will be the total real output demanded by the economy, everything else staying constant.

Let's take the year 1996. Looking at U.S. Department of Commerce preliminary statistics will reveal the following information:

- GDP was $7,566.9 billion.
- The price level as measured by GDP deflator was 109.21 (base year 1992, when the index equals 100).
- Real GDP (output) was $6,928.8 billion in 1992 dollars.

What can we say about 1996? Given the dollar cost of buying goods and services and all of the other factors that go into spending decisions by individuals, firms, governments, and foreigners, the total amount of real domestic output demanded by firms, individuals, governments, and foreigners was $6,928.8 billion in 1996 (in terms of 1992 dollars).

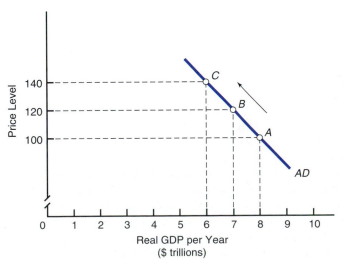

FIGURE 10-1

The Aggregate Demand Curve
Because of the real-balance, interest rate, and open economy effects, the aggregate demand curve, *AD*, slopes downward. If the price level is 100, we will be at point *A* with $8 trillion of real GDP demanded per year. As the price level increases to 120 and 140, we will move up the aggregate demand curve to points *B* and *C*.

What Happens When the Price Level Rises?

What if the price level in the economy rose to 160 tomorrow? What would happen to the amount of real goods and services that individuals, firms, governments, and foreigners wish to purchase in the United States? When we asked that question about individual commodities in Chapter 3, the answer was obvious: The quantity demanded would fall if the price went up. Now we are talking about the *price level*—the average price of *all* goods and services in the economy. The answer is still that the total quantities of real goods and services demanded would fall, but the reasons are different. Remember that in Chapter 3, when the price of one good or service went up, the consumer would substitute other goods and services. For the entire economy, when the price level goes up, the consumer doesn't simply substitute one good for another, for now we are dealing with the demand for all goods and services in the entire nation. There are *economywide* reasons that cause the aggregate demand curve to slope downward. They involve at least three distinct forces: the *real-balance effect,* the *interest rate effect,* and the *open economy effect.*

The Direct Effect: The Real-Balance Effect.

A rise in the price level will have a direct effect on spending. Individuals, firms, governments, and foreigners carry out transactions using money. Money in this context only consists of currency and coins that you have in your pocket (or stashed away) right now. Because people use money to purchase goods and services, the amount of money that people have influences the amount of goods and services they want to buy. For example, if you found a $10 bill on the sidewalk, the amount of money you had would rise. This would likely have a *direct* effect on the amount of spending in which you would engage. Given your greater level of money balances— currency in this case—you would almost surely increase your spending on goods and services. Similarly, if while on a trip downtown you had your pocket picked, there would be a direct effect on your desired spending. For example, if your wallet had $30 in it when it was stolen, the reduction in your cash balances—in this case currency—would no doubt cause you to reduce your planned expenditures. You would ultimately buy fewer goods and services. This response is sometimes called the **real-balance effect** (or *wealth effect*) because it relates to the real value of your cash balances. While your nominal cash balances may remain the same, any change in the price level will cause a change in the real value of those cash balances—hence the real-balance effect on the quantity of aggregate goods and services demanded.

> **Real-balance effect**
> The change in the real value of money balances when the price level changes, all other things held constant. Also called the *wealth effect.*

When you think of the real-balance effect, just think of what happens to your real wealth if you have, say, a $100 bill hidden under your mattress. If the price level increases by 10 percent, the purchasing power of that $100 bill drops by 10 percent, so not only may you feel less wealthy, you actually are. This will reduce your spending on all goods and services by some small amount.

The Indirect Effect: The Interest Rate Effect.

There is a more subtle, but equally important, *indirect* effect on your desire to spend. As we said before, when the price level goes up, the real value of your money balances declines. You end up with too few real money balances relative to other things that you own. After all, we all own a bit of many things—clothes, money balances, bicycles, cars, CD players, and perhaps houses and stocks and bonds. If, because of the price level increase, you find out that you have too few real money balances, you might actually go out to borrow to replenish them. When there are more people going in the front door of lending institutions to borrow money than there are people coming in the back door, as it were, to lend the money, the price of borrowing is going to go up. The price you pay to borrow money is the interest rate you have to pay. Because more people want to borrow now to replenish their real cash balances, interest rates will rise, and this is where the indirect effect—the **interest rate effect**—on total spending comes in.

Higher interest rates make it less attractive for people to buy houses and cars. Higher interest rates also make it less profitable for firms to install new equipment and to erect new office buildings. Whether we are talking about individuals or firms, the indirect effect of a rise in the price level will cause a higher level of interest rates, which in turn reduces the amount of goods and services that people are willing to purchase when the price level rises. Therefore, an increase in the price level will tend to reduce the quantity of aggregate goods and services demanded. (The opposite occurs if the price level declines.)

The Open Economy Effect: The Substitution of Foreign Goods. Remember from Chapter 8 that GDP includes net exports—the difference between exports and imports. In an open economy, we buy imports from other countries and ultimately pay for them through the foreign exchange market. The same is true for foreigners who purchase our goods (exports). Given any set of exchange rates between the U.S. dollar and other currencies, an increase in the price level in the United States makes American goods more expensive relative to foreign goods. Foreigners have downward-sloping demand curves for American goods. When the relative price of American goods goes up, foreigners buy fewer American goods and more of their own. In America, the cheaper-priced foreign goods now result in Americans wanting to buy more foreign goods rather than American goods. The result is a fall in exports and a rise in imports when the domestic price level rises. That means that a price level increase tends to reduce net exports, thereby reducing the amount of real goods and services purchased in the United States. This is known as the **open economy effect.**

What Happens When the Price Level Falls?

What about the reverse? Suppose now that the GDP deflator falls to 100 from an initial level of 120. You should be able to trace the three effects on desired purchases of goods and services. Specifically, how do the real-balance, interest rate, and open economy effects cause people to want to buy more? You should come to the conclusion that the lower the price level, the greater the quantity of output of goods and services demanded.

The aggregate demand curve, *AD*, shows the quantity of aggregate output that will be demanded at alternative price levels. It is downward-sloping, as is the demand curve for individual goods. The higher the price level, the lower the quantity of aggregate output demanded, and vice versa.

Aggregate Demand Versus *Individual* Demand

Even though the aggregate demand curve, *AD*, in Figure 10-1 on page 209 looks quite similar to the individual demand curve, *D*, to which you were introduced in Chapters 3 and 4, it is not the same. When we derive the aggregate demand curve, we are looking at the entire economic system. The aggregate demand curve, *AD*, differs from an individual demand curve, *D*, because we are looking at the *entire* circular flow of income and product when we construct *AD*.

Interest rate effect
One of the reasons that the aggregate demand curve slopes downward is because higher price levels indirectly increase the interest rate, which in turn causes businesses and consumers to reduce desired spending due to the higher cost of borrowing.

Open economy effect
One of the reasons that the aggregate demand curve slopes downward is because higher price levels result in foreigners' desiring to buy fewer American-made goods while Americans now desire more foreign-made goods, thereby reducing net exports, which is equivalent to a reduction in the amount of real goods and services purchased in the United States.

SHIFTS IN THE AGGREGATE DEMAND CURVE

In Chapter 3 you learned that any time a nonprice determinant of demand changed, the demand curve shifted inward to the left or outward to the right. The same analysis holds for the aggregate demand curve, except we are now talking about the non-price-level determinants of aggregate demand. So when we ask the question, "What determines the position of the aggregate demand curve?" the fundamental proposition is as follows:

> Any non-price-level change that increases aggregate spending (on domestic goods) shifts *AD* to the right. Any non-price-level change that decreases aggregate spending (on domestic goods) shifts *AD* to the left.

The list of potential determinants of the position of the aggregate demand curve is virtually without limit. Some of the most important "curve shifters" with respect to aggregate demand are presented in Table 10-1.

TABLE 10-1

Determinants of Aggregate Demand
Aggregate demand consists of the demand for domestically produced consumption goods, investment goods, government purchases, and net exports. Consequently, any change in the demand for any one of these components of real GDP will cause a change in aggregate demand. Here are listed some possibilities.

Changes That Cause an Increase in Aggregate Demand	Changes That Cause a Decrease in Aggregate Demand
A drop in the foreign exchange value of the dollar	A rise in the foreign exchange value of the dollar
Increased security about jobs and future income	Decreased security about jobs and future income
Improvements in economic conditions in other countries	Declines in economic conditions in other countries
A reduction in real interest rates (nominal interest rates corrected for inflation) not due to price level changes	A rise in real interest rates (nominal interest rates corrected for inflation) not due to price level changes
Tax decreases	Tax increases
An increase in the amount of money in circulation	A decrease in the amount of money in circulation

CONCEPTS IN BRIEF

- Aggregate demand is the total of all planned expenditures in the economy, and aggregate supply is the total of all planned production in the economy. The aggregate demand curve shows the various quantities of all commodities demanded at various price levels; it is downward-sloping.

- There are three reasons why the aggregate demand curve is downward-sloping: the direct effect, the indirect effect, and the open economy effect.

- The direct effect, sometimes called the real-balance effect, occurs because price level changes alter the real value of cash balances, thereby directly causing people to desire to spend more or less, depending on whether the price level decreases or increases.

- The indirect, or interest rate, effect is caused via interest rate changes that mimic price level changes. At higher interest rates, people desire to buy fewer houses and cars, and vice versa.

- The open economy effect occurs because of the substitution toward foreign goods when the domestic price level increases and a shift away from foreign goods when the domestic price level decreases.

THE AGGREGATE SUPPLY CURVE

The aggregate demand curve tells us how much output will be demanded given the price level. It also indicates the point toward which the price level will gravitate for any *given* total output. Knowing the position and shape of the aggregate demand curve does not tell us anything about how the *total* dollar value of spending will ultimately be divided between output—real goods and services—and prices. To determine this and thus the equilibrium level of real GDP, we must introduce supply conditions.

When we talk about aggregate supply, we have to distinguish between the long run, when all adjustments to changes in the price level can be made, and the short run, when all adjustments to changes in the price level cannot be made. Therefore, we must derive two different aggregate supply curves.

Long-Run Aggregate Supply Curve

In Chapter 2 we showed the derivation of the production possibilities curve. At any point in time, the economy can be inside or on the production possibilities curve but never outside it. The only way we can have more of everything is through economic growth—the production possibilities curve moves outward as shown in panel (a) of Figure 10-2. The idea behind the production possibilities curve can be translated into what we call the **long-run aggregate supply curve** *(LRAS)*.

Put yourself in a world in which nothing has been changing, year in and year out. The price level has not changed. Technology has not changed. The prices of inputs that firms must purchase have not changed. Labor productivity has not changed. This is a world that is fully adjusted and in which people have all the information they are ever going to get about that world. The long-run aggregate supply curve in this world is some amount of output of real goods and services, say, $7 trillion of real GDP. We can show long-run aggregate supply simply by a vertical line at $7 trillion of real GDP. This is what you see in

Long-run aggregate supply curve

A vertical line representing real output of goods and services based on full information and after full adjustment has occurred. Can also be viewed as representing the real output of the economy under conditions of full employment—the full-employment level of real GDP.

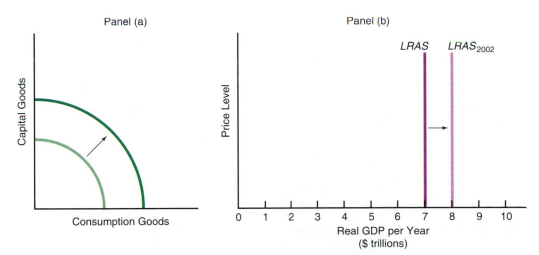

FIGURE 10-2

The Long-Run Aggregate Supply Curve and Shifts in It

In panel (a), we repeat a diagram that we used in Chapter 2 to show the meaning of economic growth. Over time, the production possibilities curve shifts outward. In panel (b), we demonstrate the same principle by showing the long-run aggregate supply curve as initially a vertical line at *LRAS* at $7 trillion of real GDP per year. As our endowments increase, the *LRAS* moves outward to *LRAS*₂₀₀₂.

panel (b) of Figure 10-2. That curve, labeled *LRAS*, is a vertical line determined by tastes, technology, and the **endowments** of resources that exist in our economy. It is the full-information and full-adjustment level of real output of goods and services. It is the level of real output that will continue being produced year after year, forever, if nothing changes.

Another way of viewing the *LRAS* is to think of it as the full-employment level of real GDP. When the economy reaches full employment, no further adjustments will occur unless a fundamental change occurs.

To understand why the long-run aggregate supply curve is vertical, think about the long run. The price level has no effect on real output (real GDP per year) because higher output prices will be accompanied by comparable changes in input prices, and suppliers will therefore have no incentive to increase or decrease output. Remember that in the long run, everybody has full information and there is full adjustment to price level changes.

Endowments
The various resources in an economy, including both physical resources and such human resources as ingenuity and management skills.

What If Non-Price-Level Variables Change? Clearly, as the years go by, things do change. Population increases, we discover more resources, and we improve technology. That means that over time, at least in a growing economy such as ours, *LRAS* will shift outward to the right, as in Figure 10-2. We have drawn *LRAS* for the year 2002 to the right of our original *LRAS* of $7 trillion of real GDP. The number we attached to $LRAS_{2002}$ is $8 trillion of real GDP, but that is only a guess; the point is that it is to the right of today's *LRAS*.

Aggregate Demand and Long-Run Output. Because *LRAS* depends on technology and endowments, aggregate demand in the long run has no bearing on the level of output of real goods and services. Draw any *AD* curve on $LRAS_{2002}$ in panel (b) of Figure 10-2, and you will see that the only thing that changes will be the price level. In the long run, the output of real goods and services is supply-side determined. Only shifts in *LRAS* will change long-run levels of output of real goods and services.

Short-Run Aggregate Supply Curve

The **short-run aggregate supply curve**, *SRAS*, represents the relationship between the price level and the real output of goods and services in the economy *without* full adjustment and full information. Just as we drew the supply curve for an individual good or service in Chapter 3 holding everything constant except the price of the good or service, we will do the same here. The short-run aggregate supply curve will be drawn under the assumption that all determinants of aggregate supply other than the price level will be held constant. Most notably, we hold constant the prices of the inputs used in the production of real goods and services. Now, what does this mean? It means that when we hold the prices of the factors of production constant in the short run, as the price level rises, it becomes profitable for all firms to expand production. Otherwise stated, changes in the price level in the short run can affect real output because some production costs might be relatively fixed in nominal terms. Therefore, an increase in the price level increases expected profits.

Short-run aggregate supply curve
The relationship between aggregate supply and the price level in the short run, all other things held constant; the curve is normally positively sloped.

Why Can Output Be Expanded in the Short Run? In the short run, if the price level rises, output can be expanded (even beyond the economist's notion of the normal capacity of a firm). That is to say, the overall economy can temporarily produce beyond its normal limits or capacity, for a variety of reasons:

1. In the short run, most labor contracts implicitly or explicitly call for flexibility in hours of work at the given wage rate. Therefore, firms can use existing workers more intensively in a variety of ways: They can get them to work harder. They can get them to

work more hours per day. And they can get them to work more days per week. Workers can also be switched from *uncounted* production, such as maintenance, to *counted* production, which generates counted output. The distinction between counted and uncounted is simply what is measured in the marketplace, particularly by government statisticians and accountants. If a worker cleans a machine, there is no measured output. But if that worker is put on the production line and helps increase the number of units produced each day, measured output will go up. That worker's production has then been counted.

2. Existing capital equipment can be used more intensively. Machines can be worked more hours per day. Some can be made to work at a faster speed. Maintenance can be delayed.

3. Finally, and just as important, if wage rates are held constant, a higher price level means that profits go up, which induces firms to hire more workers. The duration of unemployment falls, and thus the unemployment rate falls. And people who were previously not in the labor force (homemakers and younger or older workers) can be induced to enter.

All these adjustments cause national output to rise as the price level increases.

The Shape of the Short-Run Supply Curve. Even if firms want to continue increasing production because the price level has risen, they cannot do this forever. That means that when we hold input prices constant, the extra output that will be forthcoming for the three reasons just listed must eventually come to an end. Individual workers get tired. Workers are more willing to work one extra weekend than they are eight extra weekends in a row. Machines cannot go forever without maintenance. Finally, as all firms are hiring more workers from the pool of unemployed, it gets harder (more costly) to find workers at the existing level of wages.

What does all this mean? Simply that the short-run aggregate supply curve at some point must get steeper and steeper.

Graphing the Short-Run Aggregate Supply Curve. Look at Figure 10-3. There you see the short-run aggregate supply curve, *SRAS*. As we have drawn it, after a real GDP of $7 trillion, it starts to become steeper and steeper, and by the time it gets close to $8 trillion,

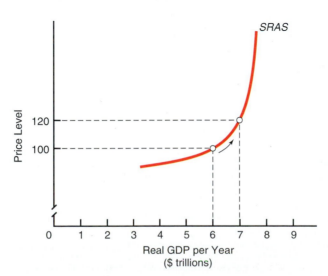

FIGURE 10-3

The Short-Run Aggregate Supply Curve

The short-run aggregate supply curve, *SRAS,* slopes upward because with fixed input prices, at a higher price level firms make more profits and desire more output. They use workers and capital more intensively. At price level 100, $6 trillion of real GDP per year is supplied. If the price level rises to 120, $7 trillion of real GDP per year will be supplied.

it is very steep indeed.[1] If the price index, as represented by the GDP deflator, is 100, the economy will supply $6 trillion per year of real GDP in Figure 10-3. If the GDP deflator increases to 120, the economy will move up the *SRAS* to $7 trillion of real GDP per year.

The Difference Between Aggregate and Individual Supply. Although the aggregate supply curve tends to look like the supply curve for an individual commodity, the two curves are not exactly the same. A commodity supply curve reflects a change in the price of an individual commodity *relative* to the prices of goods, whereas the aggregate supply curve shows the effects of changes in the price *level* for the entire economy.

SHIFTS IN THE AGGREGATE SUPPLY CURVE

Just as there were non-price-level factors that could cause a shift in the aggregate demand curve, there are non-price-level factors that can cause a shift in the aggregate supply curve. The analysis here is not quite so simple as the analysis for the non-price-level determinants for aggregate demand, for here we are dealing with both the short run and the long run—*SRAS* and *LRAS*. Still, anything other than the price level that affects supply will shift aggregate supply curves.

Shifts in Both Short- and Long-Run Aggregate Supply

There is a core class of events that causes a shift in both the short-run aggregate supply curve and the long-run aggregate supply curve. These include any change in our endowments of the factors of production.[2] Any change in land, labor, or capital will shift *SRAS* and *LRAS*. Furthermore, any change in the level of our technology or knowledge will also shift *SRAS* and *LRAS*. Look at Figure 10-4. Initially, the two curves are *SRAS*₁ and *LRAS*₁. Now consider a big oil discovery in Tennessee in an area where no one thought oil existed.

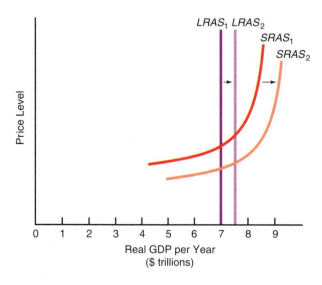

FIGURE 10-4

Shifts in Both Short- and Long-Run Aggregate Supply
Initially, the two supply curves are *SRAS*₁ and *LRAS*₁. Now consider a big oil find in Tennessee in an area where no one thought oil existed. This shifts *LRAS*₁ to *LRAS*₂ at $7.5 trillion of real GDP. *SRAS*₁ also shifts outward horizontally to *SRAS*₂.

[1]If there is a maximum short-run amount of output, at some point the *SRAS* becomes vertical. However, there is always some way to squeeze a little bit more out of an economic system, so the *SRAS* does not necessarily have to become vertical, just extremely steep.

[2]There is a complication here. A big enough increase in natural resources not only shifts aggregate supply outward but also affects aggregate demand. Aggregate demand is a function of people's wealth, among other things. A big oil discovery in America will make enough people richer that desired total spending will increase. For the sake of simplicity, we ignore this complication.

This shifts $LRAS_1$ to $LRAS_2$ at \$7.5 trillion of real GDP. $SRAS_1$ also shifts outward horizontally to $SRAS_2$.

Shifts in *SRAS* Only

Some events, particularly those that are short-lived, will temporarily shift *SRAS* but not *LRAS*. One of the most obvious is a temporary shift in input prices, particularly those caused by external events that are not expected to last forever. Consider the possibility of an announced 90-day embargo of oil from the Middle East to the United States. Oil is an important input in many production activities. The 90-day oil embargo will cause at least a temporary increase in the price of this input. You can see what happens in Figure 10-5. *LRAS* remains fixed, but $SRAS_1$ shifts to $SRAS_2$ reflecting the increase in input prices—the higher price of oil. This is because the rise in costs at each level of real GDP per year requires a higher price level to cover those costs.

We summarize the possible determinants of aggregate supply in Table 10-2 on page 218. These determinants will cause a shift in either the short-run or the long-run aggregate supply curve, or both, depending on whether they are temporary or permanent.

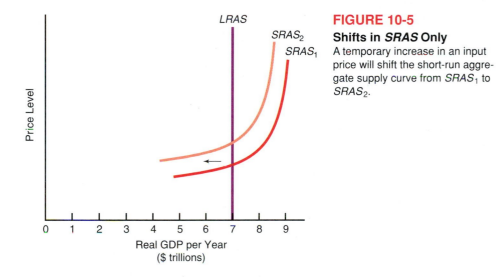

FIGURE 10-5

Shifts in *SRAS* Only

A temporary increase in an input price will shift the short-run aggregate supply curve from $SRAS_1$ to $SRAS_2$.

CONCEPTS IN BRIEF

- The long-run aggregate supply curve, *LRAS,* is a vertical line determined by technology and endowments of natural resources in an economy. It is the full-information and full-adjustment level of real output of goods and services.

- If population increases, more resources are discovered, or technology improves, *LRAS* will shift outward to the right.

- The short-run aggregate supply curve, *SRAS,* shows the relationship between the price level and the real output of goods and services in the economy without full adjustment or full information. It is upward-sloping.

- Output can be expanded in the short run because firms can use existing workers and capital equipment more intensively. Also, in the short run, when input prices are fixed, a higher price level means higher profits, which induces firms to hire more workers.

- Any change in land, labor, or capital will shift both *SRAS* and *LRAS*. A temporary shift in input prices, however, will shift only *SRAS*.

Changes That Cause an Increase in Aggregate Supply	Changes That Cause a Decrease in Aggregate Supply
Discoveries of new raw materials	Depletion of raw materials
Increased competition	Decreased competition
A reduction in international trade barriers	An increase in international trade barriers
Fewer regulatory impediments to business	More regulatory impediments to business
An increase in labor supplied	A decrease in labor supplied
Increased training and education	Decreased training and education
A decrease in marginal tax rates	An increase in marginal tax rates
A reduction in input prices	An increase in input prices

TABLE 10-2

Determinants of Aggregate Supply
The determinants listed here can affect short-run or long-run aggregate supply (or both), depending on whether they are temporary or permanent.

EQUILIBRIUM

As you discovered in Chapter 3, equilibrium occurs where demand and supply curves intersect. It is a little more complicated here because we have two types of aggregate supply curves, long-run and short-run. Let's look first at short-run equilibrium. It occurs at the intersection of aggregate demand, *AD*, and short-run aggregate supply, *SRAS*, as shown in Figure 10-6. The equilibrium price level is 120, and the equilibrium annual level of real GDP is $7 trillion. If the price level increased to 140, there would be an excess quantity of real goods and services supplied in the entire economy, and the price level would tend to fall. If the price level were 100, aggregate quantity demanded would be greater than aggregate quantity supplied, and buyers would bid up prices so that the price level would move toward 120.

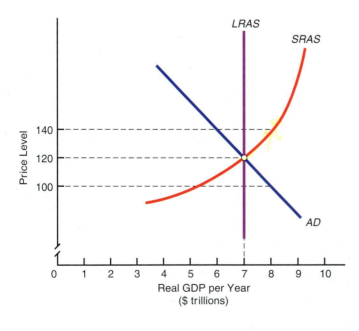

FIGURE 10-6

Equilibrium
Equilibrium will occur where the aggregate demand curve intersects the short-run aggregate supply curve and the long-run aggregate supply curve. In this diagram it is at price level 120 and a real GDP of $7 trillion per year.

Can Recessions Be Good for the Economy?

Every time there is a recession, or a period when a contractionary gap exists in the U.S. economy, some business commentators proclaim that it is good for the economy. Why? Because a minor recession, according to them, forces firms to "cut out the fat," to become more efficient and generally make themselves more fit, the better to compete in a competitive world. By definition, though, a recession is a period when the nation's full productive potential is not being used. That means that every time we experience a recession, we permanently give up billions of dollars of output and hence some significant amount of welfare to our society.

In Figure 10-6 you see that we have drawn the long-run aggregate supply curve, LRAS, so that there is full equilibrium in both the short run and the long run at price level 120. At price level 120 this economy can operate forever at $7 trillion without the price level changing.

In the short run, it is possible for us to be on SRAS to the right and above the intersection with AD and LRAS. Why? Because more can be squeezed out of the economy in the short run than would occur in the long-run, full-information, full-adjustment situation. Although in this economy a real GDP greater than $7 trillion per year is possible, it is not consistent with long-run aggregate supply. Firms would be operating beyond long-run desired capacity, and inputs would be working too long and too hard for too little money. Input prices would begin to rise. When this happens, we can no longer stay with the same SRAS, because it was drawn with input prices held constant.

If the economy finds itself on SRAS below and to the left of the intersection of AD and LRAS, the opposite will occur. Firms are operating well below long-run capacity, and there are too many unemployed inputs. Input prices will begin to fall. We can no longer stay with the same SRAS, because it was drawn with constant input prices. SRAS will shift down.

CONSEQUENCES OF CHANGES IN AGGREGATE SUPPLY AND DEMAND

We now have a basic model of the entire economy. We can trace the movement of the equilibrium price level and the equilibrium real GDP when there are shocks to the economy. Whenever there is a shift in our economy's curves, the equilibrium price level or real GDP level (or both) may change. These shifts are called **aggregate demand shocks** on the demand side and **aggregate supply shocks** on the supply side.

In Chapter 4 you learned what happened to the equilibrium price and quantity when there was a shift in demand, then a shift in supply, and then shifts in both curves. In the analysis that follows, we will be using the same basic analysis, but you should remember that we are now talking about changes in the overall price level and changes in the equilibrium level of real GDP per year.

Aggregate demand shock
Any shock that causes the aggregate demand curve to shift inward or outward.

Aggregate supply shock
Any shock that causes the aggregate supply curve to shift inward or outward.

Contractionary gap
The gap that exists whenever the equilibrium level of real national income per year is less than the full-employment level as shown by the position of the long-run aggregate supply curve.

Aggregate Demand Shifts While Aggregate Supply Is Stable

Now we can show what happens when aggregate supply remains stable but aggregate demand falls. The outcome may be the possible cause of a recession and can under certain circumstances explain a rise in the unemployment rate. In Figure 10-7 on the next page you see that with AD_1, both long-run and short-run equilibrium are at $7 trillion of real GDP per year (because SRAS and LRAS also intersect AD_1 at that level of real GDP). The long-run equilibrium price level is 120. A reduction in aggregate demand shifts the aggregate demand curve to AD_2. The new intersection with SRAS is at $6.8 trillion per year, which is below the economy's long-run aggregate supply. The difference between $7 trillion and $6.8 trillion is called the **contractionary gap,** which is defined as the difference between the short-run equilibrium level of real GDP and how much the economy could be producing if it were operating at full employment on its LRAS.

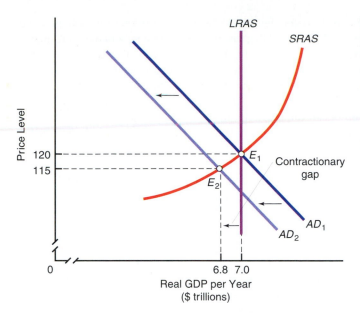

FIGURE 10-7

The Effects of Stable Aggregate Supply and a Decrease in Aggregate Demand: The Contractionary Gap

If the economy is at equilibrium at E_1, with price level 120 and real GDP per year of $7 trillion, a shift inward of the aggregate demand curve to AD_2 will lead to a new short-run equilibrium at E_2. The equilibrium price level will fall to 115, and the short-run equilibrium level of real GDP per year will fall to $6.8 trillion. There will be a contractionary gap.

Effect on the Economy of an Increase in Aggregate Demand

We can reverse the situation and have aggregate demand increase to AD_2, as is shown in Figure 10-8. The initial equilibrium conditions are exactly the same as in Figure 10-7. The move to AD_2 increases the short-run equilibrium from E_1 to E_2 such that the economy is operating at $7.2 trillion of real GDP per year, which exceeds *LRAS*. This is a condition of an overheated economy, typically called an **expansionary gap.**

Expansionary gap
The gap that exists whenever the equilibrium level of real national income per year is greater than the full-employment level as shown by the position of the long-run aggregate supply curve.

FIGURE 10-8

The Effects of Stable Aggregate Supply with an Increase in Aggregate Demand: The Expansionary Gap

The economy is at equilibrium at E_1. An increase in aggregate demand of AD_2 leads to a new short-run equilibrium at E_2 with the price level rising from 120 to 125 and the equilibrium level of real GDP per year rising from $7 trillion to $7.2 trillion. The difference is called the expansionary gap.

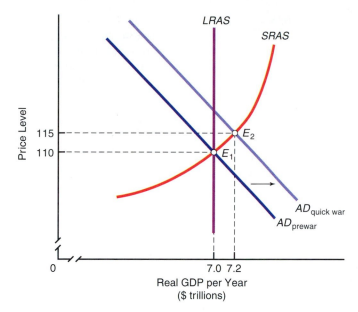

FIGURE 10-9
The Effects of War on Equilibrium
A quick temporary war will shift aggregate demand to $AD_{quick\ war}$. Equilibrium will move from E_1 to E_2 temporarily.

EXAMPLE
The Effects of a Short-Lived War

One way we can show what happens to the equilibrium price level and the equilibrium real GDP level with an aggregate demand shock is to consider a short-lived war (we actually had one in the Persian Gulf from August 1990 to early 1991). In Figure 10-9 you see the equilibrium price level of 110 and the equilibrium real GDP level of $7 trillion at the long-run aggregate supply curve. The quick war shifts aggregate demand from AD_{prewar} to $AD_{quick\ war}$. Equilibrium moves from E_1 to E_2, and the price level moves from 110 to 115. The short-run equilibrium real GDP increases to $7.2 trillion per year. The government's spending for the short-lived war caused AD to shift outward to the right. Also notice that the quick war temporarily pushed the economy above its long-run aggregate supply curve.

FOR CRITICAL ANALYSIS: *What would happen if the short-lived war became permanent? How would you show it in Figure 10-9?* •

EXPLAINING INFLATION: DEMAND-PULL OR COST-PUSH?

When you first examined inflation in Chapter 7, no theory was given for why the general level of prices might rise. You can use the *AD-AS* framework to explain inflation. Indeed, Figure 10-8 is what is known as a theory of demand-side inflation, sometimes called *demand-pull inflation*. Whenever the general level of prices rises because of continual increases in aggregate demand, we say that the economy is experiencing **demand-pull inflation**—inflation caused by increases in aggregate demand. (Some economists argue that generally economywide increases in demand—increased aggregate demand—often

Demand-pull inflation
Inflation caused by increases in aggregate demand not matched by increases in aggregate supply.

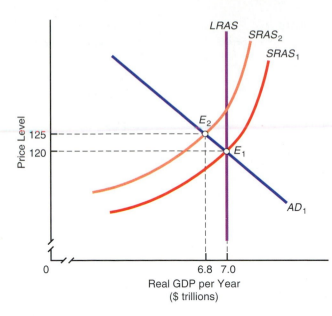

The Effects of Stable Aggregate Demand and a Decrease in Aggregate Supply: Supply-Side Inflation
If aggregate demand remains stable but $SRAS_1$ shifts to $SRAS_2$, equilibrium changes from E_1 to E_2. The price level rises from 120 to 125. If there are continual decreases in aggregate supply of this nature, the situation is called cost-push inflation.

occur when the amount of money in circulation increases faster than the growth in the economy. You will read more about this subject in Chapter 17.)

An alternative explanation comes from the supply side. Look at Figure 10-10. The initial equilibrium conditions are the same as in Figures 10-8 and 10-9. Now, however, there is a decrease in the aggregate supply curve, from $SRAS_1$ to $SRAS_2$. Equilibrium shifts from E_1 to E_2. The price level has increased from 120 to 125, too, while the equilibrium level of real GDP per year decreased from $7 trillion to $6.8 trillion. If there are continual decreases in aggregate supply, the situation is called **cost-push inflation.**

As the example of cost-push inflation shows, if the economy is initially in equilibrium on its *LRAS*, a decrease in *SRAS* will lead to a rise in the price level. Thus any abrupt change in one of the factors that determine aggregate supply will shift the equilibrium level of real GDP and the equilibrium price level. If the economy for some reason is operating to the left of its *LRAS*, an increase in *SRAS* will lead to a simultaneous *increase* in the equilibrium level of real GDP per year and a *decrease* in the price level. You should be able to show this in a graph similar to Figure 10-10.

EXAMPLE
The Oil Price Shock of the 1970s

One of the best examples of an aggregate supply shock occurred in the 1970s. During several instances, the supply of crude oil to the United States was restricted.

THINKING CRITICALLY ABOUT THE MEDIA

The Real Price of Gas

Since the 1970s, the media have made references to the "high price of gas." A typical comment by some senior citizens interviewed on TV might be, "When I was a kid, gas cost only 25 cents a gallon." The interviewee is obviously referring to the *nominal* price of gasoline. References to nominal prices during periods of inflation are virtually meaningless. Only after a nominal price is corrected for general price level changes can we make a meaningful comparison to the price of the same product or service today. In the case of gas, the price of a gallon in the late 1990s, in real terms, is about where it was a few years after World War II.

Cost-push inflation
Inflation caused by a continually decreasing short-run aggregate supply curve.

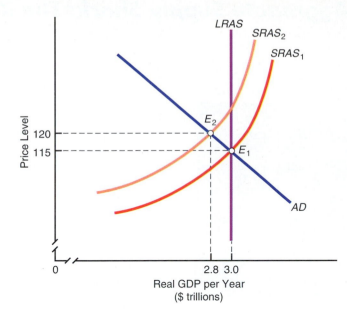

FIGURE 10-11

The Effects of Oil Price Shocks on the Economy
In the 1970s, the supply of crude oil to the United States was restricted. Higher oil prices raised the cost of production. $SRAS_1$ shifted to $SRAS_2$, and equilibrium went from E_1 to E_2 with a higher price level and a lower equilibrium real GDP per year.

These restrictions were the result of actions taken by the Organization of Petroleum Exporting Countries (OPEC). The oil embargo had an almost immediate impact on the price of oil and petroleum products, mainly gasoline and heating oil. Higher oil prices raised the cost of production in many U.S. industries that relied on petroleum. The result was a shift in the aggregate supply curve as shown in Figure 10-11. The equilibrium shifted from E_1—$3 trillion of real GDP per year and a price level of 115—to E_2—equilibrium real GDP of $2.8 trillion and a price level of 120.

FOR CRITICAL ANALYSIS: *If the price of oil had remained permanently high, what would have happened to LRAS in Figure 10-11?* ●

CONCEPTS IN BRIEF

- Short-run equilibrium occurs at the intersection of the aggregate demand curve, *AD*, and the short-run aggregate supply curve, *SRAS*. Long-run equilibrium occurs at the intersection of AD and the long-run aggregate supply curve, *LRAS*. Any unanticipated shifts in aggregate demand or supply are called aggregate demand shocks or aggregate supply shocks.

- When aggregate demand shifts while aggregate supply is stable, a contractionary gap can occur, defined as the difference between the equilibrium level of real GDP and how much the economy could be producing if it were operating on its *LRAS*. The reverse situation leads to an expansionary gap.

- With stable aggregate supply, an abrupt shift in *AD* may lead to what is called demand-pull inflation. With a stable aggregate demand, an abrupt shift inward in *SRAS* may lead to what is called cost-push inflation.

The Ultimate Aggregate Supply Shock: The Kobe Earthquake

Concepts Applied: Aggregate demand, aggregate supply, long-run aggregate supply, aggregate supply shock, equilibrium, real GDP

The Kobe earthquake in Japan was devastating in terms of casualties and property. Property damages were estimated at over $100 billion, roughly 0.8% of Japan's total wealth.

When the worst earthquake to hit Japan since 1923 occurred, the Japanese economy had already suffered more than four years of hard times—a recession during which the economy was operating to the left of its *LRAS*. This situation is similar to the contractionary gap illustrated in Figure 10-7.

Human and Physical Cost of the Kobe Earthquake

The human suffering caused by Japan's most serious earthquake in decades was enormous. More than 6,000 people were killed, and tens of thousands more were injured. Over 115,000 buildings were completely destroyed, and tens of thousands of others were damaged. All in all, the earthquake wiped out .8 percent of Japan's total wealth. The final estimated cost of the destruction was almost 10 trillion yen, or about $100 billion, considerably more damage than that caused by Hurricane Andrew in southern Florida in 1992 ($30 billion) or the earthquake in the Los Angeles–San Fernando Valley in 1994 ($15 billion).

At First Blush: Reconstruction Equals Increased Employment

After the Kobe earthquake, a number of economists throughout the world argued that the quake would revive the stagnating Japanese economy. After all, if factory people are unemployed, the reconstruction after the disaster would create income from resources that would otherwise remain unused. The problem with such an analysis, however, is that it ignores what has happened to the *wealth* of the Japanese economy. A loss of $100 billion in wealth can never be a benefit to a nation. Although it is true that employment may have increased because of reconstruction after the Kobe earthquake, as a nation, Japan has permanently lost $110 billion.

Using *AD-AS* Analysis

In Figure 10-12 you see that *LRAS* before the earthquake was $5 trillion. The economy was operating with the contractionary gap at E_1, the price level at 100, and the equi-

FIGURE 10-12

The Effects of the Kobe Earthquake in Japan
Japan was already operating below its *LRAS* at E_1 when the earthquake hit Kobe. Its $LRAS_{postquake}$ dropped to $4.9 trillion of real GDP per year from $5 trillion. Even if aggregate demand shifted to AD_2, the new equilibrium at E_2 would be below $5 trillion per year.

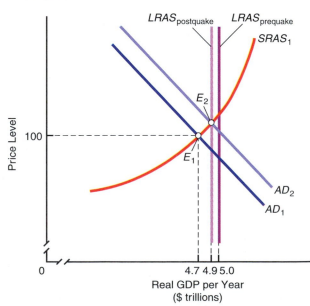

librium level of real GDP at $4.7 trillion per year. The earthquake shifted *LRAS* to *LRAS*$_{postquake}$ at $4.9 trillion, which means that even if the contractionary gap were completely eliminated, the Japanese would be worse off in the long run.

What About Aggregate Demand?

Remember that increases in aggregate demand can develop through government spending increases. It is possible, then, that aggregate demand could shift from AD_1 to AD_2.

The new equilibrium would shift to E_2, at $4.9 trillion per year. Notice, however, that it is below the equilibrium level of real GDP per year that could have been achieved prior to the earthquake.

FOR CRITICAL ANALYSIS

1. Which sectors in the Japanese labor market were most affected by the Kobe earthquake?
2. Are there any circumstances under which a natural disaster could actually be good for an economy?

CHAPTER SUMMARY

1. Aggregate demand is the total of all planned expenditures on final goods and services, and aggregate supply is the total of all planned production.
2. The aggregate demand curve gives the various quantities of all commodities demanded at various price levels. It slopes downward due to the real-balance effect, the interest rate effect, and the open economy effect.
3. Aggregate demand is not the same thing as individual demand because individual demand curves are drawn holding income, among other things, constant. The aggregate demand curve reflects the entire circular flow of income and product.
4. Any non-price-level change that increases aggregate spending on domestic goods shifts the aggregate demand curve to the right. Any non-price-level change that decreases aggregate spending on domestic goods shifts the aggregate demand curve to the left.
5. There are two aggregate supply curves. The long-run aggregate supply curve is a vertical line, the location of which depends on tastes, technology, and endowments of natural resources; it assumes full information and full adjustment. The short-run aggregate supply curve is drawn without full information and full adjustment and slopes upward, but it is not vertical.
6. Output can be expanded in the short run because firms can work both capital and labor more intensively and because firms with fixed input prices experience higher profits as the price level increases and therefore desire to hire more workers. The closer to capacity the economy is running, the steeper the short-run aggregate supply curve becomes.
7. There are events that shift both the long-run and short-run aggregate curves simultaneously. These include any change in the endowments of factors of production (land, labor, or capital). A temporary change in an input price, by contrast, shifts only the short-run aggregate supply curve.
8. Equilibrium occurs at the intersection of aggregate demand, short-run aggregate supply, and long-run aggregate supply.
9. The economy may experience shifts in aggregate demand and supply, called aggregate demand shocks and aggregate supply shocks. The impacts of such shocks on the equilibrium level of real output depend on the time period under study and other factors.

DISCUSSION OF PREVIEW QUESTIONS

1. Why does the aggregate demand curve slope downward?

There are three reasons for believing that the quantity demanded for real output rises as the price level falls, and vice versa. A decrease in the price level leads to higher *real* money balances, all other things held constant. This increased real wealth causes a direct effect on consumers' spending decisions.

There is an indirect effect via interest rates, which move with price level changes. As the price level falls, the interest rate will fall, and consumers will want to spend more on houses and cars. Finally, in an open economy, if the price level falls, people will want domestic goods rather than imports, and foreigners will want to buy more of our goods.

2. Why does the short-run aggregate supply curve slope upward?

As the price level increases, firms presumably face fixed input prices in the short run. Their profits go up, and will rise even more if they increase production. They do so by working their labor force and their capital equipment more intensively, thereby generating more output.

3. Why is the long-run aggregate supply curve vertical?

The definition of the long-run aggregate supply curve is the amount of real output of goods and services that will be produced in the long run with full information and full adjustment. With full information and full adjustment, changes in the price level do not affect real output. Real output in the long run is solely a function of tastes, technology, and endowments of land, labor, and capital. Hence the long-run aggregate supply curve is a vertical line.

4. How can we show improvements in technology using aggregate demand and aggregate supply analysis?

Improvements in technology shift both the long-run aggregate supply curve and the short-run aggregate supply curve outward. Essentially, you can show this using aggregate supply and aggregate demand analysis by drawing the curves that are shown in Figure 10-4.

PROBLEMS

(Answers to the odd-numbered problems appear at the back of the book.)

10-1. Given the curves in the accompanying graph, discuss why the equilibrium price level will be at P_e and not at P_1 or P_2.

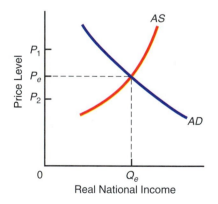

10-2. In the discussion of why the *AD* curve slopes downward from left to right, notice that nothing was said about what happens to the quantity of real output demanded when the price level rises and causes wealth to fall for people in businesses who own mortgages on houses and buildings. Why not? (Hint: What is the *net* effect to the whole economy when the price level rises and causes a wealth loss to lenders who get paid back in fixed nominal dollars?)

10-3. Distinguish between short-run and long-run supply curves.

10-4. How is aggregate demand affected when the price level in *other* economies decreases? What happens to aggregate demand when the price level in *this* economy falls?

10-5. Suppose that aggregate supply decreases while aggregate demand is held constant.

a. What happens to the price level?
b. What happens to national output?

COMPUTER-ASSISTED INSTRUCTION

When the price level falls, what happens to (1) mortgage owners and (2) holders of $1,000 bills? The differential impact of a lower price level on these two groups helps explain the real-balance effect. That effect can in turn help explain a negatively sloped aggregate demand curve.

Complete problem and answer appear on disk.

CHAPTER

CLASSICAL AND KEYNESIAN MACRO ANALYSES

Since the 1930s, the United States has flirted with annual double-digit unemployment rates (but did not actually reach them) only in 1982 and 1983. In the 1990s, Americans have come to expect a level of around 5.5 to 6.0 percent, although unemployment did reach 7.4 percent in 1992. In contrast, the 380 million individuals who comprise the European Union (EU) of 15 nations in Western Europe have learned to live with average unemployment rates that exceed 11 percent. Even when European countries expand out of a recession, their unemployment rates remain stubbornly in the double digits. To understand why unemployment remains so high in Europe, but not in the United States, you need to learn about equilibrium in the labor market and how it fits in with classical and Keynesian views of macroeconomics.

PREVIEW QUESTIONS

1. What are the assumptions of the classical macro model?

2. What determines the rate of interest in the classical model?

3. Why do Keynesian economists believe that the short-run aggregate supply curve is horizontal?

4. Why is real GDP said to be demand-determined when the short-run aggregate supply curve is horizontal?

Did **You Know That . . .** in spite of continuing general inflation, magazine publishers tend to keep the same magazine prices for more than a year? According to one study by economist Stephen G. Cecchetti, the typical magazine publisher lets inflation eat away at a fourth of the magazine's price before a new price is printed on the magazine. This common example of "sticky" prices gives just a hint that our economy may not instantaneously adapt itself to changes in macroeconomic variables such as an increase in the rate of inflation. Economists want to know what causes fluctuations in employment, output, and the price level. The fact that magazine prices are sticky is just one empirical observation that would lead researchers to develop macroeconomic models that somehow reflect the less flexible nature of certain prices. Such was not the case with the classical economists, who had a different view of how the macroeconomy operated. We will start this chapter with a look at the classical model of the economy and then examine a model developed in the twentieth century.

THE CLASSICAL MODEL

The classical model, which traces its origins to the 1770s, was the first systematic attempt to explain the determinants of the price level and the national levels of output, income, employment, consumption, saving, and investment. The term *classical model* was coined by John Maynard Keynes (pronounced "kainz"), a Cambridge University economist, who used the term to refer to the way in which earlier economists had analyzed economic aggregates. Classical economists—Adam Smith, J. B. Say, David Ricardo, John Stuart Mill, Thomas Malthus, and others—wrote from the 1770s to the 1870s. They assumed, among other things, that all wages and prices were flexible and that competitive markets existed throughout the economy. Starting in the 1870s, so-called neoclassical economists, including Alfred Marshall, introduced a mathematical approach that allowed them to refine earlier economists' models.

Say's Law

Every time you produce something for which you receive income, you generate the income necessary to make expenditures on other goods and services. That means that an economy producing $7 trillion of GDP (final goods and services) simultaneously produces the income with which these goods and services can be supplied. As an accounting identity, *actual* aggregate income always equals *actual* aggregate expenditures. Classical economists took this accounting identity one step further by arguing that total national supply creates its own demand. They asserted what has become known as **Say's law:**

> **Supply creates its own demand; hence it follows that** *desired* **expenditures will equal** *actual* **expenditures.**

What does Say's law really mean? It states that the very process of producing specific goods (supply) is proof that other goods are desired (demand). People produce more goods than they want for their own use only if they seek to trade them for other goods. Someone offers to supply something only because he or she has a demand for something else. The implication of this, according to Say, is that no general glut, or overproduction, is possible in a market economy. From this reasoning, it seems to follow that full employment of labor and other resources would be the normal state of affairs in such an economy.

Say's law
A dictum of economist J. B. Say that supply creates its own demand; producing goods and services generates the means and the willingness to purchase other goods and services.

Underlying Say's law is the premise that wants are unlimited and, further, that the primary goal of economic activity is consumption for oneself or one's family, either in the present or in the future. If a more or less self-sufficient family wants to increase its consumption, it can do so by producing more and trading its surplus of one good to get more of another good.

Say indicated that an oversupply of some goods might occur in particular markets. He argued that such surpluses would simply cause prices to fall, thereby decreasing production in the long run. The opposite would occur in markets in which shortages temporarily appeared.

All this seems reasonable enough in a simple barter economy in which households produce most of the goods they need and trade for the rest. This is shown in Figure 11-1, where there is a simple circular flow. But what about a more sophisticated economy in which people work for others and there is no barter but rather the use of money? Can these complications create the possibility of unemployment? And does the fact that laborers receive money income, some of which can be saved, lead to unemployment? No, said the classical economists to these last two questions. They based their reasoning on a number of key assumptions.

Assumptions of the Classical Model

The classical model makes four major assumptions:

1. *Pure competition exists.* No single buyer or seller of a commodity or an input can affect its price.
2. *Wages and prices are flexible.* The assumption of pure competition leads to the notion that prices, wages, interest rates, and the like are free to move to whatever level supply and demand dictate (in the long run). Although no *individual* buyer can set a price, the community of buyers or sellers can cause prices to rise or to fall to an equilibrium level.
3. *People are motivated by self-interest.* Businesses want to maximize their profits, and households want to maximize their economic well-being.
4. *People cannot be fooled by money illusion.* Buyers and sellers react to changes in relative prices. That is to say, they do not suffer from **money illusion.** For example, a worker will not be fooled into thinking that he or she is better off by a doubling of wages if the price level has also doubled during the same time period.

Money illusion
Reacting to changes in money prices rather than relative prices. If a worker whose wages double when the price level also doubles thinks he or she is better off, the worker is suffering from money illusion.

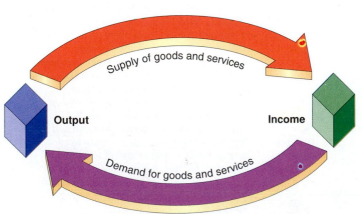

FIGURE 11-1

Say's Law and the Circular Flow
Here we show the circular flow of income and output. The very act of supplying a certain level of goods and services necessarily equals the level of goods and services demanded, in Say's simplified world.

Supply of goods and services

Output

Income

Demand for goods and services

The classical economists concluded, after taking account of the four major assumptions, that the role of government in the economy should be minimal. If all prices, wages, and markets are flexible, any problems in the macroeconomy will be temporary. The market will come to the rescue and correct itself.

The Problem of Saving

When income is saved, it is not reflected in product demand. It is a type of *leakage* in the circular flow of income and output because saving withdraws funds from the income stream. Consumption expenditures can fall short of total output now. In such a situation, it does not appear that supply necessarily creates its own demand.

The classical economists did not believe that the complicating factor of saving in the circular flow model of income and output was a problem. They contended that each dollar saved would be invested by businesses so that the leakage of saving would be matched by the injection of business investment. *Investment* here refers only to additions to the nation's capital stock. The classical economists believed that businesses as a group would intend to invest as much as households wanted to save. Equilibrium between the saving plans of consumers and the investment plans of businesses comes about, in the classical economists' world, through the working of the credit market. In the credit market, the *price* of credit is the interest rate. At equilibrium, the price of credit—the interest rate—is such that the quantity of credit demanded equals the quantity of credit supplied. Planned investment just equals planned saving, for saving represents the supply of credit and investment represents the demand for credit.

The Interest Rate: Equating Desired Saving and Investment. In Figure 11-2, the vertical axis measures the rate of interest in percentage terms; on the horizontal axis are the

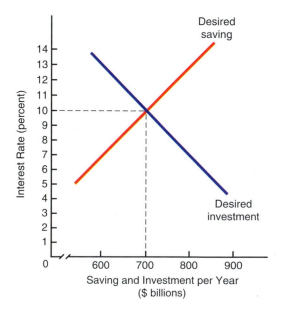

Saving and Investment per Year ($ billions)

FIGURE 11-2

Equating Desired Saving and Investment in the Classical Model
The demand curve for investment is labeled "Desired investment." The supply of resources used for investment occurs when individuals do not consume but save instead. The desired saving curve is shown as an upward-sloping supply curve of saving. The equilibrating force here is, of course, the interest rate. At higher interest rates, people desire to save more. But at higher interest rates, businesses demand less investment because it is more expensive to invest. In this model, at an interest rate of 10 percent, the quantity of investment desired just equals the quantity of saving desired (supply), which is $700 billion per year.

quantities of desired saving and desired investment per unit time period. The desired saving curve is really a supply curve of saving. It shows how much individuals and businesses wish to save at various interest rates. People wish to save more at higher interest rates than at lower interest rates.

Investment, primarily desired by businesses, responds in a predictable way. The higher the rate of interest, the more expensive it is to invest and the lower the level of desired investment. The desired investment curve slopes downward. In this simplified model, the equilibrium rate of interest is 10 percent, and the equilibrium quantity of saving and investment is $700 billion per year.

INTERNATIONAL EXAMPLE
High Interest Rates and Loan Sharks in Naples

Although the simple diagram shown in Figure 11-2 reveals an equilibrium rate of interest of 10 percent, people who seek loans often have to pay much more than 10 percent. Someone who wishes to borrow purchasing power from a creditor may not always have access to regular banks and other lending facilities that charge "normal" equilibrium interest rates. In Naples, Italy, more than 20 percent of the citizens lack a regular income. When they go to a bank to borrow, they are often denied. They turn to alternative moneylenders, of which there are about 40,000 today. These so-called loan sharks sometimes charge as high as 400 percent a year.

The Jesu Nuovo church, under the direction of Father Massimo Rastrelli, decided to fight back against the loan sharks. He founded the St. Joseph Moscati Foundation Antiusury Solidarity Fund. (*Usury* means lending at exorbitant interest rates.) Over a four-year period, Father Rastrelli obtained 16 million lire (about $10,000 at the prevailing exchange rate), which he deposited in local banks as collateral (security) for loans. Individuals in the clutches of loan sharks are able to borrow money from the fund at reasonable interest rates to pay off their debts to the loan sharks.

FOR CRITICAL ANALYSIS: *People in the business world in the United States rarely, if ever, turn to loan sharks to obtain funds to start new businesses or expand existing ones. Why don't they use the services of loan sharks?* ●

Equilibrium in the Labor Market

Now consider the labor market. If an excess quantity of labor is supplied at a particular wage level, the wage level is above equilibrium. By accepting lower wages, unemployed workers will quickly be put back to work. We show equilibrium in the labor market in Figure 11-3 on page 232.

Equilibrium of $12 per hour and 135 million workers employed represents full-employment equilibrium. If the wage rate were $14 an hour, there would be unemployment—145 million workers would want to work, but businesses would want to hire only 125 million. In the classical model, this unemployment is eliminated rather rapidly by wage rates dropping back to $12 per hour. As you will see in the Issues and Applications section at the end of this chapter, there are forces that may prevent workers from offering to work at the lower wage rates that would lead to full employment.

The Relationship Between Employment and Real GDP. Employment is not to be regarded simply as some isolated figure that government statisticians estimate. Rather, the level of employment in an economy determines its real GDP (output), other things held

FIGURE 11-3

Equilibrium in the Labor Market
The demand for labor is downward-sloping; at higher wage rates, firms will employ fewer workers. The supply of labor is upward-sloping; at higher wage rates, more workers will work longer and more people will be willing to work. The equilibrium wage rate is $12 with an equilibrium employment per year of 135 million workers.

constant. A hypothetical relationship between input (number of employees) and output (rate of real GDP per year) is shown in Table 11-1. We have highlighted the row that has 135 million workers per year as the labor input. That might be considered a hypothetical level of full employment, and it is related to a rate of real GDP of $7 trillion per year.

Classical Theory, Vertical Aggregate Supply, and the Price Level

In the classical mold of reasoning, long-term unemployment is impossible. Say's law, coupled with flexible interest rates, prices, and wages, would always tend to keep workers fully employed so that the aggregate supply curve, as shown in Figure 11-4, is vertical at Q_0. We

TABLE 11-1

The Relationship Between Employment and Real GDP

Labor Input per Year (millions of workers)	Real GDP per Year ($ trillions)
98	4
104	5
120	6
135	7
145	8
160	9

FIGURE 11-4

Classical Theory and Increases in Aggregate Demand
The classical theorists believed that Say's law, flexible interest rates, prices, and wages would always lead to full employment at Q_0 along the vertical aggregate supply curve, *LRAS*, was vertical. With aggregate demand, AD_1, the price level is 100. An increase in aggregate demand shifts AD_1 to AD_2. At price level 100, the quantity of real GDP per year demanded is *A* on AD_2, or Q_1. But this is greater than at full employment. Prices rise, and the economy quickly moves from E_1 to E_2 at the higher price level of 110.

have labeled the supply curve *LRAS*, consistent with the long-run aggregate supply curve introduced in Chapter 10. It was defined there as the quantity of output that would be produced in an economy with full information and full adjustment of wages and prices year in and year out. In the classical model, this happens to be the *only* aggregate supply curve that exists in equilibrium. Everything adjusts so fast that we are essentially always on or quickly moving toward *LRAS*. Furthermore, because the labor market is working well, Q_0 is always at, or soon to be at, full employment. Full employment is defined as the amount of employment that would exist year in and year out if all parties in the labor market fully anticipated any inflation or deflation that was occurring. Full employment does not mean zero unemployment because there is always some frictional unemployment (discussed in Chapter 7), even in the classical world.

Effect of an Increase in Aggregate Demand in the Classical Model. In this model, any change in aggregate demand will soon cause a change in the price level. Consider starting at E_1, at price level 100. If the aggregate demand shifts to AD_2, at price level 100, output would increase to Q_1. But that is greater than the full-employment level of output of real GDP, Q_0. The economy will attempt to get to point *A*, but because this is beyond full employment, prices will rise, and the economy will find itself back on the vertical *LRAS* at point E_2 at a higher price level, 110. The price level will increase at output rates in excess of the full-employment level of output because employers will end up bidding up wages for now more relatively scarce workers. In addition, factories will be bidding up the price of other inputs at this greater-than-full-employment rate of output.

The level of real GDP per year clearly does not depend on any changes in aggregate demand. Hence we say that in the classical model, the equilibrium level of real GDP per year is completely *supply-determined*. Changes in aggregate demand affect only the price level, not the output of real goods and services.

FIGURE 11-5

Effect of a Decrease in Aggregate Demand in the Classical Model

Effect of a Decrease in Aggregate Demand in the Classical Model. The effect of a decrease in aggregate demand in the classical model is the converse of the analysis just presented for an increase in aggregate demand. You can simply reverse AD_2 and AD_1 in Figure 11-4. To help you see how this analysis works, consider the flowchart in Figure 11-5.

CONCEPTS IN BRIEF

- Say's law states that supply creates its own demand and therefore *desired* expenditures will equal *actual* expenditures.

- The classical model assumes that (1) pure competition exists, (2) wages and prices are completely flexible, (3) individuals are motivated by self-interest, and (4) they cannot be fooled by money illusion.

- When saving is introduced into the model, equilibrium occurs in that market through changes in the interest rate such that desired saving equals desired investment at the equilibrium rate of interest.

- In the labor market, full employment occurs at a wage rate at which quantity demanded equals quantity supplied. That particular level of employment is associated with a certain value of real GDP per year.

- In the classical model, because the *LRAS* is vertical, the equilibrium level of real GDP is supply-determined. Any changes in aggregate demand simply change the price level.

KEYNESIAN ECONOMICS AND THE KEYNESIAN SHORT-RUN AGGREGATE SUPPLY CURVE

The classical economists' world was one of fully utilized resources. There would be no unused capacity and no unemployment. However, post–World War I Europe entered a period of long-term economic decline that could not be explained by the classical model. John Maynard Keynes developed an explanation that has since become known as the Keynesian model, which presented an explanation of the Great Depression in the 1930s. Keynes argued that if we are in a world in which there are large amounts of excess capacity and unemployment, a positive aggregate demand shock will not raise prices and a negative aggregate demand shock will not cause firms to lower prices. This situation is depicted in Figure 11-6. The short-run aggregate supply curve is labeled as the horizontal line *SRAS*. If we start out in equilibrium with aggregate demand at AD_1, the equilibrium level of real

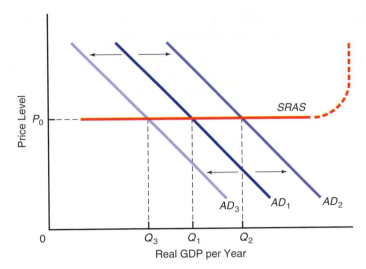

FIGURE 11-6

Demand-Determined Income Equilibrium

If we assume that prices will not fall when aggregate demand falls and that there is excess capacity so that prices will not rise when aggregate demand increases, the short-run aggregate supply curve is simply a horizontal line at the given price level, P_0, represented by *SRAS*. An aggregate demand shock that increases aggregate demand to AD_2 will increase the equilibrium level of real national income per year to Q_2. An aggregate demand shock that decreases aggregate demand to AD_3 will decrease the equilibrium level of real national income to Q_3. The equilibrium price level will not change.

GDP per year will be Q_1 and the equilibrium price level will be P_0. If there is an aggregate demand shock such that the aggregate demand curve shifts outward to the right to AD_2, the equilibrium price level will not change; only the equilibrium level of real GDP per year will increase, to Q_2. Conversely, if there is an aggregate demand shock that shifts the aggregate demand curve to AD_3, the equilibrium price level will again remain at P_0, but the equilibrium level of real GDP per year will fall to Q_3.

Under such circumstances, the equilibrium level of real GDP per year is completely *demand-determined*.

The horizontal short-run aggregate supply curve represented in Figure 11-6 is often called the **Keynesian short-run aggregate supply curve.** It is so named because Keynes hypothesized that many prices, especially the price of labor (wages), are "sticky downward." According to Keynes, the existence of unions and of long-term contracts between workers are real-world factors that can explain the downward inflexibility of *nominal* wage rates. Such "stickiness" of wages makes *involuntary* unemployment of labor a distinct possibility. The classical assumption of everlasting full employment no longer holds.

Further, even in situations of excess capacity and large amounts of unemployment, we will not necessarily see the price level falling; rather, all we will see is continuing unemployment and a reduction in the equilibrium level of real GDP per year. Thus general economywide equilibrium can occur and endure even if there is excess capacity. Keynes and his followers argued that capitalism was therefore not necessarily a self-regulating system sustaining full employment. At the time, Keynes was attacking the classical view of the world, which argued that markets would all eventually be in equilibrium—prices and wages would adjust—so that full employment would never be far away.

A pretty good example of a horizontal short-run aggregate supply curve can be seen by examining data from the aftermath of the Great Depression of the 1930s. Look at Figure 11-7 on page 236, where you see real GDP in billions of 1992 dollars on the horizontal axis and the price level index on the vertical axis. From the early days of recovery from the Great Depression to the outbreak of World War II, real GDP increased without much rise in the price level. During this period the economy experienced neither supply

Keynesian short-run aggregate supply curve
The horizontal portion of the aggregate supply curve in which there is unemployment and unused capacity in the economy.

FIGURE 11-7

Real GDP and the Price Level, 1934–1940

In a depressed economy, increased aggregate spending can increase output without raising prices. This is what John Maynard Keynes believed, and the data for the United States's recovery from the Great Depression seem to bear this out. In such circumstances, the level of real output is demand-determined.

constraints nor any dramatic changes in the price level. The most simplified Keynesian model in which prices do not change is essentially an immediate post-Depression model that fits the data very well during this period.

INCOME DETERMINATION USING AGGREGATE DEMAND AND AGGREGATE SUPPLY: FIXED VERSUS CHANGING PRICE LEVELS

The underlying assumption of the simplified Keynesian model is that the relevant range of the short-run aggregate supply schedule *(SRAS)* is horizontal, as depicted in panel (a) of Figure 11-8. There you see that short-run aggregate supply is fixed at price level 120. If

Panel (a)

Panel (b)

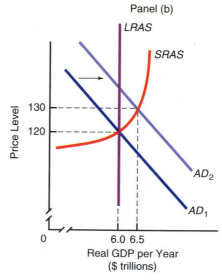

FIGURE 11-8

Income Determination with Fixed vs. Flexible Prices

In panel (a), the price level index is fixed at 120. An increase in aggregate demand from AD_1 to AD_2 moves the equilibrium level of real GDP from $6 trillion per year to $7 trillion per year. In panel (b), *SRAS* is upward-sloping. The same shift in aggregate demand yields an equilibrium level of real GDP of only $6.5 trillion per year and a higher price level index at 130.

aggregate demand is AD_1, the equilibrium level of real GDP is at $6 trillion per year. If aggregate demand increases to AD_2, the equilibrium level of real GDP increases to $7 trillion per year. Compare this situation with the standard upward-sloping short-run aggregate supply curve presented in Chapter 10. In panel (b) of Figure 11-8, $SRAS$ is upward-sloping, with its slope becoming steeper and steeper after it crosses long-run aggregate supply, $LRAS$. Recall that $LRAS$ is the level of real GDP that the economy would produce year in and year out with full information and full adjustment. It is sometimes called the full-employment level of real GDP because, presumably, full employment occurs when there is full information and full adjustment possible in the economy. If aggregate demand is AD_1, the equilibrium level of real GDP in panel (b) is also $6 trillion per year, also at a price level of 120. A similar increase in aggregate demand to AD_2 as occurred in panel (a) produces a different equilibrium, however. Equilibrium real GDP increases to $6.5 trillion per year, which is less than in panel (a) because part of the increase in *nominal* GDP has occurred through an increase in the price level to 130.

EXAMPLE
Keynesian Analysis of the Great Depression

At the beginning of 1929, the American economy was doing quite well, with the unemployment rate hovering around 3 percent. A year later it was almost 9 percent, and by 1933 it had reached an astonishing 25 percent. The real GDP of 1929 was not reached again until 1937, when another business downturn hit the economy. We can use the Keynesian analysis presented in Figure 11-9 to describe what happened. Aggregate demand to start with is AD_{1929}. According to Keynes and his followers, the economy experienced a dramatic reduction in aggregate demand, represented by a shift to AD_{1933}. To prevent massive unemployment, wages and prices would have to have fallen such that a new equilibrium would have been at point A on $LRAS$. Even though many wages and prices did fall, they didn't fall sufficiently. Consequently, a new equilibrium was established at E_2.

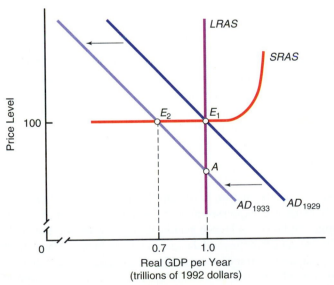

FIGURE 11-9

Keynesian Analysis of the Great Depression
Aggregate demand dropped from AD_{1929} to AD_{1933}. The price level would have had to drop to point A on $LRAS$ in order to avoid unemployment. In reality, it did not, so that the new equilibrium shifted from E_1 to E_2. By 1933, the economy was operating at 30 percent below its potential output.

Real GDP fell from about $1 trillion dollars to $700 billion (expressed in 1992 dollars). By 1933, the economy was operating at 30 percent below its potential output represented by *LRAS*.

FOR CRITICAL ANALYSIS: *If the equilibrium stayed at E_2, what do you expect would eventually happen to LRAS?* ●

CONCEPTS IN BRIEF

- If we assume that we are operating on a horizontal short-run aggregate supply curve, the equilibrium level of real GDP per year is completely demand-determined.
- The horizontal short-run aggregate supply curve has been called the Keynesian short-run aggregate supply curve because Keynes believed that many prices, especially wages, would not be reduced even when aggregate demand decreased.

AGGREGATE DEMAND AND SUPPLY IN AN OPEN ECONOMY

In many of the international examples in the preceding chapters, we had to translate foreign currencies into dollars when the open economy was discussed. We used the exchange rate, or the price of the dollar relative to other currencies. In Chapter 10 you also discovered that the open economy effect was one of the reasons why the aggregate demand curve slopes downward. When the domestic price level rises, Americans want to buy cheaper-priced foreign goods. The opposite occurs when the American domestic price level falls. Currently, the foreign sector of the American economy constitutes over 12 percent of all economic activities.

How a Stronger Dollar Affects Aggregate Supply

Assume that the dollar becomes stronger in international foreign exchange markets. If last week the dollar could buy 4 francs but this week it now buys 5 francs, it has become stronger. To the extent that American companies import raw and partially processed goods from abroad, a stronger dollar can lead to lower input prices. This will lead to a shift outward to the right in the short-run aggregate supply curve as shown in panel (a) of Figure 11-10. In that simplified model, equilibrium GDP would rise and the price level would fall. The result might involve increased employment and lower inflation.

How a Stronger Dollar Affects Aggregate Demand

There is another effect of a stronger dollar that we must consider. Foreigners will find that American goods are now more expensive, expressed in their own currency. After all, a $10 compact disc before the stronger dollar cost a French person 40 francs when the exchange rate was 4 to 1. After the dollar became stronger and the exchange rate increased to 5 to 1, that same $10 compact disc would cost 50 francs. Conversely, Americans will find that the stronger dollar makes imported goods cheaper. The result for Americans is fewer exports

Panel (a)

Panel (b)

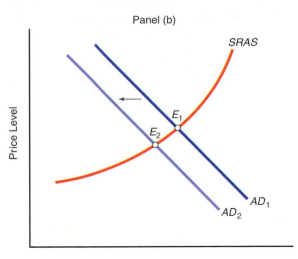

FIGURE 11-10

The Effects of a Stronger Dollar

When the dollar increases in value in the international currency market, lower prices for imported inputs result, causing a shift outward to the right in the short-run aggregate supply schedule from $SRAS_1$ to $SRAS_2$ in panel (a). If nothing else changes, equilibrium shifts from E_1 to E_2 at a lower price level and a higher equilibrium real GDP per year. A stronger dollar can also affect the aggregate demand curve because it will lead to fewer net exports and cause AD_1 to fall to AD_2 in panel (b). Equilibrium would move from E_1 to E_2, a lower price level, and a lower equilibrium real GDP per year.

and more imports, or lower net exports (exports minus imports). If net exports fall, employment in export industries will fall: This is represented in panel (b) of Figure 11-10. After the dollar becomes stronger, the aggregate demand curve shifts inward from AD_1 to AD_2. The result is a tendency for equilibrium real GDP and the price level to fall, and unemployment to rise.

The Net Effect

We have learned, then, that a stronger dollar *simultaneously* leads to an increase in *SRAS* and a decrease in *AD*. Remember from Chapter 4 that in such situations, the result depends on which curve shifts more. If the aggregate demand curve shifts more than the short-run aggregate supply curve, equilibrium real GDP will fall. Conversely, if the aggregate supply curve shifts more than the aggregate demand curve, equilibrium real GDP will rise.

You should be able to redo this entire analysis for a weaker dollar.

ECONOMIC GROWTH IN AN AGGREGATE DEMAND AND SUPPLY FRAMEWORK

Much (not all) of the Keynesian macroeconomic analysis to which you have been introduced in this chapter, and which you will examine in the next chapter, relates to short-run fluctuations in unemployment, inflation, and other macroeconomic variables. Whether one

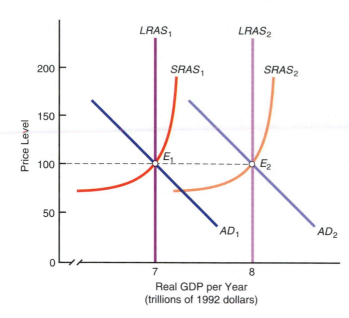

FIGURE 11-11

Economic Growth, Aggregate Demand, and Aggregate Supply
Economic growth can be shown using short-run and long-run aggregate demand and supply curves. Aggregate demand, AD_1, intersects short-run aggregate supply, $SRAS_1$, at E_1, yielding $7 trillion of real GDP per year at a price level of 100. This yearly real GDP is consistent with full employment. The long-run aggregate supply curve is vertical at $7 trillion and is labeled $LRAS_1$. With economic growth, $LRAS_1$ moves outward to $8 trillion per year. Short-run aggregate supply shifts to $SRAS_2$, and aggregate demand increases to AD_2. New equilibrium is at E_2, still at a price level of 100. There is no inflation.

uses some variant of classical macroeconomic analysis or the Keynesian analysis, over time, short-term business fluctuations tend to iron out. We are left with economic growth, which can occur with or without inflation.

Economic Growth Without Inflation

Look at Figure 11-11. We start in equilibrium with AD_1 and $SRAS_1$ intersecting at the long-run aggregate supply curve, $LRAS_1$, at a price level of 100. Real GDP per year is $7 trillion. Economic growth occurs due to labor force expansion, capital investments, and other occurrences. The result is a rightward shift in the long-run aggregate supply curve to $LRAS_2$. As the long-run productive capacity of the nation grows, the economy doesn't stay on its short-run aggregate supply curve, $SRAS$. Rather, $SRAS$ shifts along with shifts in aggregate demand due to population increases and rising per capita income. It is thus possible for us to achieve real GDP of $8 trillion without any increase in the price level. The short-run aggregate supply curve moves outward to $SRAS_2$ and intersects AD_2 at E_2 where the new long-run aggregate supply curve, $LRAS_2$, has moved.

In the world just hypothesized, aggregate demand shifts outward so that at the same price level, 100, it intersects the new short-run aggregate supply curve, $SRAS_2$ at the rate of real GDP that is consistent with more or less full employment (on $LRAS_2$). Firms sell all the output produced at the new level without changing prices. In some situations, however, inflation may accompany growth.

EXAMPLE
The U.S. Record over the Past Few Decades

What has been the United States's experience regarding economic growth and the rate of inflation over the past few decades? Has it resembled Figure 11-11? The answer can be seen in Figure 11-12, which reflects the U.S. experience from 1970 to 1996. In essence, each of the points represents the intersection of aggregate supply and aggregate demand for that year. Since 1970, the price level has clearly risen. So, too, has real GDP.

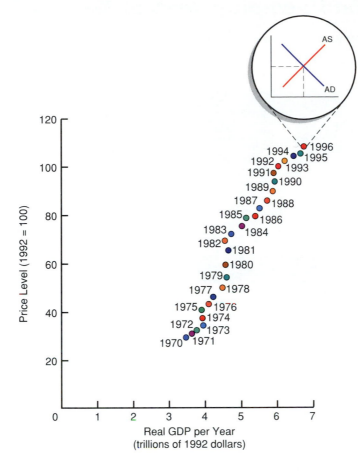

FIGURE 11-12

Economic Growth and Inflation in the United States

This figure shows the points where aggregate demand and aggregate supply have intersected each year from 1970 to the present. The United States has experienced economic growth over this period, but not without inflation.

Sources: Economic Report of the President; Economic Indicators, various issues.

Apparently, the American economy has been unable to experience economic growth without inflation.

FOR CRITICAL ANALYSIS: As an individual, should you care whether the United States has economic growth with or without inflation? Explain your answer. ●

CONCEPTS IN BRIEF

- A change in the international value of the dollar can affect both the *SRAS* and aggregate demand.

- A stronger dollar will reduce the cost of imported inputs, thereby causing the *SRAS* to shift outward to the right, leading to a lower price level and a higher equilibrium real GDP per year, given no change in aggregate demand.

- In contrast, a stronger dollar will lead to lower net exports, causing the aggregate demand curve to shift inward, leading to a lower price level and a lower equilibrium real GDP per year. The net effect depends on which shift is more important. The opposite analysis applies to a weakening dollar in international currency markets.

- It is possible to have economic growth with and without inflation. If the aggregate demand curve shifts outward to the right at the same speed as the aggregate supply curve, there will be no inflation accompanying economic growth.

High European Unemployment, or Keynes Revisited?

Concepts Applied: Employment and unemployment, equilibrium, sticky wages, wait unemployment, unemployment duration, marginal tax rate

The unemployment rate in France and other European countries hovers around 11 percent, compared to less than 6 percent in the United States. One reason for such a high rate of unemployment in the EU is the disincentive to find work, due to social programs that provide generous unemployment benefits.

At the beginning of the 1970s, the U.S. unemployment rate was a little less than 5 percent. The average rate for all of Europe was half that—about 2.4 percent. Since then, unemployment rates in the United States have gone up and down, but the average has remained only a bit less than 6 percent. Moreover, for at least a decade, there has been no evidence that U.S. unemployment is rising significantly. Such is not the case in the European Union (EU), where the average unemployment rate has risen from about 2.4 percent in 1970 to over 11 percent in the 1990s—more than a fourfold increase!

Keynes Revisited

Remember that at the heart of Keynesian macroeconomic analysis is the concept of persistent unemployment in a deep recession or a great depression. This is because wages tend to be sticky downward. Keynes postulated that because of union and other contracts, a decrease in aggregate demand would not lead to a reduction in wages and other prices. Consequently, aggregate demand would be insufficient, and unemployment would result. In Europe today, not only are there union contracts that prevent wages from falling, but there are a host of other impediments to the classical economists' view of a freely functioning employment market.

The Duration of Unemployment

First, one must note that part of the reason Europe's high unemployment rate exists is because over half of the unemployed are out of work for a year or more. In the United States, less than 10 percent of the unemployed have been out of work for more than a year. Remember from Chapter 7 that an increase in the duration of unemployment, with the same absolute number of people being fired or laid off for any given time period, will of necessity increase the rate of unemployment. Thus one of the major reasons that Europe suffers from such high unemployment is that workers take so long to find other jobs.

The Incentive to Work or Not Work

The simple supply and demand diagram for employment shown in Figure 11-3 ignores any incentives for remaining unemployed. Otherwise stated, it ignores any disincentive to return to work once unemployed. In general, the EU countries offer generous unemployment benefits. For example, in France one can receive over 60 percent of previous (gross) pay for several years, no matter how much one was earning. In general, EU countries offer minimum income compensation and other benefits to the unemployed. In certain countries, a formerly low-income-earning individual who becomes unemployed will actually face a marginal tax rate of over 100 percent if he or she goes back to work, because benefits are withdrawn if income is earned. Consequently, the rewards for reentering the labor market are so minimal that they provide little incentive to look for a job.

Employers' Full Cost of Hiring

On the employers' side of the ledger, there are numerous costs associated with hiring a new worker. These include the so-called social charges, which in some countries equal twice the hourly pay of low-income employees. Also, in many EU countries, employers are required to give severance pay if the employer decides to fire a recently hired employee. This means that employers have diminished incentives to hire new workers, even during an economic expansion.

The only way that workers can effectively offer their services at a lower wage rate, thereby complying with the classical economists' view of the labor market, is by agreeing to work off the books. Of course, as we pointed out in Chapter 7, they still are nonetheless counted as unemployed.

Wait Unemployment

Rather than having a flexible labor market, as the classical economists assumed, Europe now has a relatively inflexible labor market. Much of the unemployment is simply wait unemployment, which we defined in Chapter 7 as unemployment due to workers' inability to offer their services at lower than prevailing wage rates. These pre-

vailing wage rates include the additional "perks" and social charges that employers by law must offer every worker in most EU countries, which make the true wage considerably higher than the apparent money wage.

FOR CRITICAL ANALYSIS

1. Why might it be difficult for European politicians to dismantle programs that result in large amounts of wait unemployment?
2. Over the past 20 years, more than 40 million new jobs have been created in the United States, whereas only a few million have been created in the European Union. What might explain this anomaly?

CHAPTER SUMMARY

1. The classical model was developed in the 1770s by such economists as Adam Smith, David Ricardo, John Stuart Mill, and Thomas Malthus. It attempted to explain the determinants of the price level and national income and employment.

2. Say's law holds that supply creates its own demand. A more complete classical model assumes (a) pure competition, (b) wage and price flexibility, (c) self-interest motivation throughout the population, and (d) no money illusion. With the introduction of saving, the classical economists believed, the market economy would still reach full employment of resources because planned saving would be met by planned investment. Saving is the supply of credit, and investment is the demand for credit. The interest rate in the credit market was assumed to be flexible, like all other prices, so equilibrium would always prevail, and therefore planned saving would always equal planned investment.

3. Because the classical model posits a vertical long-run aggregate supply curve, any changes in aggregate demand simply change the equilibrium price level. The equilibrium level of real GDP per year is completely supply-determined.

4. Whenever we are operating on a horizontal short-run aggregate supply curve, the equilibrium level of real GDP is completely demand-determined by the position of the aggregate demand curve. The Keynesian short-run aggregate supply curve is typically given as horizontal because Keynes assumed that wages and

prices would not be reduced even if aggregate demand decreased substantially.

5. If we relax the assumption of a fixed price level, we are then operating on the upward-sloping portion of the short-run aggregate supply curve. Hence an increase in aggregate demand will lead to some increase in the price level. This increase in the price level will have an offsetting effect on equilibrium total planned expenditures because of wealth, interest rate, and foreign goods substitution effects. Under such circumstances, any increase in aggregate demand will lead to both an increase in the price level and an increase in output.

6. A stronger dollar will reduce the cost of imported inputs, thereby causing the *SRAS* to shift outward to the right, leading to a lower price level and a higher equilibrium real GDP per year, given no change in aggregate demand.

7. In contrast, a stronger dollar will lead to lower net exports, causing the aggregate demand curve to shift inward, leading to a lower price level and a lower equilibrium real GDP per year. The net effect depends on which shift is more important. The opposite analysis applies to a weakening dollar in international currency markets.

8. It is possible to have economic growth with or without inflation. If the aggregate demand curve shifts outward to the right at the same speed as the aggregate supply curve, there will be no inflation accompanying economic growth.

DISCUSSION OF PREVIEW QUESTIONS

1. **What are the assumptions of the classical macro model?**
   In the classical model, the following four assumptions are made: (a) the existence of pure competition, (b) complete wage and price flexibility, (c) individuals motivated by self-interest, and (d) individuals not fooled by money illusion.

2. **What determines the rate of interest in the classical model?**
   In the classical model, the interaction between desired investment and desired saving determines the equilibrium rate of interest in the economy. Otherwise stated, the equilibrium rate of interest is determined at the intersection of the desired investment curve and the desired saving curve.

3. **Why do Keynesian economists believe that the short-run aggregate supply curve is horizontal?**
   In the horizontal range of the *SRAS* curve, changes in real GDP (output) occur without changes in the price level. This pure quantity response (no price response) to changes in *AD* reflects Keynes's assumption that during a depression or a very deep recession, businesses have so much excess capacity that *increases* in *AD* will elicit only an increase in output; businesses

that try to increase prices in such a situation discover that they lose sales to competitors. Similarly, a *reduction* in *AD* will lead only to a reduction in output; businesses won't reduce prices. Keynes assumed that in modern economies the existence of unions and contracts to support the unemployed imply that wages are "sticky downward"—wages aren't likely to fall even during periods of significant unemployment. Businesses have a certain control over prices and, confronting wages that are sticky, prefer to reduce output instead of price.

4. **Why is real GDP said to be demand-determined when the short-run aggregate supply curve is horizontal?**
   When the *SRAS* curve is horizontal, real GDP will change only in response to a change in *AD*. If *AD* increases, real GDP rises; if *AD* decreases, real GDP falls. Therefore, real GDP merely responds to changes in *AD*, which is therefore the primary mover in the economy. According to Keynes, businesses are prepared to produce *any* output level; the output level that they do produce is the most profitable one, and that depends on *AD*. This theory says that if you want to predict what real GDP and national employment will be in the future, discover what is happening to *AD* now.

PROBLEMS

(Answers to the odd-numbered problems appear at the back of the book.)

11-1. The desired investment curve intersects the desired saving curve in the economy at an interest rate of 8 percent. The current market rate of interest is 9 percent. Outline what will now take place in the economy so that the saving and investment market is in equilibrium.

11-2. Look at Figure 11-3 on page 232 again. At a wage rate of $12 per hour, 135 million workers are employed. This is called full-employment equilibrium. Does that mean there is no unemployment?

11-3. Show the effects of a decrease in aggregate demand in the classical model.

11-4. On one graph, show economic growth with concomitant increases in the price level.

COMPUTER-ASSISTED INSTRUCTION

The sharp contrast between the classical and Keynesian models is illustrated.

CHAPTER 12

CONSUMPTION, INCOME, AND THE MULTIPLIER

Some people refer to baseball as America's national sport. Not everyone agrees with that assessment; nonetheless, when the baseball players went on strike a few years ago, there were repercussions throughout the entire economy, causing job losses and financial ruin for many people. To comprehend how the interruption of major league baseball could do so much damage to the economy, you need an understanding of the relationship between income, consumption, and the multiplier, the subject matter of this chapter.

PREVIEW QUESTIONS

1. What does the total planned expenditures curve indicate?

2. How do we interpret the 45-degree reference line?

3. What is the concept of the multiplier, how does it work, and what is its main determinant?

4. What might cause shifts in the total planned expenditures curve?

Did **You Know That . . .** personal consumption expenditures in the United States have averaged about two-thirds of gross domestic product for decades? Each year, Americans purchase millions of television sets, millions of pairs of shoes, millions of compact discs, and billions of stress-reducing pills, among other products and services. We are a nation of spenders, and our personal consumption expenditures keep the American economic machine moving day in and day out. As it turns out, John Maynard Keynes focused much of his research on what determines how much you and I decide to spend each year. Remember that aggregate demand consists of consumption expenditures, plus expenditures for investment purposes, what the government spends, and what foreigners spend on domestically produced output. As you will learn in this chapter, Keynes focused on the relationship between how much people earn and their willingness to engage in personal consumption expenditures. In this chapter you will learn about that relationship as well as the influence of investment, government, and the foreign sector on the economy's equilibrium level of real output per year.

SOME SIMPLIFYING ASSUMPTIONS IN A KEYNESIAN MODEL

Continuing in the Keynesian tradition, we will assume that the short-run aggregate supply curve within the relevant range is horizontal. That is to say, we assume that it is similar to Figure 11-6 on page 235, meaning that the equilibrium level of real GDP is demand-determined. That is why Keynes wished to examine the elements of desired aggregate expenditures.

Also, for the time being we will not be concerned with the problem of inflation, because by definition, along the Keynesian short-run aggregate supply curve, inflation is impossible. Finally, given that the price level is assumed to be unchanging, all of the variables with which we will be dealing will be expressed in real terms. After all, with no change in the price level, any change in the magnitude of an economic variable, such as income, will be equivalent to a real change in terms of purchasing power. Hence we will be examining Keynes's income-expenditure model of real GDP determination in a world of inflexible prices.

To simplify the income determination model that follows, a number of assumptions are made:

1. Businesses pay no indirect taxes (for example, sales taxes).
2. Businesses distribute all of their profits to shareholders.
3. There is no depreciation (capital consumption allowance), so gross private domestic investment equals net investment.
4. The economy is closed—that is, there is no foreign trade.

Given all these simplifying assumptions, real disposable income will be equal to real national income minus taxes.[1]

Definitions and Relationships Revisited

You can do only two things with a dollar of income (in the absence of taxes): consume it or save it. If you consume it, it is gone forever. If you save the entire dollar, however, you will

---

[1]Strictly speaking, we are referring here to net taxes—that is, the difference between taxes paid and transfer payments received. If taxes are $1 trillion but individuals receive transfer payments—Social Security, unemployment benefits, and so forth—of $300 billion, net taxes are equal to $700 billion.

be able to consume it (and perhaps more if it earns interest) at some future time. That is the distinction between **consumption** and **saving.** Consumption is the act of using income for the purchase of consumption goods. **Consumption goods** are goods purchased by households for immediate satisfaction. Consumption goods are such things as food, clothing, and movies. By definition, whatever you do not consume you save and can consume at some time in the future.

Stocks and Flows: The Difference Between Saving and Savings.

It is important to distinguish between *saving* and *savings*. *Saving* is an action that occurs at a particular rate—for example, $10 a week or $520 a year. This rate is a flow. It is expressed per unit of time, usually a year. Implicitly, then, when we talk about saving, we talk about a *flow* or rate of saving. *Savings*, by contrast, is a *stock* concept, measured at a certain point or instant in time. Your current *savings* are the result of past *saving*. You may presently have *savings* of $2,000 that are the result of four years' *saving* at a rate of $500 per year. Consumption, being related to saving, is also a flow concept. You consume from after-tax income at a certain rate per week, per month, or per year.

Relating Income to Saving and Consumption.

Obviously, a dollar of take-home income can be either consumed or not consumed. Realizing this, we can see the relationship among saving, consumption, and disposable income:

$$\text{Consumption} + \text{saving} \equiv \text{disposable income}$$

This is called an *accounting identity*. It has to hold true at every moment in time. From it we can derive the definition of saving:

$$\text{Saving} \equiv \text{disposable income} - \text{consumption}$$

Recall that disposable income is what you actually have left to spend after you pay taxes.

Investment

Investment is also a flow concept. *Investment* as used in economics differs from the common use of the term, as we have already pointed out. In common speech, it is often used to describe putting money into the stock market or real estate. In economic analysis, investment is defined as expenditures by firms on new machines and buildings—**capital goods**—that are expected to yield a future stream of income. This we have already called *fixed investment*. We also included changes in business inventories in our definition. This we have already called *inventory investment*.

Consumption
Spending on new goods and services out of a household's current income. Whatever is not consumed is saved. Consumption includes such things as buying food and going to a concert.

Saving
The act of not consuming all of one's current income. Whatever is not consumed out of spendable income is, by definition, saved. *Saving* is an action measured over time (a flow), whereas *savings* are a stock, an accumulation resulting from the act of saving in the past.

Consumption goods
Goods bought by households to use up, such as food, clothing, and movies.

Investment
The spending by businesses on things such as machines and buildings, which can be used to produce goods and services in the future. The investment part of total income is the portion that will be used in the process of producing goods in the future.

Capital goods
Producer durables; nonconsumable goods that firms use to make other goods.

CONCEPTS IN BRIEF

- If we assume that we are operating on a horizontal short-run aggregate supply curve, the equilibrium level of real GDP per year is completely demand determined.

- *Saving* is a flow, something that occurs over time. It equals disposable income minus consumption. *Savings* are a stock. They are the accumulation resulting from saving.

- Investment is also a flow. It includes expenditures on new machines, buildings, and equipment and changes in business inventories.

DETERMINANTS OF PLANNED CONSUMPTION AND PLANNED SAVING

In the classical model, the supply of saving was determined by the rate of interest: The higher the rate of interest, the more people wanted to save and therefore the less people wanted to consume. According to Keynes, the interest rate is not the primary determinant of an individual's saving and consumption decisions.

Keynes argued that saving and consumption decisions depend primarily on an individual's real current income.

The relationship between planned consumption expenditures of households and their current level of real income has been called the **consumption function.** It shows how much all households plan to consume per year at each level of real disposable income per year. Using for the moment only columns 1, 2, and 3 of Table 12-1, we will present a consumption function for a hypothetical household.

We see from Table 12-1 that as real disposable income rises, planned consumption also rises, but by a smaller amount, as Keynes suggested. Planned saving also increases with disposable income. Notice, however, that below an income of $10,000, the planned saving of this hypothetical family is actually negative. The further that income drops below that

Consumption function
The relationship between amount consumed and disposable income. A consumption function tells us how much people plan to consume at various levels of disposable income.

TABLE 12-1
Real Consumption and Saving Schedules: A Hypothetical Case
Column 1 presents real disposable income from zero up to $20,000 per year; column 2 indicates planned consumption per year; column 3 presents planned saving per year. At levels of disposable income below $10,000, planned saving is negative. In column 4, we see the average propensity to consume, which is merely planned consumption divided by disposable income. Column 5 lists average propensity to save, which is planned saving divided by disposable income. Column 6 is the marginal propensity to consume, which shows the proportion of *additional* income that will be consumed. Finally, column 7 shows the proportion of *additional* income that will be saved, or the marginal propensity to save.

Combination	(1) Real Disposable Income per Year (Y_d)	(2) Planned Real Consumption per Year (C)	(3) Planned Real Saving Per Year ($S \equiv Y_d - C$) (1) − (2)	(4) Average Propensity to Consume (APC $\equiv C/Y_d$) (2) ÷ (1)	(5) Average Propensity to Save (APS $\equiv S/Y_d$) (3) ÷ (1)	(6) Marginal Propensity to Consume (MPC $\equiv \Delta C/\Delta Y_d$)	(7) Marginal Propensity to Save (MPS $\equiv \Delta S/\Delta Y_d$)
A	$ 0	$ 2,000	$−2,000	—	—	—	—
B	2,000	3,600	−1,600	1.8	−.8	.8	.2
C	4,000	5,200	−1,200	1.3	−.3	.8	.2
D	6,000	6,800	− 800	1.133	−.133	.8	.2
E	8,000	8,400	− 400	1.05	−.05	.8	.2
F	10,000	10,000	0	1.0	.0	.8	.2
G	12,000	11,600	400	.967	.033	.8	.2
H	14,000	13,200	800	.943	.057	.8	.2
I	16,000	14,800	1,200	.925	.075	.8	.2
J	18,000	16,400	1,600	.911	.089	.8	.2
K	20,000	18,000	2,000	.9	.1	.8	.2

Dissaving
Negative saving; a situation in which spending exceeds income. Dissaving can occur when a household is able to borrow or use up existing owned assets.

==level, the more the family engages in **dissaving,** either by going into debt or by using up some of its existing wealth.==

Graphing the Numbers

When we constructed demand and supply curves in Chapter 3, we merely plotted the points from a table showing price-quantity pairs onto a diagram whose axes were labeled "Price" and "Quantity." We will graph the consumption and saving relationships presented in Table 12-1 in the same manner. In the upper part of Figure 12-1, the vertical axis measures the level of planned real consumption per year, and the horizontal axis measures the level of real disposable income per year. In the lower part of the figure, the horizontal axis is again real disposable income per year, but now the vertical axis is planned real saving per year. All of these are on a dollars-per-year basis, which emphasizes the point that we are measuring flows, not stocks.

As you can see, we have taken income-consumption and income-saving combinations A through K and plotted them. In the upper part of Figure 12-1, the result is called the

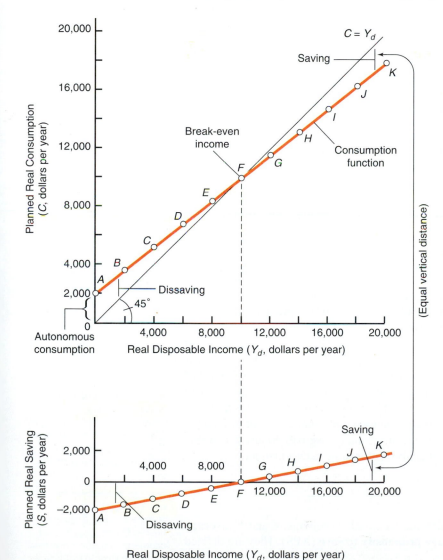

FIGURE 12-1

The Consumption and Saving Functions

If we plot the combinations of real disposable income and planned real consumption from columns 1 and 2 in Table 12-1, we get the consumption function. At every point on the 45-degree line, a vertical line drawn to the income axis is the same distance from the origin as a horizontal line drawn to the consumption axis. Where the consumption function crosses the 45-degree line at F, we know that consumption equals real disposable income and there is zero saving. The vertical distance between the 45-degree line and the consumption function measures the rate of saving or dissaving at any given income level. If we plot the relationship between column 1, real disposable income, and column 3, planned real saving, from Table 12-1, we arrive at the saving function shown in the lower part of this diagram. It is the complement of the consumption function presented above it.

consumption function. In the lower part, the result is called the *saving function*. Mathematically, the saving function is the *complement* of the consumption function because consumption plus saving always equals disposable income. What is not consumed is, by definition, saved. The difference between actual disposable income and the planned level of consumption per year *must* be the planned level of saving per year.

How can we find the rate of saving or dissaving in the upper part of Figure 12-1? We draw a line that is equidistant from both the horizontal and the vertical axes. This line is 45 degrees from either axis and is often called the **45-degree reference line.** At every point on the 45-degree reference line, a vertical line drawn to the income axis is the same distance from the origin as a horizontal line drawn to the consumption axis. Thus at point *F,* where the consumption function intersects the 45-degree line, real disposable income equals planned consumption. Point *F* is sometimes called the *break-even income point* because there is neither positive nor negative saving. This can be seen in the lower part of Figure 12-1 as well. The planned annual rate of saving at a real disposable income level of $10,000 is indeed zero.

Dissaving and Autonomous Consumption

To the left of point *F* in either part of Figure 12-1, this hypothetical family engages in dissaving, either by going into debt or by consuming existing assets, including savings. The amount of saving or dissaving in the upper part of the figure can be found by measuring the vertical distance between the 45-degree line and the consumption function. This simply tells us that if our hypothetical family starts above $10,000 of real disposable income per year and then temporarily finds its real disposable income below $10,000, it will not cut back its consumption by the full amount of the reduction. It will instead go into debt or consume existing assets in some way to compensate for part of the loss.

Now look at the point on the diagram where real disposable income is zero but planned consumption per year is $2,000. This amount of planned consumption, which does not depend at all on actual disposable income, is called **autonomous consumption.** The autonomous consumption of $2,000 is *independent* of the level of disposable income. That means that no matter how low the level of income of our hypothetical family falls, the family will always attempt to consume at least $2,000 per year. (We are, of course, assuming here that the family's real disposable income does not equal zero year in and year out. There is certainly a limit to how long our hypothetical family could finance autonomous consumption without any income.) That $2,000 of yearly consumption is determined by things other than the level of income. We don't need to specify what determines autonomous consumption; we merely state that it exists and that in our example it is $2,000 per year. Just remember that the word *autonomous* means "existing independently." In our model, autonomous consumption exists independently of the hypothetical family's level of real disposable income. (Later we will review some of the non-real-disposable-income determinants of consumption.) There are many possible types of autonomous expenditures. Hypothetically, we can consider that investment is autonomous—independent of income. We can assume that government expenditures are autonomous. We will do just that at various times in our discussions to simplify our analysis of income determination.

Average Propensity to Consume and to Save

Let's now go back to Table 12-1, and this time let's look at columns 4 and 5: **average propensity to consume (APC)** and **average propensity to save (APS).** They are defined as follows:

45-degree reference line
The line along which planned real expenditures equal real national income per year.

Autonomous consumption
The part of consumption that is independent of (does not depend on) the level of disposable income. Changes in autonomous consumption shift the consumption function.

Average propensity to consume (APC)
Consumption divided by disposable income; for any given level of income, the proportion of total disposable income that is consumed.

Average propensity to save (APS)
Saving divided by disposable income; for any given level of income, the proportion of total disposable income that is saved.

$$APC \equiv \frac{consumption}{real\ disposable\ income}$$

$$APS \equiv \frac{saving}{real\ disposable\ income}$$

Notice from column 4 in Table 12-1 that for this hypothetical family, the average propensity to consume decreases as real disposable income increases. This decrease simply means that the fraction of the family's real disposable income going to saving rises as income rises. The same fact can be found in column 5. The average propensity to save (APS), which at first is negative, finally hits zero at an income level of $10,000 and then becomes positive. In this example, the APS reaches a value of .1 at income level $20,000. This means that the household saves 10 percent of a $20,000 income.

It's quite easy for you to figure out your own average propensity to consume or to save. Just divide your total real disposable income for the year into what you consumed and what you saved. The result will be your personal APC and APS, respectively, at your current level of income. This gives the proportions of total income that are consumed and saved.

Marginal Propensity to Consume and to Save

Now we go to the last two columns in Table 12-1: **marginal propensity to consume (MPC)** and **marginal propensity to save (MPS).** We have used the term *marginal* before. It refers to a small incremental or decremental change (represented by Δ in Table 12-1). The marginal propensity to consume, then, is defined as

$$MPC \equiv \frac{change\ in\ consumption}{change\ in\ real\ disposable\ income}$$

The marginal propensity to save is defined similarly as

$$MPS \equiv \frac{change\ in\ saving}{change\ in\ real\ disposable\ income}$$

What do MPC and MPS tell you? They tell you what percentage of a given increase or decrease in income will go toward consumption and saving, respectively. The emphasis here is on the word *change*. The marginal propensity to consume indicates how much you will change your planned rate of consumption if there is a change in your real disposable income. If your marginal propensity to consume is .8, that does not mean that you consume 80 percent of *all* disposable income. The percentage of your real disposable income that you consume is given by the average propensity to consume, or APC, which is not, in Table 12-1, equal to .8. In contrast, an MPC of .8 means that you will consume 80 percent of any *increase* in your disposable income. In general, we assume that the marginal propensity to consume is between zero and one. We assume that individuals increase their planned consumption by more than zero and less than 100 percent of any increase in real disposable income that they receive.

Consider a simple example in which we show the difference between the average propensity to consume and the marginal propensity to consume. Assume that your consumption behavior is exactly the same as our hypothetical family's behavior depicted in Table 12-1. You have an annual real disposable income of $18,000. Your planned consumption rate, then, from column 2 of Table 12-1 is $16,400. So your average propensity to consume is $16,400 \div $18,000 = .911. Now suppose that at the end of the year your boss gives you an after-tax bonus of $2,000. What would you do with that additional

Marginal propensity to consume (MPC)
The ratio of the change in consumption to the change in disposable income. A marginal propensity to consume of .8 tells us that an additional $100 in take-home pay will lead to an additional $80 consumed.

Marginal propensity to save (MPS)
The ratio of the change in saving to the change in disposable income. A marginal propensity to save of .2 indicates that out of an additional $100 in take-home pay, $20 will be saved. Whatever is not saved is consumed. The marginal propensity to save plus the marginal propensity to consume must always equal 1, by definition.

$2,000 in real disposable income? According to the table, you would consume $1,600 of it and save $400. In that case, your *marginal* propensity to consume would be $1,600 ÷ $2,000 = .8, and your marginal propensity to save would be $400 ÷ $2,000 = .2. What would happen to your *average* propensity to consume? To find out, we add $1,600 to $16,400 of planned consumption, which gives us a new consumption rate of $18,000. The average propensity to consume is then $18,000 divided by the new higher salary of $20,000. Your APC drops from .911 to .9. By contrast, your MPC remains in our simplified example .8 all the time. Look at column 6 in Table 12-1. The MPC is .8 at every level of income. (Therefore, the MPS is always equal to .2 at every level of income.) Underlying the constancy of MPC is the assumption that the amount that you are willing to consume out of additional income will remain the same in percentage terms no matter what level of real disposable income is your starting point.

Some Relationships

Consumption plus saving must equal income. Both your total real disposable income and the change in total real disposable income are either consumed or saved. The proportions of either measure must equal 1, or 100 percent. This allows us to make the following statements:

$$APC + APS = 1 \ (= 100 \text{ percent of total income})$$

$$MPC + MPS = 1 \ (= 100 \text{ percent of the } \textit{change} \text{ in income})$$

The average propensities as well as the marginal propensities to consume and save must total 1, or 100 percent. Check the two statements by adding the figures in columns 4 and 5 for each level of real disposable income in Table 12-1. Do the same for columns 6 and 7.

Causes of Shifts in the Consumption Function

A change in any other relevant economic variable besides real disposable income will cause the consumption function to shift. There is a virtually unlimited number of such non-income determinants of the position of the consumption function. When population increases or decreases, for example, the consumption function will shift up or down, respectively. Changes in expectations can also shift the consumption function. If the average household believes that the rate of inflation is going to fall dramatically in the years to come, the current consumption function will probably shift down: Planned consumption would be less at every level of real disposable income than before this change in expectations. Real household **wealth** is also a determinant of the position of the consumption function. An increase in real wealth of the average household will cause the consumption function to shift upward. A decrease in real wealth will cause it to shift downward.

Wealth
The stock of assets owned by a person, household, firm, or nation. For a household, wealth can consist of a house, cars, personal belongings, bank accounts, and cash.

CONCEPTS IN BRIEF

- The consumption function shows the relationship between planned rates of consumption and real disposable income per year. The saving function is the complement of the consumption function because saving plus consumption must equal real disposable income.

- The average propensity to consume (APC) is equal to consumption divided by real disposable income. The average propensity to save (APS) is equal to saving divided by real disposable income.

- The marginal propensity to consume (MPC) is equal to the change in planned consumption divided by the change in real disposable income. The marginal propensity to save (MPS) is equal to the change in planned saving divided by the change in real disposable income.

- Any change in real disposable income will cause the planned rate of consumption to change; this is represented by a movement along the consumption function. Any change in a nonincome determinant of consumption will shift the consumption function.

DETERMINANTS OF INVESTMENT

Investment, you will remember, is defined as expenditures on new buildings and equipment and changes in business inventories. Real gross private domestic investment in the United States has been extremely volatile over the years relative to real consumption. If we were to look at net private domestic investment (investment after depreciation has been deducted), we would see that in the depths of the Great Depression and at the peak of the World War II effort, the figure was negative. In other words, we were eating away at our capital stock—we weren't even maintaining it by completely replacing depreciated equipment.

If we compare real investment expenditures historically with real consumption expenditures, we find that the latter are relatively less variable over time than the former. Why is this so? The answer is that the real investment decisions of businesspeople are based on highly variable, subjective estimates of how the economic future looks. We just discussed the role of expectations in determining the position of the consumption function. Expectations play an even greater role in determining the position of the investment function. This could account for much of the instability of investment over time.

The Planned Investment Function

Consider that at all times, businesses perceive an array of investment opportunities. These investment opportunities have rates of return ranging from zero to very high, with the number (or dollar value) of all such projects inversely related to the rate of return. Because a project is profitable only if its rate of return exceeds the opportunity cost of the investment—the rate of interest—it follows that as the interest rate falls, planned investment spending increases, and vice versa. Even if firms use retained earnings (internal financing) to fund an investment, the higher the market rate of interest, the greater the *opportunity cost* of using those retained earnings. Thus it does not matter in our analysis whether the firm must seek financing from external sources or can obtain such financing by using retained earnings. Just consider that as the interest rate falls, more investment opportunities will be profitable, and planned investment will be higher.

It should be no surprise, therefore, that the investment function is represented as an inverse relationship between the rate of interest and the value of planned investment. A hypothetical investment schedule is given in panel (a) of Figure 12-2 on page 254 and plotted in panel (b). We see from this schedule that if, for example, the rate of interest is 13 percent, the dollar value of planned investment will be $400 billion per year. Notice, by the way, that planned investment is also given on a per-year basis, showing that it represents a flow, not a stock. (The stock counterpart of investment is the stock of capital in the economy measured in dollars at a point in time.)

Panel (a)	
Rate of Interest (percent per year)	Planned Investment per Year ($ trillions)
15	.2
14	.3
13	.4
12	.5
11	.6
10	.7
9	.8
8	.9
7	1.0
6	1.1

FIGURE 12-2

Planned Investment

In the hypothetical planned investment schedule in panel (a), the rate of planned investment is asserted to be inversely related to the rate of interest. If we plot the data pairs from panel (a), we obtain the investment function, *I,* in panel (b). It is negatively sloped.

What Causes the Investment Function to Shift?

Because planned investment is assumed to be a function of the rate of interest, any non-interest-rate variable that changes can have the potential of shifting the investment function. Expectations of businesspeople is one of those variables. If higher future sales are expected, more machines and bigger plants will be planned for the future. More investment will be undertaken because of the expectation of higher future profits. In this case the investment schedule, *I,* would shift outward to the right, meaning that more investment would be desired at all rates of interest. Any change in productive technology can potentially shift the investment function. A positive change in productive technology would stimulate demand for additional capital goods and shift the investment schedule, *I,* outward to the right. Changes in business taxes can also shift the investment schedule. If they increase, we predict a leftward shift in the planned investment function.

CONCEPTS IN BRIEF

- The planned investment schedule shows the relationship between investment and the rate of interest; it slopes downward.

- The non-interest-rate determinants of planned investment are expectations, innovation and technological changes, and business taxes.

- Any change in the non-interest-rate determinants of planned investment will cause the planned investment function to shift so that at each and every rate of interest a different amount of planned investment will be obtained.

CONSUMPTION AS A FUNCTION OF REAL NATIONAL INCOME

We are interested in determining the equilibrium level of real national income per year. But when we examined the consumption function earlier in this chapter, it related planned consumption expenditures to the level of real disposable income per year. We have already shown where adjustments must be made to GDP in order to get real disposable income (see Table 8-2 in Chapter 8). Real disposable income turns out to be less than real national income because net taxes (taxes minus government transfer payments) are usually about 11 to 18 percent of national income. A representative average in the 1990s is about 15 percent, so disposable income, on average, has in recent years been around 85 percent of national income.

If we are willing to assume that real disposable income, Y_d, differs from real national income by an amount T every year, we can relatively easily substitute real national income for real disposable income in the consumption function.

We can now plot any consumption function on a diagram in which the horizontal axis is no longer real disposable income but rather real national income, as in Figure 12-3. Notice that there is an autonomous part of consumption that is so labeled. The difference between this graph and the graphs presented earlier in this chapter is the change in the horizontal axis from real disposable income to real national income per year. For the rest of this chapter, assume that this calculation has been made, and the result is that the MPC out of real national income equals .8, suggesting that 20 percent of changes in real national income are either saved or paid in taxes: In other words, of an additional $100 earned, an additional $80 will be consumed.

The 45-Degree Reference Line

Like the earlier graphs, Figure 12-3 shows a 45-degree reference line. The 45-degree line bisects the quadrant into two equal spaces. Thus along the 45-degree reference line, planned consumption expenditures, C, equal real national income per year, Y. One can see, then, that at any point where the consumption function intersects the 45-degree reference line, planned consumption expenditures will be exactly equal to real national income per year, or $C = Y$. Note that in this graph, because we are looking only at planned consumption on the vertical axis, the 45-degree reference line is where planned consumption, C, is always equal to real

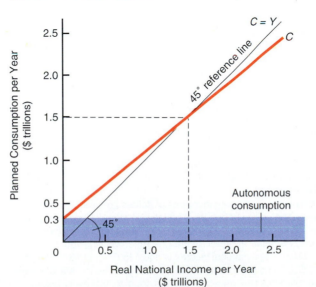

FIGURE 12-3

Consumption as a Function of Real National Income
This consumption function shows the rate of planned expenditures for each level of real national income per year. There is an autonomous component in consumption equal to $0.3 trillion. Along the 45-degree reference line, planned consumption expenditures per year, C, are identical to real national income per year, Y. The consumption curve intersects the 45-degree reference line at a value of $1.5 trillion per year.

national income per year, *Y*. Later, when we add investment, government spending, and net exports to the graph, the 45-degree reference line with respect to *all* planned expenditures will be labeled as such on the vertical axis. In any event, consumption and real national income are equal at $1.5 trillion per year. That is where the consumption curve, *C*, intersects the 45-degree reference line. At that income level, all income is consumed.

Adding the Investment Function

Another component of private aggregate demand is, of course, investment spending, *I*. We have already looked at the planned investment function, which related investment to the rate of interest. You see that as the downward-sloping curve in panel (a) of Figure 12-4. Recall from Figure 11-2 that the equilibrium rate of interest is determined at the intersection of the desired savings schedule, which is labeled *S* and is upward-sloping. The equilibrium rate of interest is 10 percent, and the equilibrium rate of investment is $700 billion per year. The $700 billion of real investment per year is *autonomous* with respect to real national income—that is, it is independent of real national income. In other words, given that we have a determinant investment level of $700 billion at a 10 percent rate of interest, we can treat this level of investment as constant, regardless of the level of national income. This is shown in panel (b) of Figure 12-4. The vertical distance of investment spending is $700 billion. Businesses plan on investing a particular amount—$700 billion per year—and will do so no matter what the level of real national income.

How do we add this amount of investment spending to our consumption function? We simply add a line above the *C* line that we drew in Figure 12-3 that is higher by the vertical distance equal to $700 billion of autonomous investment spending. This is shown by the arrow in panel (c) of Figure 12-4. Our new line, now labeled *C* + *I*, is called the *consumption plus investment line*. In our simple economy without government expenditures and net exports, the *C* + *I* curve represents total planned expenditures as they relate to different levels of real national income per year. Because the 45-degree reference line shows all

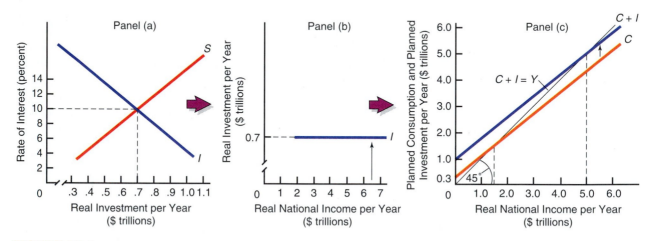

FIGURE 12-4

Combining Consumption and Investment
In panel (a), we show the determination of real investment in trillions of dollars per year. It occurs where the investment schedule intersects the saving schedule at an interest rate of 10 percent and is equal to $700 billion per year. In panel (b), investment is a constant $700 billion per year. When we add this amount to the consumption line, we obtain in panel (c) the *C* + *I* line, which is vertically higher than the *C* line by exactly $700 billion. Real national income is equal to *C* + *I* at $5 trillion per year where total planned expenditure, *C* + *I*, is equal to actual real national income, for this is where the *C* + *I* line intersects the 45-degree reference line, on which *C* + *I* is equal to *Y* at every point.

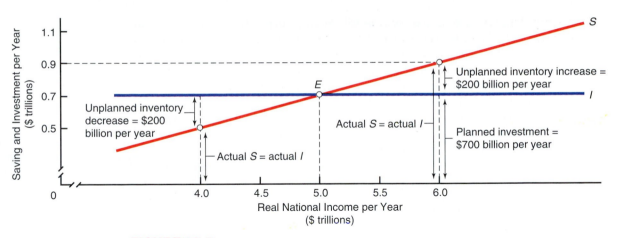

FIGURE 12-5

Planned and Actual Rates of Saving and Investment
Only at the equilibrium level of real national income of $5 trillion per year will planned saving equal actual saving, planned investment equal actual investment, and hence planned saving equal planned investment.

the points where planned expenditures (now $C + I$) equal real national income, we label it $C + I = Y$. Equilibrium Y equals $5 trillion per year. Equilibrium occurs when total planned expenditures equal total planned production (given that any amount of production in this model in the short run can occur without a change in the price level).

SAVING AND INVESTMENT: PLANNED VERSUS ACTUAL

Figure 12-5 shows the planned investment curve as a horizontal line at $700 billion per year. Investment is completely autonomous in this simplified model—it does not depend on the level of income.

The planned saving curve is represented by S. Because in our model whatever is not consumed is, by definition, saved, the planned saving schedule is the complement of the planned consumption schedule, represented by the C line in Figure 12-3. For better exposition, we look at only a small part of the saving and investment schedules—real national incomes between $4 and $6 trillion per year.

Why does equilibrium have to occur at the intersection of the planned saving and planned investment schedules? If we are at E in Figure 12-5, planned saving equals planned investment. All anticipations are validated by reality. There is no tendency for businesses to alter the rate of production or the level of employment because they are neither increasing nor decreasing their inventories in an unplanned way.

If we are producing at a real national income level of $6 trillion instead of $5 trillion, planned investment, as usual, is $700 billion per year, but it is exceeded by planned saving, which is $900 billion per year. This means that consumers will purchase less of total output than businesses had anticipated. Unplanned business inventories will now rise at the rate of $200 billion per year, bringing actual investment into line with actual saving because the $200 billion increase in inventories is included in actual investment. But this rate of output cannot continue for long. Businesses will respond to this unplanned increase in inventories by cutting back production and employment, and we will move toward a lower level of real national income.

Conversely, if the real national income is $4 trillion per year, planned investment continues annually at $700 billion; but at that output rate, planned saving is only $500 billion. This means that households and businesses are purchasing more of real national income than businesses had planned. Businesses will find that they must draw down their inventories below the planned level by $200 billion (business inventories will fall now at the unplanned rate of $200 billion per year), bringing actual investment into equality with actual saving because the $200 billion decline in inventories is included in actual investment (thereby decreasing it). But this situation cannot last forever either. In their attempt to increase inventories to the desired previous level, businesses will increase output and employment, and real national income will rise toward its equilibrium value of $5 trillion per year. Figure 12-5 demonstrates the necessary equality between actual saving and actual investment. Inventories adjust so that saving and investment, after the fact, are *always* equal in this simplified model. (Remember that changes in inventories count as part of investment.)

Every time the saving rate planned by households differs from the investment rate planned by businesses, there will be a shrinkage or an expansion in the circular flow of income and output (introduced in Chapter 8) in the form of unplanned inventory changes. Real national income and employment will change until unplanned inventory changes are again zero—that is, until we have attained the equilibrium level of real national income.

CONCEPTS IN BRIEF

- We assume that the consumption function has an autonomous part that is independent of the level of real national income per year. It is labeled "autonomous consumption."

- For simplicity, we assume that investment is autonomous with respect to real national income and therefore unrelated to the level of real national income per year.

- The equilibrium level of real national income can be found where planned saving equals planned investment.

- Whenever planned saving exceeds planned investment, there will be unplanned inventory accumulation, and national income will fall as producers reduce output. Whenever planned saving is less than planned investment, there will be unplanned inventory depletion, and national income will rise as producers increase output.

THINKING CRITICALLY ABOUT THE MEDIA

Small Businesses and New Jobs

One of the darlings of both politicians and the media is small businesses. According to a common explanation of job creation, small businesses are the source of all new jobs. In recent years, there has been a lot of talk concerning major corporate "restructuring" and the subsequent laying off of thousands of workers. Yet an examination of all of the available data does not support the conclusion that only small firms are hiring. Although it is true that small businesses hire at twice the rate, relative to their total employment, as midsized and big businesses, small businesses also *eliminate* jobs at a far higher rate. In other words, hiring is not the same as job creation because we have to look at the difference between hirings and firings. Indeed, while some big businesses are in the news because of layoffs, others are hiring and are not getting news coverage. For instance, one year, the media reported that Sears and Woolworth had laid off 80,000 workers; that same year, however, Wal-Mart quietly created almost 90,000 new jobs. The moral of the story is that headlines are not always based on the overall economic picture.

KEYNESIAN EQUILIBRIUM WITH GOVERNMENT AND THE FOREIGN SECTOR ADDED

Government

We have to add government spending, *G,* to our macroeconomic model. We assume that the level of resource-using government purchases of goods and services (federal, state, and local), *not* including transfer payments, is determined by the political process. In other words, *G* will be considered autonomous, just like investment (and a certain component of consumption). In the United States, resource-using government expenditures are around 25 percent of real national income. The other side of the coin, of course, is that there are taxes, which are used to pay for much of government spending. We will simplify our model greatly

Lump-sum tax

A tax that does not depend on income or the circumstances of the taxpayer. An example is a $1,000 tax that every family must pay, irrespective of its economic situation.

by assuming that there is a constant **lump-sum tax** of $1 trillion a year to finance $1 trillion of government spending. This lump-sum tax will reduce disposable income and consumption by the same amount. We show this in Table 12-2 (column 2), where we give the numbers for a complete model.

The Foreign Sector

Not a week goes by without a commentary in the media about the problem of our foreign trade deficit. For many years, we have been buying merchandise from foreigners—imports—the value of which exceeds the value of the exports we have been selling to them and service. The difference between exports and imports is *net exports,* which we label X in our graphs. The level of exports depends on international economic conditions, especially in the countries that buy our products. Imports depend on economic conditions here at home. For simplicity, let us assume that exports exceed imports (net exports, X, is positive) and furthermore that the level of net exports is autonomous—independent of national income. Assume a level of X of $100 billion per year. In Table 12-2, net exports is shown in column 8 as $100 billion per year.

Determining the Equilibrium Level of Real National Income per Year

We are now in a position to determine the equilibrium level of real national income per year under the continuing assumptions that the short-run aggregate supply curve is horizontal; that investment, government, and the foreign sector are autonomous; and that planned consumption expenditures are determined by the level of real national income. As can be seen in Table 12-2, total planned expenditures of $6.5 trillion per year equal real national income of $6.5 trillion per year, and this is where we reach equilibrium.

Remember that equilibrium *always* occurs when total planned expenditures equal total production (given that any amount of production in this model in the short run can occur without a change in the price level).

TABLE 12-2

The Determination of Equilibrium Real National Income with Net Exports

Figures are trillions of dollars.

(1) Real National Income	(2) Taxes	(3) Real Disposable Income	(4) Planned Consumption	(5) Planned Saving	(6) Planned Investment	(7) Government Spending	(8) Net Exports (exports − imports)	(9) Total Planned Expenditures (4) + (6) + (7) + (8)	(10) Unplanned Inventory Changes	(11) Direction of Change in Real National Income
2.0	1.0	1.0	1.1	−.1	.7	1.0	.1	2.9	−.9	Increase
2.5	1.0	1.5	1.5	0	.7	1.0	.1	3.3	−.8	Increase
3.0	1.0	2.0	1.9	.1	.7	1.0	.1	3.7	−.7	Increase
4.0	1.0	3.0	2.7	.3	.7	1.0	.1	4.5	−.5	Increase
5.0	1.0	4.0	3.5	.5	.7	1.0	.1	5.3	−.3	Increase
6.0	1.0	5.0	4.3	.7	.7	1.0	.1	6.1	−.1	Increase
6.5	1.0	5.5	4.7	.8	.7	1.0	.1	6.5	0	Neither (equilibrium)
7.0	1.0	6.0	5.1	.9	.7	1.0	.1	6.9	+.1	Decrease
8.0	1.0	7.0	5.9	1.1	.7	1.0	.1	7.7	+.3	Decrease

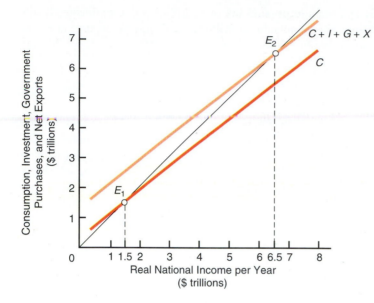

FIGURE 12-6

The Equilibrium Level of Real National Income

The consumption function, with no government and thus no taxes, is shown as C. When we add autonomous investment, government, taxes, and net exports, we obtain $C + I + G + X$. We move from E_1 to E_2. The equilibrium level of real national income is $6.5 trillion per year.

Now look at Figure 12-6, which shows the equilibrium level of real national income. There are two curves, one showing the consumption function, which is the exact duplicate of the one shown in Figure 12-3, and the other being the $C + I + G + X$ curve, which intersects the 45-degree reference line (representing equilibrium) at $6.5 trillion per year. Whenever total planned expenditures differ from real national income, there are unplanned inventory changes. When total planned expenditures are greater than real national income, inventory levels drop in an unplanned manner. To get them back up, firms seek to expand their production, which increases real national income. Real national income rises toward its equilibrium level. Whenever total planned expenditures are less than real national income, the opposite occurs. There are unplanned inventory increases, causing firms to cut back on their production. The result is a drop in real national income toward the equilibrium level.

CONCEPTS IN BRIEF

- When we add autonomous investment, I, and autonomous government spending, G, to the consumption function, we obtain the $C + I + G$ curve, which represents total planned expenditures for a closed economy. In an open economy, we add the foreign sector, which consists of exports minus imports, or net exports, X. Total planned expenditures are thus represented by the $C + I + G + X$ curve.

- The equilibrium level of real national income can be found by locating the intersection of the total planned expenditures curve with the 45-degree reference line. At that level of real national income per year, planned consumption plus planned investment plus government expenditures plus net exports will equal real national income.

- Whenever total planned expenditures exceed real national income, there will be unplanned decreases in inventories; the size of the circular flow of income will increase, and a higher level of equilibrium real national income will prevail. Whenever planned expenditures are less than real national income, there will be unplanned increases in inventories; the size of the circular flow will shrink, and a lower equilibrium level of real national income will prevail.

THE MULTIPLIER

Look again at panel (c) of Figure 12-4. Assume for the moment that the only expenditures included in real national income are consumption expenditures. Where would the equilibrium level of income be in this case? It would be where the consumption function (C) intersects the 45-degree reference line, which is at $1.5 trillion per year. Now we add the autonomous amount of planned investment, or $700 billion, and then determine what the new equilibrium level of income will be. It turns out to be $5 trillion per year. Adding $700 billion per year of investment spending increased the equilibrium level of income by *five* times that amount, or by $3.5 trillion per year.

What is operating here is the multiplier effect of changes in autonomous spending. The multiplier is the number by which a permanent change in autonomous investment or autonomous consumption is multiplied to get the change in the equilibrium level of real national income. Any permanent increases in autonomous investment or in any autonomous component of consumption will cause an even larger increase in real national income. Any permanent decreases in autonomous spending will cause even larger decreases in the equilibrium level of real national income per year. To understand why this multiple expansion (or contraction) in the equilibrium level of real national income occurs, let's look at a simple numerical example.

We'll use the same figures we used for the marginal propensity to consume and to save. MPC will equal .8, or $\frac{4}{5}$, and MPS will equal .2, or $\frac{1}{5}$. Now let's run an experiment and say that businesses decide to increase planned investment permanently by $100 billion a year. We see in Table 12-3 that during what we'll call the first round in column 1, investment is

Multiplier
The ratio of the change in the equilibrium level of real national income to the change in autonomous expenditures; the number by which a change in autonomous investment or autonomous consumption, for example, is multiplied to get the change in the equilibrium level of real national income.

TABLE 12-3

The Multiplier Process
We trace the effects of a permanent $100 billion increase in autonomous investment spending on the equilibrium level of real national income. If we assume a marginal propensity to consume of .8, such an increase will eventually elicit a $500 billion increase in the equilibrium level of real national income per year.

	Assumption: MPC = .8, or $\frac{4}{5}$		
(1) Round	(2) Annual Increase in Real National Income ($ billions per year)	(3) Annual Increase in Planned Consumption ($ billions per year)	(4) Annual Increase in Planned Saving ($ billions per year)
1 ($100 billion per year increase in *I*)	100.00	80.000	20.000
2	80.00	64.000	16.000
3	64.00	51.200	12.800
4	51.20	40.960	10.240
5	40.96	32.768	8.192
.	.	.	.
All later rounds	163.84	131.072	32.768
Totals (*C + I + G*)	500.00	400.000	100.000

increased by $100 billion; this also means an increase in real national income of $100 billion, because the spending by one group represents income for another, shown in column 2. Column 3 gives the resultant increase in consumption by households that received this additional $100 billion in real income. This is found by multiplying the MPC by the increase in real income. Because the MPC equals .8, consumption expenditures during the first round will increase by $80 billion.

But that's not the end of the story. This additional household consumption is also spending, and it will provide $80 billion of additional real income for other individuals. Thus during the second round, we see an increase in real income of $80 billion. Now, out of this increased real income, what will be the resultant increase in consumption expenditures? It will be .8 times $80 billion, or $64 billion. We continue these induced expenditure rounds *ad infinitum* and find that because of an initial increase in autonomous investment expenditures of $100 billion, the equilibrium level of real national income has increased by $500 billion. A permanent $100 billion increase in autonomous investment spending has induced an additional $400 billion increase in consumption spending, for a total increase in real national income of $500 billion. In other words, the equilibrium level of real national income has changed by an amount equal to five times the change in investment.

The Multiplier Formula

It turns out that the autonomous spending multiplier is equal to the reciprocal of the marginal propensity to save. In our example, the MPC was $\frac{4}{5}$; therefore, because MPC + MPS = 1, the MPS was equal to $\frac{1}{5}$. The reciprocal is 5. That was our multiplier. A $100 billion increase in planned investment led to a $500 billion increase in the equilibrium level of real income. Our multiplier will always be the following:

$$\text{Multiplier} \equiv \frac{1}{1 - \text{MPC}} \equiv \frac{1}{\text{MPS}}$$

You can always figure out the multiplier if you know either the MPC or the MPS. Let's take some examples. If MPS $= \frac{1}{4}$,

$$\text{Multiplier} = \frac{1}{\frac{1}{4}} = 4$$

Repeating again that MPC + MPS = 1, then MPS = 1 − MPC. Hence we can always figure out the multiplier if we are given the marginal propensity to consume. In this example, if the marginal propensity to consume were given as $\frac{3}{4}$,

$$\text{Multiplier} = \frac{1}{1 - \frac{3}{4}} = \frac{1}{\frac{1}{4}} = 4$$

By taking a few numerical examples, you can demonstrate to yourself an important property of the multiplier:

The smaller the marginal propensity to save, the larger the multiplier.

Otherwise stated:

The larger the marginal propensity to consume, the larger the multiplier.

Demonstrate this to yourself by computing the multiplier when the marginal propensities to save equal $\frac{3}{4}$, $\frac{1}{2}$, and $\frac{1}{4}$. What happens to the multiplier as the MPS gets smaller?

When you have the multiplier, the following formula will then give you the change in the equilibrium level of real national income due to a permanent change in autonomous spending:

Multiplier $\times$ change in autonomous spending =
change in equilibrium level of real national income

The multiplier, as we have mentioned, works for a permanent increase or permanent decrease in autonomous spending. In our earlier example, if the autonomous component of consumption had fallen by $100 billion, the reduction in the equilibrium level of real national income per year would have been $500 billion per year.

Significance of the Multiplier

Depending on the size of the multiplier, it is possible that a relatively small change in planned investment or autonomous consumption can trigger a much larger change in the equilibrium level of real national income per year. In essence, the multiplier magnifies the fluctuations in the equilibrium level of real national income initiated by changes in autonomous spending.

As was just stated, the larger the marginal propensity to consume, the larger the multiplier. If the marginal propensity to consume is $\frac{1}{2}$, the multiplier is 2. In that case, a $1 billion decrease in (autonomous) investment will elicit a $2 billion decrease in the equilibrium level of real national income per year. Conversely, if the marginal propensity to consume is $\frac{9}{10}$, the multiplier will be 10. That same $1 billion decrease in planned investment expenditures with a multiplier of 10 will lead to a $10 billion decrease in the equilibrium level of real national income per year.

EXAMPLE
Changes in Investment and the Great Depression

Changes in autonomous spending lead to shifts in the total expenditures $(C + I + G + X)$ curve and, as you have seen, cause a multiplier effect on the equilibrium level of real GDP per year. A classic example apparently occurred during the Great Depression. Indeed, some economists believe that it was an autonomous downward shift (collapse) in the investment function that provoked the Great Depression. Look at panel (a) of Figure 12-7 on page 264. There you see the net investment in the United States from 1929 to 1941 (expressed in 1992 dollars). Clearly, during business contractions, decision makers in the business world can and do decide to postpone long-range investment plans for buildings and equipment. This causes the business recovery to be weak unless those business plans are revised. If you examine real GDP in panel (b) of Figure 12-7, you see that the contraction that started in 1929 reached its trough in 1933. The expansion was relatively strong for the following four years, and then there was another contraction from 1937 to 1938. Some researchers argue that even though the 1937–1938 contraction was more severe than the initial one that started in 1929, it was short-lived because long-range investment plans were revised upward by the end of 1938.

FOR CRITICAL ANALYSIS: *Relatively speaking, how healthy was the national economy in 1941? [Hint: Look at panel (b) of Figure 12-7.]* ●

Panel (a)	
Year	Net Private Domestic Investment (billions of 1992 dollars)
1929	85.96
1930	24.48
1931	−26.89
1932	−83.34
1933	−80.20
1934	−43.51
1935	− 6.13
1936	18.39
1937	54.20
1938	− 9.54
1939	24.27
1940	66.89
1941	107.71

FIGURE 12-7

Net Private Domestic Investment and Real GDP During the Great Depression

In panel (a), you see how net private investment expressed in billions of 1992 dollars became negative starting in 1931 and stayed negative for several years. It became positive in 1936 and 1937, only to become negative again in 1938. Look at panel (b). There you see how changes in GDP seem to mirror changes in net private domestic investment.

Source: U.S. Bureau of the Census.

THE MULTIPLIER EFFECT WHEN THE PRICE LEVEL CAN CHANGE

Clearly, the multiplier effect on the equilibrium overall level of *real* national income will not be as great if part of the increase in *nominal* national income occurs because of increases in the price level. We show this in Figure 12-8. The intersection of AD_1 and *SRAS* is at a price level of 120 with equilibrium real national income of $5 trillion per year. An increase in autonomous spending shifts the aggregate demand curve outward to the right to AD_2. If price level remained at 120, the short-run equilibrium level of real GDP would increase to $5.5 trillion per year because, for the $100 billion increase in autonomous spending, the multiplier would be 5, as it was in Table 12-3. But the price level does not stay fixed because ordinarily *SRAS* is positively sloped. In this diagram, the new short-run equilibrium level of real national income is hypothetically $5.3 trillion of real national income per year. Instead of the multiplier being 5, the multiplier with respect to the equilibrium changes in the output of real goods and services—real national income—is only 3. The multiplier is smaller because part of the additional income is used to pay higher prices; not all is spent on increased output, as is the case when the price level is fixed.

If the economy is at an equilibrium level of real national income that is greater than *LRAS*, the implications for the multiplier are even more severe. Look again at Figure 12-8. The *SRAS* curve starts to slope upward more dramatically after $5 trillion of real national income per year. Therefore, any increase in aggregate demand will lead to a proportionally greater increase in the price level and a smaller increase in the equilibrium level of real national income per year. The multiplier effect of any increase in autonomous spending will be relatively small because most of the changes will be in the price level. Moreover,

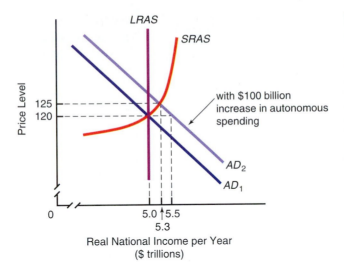

Multiplier Effect on Equilibrium of Real National Income
A $100 billion increase in autonomous spending (investment, government, or net exports), which moves AD_1 to AD_2, will yield a full multiplier effect only if prices are constant. If the price index increases from 120 to 125, the multiplier effect is less, and the equilibrium level of real national income goes up only to, say, $5.3 trillion per year instead of $5.5 trillion per year.

any increase in the short-run equilibrium level of real national income will tend to be temporary because the economy is temporarily above *LRAS*—the strain on its productive capacity will raise prices.

THE RELATIONSHIP BETWEEN AGGREGATE DEMAND AND THE *C + I + G + X* CURVE

There is clearly a relationship between the aggregate demand curves that you studied in Chapters 10 and 11 and the *C + I + G + X* curve developed in this chapter. After all, aggregate demand consists of consumption, investment, and government purchases, plus the foreign sector of our economy. There is a major difference, however, between the aggregate demand curve, *AD,* and the *C + I + G + X* curve: The latter is drawn with the price level held constant, whereas the former is drawn, by definition, with the price level changing. In other words, the *C + I + G + X* curve shown in Figure 12-6 on page 260 is drawn with the price level fixed. To derive the aggregate demand curve, we must now allow the price level to change. Look at the upper part of Figure 12-9 on page 266. Here we show the *C + I + G + X* curve at a price level equal to 100 and equilibrium at $8 trillion of income per year. This gives us point *A* in the lower graph, for it shows what real income would be at a price level of 100.

Now let's assume that in the upper graph, the price level doubles to 200. What are the effects?

1. A higher price level can decrease the purchasing power of any cash that people hold (the real-balance effect). This is a decrease in real wealth, and it causes consumption expenditures, *C*, to fall, thereby putting downward pressure on the *C + I + G + X* curve.
2. Because individuals attempt to borrow more to replenish their real cash balances, interest rates will rise, which will make it more costly for people to buy houses and cars (the interest rate effect). Higher interest rates make it more costly, for example, to install new equipment and to erect new buildings. Therefore, the rise in the price level indirectly causes a reduction in the quantity of aggregate goods and services demanded.
3. In an open economy, our higher price level causes the foreign demand for our goods to fall (the open economy effect). Simultaneously, it increases our demand for others' goods. If the foreign exchange price of the dollar stays constant for a while, there will

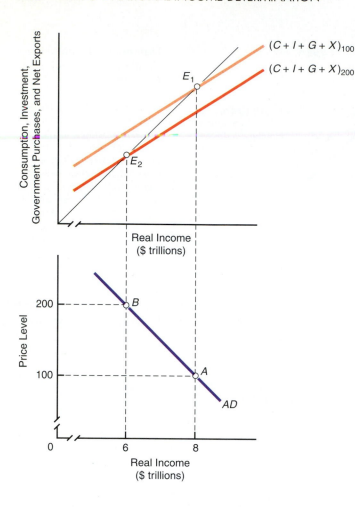

FIGURE 12-9

The Relationship Between *AD* and the *C + I + G + X* curve
In the upper graph, the *C + I + G + X* curve at a price level equal to 100 intersects the 45-degree reference line at E_1, or $8 trillion of real income per year. That gives us point *A* (price level = 100; real income = $8 trillion) in the lower graph. When the price level increases to 200, the *C + I + G + X* curve shifts downward, and the new equilibrium level of real income is at E_2 at $6 trillion per year. This gives us point *B* in the lower graph. Connecting points *A* and *B*, we obtain the aggregate demand curve.

be an increase in imports and a decrease in exports, thereby reducing the size of *X*, again putting downward pressure on the *C + I + G + X* curve.

The result is that a new *C + I + G + X* curve at a price level equal to 200 generates an equilibrium at E_2 at $6 trillion of real income per year. This gives us point *B* in the lower part of Figure 12-9. When we connect points *A* and *B*, we obtain the aggregate demand curve, *AD*.

CONCEPTS IN BRIEF

- Any change in autonomous spending shifts the expenditure curve and causes a multiplier effect on the equilibrium level of real national income per year.
- The multiplier is equal to the reciprocal of the marginal propensity to save.
- The smaller the marginal propensity to save, the larger the multiplier. Otherwise stated, the larger the marginal propensity to consume, the larger the multiplier.
- The *C + I + G + X* curve is drawn with the price level held constant, whereas the *AD* curve allows the price level to change. Each different price level generates a new *C + I + G + X* curve.

Can Professional Baseball Have a Multiplier Effect?

Concepts Applied: Consumption, multiplier, equilibrium level of real GDP

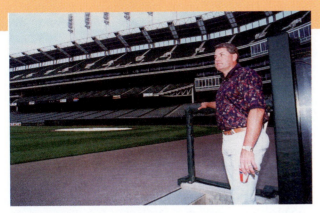

Baseball fans, owners, and players were not the only people who suffered during the 1994 strike. The economy also felt its impact—baseball card sales, hot dog and souvenir vendors, and hotels lost millions of dollars in revenues.

When the major league baseball players went on strike in 1994, they were repeating a ploy they had used 13 years earlier. In June 1981, the players declared a strike that went on for 50 days. About a month later, the U.S. economy went into a deep recession, sending the unemployment rate skyrocketing to around 10 percent 18 months later. Does that mean that baseball can actually affect the equilibrium level of real GDP? Certainly not as much as the apparent correlation between the 1981 strike and the subsequent recession would imply. Nonetheless, the even longer 1994 strike did have an impact on certain segments of the economy.

A Reduction in Spending

Sales of baseball cards, which normally represent about $1 billion of the almost $2 billion sports trading card industry, suffered dramatically due to the strike. Baseball fans canceled tens of thousands of stays at various hotels around the country, costing innkeepers billions of dollars. Thousands of beer, hot dog, and souvenir vendors lost tens of millions of dollars in sales. The TV networks lost out on millions of dollars of advertising revenues.

Owners and Players Lost Income, Too

The strike wiped out the season. Team owners lost a total of $442 million in revenues. Of course, the players lost income during the strike because they were not paid. The total amount of salaries given up was estimated at almost $250 million. Many players and owners canceled commitments to buy cars, houses, and other major purchases.

Keynesian Analysis and the Multiplier

One could imagine a multiplier effect of the baseball strike, given all of the statistics just mentioned. After all, players who lost $250 million in salaries and team owners who lost $442 million in revenues would certainly end up reducing their consumption. That means that the people who would have received income from that consumption would also have to decrease their consumption, and so on.

A Classical View

The classical economists (if they were still alive) would predict that the shrinkage of the professional baseball industry during the strike would simply cause individuals to earn income elsewhere and spend elsewhere. Indeed, there is some evidence that professional *football* team owners' revenues increased substantially during the baseball strike. Also, individuals who might have attended a baseball game certainly spent that income elsewhere, such as going to the movies, going to see other professional sports games, or buying interactive video games. Ultimately, the issue is how long it took businesses and individuals to reorient themselves because of the changes inflicted by the baseball strike. On a national level, the data on unemployment and real GDP didn't show a significant effect of the baseball strike.

FOR CRITICAL ANALYSIS

1. "There is a real economic impact for the owners, the players, and the people who work for the clubs or around the ball park." This quote is from the chief economist of the Federal National Mortgage Association. Is this statement relevant for the overall economy? Why or why not?
2. What percentage of the $6.5 trillion economy that existed during the baseball strike do you think professional baseball accounts for?

CHAPTER SUMMARY

1. If we assume that there are large amounts of excess capacity and labor unemployment, we can use the horizontal portion of the short-run aggregate supply curve. Therefore, prices are assumed to be constant, and nominal values are equivalent to real values.

2. A consumption function, in its simplest form, shows that current real consumption is directly related to current real disposable income. The complement of a consumption function is a saving function. A saving function shows the relationship between current real saving and current real disposable income.

3. The marginal propensity to consume shows how much additional income is devoted to consumption. The marginal propensity to save is the difference between 1 and the marginal propensity to consume. Otherwise stated, the marginal propensity to save plus the marginal propensity to consume must equal 1.

4. We must be careful to distinguish between average and marginal propensities. The average propensity to consume is the amount of total real consumption divided by total real disposable income. The average propensity to save is the total amount of real saving divided by total real disposable income. The marginal propensities relate to changes in consumption and saving resulting from changes in income.

5. Some nonincome determinants of planned consumption are wealth, expectations, and population.

6. Investment is made by the business sector of the economy. Investment is the spending by businesses on such things as new machines and buildings that can be used later in the production of goods and services. Investment is the use of resources to provide for future production. There are numerous determinants of investment, including the rate of interest, changes in expectations, innovation and technology, and business taxes.

7. When we add the consumption function, autonomous investment, autonomous government spending, and the autonomous net exports function, we obtain the $C + I + G + X$ curve, which gives us total planned expenditures per year. The equilibrium level of real national income occurs where the $C + I + G + X$ curve intersects the 45-degree reference line, or where total planned expenditures exactly equal real national income (total production).

8. When total planned expenditures exceed real national income, inventories will be drawn down more rapidly than planned. As a result, firms will expand production and, in the process, hire more workers, thus leading to an increase in output and employment. The opposite occurs when total planned expenditures are less than real national income.

9. Planned saving and planned investment must be equal at the equilibrium rate of real national income (ignoring government and foreign transactions). Whenever the actual level of real national income exceeds the equilibrium level, an unplanned inventory increase will trigger production cuts and layoffs. Whenever actual real national income is less than the equilibrium level of real national income, an unplanned inventory decrease will cause increased production and employment.

10. A key aspect of simplified Keynesian analysis is that a change in investment will result in a multiple change in equilibrium income. The size of the multiplier effect of a change in autonomous investment is positively related to the marginal propensity to consume. The higher the marginal propensity to consume, the greater the autonomous investment multiplier. We find the autonomous investment multiplier by first finding the marginal propensity to save (1 minus the marginal propensity to consume), expressed as a fraction, and taking the inverse of that fraction. A marginal propensity to consume of .8 means that the marginal propensity to save is .2 or $\frac{1}{5}$. The inverse of $\frac{1}{5}$ is 5; thus the investment multiplier is 5.

DISCUSSION OF PREVIEW QUESTIONS

1. What does the total planned expenditures curve indicate?
The total planned expenditures curve indicates what the community intends to spend at every level of real national income. In a closed (omitting international transactions), private (omitting government transactions) economy, the total planned expenditures curve equals the value of consumption expenditures plus

the value of investment expenditures at every level of real national income.

2. How do we interpret the 45-degree reference line?
Because the 45-degree reference line bisects the total planned expenditures/real national income quadrant, total planned expenditures *exactly* equal real national income at all points on this line. Hence equilibrium is possible at any point on the 45-degree reference line.

3. What is the concept of the multiplier, how does it work, and what is its main determinant?
The multiplier concept says, simply, that a $1 shift in the total planned expenditures curve will cause the equilibrium level of national income to change by more than $1. In particular, a $1 increase (shift upward) in the total planned expenditures curve will cause the equilibrium level of national income to rise by more than $1; a $1 decrease (shift downward) in the total planned expenditures curve will cause the equilibrium level of national income to fall by more than $1. In a closed, private economy, changes (shifts) in the total planned expenditures curve are caused by changes (shifts) in autonomous consumption and autonomous investment.

Let's take an example. Suppose that we start from an equilibrium position and then autonomous net investment rises by $1 due to an increase in the output and sale of one machine priced at $1. The people who produced this machine receive an extra $1 in income (above last year's income). Thus income already rises by $1 in the first round. The people who produced the machine will spend some of the increase in their income and save some of it. Because one person's expenditure is another's income, income will rise again.

Thus if the MPC is $\frac{3}{4}$, the group that produced the machine (and received a $1 increase in income) will spend 75 cents on goods and services and will save 25 cents. The 75 cents spent becomes income for the people who produced the 75 cents' worth of consumer goods. Note that after two rounds, national income has already increased by $1.75 ($1 + $.75); we already have a multiplier effect. Moreover, there is no reason why this process should stop here; the people who just received an increase in income of 75 cents will spend some and save some. The amount they spend becomes income for others. Thus the multiplier effect exists because increases in income lead to increases in consumption expenditures, which in turn lead to further income increases. Because one person's expenditure is another's income, it follows that the higher the MPC, the more the equilibrium level of income will change for given changes in autonomous expenditures.

4. What might cause shifts in the total planned expenditures curve?
In our model, total planned expenditures equal consumption *(C)*, investment *(I)*, government purchases of goods and services *(G)*, and net exports *(X)*. For simplicity, we have made the last three components of total planned expenditures autonomous—that is, independent of the level of real disposable income. Consumption also has an autonomous component. Therefore, any change in the nonincome determinants of consumption—for example, changes in expectations—will shift the $C + I + G + X$ curve. Furthermore, because *I, G,* and *X* are all considered autonomous, any change in those functions will also shift the $C + I + G + X$ curve.

PROBLEMS

(Answers to the odd-numbered problems appear at the back of the book.)

12-1. Complete the accompanying table.
   a. Plot the consumption and saving schedules on graph paper.
   b. Determine the marginal propensity to consume and the marginal propensity to save.
   c. Determine the average propensity to consume and the average propensity to save for each level of income.

Disposable Income	Consumption	Saving
$ 500	$510	$_____
600	600	_____
700	690	_____
800	780	_____
900	870	_____
1,000	960	_____

Real National Income	Consumption Expenditures	Saving	Investment	APC	APS	MPC	MPS
$1,000	$1,100	$ ~100	$100	_____	_____	_____	_____
2,000	2,000	_____		_____	_____	_____	_____
3,000		_____		_____	_____	_____	_____
4,000		_____		_____	_____	_____	_____
5,000		_____		_____	_____	_____	_____
6,000		_____		_____	_____	_____	_____

12-2. Make a list of determinants, other than income, that might affect your personal MPC.

12-3. List each of the following under the heading "Stock" or "Flow."

    a. The Chens have $100 of savings in the bank.

    b. Smith earns $200 per week.

    c. General Electric owns 2,000 autos.

    d. Inventories rise at 400 units per year.

    e. Lopez consumes $80 per week out of income.

    f. The equilibrium quantity is 1,000 per day.

    g. The corporation spends $1 billion per year on investments.

12-4. The rate of return on an investment on new machinery is 9 percent.

    a. If the market interest rate is 9.5 percent, will the investment be carried out?

    b. If the interest rate is 8 percent, will the machinery be purchased?

    c. If the interest rate is 9 percent, will the machinery be purchased?

12-5. The data in the table above apply to a hypothetical economy. Assume that the marginal propensity to consume is constant at all levels of income. Further assume that investment is autonomous.

    a. Draw a graph of the consumption function. Then add the investment function, giving you $C + I$.

    b. Right under the first graph, draw in the saving and investment curves. Does the $C + I$ curve intersect the 45-degree line in the upper graph at the same level of real national income as where saving equals investment in the lower graph? (If not, redraw your graphs.)

    c. What is the multiplier effect from the inclusion of investment?

    d. What is the numerical value of the multiplier?

    e. What is the equilibrium level of real national income and output without investment? With investment?

    f. What will happen to income if autonomous investment increases by $100?

    g. What will the equilibrium level of real national income be if autonomous consumption increases by $100?

12-6. Assume a closed, private economy.

    a. If the MPC = 0, what is the multiplier?

    b. What is the multiplier if the MPC = $\frac{1}{2}$? If the MPC = $\frac{3}{4}$? If the MPC = $\frac{9}{10}$? If the MPC = 1?

    c. What happens to the multiplier as the MPC rises?

    d. In what range does the multiplier fall?

12-7. Calculate the multiplier for the following cases.

    a. MPC = .9 $\frac{9}{10}$

    b. MPS = .3

    c. MPS = .15

    d. $C = \$100 + .65Y$

COMPUTER-ASSISTED INSTRUCTION

Consumption spending is the single most important component of desired aggregate demand. This computer session examines the determinants of consumption spending and saving, as well as the link between the marginal and average propensities to consume. In addition, a blend of numerical and graphical exercises is used to examine the basics of income determination, emphasizing the central role of the multiplier.

Complete problem and answer appear on disk.

A PPENDIX B

THE KEYNESIAN CROSS AND THE MULTIPLIER

We can see the multiplier effect more clearly if we look at Figure B-1, in which we see only a small section of the graphs that we used in Chapter 12. We start with an equilibrium level of real national income of $6.5 trillion per year. This equilibrium occurs with total planned expenditures represented by $C + I + G + X$. The $C + I + G + X$ curve intersects the 45-degree reference line at $6.5 trillion per year. Now we increase investment, I, by $100 billion. This increase in investment shifts the entire $C + I + G + X$ curve vertically to $C + I' + G + X$. The vertical shift represents that $100 billion increase in autonomous investment. With the higher level of planned expenditures per year, we are no longer in equilibrium at E. Inventories are falling. Production will increase. Eventually, planned production will catch up with total planned expenditures. The new equilibrium level of real national income is established at E' at the intersection of the new $C + I' + G + X$ curve and the 45-degree reference line, along which $C + I + G + X = Y$ (total planned expenditures equal real national income). The new equilibrium level of real national income is $7 trillion per year. Thus the increase in equilibrium real national income is equal to five times the permanent increase in planned investment spending.

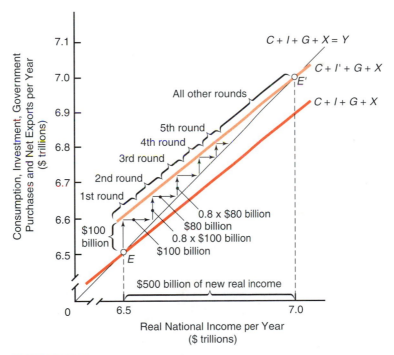

FIGURE B-1

Graphing the Multiplier
We can translate Table 12-3 on page 261 into graphic form by looking at each successive round of additional spending induced by an autonomous increase in planned investment of $100 billion. The total planned expenditures curve shifts from $C + I + G + X$, with its associated equilibrium level of real national income of $6.5 trillion, to a new curve labeled $C + I' + G + X$. The new equilibrium level of real national income is $7 trillion. Equilibrium is again established.

PART 4

FISCAL POLICY AND DEFICIT SPENDING

13

FISCAL POLICY

At certain times during the past few years, the economy has experienced a slowdown, and the same thing will surely occur again in the future. If that economic downturn coincides with the campaign period for a presidential election, you can be sure that every politician will have an opinion on what should be done to get the country moving again. If the past is any predictor of the future, such political references will invariably lead to discussions about stimulating the national economy by having the federal government either increase spending or decrease taxes (or both). But are such changes in government policy possible within the confines of the way the U.S. government actually works? To understand the importance of this question and its answer, you need to study what is generally called fiscal policy.

PREVIEW QUESTIONS

1. What is fiscal policy?

2. What is automatic fiscal policy, and how does it lend stability to an economy?

3. How does the crowding-out effect offset expansionary fiscal policy?

4. What types of time lags exist between the need for fiscal stimulus and the time when such stimulus actually affects the national economy?

Did You Know That ... the first type of income tax was probably established in the 1200s and 1300s during times of war in the Italian city-states? America's first income tax, enacted in 1861 to help pay for the Civil War, was 3 percent on incomes over $800 a year. The following year it was raised to 5 percent on incomes over $10,000 a year. It was not until the Sixteenth Amendment to the Constitution was ratified in 1913 that most Americans came to know of the federal income tax, and even then very few had to pay it. Today, federal income taxes are taken for granted. More important for this chapter, the federal tax system is now viewed as being capable of affecting the equilibrium level of real GDP. On the spending side of the budget, changes in the federal government's expenditures are also viewed as potentially capable of changing the equilibrium level of real GDP.

FISCAL POLICY

Deliberate, discretionary changes in government expenditures and/or taxes in order to achieve certain national economic goals is the realm of **fiscal policy.** Some national goals are high employment (low unemployment), price stability, economic growth, and improvement in the nation's international payments balance. Fiscal policy can be thought of as a deliberate attempt to cause the economy to move to full employment and price stability more quickly than it otherwise might.

Fiscal policy
The discretionary changing of government expenditures and/or taxes in order to achieve national economic goals, such as high employment with price stability.

Fiscal policy has typically been associated with the economic theories of John Maynard Keynes and what is now called *traditional* Keynesian analysis. Recall from Chapter 11 that Keynes's explanation of the Great Depression was that there was insufficient aggregate demand. Because he believed that wages and prices were "sticky downward," he argued that the classical economists' view of the economy automatically moving toward full employment was inaccurate. To Keynes and his followers, government had to step in to increase aggregate demand. In other words, expansionary fiscal policy initiated by the federal government was the way to ward off recessions and depressions.

Traditional Keynesian economics dominated academic and government policymaking debates (and often actions) in the 1960s and 1970s. Perhaps the best-known policy action based on traditional Keynesian theory was the Kennedy-Johnson tax cut of 1964. When John Kennedy took office in 1961 with the claim that he wanted to "get the country moving again," his advisers recommended a tax cut. The tax cut did not occur until after Kennedy's death, when Lyndon Johnson was in office. In 1964, federally collected taxes were cut by $11 billion. From 1964 to 1965, the unemployment rate fell from 5.2 percent to 4.5 percent.

As you will see in Chapter 18, modern-day variants of Keynesian analysis are now taking center stage in policymaking discussions.

Changes in Government Spending

Recall that in Chapter 10 (Figures 10-8 and 10-9 on pages 220 and 221), we looked at the contractionary gap and the expansionary gap. The former was defined as the amount by which the current level of real GDP fell short of how much the economy could be producing if it were operating on its *LRAS*. The latter was defined as the amount by which the equilibrium level of real GDP exceeds the long-run equilibrium level as given by *LRAS*. In this section we examine fiscal policy in the context of a contractionary gap.

When There Is a Contractionary Gap. The government, along with firms, individuals, and foreigners, is one of the spending agents in the economy. When the government

Panel (a)

Panel (b)

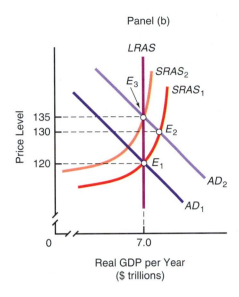

FIGURE 13-1

Expansionary Fiscal Policy: Two Scenarios

If there is a contractionary gap and equilibrium is at E_1 in panel (a), fiscal policy can presumably increase aggregate demand to AD_2. The new equilibrium is at E_2 at higher real GDP per year and a higher price level. If, though, we are already on *LRAS* as in panel (b), expansionary fiscal policy will simply lead to a temporary equilibrium at E_2 and a final equilibrium at E_3, again at *LRAS* of $7 trillion of real GDP per year but at a higher price level of 135.

decides to spend more, all other things held constant, the dollar value of total spending must rise. Look at panel (a) of Figure 13-1. We start at short-run equilibrium with AD_1 intersecting *SRAS* at $6.5 trillion of real GDP per year. There is a contractionary gap of $500 billion of real GDP per year—the difference between *LRAS* (the economy's long-run potential) and the short-run equilibrium level of real GDP per year. When the government decides to spend more, the aggregate demand curve shifts to the right to AD_2. Here we assume that the government knows exactly how much more to spend so that AD_2 intersects *SRAS* at $7 trillion, or at *LRAS*. Because of the upward-sloping *SRAS*, the price level has risen from 120 to 130. Real GDP has gone to $7 trillion per year. (Nominal GDP has gone up by even more because it consists of the price level index times real GDP. Here the GDP deflator has gone up by $10 \div 120 = 8.33$ percent.)[1]

When the Economy Is Operating on Its *LRAS*. Suppose that the economy is operating on *LRAS*, as in panel (b) of Figure 13-1. An increase in government spending shifts the aggregate demand curve from AD_1 to AD_2. Both prices and real output of goods and services begin to rise toward the intersection of E_2. But this rate of real GDP per year is untenable in the long run because it exceeds *LRAS*. In the long run, expectations of input owners—workers, owners of capital and raw materials, and so on—are revised. The short-run aggregate supply curve shifts from $SRAS_1$ to $SRAS_2$ because of higher prices and higher resource costs. Real GDP returns to the *LRAS* level of $7 trillion per year. The full impact of the increased government expenditures is on the price level only, which increases to 135. Therefore, an attempt to increase real GDP above its long-run equilibrium can be accomplished only in the short run.

Reductions in Government Spending. The entire process shown in Figure 13-1 can be reversed. Government can reduce spending, thereby shifting the aggregate demand curve inward. You should be able to show how this affects the equilibrium level of the price index and the real output of goods and services (real GDP) on similar diagrams.

---

[1]Percent change in price index $= \dfrac{\text{change in price index}}{\text{price index}} = \dfrac{130 - 120}{120} = 8.33$ percent

Changes in Taxes

The spending decisions of firms, individuals, and foreigners depend on the taxes levied on them. Individuals in their role as consumers look to their disposable (after-tax) income when determining their desired rate of consumption. Firms look at their after-tax profits when deciding on the level of investment to undertake. Foreigners look at the tax-inclusive cost of goods when deciding whether to buy in the United States or elsewhere. Therefore, holding all other things constant, a rise in taxes causes a reduction in aggregate demand for three reasons: (1) It reduces consumption, (2) it reduces investment, and (3) it reduces net exports. What actually happens depends, of course, on whom the taxes are levied.

When the Current Short-Run Equilibrium Is Greater than *LRAS*. Assume that aggregate demand is AD_1 in panel (a) of Figure 13-2. It intersects *SRAS* at E_1, which is at a level greater than *LRAS*. In this situation, an increase in taxes shifts the aggregate demand curve inward to the left. For argument's sake, assume that it intersects *SRAS* at E_2, or exactly where *LRAS* intersects AD_2. In this situation, the equilibrium level of real GDP falls from $7.5 trillion per year to $7 trillion per year. The price level index falls from 120 to 100.

If the Economy Is in Long-Run Equilibrium. Assume that the economy is already at short-run and long-run equilibrium as shown in panel (b) of Figure 13-2. The aggregate demand curve, AD_1, intersects both *LRAS* and *SRAS* at $7 trillion of real GDP per year. If aggregate demand decreases to AD_2, a new temporary equilibrium will occur at E_2 with the price level at 110 and real equilibrium GDP at $6.5 trillion per year. That means that in the short run, prices and the real output of goods and services fall. Input suppliers revise their expectations downward. The short-run aggregate supply curve shifts to $SRAS_2$. The real level of equilibrium GDP returns to the *LRAS* level of $7 trillion per year. The full *long-run* impact of fiscal policy in this situation is solely on the price level, which falls to 100.

Effects of a Reduction in Taxes. The effects of a reduction in taxes are exactly the reverse of the effects of an increase in taxes. Figure 13-1 on page 277 and the accompanying discussion of the effects of an increase in government expenditures provide the full analysis.

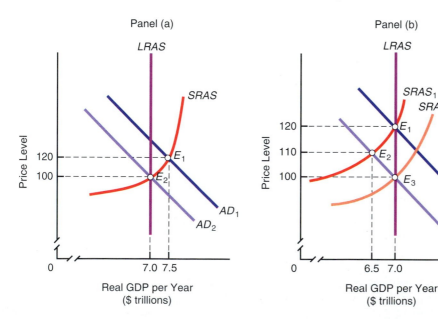

Panel (a)

Panel (b)

FIGURE 13-2

Contractionary Fiscal Policy: Two Scenarios

In panel (a), the economy is initially at E_1, which exceeds *LRAS*. Contractionary fiscal policy can move aggregate demand to AD_2 so the new equilibrium is at E_2 at a lower price level and now at *LRAS*. In panel (b), similar contractionary fiscal policy initially moves equilibrium from E_1 to E_2, but then it goes to E_3 at *LRAS*. The only long-run effect is to lower the price level to 100.

Tax Rates and Tax Revenues

Every time the federal government—or state and local governments, for that matter—announces a change in tax rates, the media are quick to pick up on projected increases or decreases in tax revenues. The arithmetic is simple: If the Treasury obtains $100 billion from the highest-earning individuals, it will garner $120 billion if their tax rates are increased by 20 percent. But tax revenues received after the tax rate increase are nowhere near those projected. Why? Because individuals and businesses are not static—they respond to higher marginal tax rates by retiring earlier, entering the job market later, engaging in the off-the-books underground economy, quitting second jobs, and compensating in other ways. The rule must be this: Never assume a static economy.

POLICY EXAMPLE
Did the New Deal Really Provide a Stimulus?

Many researchers have pointed out that Roosevelt's New Deal was influenced by Keynes's view that government had to increase "effective" aggregate demand. To be sure, Roosevelt's New Deal included what appeared on the surface to be large federal government expenditures and numerous government jobs programs. We have to look at the total picture, however. During the Great Depression, taxes were raised repeatedly. The Revenue Act of 1932, for example, passed during the depths of the Depression, brought the largest percentage increase in federal taxes in the history of the United States in peacetime—it almost doubled total federal tax revenues. Federal government deficits during the Depression years were small. In fact, in 1937 the total government budget—including federal, state, and local levels—was in surplus by $300 million. That means that at the same time that the federal government was increasing expenditures, local and state governments were decreasing them. If we measure the total of federal, state, and local fiscal policies, we find that they were truly expansive only in 1931 and 1936 compared to what the government was doing prior to the Great Depression. These two years were expansive only because of large veterans' payments, passed by Congress in both years over the vigorous opposition of the president.

FOR CRITICAL ANALYSIS: *What other aspects of Roosevelt's New Deal might be studied to see if they had expansionary effects on the national economy?* ●

CONCEPTS IN BRIEF

- Fiscal policy is defined as the discretionary change in government expenditures and/or taxes in order to achieve such national goals as high employment or reduced inflation.

- If there is a contractionary gap and the economy is operating at less than long-run average supply (*LRAS*), an increase in government spending can shift the aggregate demand curve to the right and perhaps lead to a higher equilibrium level of real GDP per year. If the economy is already operating on *LRAS*, in contrast, expansionary fiscal policy in the long run simply leads to a higher price level.

- Changes in taxes can have similar effects on the equilibrium rate of real GDP and the price level. A decrease in taxes can lead to an increase in real GDP, but if the economy is already operating on its *LRAS*, eventually such decreases in taxes will lead only to increases in the price level.

POSSIBLE OFFSETS TO FISCAL POLICY

Fiscal policy does not operate in a vacuum. Important questions have to be answered: If government expenditures increase, how are those expenditures financed, and by whom? If taxes are increased, what does the government do with the taxes? What will happen if individuals worry about increases in *future* taxes because there is more government spending today with no increased taxes? All of these questions involve *offsets* to the effects of fiscal policy. We will look at each of them and others in detail.

Indirect Crowding Out

Let's take the first example of fiscal policy in this chapter, an increase in government expenditures. If government expenditures rise and taxes are held constant, something has to give. Our government does not simply take goods and services when it wants them. It has to pay for them. When it pays for them and does not simultaneously collect the same amount in taxes, it must borrow. That means that an increase in government spending without raising taxes creates additional government borrowing from the private sector (or from foreigners).

The Interest Rate Effect. Holding everything else constant, if the government attempts to borrow more from the private sector to pay for its increased budget deficit, it is not going to have an easy time selling its bonds. If the bond market is in equilibrium, when the government tries to sell more bonds, it is going to have to offer a better deal in order to get rid of them. A better deal means offering a higher interest rate. This is the interest rate effect of expansionary fiscal policy financed by borrowing from the public. In this sense, when the federal government finances increased spending by additional borrowing, it may push interest rates up. When interest rates go up, it is more expensive for firms to finance new construction, equipment, and inventories. It is also more expensive for individuals to finance their cars and homes. Thus a rise in government spending, holding taxes constant (in short, deficit spending), tends to crowd out private spending, dampening the positive effect of increased government spending on aggregate demand. This is called the **crowding-out effect.** In the extreme case, the crowding out may be complete, with the increased government spending having no net effect on aggregate demand. The final result is simply more government spending and less private investment and consumption. Figure 13-3 shows how the crowding-out effect occurs.

Crowding-out effect
The tendency of expansionary fiscal policy to cause a decrease in planned investment or planned consumption in the private sector; this decrease normally results from the rise in interest rates.

The Firm's Investment Decision. To understand the interest rate effect better, consider a firm that is contemplating borrowing $100,000 to expand its business. Suppose that the interest rate is 9 percent. The interest payments on the debt will be 9 percent times $100,000, or $9,000 per year ($750 per month). A rise in the interest rate to 12 percent will push the payments to 12 percent of $100,000, or $12,000 per year ($1,000 per month). The extra $250 per month in interest expenses will discourage some firms from making the investment. Consumers face similar decisions when they purchase houses and cars. An increase in the interest rate causes their monthly payments to go up, thereby discouraging some of them from purchasing cars and houses.

Graphical Analysis. You see in Figure 13-4 that the initial equilibrium, E_1, is below *LRAS*. But suppose that government expansionary fiscal policy in the form of increased

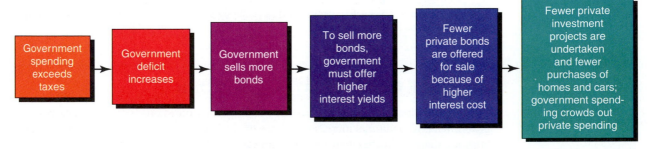

FIGURE 13-3
The Crowding-out Effect in Words

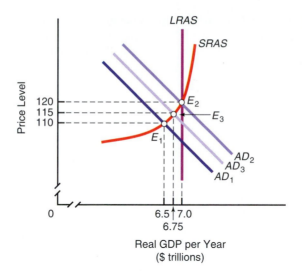

FIGURE 13-4

The Crowding-out Effect
Expansionary fiscal policy that causes deficit financing initially shifts AD_1 to AD_2. Equilibrium initially moves toward E_2. But because of crowding out, the aggregate demand curve shifts inward to AD_3, and the new short-run equilibrium is at E_3.

government spending (without increasing taxes) shifts aggregate demand from AD_1 to AD_2. In the absence of the crowding-out effect, the real output of goods and services would increase to $7 trillion per year, and the price level would rise to 120 (point E_2). With the (partial) crowding-out effect, however, as investment and consumption decline, partly offsetting the rise in government spending, the aggregate demand curve shifts inward to the left to AD_3. The new equilibrium is now at E_3, with real GDP of $6.75 trillion per year at a price level of 115.

Planning for the Future: The New Classical Economics

Economists have implicitly assumed that people look at changes in taxes or changes in government spending only in the present. What if people actually think about the size of *future* tax payments? Does this have an effect on how they react to an increase in government spending with no tax increases? Some economists, who call themselves the *new classical economists,* believe that the answer is yes. What if people's horizons extend beyond this year? Don't we then have to take into account the effects of today's government policies on the future?

Consider an example. If the government wants to spend $1 today, it can raise tax revenues by $1 and the public's responsibility to the government for that particular dollar has now been met and will never return. Alternatively, the government can borrow $1 today and the public will owe $1 plus interest later. Realizing that $1 today is mathematically equivalent to $1 plus interest next year, people may save the $1 to meet the future tax liabilities. Therefore, whether the $1 spending is financed by taxation or by borrowing, the two methods of finance are equivalent.

Increased government spending without an increase in taxes, according to the new classical economists, will not necessarily have a large impact on aggregate demand. In terms of Figure 13-4, the aggregate demand curve will shift inward from AD_2 to AD_3. In the extreme case, if consumers fully compensate for a higher tax liability in the future by saving more, the aggregate demand curve shifts all the way back to AD_1 in Figure 13-4. This is the case of individuals fully discounting their increased tax liabilities. The result is that an increased budget deficit created entirely by a current tax cut has literally no effect on the economy. This is known as the **Ricardian equivalence theorem,** after the nineteenth-century economist David Ricardo, who first developed the argument publicly.

Ricardian equivalence theorem
The proposition that an increase in the government budget deficit has no effect on aggregate demand.

Though the Ricardian equivalence theorem has generated much theoretical excitement, recent empirical studies cast some doubt on its relevance. During the 1980s, government spending exceeded government taxes by over $100 billion every year. There is little evidence that, in response, private saving rates increased during that same time period.

Direct Crowding Out

Government has a distinct comparative advantage over the private sector in certain activities such as diplomacy and national defense. Otherwise stated, certain resource-using activities in which the government engages do not compete with the private sector. In contrast, some of what government does competes directly with the private sector, such as education. When government competes with the private sector, **direct expenditure offsets** to fiscal policy may occur. For example, if the government starts providing milk at no charge to students who are already purchasing milk, there is a direct expenditure offset. Households spend less directly on milk, but government spends more.

The normal way to analyze the impact of an increase in government spending on aggregate demand is implicitly to assume that government spending is *not* a substitute for private spending. This is clearly the case for an ICBM missile. Whenever government spending is a substitute for private spending, however, a rise in government spending causes a direct reduction in private spending to offset it.

Direct expenditure offsets
Actions on the part of the private sector in spending money that offset government fiscal policy actions. Any increase in government spending in an area that competes with the private sector will have some direct expenditure offset.

The Extreme Case. In the extreme case, the direct expenditure offset is dollar for dollar, so we merely end up with a relabeling of spending from private to public. Assume that you have decided to spend $100 on groceries. Upon your arrival at the checkout counter, you are met by a U.S. Department of Agriculture official. She announces that she will pay for your groceries—but only the ones in the cart. Here increased government spending is $100. You leave the store in bliss. But just as you are deciding how to spend the $100, an Internal Revenue Service agent meets you. He announces that as a result of the current budgetary crisis, your taxes are going to rise by $100. You have to pay right now. Increases in taxes have now been $100. We have a balanced-budget increase in government spending. Under the assumption of a complete direct expenditure offset, there would be no change in total spending. We simply end up with higher government spending, which directly crowds out exactly the same amount of consumption. Aggregate demand and GDP are unchanged. Otherwise stated, if there is a full direct expenditure offset, the government spending multiplier is zero.

The Less Extreme Case. Much government spending has a private-sector substitute. When government expenditures increase, there is a tendency for private spending to decline somewhat (but not in proportion), thereby mitigating the upward impact on total aggregate demand. To the extent that there are some direct expenditure offsets to expansionary fiscal policy, predicted changes in aggregate demand will be lessened. Consequently, real output and the price level will be less affected.

INTERNATIONAL POLICY EXAMPLE
French Policymakers Ignore Crowding-out Effects

In the past few years, Europe's persistent high unemployment rates have been a major campaign topic in virtually every national election in the European Union. It came as no surprise, therefore, that the latest president of France, Jacques Chirac, chose a "pro-employment" prime minister, Alain Juppé. Juppé quickly put into effect the French government's plan to increase jobs. At the heart of the plan was a 50-billion-franc sum (about $10 billion) to create jobs at small and medium-sized companies. This was done by reducing some of the employer taxes owed on low-salaried employees. In addition, the government offered subsidies to companies that hired long-term unemployed persons. The French government projected that 700,000 jobs would be created from mid-1995 through the beginning of 1997. Clearly, French government policymakers do not believe that much, if any, crowding out will occur.

At the same time, though, the French government increased marginal tax rates on corporations, increased the value-added tax on virtually everything sold in France from 18.6 percent to 20.6 percent, and imposed a "temporary" 10 percent tax surcharge on "large fortunes."

FOR CRITICAL ANALYSIS: Soon after the new French policy was announced, the head of the forecasting unit of the Paris Chamber of Commerce argued that the government would need to spend as much as 80 billion francs (about $16 billion) if it were "really serious" about fighting unemployment. What does this criticism ignore? ●

The Open Economy Effect

The last offset to fiscal policy that we will discuss involves the open economy effect. It is a variant of the crowding-out effect, but one that now works its way through changes in net exports. If government spending is increased without a rise in taxes or if taxes are decreased without a reduction in government spending, the federal government must borrow more. As we pointed out, the government has to offer more attractive interest rates, so overall interest rates go up. When interest rates go up in the United States, foreigners demand more securities such as U.S. government bonds. When they do this, they have to pay for the bonds with dollars. After all, the typical Japanese stock and bond firm cannot buy more U.S. government bonds without getting its hands on more U.S. dollars. This increases the demand for dollars at the same time that it increases the supply of yen. The value of the yen falls relative to the value of the dollar in international transactions. When this occurs, Japanese-made goods become cheaper in America, and American-made goods become more expensive in Japan. Americans want to buy more Japanese goods, and the Japanese want to buy fewer American goods. This causes a reduction in net exports *(X)* and cuts into any increase in aggregate demand. In sum, to the extent that federal deficit spending reduces net exports, the effect of expansionary fiscal policy will be less.

The Supply-Side Effects of Changes in Taxes

We have talked about changing taxes and changing government spending, the traditional tools of fiscal policy. We have not really talked about the possibility of changing marginal tax rates. Recall from Chapter 5 that the marginal tax rate is the rate applied to the last bracket of taxable income. In our federal tax system, rising marginal tax rates are applied to rising income. In that sense, the United States has a progressive federal individual income tax system. Expansionary fiscal policy might involve reducing marginal tax rates. Advocates of such changes argue that (1) lower tax rates will lead to an increase in productivity because individuals will work harder and longer, save more, and invest more; and (2) increased productivity will lead to more economic growth, which will lead to higher real GDP. The government, by applying lower marginal tax rates, will not necessarily lose tax revenues, for the lower marginal tax rates will be applied to a growing tax base because of economic growth—after all, tax revenues are the product of a tax rate times a tax base.

People who support this notion are called supply-side economists. **Supply-side economics** involves changing the tax structure to create incentives to increase productivity. Due to a shift outward to the right in the aggregate supply curve, there can be greater output without upward pressure on the price level.

Supply-side economics
The notion that creating incentives for individuals and firms to increase productivity will cause the aggregate supply curve to shift outward.

Effect of Changes in Tax Rates on Labor. Consider the supply-side effects of taxes on labor. An increase in tax rates reduces the opportunity cost of leisure, thereby inducing individuals (at least on the margin) to reduce their work effort and to consume more leisure. But an increase in tax rates will also reduce spendable income, thereby shifting the demand for leisure curve inward to the left. Here a reduction in real spendable income shifts the demand curve for all goods and services, including leisure, inward to the left. The outcome of these two effects depends on which of them is stronger. Supply-side economists argue that in the 1970s and 1980s the first effect dominated: increases in marginal tax rates caused workers to work less and decreases in marginal tax rates caused workers to work more.

INTERNATIONAL EXAMPLE
Islam and Supply-Side Economics

Supply-side economics has a long history, dating back to at least the fourteenth century. The greatest of medieval Islamic historians, Abu Zayd Abd-Ar-Rahman Ibn Khaldun (1332–1406) included an Islamic view of supply-side economics in his monumental book, *The Muqaddamh* (1377). He pointed out that "When tax assessments . . . upon the subjects are low, the latter have the energy and desire to do things. Cultural enterprises grow and increase. . . . [Therefore] the number of individual imposts [taxes] and assessments mounts." If taxes are increased both in size and rates, "the result is that the interest of subjects in cultural enterprises disappears, because when they compare expenditures and taxes with their income and gain and see little profit they make, they lose all hope." Khaldun concluded that "At the beginning of a dynasty, taxation yields a large revenue from small assessments. At the end of a dynasty, taxation yields a small revenue from large assessments."

FOR CRITICAL ANALYSIS: How do this Islamic scholar's economic theories apply to the modern world? •

CONCEPTS IN BRIEF

- Indirect crowding out occurs because of an interest effect in which the government's efforts to finance its deficit spending cause interest rates to rise, thereby crowding out private investment and spending, particularly on cars and houses. This is called the crowding-out effect.

- Many new classical economists believe in the Ricardian equivalence theorem, which argues that an increase in the government budget deficit has no effect on aggregate demand because individuals correctly perceive their increased future taxes and therefore save more today to pay for them.

- Direct crowding out occurs when government spending competes with the private sector and is increased. Direct expenditure offsets to fiscal policy may occur.

- There is an open economy effect that offsets fiscal policy. Like the crowding-out effect, it occurs because the government's increased deficit causes interest rates to rise. This encourages foreigners to invest more in American securities. When they do so, they demand more dollars, thereby increasing the international value of the dollar. As a result, American-made goods become more expensive abroad and foreign goods cheaper here, so America exports fewer goods and imports more.

- Changes in marginal tax rates may cause supply-side effects if a reduction in marginal tax rates induces enough additional work, saving, and investing. Government tax receipts can actually increase. This is called supply-side economics.

DISCRETIONARY FISCAL POLICY IN PRACTICE

We can discuss fiscal policy in a relatively precise way. We draw graphs with aggregate demand and supply curves to show what we are doing. We could even in principle estimate the offsets that were just discussed. However, even if we were able to measure all of these offsets exactly, would-be fiscal policymakers still face problems: which fiscal policy mix to choose and the various time lags involved in conducting fiscal policy.

Fiscal Policy Mix

Suppose that it is agreed that fiscal policy is desirable. What is the proper mix of taxes and government expenditures? Let's say that policymakers decide that a change in taxes is desirable. At least seven options are available:

1. Permanent change in personal income taxes
2. Permanent change in corporate income taxes
3. Temporary change in personal income taxes
4. Temporary change in corporate income taxes
5. Change in employment subsidies
6. Change in depreciation allowance on investment expenditures
7. Change in specific consumption tax, such as on oil

Note that all of these are tax changes, but their effects on individual groups will be different, and special-interest groups will be lobbying powerful politicians to protect specific interests.

Alternatively, assume that policymakers decide that a change in government expenditures is desirable. There are disadvantages to these changes. Political wrangling will arise over the amount, type, and geographic location of the expenditure change ("spend more in my district or state, less in someone else's"). Furthermore, if the expenditure is to be made on a capital goods project, such as a highway, a dam, or a public transportation system, the problem of timing arises. If started during a recession, should or could such a project be abandoned or delayed if inflation emerges before the project is finished? Are delays or reversals politically feasible, even if they are economically sensible?

Time Lags

Recognition time lag
The time required to gather information about the current state of the economy.

Policymakers must be concerned with various time lags. Quite apart from the fact that it is difficult to measure economic variables, it takes time to collect and assimilate such data. Thus policymakers must be concerned with the **recognition time lag,** the period of months that may elapse before economic problems can be identified.[2]

---

[2]Final annual data for GDP, after various revisions, are not forthcoming for three to six months after the year's end.

After an economic problem is recognized, a solution must be formulated; thus there will be an **action time lag,** the period between the recognition of a problem and the implementation of policy to solve it. For fiscal policy, the action time lag is particularly long. It must be approved by Congress, and much political wrangling and infighting accompany congressional fiscal policy decision making. It is not at all unusual for the action time lag to last a year or two. Then it takes time to put the policy into effect. After Congress enacts a fiscal policy as legislation, it takes time to decide, for example, who gets the new federal construction contract, and so on.

When we add the recognition time lag to the action time lag, we get what is known as the *inside lag.* That is how long it takes to get a policy from inside the institutional structure of our federal government.

Finally, there is the **effect time lag:** After fiscal policy is enacted, it takes time for it to affect the economy. Multiplier effects take more time to work through the economy than it takes an economist to shift a curve on a chalkboard.

Because the various fiscal policy time lags are long, a policy designed to combat a recession might not produce results until the economy is experiencing inflation, in which case the fiscal policy would worsen the situation. Or a fiscal policy designed to eliminate inflation might not produce effects until the economy is in a recession; in that case, too, fiscal policy would make the economic problem worse rather than better.

Furthermore, because fiscal policy time lags tend to be *variable* (anywhere from one to three years), policymakers have a difficult time fine-tuning the economy. Clearly, fiscal policy is more an art than a science.

AUTOMATIC STABILIZERS

Not all changes in taxes (or in tax rates) or in government spending (including government transfers) constitute discretionary fiscal policy. There are several types of automatic (or nondiscretionary) fiscal policies. Such policies do not require new legislation on the part of Congress. Specific automatic fiscal policies—called **automatic,** or **built-in, stabilizers**—include the progressive federal income tax system itself and the government transfer system; the latter includes unemployment compensation.

The Progressive Income Tax

We have in the United States a progressive income tax that reaches a maximum rate of around 40 percent. For an individual, as taxable income rises, the marginal tax rate rises, and as taxable income falls, so does the marginal tax rate. Think about this now in terms of the entire economy. If the nation is at full employment, personal income taxes may yield the government, say, $600 billion per year. Now suppose that, for whatever reason, business activity suddenly starts to slow down. Workers are not allowed to put in as much overtime as before. Some workers are laid off, and some must change to jobs that pay less. Some workers and even some executives might take voluntary pay cuts. What happens to federal income taxes when wages and salaries go down? Taxes are still paid, but at a lower marginal rate than before, because the tax schedule is progressive. As a result of these decreased taxes, disposable income—the amount remaining after taxes—doesn't fall by the same percentage as before-tax income. In other words, the individual doesn't feel the pinch of recession as much as we might think if we ignored the progressive nature of our tax schedule. The *average* tax rate falls when less is earned.

Conversely, when the economy suddenly comes into a boom period, people's incomes tend to rise. They can work more overtime and can change to higher-paying jobs. Their *disposable* income does not, however, go up as rapidly as their total income because their

---

Action time lag
The time required between recognizing an economic problem and putting policy into effect. The action time lag is short for monetary policy but quite long for fiscal policy, which requires congressional approval.

Effect time lag
The time that elapses between the onset of policy and the results of that policy.

Automatic, or **built-in, stabilizers**
Special provisions of the tax law that cause changes in the economy without the action of Congress and the president. Examples are the progressive income tax system and unemployment compensation.

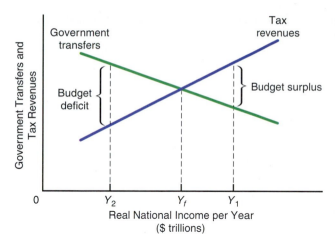

FIGURE 13-5

Automatic Stabilizers
Here we assume that as real national income rises, tax revenues rise and government transfers fall, other things remaining constant. Thus as the economy expands from Y_f to Y_1, a budget surplus automatically arises; as the economy contracts from Y_f to Y_2, a budget deficit automatically arises. Such automatic changes tend to drive the economy back toward its full-employment output level.

average tax rates are rising at the same time. Uncle Sam ends up taking a bigger bite. In this situation, the progressive income tax system tends to stabilize any abrupt changes in economic activity. (Actually, the progressive tax structure simply magnifies any stabilization effect that might exist.)

Unemployment Compensation

Like the progressive income tax, unemployment compensation stabilizes aggregate demand. Throughout the business cycle, it reduces changes in people's disposable income. When business activity drops, most laid-off workers automatically become eligible for unemployment compensation from their state governments. Their disposable income therefore remains positive, although certainly it is less than when they were employed. During boom periods there is less unemployment, and consequently fewer unemployment payments are made to the labor force. Less purchasing power is being added to the economy because fewer unemployment checks are paid out. Historically, the relationship between the unemployment rate and unemployment compensation payments has been strongly positive.

Stabilizing Impact

The key stabilizing impact of the progressive income tax and unemployment compensation is their ability to mitigate changes in disposable income, consumption, and the equilibrium level of national income. If disposable income is prevented from falling as much as it would during a recession, the downturn will be moderated. In contrast, if disposable income is prevented from rising as rapidly as it would during a boom, the boom will not get out of hand. The progressive income tax and unemployment compensation thus provide automatic stabilization to the economy. We present the argument graphically in Figure 13-5.

WHAT DO WE REALLY KNOW ABOUT FISCAL POLICY?

There are two ways of looking at fiscal policy, one that prevails during normal times and the other during abnormal times.

Fiscal Policy During Normal Times

During normal times (without "excessive" unemployment, inflation, or problems in the national economy), we know that given the time lag between the recognition of the need to increase aggregate demand and the impact of any expansionary fiscal policy, and given the very modest size of any fiscal policy action that Congress actually will take, discretionary fiscal policy is probably not very effective. Congress ends up doing too little too late to help in a minor recession. Moreover, fiscal policy that generates repeated tax changes (as it has done) creates uncertainty, which may do more harm than good. To the extent that fiscal policy has any effect during normal times, it probably achieves this by way of automatic stabilizers rather than by way of discretionary policy.

Fiscal Policy During Abnormal Times

During abnormal times, fiscal policy can be effective. Consider some classic examples: the Great Depression and war periods.

The Great Depression. When there is a substantial catastrophic drop in real GDP, as there was during the Great Depression, fiscal policy probably can do something to stimulate aggregate demand. Because so many people are cash-constrained, government spending is a good way during such periods to get cash into their hands.

Wartime. Wars are in fact reserved for governments. War expenditures are not good substitutes for private expenditures—they have little or no direct expenditure offsets. Consequently, war spending as part of expansionary fiscal policy usually has noteworthy effects, such as occurred while we were waging World War II, during which real GDP increased dramatically.

The "Soothing" Effect of Keynesian Fiscal Policy

One view of traditional Keynesian fiscal policy does not relate to its being used on a regular basis. As you have learned in this chapter, there are many problems associated with attempting to use fiscal policy. But if we should encounter a severe downturn, fiscal policy is available. Knowing this may reassure consumers and investors. After all, the ability of the federal government to prevent another great depression—given what we know about how to use fiscal policy today—may take some of the large risk out of consumers' and particularly investors' calculations. This may induce more buoyant and stable expectations of the future, thereby smoothing investment spending.

CONCEPTS IN BRIEF

- Time lags of various sorts reduce the effectiveness of fiscal policy. These include the recognition time lag, the action time lag, and the effect time lag.

- Two automatic, or built-in, stabilizers are the progressive income tax and unemployment compensation.

- Built-in stabilizers tend automatically to moderate changes in disposable income resulting from changes in overall business activity.

- Though discretionary fiscal policy may not necessarily be a useful policy tool in normal times because of time lags, it may work well during abnormal times, such as depressions and wartime. In addition, the existence of fiscal policy may have a soothing effect on consumers and investors.

The Real-World Political Constraints on Fiscal Policy

Concepts Applied: *Fiscal policy, government spending, marginal tax rates, time lags*

Implementing a new fiscal policy can be a lengthy and tedious process. Disagreement is common not only between Congress and the president, but also among members of Congress.

It's 1999, and the president wants to institute a new fiscal policy. There is one problem, however: The president is only one of the participants in the fiscal policy-making process. No single governmental body designs and implements fiscal policy.

The Inherent Political Conflict

The president, with the aid of the director of the Office of Management and Budget, the secretary of the Treasury, and the Council of Economic Advisers, designs a desired mix of taxes and government expenditures. But they can only *recommend* this mix (and level). Congress, with the aid of many committees (the House Ways and Means Committee, the Senate Finance Committee, and the Senate Budget Committee, to name a few) enacts fiscal policy. The president can veto congressional fiscal policy, but then Congress can override the president's veto.

Thus an inherent organizational problem exists with respect to fiscal policy right from the start—the power to enact fiscal policy does not rest with one institution. Disagreement as to proper fiscal policy normally emerges among members of Congress and between Congress and the president. Although the procedure required for an ulti-

mate solution is clearly spelled out in the U.S. Constitution, in reality it is often a tedious and time-consuming process.

The Budget Preparation and Enactment Process

The U.S. government follows a fairly well defined budget cycle, as illustrated in Figure 13-6 on page 291. About 18 months before the start of the federal government's fiscal year (October 1), the executive branch begins preparing the budget. Every year, the Office of Management and Budget (OMB) kicks off the process with a *spring review* in which it requires all agencies and departments to reexamine their programs, activities, and goals. This is followed by the *fall review,* during which the OMB looks at budget requests. The president's budget must be completed by January so that it can go to the printer to be included in the annual *Economic Report of the President* for submission to Congress. The legislature takes about five months to develop its *first budget resolution* in May. Then it proceeds to a *second budget resolution,* which is supposed to be ready by October 1. That normally does not happen, so every agency operates on *continuing resolutions.*

No wonder there is a lag between when government wants to institute fiscal policy and when it actually gets instituted!

What About a Special Tax or Spending Bill?

To avoid the standard 18-month budget cycle, the president can attempt to get Congress to pass a special tax bill, for example. But doing so is not easy either. Figure 13-7 on page 290 illustrates the intricate steps involved in how a bill becomes a law.

FOR CRITICAL ANALYSIS

1. Under what circumstances would fiscal policy be enacted most rapidly?
2. Would you ever expect Congress to change the way it deals with fiscal policy in order to reduce the time lags? Why or why not?

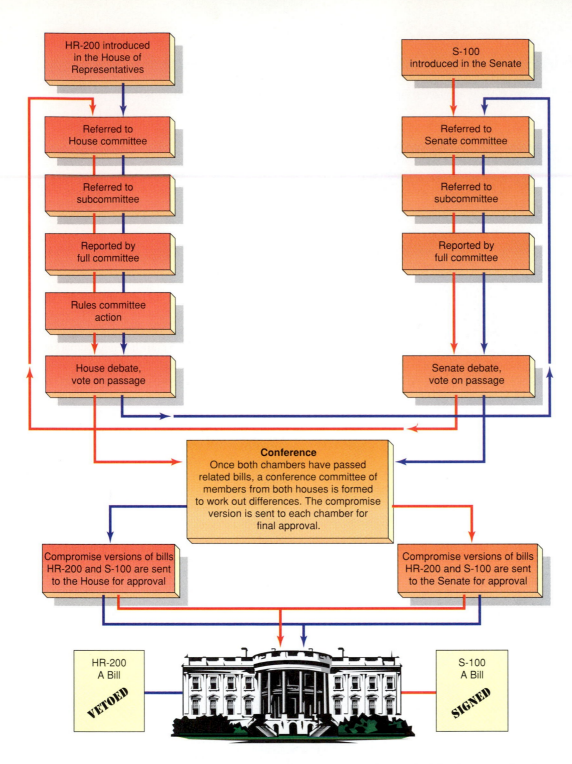

The compromise bill, approved by both houses, is sent to the president, who can sign it into law or veto it and return it to Congress. Congress may override a veto by a two-thirds majority vote in both houses; the bill then becomes law without the president's signature.

FIGURE 13-7

How a Bill Becomes Law

This illustration shows the most typical way in which proposed legislation is enacted into law. The process is illustrated with two hypothetical bills. House bill 200 (HR-200) and Senate bill 100 (S-100). Bills must be passed by both houses in identical form before they can be sent to the president. The path of HR-200 is traced by a blue line, that of S-100 by a red line. In practice, most bills begin as similar proposals in both houses.

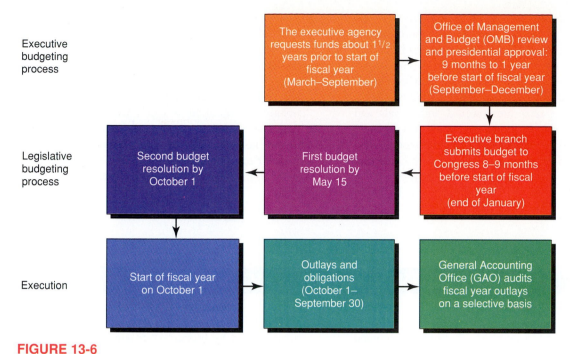

FIGURE 13-6
The Budget Cycle

CHAPTER SUMMARY

1. Fiscal policy involves deliberate discretionary changes in government expenditures and personal income taxes. Typically, policymakers argue in favor of fiscal policy during a contractionary gap.

2. Increased government spending when there is a contractionary gap can lead to a shift outward in the aggregate demand curve such that the equilibrium level of real GDP per year increases. If, however, the economy is already operating on its long-run aggregate supply curve *(LRAS),* the increase in aggregate demand will simply lead in the long run to a rise in the price level, all other things held constant.

3. Individuals respond to changes in after-tax profits, after-tax (disposable) income, and the tax-inclusive cost of foreign goods. Consequently, changes in taxes will change aggregate demand by changing consumption, investment, and net exports.

4. A decrease in taxes can lead to an increase in aggregate demand and in the equilibrium level of real GDP per year, provided that the economy is not already on its long-run aggregate supply curve. If it is, such tax decreases will simply lead to a higher price level.

5. There are numerous possible offsets to any fiscal policy. Indirect crowding out occurs when increased deficit spending requires the government to borrow more and drives interest rates up. Increased interest rates cause private firms to undertake fewer investments. This is called the crowding-out effect.

6. The new classical economists believe in the Ricardian equivalence theorem, a proposition stating that an increase in the government budget deficit has no effect on aggregate demand because individuals properly discount increased future tax liabilities and therefore increase saving when the government engages in new deficit spending.

7. Direct crowding out occurs when the government competes with the private sector and then increases spending in those areas of competition. There is a direct expenditure offset. This occurs, for example, when the government increases direct payments for school lunches that students' parents have been paying for anyway.

8. There is a possible open economy effect offsetting fiscal policy. Deficit spending that leads to increased

interest rates causes foreigners to invest more in the United States. To do so, they demand more dollars, thereby increasing the international price of our currency. Our goods become more expensive to foreigners, they buy less, and the result is a reduction in net exports that offsets the fiscal policy stimulus.

9. If marginal tax rates are lowered, individuals and firms may react by increasing work, saving, and investing. People who believe this favor supply-side economics, which involves changing the tax structure to create incentives to increase productivity.

10. Time lags, including the recognition time lag, the action time lag, and the effect time lag, tend to reduce the effectiveness of fiscal policy. When we add the recognition time lag to the action time lag, we get what is known as the inside lag, because this is how long it takes to get a policy from inside the institutional structure of our federal government.

11. Automatic stabilizers include personal and corporate income taxes and unemployment insurance. Automatic stabilizers counter ups and downs in fiscal activity without the necessity for legislative action.

DISCUSSION OF PREVIEW QUESTIONS

1. What is fiscal policy?

Fiscal policy refers to the changing of governmental expenditures and/or taxes in order to eliminate expansionary and contractionary gaps. Proponents of fiscal policy make the value judgment that price stability and full employment are worthwhile goals. Proponents also assume that our knowledge of positive economics is sufficient to achieve these normative goals.

2. What is automatic fiscal policy, and how does it lend stability to an economy?

With discretionary fiscal policy, government spending and taxing policies are consciously applied to stabilize an economy. Automatic fiscal policy, by contrast, does not require conscious policy or congressional legislation; automatic fiscal policy results from institutional characteristics in the economy. Thus a progressive tax structure and an unemployment compensation system (which are already in force) automatically change taxes and government outlays as national income changes. In particular, as national income falls in a recession, government outlays for unemployment automatically increase, and tax revenues fall as lower incomes push people into lower marginal tax brackets. These automatic stabilizers counteract declining national income. Similarly, in an expansionary period, tax revenues automatically rise (as people are forced into higher marginal tax brackets), and unemployment compensation out-

lays fall. Thus aggregate demand is automatically counteracted by higher tax revenues and decreased government outlays. Because income increases or decreases are automatically countered to a certain extent by a progressive tax system and an unemployment compensation program, we say that automatic fiscal policy lends stability to the U.S. economy.

3. How does the crowding-out effect tend to offset expansionary fiscal policy?

When the government spends more without increasing taxes or taxes less without reducing spending, it increases the government budget deficit. When the government attempts to sell more bonds to finance the increased deficit, it may end up increasing interest rates. Higher interest rates induce private businesses to reduce investment projects and also cause consumers to reduce their purchases of houses and cars. Therefore, expansionary fiscal policy tends to crowd out private investment and spending.

4. What types of time lags exist between the need for fiscal stimulus and the time when such stimulus actually affects the national economy?

There is a lag between the start of a recession and the availability of relevant data—the recognition time lag. There is a lag between the recognition of a need for a fiscal policy and putting one in motion—the action time lag. And there is a lag between policy implementation and tangible results—the effect time lag.

PROBLEMS

(Answers to the odd-numbered problems appear at the back of the book.)

13-1. What is *discretionary fiscal policy?* What are *automatic stabilizers?* Give examples of each.

13-2. Assume that you are a new member of Congress. You believe that expansionary government fiscal policy will pull the country rapidly out of its recession. What are some of the possible tax and spending changes you could recommend? What are the possible mixes?

13-3. Given the existence of automatic stabilizers, a recession is expected to generate a budget deficit, and an expansion is expected to generate a budget surplus. If the generation of such budget deficits or surpluses is to be countercyclical, what assumptions must be made about how consumers react to such budget deficits or surpluses?

13-4. How do economists distinguish between budget deficits or surpluses that occur automatically and those that are the result of discretionary policy?

COMPUTER-ASSISTED INSTRUCTION

Key elements of successful and unsuccessful fiscal policy are illustrated in a series of exercises that examine the implications of changes in both taxes and government expenditures.

Complete problem and answer appear on disk.

INTERACTING WITH THE INTERNET

A nice description of the U.S. federal budget (with both detailed and summary information) can be found at

gopher://sunny.stat-usa.gov/11/BudgetFY96

(future budgets should have a similar name). The University of California at Berkeley's Center for Community Economic Research (CCER) sponsors a good simulation of the effects of changing government spending. It can be found at

http://garnet.berkeley.edu:3333/budget/budget.html

APPENDIX C

FISCAL POLICY: A KEYNESIAN PERSPECTIVE

The traditional Keynesian approach to fiscal policy differs in three ways from that presented in Chapter 13. First, it emphasizes the underpinnings of the components of aggregate demand. Second, it assumes that government expenditures are not substitutes for private expenditures and that current taxes are the only taxes taken into account by consumers and firms. Third, the traditional Keynesian approach focuses on the short run and so assumes that as a first approximation, the price level is constant.

CHANGES IN GOVERNMENT SPENDING

Figure C-1 measures real national income along the horizontal axis and total planned expenditures (aggregate demand) along the vertical axis. The components of aggregate demand are consumption *(C)*, investment *(I)*, government spending *(G)*, and net exports *(X)*. The height of the schedule labeled $C + I + G + X$ shows total planned expenditures (aggregate demand) as a function of income. This schedule slopes upward because consumption depends positively on income. Everywhere along the 45-degree reference line, planned spending equals income. At the point Y^*, where the $C + I + G + X$ line intersects the 45-degree line, planned spending is consistent with real national income. At any income less than Y^*, spending exceeds income, and so income and thus spending will tend to rise. At any level of income greater than Y^*, planned spending is less than income, and so income and thus spending will tend to decline. Given the determinants of $C, I, G,$ and X, total spending (aggregate demand) will be Y^*.

The Keynesian approach assumes that changes in government spending cause no direct offsets in either consumption or investment spending because G is not a substitute for $C, I,$ or X. Hence a rise in government spending from G to G' causes the $C + I + G + X$ line to shift upward by the full amount of the rise in government spending, yielding the line $C + I + G' + X$. The rise in government spending causes income to rise, which in turn causes consumption spending to rise, which further increases income. Ultimately, aggregate demand rises to Y^{**}, where spending again equals income. A key conclusion of the Keynesian analysis is that total spending rises by *more* than the original rise in government spending because consumption spending depends positively on income.

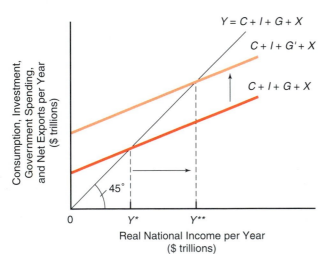

FIGURE C-1

The Impact of Higher Government Spending on Aggregate Demand
Government spending increases, causing $C + I + G + X$ to move to $C + I + G' + X$. Equilibrium increases to Y^{**}.

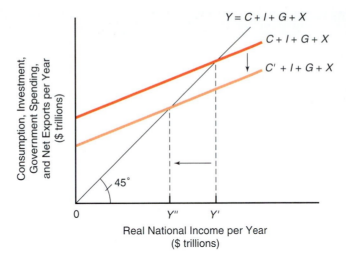

FIGURE C-2

The Impact of Higher Taxes on Aggregate Demand
Higher taxes cause consumption to fall to C'. Equilibrium decreases to Y''.

CHANGES IN TAXES

According to the Keynesian approach, changes in current taxes affect aggregate demand by changing the amount of disposable (after-tax) income available to consumers. A rise in taxes reduces disposable income and thus reduces consumption; conversely, a tax cut raises disposable income and thus causes a rise in consumption spending. The effects of a tax increase are shown in Figure C-2. Higher taxes cause consumption spending to decline from C to C', causing total spending to shift downward to $C' + I + G + X$. In general, the decline in consumption will be less than the increase in taxes because people will also reduce their saving to help pay the higher taxes. Thus although aggregate demand declines to Y'', the decline is *smaller* than the tax increase.

THE BALANCED-BUDGET MULTIPLIER

One interesting implication of the Keynesian approach concerns the impact of a balanced-budget change in government spending. Suppose that the government increases spending by $1 billion and pays for it by raising current taxes by $1 billion. Such a policy is called a *balanced-budget increase in spending*. Because the higher spending tends to push aggregate demand *up* by *more* than $1 billion while the higher taxes tend to push aggregate demand *down* by *less* than $1 billion, a most remarkable thing happens: A balanced-budget increase in G causes total spending to rise by *exactly* the amount of the rise in G—in this case, $1 billion. We say that the *balanced-budget multiplier* is equal to 1. Similarly, a balanced-budget reduction in spending will cause total spending to fall by exactly the amount of the spending cut.

THE FIXED PRICE LEVEL ASSUMPTION

The final key feature of the Keynesian approach is that it typically assumes that as a first approximation, the price level is fixed. Recall that nominal income equals the price level multiplied by real output. If the price level is fixed, an increase in government spending that causes nominal income to rise will show up exclusively as a rise in *real* output. This will in turn be accompanied by a decline in the unemployment rate because the additional output can be produced only if additional factors of production, such as labor, are utilized.

PROBLEMS

C-1. In this problem, equilibrium income is $1.1 trillion and full-employment equilibrium is $1.45 trillion. The marginal propensity to save is $\frac{1}{7}$. Answer the questions using the data in the following graph.

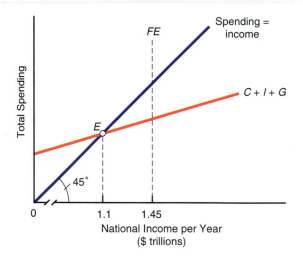

a. What is the marginal propensity to consume?

b. By how much must new investment or government spending increase to bring the economy up to full employment?

c. By how much must government cut personal taxes to stimulate the economy to the full-employment equilibrium?

C-2. Consider the following model; then answer the questions.

If $C = 30 + \frac{3}{4}Y$ and $I_n = 25$, equilibrium $Y = \$220$.

a. If government expenditures equal $5, what will be the new equilibrium level of national income? (Hint: Aggregate spending $\equiv C + I + G$.)

b. What was the government spending multiplier in this example?

C-3. Assume that MPC $= \frac{9}{10}$; then answer the following questions.

a. If government expenditures fall by $500, by how much will the aggregate expenditure curve shift downward? By how much will equilibrium income change?

b. If taxes fall by $500, by how much will the aggregate expenditure curve shift upward? By how much will equilibrium income change?

C-4. Assume that MPC $= \frac{3}{4}$; then answer the following questions.

a. If government expenditures rise by $1 billion, by how much will the aggregate expenditure curve shift upward?

b. If taxes rise by $1 billion, by how much will the aggregate expenditure curve shift downward?

c. If both taxes and government expenditures rise by $1 billion, by how much will the aggregate expenditure curve shift? What will happen to the equilibrium level of income?

d. How does our conclusion in the second part of (c) change if MPC $= \frac{9}{10}$? If MPC $= \frac{1}{2}$?

CHAPTER 14

DEFICIT SPENDING AND THE PUBLIC DEBT

It is conceivable that at some point during your life, you may experience some form of debt. If this happens, you will most likely pay off your debt. Many families are most comfortable when their yearly expenditures do not exceed their yearly income. That has not been the case with the federal government, which has been running a deficit almost every year for decades. Consequently, concerned citizens and many politicians are determined to pass an amendment to the U.S. Constitution that requires the federal government to have a balanced budget. Is such an amendment important? To answer that question, you will need to know more about deficit financing and the public debt.

PREVIEW QUESTIONS

1. By what methods can the U.S. federal government obtain purchasing power?

2. What are some suggested ways to reduce the federal government deficit?

3. What is the difference between the gross public debt and the net public debt?

4. What is the burden of the public debt?

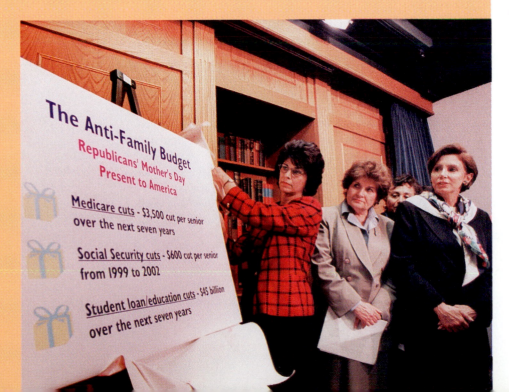

Did You Know That . . . every year your federal government has so consistently spent more than it receives that by the time you read this, the total accumulated net public debt will be around $4 trillion! Here is what $4 trillion could buy: about 1.4 trillion dozen Dunkin Donuts or 3.7 trillion cheeseburgers or 450 textbooks for every man, woman, and child in the United States. Your individual share of what the federal government owes is around $15,000. Should you be worried? The answer is both yes and no, as you will see in this chapter. First, let's examine what the government actually does when it spends more than it receives.

GOVERNMENT FINANCE: FILLING THE GAP

When the government spends more than it receives, its spending exceeds its tax revenues. Life must go on, though, so the government has to finance this shortfall somehow. Barring any resort to money creation (the subject matter of Chapters 15, 16, and 17), the U.S. Treasury sells IOUs on behalf of the U.S. government, in the form of securities that are normally called bonds. In effect, the federal government asks Americans and others to lend money to the government to cover its deficit. For example, if the federal government spends $100 billion more than it receives in revenues, the Treasury will raise that $100 billion by selling $100 billion of new Treasury bonds. The people who buy the Treasury bonds (lend money to the U.S. government) will receive interest payments over the life of the bond. In return, the Treasury receives immediate purchasing power.

The Historical Record of Deficit Financing

The process of how the government finances the deficit is relatively straightforward. So, too, are the data that show the historical record of deficit financing in the United States. In panel (a) of Figure 14-1, you can see that while federal government tax revenues have remained less than 20 percent of GDP, federal government expenditures in recent years have consistently been greater. The difference in the two curves in panel (a) represents the federal budget deficit expressed as a percentage of GDP since 1950. In panel (b), you see the absolute growth in federal government tax revenues and expenditures. The shaded red area represents the actual dollar size of the deficit since 1975.

Deficits Versus Debt: The Distinction Between Stocks and Flows

You have already learned the distinction between stocks and flows. The same analysis can be applied to the difference between the federal budget deficit and the total accumulated **public debt.** The public debt is a stock. At any point in time, it is some number, such as $4 trillion. The federal budget deficit, in contrast, is a flow. If it is $200 billion, that means that the federal government is spending at a rate of $200 billion per year more than it is receiving in taxes and other revenues. Hence if this year the public debt is $4 trillion and each year the federal government has a deficit of $200 billion, then next year the public debt will be $4.2 trillion, the year after that it will be $4.4 trillion, and so on.

Public debt
The total value of all outstanding federal government securities.

The Relative Size of the Federal Deficit

The problem with looking at panel (b) of Figure 14-1 is that the annual deficit is expressed as a current dollar figure. In a growing economy (both through real output increases and

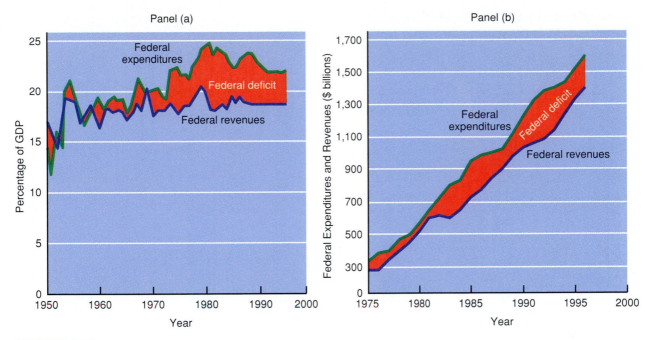

FIGURE 14-1

Two Ways of Viewing the Historical Record of Federal Deficit Financing
In panel (a), federal expenditures and revenues are expressed as a percentage of GDP. The difference is the federal deficit, also expressed as a percentage of GDP. Since the 1980s, the federal deficit has averaged about 3 percent of GDP. In panel (b), we express federal expenditures and federal revenues in nominal dollar terms. The difference is, of course, the nominal dollar deficit.
Sources: Economic Report of the President; Economic Indicators, various issues.

inflation), what is perhaps more important is the relative size of the federal budget deficit expressed as a percentage of GDP. This is shown in Figure 14-2. You can see that the federal budget deficit expressed as a percentage of GDP reached its most recent peak of nearly 6 percent early in the Reagan administration before falling back, again rose substantially during the Bush administration, and has been falling ever since.

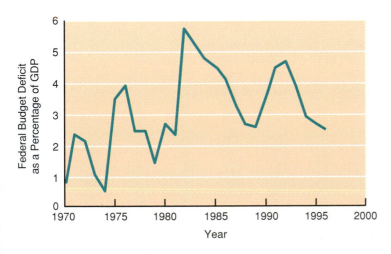

FIGURE 14-2

The Federal Budget Deficit Expressed as a Percentage of GDP
The budget deficit reached its peak during the Reagan administration and hit another peak during the Bush administration, but has fallen ever since.
Sources: Economic Report of the President; Economic Indicators, various issues.

INTERNATIONAL POLICY EXAMPLE
Will the European Union Have Its Way?

The European Union has outlined a policy strategy that requires all of its 15 members to have government deficits that do not exceed 3 percent of GDP. Each country must reach this goal by the year 1999 in order for all EU countries to adopt a common currency. As you see in Figure 14-3, by 1996, only 7 of the 15 EU countries had met that goal.

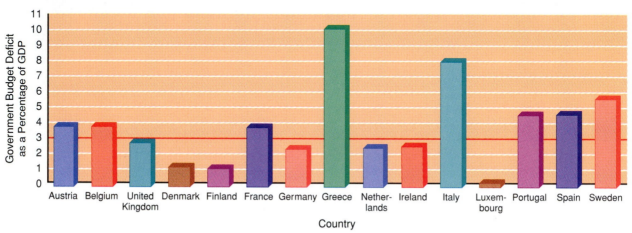

FIGURE 14-3

European Union Budget Deficits
Only 7 of the 15 EU countries have deficits that fall below 3 percent of GDP.

Source: European Commission.

FOR CRITICAL ANALYSIS: *If the United States were part of the European Union, how would its annual government budget deficit stack up against the deficits of other members?* •

CONCEPTS IN BRIEF

• Whenever the federal government spends more than it receives, it runs a budget deficit.

• The budget deficit is a flow, whereas the accumulated budget deficits are a stock, called the public debt.

• The federal deficit expressed as a percentage of GDP hit a peak of around 6 percent in the Reagan administration in the 1980s, fell back, rose to another peak during the Bush administration, and has been falling ever since.

ACCUMULATED DEFICITS: THE PUBLIC DEBT AND INTEREST PAYMENTS ON IT

As you have already learned, every time the federal government runs a deficit, it must borrow from the private sector and foreigners, thereby increasing its debt.

The Public Debt

Gross public debt
All federal government debt irrespective of who owns it.

Net public debt
Gross public debt minus all government interagency borrowing.

All federal public debt, taken together, is called the **gross public debt.** When we subtract from the gross public debt the portion that is held by government agencies (what the federal government owes to itself), we arrive at the **net public debt.** The net public debt normally increases whenever the federal government runs a budget deficit—that is, whenever total government outlays are greater than total government revenues. Look at column 3 in Table 14-1. The total net public debt has been growing continuously for many years.

TABLE 14-1

The Federal Deficit, Our Public Debt, and the Interest We Pay on It
Net public debt in column 3 is defined as total federal debt excluding all loans between federal government agencies. Per capita net public debt is obtained by dividing population into the net public debt.

(1) Year	(2) Federal Budget Deficit (billions of current dollars)	(3) Net Public Debt (billions of current dollars)	(4) Per Capita Net Public Debt (current dollars)	(5) Net Interest Costs (billions of current dollars)	(6) Net Interest as a Percentage of GDP
1940	3.9	42.7	323.2	0.9	0.90
1945	53.9	235.2	1,681.2	3.1	1.45
1950	3.1	219.0	1,438.0	4.8	1.68
1955	3.0	226.6	1,365.9	4.9	1.23
1960	0.3	237.2	1,312.7	6.9	1.37
1965	1.6	261.6	1,346.4	8.6	1.26
1970	2.8	284.9	1,389.1	14.4	1.47
1975	45.1	396.9	1,837.5	23.3	1.52
1980	73.8	709.3	3,140.5	52.5	1.92
1981	78.9	804.7	3,501.7	68.7	2.25
1982	127.9	929.3	4,003.9	85.0	2.68
1983	207.8	1,141.8	4,875.3	89.8	2.63
1984	185.3	1,312.6	5,538.4	111.1	2.94
1985	212.3	1,499.4	6,322.9	129.4	3.22
1986	221.2	1,736.2	7,357.2	136.0	3.21
1987	149.7	1,888.1	7,867.8	138.6	3.06
1988	155.1	2,050.2	8,473.6	151.7	3.23
1989	152.5	2,189.3	8,941.3	169.1	3.23
1990	221.4	2,410.4	9,641.6	175.6	3.23
1991	269.5	2,687.4	10,664.2	173.0	3.22
1992	290.2	2,998.6	11,759.2	177.9	3.21
1995	163.8	3,603.3	13,711.1	232.2	3.19
1996	174.8	3,767.1	14,215.3	—	—
1997	160.4	3,927.5	14,765.6	—	—

Sources: U.S. Department of the Treasury and Office of Management and Budget. Data for 1997 are estimates.

FIGURE 14-4

Net U.S. Public Debt as a Percentage of GDP
During World War II, the net public debt grew dramatically. It fell until the 1970s, then started rising again.

Source: U.S. Department of the Treasury.

Expressed in terms of per capita figures, however, it has not grown so rapidly. (We should also take account of inflation.) Perhaps a better way to look at the U.S. national debt is to examine it as a percentage of GDP, which we do in Figure 14-4. We see that after World War II, this ratio fell steadily until the early 1970s (except for a small rise in the late 1950s) and then leveled off until the 1980s. Since then, the ratio of net public debt to annual income has more or less continued to rise and now hovers around 50 percent of GDP.

INTERNATIONAL EXAMPLE
Public Debt Around the World

Whereas our net public debt as a percentage of GDP now exceeds 50 percent, many other industrialized nations have a much greater debt ratio. Figure 14-5 shows predicted public debt as a percentage of GDP for several of the United States's important trading partners. It is clear from the graph that none of the countries depicted plans to reduce the size of its public debt-to-annual GDP ratio.

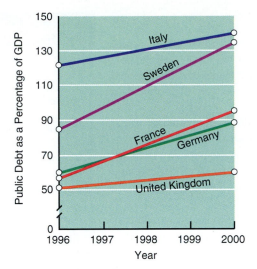

FIGURE 14-5
Rising Debt in Europe
Over the next few years, the public debt of many EU countries is expected to rise.
Source: European Commission.

FOR CRITICAL ANALYSIS: What does Figure 14-5 tell you about projected annual budget deficits in Italy, Sweden, France, Germany, and the United Kingdom? ●

Annual Interest Payments on the Public Debt

Consider the size of interest payments on the public debt as shown in column 5 of Table 14-1. Those interest payments started rising dramatically around 1975. Expressed as a percentage of GDP, today they are more than twice what they were a half century ago. The true size of the government deficit each year has not fallen as planned. Therefore, it is possible that interest payments expressed as a percentage of national income will rise, as is apparent in column 6 in Table 14-1. As long as the government borrows from Americans, the interest payments will be made to Americans. In other words, we owe the debt to ourselves; some people are taxed so that the government can pay interest to others (or themselves). But we have seen a rising share of the public debt owned by foreigners, reaching its peak in 1978 at 22 percent. Foreigners still own around 16 percent of the U.S. public debt. So we don't just owe it to ourselves.

INTERNATIONAL POLICY EXAMPLE
Belgium's Diminishing Policy Options

Belgium's public debt is approaching 150 percent of GDP. This figure has little meaning until one examines its effect on the Belgian government's policy options. Today in the United States, the interest cost of our public debt is about 17 percent of the federal government budget; in Belgium, it exceeds 40 percent. This increasing net interest cost of the public debt in Belgium is steadily crowding out everything else the government wants to do. Recently, it stopped maintaining its national road system. If Belgium continues to add to its public debt through annual budget deficits the way it has done in the past, the net interest payment on that public debt will eventually crowd out every other government expenditure!

FOR CRITICAL ANALYSIS: What policy options are available to the Belgian government to prevent the doomsday prediction just mentioned from coming true? ●

The Burden of the Public Debt

From 1984 to 1997, the net public debt of the United States almost tripled, to nearly $4 trillion. The public debt is the total of all the outstanding debt owed by the Treasury to its individual and institutional lenders. Whenever the federal government is in deficit, the public debt rises; for example, in fiscal 1996, the federal government deficit was about $170 billion, so the public debt increased by that amount in that fiscal year. Because of the large deficits incurred by the federal government in the 1980s and 1990s, the public debt rose dramatically—at least in nominal values. We shall now analyze whether federal deficits, and the accompanying increase in the public debt that they generate, impose a burden on future generations or are irrelevant.

As you read the remainder of this chapter, try to keep two things in mind. First, given the level of government expenditures, the main alternative to the deficit is higher taxes; therefore, the costs of a deficit should be compared to the costs of higher taxes, not to zero. Second, it is important to distinguish between the effects of deficits when full employment exists and when substantial unemployment exists.

Federal Budget Deficits: A Burden on Future Generations?

Assume that the federal government decides to increase government expenditures on final goods and services by $100 billion and that it can finance such expenditures either by raising taxes by $100 billion or by selling $100 billion of bonds. Many economists maintain that the second option, deficit spending, would lead to a higher level of national consumption and a lower level of national private saving than the first option.

The reason this is so, say these economists, is that if people are taxed, they will have to forgo private consumption now as they substitute government goods for private goods. Suppose that taxes are not raised, but instead the public buys bonds to finance the $100 billion in government expenditures. The community's disposable income is the same, and it has increased its assets by $100 billion in the form of bonds. The community will either (1) fail to realize that its liabilities (in the form of future taxes due to an increased public debt that must eventually be paid) have *also* increased by $100 billion or (2) believe that it can consume the governmentally provided goods and simultaneously purchase the same quantity of privately provided consumer goods because the bill for the currently governmentally provided goods will be paid by *future* taxpayers.

If full employment exists, then as people raise their present consumption (the same quantity of private consumption goods, but more public consumption goods), something must be crowded out. In a closed economy, investment (spending on capital goods) is crowded out. The mechanism by which this crowding out occurs is an increase in the interest rate: Deficit spending increases the total demand for credit but leaves the total supply of credit unaltered. The rise in interest rates that causes a reduction in the growth of investment and capital formation in turn slows the growth of productivity and improvement in the community's living standard.

The foregoing analysis suggests that deficit spending can impose a burden on future generations in two ways. First, unless income grows dramatically, future generations will have to be taxed at a higher rate to retire the higher public debt resulting from the present generation's increased consumption of governmentally provided goods. Second, the increased level of consumption by the present generation crowds out investment and reduces the growth of capital goods; this leaves future generations with a smaller capital stock and thereby reduces their wealth.

Paying Off the Public Debt in the Future. Suppose that after 50 years of running deficits, the public debt becomes so large that each adult person's tax liability is $50,000. Suppose further that the government chooses (or is forced) to pay off the debt at that time. Will that generation be burdened with our generation's overspending? The debt is, after all, owed (mostly) to ourselves. It's true that every adult will have to come up with $50,000 in taxes to pay off the debt; but then the government will use that money to pay off bondholders, who are (mostly) the same people. Thus *some* people will be burdened because they owe $50,000 and own less than $50,000 in government bonds. But others will receive more than $50,000 for the bonds they own. As a generation or a community, they will pay and receive about the same amount of money.

Of course, there could be a burden on some low-income adults who will find it difficult or impossible to obtain $50,000 to pay the tax liability. Still, nothing says that taxes to pay off the debt must be assessed equally; it seems likely that a special tax would be levied, based on the ability to pay.

Our Debt to Foreigners. We have been assuming that most of the debt is owed to ourselves. What about the 16 percent of our public debt that is owned by foreigners?

It is true that if foreigners buy U.S. government bonds, we do not owe that debt to ourselves, and a potential burden on future generations may result. But not necessarily. Foreigners will buy our government's debt if the inflation-adjusted, risk-adjusted, after-tax rate of return on such bonds exceeds what the investors can earn in their own country or some other country. If they buy U.S. bonds voluntarily, they perceive a benefit in doing so.

It is important to realize that not all government expenditures can be viewed as consumption; government expenditures on such things as highways, bridges, dams, research and development, and education might properly be perceived as investments. If the rate of return on such investments exceeds the interest rate paid to foreign investors, both foreigners and future Americans will be economically better off. What really matters is on what the government spends its money. If government expenditures financed by foreigners are made on wasteful projects, a burden may well be placed on future generations.

We can use the same reasoning to examine the problem of current investment and capital creation being crowded out by current deficits. If deficits lead to slower growth rates, future generations will be poorer. But if the government expenditures are really investments, and if the rate of return on such public investments exceeds the interest rate paid on the bonds, both present and future generations will be economically richer.

The Effect of Unemployment. If the economy is operating at a level substantially below full-employment real GDP, crowding out need not take place. In such a situation, an expansionary fiscal policy via deficit spending can increase current consumption (of governmentally provided goods) without crowding out investment. Indeed, if some government spending is in the form of high-yielding public investments, both present and future generations can be economically richer; such public investments will provide positive benefits in the future.

Not All Borrowing Is Bad. Don't get the impression that the government should never borrow. After all, borrowing is not always bad. Consider an example of a student who has a choice of borrowing money for one of two purposes: the purchase of a home entertainment center or tuition payments to attend college. Borrowing for the first purpose may prove to be burdensome; borrowing for the second purpose—building human capital—

may allow the student to reap greater returns in the form of higher income later. The same analysis can be applied to government borrowing. There is a difference between government borrowing to purchase Fourth of July fireworks shows and government borrowing to invest in the interstate highway system. One can conclude, therefore, that increased public debt is not necessarily bad if it creates a net investment for the future.

Are Deficits Relevant?

Much of the analysis to this point has assumed that deficit spending increases the demand for credit, while the supply of credit remains constant. Hence the interest rate rises and investment is crowded out. But what if the community realizes that an increase in the public debt also represents an increase in its future tax liabilities—the Ricardian equivalence theorem? Further, what if people wish not to burden their own children with an increased public debt? Because the deficit has increased, they would increase their current saving in order to enable their children to meet future debt obligations. In fact, because their taxes do not rise, their disposable income is higher, and they can save by purchasing the new government bonds. In the process, interest rates will not rise. Deficit spending may not lead to crowding out.

Many people plan to (and do) bestow wealth on others. The latest research shows that from 25 to 50 percent of all saving is undertaken in order to transfer wealth to relatives (usually children) during an individual's lifetime. And most people also bestow wealth on their heirs at death. To illustrate the point, assume that parents intend to leave $200,000 to their descendants and that they have saved sufficiently to achieve that goal. Then suppose that the government engages in deficit spending so that their heirs' future tax liabilities rise by $20,000. Realizing that they no longer have achieved their goal, the parents might increase the amount they save now so as to cover their heirs' additional future $20,000 tax liability.

If both the supply of credit (saving) and the demand for credit rise, there is no theoretical reason for believing that the interest rate will rise. If that is so, crowding out won't occur; the growth of investment and capital production won't be retarded, and future generations need not have lower living standards.

CONCEPTS IN BRIEF

- When we subtract the money government agencies borrow from each other from the gross public debt, we obtain the net public debt.

- There may be a burden of the public debt on future generations if they have to be taxed at higher rates to pay for the current generation's increased consumption of governmentally provided goods; also there may be a burden if there is crowding out of current investment, resulting in less capital formation and hence a lower economic growth rate.

- If a significant part of our public debt is bought by foreigners, then we no longer "owe it to ourselves." If the rate of return on the borrowed funds is higher than the interest to be paid, future generations can be made better off by government borrowing, but will be worse off if the opposite is true.

FEDERAL BUDGET DEFICITS IN AN OPEN ECONOMY

Many economists, and most noneconomists, believe that the U.S. trade deficit (a situation in which the value of the nation's imports of goods and services exceeds the value of its exports) is just as serious a problem as its government budget deficit. The U.S. trade deficit went from a surplus of $32 billion in 1980 to a deficit of $119.9 billion in 1987; in 1996 the U.S. trade deficit was an estimated $123.6 billion.

By virtue of such trade deficits, foreigners have accumulated U.S. dollars and purchased U.S. assets (real estate, corporate stocks, bonds, and so on). If this country continues to incur huge trade deficits, foreigners will continue to purchase assets here.

Let us examine the link between federal budget deficits and trade deficits.

What the Evidence Says

Figure 14-6 shows U.S. international trade deficits and surpluses compared to federal budget deficits and surpluses. The year 1983 appears to be a watershed year, for that is when imports began to consistently exceed exports on an annual basis in the United States. Concurrently, the federal budget fiscal deficit moved progressively into new territory.

On the basis of the evidence presented in Figure 14-6, it appears that there is a close relationship between the trade and fiscal deficits: Larger trade deficits accompany larger fiscal deficits.

Why the Two Deficits Are Related

Intuitively, there is a reason why we would expect federal budget deficits to lead to trade deficits. You might call this the unpleasant arithmetic of trade and federal budget deficits.

Assume that the federal government runs a budget deficit. Assume further that domestic consumption and domestic investment haven't decreased relative to GDP. Where, then, does the money come from to finance the federal government deficit? Part of it must come from abroad. That is to say, dollar holders abroad are buying our newly created federal government–issued bonds. If that's the case, dollar holders abroad have fewer dollars to spend on our goods, that is, our exports. Hence when we run large federal government deficits, we should expect to see foreign dollar holders spending more on U.S. government securities (bonds) and less on U.S.-produced goods and services (exports).

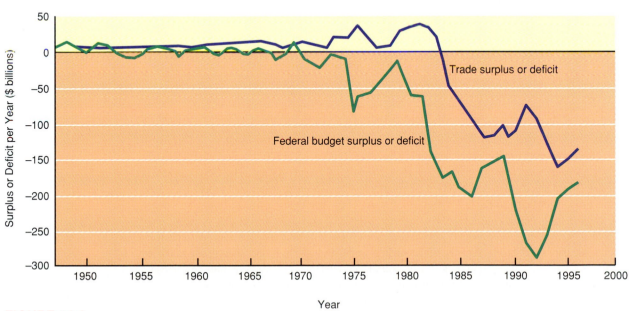

FIGURE 14-6

America's Twin Deficits

The United States exported more than it imported until 1983. Then it started running large trade deficits, as shown in this diagram. The federal budget has been in deficit for many years, starting in earnest in the late 1960s. The question is, has the federal budget deficit created the trade deficit?

Source: Economic Indicators, various issues.

The reason that foreign dollar holders are induced to buy U.S. government securities is that domestic U.S. interest rates will normally rise, all other things held constant, whenever there is an increase in government deficits financed by increased borrowing.

HAS THE DEFICIT BEEN MEASURED CORRECTLY?

Part of the problem, according to some economists, is that we are measuring the deficit incorrectly. One such economist is Robert Eisner of Northwestern University, who claims that we need to change the government accounting system to come up with a better measure of the deficit.

Capital Budgeting Theory

The federal government has only one budget to guide its spending and taxing each fiscal year. It does not distinguish between current spending for upkeep on the White House, for example, and spending for a new park that's going to last for many years to come. By contrast, businesses, as well as state and local governments, have two budgets. One, called the *operating budget,* includes expenditures for current operations, such as salaries and interest payments. The other is called a *capital budget,* which includes expenditures on investment items, such as machines, buildings, roads, and dams. With municipal governments, for example, expenditures on the capital budget may be paid for by long-term borrowing.

The Office of Management and Budget (OMB) estimated that in fiscal 1996, investment-type outlays such as military equipment and loans for research and development exceeded $150 billion. Given an estimated budget deficit of over $170 billion, then, if a capital budgeting system were used, we would simply see that most of the deficit was being used to finance activities or assets yielding long-term returns.

Eisner and others recommend that Congress should set up a capital budget, thereby removing investment outlays from its operating budget. Opponents of such a change in the accounting rules for the federal government point out that such an action would allow the government to grow even faster than currently because many new expenditures could be placed in the capital budget, thereby reducing the operating budget deficit and reducing the pressure on Congress to cut the growth in federal government spending.

Pick a Deficit, Any Deficit

Even using standard accounting techniques, the federal budget deficit that is "officially" announced can vary dramatically, depending on what is included or is not included. The OMB comes up each year with its predictions about the federal budget deficit. The Congressional Budget Office has its own set of deficit calculations. The two budget agencies produce a minimum of eight deficit estimates for each fiscal year. They give them such names as the "baseline deficit," the "policy deficit," the "on-budget deficit," and the "deficit that includes the bailout to save failing savings and loan associations." There is also a deficit that includes the Social Security surplus plus the cost of the savings and loan bailout. Rather than going into the details to explain each of these deficits, the point to understand is that no one number gives a complete picture of how much the government is spending over and above what it is receiving.

Liabilities That Aren't Showing Up

Even the highest figures shown for the federal budget deficit do not include liabilities that the federal government is incurring each year. In particular, the federal government has increasingly become liable for civilian and military employee pension plans. These are as much an obligation as a formal bond contract that is sold to finance the federal budget deficit. One estimate by economist Henning Bohn of the University of California, Santa Barbara, shows that the federal government is liable for over $1.2 trillion for just the pension obligations for government employees. The federal government is also incurring liabilities for private pension plans, savings and loan and bank deposits, and shareholders' brokerage accounts. Economist Jean-Michel Paul of the University of California, Berkeley, has estimated that the net pension liabilities of the U.S. government amount to almost 70 percent of GDP.

INTERNATIONAL EXAMPLE
Pension Liabilities Around the World

Table 14-2 shows net pension liabilities for various countries expressed as a percentage of GDP.

If you add a country's net pension liabilities to its existing public debt, you come up with some impressive numbers. In Italy, the combined liabilities of the government equal 350 percent of GDP.

TABLE 14-2

Net Pension Liabilities of the National Government as a Percentage of GDP

Country	Net Pension Liabilities as a Percentage of GDP
United States	66
Germany	160
Belgium	165
United Kingdom	186
France	216
Japan	218
Italy	233
Canada	250

Sources: Organization of Economic Cooperation and Development; Jean-Michel Paul, "Belgium's Debt Crisis Is Europe's Too," *Wall Street Journal Europe*, May 22, 1995, p. A-17.

FOR CRITICAL ANALYSIS: Does it matter what the government's net pension liabilities are relative to its GDP? Why or why not? ●

SUGGESTIONS FOR REDUCING THE DEFICIT

There have been many suggestions about how to reduce the government deficit. The most obvious way to reduce the deficit is to increase taxes.

Increasing Taxes

From an arithmetic point of view, a federal budget deficit can be wiped out by simply increasing the amount of taxes collected. Let's see what this would require. The data for 1996 are instructive. The Office of Management and Budget estimated the 1996 federal budget deficit at about $170 billion. This is as much as Americans paid in total individual income taxes to the federal government in all of 1978. That deficit in 1996 shows that for the year, the federal government spent about $700 more than it had in tax revenues for every person in the country. To eliminate the deficit by raising taxes, we need $1400 more in taxes every year from *every worker* in America just to balance the budget. In 1996, Americans paid about $600 billion in personal income taxes. Every taxpayer would have to pay 30 percent more in income taxes to balance the budget. Needless to say, reality is such that we will never see a simple tax increase that will wipe out the annual federal budget deficit.

Taxing the Rich. Some people suggest that the way to eliminate the deficit is to raise taxes on the rich. Currently, over 70 percent of all federal income taxes are already being paid by the top 20 percent of families. The entire bottom 60 percent of families (those earning below $45,000 per year) pay only slightly more than 11 percent of federal income taxes. Families earning below $30,000 pay less than 3 percent of federal income taxes. Currently, families whose income are in the top 5 percent pay about 45 percent of all federal income taxes paid. The richest 1 percent pay about 25 percent of all income taxes paid. What does it mean to tax the rich more? If you talk about taxing "millionaires," you are referring to those who pay taxes on more than $1 million income per year. There are only around 57,000 of them. Even if you doubled the taxes they paid, the reduction in the deficit would be relatively trivial. Changing marginal tax rates at the upper end will show similarly unimpressive results. An increase in the top marginal tax rate from 39.6 percent to 45 percent will raise, at best, only about $20 billion in additional taxes (assuming that people do not figure out a way to avoid the higher tax rate). This $20 billion per year in extra tax revenues represented only 12 percent of the estimated 1996 federal budget deficit.

The Historical Reality. The data do not support the notion that tax increases can reduce deficits. Though it is possible arithmetically, politically just the opposite has occurred. Since World War II, for every dollar increase in taxes legislated, federal government spending has increased $1.59.

Reducing Expenditures, Particularly on Entitlements

Reducing expenditures is another way to reduce the federal budget deficit. Figure 14-7 shows spending on the military as a percentage of GDP. There you see that the military budget will be shrinking in real terms at least through 1997.

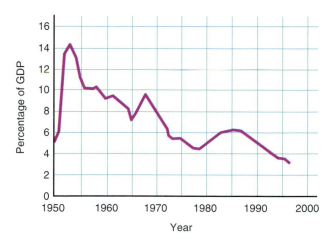

FIGURE 14-7

Defense Outlays as a Percentage of GDP
Defense spending as a percentage of GDP continues to fall.
Source: Office of Management and Budget.

TABLE 14-3
Federal Domestic Spending

Year	Social Security, Medicare, and Medicaid (billions of 1992 dollars)	All Other Domestic Programs (billions of 1992 dollars)
1953	17.93	87.82
1963	74.01	136.52
1973	183.65	255.63
1983	325.29	340.95
1995	544.27	423.81
1996	587.65	448.69

Entitlements
Guaranteed benefits under a government program such as Social Security, Medicare, or Medicaid.

During the Cold War, the military budget was the most important aspect of the federal budget; it no longer is. **Entitlements** are now the most important aspect of the federal budget. These include payments for Social Security, welfare, Medicare, and Medicaid. Entitlements are legislated federal government payments; anybody who qualifies is entitled to them. They are consequently often called noncontrollable expenditures. They represent about 50 percent of the total federal budget today. In 1960, they represented only 10 percent. Let's look at Social Security, Medicaid, and Medicare in Table 14-3. In constant 1992 dollars, in 1996 Social Security, Medicaid, and Medicare represented about $588 billion of federal government expenditures, compared to almost $449 billion of other domestic federal government expenditures. (These exclude military and international payments and interest on the public debt.)

Entitlement payments on Social Security, Medicaid, and Medicare now exceed all other domestic spending. Entitlements are growing faster than any other part of the federal government budget. In the past two decades, real spending on entitlements (adjusted for inflation) grew between 6 and 7 percent a year, while the economy grew by less than 3 percent per year. Social Security payments are growing in real terms at about 6 percent a year, but Medicare and Medicaid are growing at double-digit rates.

Entitlement programs are believed to be necessary. Interest on the public debt must be paid, but just about every other federal expenditure that is labeled necessary can be changed by Congress. The federal deficit is not expected to drop in the near future because entitlement programs are not likely to be eliminated. It is difficult to cut government benefits once they are established.

CONCEPTS IN BRIEF

- Some people argue that the federal budget deficit is measured incorrectly because it lumps together spending on capital and spending on consumption. It is therefore argued that there should be an operating budget and a capital budget.

- Some observers see a close correlation between foreign trade deficits and federal budget deficits.

- There are many deficits measured and announced by various government offices. Also, there are many liabilities that are not shown, such as future pension obligations.

- Suggested ways to reduce the deficit are to increase taxes, particularly on the rich, and to reduce expenditures, particularly on entitlements, defined as guaranteed benefits under a government program such as Social Security or Medicare.

Would a Balanced-Budget Amendment Make a Difference?

Concepts Applied: *Deficit, deficit financing, public debt*

The federal government has been running a deficit for decades, and each year politicians propose an amendment requiring the government to pass a balanced budget. In an attempt to balance the budget, some politicians suggest cuts be made to entitlements such as Medicare and Social Security.

It has become almost a ritual in Congress each year. A senator or representative, or a group of them, proposes a bill to amend the Constitution requiring the federal government to run a balanced budget each year. So far, all such bills have failed, even the one promised by the Republican-dominated 104th Congress.

Ratification Required

Even if Congress eventually passes a balanced-budget amendment, 38 states have to ratify it. As of the mid-1990s, Congress has considered more than 7,000 amendments; only 33 have been submitted to the states, and of these, 27 have become law. The probability that 38 state legislatures (or conventions) will pass a balanced-budget amendment within the traditional seven-year period is small.

Playing with the Numbers

Even if there were to be a balanced-budget law, the federal government has the ability to play all sorts of tricks with its accounting system. It has the right, for example, to place certain items in a category known as "off budget." The government has set up off-budget agencies that it owns and controls but whose lending activities do not

appear on the official federal budget. Examples of off-budget agencies are the Federal Financing Bank, the Pension Benefit Guarantee Corporation, and the Rural Electrification and Telephone Revolving Fund. By law, these agencies' transactions are excluded from the regular federal budget. Also, the federal government often guarantees loans or mortgage pools. Such federal loan guarantees also do not appear in the regular federal budget.

What Is the Real Issue?

Consider a hypothetical situation: A balanced budget amendment is passed, and Congress takes it seriously. It does its job well by raising taxes and user fees, resulting in a balanced budget every year. Is the nation better off? The answer depends on the level at which the federal budget is balanced, or more precisely, at what percentage of gross domestic product (GDP) the federal budget is balanced. Currently, the federal government controls slightly less than 25 percent of annual GDP. (There is always some disagreement about the exact size of federal government outlays.)

Federal government revenues (mainly taxes) account for 19 to 20 percent of GDP. The difference is, of course, the annual deficit. The question now to ask is this: Would you, your family, your friends, or anybody else necessarily be better off if federal government outlays remained the same while taxes and other revenues increased to match those outlays? The federal government would still be controlling the same percentage of GDP each year.

To make the hypothetical query even more persuasive, consider this: What if the federal government a decade from now balanced the budget while it was controlling 50 percent of GDP? Or even 60 or 70 percent? Would a balanced budget make any of us better off then?

Full Disclosure May Help, Though

A balanced budget might force the federal government to tax Americans explicitly and directly for everything they spend on the federal government. Then the true size of the federal government cannot be hidden from the average citizen-taxpayer. That the relative size of the federal government will become smaller is not obvious, however. The electorate could decide in the future that the work of government is even more important than it has been in the past.

FOR CRITICAL ANALYSIS

1. As an individual, does it matter to you how the government pays for its spending—through taxation or through deficit financing?
2. "The federal government can't run in the red forever." Is this statement correct? Explain your answer.

CHAPTER SUMMARY

1. Whenever government expenditures exceed government revenues, a budget deficit occurs. Federal deficit spending as a share of GDP reached its peak right after World War II. In recent years, it has been running at about 50 percent of GDP.

2. The federal government will not go bankrupt just because the public debt is rising, for it has its taxing authority to cover interest payments on the debt, which is constantly rolled over.

3. Government use of resources today must be paid for by people living today, because there is a trade-off between private use of resources and government use of resources in any one year.

4. To the extent that the existence of the federal deficit encourages foreigners to purchase American assets, there is a potential problem that we no longer owe the public debt to ourselves. To the extent that the capital invested by foreigners in the United States has been

productively used, however, future generations will be no worse off and in fact may be better off by the fact that foreigners have invested in this country.

5. If all taxpayers perfectly anticipate increased future tax liabilities due to higher deficits, saving will increase to cover those tax liabilities. Future productivity will therefore not be affected, nor will interest rates rise; there will be no crowding-out effect.

6. Some people argue that the federal budget deficit is measured incorrectly because it lumps together spending on capital and spending on consumption. It is therefore argued that there should be an operating budget and a capital budget.

7. Suggested ways to reduce the deficit are to increase taxes, particularly on the rich, and to reduce expenditures, particularly on entitlements, defined as guaranteed benefits under a government program such as Social Security or Medicare.

DISCUSSION OF PREVIEW QUESTIONS

1. **By what methods can the U.S. federal government obtain purchasing power?**
   In the United States, the federal government is able to obtain purchasing power by selling bonds, taxing, or creating money. State and local governments can also obtain purchasing power by selling bonds and by taxing, but only the federal government has the power to create money in the United States. Perhaps surprisingly, regardless of how government expenditures are financed, most of the burden of government expendi-

tures falls on the present generation; the effects of government money creation and bond sales are similar to the effects of taxation. All of the methods of financing government expenditures require the present generation to consume fewer consumer goods now in order to get more governmentally provided goods. Taxation does so in an obvious way; government bond sales compete with private industry bond sales, thereby contracting the private sector.

2. **What are some suggested ways to reduce the federal government deficit?**

The two most obvious ways to reduce the federal budget deficit are increasing taxes and reducing expenditures. Historically, though, for every dollar increase in federal taxes there has been $1.59 increase in federal government spending. Reductions in federal spending face political problems because of the difficulty of reducing entitlements.

3. **What is the difference between the gross public debt and the net public debt?**

The gross public debt is all federal government debt irrespective of who owns it. The net public debt eliminates all government interagency borrowing. In other words, if we subtract what government agencies borrow from each other from the gross public debt, we obtain the net public debt.

4. **What is the burden of the public debt?**

If federal spending that increases the public debt crowds out private investment, future generations will be burdened with a lower capital stock and lower incomes. If the Ricardian equivalence theorem holds—if people in fact increase saving today to pay for higher tax liabilities in the future when there is deficit spending—crowding out is not inevitable, and this burden may not be as great as presumed.

PROBLEMS

(Answers to the odd-numbered problems appear at the back of the book.)

14-1. In 1999, government spending is $8 trillion and taxes collected are $7.7 trillion. What is the federal budget deficit in that year?

14-2. Look at the accompanying table showing federal budget spending and federal budget receipts. Calculate the federal budget deficit as a percentage of GDP for each year.

Year	Federal Budget Receipts ($ billions)	Federal Budget Spending ($ billions)	GDP ($ trillions)
1988	972.3	1,109.0	4,900.4
1989	1,059.3	1,181.6	5,250.8
1990	1,107.4	1,273.6	5,522.2
1991	1,122.2	1,332.7	5,677.5

14-3. It may be argued that the effects of a higher public debt are the same as the effects of higher taxes. Why?

14-4. To reduce the size of the deficit (and reduce the growth in the net public debt), a politician suggests that "we should tax the rich." The politician makes a simple arithmetic calculation in which he applies the increased tax rate to the total income reported by "the rich" in a previous year. He says that this is how much the government could receive from the increased taxes on "the rich." What is the major fallacy in such calculations?

14-5. Proponents of capital budgeting theory argue that whenever the government invests in capital expenditures, such as roads and dams, such government spending should be put in a separate budget called the capital budget. In doing so, the federal government's budget deficit would thereby be reduced by the amount of government capital spending. Would such a change in measuring the government deficit change anything? Explain.

14-6. What is the relationship between the gross public debt and the net public debt? What is the relationship between the annual federal government budget deficit and the net public debt?

COMPUTER-ASSISTED INSTRUCTION

A series of conceptual and numerical exercises illustrates the links among taxation, government spending, and the size of the public debt.

Complete problem and answer appear on disk.

INTERACTING WITH THE INTERNET

A great amount of information on the U.S. federal budget can be found at
   gopher://sunny.stat-usa.gov/11/BudgetFY96
(future budgets should have a similar name). You can also find detailed material on the federal debt there; see
   gopher://sunny.stat-usa.gov/00/BudgetFY96/Historical/bud96h07.txt
   You can try to balance the budget yourself at
   http://garnet.berkeley.edu:3333/budget/budget.html

PART 5

MONEY, MONETARY POLICY, AND STABILIZATION

CHAPTER

15

MONEY AND THE BANKING SYSTEM

Worldwide telecommunications are growing at such a rapid pace that it's hard to keep up with the changes. The Internet is accessed by over 40 million individuals, and millions more are logging on each year. It is now possible to do business on the Internet—to buy and to sell. But how do you pay for those purchases? Many people use credit card numbers, now that safeguards exist to prevent the numbers from being accessed by crooks. But something else is starting to happen—the advent of *e-cash,* or digital money. Will digital money have an effect on our banking system? To answer this question, you need to know what money is and how it relates to what banks do today.

PREVIEW QUESTIONS

1. What is money?

2. What "backs" the U.S. dollar?

3. What are the functions of the Federal Reserve System?

4. Who is involved in the process of transferring funds from savers to investors?

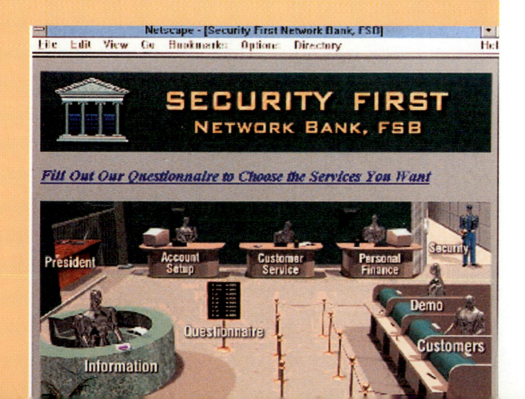

Did You Know That . . . the typical dollar bill changes hands 50 times a year? Cash, of course, is not the only thing we use as money. As you will see in this chapter, our definition of money is much broader. Money has been important to society for thousands of years. In 300 B.C., Aristotle claimed that everything had to "be accessed in money, for this enables men always to exchange their services, and so makes society possible." Money is indeed a part of our everyday existence. We have to be careful, though, when we talk about money because it means two different things. Most of the time when people say "I wish I had more money," they mean that they want more income. Thus the normal use of the term *money* implies the ability to purchase goods and services. In this chapter, in contrast, you will use the term **money** to mean anything that people generally accept in exchange for goods and services. Most people think of money as the paper bills and coins they carry. But as you will see in this chapter, the concept of money is normally more inclusive. Table 15-1 provides a list of the types of money that have been used throughout the history of civilization. The best way to understand money is to examine its functions.

THE FUNCTIONS OF MONEY

Money traditionally serves four functions. The one that most people are familiar with is money's function as a *medium of exchange*. Money also serves as a *unit of accounting,* a *store of value* or *purchasing power,* and a *standard of deferred payment*. Anything that serves these four functions is money. Anything that could serve these four functions could be considered money.

Money as a Medium of Exchange

When we say that money serves as a **medium of exchange,** what we mean is that sellers will accept it as payment in market transactions. Without some generally accepted medium of exchange, we would have to resort to *barter*. In fact, before money was used, transactions took place by means of barter. **Barter** is simply a direct exchange—no intermediary

Money
Any medium that is universally accepted in an economy both by sellers of goods and services as payment for those goods and services and by creditors as payment for debts.

Medium of exchange
Any asset that sellers will accept as payment.

Barter
The direct exchange of goods and services for other goods and services without the use of money.

Iron	Boar tusk	Playing cards
Copper	Red woodpecker scalps	Leather
Brass	Feathers	Gold
Wine	Glass	Silver
Corn	Polished beads (wampum)	Knives
Salt	Rum	Pots
Horses	Molasses	Boats
Sheep	Tobacco	Pitch
Goats	Agricultural implements	Rice
Tortoise shells	Round stones with centers removed	Cows
Porpoise teeth	Crystal salt bars	Paper
Whale teeth	Snail shells	Cigarettes

TABLE 15-1
Types of Money
This is a partial list of things that have been used as money. Native Americans used wampum, beads made from shells. Fijians used whale teeth. The early colonists in North America used tobacco. And cigarettes were used in prisoner-of-war camps during World War II and in post–World War II Germany.

Source: Roger LeRoy Miller and David D. VanHoose, *Modern Money and Banking,* 3d ed. (New York: McGraw-Hill, 1993), p. 13.

good called money is used. In a barter economy, the shoemaker who wants to obtain a dozen water glasses must seek out a glassmaker who at exactly the same time is interested in obtaining a pair of shoes. For this to occur, there has to be a *double coincidence of wants*. If there isn't, the shoemaker must go through several trades in order to obtain the desired dozen glasses—perhaps first trading shoes for jewelry, then jewelry for some pots and pans, and then the pots and pans for the desired glasses.

Money facilitates exchange by reducing the transaction costs associated with means-of-payment uncertainty—that is, with regard to goods that the partners in any exchange are willing to accept. The existence of money means that individuals no longer have to hold a diverse collection of goods as an exchange inventory. As a medium of exchange, money allows individuals to specialize in any area in which they have a comparative advantage and to receive money payments for their labor. Money payments can then be exchanged for the fruits of other people's labor. The use of money as a medium of exchange permits more specialization and the inherent economic efficiencies that come with it (and hence greater economic growth). Money is even more important when used for large amounts of trade.

Money as a Unit of Accounting

Unit of accounting
A measure by which prices are expressed; the common denominator of the price system; a central property of money.

A **unit of accounting** is a way of placing a specific price on economic goods and services. Thus as a unit of accounting, the monetary unit is used to measure the value of goods and services *relative to* other goods and services. It is the common denominator, or measure, the commonly recognized unit of value measurement. The dollar is the monetary unit in the United States. It is the yardstick that allows individuals easily to compare the relative value of goods and services. Accountants at the U.S. Department of Commerce use dollar prices to measure national income and domestic product, a business uses dollar prices to calculate profits and losses, and a typical household budgets regularly anticipated expenses using dollar prices as its unit of accounting.

Another way of describing money as a unit of accounting is to say that it serves as a *standard of value* that allows economic actors to compare the relative worth of various goods and services. It allows for comparison shopping, for example.

Money as a Store of Value

Store of value
The ability to hold value over time; a necessary property of money.

One of the most important functions of money is that it serves as a **store of value** or purchasing power. The money you have today can be set aside to purchase things later on. In the meantime, money retains its nominal value, which you can apply to those future purchases. If you have $1,000 in your checking account, you can either spend it today on goods and services, spend it tomorrow, or spend it a month from now. In this way, money provides a way to transfer value (wealth) into the future.

Money as a Standard of Deferred Payment

Standard of deferred payment
A property of an asset that makes it desirable for use as a means of settling debts maturing in the future; an essential property of money.

The fourth function of the monetary unit is as a **standard of deferred payment.** This function involves the use of money both as a medium of exchange and as a unit of accounting. Debts are typically stated in terms of a unit of accounting; they are paid with a monetary

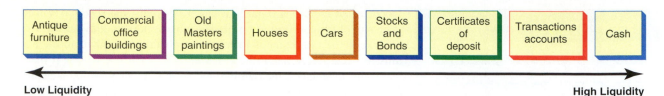

Low Liquidity   High Liquidity

FIGURE 15-1
Degrees of Liquidity
The most liquid asset is, of course, cash. Liquidity decreases as you move from right to left.

medium of exchange. That is to say, a debt is specified in a dollar amount and paid in currency (or by check). A corporate bond, for example, has a face value—the dollar value stated on it, which is to be paid upon maturity. The periodic interest payments on that corporate bond are specified and paid in dollars, and when the bond comes due (at maturity), the corporation pays the face value in dollars to the holder of the bond.

Not all countries, or the firms and individuals in those countries, will specify that debts owed must be paid in their own national monetary unit. For example, individuals, private corporations, and governments in other countries incur debts in terms of the U.S. dollar, even though the dollar is neither the medium of exchange nor the monetary unit in those countries. Also, contracts for some debts specify repayment in gold rather than in a nation's currency.

Liquidity

Money is an asset—something of value—that accounts for part of personal wealth. Wealth in the form of money can be exchanged later for some other asset. Although it is not the only form of wealth that can be exchanged for goods and services, it is the one most widely and readily accepted. This attribute of money is called **liquidity.** We say that an asset is liquid when it can easily be acquired or disposed of without high transaction costs and with relative certainty as to its value. Money is by definition the most liquid asset there is. Just compare it, for example, with a share of stock listed on the New York Stock Exchange. To buy or sell that stock, you usually call a stockbroker, who will place the buy or sell order for you. This generally must be done during normal business hours. You have to pay a commission to the broker. Moreover, there is a distinct probability that you will get more or less for the stock than you originally paid for it. This is not the case with money. Money can be easily converted to other asset forms. Therefore, most individuals hold at least a part of their wealth in the form of the most liquid of assets, money. You can see how assets rank in liquidity relative to one another in Figure 15-1.

When we hold money, however, we pay a price for this advantage of liquidity. That price is the interest yield that could have been obtained had the asset been held in another form—for example, in the form of stocks and bonds.

> **The cost of holding money (its opportunity cost) is measured by the alternative interest yield obtainable by holding some other asset.**

MONETARY STANDARDS, OR WHAT BACKS MONEY

Today in the United States, all of us accept coins, paper currency, and balances in **transactions accounts** (checking accounts with banks and other financial institutions) in exchange for items sold, including labor services. The question remains, why are we willing to accept as payment something that has no intrinsic value? After all, you could not sell checks to

Liquidity
The degree to which an asset can be acquired or disposed of without much danger of any intervening loss in *nominal* value and with small transaction costs. Money is the most liquid asset.

Transactions accounts
Checking account balances in commercial banks and other types of financial institutions, such as credit unions and mutual savings banks; any accounts in financial institutions on which you can easily write checks without many restrictions.

Fiduciary monetary system
A system in which currency is issued by the government and its value is based uniquely on the public's faith that the currency represents command over goods and services.

anybody for use as a raw material in manufacturing. The reason is that in this country the payments arise from a **fiduciary monetary system.** This means that the value of the payments rests on the public's confidence that such payments can be exchanged for goods and services. *Fiduciary* comes from the Latin *fiducia,* which means "trust" or "confidence." In our fiduciary monetary system, money, in the form of currency or transactions accounts, is not convertible to a fixed quantity of gold, silver, or some other precious commodity. The paper money that people hold cannot be exchanged for a specified quantity of some specified commodity. The bills are just pieces of paper. Coins have a value stamped on them that is normally greater than the market value of the metal in them. Nevertheless, currency and transactions accounts are money because of their acceptability and predictability of value.

Acceptability

Transactions accounts and currency are money because they are accepted in exchange for goods and services. They are accepted because people have confidence that they can later be exchanged for other goods and services. This confidence is based on the knowledge that such exchanges have occurred in the past without problems. Even during a period of relatively rapid inflation, we would still be inclined to accept money in exchange for goods and services because it is so useful. Barter is a costly and time-consuming alternative.

Realize always that money is socially defined. Acceptability is not something that you can necessarily predict. For example, the U.S. government has tried to circulate types of money that were socially unacceptable. How many $2 bills have you seen lately? The answer is probably none. No one wanted to make room for $2 bills in register tills or billfolds.

Predictability of Value

The purchasing power of the dollar (its value) varies inversely with the price level. The more rapid the rate of increase of some price level index, such as the Consumer Price Index, the more rapid the decrease in the value, or purchasing power, of a dollar. Money still retains its usefulness even if its value—its purchasing power—is declining year in and year out, as in periods of inflation, because it still retains the characteristic of predictability of value. If you believe that the inflation rate is going to be around 10 percent next year, you know that any dollar you receive a year from now will have a purchasing power equal to 10 percent less than that same dollar this year. Thus you will not necessarily refuse to use money or accept it in exchange simply because you know that its value will decline by the rate of inflation next year.

CONCEPTS IN BRIEF

- Money is defined by its functions, which are as a medium of exchange, a unit of accounting or standard of value, a store of value or purchasing power, and a standard of deferred payment.

- Because money is a highly liquid asset, it can be disposed of without high transaction costs and with relative certainty as to its value.

- The United States has a fiduciary monetary system—our money is not convertible into a fixed quantity of a commodity such as gold or silver.

- Money is accepted in exchange for goods and services because people have confidence that it can later be exchanged for other goods and services. Another reason for this is that it has a predictable value.

DEFINING THE U.S. MONEY SUPPLY

Money is important. Changes in the total **money supply**—the amount of money in circulation—and changes in the rate at which the money supply increases or decreases affect important economic variables, such as the rate of inflation, interest rates, employment, and the equilibrium level of real national income. Although there is widespread agreement among economists that money is indeed important, they have never agreed on how to define or measure it. There are two approaches to defining and measuring money: the **transactions approach,** which stresses the role of money as a medium of exchange, and the **liquidity approach,** which stresses the role of money as a temporary store of value.

Money supply
The amount of money in circulation.

Transactions approach
A method of measuring the money supply by looking at money as a medium of exchange.

Liquidity approach
A method of measuring the money supply by looking at money as a temporary store of value.

The Transactions Approach to Measuring Money: M1

Using the transactions approach to measuring money, the money supply consists of the following:

1. Currency
2. Checkable deposits
3. Traveler's checks

The official designation of the money supply, including currency, checkable deposits, and traveler's checks not issued by banks is **M1.** The various elements of M1 for a typical year are presented in panel (a) of Figure 15-2.

M1
The money supply, taken as the total value of currency plus checkable deposits plus traveler's checks not issued by banks.

Currency. Currency includes coins minted by the U.S. Treasury and paper currency, usually in the form of Federal Reserve notes, issued by the Federal Reserve banks (to be discussed shortly). Although nowhere near as important as checkable deposits as a percent-

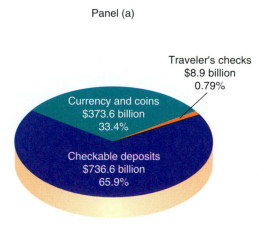

Panel (a)

Traveler's checks
$8.9 billion
0.79%

Currency and coins
$373.6 billion
33.4%

Checkable deposits
$736.6 billion
65.9%

M1 = $1,119.1 billion

Panel (b)

Overnight repurchase agreements
and Eurodollars
$118.6 billion
3.2%

Small time
deposits at all
depository
institutions
$1, 972.3 billion
53.5%

M1 =
$1,119.1 billion
30.3%

Retail money market mutual fund shares
$479.0 billion
13.0%

M2 = $3,689.0 billion

FIGURE 15-2

Composition of the U.S. M1 and M2 Money Supply, 1996

Panel (a) shows the M1 money supply, of which the greatest component is checkable deposits (over 65 percent). M2 consists of M1 plus three other components, the most important of which is small time deposits at all depository institutions (over 50 percent).

Sources: Federal Reserve Bulletin; Economic Indicators, various issues. Data are for 1996.

age of the money supply, currency has increased in significance in the United States. One of the major reasons for the increased use of currency in the U.S. economy is the growing number of illegal transactions, especially illegal drug transactions.

POLICY EXAMPLE
Should the Penny and the Dollar Bill Be Eliminated?

The U.S. Mint started making the penny over 200 years ago. When first put into circulation, the penny could be exchanged for coffee, a loaf of bread, and many other goods. Today, you can buy virtually nothing with one penny. The American government spends millions of dollars a year minting pennies because Americans lose them, throw them out, or just keep them at home. On average, Americans have almost $10 worth of pennies in each household.

The Bureau of Engraving and Printing also spends over $300 million a year printing $1 bills.

Some members of Congress have proposed that the dollar bill be phased out and replaced with a coin. After all, few industrialized countries have a bill that is worth so little. Indeed, in the 1980s and 1990s, Australia, Canada, France, Japan, New Zealand, Norway, Spain, and the United Kingdom each replaced its lowest denomination bills with coins. The British, for example, replaced the one-pound note with a one-pound coin (worth about $1.60). Although coins cost more to produce, they last 30 years compared to a bill, which lasts only 17 months. On a per-year basis, dollar bills cost 10 times more than dollar coins would to keep in circulation.

Not everyone is in favor of replacing dollars with coins, however. There is a social cost to be incurred by carrying around bulky, heavy change. Paper is lighter and often more convenient, although not in vending machines, to be sure.

FOR CRITICAL ANALYSIS: *In 1979, the Susan B. Anthony dollar coin was introduced. It flopped. Can you guess why?* ●

Checkable deposits
Any deposits in a thrift institution or a commercial bank on which a check may be written.

Thrift institutions
Financial institutions that receive most of their funds from the savings of the public; they include mutual savings banks, savings and loan associations, and credit unions.

Traveler's checks
Financial instruments purchased from a bank or a nonbanking organization and signed during purchase that can be used as cash upon a second signature by the purchaser.

Checkable Deposits. Most major transactions today are done with checks. The convenience and safety of using checks has made checking accounts the most important component of the money supply. For example, in 1997 it is estimated that currency transactions accounted for only .5 percent of the *dollar* amount of all transactions. The rest (excluding barter) involved checks. Checks are a way of transferring the ownership of deposits in financial institutions. They are normally acceptable as a medium of exchange. The financial institutions that offer **checkable deposits** are numerous and include virtually all **thrift institutions**—mutual savings banks, savings and loan associations (S&Ls), and credit unions. Regular banks, called commercial banks, used to be the only financial institutions that could offer checkable deposits.

Traveler's Checks. **Traveler's checks** are paid for by the purchaser at the time of transfer. The total quantity of traveler's checks outstanding issued by institutions other than banks is part of the M1 money supply.[1] American Express, Citibank, Cook's, and other institutions issue traveler's checks.

---

[1]Banks place the funds that are to be used to redeem traveler's checks in a special deposit account, and they are therefore already counted as checkable accounts. Nonbank issuers, however, do not place these funds in checkable accounts. Improvements in data collection have made it possible to estimate the total amount of nonbank traveler's checks, and since June 1981 they have been included in M1.

INTERNATIONAL EXAMPLE
Greenbacks Abroad

For years, estimates of the M1 money supply have seemed at odds with the amount of dollars that are printed each year. Of the almost $400 billion in currency and coins circulating outside the banking system, over 85 percent could not be accounted for. University of Wisconsin economist Edgar L. Feige discovered that fully 45 percent is held abroad. Indeed, the dollar is a de facto currency in many developing countries. Feige further discovered that U.S. citizens admit to hoarding another 12 percent of the missing currency and businesses another 10 percent. The underground economy accounts for between 4 and 6 percent.

FOR CRITICAL ANALYSIS: *Foreigners hold lots of our currency. Why don't we generally hold any of their currency?* •

What About Credit Cards?

Even though a large percentage of transactions are accomplished by using a plastic credit card, we do not consider the credit card itself money. Remember the functions of money. A credit card is not a unit of accounting, a store of value, or a standard of deferred payment. The use of your credit card is really a loan to you by the issuer of the card, be it a bank, a retail store, a gas company, or American Express. The proceeds of the loan are paid to the business that sold you something. You must pay back the loan to the issuer of the credit card, either when you get your statement or with interest throughout the year if you don't pay off your balance. (We ignore those with credit card debt who become "deadbeats.") It is not a store of value. Credit cards *defer* rather than complete transactions that ultimately involve the use of money.

A relative newcomer, the *debit card* automatically withdraws money from a transactions account. When you use your debit card to purchase something, you are giving an instruction to your bank to transfer money directly from your bank account to the store's bank account. If the store in which you are shopping has a direct electronic link to the bank, that transfer may be made instantaneously. Use of a debit card does not create a loan. A debit card is therefore not a new type of "money."

The Liquidity Approach to Measuring Money: M2

The liquidity approach to defining and measuring the U.S. money supply involves taking into account not only the most liquid assets that people use as money, which are already included in the definition of M1, but also other assets that are highly liquid—that is, that can be converted into money quickly without loss of nominal dollar value and without much cost. Any (non-M1) assets that come under this definition have been called **near monies.** Thus the liquidity approach to the definition of the money supply will include M1 plus near monies. Also consider that the liquidity approach views money as a temporary store of value and thus includes all of M1 plus all near monies. Panel (b) of Figure 15-2 on page 324 shows the components of **M2**—money as a temporary store of value. We examine each of these components in turn.

Savings Deposits. **Savings deposits** in all **depository institutions** (such as commercial banks, mutual savings banks, savings and loan associations, and credit unions) are part of the M2 money supply. A savings deposit is distinguishable from a time deposit because savings funds may be withdrawn without payment of a penalty. Funds are fully protected against loss in their nominal value. There are two types of savings deposits, statement and passbook.

Near monies
Assets that are almost money. They have a high degree of liquidity; they can be easily converted into money without loss in value. Time deposits and short-term U.S. government securities are examples.

M2
M1 plus (1) savings and small-denomination time deposits at all depository institutions, (2) overnight repurchase agreements at commercial banks, (3) overnight Eurodollars held by U.S. residents other than banks at Caribbean branches of member banks, (4) balances in retail money market mutual funds, and (5) money market deposit accounts (MMDAs).

Savings deposits
Interest-earning funds that can be withdrawn at any time without payment of a penalty.

Depository institutions
Financial institutions that accept deposits from savers and lend those deposits out at interest.

1. *Statement savings deposit.* A statement savings deposit is similar to a checking account because the owner (depositor) receives a monthly statement or record of the deposits and withdrawals and the interest earned during the month. Deposits and withdrawals from a statement savings account can be made by mail.

2. *Passbook savings account.* A passbook savings account requires that the owner present a physical passbook at the time of each deposit or withdrawal. Deposits, withdrawals, and interest are recorded in the passbook.

Time Deposits. A basic distinction has always been made between a checkable deposit, which is a checking account, and a **time deposit,** which theoretically requires notice of withdrawal and on which the financial institution pays the depositor interest. The name indicates that there is an agreed period during which the funds must be left in the financial institution. If they are withdrawn prior to the end of that period, a penalty may be applied. The distinction between checkable and time deposits has been blurred over time, but it is still used in the official definition of the money supply.

Small-Denomination Time Deposits. Time deposits include savings certificates and small **certificates of deposit (CDs).** To be included in the M2 definition of the money supply, such time deposits must be less than $100,000—hence the name *small-denomination time deposits.* The owner of a savings certificate is given a receipt indicating the amount deposited, the interest rate to be paid, and the maturity date. A CD is an actual certificate that indicates the date of issue, its maturity date, and other relevant contractual matters.

A variety of small-denomination time deposits are available from depository institutions, ranging in maturities from one month to 10 years.

Money Market Deposit Accounts (MMDAs). Since 1982, banks and thrift institutions have offered **money market deposit accounts (MMDAs),** which usually require a minimum balance and set limits on the number of monthly transactions (deposits and withdrawals by check).

Overnight Repurchase Agreements at Commercial Banks (REPOs, or RPs). A **repurchase agreement (REPO,** or **RP)** is made by a bank to sell Treasury or federal agency securities to its customers, coupled with an agreement to repurchase them at a price that includes accumulated interest. REPOs fill a gap in that depository institutions are not yet allowed to offer to businesses interest-bearing commercial checking accounts. Therefore, REPOs can be thought of as a financial innovation that bypasses regulation because businesses can deposit their excess cash in REPOs instead of leaving it in non-interest-bearing commercial checking accounts.

Overnight Eurodollars. **Eurodollar deposits** are dollar-denominated deposits in foreign commercial banks and in foreign branches of U.S. banks. *Dollar-denominated* simply means that although the deposit might be held at a Caribbean commercial bank, its value is stated in terms of U.S. dollars rather than in terms of the local currency. The term *Eurodollar* is inaccurate because banks outside continental Europe participate in the so-called Eurodollar market and also because banks in some countries issue deposits denominated in German marks, Swiss francs, British sterling, and Dutch guilders.

Money Market Mutual Fund Balances. Many individuals keep part of their assets in the form of shares in **money market mutual funds.** These retail mutual funds invest only in short-term credit instruments. The majority of these money market funds allow check-writing privileges, provided that the size of the check exceeds some minimum.

Time deposit
A deposit in a financial institution that requires notice of intent to withdraw or must be left for an agreed period. Withdrawal of funds prior to the end of the agreed period may result in a penalty.

Certificate of deposit (CD)
A time deposit with a fixed maturity date offered by banks and other financial institutions.

Money market deposit accounts (MMDAs)
Accounts issued by banks yielding a market rate of interest with a minimum balance requirement and a limit on transactions. They have no minimum maturity.

Repurchase agreement (REPO, or RP)
An agreement made by a bank to sell Treasury or federal agency securities to its customers, coupled with an agreement to repurchase them at a price that includes accumulated interest.

Eurodollar deposits
Deposits denominated in U.S. dollars but held in banks outside the United States, often in overseas branches of U.S. banks.

Money market mutual funds
Funds of investment companies that obtain funds from the public that are held in common and used to acquire short-maturity credit instruments, such as certificates of deposit and securities sold by the U.S. government.

M2 and Other Money Supply Definitions. When all of these assets are added together, the result is M2. The composition of M2 is given in panel (b) of Figure 15-2 (page 324).

Economists and researchers have come up with even broader definitions of money than M2.[2] More assets are simply added to the definition. Just remember that there is no one best definition of the money supply. For different purposes, different definitions are appropriate. If we want to use a definition that seems to correlate best with economic activity on an economywide basis, M2 is probably best.

THE U.S. BANKING STRUCTURE

The United States's banking system consists of a **central bank** called the Federal Reserve System, or **the Fed.** In addition, there are a large number of commercial banks, which are privately owned, profit-seeking institutions, and thrift institutions (savings and loan associations, mutual savings banks, and credit unions).

Financial Intermediaries: Sources and Uses of Funds

The financial institutions in our banking system are all in the same business—transferring funds from savers to investors. This process has become known as **financial intermediation,** and its participants are called **financial intermediaries.** Savers lend funds through financial intermediaries (banks, savings and loans, etc.) to borrowers such as businesses, governments, and home buyers. The process of financial intermediation is illustrated in Figure 15-3.

Central bank
A banker's bank, usually an official institution that also serves as a country's treasury's bank. Central banks normally regulate commercial banks.

The Fed
The Federal Reserve System; the central bank of the United States.

Financial intermediation
The process by which financial institutions accept savings from businesses, households, and governments and lend the savings to other businesses, households, and governments.

Financial intermediaries
Institutions that transfer funds between ultimate lenders (savers) and ultimate borrowers.

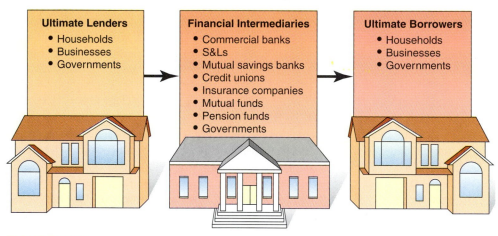

FIGURE 15-3

The Process of Financial Intermediation
The process of financial intermediation is depicted here. Note that ultimate lenders and ultimate borrowers are the same economic units—households, businesses, and governments—but not necessarily the same individuals. Whereas individual households can be net lenders or borrowers, households as an economic unit are net lenders. Specific businesses or governments similarly can be net lenders or borrowers; as economic units, both are net borrowers.

---

[2]They include M3, which is equal to M2 plus large-denomination time deposits and REPOs (in amounts over $100,000) issued by commercial banks and thrift institutions, Eurodollars held by U.S. residents and foreign branches of U.S. banks worldwide and all banking offices in the United Kingdom and Canada, and the balances in both taxable and tax-exempt institution-only money market mutual funds. An even broader definition is called L, for liquidity. It is defined as M3 plus nonbank public holdings of U.S. savings bonds, short-term Treasury securities, commercial paper, and bankers' acceptances.

TABLE 15-2
Financial Intermediaries and Their Assets and Liabilities

Financial Intermediary	Assets	Liabilities
Commercial banks	Car loans and other consumer debt, business loans, government securities, home mortgages	Transactions accounts, savings deposits, various other time deposits, money market deposit accounts
Savings and loan associations	Home mortgages, some consumer and business debt	Savings and loan shares, transactions accounts, various time deposits, money market deposit accounts
Mutual savings banks	Home mortgages, some consumer and business debt	Transactions accounts, savings accounts, various time deposits, money market deposit accounts
Credit unions	Consumer debt, long-term mortgage loans	Credit union shares, transactions accounts
Insurance companies	Mortgages, stocks, bonds, real estate	Insurance contracts, annuities, pension plans
Pension and retirement funds	Stocks, bonds, mortgages, time deposits	Pension plans
Money market mutual funds	Short-term credit instruments such as large-bank CDs, Treasury bills, and high-grade commercial paper	Fund shares with limited checking privileges

Liabilities
Amounts owed; the legal claims against a business or household by nonowners.

Assets
Amounts owned; all items to which a business or household holds legal claim.

Each financial intermediary in the U.S. system has its own primary source of funds, which are called **liabilities.** When you deposit $100 in your checking account in the bank, the bank creates a liability—it owes you $100—in exchange for the funds deposited. A commercial bank gets its funds from checking and savings accounts; an insurance company gets its funds from insurance policy premiums.

Each financial intermediary normally has a different primary use of its **assets.** For example, a credit union usually makes small consumer loans, whereas a mutual savings bank makes mainly home mortgage loans. Table 15-2 lists the assets and liabilities of financial intermediaries. Be aware, though, that the distinction between different financial institutions is becoming more and more blurred. As the laws and regulations change, there will be less need to make any distinction. All may ultimately be treated simply as financial intermediaries.

CONCEPTS IN BRIEF

- The money supply can be defined in a variety of ways, depending on whether we use the transactions approach or the liquidity approach. Using the transactions approach, the money supply consists of currency, checkable deposits, and traveler's checks. This is called M1.
- Checkable deposits (transactions accounts) are any deposits in financial institutions on which the deposit owner can write checks.
- Credit cards are not part of the money supply, for they simply defer transactions that ultimately involve the use of money.

- When we add savings deposits, time deposits, small-denomination time deposits (certificates of deposit), money market deposit accounts, overnight REPOs, overnight Eurodollars, and retail money market mutual fund balances to M1, we obtain the measure known as M2.

- Financial intermediaries transfer funds from ultimate lenders (savers) to ultimate borrowers. This process of financial intermediation is undertaken by commercial banks, savings and loan associations, mutual savings banks, credit unions, insurance companies, mutual funds, pension funds, and governments.

THE FEDERAL RESERVE SYSTEM

The Federal Reserve System is the most important regulatory agency in our monetary system and is usually considered the monetary authority. Our central bank was established by the Federal Reserve Act, signed on December 23, 1913, by President Woodrow Wilson. The act was the outgrowth of recommendations from the National Monetary Commission, which had been authorized by the Aldridge-Vreeland Act of 1908. Basically, the commission had attempted to find a way to counter the periodic financial panics that had occurred in our country. The Federal Reserve System was established to aid and supervise banks and also to provide banking services for the U.S. Treasury.

Organization of the Federal Reserve System

Figure 15-4 shows how the Federal Reserve is organized. It is run by the Board of Governors, composed of seven full-time members appointed by the nation's president with the approval of the Senate. The 12 Federal Reserve district banks have a total of 25 branches. The boundaries of the 12 federal reserve districts and the cities in which a Federal Reserve bank is located are shown in Figure 15-5 on page 332. The Federal Open Market Committee (FOMC) determines monetary policy actions for the Fed. This committee is composed of the members of the Board of Governors, the president of the New York Federal Reserve Bank, and representatives of four other reserve banks, rotated periodically. The FOMC determines the future growth of the money supply and other important variables.

Depository Institutions

The banks and other depository institutions—all financial institutions that accept deposits—that comprise our monetary system consist of approximately 10,000 commercial banks, 2,100 savings and loan associations, 12,000 credit unions, and 500 mutual savings banks. No one financial institution dominates the marketplace. For example, the largest bank holds only 6 percent of total banking system deposits. All depository institutions, including member and nonmember commercial banks, as well as savings and loan associations, credit unions, and mutual savings banks, may purchase services from the Federal Reserve System on an equal basis. Also, almost all depository institutions are required to keep a certain percentage of their deposits in reserve at the Federal Reserve district banks or as vault cash. This percentage depends on the bank's volume of business. (For further discussion, see Chapter 16.)

Functions of the Federal Reserve System

Here we will present in detail what the Federal Reserve does in this country.

1. *The Fed supplies the economy with fiduciary currency.* The Federal Reserve banks must supply the economy with paper currency called Federal Reserve notes. For example,

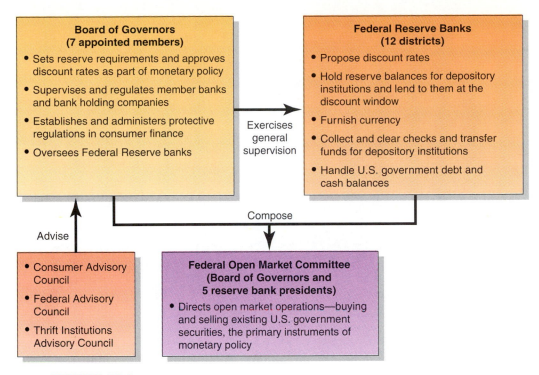

FIGURE 15-4

Organization of the Federal Reserve System

The 12 Federal Reserve district banks are headed by 12 separate presidents. The main authority of the Fed resides with the Board of Governors of the Federal Reserve System, whose seven members are appointed for 14-year terms by the president and confirmed by the Senate. Open market operations are carried out through the Federal Open Market Committee (FOMC), consisting of the seven members of the Board of Governors plus five presidents of the district banks (always including the president of the New York bank, with the others rotating).

Source: Board of Governors of the Federal Reserve System, *The Federal Reserve System: Purposes and Functions,* 7th ed. (Washington, D.C., 1984), p. 5.

at Christmastime, when there is an abnormally large number of currency transactions, more paper currency is desired. Commercial banks find this out as deposit holders withdraw large amounts of cash from their accounts. Commercial banks then turn to the Federal Reserve banks to replenish vault cash. Hence the Federal Reserve banks must have on hand a sufficient amount of cash to accommodate the demands for paper currency at different times of the year. Note that even though all Federal Reserve notes are printed at the Bureau of Printing and Engraving in Washington, D.C., each note is assigned a code indicating from which of the 12 Federal Reserve banks it "originated."

2. *The Fed provides a system for check collection and clearing.* The Federal Reserve System has established a clearing mechanism for checks. Suppose that John Smith in Chicago writes a check to Jill Jones, who lives in San Francisco. When Jill receives the check in the mail, she deposits it at her commercial bank. Her bank then deposits the check in the Federal Reserve Bank of San Francisco. In turn, the Federal Reserve Bank of San Francisco sends the check to the Federal Reserve Bank of Chicago. The Chicago Fed then sends the check to John Smith's commercial bank, where the amount of the check is deducted from John's account. The schematic diagram in Figure 15-6 on page 333 illustrates this check-clearing process. All member banks and

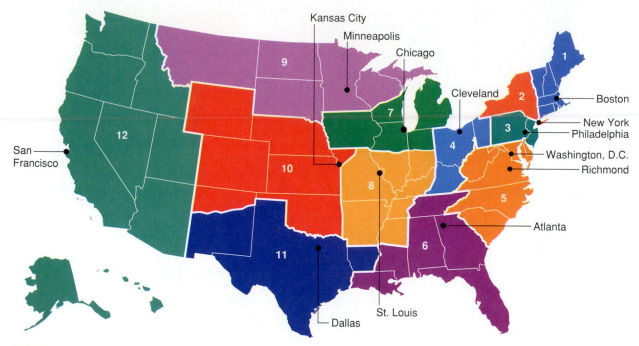

FIGURE 15-5

The Federal Reserve System
The Federal Reserve System is divided into 12 districts, each served by one of the Federal Reserve district banks, located in the cities indicated. The Board of Governors meets in Washington, D.C.

depository institutions in a particular Federal Reserve district can send deposited checks to one location—their district bank—thereby reducing the cost of check clearing. (The Fed's check collection and clearing operations compete with private clearinghouses. Since the Fed began charging for these services, some of this business has shifted back to the private sector.)

3. *The Fed holds depository institutions' reserves*. The 12 Federal Reserve district banks hold the reserves (other than vault cash) of depository institutions. As you will see in Chapter 16, depository institutions are required by law to keep a certain percentage of their deposits in reserves. Even if they weren't required to do so by law, they would still wish to keep some reserves. Depository institutions act just like other businesses. A firm would not try to operate with a zero balance in its checking account, would it? It would keep a positive balance on hand from which it could draw for expected and unexpected transactions. So, too, would a depository institution desire to have reserves in its banker's bank (the Federal Reserve) on which it could draw funds needed for expected and unexpected transactions.

4. *The Fed acts as the government's fiscal agent*. The Federal Reserve is the banker and fiscal agent for the federal government. The government, as we are all aware, collects large sums of money through taxation. The government also spends and distributes equally large sums. Consequently, the U.S. Treasury has a checking account with the Federal Reserve. Thus the Fed acts as the government's banker, along with commercial banks that hold government deposits. The Fed also helps the government collect certain tax revenues and aids in the purchase and sale of government securities.

FIGURE 15-6

How a Check Clears
The check-clearing process for an out-of-town check normally involves four steps, including two with Federal Reserve district banks.

5. *The Fed supervises member banks.* The Fed (along with the Comptroller of the Currency and the Federal Deposit Insurance Corporation) is the supervisor and regulator of depository institutions. (All banks are regulated by some agency. No bank, savings and loan association, or credit union in the United States is unregulated.) The Fed will periodically and without warning examine member commercial banks to see what kinds of loans have been made, what has been used to back the loans, and who has received them. Whenever such an examination indicates that a member bank is not conforming to current banking rules and standards, the Fed can exert pressure on the bank to alter its banking practices.

6. *The Fed acts as the "lender of last resort."* As our central bank, the Fed stands ready to temporarily assist any part of the banking system that is in trouble. In this sense, it acts as a lender of last resort to depository institutions that it has decided should not fail.

7. *The Fed regulates the money supply.* Perhaps the Fed's most important task is its ability to regulate the nation's money supply. To understand how the Fed manages the money supply, we must examine more closely its reserve-holding function and the way in which depository institutions aid in expansion and contraction of the money supply. We will do this in Chapter 16.

EXAMPLE
Cashing Your Check at a Nonbank

One of the fastest-growing banking industries in the United States is the check-cashing business. As America's large banks continue to shy away from low-income areas, the number of private check cashers has skyrocketed. In 1990, there were approximately 2,000 check-cashing outlets; today, they number well over 5,000. Shares of some check-cashing chains are even traded on major stock exchanges.

One reason that check cashers have become so popular is that the percentage of American families without a bank account has increased from 9 percent in 1980 to almost 15 percent today. Consider South Central Los Angeles with a population close to that of Washington, D.C. At most times there are fewer than 20 banks in all of South Central, yet there are more than 20 in a half-mile stretch of downtown D.C. Approximately 140 fee-charging, check-cashing outlets compensate for the absence of banks in this Los Angeles neighborhood.

Forty-two states have no regulations on check-cashing fees. These services generally charge anywhere from 2 to 10 percent of the amount of the check cashed. Some check cashers also have entered the lending business by cashing a postdated check for customers. The annualized interest rate on these short-term loans often exceeds 1,000 percent. According to University of Illinois economist John Binder, check cashers earn 10 to 20 times more on their initial investment than banks do. Check cashers argue that Binder's figures are inflated because they do not take into account the high security and insurance costs that check-cashing outlets must pay.

FOR CRITICAL ANALYSIS: *How can check cashers get away with charging such high fees?* ●

CONCEPTS IN BRIEF

- The central bank in the United States is the Federal Reserve System, which was established on December 13, 1913.

- There are 12 Federal Reserve district banks, with 25 branches. The Federal Reserve is run by the Board of Governors in Washington, D.C.

- The Fed has control over virtually all depository institutions in the United States, including commercial banks, savings and loan associations, credit unions, and mutual savings banks. Most must keep a certain percentage of their deposits on reserve with the Fed.

- The functions of the Federal Reserve are to supply fiduciary currency, provide for check collection and clearing, hold depository institution reserves, act as the government's fiscal agent, supervise member banks, act as the lender of last resort, and regulate the supply of money.

ISSUES AND APPLICATIONS

Watch Out for E-Cash

Concepts Applied: Money, money supply, transactions accounts

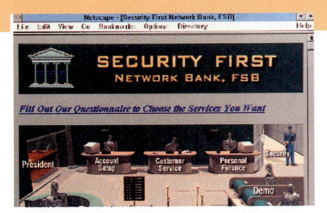

On-line banking and other Internet services introduce the advent of a growing e-cash economy. But the convenience of electronic commerce raises other issues, such as electronic counterfeiting, tax evasion, and money laundering.

It began with seashells and beads. Objects that were once used as money were gradually replaced by standardized commodities, such as gold and silver. Then came paper money and next checking accounts. With checking accounts and new technology have come electronic means of handling money, such as ATMs and debit cards.

Enter Mondex

Two British banks, National Westminster and Midland, started a plastic-and-silicone cash substitute called Mondex cards. They resemble ATM cards but carry a computer chip inside. This is *data money*. Bank customers can transfer data money onto their cards over the phone if they have a "smart" phone in their house. Although Mondex marks the beginning of the true cashless society, banks still play a large role.

Now there's e-money too. Companies other than banks have started their own forms of electronic money called *e-cash*. E-cash operates completely outside the network of banks, checks, and paper currency. In other words, accounts are debited and credited without cash or checks changing hands (just as banks have begun to do among themselves). Some of the companies in the e-cash game, such as Microsoft and Xerox, are well known; others, such as CyberCash and DigiCash, are less well known. Perhaps e-cash's biggest opportunity for success will be on the Internet, where electronic commerce is growing daily. People will be able to download money to their PC or to palm-sized electronic wallets or transfer money instantly to Internet merchants.

The Benefits of E-Cash

E-cash may turn out to be more convenient than traditional money, particularly on the Internet. Banks that decide to issue e-cash may find it cheaper than handling checks and paper records.

The Risks of E-Cash

The traditional definition of money will certainly no longer hold if e-cash becomes the preferred method of carrying out transactions. The Federal Reserve will have less ability to control the money supply. Furthermore, e-cash may present problems if it is stored in computer systems. What if the systems crash? Furthermore, electronic counterfeiting may turn out to be a serious problem. Computer hackers who break into an e-cash system might be able to steal money from thousands or even hundreds of thousands of individuals all at once. Finally, e-cash may allow for more tax evasion and money laundering.

FOR CRITICAL ANALYSIS

1. Will there be any way to measure the size of the e-cash element of the money supply in the future?
2. What is the disadvantage of having a Mondex card instead of cash?

CHAPTER SUMMARY

1. The functions of money are as a medium of exchange, a unit of accounting (standard of value), a store of value or purchasing power, and a standard of deferred payment.

2. We have a fiduciary monetary system in the United States—our money, whether in the form of currency or checkable accounts, is not convertible into a fixed quantity of a commodity, such as gold or silver.

3. Our money is exchangeable for goods and services because it has acceptability: People have confidence that whatever money they receive can be exchanged for other goods and services later. Our money also has a predictable value.

4. There are numerous ways to define the U.S. money supply. One method is called the transactions approach, which stresses the role of money as a medium of exchange. The other method is the liquidity approach, which stresses the role of money as a temporary store of value.

5. The transactions approach generates the M1 definition of money, which includes currency, checkable deposits, and traveler's checks not issued by banks.

6. The liquidity approach generates the M2 definition of money, which includes M1 plus such near monies as savings deposits, overnight repurchase agreements, retail money market mutual fund balances, money market deposit accounts, and overnight Eurodollars.

7. Our central bank is the Federal Reserve System, which consists of 12 district banks with 25 branches. The governing body of the Federal Reserve System is the Board of Governors. The group that makes monetary policy decisions is the Federal Open Market Committee.

8. The basic functions of the Federal Reserve System are supplying the economy with fiduciary currency, providing a system for check collection and clearing, holding depository institutions' reserves, acting as the government's fiscal agent, supervising member banks, acting as a lender of last resort, and regulating the money supply.

DISCUSSION OF PREVIEW QUESTIONS

1. **What is money?**
Money is defined by its functions. Thus money is whatever is generally accepted for use as a medium of exchange, a unit of accounting, a store of value or purchasing power, and a standard of deferred payment. In various places in the world, throughout history, different items have performed these functions: wampum, gold, silver, cows, stones, paper, diamonds, salt, cigarettes, and many others.

2. **What "backs" the U.S. dollar?**
Some students think that the U.S. dollar is "backed" by gold, but alas (some experts say fortunately), this is not the case. The United States is presently on a fiduciary monetary standard, and as such the U.S. dollar is backed only by faith—the public's confidence that it can be exchanged for goods and services. This confidence comes from the fact that other people will accept the dollar in transactions because our government has declared it legal tender and because, despite inflation, it still retains the characteristic of predictability of value.

3. **What are the functions of the Federal Reserve System?**
The Fed's most important function is to regulate the U.S. money supply, a topic covered in the next several chapters. The Fed also holds depository institutions' reserves, acts as the U.S. government's fiscal agent, supervises member banks, serves as a lender of last resort, clears checks, and supplies fiduciary currency to the public.

4. **Who is involved in the process of transferring funds from savers to investors?**
Financial intermediation involves the transfer of funds from savers to investors. The ultimate lenders are the savers—households, businesses, and governments, including the federal government and state

and local governments. The ultimate borrowers are also households, businesses, and governments—the same economic units but not necessarily the same individuals. Between ultimate lenders and ultimate borrowers are financial intermediaries, including commercial banks, savings and loans, mutual savings banks, credit unions, insurance companies, mutual funds, pension funds, and governments.

PROBLEMS

(Answers to the odd-numbered problems appear at the back of the book.)

15-1. Consider each type of asset in terms of its potential use as a medium of exchange, a unit of accounting, and a store of value or purchasing power. Indicate which use is most appropriately associated with each asset.

   a. A painting by Renoir
   b. A 90-day U.S. Treasury bill
   c. A time deposit account with a savings and loan association in Reno, Nevada
   d. One share of IBM stock
   e. A $50 Federal Reserve note
   f. A MasterCard credit card
   g. A checkable account in a mutual savings bank in New England
   h. A lifetime pass to the Los Angeles Dodgers' home baseball games

15-2. The value of a dollar bill is the reciprocal of the price index. In 1983 the CPI had a value of 1; hence the value of a dollar in 1983 equaled $1. If the price index now is 2, what is the value of the dollar in 1983 prices? If the price index is 2.5?

15-3. What are the components of M2?

15-4. How have technological changes altered the form of money?

15-5. Elsa Lee can make several uses of her money. Indicate for each case whether her money is being used as a medium of exchange (E), a unit of accounting (A), a store of value (V), or a standard of deferred payment (P).

   a. Lee has accumulated $600 in her checking account at a depository institution.
   b. Lee decides to use this $600 to purchase a new washing machine and goes shopping to compare the prices being charged by different dealers for the machine she wishes to buy.

   c. Lee finds that the lowest price at which she can purchase the machine she wants is $498.50. She has the dealer deliver the machine and agrees to pay the dealer in 30 days.
   d. Thirty days later, Lee sends the dealer a check drawn on her checking account to pay for the washer.

15-6. Explain why a debit card is not a new form of money.

15-7. Consider a barter economy in which 10 goods and services are produced and exchanged. How many exchange rates exist in that economy, which does not use money?

15-8. Use the data in the table to compute M1.

Components	Amount ($ billions)
Currency outside of the Treasury, Federal Reserve banks, and vaults of depository institutions	193.2
Checkable accounts other than those owned by depository institutions, the U.S. government, foreign banks, and foreign institutions	541.9
Large time deposits, short-term REPOs, liabilities, and overnight Eurodollars	743.4
Nonbank public holdings of U.S. savings bonds	643.0
Nonbank traveler's checks	8.1

15-9. Cash and checks account for nearly 98 percent of the total *number* of all payments in the United States, but wire transfers account for over 82 percent of the dollar *value* of all payments in the United States. How can both situations be true simultaneously?

COMPUTER-ASSISTED INSTRUCTION

The key conceptual and institutional features of our monetary and banking systems are illuminated with the aid of real-world questions.

Complete problem and answer appear on disk.

INTERACTING WITH THE INTERNET

Extensive Fed information can be found at

> **gopher://una.hh.lib.umich.edu/11/ebb/monetary**

It includes current and past monetary statistics, as well as other information. In addition, different Federal Reserve banks have sites on the Net; see the Boston Federal Reserve Bank,

> **gopher://neeedc.umesbs.maine.edu/**

for material on that region; the Philadelphia Federal Reserve Bank,

> **http://www.libertynet.org/~fedresrv/fedpage.html**

for some of its publications; the Chicago Federal Reserve Bank,

> **gopher://gopher.great-lakes.net:2200/11/partners/ChicagoFed**

for guides to the Fed and some macro data in an easy-to-use format; the Minneapolis Federal Reserve Bank,

> **http://woodrow.mpls.frb.fed.us/**

for material on that region. Finally, a number of banks on the Internet can be found at

> **http://www.yahoo.com/Business_and_Economy/Companies/Financial_Services/Banks/**

CHAPTER 16

MONEY CREATION AND DEPOSIT INSURANCE

Life used to be simple for persons wishing to finance the purchase of a house, acquire stocks and bonds, take out insurance, or obtain a credit card. Each of those decisions involved going to any of a well-defined set of separate institutions. Insurance was always bought from an insurance company, for example; stocks and bonds were sold only by brokerage firms; and money for a house was borrowed from a savings and loan association or a mutual savings bank. Today, the choices are much more complicated and the distinctions between banks and nonbanks is getting ever more blurred. All of this comes about in an era of deregulation of depository institutions. To understand the effects of deregulation, you need to learn about the regulation of such institutions and, before that, how money is created in our economy.

PREVIEW QUESTIONS

1. What is a fractional reserve banking system?

2. What happens to the total money supply when a person deposits in one depository institution a check drawn on another depository institution?

3. What happens to the overall money supply when a person who sells a U.S. government security to the Federal Reserve places the proceeds in a depository institution?

4. How does the existence of deposit insurance affect a financial institution's choice of risky versus nonrisky assets?

Did You Know That . . . virtually overnight, Nick Leeson, a 27-year-old manager in the Singapore branch of Barings Bank, was able to inflict losses of several billion dollars on the institution? Barings was founded in 1762. In 1803, it helped the United States purchase the Louisiana Territory from France. It provided credit to the British government during the Napoleonic Wars (1803–1815). When Barings collapsed in 1995, it was bought by former competitors, thereby ending the life of one of the longest-running financial institutions in the world. Could the collapse of such an important bank lead to serious problems in the world's banking sector? A lot depends on whether the losses suffered by Barings's depositors would cause other banks to contract. That, in turn, depends on the relationship between deposits in different banks.

If you were to attend a luncheon of local bankers and ask the question, "Do you as bankers create money?" you would get a uniformly negative response. Bankers are certain that they do not create money. Indeed, no individual bank can create money. But along with the Federal Reserve System, depository institutions do create money; they determine the total deposits outstanding. In this chapter we will examine the **money multiplier process,** which explains how an injection of new money into the banking system leads to an eventual multiple expansion in the total money supply. We will also take a look at federal deposit insurance and its role in provoking the past crisis in the savings and loan industry.

LINKS BETWEEN CHANGES IN THE MONEY SUPPLY AND OTHER ECONOMIC VARIABLES

How fast the money supply grows or does not grow is important because no matter what model of the economy is used, theories link the money supply growth rate to economic growth or to business fluctuations. There is in fact a long-standing relationship between changes in the money supply and changes in GDP. Some economists use this historical evidence to argue that money is an important determinant of the level of economic activity in the economy.

Another key economic variable in our economy is the price level. At least one theory attributes changes in the rate of inflation to changes in the growth rate of money in circulation. Figure 16-1 shows the relationship between the rate of growth of the money supply and the inflation rate. There seems to be a loose, albeit consistent, direct relationship between changes in the money supply and changes in the rate of inflation. Increases in the money supply growth rate seem to lead to increases in the inflation rate, after a time lag.

THE ORIGINS OF FRACTIONAL RESERVE BANKING

As early as 1000 B.C., uncoined gold and silver were being used as money in Mesopotamia. Goldsmiths weighed and assessed the purity of those metals; later they started issuing paper notes indicating that the bearers held gold or silver of given weights and purity on deposit with the goldsmith. These notes could be transferred in exchange for goods and became the first paper currency. The gold and silver on deposit with the goldsmiths were the first bank deposits. Eventually, goldsmiths realized that the amount of gold and silver on deposit always exceeded the amount of gold and silver withdrawn—often by a predictable ratio. These goldsmiths started issuing to borrowers paper notes that exceeded in value the amount of gold and silver they actually kept on hand. They charged interest on these loans. This constituted the earliest form of what is now called **fractional reserve banking.** We know that goldsmiths operated this way in Delphi, Didyma, and Olympia in

Money multiplier process
The process by which an injection of new money into the banking system leads to a multiple expansion in the total money supply.

Fractional reserve banking
A system in which depository institutions hold reserves that are less than the amount of total deposits.

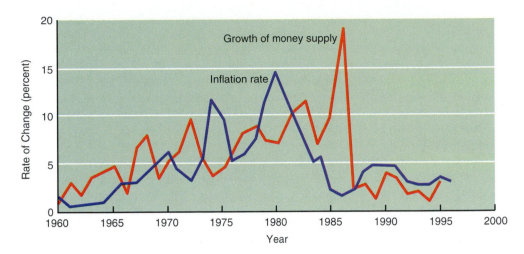

FIGURE 16-1

Money Supply Growth Versus the Inflation Rate
These time-series curves indicate a loose correspondence between money supply growth and the inflation rate. Actually, closer inspection reveals a direct relationship between changes in the growth rate of money and changes in the inflation rate *in a later period.* Increases in the rate of growth of money seem to lead to subsequent increases in the inflation rate; decreases in the rate of money growth seem to lead to subsequent reductions in the inflation rate.
Sources: Economic Report of the President; Federal Reserve Bulletin; Economic Indicators, various issues.

Greece as early as the seventh century B.C. In Athens, fractional reserve banking was well developed by the sixth century B.C.

In a fractional reserve banking system, banks do not keep sufficient reserves on hand to cover 100 percent of their depositors' accounts. And the reserves that are held by depository institutions in the United States are not kept in gold and silver, as they were with the early goldsmiths, but rather in the form of deposits on reserve with Federal Reserve district banks and in vault cash.

RESERVES

Depository institutions are required by the Fed to maintain a specified percentage of their customer deposits as **reserves.** Different types of depository institutions are required to hold different percentages of reserves. Also, within one type of depository institution, the larger the institution, the larger the reserve requirements. On checkable accounts, most depository institutions have to keep 10 percent as reserves.

Take a hypothetical example. If the required level of reserves is 10 percent and the bank[1] has $1 billion in customer checkable deposits, it must hold at least $100 million as reserves. These can be either deposits with the Federal Reserve district bank or vault cash. There are three distinguishable types of reserves: legal, required, and excess.

1. *Legal reserves.* For depository institutions, **legal reserves** constitute anything that the law permits them to claim as reserves. Today, that consists only of deposits held at the

Reserves
In the U.S. Federal Reserve System, deposits held by Federal Reserve district banks for depository institutions, plus depository institutions' vault cash.

Legal reserves
Reserves that depository institutions are allowed by law to claim as reserves—for example, deposits held at Federal Reserve district banks and vault cash.

---

[1]The term *bank* will be used interchangeably with the term *depository institution* in this chapter because distinctions among financial institutions are becoming less and less meaningful.

Federal Reserve district bank plus vault cash. Government securities, for example, are not legal reserves, even though the owners and managers of the depository institutions may consider them such because they can easily be turned into cash, should the need arise, to meet unusually large net withdrawals by customers.

2. *Required reserves*. **Required reserves** are the *minimum* amount of legal reserves—vault cash plus deposits with the Fed—that a depository institution must have to back its checkable deposits. They are expressed as a ratio of required reserves to total checkable deposits (banks need hold no reserves on noncheckable deposits). The **required reserve ratio** is currently 10 percent.

3. *Excess reserves*. Depository institutions often hold reserves in excess of what is required by law. This difference between actual (legal) reserves and required reserves is called **excess reserves.** (Excess reserves can be negative, but they rarely are. Negative excess reserves indicate that depository institutions do not have sufficient reserves to meet their required reserves. When this happens, they borrow from other depository institutions or from a Federal Reserve district bank, sell assets such as securities, or call in loans.) Excess reserves are an important potential determinant of the rate of growth of the money supply, for as we shall see, it is only to the extent that depository institutions have excess reserves that they can make new loans. Because reserves produce no income, profit-seeking financial institutions have an incentive to minimize excess reserves. They use them either to purchase income-producing securities or to make loans with which they earn income through interest payments received. In equation form, we can define excess reserves in this way:

$$\text{Excess reserves} = \text{legal reserves} - \text{required reserves}$$

In the analysis that follows, we examine the relationship between the level of reserves and the size of the money supply. This analysis implies that factors influencing the level of the reserves of the banking system as a whole will ultimately affect the level of the money supply, other things held constant. We show first that when someone deposits in one depository institution a check that is written on another depository institution, the two depository institutions involved are individually affected, but the overall money supply does not change. Then we show that when someone deposits in a depository institution a check that is written on the Fed, a multiple expansion in the money supply results.

Required reserves
The value of reserves that a depository institution must hold in the form of vault cash or deposits with the Fed.

Required reserve ratio
The percentage of total deposits that the Fed requires depository institutions to hold in the form of vault cash or deposits with the Fed.

Excess reserves
The difference between legal reserves and required reserves.

CONCEPTS IN BRIEF

- Ours is a fractional reserve banking system in which depository institutions must hold only a percentage of their deposits as reserves, either on deposit with a Federal Reserve district bank or as vault cash.

- Required reserves are usually expressed as a ratio, in percentage terms, of legal reserves to total deposits.

THE RELATIONSHIP BETWEEN RESERVES AND TOTAL DEPOSITS

To show the relationship between reserves and depository institution deposits, we first analyze a single bank (existing alongside many others). A single bank is able to make new loans to its customers only to the extent that it has reserves above the level legally required to cover the new deposits. When an individual bank has no excess reserves, it cannot make loans.

How a Single Bank Reacts to an Increase in Reserves

Balance sheet
A statement of the assets and liabilities of any business entity, including financial institutions and the Federal Reserve System. Assets are what is owned; liabilities are what is owed.

To examine the **balance sheet** of a single bank after its reserves are increased, the following assumptions are made:

1. The required reserve ratio is 10 percent for all checkable deposits; that is, the federal government requires that an amount equal to 10 percent of all checkable deposits be held in reserve in a Federal Reserve district bank or in vault cash.
2. Checkable deposits are the bank's only liabilities; reserves at a Federal Reserve district bank and loans are the bank's only assets. Loans are promises made by customers to repay some amount in the future; that is, they are IOUs and as such are assets to the bank.
3. An individual bank can lend all it wants at current market interest rates.
4. Every time a loan is made to an individual (consumer or business), all the proceeds from the loan are put into a checkable account; no cash (currency or coins) is withdrawn.
5. Depository institutions seek to keep their excess reserves at a zero level because reserves at the Federal Reserve district bank do not earn interest. (Depository institutions are run to make profits; we assume that all depository institutions wish to convert excess reserves that do not pay interest into interest-bearing loans.)

Look at the simplified initial position of the bank in Balance Sheet 16-1. Liabilities consist of $1 million in checkable deposits. Assets consist of $100,000 in reserves, which you can see are required reserves in the form of vault cash or deposits in the institution's reserve account at the Federal Reserve district branch, and $900,000 in loans to customers. Total assets of $1 million equal total liabilities of $1 million. With a 10 percent reserve requirement and $1 million in checkable deposits, the bank has the actual required reserves of $100,000 and no excess reserves. The simplifying assumption here is that the bank has a zero **net worth.** A depository institution rarely has a net worth of more than a small percentage of its total assets.

Net worth
The difference between assets and liabilities.

BALANCE SHEET 16-1
Bank 1

ASSETS			LIABILITIES	
Total reserves		$100,000	Checkable deposits	$1,000,000
Required reserves	$100,000			
Excess reserves	0			
Loans		900,000		
Total		$1,000,000	Total	$1,000,000

Assume that a *new* depositor writes a $100,000 check drawn on another depository institution and deposits it in Bank 1. Checkable deposits in Bank 1 immediately increase by $100,000, bringing the total to $1.1 million. Once the check clears, total reserves of Bank 1 increase to $200,000. A $1.1 million total in checkable deposits means that required reserves will have to be 10 percent of $1.1 million, or $110,000. Bank 1 now has excess reserves equal to $200,000 minus $110,000, or $90,000. This is shown in Balance Sheet 16-2.

BALANCE SHEET 16-2
Bank 1

ASSETS			LIABILITIES	
Total reserves		$200,000	Checkable deposits	$1,100,000
Required reserves	$110,000			
Excess reserves	90,000			
Loans		900,000		
Total		$1,100,000	Total	$1,100,000

Look at excess reserves in Balance Sheet 16-2. Excess reserves were zero before the $100,000 deposit, and now they are $90,000—that's $90,000 worth of assets not earning any income. By assumption, Bank 1 will now lend out this entire $90,000 in excess reserves in order to obtain interest income. Loans will increase to $990,000. The borrowers who receive the new loans will not leave them on deposit in Bank 1. After all, they borrow money to spend it. As they spend it by writing checks that are deposited in other banks, actual reserves will fall to $110,000 (as required), and excess reserves will again become zero, as indicated in Balance Sheet 16-3.

BALANCE SHEET 16-3
Bank 1

ASSETS			LIABILITIES	
Total reserves		$110,000	Checkable deposits	$1,100,000
Required reserves	$110,000			
Excess reserves	0			
Loans		990,000		
Total		$1,100,000	Total	$1,100,000

In this example, a person deposited an additional $100,000 check drawn on another bank. That $100,000 became part of the reserves of Bank 1. Because that deposit immediately created excess reserves in Bank 1, further loans were possible for Bank 1. The excess reserves were lent out to earn interest. A bank will not lend more than its excess reserves because, by law, it must hold a certain amount of required reserves.

Effect on the Money Supply. A look at the balance sheets for Bank 1 might give the impression that the money supply increased because of the new customer's $100,000 deposit. Remember, though, that the deposit was a check written on *another* bank. Therefore, the other bank suffered a *decline* in its checkable deposits and its reserves. While total assets and liabilities in Bank 1 have increased by $100,000, they have *decreased* in the other bank by $100,000. The *total* amount of money and credit in the economy is unaffected by the transfer of funds from one depository institution to another.

Each individual depository institution can create new loans (and deposits) only to the extent that it has excess reserves. In our example, Bank 1 had $90,000 of excess reserves after the deposit of the $100,000. But the bank on which the check was written found that its excess reserves were now a *negative* $90,000 (assuming that it had zero excess reserves previously). That bank now has fewer reserves than required by law. It will have to call in loans or sell assets to make actual reserves meet required reserves.

The thing to remember is that new reserves are not created when checks written on one bank are deposited in another bank. The Federal Reserve System can, however, create new reserves; that is the subject of the next section.

THE FED'S DIRECT EFFECT ON THE OVERALL LEVEL OF RESERVES

Now we shall examine the Fed's direct effect on the level of reserves. An explanation of how a change in the level of reserves causes a multiple change in the total money supply follows. Consider the Federal Open Market Committee (FOMC), whose decisions essentially determine the level of reserves in the monetary system.

Federal Open Market Committee

Open market operations are the purchase and sale of *existing* U.S. government securities in the open market (the private secondary U.S. securities market) by the FOMC in order to change the money supply. If the FOMC decides that the Fed should buy or sell bonds, it instructs the New York Federal Reserve Bank trading desk to do so.[2]

Open market operations
The purchase and sale of existing U.S. government securities (such as bonds) in the open private market by the Federal Reserve System.

A Sample Transaction

Assume that the trading desk at the New York Fed has received an order from the FOMC to purchase $100,000 worth of U.S. government securities.[3] The Fed pays for these securities by writing a check on itself for $100,000. This check is given to the bond dealer in exchange for the $100,000 worth of bonds. The bond dealer deposits the $100,000 check in its checkable account at a bank, which then sends the $100,000 check back to the Federal Reserve. When the Fed receives the check, it adds $100,000 to the reserve account of the bank that sent it the check. The Fed has created $100,000 of reserves. The Fed can create reserves because it has the ability to "write up" (add to) the reserve accounts of depository institutions whenever it buys U.S. securities. When the Fed buys a U.S. government security in the open market, it initially expands total reserves and the money supply by the amount of the purchase.

Using Balance Sheets. Consider the balance sheets of the Fed and of the depository institution, such as a typical bank, receiving the check. Balance Sheet 16-4 shows the results for the Fed after the bond purchase and for the bank after the bond dealer deposits the $100,000 check.[4] The Fed's balance sheet (which here reflects only account *changes*) shows that after the purchase, the Fed's assets have increased by $100,000 in the form of U.S. government securities. Liabilities have also increased by $100,000 in the form of an increase in the reserve account of the bank. The balance sheet for the bank shows an increase in assets of $100,000 in the form of reserves with its Federal Reserve district bank. The bank also has an increase in its liabilities in the form of $100,000 in the checkable account of the bond dealer; this is an immediate $100,000 increase in the money supply.

BALANCE SHEET 16-4

Balance Sheets for the Fed and the Bank When a U.S. Government Security Is Purchased by the Fed, Showing Changes in Assets and Liabilities

The Fed		Bank	
ASSETS	LIABILITIES	ASSETS	LIABILITIES
+$100,000 U.S. government securities	+$100,000 depository institution's reserves	+$100,000 reserves	+$100,000 checkable deposit owned by bond dealer

---

[2] Actually, the Fed usually deals in Treasury bills that have a maturity date of one year or less.

[3] In practice, the trading desk is never given a specific dollar amount to purchase or to sell. The account manager uses personal discretion in determining what amount should be purchased or sold in order to satisfy the FOMC's latest directive. For expositional purposes, assume nonetheless that the account manager is directed to make a specific transaction.

[4] Strictly speaking, the balance sheets that we are showing should be called the *consolidated balance sheets* for the 12 Federal Reserve district banks. We will simply refer to these banks as the Fed, however.

Sale of a $100,000 U.S. Government Security by the Fed

The process is reversed when the account manager at the New York Fed trading desk sells a U.S. government security from the Fed's portfolio. When the individual or institution buying the security from the Fed writes a check for $100,000, the Fed reduces the reserves of the bank on which the check was written. The $100,000 sale of the U.S. government security leads to a reduction in reserves in the banking system.

Using Balance Sheets Again. Balance Sheet 16-5 shows the results for the sale of a U.S. government security by the Fed. When the $100,000 check goes to the Fed, the Fed reduces by $100,000 the reserve account of the bank on which the check is written. The Fed's assets are also reduced by $100,000 because it no longer owns the U.S. government security. The bank's liabilities are reduced by $100,000 when that amount is deducted from the account of the bond purchaser, and the money supply is thereby reduced by that amount. The bank's assets are also reduced by $100,000 because the Fed has reduced its reserves by that amount.

The Fed		Bank	
ASSETS	LIABILITIES	ASSETS	LIABILITIES
−$100,000 U.S. government securities	−$100,000 depository institution's reserves	−$100,000 reserves	−$100,000 checkable deposit balances

BALANCE SHEET 16-5
Balance Sheets After the Fed Has Sold $100,000 of U.S. Government Securities, Showing Changes Only

CONCEPTS IN BRIEF

- If a check is written on one depository institution and deposited in another, there is no change in total deposits or in the total money supply. No new reserves have been created.

- The Federal Reserve, through its Federal Open Market Committee (FOMC), can directly increase depository institutions' reserves by purchasing U.S. government securities in the open market; it can decrease depository institutions' reserves by selling U.S. government securities in the open market.

MONEY EXPANSION BY THE BANKING SYSTEM

Consider now the entire banking system. For practical purposes, we can look at all depository institutions taken as a whole. To understand how money is created, we must understand how depository institutions respond to Fed actions that increase reserves in the entire system.

Fed Purchases of U.S. Government Securities

Assume that the Fed purchases a $100,000 U.S. government security from a bond dealer. The bond dealer deposits the $100,000 check in Bank 1 (which started out in the position depicted in Balance Sheet 16-1 on page 343). The check, however, is not written on another depository institution; rather, it is written on the Fed itself.

Look at the balance sheet for Bank 1 shown in Balance Sheet 16-6. It is the same as Balance Sheet 16-2. Reserves have been increased by $100,000 to $200,000, and checkable deposits have also been increased by $100,000. Because required reserves on $1.1 million of checkable deposits are only $110,000, there is $90,000 in excess reserves.

BALANCE SHEET 16-6
Bank 1

ASSETS			LIABILITIES	
Total reserves		$200,000	Checkable deposits	$1,100,000
Required reserves	$110,000			
Excess reserves	90,000			
Loans		90,000		
Total		$1,100,000	Total	$1,100,000

Effect on the Money Supply. The major difference between this example and the one given previously is that here the money supply has increased by $100,000 immediately. Why? Because checkable deposits held by the public—the bond dealers are members of the public—are part of the money supply, *and no other bank has lost reserves.* Thus the purchase of a $100,000 U.S. government security by the Federal Reserve from the public (a bond dealer or a bank) increases the money supply immediately by $100,000.

Not the End of the Process. The process of money creation does not stop here. Look again at Balance Sheet 16-6. Bank 1 has excess reserves of $90,000. No other depository institution (or combination of depository institutions) has negative excess reserves of $90,000 as a result of the Fed's bond purchase. (Remember, the Fed simply created the money to pay for the bond purchase.)

Bank 1 will not wish to hold non-interest-bearing excess reserves. It will expand its loans by creating deposits equal to $90,000. This is shown in Balance Sheet 16-7, which is exactly like Balance Sheet 16-3, except there has been no corresponding reduction in loans at any other depository institution.

BALANCE SHEET 16-7
Bank 1

ASSETS			LIABILITIES	
Total reserves		$110,000	Checkable deposits	$1,100,000
Required reserves	$110,000			
Excess reserves	0			
Loans		990,000		
Total		$1,100,000	Total	$1,100,000

The individuals who have received the $90,000 of new loans will spend (write checks on) these funds, which will then be deposited in other banks. To make this example simple, assume that the $90,000 in excess reserves was lent to a single firm for the purpose of buying a Burger King franchise. After the firm buys the franchise, Burger King deposits the

$90,000 check in its account at Bank 2. For the sake of simplicity, ignore the previous assets and liabilities in Bank 2 and concentrate only on the balance sheet *changes* resulting from this new deposit, as shown in Balance Sheet 16-8. A plus sign indicates that the entry has increased, and a minus sign indicates that the entry has decreased. For the depository institution, Bank 2, the $90,000 deposit, after the check has been sent to the Fed, becomes an increase in reserves (assets) as well as an increase in checkable deposits (liabilities) and hence the money supply. Because the reserve requirement is 10 percent, or $9,000, Bank 2 will have excess reserves of $81,000. But, of course, excess reserves are not income-producing, so Bank 2 will reduce them to zero by making loans of $81,000 (which will earn interest income) by creating deposits for borrowers equal to $81,000. This is shown in Balance Sheet 16-9.

ASSETS			LIABILITIES	
Total reserves		+$90,000	New checkable deposits	+$90,000
Required reserves	$9,000			
Excess reserves	+81,000			
Total		+$90,000	Total	+$90,000

BALANCE SHEET 16-8
Bank 2 (Changes Only)

ASSETS			LIABILITIES	
Total reserves		$9,000	Checkable deposits	$90,000
Required reserves	$9,000			
Excess reserves	0			
Loans		+81,000		
Total		$90,000	Total	$90,000

BALANCE SHEET 16-9
Bank 2 (Changes Only)

Remember that in this example, the original $100,000 deposit was a check issued by a Federal Reserve bank to the bond dealer. That $100,000 constituted an immediate increase in the money supply of $100,000 when deposited in the bond dealer's checkable account. The deposit creation process (in addition to the original $100,000) occurs because of the fractional reserve banking system, coupled with the desire of depository institutions to maintain a minimum level of excess reserves.

Continuation of the Deposit Creation Process. Assume that the company that has received the $81,000 loan from Bank 2 wants to buy into an oil-drilling firm. This oil-drilling firm has an account at Bank 3. Look at Bank 3's simplified account in Balance Sheet 16-10, where, again, only changes in the assets and liabilities are shown. When the firm borrowing from Bank 2 pays the $81,000 to the oil-drilling firm's owner, the owner deposits the check in Bank 3; checkable deposits and the money supply increase by $81,000. Total reserves of Bank 3 rise by that amount when the check is sent to the Fed.

ASSETS			LIABILITIES	
Total reserves		+$81,000	New checkable deposits	+$81,000
Required reserves	$8,100			
Excess reserves	+72,900			
Total		+$81,000	Total	+$81,000

BALANCE SHEET 16-10
Bank 3 (Changes Only)

Because the reserve requirement is 10 percent, required reserves rise by $8,100, and excess reserves are therefore $72,900. Bank 3 will want to lend those non-interest-earning assets (excess reserves). When it does, loans (in the form of created checkable deposits) will increase by $72,900. This bank's total reserves will fall to $8,100, and excess reserves become zero as the oil-drilling firm's manager writes checks on the new deposit. This is shown in Balance Sheet 16-11.

BALANCE SHEET 16-11

Bank 3 (Changes Only)

ASSETS			LIABILITIES	
Total reserves		$8,100	Checkable deposits	$81,000
Required reserves	$8,100			
Excess reserves	0			
Loans		+72,900		
Total		$81,000	Total	$81,000

Progression to Other Banks. This process continues to Banks 4, 5, 6, and so forth. Each bank obtains smaller and smaller increases in deposits because 10 percent of each deposit must be held in reserves; therefore, each succeeding depository institution makes correspondingly smaller loans. Table 16-1 shows the new deposits, possible loans, and required reserves for the remaining depository institutions in the system.

Effect on Total Deposits. In this simple example, deposits increased initially by the $100,000 that the Fed paid the bond dealer in exchange for a bond. They were further increased by a $90,000 deposit in Bank 2, and they were again increased by an $81,000 deposit in Bank 3. Eventually, total deposits will increase by $1 million, as shown in Table 16-1. The money multiplier process is portrayed graphically in Figure 16-2 on page 350.

Increase in Overall Reserves

Even with fractional reserve banking, if there are zero excess reserves, deposits cannot expand unless overall reserves are increased. The original new deposit in Bank 1, in our

TABLE 16-1

Maximum Money Creation with 10 Percent Required Reserves
This table shows the maximum new loans plus investments that banks can make, given the Fed's deposit of a $100,000 check in Bank 1. The required reserve ratio is 10 percent. We assume that all excess reserves in each bank are used for new loans or investments.

Bank	New Deposits (new reserves)	New Required Reserves	Maximum New Loans plus Investments (excess reserves)
1	$100,000 (from Fed)	$10,000	$90,000
2	90,000	9,000	81,000
3	81,000	8,100	72,900
4	72,900	7,290	65,610
.	.	.	.
.	.	.	.
.	.	.	.
All other banks	656,100	65,610	590,490
Totals	$1,000,000	$100,000	$900,000

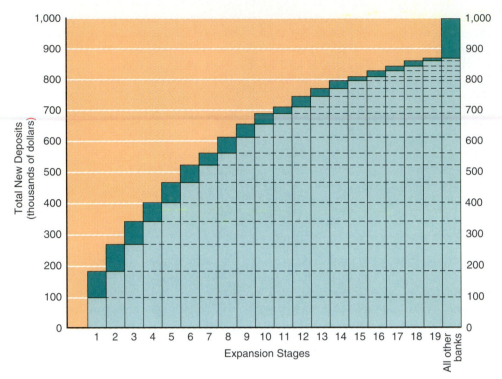

FIGURE 16-2

The Multiple Expansion in the Money Supply Due to $100,000 in New Reserves When the Required Reserve Ratio is 10 Percent

The banks are all aligned in decreasing order of new deposits created. Bank 1 receives the $100,000 in new reserves and lends out $90,000. Bank 2 receives the $90,000 and lends out $81,000. The process continues through banks 3 to 19 and then the rest of the banking system. Ultimately, assuming no leakages, the $100,000 of new reserves results in an increase in the money supply of $1,000,000, or 10 times the new reserves, because the required reserve ratio is 10 percent.

example, was in the form of a check written on a Federal Reserve district bank. It therefore represented new reserves to the banking system. Had that check been written on Bank 3, by contrast, nothing would have happened to the total amount of checkable deposits; there would have been no change in the total money supply. To repeat: Checks written on banks within the system represent assets and liabilities that simply cancel each other out. Only when excess reserves are created by the Federal Reserve System can the money supply increase.

In our example, the depository institutions use their excess reserves to make loans. It is not important how they put the money back into the system. If they bought certificates of deposit or any other security, the analysis would be the same because the party they bought those securities from would receive a check from the purchasing depository institution. The recipient of the check would then deposit it into his or her own depository institution. The deposit expansion process would be the same as we have already outlined.

You should be able to work through the foregoing example to show the reverse process when there is a decrease in reserves because the Fed sells a $100,000 U.S. government security. The result is a multiple contraction of deposits and therefore of the total money supply in circulation.

CONCEPTS IN BRIEF

• When reserves are increased by the Fed through a purchase of U.S. government securities, the result is a multiple expansion of deposits and therefore of the supply of money.

• When the Fed reduces the banking system's reserves by selling U.S. government securities, the result is a multiple contraction of deposits and therefore of the money supply.

THE MONEY MULTIPLIER

In the example just given, a $100,000 increase in excess reserves generated by the Fed's purchase of a security yielded a $1 million increase in total deposits; deposits increased by a multiple of 10 times the initial $100,000 increase in overall reserves. Conversely, a $100,000 decrease in excess reserves generated by the Fed's sale of a security will yield a $1 million decrease in total deposits; they will decrease by a multiple of 10 times the initial $100,000 decrease in overall reserves. We can now make a generalization about the extent to which the money supply will change when the banking system's reserves are increased or decreased. If we assume that no excess reserves are kept and that all loan proceeds are deposited in depository institutions in the system, the following equation applies:

$$\text{Potential money multiplier} = \frac{1}{\text{required reserve ratio}}$$

(handwritten in margin: $Mult = \frac{1}{.1} = 10$)

Money multiplier
The reciprocal of the required reserve ratio, assuming no leakages into currency and no excess reserves. It is equal to 1 divided by the required reserve ratio.

The **money multiplier** gives the *maximum* potential change in the money supply due to a change in reserves. The actual change in the money supply—currency plus checkable account balances—will be equal to the following:

Actual change in money supply = actual money multiplier × change in excess reserves

Now we examine why there is a difference between the *potential* money multiplier—1/required reserve ratio—and the actual multiplier.

Forces That Reduce the Money Multiplier

We made a number of simplifying assumptions to come up with the potential money multiplier. In the real world, the actual money multiplier is considerably smaller. Several factors account for this.

Leakages. The entire loan (check) from one bank is not always deposited in another bank. At least two leakages can occur:

- *Currency drains.* When deposits increase, the public may want to hold more currency. Currency that is kept in a person's wallet remains outside the banking system and cannot be held by banks as reserves from which to make loans. The greater the amount of cash leakage, the smaller the actual money multiplier.
- *Excess reserves.* Depository institutions may wish to maintain excess reserves. Depository institutions do not, in fact, always keep excess reserves at zero. To the extent that they want to keep positive excess reserves, the money multiplier will be smaller. A bank receiving $1 million in new deposits might, in our example with the 10 percent required reserve, keep more than $100,000 as reserves. The greater the excess reserves, the smaller the actual money multiplier. Empirically, the currency drain is more significant than the effect of excess reserves.

Real-World Money Multipliers. The required reserve ratio determines the maximum potential money multiplier because the reciprocal of the required reserve ratio tells us what that is. The maximum is never attained for the money supply as a whole because of currency drains and excess reserves. Also, each definition of the money supply, M1 or M2, will yield different results for money multipliers. For several decades, the M1 multiplier has varied between 2.5 and 3.0. The M2 multiplier, however, has shown a trend upward, ranging from 6.5 at the beginning of the 1960s to over 12 in the 1990s.

WAYS IN WHICH THE FEDERAL RESERVE CHANGES THE MONEY SUPPLY

As we have just seen, the Fed can change the money supply by directly changing reserves available to the banking system. It does this by engaging in open market operations. To repeat: The purchase of a U.S. government security by the Fed results in an increase in reserves and leads to a multiple expansion in the money supply. A sale of a U.S. government security by the Fed results in a decrease in reserves and leads to a multiple contraction in the money supply.

The Fed changes the money supply in two other ways, both of which will have multiplier effects similar to those outlined earlier in this chapter.

Borrowed Reserves and the Discount Rate

If a depository institution wants to increase its loans but has no excess reserves, it can borrow reserves. One place it can borrow reserves is from the Fed itself. The depository institution goes to the Federal Reserve and asks for a loan of a certain amount of reserves. The Fed charges these institutions for any reserves that it lends them. The interest rate that the Fed charges used to be called the *rediscount rate* but is now called the **discount rate.** In most other English-speaking countries, it is called the *bank rate.* When newspapers report that the Fed has decreased the discount rate from 6 to 5 percent, you know that the Fed has decreased its charge for lending reserves to depository institutions. Borrowing from the Fed increases reserves and thereby enhances the ability of the depository institution to engage in deposit creation, thus increasing the money supply.

Often the Federal Reserve System makes changes in the discount rate not necessarily to encourage or discourage depository institutions from borrowing from the Fed but rather as a signal to the banking system and financial markets that there has been a change in the Fed's monetary policy. We discuss monetary policy in more detail in Chapter 17.

Depository institutions actually do not often go to the Fed to borrow reserves because the Fed will not lend them all they want. Indeed, the Fed can even refuse to lend reserves when the depository institutions need the reserves to make their reserve accounts meet legal requirements. There are, however, alternative sources for the banks to tap when they want to expand their reserves or when they need reserves to meet a requirement. The primary source is the **federal funds market.** The federal funds market is an interbank market in reserves, with one bank borrowing the excess reserves of another. The generic term *federal funds market* refers to the borrowing or lending (purchase or sale) of reserve funds repaid within the same 24-hour period.

Depository institutions that borrow in the federal funds market pay the **federal funds rate.** Because the federal funds rate is a ready measure of the price that banks must pay to raise funds, the Federal Reserve often uses it as a yardstick by which to measure the effects of its policies. Consequently, the federal funds rate is a closely watched indicator of the Fed's anticipated intentions.

Discount rate
The interest rate that the Federal Reserve charges for reserves that it lends to depository institutions. It is sometimes referred to as the rediscount rate or, in Canada and England, as the bank rate.

Federal funds market
A private market (made up mostly of banks) in which banks can borrow reserves from other banks that want to lend them. Federal funds are usually lent for overnight use.

Federal funds rate
The interest rate that depository institutions pay to borrow reserves in the interbank federal funds market.

Reserve Requirement Changes

Another method by which the Fed can alter the money supply is by changing reserve requirements. Earlier we assumed that reserve requirements were given. Actually, these requirements are set by the Fed within limits established by Congress. Reserve requirements are set according to the net amount of checkable deposits in a given bank. Fed reserve requirements were initially imposed only on member banks, but now they are imposed on all depository institutions.

What would a change in reserve requirements from 10 to 20 percent do (if there were no excess reserves)? We already discovered that the maximum money multiplier was the reciprocal of the required reserve ratio. If reserve requirements are 10 percent, the maximum money multiplier would be the reciprocal of $\frac{1}{10}$, or 10 (assuming no leakages). If, for some reason, the Fed decided to increase reserve requirements to 20 percent, the maximum money multiplier would equal the reciprocal of $\frac{1}{5}$, or 5. The maximum money multiplier is therefore inversely related to the required reserve ratio. If the Fed decides to increase reserve requirements, there will be a decrease in the maximum money multiplier. With any given level of legal reserves already in existence, the money supply will therefore contract.

Notice the difference between this method and the first method the Federal Reserve has for changing the total money supply in circulation. When the Fed makes open market purchases or sales of bonds, it directly alters reserves. When the Fed alters reserve *requirements,* however, it does not change reserves as we have defined them. When the Fed lowers reserve requirements, it "liberates" a certain portion of required reserves and converts them into excess reserves, which the banks can then lend out. An increase in total deposits and in the money supply will result. In contrast, if the Fed increases reserve requirements, it reduces excess reserves and causes banks to contract their deposits, thereby decreasing the money supply.

Open market operations allow the Federal Reserve to control the money supply much more precisely than changes in reserve requirements do, and they also allow the Fed to reverse itself quickly. In contrast, a small change in reserve requirements can result in a very large change in the money supply. That is why the Federal Reserve does not change reserve requirements very often.

POLICY EXAMPLE
Changing Reserve Requirements and the Tax on Banks

Changing reserve requirements is a policy decision that the Federal Reserve does not make casually. But over the past two decades, the Fed has reduced reserve requirements as a way to reduce the implicit tax on banks. Realize that reserves held by banks do not earn interest; therefore, the cost of holding reserves is the interest forgone, which can be considered a tax on banks. Obviously, banks would hold some cautionary reserves even if the Fed did not require them. But the Fed has probably caused them to hold more than they would have otherwise. That is how they have been taxed. This decreased as reserve requirements fell from 18 percent in 1974 to 10 percent in 1992, where they are today.

FOR CRITICAL ANALYSIS: How has the reduction of the reserve requirements affected the sensitivity of the money supply to changes in Federal Reserve open market operations? •

CONCEPTS IN BRIEF

- The maximum money multiplier is equal to the reciprocal of the required reserve ratio.

- The actual multiplier is much less than the maximum money multiplier because of currency drains and excess reserves voluntarily held by banks.

- The Fed changes the money supply in three ways: (1) It can change reserves and hence the money supply through open market operations in which it buys and sells existing U.S. government securities. Open market operations are the primary form of monetary policy. (2) It can encourage changes in reserves by changing the discount rate. (3) It can change the amount of deposits created from reserves by changing reserve requirements.

DEPOSIT INSURANCE AND FLAWED BANK REGULATION

When businesses fail, they create hardships for creditors, owners, workers, and customers. But when a depository institution fails, an even greater hardship results because many individuals and businesses depend on the safety and security of banks. Figure 16-3 indicates that during the 1920s, an average of about 600 banks failed each year. In the 1930s, during

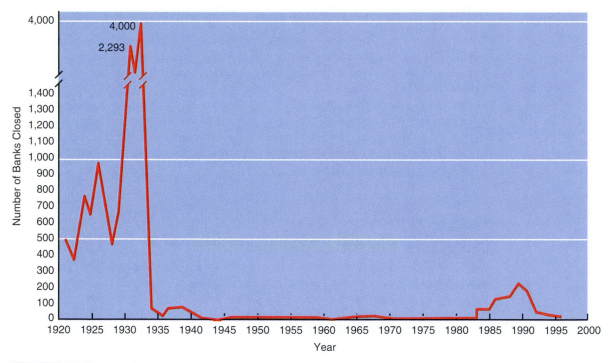

FIGURE 16-3
Commercial Bank Closings
During the Great Depression, a tremendous number of commercial banks were closed. Federal deposit insurance was created in 1933. Thereafter, bank closures were few until around 1984. Failures peaked at over 200 in 1989 and are now fewer than a dozen per year.
Source: Federal Deposit Insurance Corporation.

Federal Deposit Insurance Corporation (FDIC)

A government agency that insures the deposits held in member banks; all members of the Fed and other banks that qualify can join.

the Great Depression, that average soared to 2,000 failures each year. In 1933, at the height of such bank failures, the **Federal Deposit Insurance Corporation (FDIC) was founded to insure the funds of depositors and remove the reason for ruinous runs on banks.** In 1934, the Federal Savings and Loan Insurance Corporation (FSLIC) was installed to insure deposits in savings and loan associations and mutual savings banks. In 1971, the National Credit Union Share Insurance Fund (NCUSIF) was created to insure deposits in credit unions. In 1989, the FSLIC was dissolved and the Savings Association Insurance Fund (SAIF) was established to protect the deposits of those institutions.

As can be seen in Figure 16-3, a tremendous drop in bank failure rates occurred after the passage of the early federal legislation. The long period from 1935 until the 1980s was relatively quiet: From World War II to 1984, fewer than nine banks failed per year. From 1985 until the beginning of 1993, however, 1,065 commercial banks failed—an annual average of nearly 120 bank failures per year, more than 10 times the average for the preceding years! We will examine the reasons shortly. But first we need to understand how deposit insurance works.

The Need for Deposit Insurance

Bank runs

Attempts by many of a bank's depositors to convert checkable and time deposits into currency out of fear for the bank's solvency.

The FDIC, FSLIC, and NCUSIF were established to mitigate the primary cause of bank failures, **bank runs**—the simultaneous rush of depositors to convert their demand deposits or time deposits into currency.

Consider the following scenario. A bank begins to look shaky; its assets may not seem sufficient to cover its liabilities. If the bank has no deposit insurance, depositors in this bank (and any banks associated with it) will all want to withdraw their money from the bank at the same time. Their concern is that this shaky bank will not have enough money to return their deposits to them in the form of currency. Indeed, this is what happens in a bank failure when insurance doesn't exist. Just as with the failure of a regular business, the creditors of the bank may not all get paid, or if they do, they will get paid less than 100 percent of what they are owed. Depositors are creditors of a bank because their funds are on loan to the bank. In a fractional reserve banking system, banks do not hold 100 percent of their depositors' money in the form of reserves. Consequently, all depositors cannot withdraw all their money simultaneously. It would be desirable to assure depositors that they can have their deposits converted into cash when they wish, no matter how serious the financial situation of the bank.

The FDIC (and later the FSLIC, NCUSIF, and SAIF) provided this assurance. By insuring deposits, the FDIC bolstered depositors' trust in the banking system and provided depositors with the incentive to leave their deposits with the bank, even in the face of widespread talk of bank failures. In 1933, it was sufficient for the FDIC to cover each account up to $2,500. The current maximum is $100,000.

How Deposit Insurance Causes Increased Risk Taking by Bank Managers

Until very recently, all insured depository institutions paid the same small fee for coverage. (In 1996, the fee was reduced to zero for most banks.) The fee that they paid was completely unrelated to how risky their assets were. A depository institution that made loans only to General Motors and Microsoft Corporation paid the same deposit insurance premium as another depository institution that made loans (at higher interest rates) only to the governments of developing countries that were teetering on the brink of financial collapse.

Although deposit insurance premiums for a while were adjusted somewhat in response to the riskiness of a depository institution's assets, they never reflected all of the relative risk. This can be considered a flaw in the deposit insurance scheme. The result is that bank managers have an incentive to invest in more assets of higher yield, and therefore higher risk, than they would if there were no deposit insurance. Thus the premium rate is artificially low, permitting institution managers to obtain deposits at less than market price (because depositors will accept a lower interest payment on insured deposits); and even if the institution's portfolio becomes riskier, its deposit insurance premium rarely rises by much. Consequently, depository institution managers can increase their net interest margin by using lower-cost insured deposits to purchase higher-yield, higher-risk assets. The gains to risk taking accrue to the managers and stockholders of the depository institutions; the losses go to the deposit insurer (and, as we will see, ultimately to taxpayers).

To combat the inherent flaws in the financial institution industry and in the deposit insurance system, a vast regulatory apparatus was installed. The FDIC was given regulatory powers to offset the risk-taking temptations to depository institution managers; those powers included the ability to require higher capital investment; the ability to regulate, examine, and supervise bank affairs; and the ability to enforce its decisions. Still higher capital requirements were imposed in the early 1990s, but the basic flaws in the system remain.

The financial industry has been organized so as to protect firms from the rigors of competition; market discipline on the behavior of financial institutions was replaced by regulatory discipline. In many respects, the system worked well until 1982. No small saver had lost a penny of insured money since federal deposit insurance was established. (Today, a few smaller banks are allowed to fail and some of their bigger depositors don't get all of their deposits back.) Furthermore, there have been no true bank runs on federally insured institutions. Nevertheless, as the 1990s began, the number of depository institution closures and insolvencies increased to record post-Depression highs, though the situation has greatly improved since then.

Deposit Insurance, Adverse Selection, and Moral Hazard

When financial transactions take place, one party often does not have all the knowledge needed about the other party to make correct decisions. This is known as the problem of **asymmetric information.** For example, borrowers generally know more than lenders about the returns and risks associated with the investment projects they intend to undertake.

Adverse Selection. **Adverse selection** arises when there is asymmetric information before a transaction takes place. In financial markets, it often occurs because individuals and firms that are worse credit risks than they appear to be are the ones most willing to borrow at any given interest rate. This willingness makes them likely to be selected by lenders, yet their inferior ability to repay (relative to the interest rate being charged) means that loans to them more often yield adverse outcomes for lenders (default). The potential risks of adverse selection make lenders less likely to lend to anyone and more inclined to charge higher interest rates when they do lend.

Adverse selection is often a problem when insurance is involved because people or firms that are relatively poor risks are sometimes able to disguise that fact from insurers. It is instructive to examine the way this works with the deposit insurance provided by the FDIC. Deposit insurance shields depositors from the potential adverse effects of risky

Asymmetric information
Information possessed by one side of a transaction but not the other. The side with more information will be at an advantage.

Adverse selection
A problem created by asymmetric information prior to a transaction. Individuals who are the most undesirable from the other party's point of view end up being the ones who are most likely to want to engage in a particular financial transaction, such as borrowing.

decisions and so makes depositors willing to accept riskier investment strategies by their banks. Clearly, this encourages more high-flying, risk-loving entrepreneurs to become managers of banks. Moreover, because depositors have so little incentive to monitor the activities of insured banks, it is also likely that the insurance actually encourages outright crooks—embezzlers and con artists—to enter the industry. The consequences for the FDIC—and often for the taxpayer—are larger losses.

Moral hazard

A situation in which, after a transaction has taken place, one of the parties to the transaction has an incentive to engage in behavior that will be undesirable from the other party's point of view.

Moral Hazard. Moral hazard arises as the result of information asymmetry after a transaction has occurred. In financial markets, lenders face the hazard that borrowers may engage in activities that are contrary to the lender's interest and thus might be said to be immoral from the lender's perspective. For example, because lenders do not share in the profits of business ventures, they generally want borrowers to agree to invest prudently. Yet once the loan has been made, borrower-investors have an incentive to invest in high-risk, high-return projects because they are able to keep all of the extra profits if the projects succeed. Such behavior subjects the lender to greater hazards than are being compensated for under the terms of the loan agreement.

Moral hazard is also an important phenomenon in the presence of insurance contracts, such as the deposit insurance provided by the FDIC. Insured depositors know that they will not suffer losses if their bank fails. Hence they have little incentive to monitor their bank's investment activities or to punish their bank by withdrawing their funds if the bank assumes too much risk. Thus insured banks have incentives to take on more risks than they otherwise would—and with those risks come higher losses for the FDIC and for taxpayers.

THINKING CRITICALLY ABOUT THE MEDIA

Bailouts That Cost Taxpayers Billions

During the savings and loan crisis in the United States in the late 1980s and early 1990s, the media bombarded us with inflated figures of how much the U.S. taxpayer was paying to bail out S&Ls. The same sorts of numbers are being bandied about for the potential bailout of banks in Japan. Although technically not inaccurate, such stories fail to point out that such bailouts always occur *after the fact*. The $200 billion or so lost by U.S. savings and loans had already occurred by the time of the bailout. That is to say, the U.S. economy had already seen a $200 billion reduction in its wealth because of bad investments by S&Ls. The same is now true for the Japanese economy. The investments made by Japanese banks that turned sour will not magically increase in value if the Japanese government decides to use taxpayers' money to bail out the banks. Banking rescue plans as such are simply a determination of who will bear losses that have already occurred.

The Results of Moral Hazard: America's Savings and Loan Debacle.
For a variety of reasons, by the mid-1980s, the savings and loan industry in the United States was facing disaster. What was occurring at that time was a perfect example of the perverse incentives that occur when government-provided deposit insurance exists. Depository institution managers undertake riskier actions than they otherwise would because of the existence of deposit insurance. Moreover, because of the existence of deposit insurance, depositors in savings and loan associations and other depository institutions have little incentive to investigate the financial dealings and stability of those institutions. After all, deposits are guaranteed by an agency of the federal government, so why worry? Hence there has been little incentive for households and firms to monitor depository institutions or even to diversify their deposits across institutions. From an S&L manager's point of view, as long as deposit insurance protected depositors, the manager could feel confident to "go for the gold." One result was the increased amount of high-risk, high-yielding assets purchased by many savings and loan associations.

The first year of the S&L crisis, 135 institutions failed. Over the next two years, another 600 went bankrupt. By the end of the crisis, 1,500 thrift institutions had gone under. Politicians chose to solve the crisis by passing the Financial Institutions Reform, Recovery and Enforcement Act (FIRREA), popularly known as the Thrift Bailout Act of 1989. The estimated cost to American taxpayers was about $200 billion.

INTERNATIONAL POLICY EXAMPLE
Will the Japanese Bail Out Their Banks?

Japan is facing a banking crisis that makes America's savings and loan fiasco look like child's play. The policy question is how the Japanese government is going to bail out the banking system there. The Japanese banks in the mid-1990s held problem loans equal to about $1 trillion, or a quarter of Japan's GDP. Japanese authorities continued to allow banks to lend problem debtors enough money to cover unpaid interest. If the Japanese government chooses to bail out its banking system the way the U.S. Congress did in 1989, the estimated cost will be close to $400 billion. Alternatively, the Japanese government could simply let the weakest banks go bankrupt. Some observers believe that a third solution will eventually come about: The Japanese government will pour in enough reserves to shore up the banking system in exchange for the nation's banks' agreeing to use all of their profits for the foreseeable future to write off bad debts. In the fall of 1995, the largest credit union in Japan, Cosmo Credit Corporation, failed. The Bank of Japan (Japan's central bank) stepped in and prevented a panic. By the time you read this, many more such interventions by the Bank of Japan will almost certainly have occurred.

FOR CRITICAL ANALYSIS: Who pays for the Japanese banking bailout if the "third way" is chosen? ●

CONCEPTS IN BRIEF

- Federal deposit insurance was created in 1933 when the Federal Deposit Insurance Corporation (FDIC) was founded. In 1934, the Federal Savings and Loan Insurance Corporation (FSLIC) was founded to insure deposits in savings and loan associations and mutual savings banks.

- The FSLIC was dissolved in 1989; deposits remain protected by the Savings Association Insurance Fund (SAIF).

- Deposit insurance was designed to prevent bank runs in which individual demand deposit and savings deposit holders attempt to turn their deposits into currency. Since the advent of federal deposit insurance, there have been no true bank runs at federally insured banks.

- Because of the way deposit insurance is set up in the United States, it encourages bank managers to invest in riskier assets to make higher rates of returns.

The Deregulation of Financial Services

Concepts Applied: *Regulation, deregulation, financial intermediaries*

As a result of Congress deregulating our nations's banking system, many large firms now offer a broad range of financial services. GMAC, a subsidiary of General Motors, provides financial services such as vehicle financing and leasing, homeowners' insurance, and residential mortgage services.

Over the years, Congress has established an array of regulatory agencies to oversee our nation's banking system. But of late, Congress has gradually deregulated the banking system. Most recently, the laws restricting depository institutions' ability to engage in insurance sales, stock market underwriting, and the like have been modified.

New technologies have further opened up the possibility of many new entries into the field of banking (as you learned in the Issues and Applications section of Chapter 15).

First Things First: Combining Industrial and Service Companies

For decades, America has been known as an industrialized economy. Not surprisingly, one of the nation's foremost business magazines, *Fortune,* has presented us with a yearly list of the top 500 industrial corporations. Starting in 1995, however, *Fortune* merged the top 500 industrial corporations with the top 500 service corporations. Its editors argued that too many industrial firms, such as General Motors, also offered services, particularly financial services.

The Blurring of Lines Across Financial Service Companies

The distinction between different types of financial service companies has become clouded. Table 16-2 bears out what *Fortune* calls the "great convergence."

TABLE 16-2

The Convergence of Financial Institutions
Companies as divergent as General Motors, Prudential Insurance, and General Electric sell many of the same financial services to the public. Each check mark indicates a service offered. For example, all listed companies offer credit/debit cards and all offer some form of insurance.

Company	FDIC Insured Depository	Consumer Loans	Credit/Debit Cards	Mortgage Banking	Commercial Lending	Mutual Funds	Securities	Insurance
American Express	✓	✓	✓			✓	✓	✓
Ford		✓	✓	✓	✓			✓
General Electric	✓	✓	✓	✓	✓	✓		✓
General Motors		✓	✓	✓	✓			✓
Merrill Lynch	✓		✓	✓	✓	✓	✓	✓
Prudential	✓	✓	✓	✓	✓	✓	✓	✓

Source: Fortune, May 15, 1995, p. 178.

Today, if you would like FDIC-insured savings, you can of course go to any bank, but you can also go to Merrill Lynch or American Express. Would you like to invest in a mutual fund? You can go to your regular brokerage firm, such as Merrill Lynch, but you can also go to American Airlines, the Bank of New York, or the John Hancock Insurance Company.

The financial services offered by a firm used to depend on what Congress and the regulatory bodies determined. Now the firms' options are defined by what consumers desire. Clearly, in the age of deregulation of financial ser-vices, state and federal regulators are going to have a tougher time keeping tabs on what is happening in financial services.

FOR CRITICAL ANALYSIS

1. The term *nonbank bank* has been used a lot recently. What do you think it means?
2. Are there any arguments against allowing banks to do everything—sell insurance, underwrite new stock offerings, invest in real estate—in addition to everything else that a bank normally does?

CHAPTER SUMMARY

1. All depository institutions are required to maintain reserves, which consist of deposits in Federal Reserve district banks plus vault cash. The Federal Reserve requires that certain reserve ratios be maintained, depending on the size of the bank and the types of deposits it has.
2. When depository institutions have more reserves than are required, they are said to have excess reserves.
3. The Federal Reserve can control the money supply through open market operations—by buying and selling U.S. government securities.
4. When the Fed buys a bond, it pays for the bond by writing a check on itself. This creates additional reserves for the banking system. The result will be an increase in the money supply that is a multiple of the value of the bond purchased by the Fed. If the Fed sells a bond, it reduces reserves in the banking system. The result will be a decrease in the money supply that is a multiple of the value of the bond sold by the Fed.
5. Single depository institutions that have no excess reserves cannot alter the money supply.
6. The banking system as a whole can change the money supply pursuant to a change in reserves brought about by a Federal Reserve purchase or sale of government bonds. The Fed can also change the money supply by changing the discount rate or the required reserve ratio.
7. The maximum money multiplier is equal to the reciprocal of the required reserve ratio.
8. The actual money multiplier will be less than the maximum because of leakages—currency drains and excess reserve holdings of some banks.
9. The Federal Deposit Insurance Corporation was created in 1933 to insure commercial bank deposits. Because of the existence of federal deposit insurance, the probability of a run on the banking system, even if a significant number of depository institutions were to fail, is quite small.
10. A major flaw in the deposit insurance system has been the relatively low price for the insurance irrespective of risk. Moral hazard under the current federal deposit insurance system has led to overly risky and fraudulent behavior on the part of numerous depository institution managers. One result was the savings and loan crisis of the late 1980s and early 1990s.

DISCUSSION OF PREVIEW QUESTIONS

1. What is a fractional reserve banking system?
A fractional reserve banking system is one in which the reserves kept by the depository institutions are only a fraction of total deposits owned by the public. In general, depository institutions accept funds from the public and offer their depositors interest or other services. In turn the depository institutions lend out some of these deposits and earn interest. Because at any given time new deposits are coming in while people are drawing down on old deposits, prudent banking does not require a 100 percent reserve-deposit ratio. Because U.S. depository institutions keep less than 100 percent of their total deposits in the form of reserves, we refer to our banking structure as a *fractional* reserve system.

2. **What happens to the total money supply when a person deposits in one depository institution a check drawn on another depository institution?**
Nothing; the total money supply is unaffected. A transfer of checks from one depository institution to another does not generate any excess reserves in the banking system; hence there will be no overall deposit (and therefore money) creation. Suppose that Gerald Wong deposits in Bank A a $1,000 check that he received for services rendered to Lisa Romano, who deals with Bank B. Wong deposits a $1,000 check in Bank A, drawn on Bank B. Note that Bank A experiences an increase in total deposits and reserves and can increase its lending. However, just the opposite happens to Bank B: It experiences a reduction in deposits and reserves and must curtail its lending. There will be no net change in excess reserves; hence no net change in deposit creation and therefore no net change in the money supply occurs.

3. **What happens to the overall money supply when a person who sells a U.S. government security to the Federal Reserve places the proceeds in a depository institution?**
Assume that Wong now sells a $1,000 bond to the Fed and in exchange receives a check for $1,000, which he deposits in Bank A. Wong has received a $1,000 checkable deposit (which is money) in exchange for a $1,000 bond (which is not money); the money supply has just increased by $1,000. Furthermore, Bank A has now increased its reserves by $1,000; of this, $900 is excess reserves (assuming a 10 percent required reserve ratio). We stress that this increase in excess reserves for Bank A is *not* offset elsewhere in the banking institution; hence a net increase in excess reserves has occurred. Bank A may well lend all $900 (create $900 in checkable deposits for borrowers), thereby increasing the overall money supply by another $900; the total change

so far is $1,900. There is no need for the process to end here, because the people who borrowed $900 from Bank A will now spend this $900 on goods or services provided by people who may well deal with Bank B—which receives $900 in deposits and reserves and now has $720 in excess reserves that it can lend. And so the process of deposit and money creation continues.

4. **How does the existence of deposit insurance affect a financial institution's choice of risky versus non-risky assets?**
The best way to answer this question is with an analogy. Assume that you are given $1 million to gamble in Las Vegas. In situation 1, you share equally with your benefactor in losses and in gains. In situation 2, your benefactor lets you share in the gains (at less than 100 percent) but incurs all losses. Will your behavior be any different in situation 1 than in situation 2 while you are in Las Vegas? The answer is, of course, yes. In situation 1, you will be much more careful—you will choose games of chance that offer less risk but lower potential payoffs. In situation 2, you might as well try to break the bank. At the roulette wheel, rather than going for odd or even or red or black, you might as well bet your benefactor's money on single numbers or groups of numbers or zero or double zero because if you hit it, you stand to gain a lot, but if you don't, you stand to lose nothing. Situation 2 is analogous to that of today's managers in depository institutions—it is a situation that involves moral hazard. When times get tough and business is bad, they have had a tendency to "go for broke." They bought risky but high-yielding assets, such as dubious real estate loans, loans at high interest rates to developing countries, and oil development loans. For those whose bets didn't pay off, the federal government has bailed out all the depositors. The few whose bets did pay off look like heroes.

PROBLEMS

(Answers to the odd-numbered problems appear at the back of the book.)

16-1. Bank 1 has received a deposit of $1 million. Assuming that the banks retain no excess reserves, answer the following questions.

a. The reserve requirement is 25 percent. Fill in the blanks in the following table on the next page. What is the money multiplier?
b. Now the reserve requirement is 5 percent. Fill in the blanks in a similar table. What is the money multiplier?

Multiple Deposit Creation

Bank	Deposits	Reserves	Loans
Bank 1	$1,000,000	$_____	$_____
Bank 2	_____	_____	_____
Bank 3	_____	_____	_____
Bank 4	_____	_____	_____
Bank 5	_____	_____	_____
All other banks	_____	_____	_____
Totals	_____	_____	_____

16-2. Arrange the following items on the proper side of a bank's balance sheet.

   a. Checkable deposits
   b. Vault cash
   c. Time deposits
   d. Deposits with the Federal Reserve district bank
   e. Loans to private businesses
   f. Loans to households
   g. Holdings of U.S. government, state, and municipal bonds
   h. Borrowings from other banks

ASSETS	LIABILITIES

16-3. If the required reserve ratio is 10 percent, what will be the maximum change in the money supply in each of the following situations?

   a. Theola Smith deposits in Bank 2 a check drawn on Bank 3.
   b. Smith buys a $5,000 U.S. government bond from the Fed by drawing down on her checking account.
   c. Smith sells a $10,000 U.S. government bond to the Fed and deposits the $10,000 in Bank 3.
   d. Smith finds $1,000 in coins and paper currency buried in her backyard and deposits it in her checking account.

   e. Smith writes a $1,000 check on her own account and takes $1,000 in currency and buries it in her backyard.

16-4. The Fed purchases a $1 million government security from Sandro Mondrone, who deposits the proceeds in Bank 1. Use balance sheets to show the immediate effects of this transaction on the Fed and on Bank 1.

16-5. Continuing the example from Problem 16-4:

   a. Indicate Bank 1's position more precisely if required reserves equal 5 percent of checkable deposits.
   b. By how much can Bank 1 increase its lending?

16-6. Assume a required reserve ratio of 8 percent. A check for $60,000 is drawn on an account in Bank B and deposited in a checkable deposit in Bank A.

   a. How much have the excess reserves of Bank A increased?
   b. How much in the form of new loans is Bank A now able to extend to borrowers?
   c. By how much have reserves of Bank B decreased?
   d. By how much have excess reserves of Bank B decreased?
   e. The money supply has increased by how much?

16-7. Assume that the required reserve ratio is 15 percent and that the Fed sells $3 million worth of government securities to a customer who pays with a check drawn on the Second National Bank.

   a. The excess reserves of the Second National Bank have changed by how much?
   b. By how much has the money supply changed?
   c. What is the maximum change in the money supply that can result from this sale?

16-8. Examine the following balance sheet of B Bank.

B Bank

ASSETS		LIABILITIES	
Total reserves	$ 50	Checkable deposits	$200
Loans	100	Capital stock	200
U.S. government securities	50		
Property	200		

Assume that the required reserve ratio is 10 percent.

a. Calculate the excess reserves of B Bank.

b. How much money can B Bank lend out?

c. If B Bank lends the money in part (b) of this problem, what are the new values for total reserves? For checkable deposits? For loans?

d. What is the maximum expansion of the money supply if B Bank lends the amount suggested in part (b) of this problem?

16-9. Assume a 5 percent required reserve ratio, zero excess reserves, no currency leakage, and a ready loan demand. The Fed buys a $1 million Treasury bill from a depository institution.

a. What is the maximum money multiplier?

b. By how much will total deposits rise?

16-10. The year is A.D. 2310. Residents of an earth colony on Titan, the largest moon of the planet Saturn, use checkable deposits at financial institutions as the only form of money. Depository institutions on Titan wish to hold 10 percent of deposits as excess reserves at all times. There are no other deposits in the banking system. If the banking system on Titan has $300 million in reserves and the total quantity of money is $1.5 billion, what is the required reserve ratio set by the Titan colony's central bank?

COMPUTER-ASSISTED INSTRUCTION

What happens to the money supply (and to the value of bank deposits) when the Fed purchases a $100,000 government security on the open market? Step-by-step calculations using balance sheets show how bank deposits (money) rise with each transaction. In the process, the mechanics of the bank deposit and money supply expansion process are revealed.

Complete problem and answer appear on disk.

INTERACTING WITH THE INTERNET

Material on the FDIC, for depositors and for others interested in the system, can be found at
http://www.fdic.gov/
It covers virtually all portions of this agency's activities.

17

MONETARY POLICY

If you follow any of the news stories about economic policies being made in Washington, D.C., you cannot fail to learn about what this nation's central bank, the Federal Reserve System, is doing to stop a recession, cool down an overheated economy, or something else of that nature. Whatever the Fed does, some part of the press or academia is apt to "bash" it for doing the wrong thing. Whenever a vacancy occurs on its Board of Governors, speculation about the political leaning of the next appointee is rampant. Some analysts argue that even though the Fed is only a quasi-government agency, it is not really independent of the administration's wishes. These commentators go further and argue that the Fed should become completely independent of the administration. Is the Fed already independent? And if not, does it matter? To answer these questions, you need to know more about how monetary policy works.

PREVIEW QUESTIONS

1. What is the demand for money curve, and how is it related to the interest rate?

2. Why is the price of existing bonds inversely related to the interest rate?

3. How do the supply of and demand for money determine the interest rate?

4. What is a monetarist

Did You Know That... the chair of the Board of Governors of the Federal Reserve System is often considered the second most important person after the president? Indeed, if the head of the Fed is seated next to the first lady while the president is delivering the State of the Union message, the media try to puzzle out what that might mean. Why is the head of the Fed considered so important? Because the Fed chair, along with the other members of the Federal Open Market Committee, determine monetary policy in the United States. A strongly worded public statement by the head of the Federal Reserve can cause instant gyrations in our financial markets and sometimes in those in the rest of the world.

This chapter deals with monetary policy—the Fed's changing of the supply of money (or the rate at which it grows) in order to achieve national economic goals. When you were introduced to aggregate demand in Chapter 10, you discovered that the position of the aggregate demand curve is determined by the willingness of firms, individuals, governments, and foreigners to purchase domestically produced goods and services. Monetary policy works in a variety of ways to change this willingness, both directly and indirectly.

Think about monetary policy in an intuitive way: An increase in the money supply adds to the amount of money that firms and individuals have on hand and so increases the amount that they wish to spend. The result is an increase in aggregate demand. A decrease in the money supply reduces the amount of money that people have on hand to spend and so decreases aggregate demand.

WHAT'S SO SPECIAL ABOUT MONEY?

By definition, monetary policy has to do, in the main, with money. But what is so special about money? Money is the product of a "social contract" in which we all agree to do two things:

1. Express all prices in terms of a common unit of account, which in the United States we call the dollar
2. Use a specific medium of exchange for market transactions

These two features of money distinguish it from all other goods in the economy. As a practical matter, money is involved on one side of every nonbarter transaction in the economy—and trillions of them occur every year. What this means is that something that changes the amount of money in circulation will have some effect on many transactions and thus on elements of GDP. If something affects the number of snowmobiles in existence, probably only the snowmobile market will be altered. But something that affects the amount of money in existence is going to affect *all* markets.

Holding Money

All of us engage in a flow of transactions. We buy and sell things all of our lives. But because we use money—dollars—as our medium of exchange, all *flows* of nonbarter transactions involve a *stock* of money. We can restate this as follows:

To use money, one must hold money.

Given that everybody must hold money, we can now talk about the *demand* to hold it. People do not demand to hold money just to look at pictures of past presidents. They hold it to be able to use it to buy goods and services.

The Demand for Money: What People Wish to Hold

People have a certain motivation that causes them to want to hold money balances. Individuals and firms could try to have zero non-interest-bearing money balances. But life is inconvenient without a ready supply of money balances. There is a demand for money by the public, motivated by several factors.

The Transactions Demand. The main reason why people hold money is that money can be used to purchase goods and services. People are paid at specific intervals (once a week, once a month, and so on), but they wish to make purchases more or less continuously. To free themselves from making expenditures on goods and services only on payday, people find it beneficial to hold money. The benefit they receive is convenience: They willingly forgo interest earnings in order to avoid the inconvenience and expense of cashing in such nonmoney assets as bonds every time they wish to make a purchase.

Thus people hold money to make regular, *expected* expenditures under the **transactions demand.** As national income rises, the community will want to hold more money. Suppose that national income rises due exclusively to price level increases. If people are making the same volume of physical purchases but the goods and services cost more due to higher prices, people will want to hold more money.

Transactions demand
Holding money as a medium of exchange to make payments. The level varies directly with nominal national income.

The Precautionary Demand. The transactions demand involves money held to make *expected* expenditures; people hold money for the **precautionary demand** to make *unexpected* purchases or to meet emergencies. It is not unreasonable to maintain that as the price level or real national income rises, people will want to hold more money. In effect, when people hold money for the precautionary demand, they incur a cost in forgone interest earnings that is offset by the benefit that the precautionary balance provides. Nonetheless, the higher the rate of interest, the lower the money balances people wish to hold for the precautionary demand.

Precautionary demand
Holding money to meet unplanned expenditures and emergencies.

The Asset Demand. Remember that one of the functions of money is a store of value. People can hold money balances as a store of value, or they can hold bonds or stocks or other interest-earning assets. The desire to hold money as a store of value leads to the **asset demand** for money. People choose to hold money rather than other assets for two reasons: its liquidity and the lack of risk. Moreover, if deflation is expected, holding money balances makes sense.

Asset demand
Holding money as a store of value instead of other assets such as certificates of deposit, corporate bonds, and stocks.

The disadvantage of holding money balances as an asset, of course, is the interest earnings forgone. Each individual or business decides how much money to hold as an asset by looking at the opportunity cost of holding money. The higher the interest rate—which is our proxy for the opportunity cost of holding money—the lower the money balances people will want to hold as assets. Conversely, the lower the interest rate offered on alternative assets, the higher the money balances people will want to hold as assets.

The Demand for Money Curve

Assume that transactions demand for money is fixed, given a certain level of income. That leaves the precautionary and asset demands for money, both determined by the opportunity cost of holding money. If we assume that the interest rate represents the cost of holding money balances, we can graph the relationship between the interest rate and the quantity of money demanded. In Figure 17-1, the demand for money curve shows a familiar downward slope. The horizontal axis measures the quantity of money demanded, and the vertical axis is the interest rate. In this sense, the interest rate is the price of holding money. At a higher price, a lower quantity of money is demanded, and vice versa.

FIGURE 17-1

The Demand for Money Curve

If we use the interest rate as a proxy for the opportunity cost of holding money balances, the demand for money curve, M_d, is downward-sloping, similar to other demand curves.

Imagine two scenarios. In the first one, you can earn 20 percent a year if you put your cash into purchases of U.S. government securities. In the other scenario, you can earn 1 percent if you put your cash into purchases of U.S. government securities. If you have $1,000 average cash balances in a non-interest-bearing checking account, in the second scenario over a one-year period, your opportunity cost would be 1 percent of $1,000, or $10. In the first scenario, your opportunity cost would be 20 percent of $1,000, or $200. Under which scenario would you hold more cash?

INTERNATIONAL EXAMPLE
The Choice Between Cash and Savings Accounts in Colombia

In countries with high inflation rates, nominal interest rates are also high. Remember from Chapter 7 that the nominal interest rate equals the real interest rate plus the expected rate of inflation. Colombia is one country that has consistently high rates of inflation. Consequently, its depository institutions usually offer high nominal interest rates to attract people's cash. In Ciudad, Bolívar, about an hour from Bogotá, the Caja Social de Ahorros (Social Savings Bank) services a low-income area of about a million people. This depository institution was started by a Jesuit priest and continues to be overseen by a board of directors appointed by the Jesuits. On passbook savings accounts, it pays 19 percent. This sounds high, but not compared to Colombia's 22 percent annual inflation. Thus its 10,000 depositors are willing to accept a *negative* real rate of interest of 3 percent. Why? In the first place, if they kept their cash as cash, they would suffer a 22 percent reduction in purchasing power every year. In the second place, the Caja Social keeps its low-income clients' money safe in a high-crime area.

FOR CRITICAL ANALYSIS: Why are nominal interest rates higher when a country experiences inflation? ●

CONCEPTS IN BRIEF

- To use money, people must hold money. Therefore, they have a demand for money balances.

- The determinants of the demand for money balances are the transactions demand, the precautionary demand, and the asset demand.

- Because holding money carries with it an opportunity cost—the interest income forgone—the demand for money curve showing the relationship between money balances and the interest rate slopes downward.

EFFECTS OF AN INCREASE IN THE MONEY SUPPLY

To understand how monetary policy works in its simplest form, we are going to run an experiment in which you increase the money supply in a very direct way. Assume that the government has given you hundreds of millions of dollars in just-printed bills that you load into a helicopter. You then go around the country, dropping the money out of the window. People pick it up and put it in their billfolds. Some deposit the money in their checking accounts. The first thing that happens is that they have too much money—not in the sense that they want to throw it away but rather in relation to other things that they own. There are a variety of ways to dispose of this "new" money.

Direct Effect

The simplest thing that people can do when they have excess money balances is to go out and spend it on goods and services. Here we have a direct impact on aggregate demand. Aggregate demand rises because with an increase in the money supply at any given price level, people now want to purchase more output of real goods and services.

Indirect Effect

Not everybody will necessarily spend the newfound money on real output. Some people may wish to deposit some or all of this excess cash in banks. The recipient banks now discover that they have higher reserves than they need to hold. As you learned in Chapter 16, one thing that banks can do to get interest-earning assets is to lend out the excess reserves. But banks cannot induce people to borrow more money than they were borrowing before unless the banks lower the interest rate that they charge on loans. This lower interest rate encourages people to take out those loans. Businesses will therefore engage in new investment with the money loaned. Individuals will engage in more consumption of such durable goods as housing, autos, and home entertainment centers. Either way, the increased loans have created a rise in aggregate demand. More people will be involved in more spending, even those who did not pick up any of the money that was originally dropped out of your helicopter.

Graphing the Effects of an Expansionary Monetary Policy

We have now established the existence of both the direct and indirect effects on aggregate demand when there is an expansion in the money supply. Look at Figure 17-2. We start out in long-run and short-run equilibrium with long-run aggregate supply at $LRAS$, short-run aggregate supply at $SRAS_1$, and aggregate demand at AD_1. All three intersect at $7 trillion of real GDP at a price level of 120, at point E_1. Because of the direct and indirect effects of the increase in the money supply, aggregate demand shifts outward to the right to AD_2. At price level 120, there is an excess demand for real goods and services equal to the horizontal distance between E_1 and A. This horizontal distance shown here is $500 billion. The excess demand for goods and services must be matched, dollar for dollar, by the corresponding excess supply of money (excess liquidity). It is this excess supply of money that has caused the aggregate demand curve to shift outward to AD_2.

In the short run, something has to give. Here the excess demand for real output induces a move to point E_2. The price level rises to 130 at an output rate of $7.25 trillion per year. In the long run, though, expectations are revised upward, and input prices are revised accordingly. Therefore, the short-run aggregate supply curve, $SRAS_1$, begins to shift

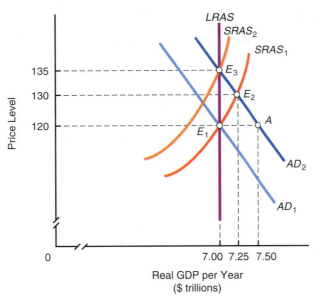

FIGURE 17-2

The Effects of Expansionary Monetary Policy
If we start with equilibrium at E_1, an increase in the money supply will cause the aggregate demand curve to shift to AD_2. There is an excess quantity of real goods and services demanded. The price level increases so that we move to E_2 at an output rate of $7.25 trillion per year and a price level of 130. But input owners revise their expectations of prices upward, and $SRAS_1$ shifts to $SRAS_2$. The new long-run equilibrium is at E_3 at the long-run aggregate supply of $7 trillion of real GDP per year and a price level of 135.

upward vertically to $SRAS_2$. Long-run equilibrium occurs at E_3, and the ultimate effect is a rise in the price level.

CONCEPTS IN BRIEF

- The direct effect of an increase in the money supply arises because people desire to spend more on real goods and services when they have excess money balances.

- The indirect effect of an increase in the money supply works through a lowering of the interest rates, which encourages businesses to make new investments with the money loaned to them. Individuals will also engage in more consumption (on consumer durables) because of lower interest rates.

MONETARY POLICY IN THE REAL WORLD

Of course, monetary policy does not consist of dropping dollar bills from a helicopter. Nonetheless, it is true that the Fed seeks to alter consumption, investment, and aggregate demand as a whole by altering the rate of growth of the money supply. The Fed uses three tools as part of its policymaking action: open market operations, discount rate changes, and reserve requirement changes.

Open Market Operations

The Fed changes the amount of reserves in the system by its purchases and sales of government bonds issued by the U.S. Treasury. To understand how the Fed does so, you must first start out in an equilibrium in which everybody, including the holders of bonds, is satisfied with the current situation. There is some equilibrium level of interest rate (and bond prices) outstanding. Now if the Fed wants to conduct open market operations, it must somehow induce individuals, businesses, and foreigners to hold more or fewer U.S. Treasury bonds. The inducement must be in the form of making people better off. So if the Fed

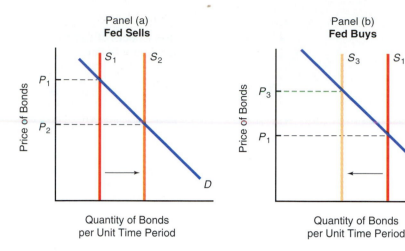

Panel (a)
Fed Sells

Panel (b)
Fed Buys

FIGURE 17-3

Determining the Price of Bonds
In panel (a), the Fed offers more bonds for sale. The price drops from P_1 to P_2. In panel (b), the Fed purchases bonds. This is the equivalent of a reduction in the supply of bonds available for private investors to hold. The price of bonds must rise from P_1 to P_3 to clear the market.

wants to buy bonds, it is going to have to offer to buy them at a higher price than exists in the marketplace. If the Fed wants to sell bonds, it is going to have to offer them at a lower price than exists in the marketplace. Thus an open market operation must cause a change in the price of bonds.

Graphing the Sale of Bonds. The Fed sells some of the bonds in its portfolio. This is shown in panel (a) of Figure 17-3. Notice that the supply of bonds is shown here as a vertical line with respect to price. The demand for bonds is downward-sloping. If the Fed offers more bonds for sale, it shifts the supply curve from S_1 to S_2. It cannot induce people to buy the extra bonds at the original price of P_1, so it must lower the price to P_2.

The Fed's Purchase of Bonds. The opposite occurs when the Fed purchases bonds. In panel (b) of Figure 17-3, the original supply curve is S_1. The new supply curve of outstanding bonds will end up being S_3 because of the Fed's purchases of bonds. You can view this purchase of bonds as a reduction in the stock of bonds available for private investors to hold. To get people to give up these bonds, the Fed must offer them a more attractive price. The price will rise from P_1 to P_3.

Relationship Between the Price of Existing Bonds and the Rate of Interest. There is an inverse relationship between the price of existing bonds and the rate of interest. Assume that the average yield on bonds is 5 percent. You decide to purchase a bond. A local corporation agrees to sell you a bond that will pay you $50 a year forever. What is the price you are willing to pay for it? $1,000. Why? Because $50 divided by $1,000 equals 5 percent. You purchase the bond. The next year something happens in the economy. For whatever reason, you can go out and obtain bonds that have effective yields of 10 percent. That is to say, the prevailing interest rate in the economy is now 10 percent. What has happened to the market price of the existing bond that you own, the one you purchased the year before? It will have fallen. If you try to sell it for $1,000, you will discover that no investors will buy it from you. Why should they when they can obtain $50 a year from someone else by paying only $500? Indeed, unless you offer your bond for sale at a price of $500, no buyers will be forthcoming. Hence an increase in the prevailing interest rate in the economy has caused the market value of your existing bond to fall.

The important point to be understood is this:

The market price of existing bonds (and all fixed-income assets) is inversely related to the rate of interest prevailing in the economy.

Contractionary Monetary Policy: Effects on Aggregate Demand, the Price Level, and Real GDP. Consider contractionary monetary policy by the Fed. When the Fed engages in contractionary monetary policy, it increases its sales of U.S. government bonds. Remember that when it does so, bond prices will fall. But lowering the price of bonds is the same thing as raising the interest rate on existing bonds. In any event, let's assume that the Fed sells bonds exclusively to banks. (This is not quite accurate because it actually deals with a small number of bond dealers.) The banks that purchase the bonds from the Fed do so with reserves. This puts banks too close to not being able to meet their reserve requirements. They replenish their reserves by reducing their lending. The way they ration available money among potential borrowers is by raising the rate of interest they charge on loans. Some borrowers, deeming the new rate too high, will eliminate themselves from the market. (The interest rate in the economy will have already gone up a bit anyway because of the initial sale of bonds to the banks.) Consequently, some borrowers who otherwise would have borrowed in order to spend no longer will do so at the higher rate of interest. The aggregate demand curve shifts from AD_1 to AD_2 in Figure 17-4. The initial equilibrium was at point E_1 with a price level of 120 and real GDP of $7 trillion per year. AD_1, $SRAS_1$, and $LRAS$ all intersect at point E_1. Now that the Fed has sold bonds, the aggregate demand curve shifts to AD_2. In the short run, we move along $SRAS_1$ to point E_2, at which the price level has dropped to 110 and real GDP has decreased to $6.5 trillion per year.

In the long run, in a fully adjusting economy, expectations adjust and so do factor (input) prices. All of the shock is absorbed in a lower price level as $SRAS_1$ moves to $SRAS_2$. The new equilibrium is at E_3, again at $7 trillion real GDP per year but at a lower price level of 100.

Expansionary Monetary Policy: Effect of a Purchase of Bonds. The Fed engages in expansionary monetary policy by purchasing bonds. Remember that for the Fed to purchase bonds, it must bid up the price it pays for bonds. That means that the interest rate on existing bonds will go down. In any event, the Fed buys the bonds from banks, which now have more reserves. Flush with excess reserves, the banks seek ways to lend them out. To induce customers to borrow more, the banks will cut interest rates even further. People who thought they were not going to be able to buy a new car, house, or whatever now find themselves able to do so. Their spending rises.

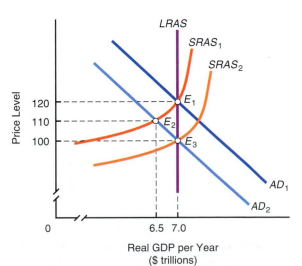

FIGURE 17-4

Contractionary Monetary Policy via Open Market Sales
If we start out in long-run and short-run equilibrium at point E_1, contractionary monetary policy by open market sales will shift aggregate demand to AD_2. The new short-run equilibrium will be at E_2. This is at a lower price level, however. Input owners will revise their expectations downward, and $SRAS_1$ will shift to $SRAS_2$. The new long-run equilibrium will be at E_3.

The graph of expansionary monetary policy was presented in Figure 17-2 on page 369; it is the opposite case to Figure 17-4.

A Real-World Caveat. Contractionary monetary policy has involved a reduction in the money supply with a consequent decline in the price level (deflation). In the real world of policymaking, contractionary monetary policy normally involves reducing the *rate of growth* of the money supply, thereby reducing the rate of increase in the price level (inflation). Similarly, real-world expansionary monetary policy typically involves increasing the rate of growth of the money supply. To show this in our diagrams, we would have to change them from static to dynamic, with a considerable amount of increased complexity.

Changes in the Discount Rate

When it was founded, the most important tool in the Fed's monetary policy kit was changes in the discount rate, discussed in Chapter 16. The Fed originally relied on the discount rate to carry out monetary policy because it had no power over reserve requirements. More important, its initial portfolio of government bonds was practically nonexistent and hence insufficient to conduct open market operations. Furthermore, the Fed did not really understand open market operations and what it could do with them until the mid-1930s. But as it has come increasingly to rely on open market operations, the Fed has used the discount rate less frequently as a tool of monetary policy—especially since the end of World War II.

Increasing the Discount Rate. Recall that the discount rate is the interest rate the Fed charges depository institutions when they borrow reserves directly from the Fed. An increase in the discount rate increases the cost of funds. In other words, depository institutions that seek loans from the Fed are now charged a higher price for those loans. That means that the price of one of their major lending inputs—the cost of money—has just gone up. Depository institutions pass at least part of this increased cost on to their borrowing customers by raising the interest rates they charge on loans.

Decreasing the Discount Rate. A reduction in the discount rate lowers depository institutions' cost of funds. It enables them to lower the rates they charge their customers for borrowing. People who thought they were not able to manage to purchase consumer durables, for example, now find themselves able to do so. The aggregate demand curve shifts outward as shown in Figure 17-2 on page 369, just as it did with expansionary open market operations (the purchase of bonds). In the short run, real output may increase without too much increase in the price index. Ultimately, though, all of the increase in demand is translated into a higher price level with output returning to its long-run equilibrium.

Changes in Reserve Requirements

Although the Fed rarely uses changes in reserve requirements as a form of monetary policy, most recently it did so in 1992, when it decreased reserve requirements on checkable deposits to 10 percent. In any event, here is how changes in reserve requirements affect the economy.

An Increase in the Required Reserve Ratio. If the Fed increases reserve requirements, this makes it more expensive for banks to meet their reserve requirements. They must replenish their reserves by reducing their lending. They induce potential borrowers not to borrow so much by raising the interest rates they charge on the loans they offer. Therefore, some borrowers who would have borrowed to purchase goods and service will no longer do so. The aggregate demand curve shifts from AD_1 to AD_2 as in Figure 17-4 on page 371. In the short run, both the price index and real GDP fall. In the long run, as expectations adjust and so do input prices, all of the shock is absorbed in a lower price level.

A Decrease in the Required Reserve Ratio. When the Fed decreases reserve requirements, as it did in 1992, some depository institutions attempt to lend their excess reserves out. To induce customers to borrow more, depository institutions cut interest rates. Individuals and firms that thought they would be unable to make new purchases now find themselves able to do so, and their spending increases. The aggregate demand curve shifts outward from AD_1 to AD_2 as in Figure 17-2 on page 369. In the short run, output increases and the price index rises moderately. In the long run, changes in expectations and input costs cause the short-run aggregate supply curve to shift so that the increase in aggregate demand is simply translated into a higher price level. (Recall from Chapter 16 that any change in the required reserve ratio changes the money multiplier.)

CONCEPTS IN BRIEF

- Monetary policy consists of open market operations, discount rate changes, and reserve requirement changes.
- When the Fed sells bonds, it must offer them at a lower price. When the Fed buys bonds, it must pay a higher price.
- There is an inverse relationship between the prevailing rate of interest in the economy and the market price of existing bonds.
- If we start out in long-run and short-run equilibrium, contractionary monetary policy first leads to a decrease in aggregate demand, resulting in a reduction in real GDP and in the price level. Eventually, though, the short-run aggregate supply curve shifts downward, and the new equilibrium is at *LRAS* but at an even lower price level. Expansionary monetary policy works the opposite way.

OPEN ECONOMY TRANSMISSION OF MONETARY POLICY

So far we have discussed monetary policy in a closed economy. When we move to an open economy, in which there is international trade and the international purchase and sale of all assets including dollars and other currencies, monetary policy becomes more complex. Consider first the effect on exports of any type of monetary policy.

The Net Export Effect

When we examined fiscal policy, we pointed out that deficit financing can lead to higher interest rates. Higher (real, after-tax) interest rates do something in the foreign sector—they attract foreign financial investment. More people want to purchase U.S. government securities, for example. But to purchase U.S. assets, people first have to obtain U.S. dollars. This means that the demand for dollars goes up in foreign exchange markets. The international price of the dollar therefore rises. This is called an *appreciation* of the dollar, and it tends to reduce net exports because it makes our exports more expensive in terms of foreign currency and imports cheaper in terms of dollars. Foreigners demand fewer of our goods and services, and we demand more of theirs. In this way, expansionary fiscal policy that creates deficit spending financed by U.S. government borrowing can lead to a reduction in net exports.

But what about expansionary monetary policy? If expansionary monetary policy reduces real, after-tax U.S. interest rates, there will be a positive net export effect because foreigners will want fewer U.S. financial instruments, demanding fewer dollars and thereby causing the international price of the dollar to fall. This makes our exports cheaper for the rest of the world, which then demands a larger quantity of our exports. It also means that foreign goods and services are more expensive in the United States, so we therefore demand fewer imports. We come up with two conclusions:

1. Expansionary fiscal policy may cause international flows of financial capital (responding to interest rate *increases*) to offset its effectiveness to some extent. The net export effect is in the opposite direction of fiscal policy.
2. Expansionary monetary policy may cause interest rates to fall. Such a fall will induce international outflows of financial capital, thereby lowering the value of the dollar and making American goods more attractive. The net export effect of expansionary monetary policy will be in the same direction as the monetary policy effect.

Contractionary Monetary Policy

Now assume that the economy is experiencing inflation and the Federal Reserve wants to contract monetary policy. In so doing, it may cause interest rates to rise. Rising interest rates will cause financial capital to flow into the United States. The demand for dollars will increase, and their international price will go up. Foreign goods will now look cheaper to Americans, and imports will rise. Foreigners will not want our exports as much, and exports will fall. The result will be a deterioration in our international trade balance. Again, the international consequences reinforce the domestic consequences of monetary policy.

Globalization of International Money Markets

On a broader level, the Fed's ability to control the rate of growth of the money supply may be hampered as U.S. money markets become less isolated. With the push of a computer button, millions or even billions of dollars can change hands halfway around the world. In the world dollar market, the Fed finds an increasing number of dollars coming from *private* institutions. If the Fed reduces the growth of the money supply, individuals and firms in the United States can increasingly obtain dollars from other sources. People in the United States who want more liquidity can obtain their dollars from foreigners or can even obtain foreign currencies and convert them into dollars in the world dollar market. Indeed, it is possible that as world markets become increasingly integrated, U.S. residents may someday conduct transactions in *foreign* currencies.

MONETARY POLICY DURING PERIODS OF UNDERUTILIZED RESOURCES

If the national economy is operating at an equilibrium output level that is below that given by the long-run aggregate supply curve, monetary policy (like fiscal policy) can generate increases in the equilibrium level of real GDP per year up to a long-run equilibrium on

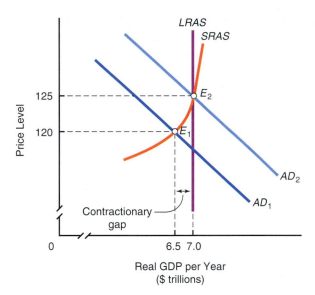

FIGURE 17-5

Expansionary Monetary Policy with Underutilized Resources
If we start out with equilibrium at E_1, expansionary monetary policy will shift AD_1 to AD_2. The new equilibrium will be at E_2.

LRAS. In Figure 17-5, you see initial aggregate demand as AD_1. It intersects *SRAS* at E_1, at an output rate of $6.5 trillion of real GDP per year and a price level of 120. There is a contractionary gap of $500 billion. That is the difference between *LRAS* and the current equilibrium. The Fed can engage in expansionary monetary policy, the direct and indirect effects of which will cause AD_1 to shift to AD_2. The new equilibrium is at E_2, at an output rate of $7 trillion of real GDP per year and a price level of 125. Note that expansionary monetary policy gets the economy to its *LRAS* sooner than otherwise.

CONCEPTS IN BRIEF

- Monetary policy in an open economy has repercussions for net exports.

- If expansionary monetary policy reduces U.S. interest rates, there is a positive net export effect because foreigners will demand fewer U.S. financial instruments, thereby demanding fewer dollars and hence causing the international price of the dollar to fall. This makes our exports cheaper for the rest of the world.

- Expansionary monetary policy during periods of underutilized resources can cause the equilibrium level of real GDP to increase (sooner than it otherwise would) to the rate of real output consistent with the vertical long-run aggregate supply curve.

MONETARY POLICY AND INFLATION

Most theories of inflation relate to the short run. The price index in the short run can fluctuate because of events such as oil price shocks, labor union strikes, or discoveries of large amounts of new natural resources. In the long run, however, empirical studies show a relatively stable relationship between excessive growth in the money supply and inflation.

Simple supply and demand can explain why the price level rises when the money supply is increased. Suppose that a major oil discovery is made, and the supply of oil increases dramatically relative to the demand for oil. The relative price of oil will fall; now it will take more units of oil to exchange for specific quantities of non-oil products. Similarly, if the supply of money rises relative to the demand for money, it will take more units of money to purchase specific quantities of goods and services. That is merely another way of stating that the price level has increased or that the purchasing power of money has fallen. In fact, the classical economists referred to inflation as a situation in which more money is chasing the same quantity of goods and services.

The Equation of Exchange and the Quantity Theory

A simple way to show the relationship between changes in the quantity of money in circulation and the price level is through the **equation of exchange,** developed by Irving Fisher:

$$M_sV \equiv PQ$$

where

M_s = actual money balances held by the nonbanking public
V = **income velocity of money,** or the number of times, on average, each monetary unit is spent on final goods and services
P = price level or price index
Q = real national output (real GDP)

Consider a numerical example involving a one-commodity economy. Assume that in this economy the total money supply, M_s, is $100; the quantity of output, Q, is 50 units of a good; and the average price, P, of this output is $10 per unit. Using the equation of exchange,

$$M_sV \equiv PQ$$

$$\$100V \equiv \$10 \times 50$$

$$\$100V \equiv \$500$$

$$V \equiv 5$$

Thus each dollar is spent an average of five times a year.

The Equation of Exchange as an Identity. The equation of exchange must always be true—it is an *accounting identity*. The equation of exchange states that the total amount of money spent on final output, M_sV, is equal to the total amount of money *received* for final output, PQ. Thus a given flow of money can be seen from either the buyers' side or the producers' side. The value of goods purchased is equal to the value of goods sold.

If Q represents real national output and P is the price level, PQ equals the dollar value of national output, or *nominal* national income. Thus

$$M_sV \equiv PQ \equiv Y$$

The Crude Quantity Theory of Money and Prices. If we now make some assumptions about different variables in the equation of exchange, we come up with the simplified theory of why prices change, called the **crude quantity theory of money and prices.** If you assume that the velocity of money, V, is constant and that real national output, Q, is basically stable, the simple equation of exchange tells you that a change in the money supply can lead only to a proportionate change in the price level. Continue with

Equation of exchange
The formula indicating that the number of monetary units times the number of times each unit is spent on final goods and services is identical to the price level times output (or nominal national income).

Income velocity of money
The number of times per year a dollar is spent on final goods and services; equal to GDP divided by the money supply.

Crude quantity theory of money and prices
The belief that changes in the money supply lead to proportional changes in the price level.

Pity Those Poor Printing Presses

An examination of stories about hyperinflation throughout the world over the past several decades yields one common media statement: "Prices are increasing so fast that the money printing presses can't keep up with the inflation." What is wrong with this statement is that the order of causation is reversed. Hyperinflation is caused by an excessive growth in the money supply—hyperactive money printing presses, if you will. Countries that have experienced hyperinflation have typically had governments that resorted to printing excessive amounts of currency. Indeed, economists have hundreds of years of empirical evidence to validate such a statement, the media notwithstanding.

our numerical example. *Q* is 50 units of the good. *V* equals 5. If the money supply increases to 200, the only thing that can happen is that the price index, *P*, has to go up from 10 to 20. Otherwise the equation is no longer in balance.

INTERNATIONAL EXAMPLE
Inflation and Money Growth Throughout the World

Is there much evidence that the rate of inflation is closely linked to the rate of monetary growth? The answer seems to be that in the long run there is a clear correlation between the two. Look at Figure 17-6. On the horizontal axis, in ratio form, is the rate of growth of the money supply. On the vertical axis is the annual rate of inflation (again, based on a ratio scale). As you can see, if you were to draw a line through the average of the points, it would slope upward: Faster monetary growth leads to a higher rate of inflation throughout different countries. This relationship appears to hold in the United States also. Decades of relatively high money supply growth are consistent with relatively higher rates of inflation and vice versa in the United States.

FOR CRITICAL ANALYSIS: Do the data shown in Figure 17-6 "prove" the crude quantity theory of money and prices? ●

Empirical Verification. There is considerable evidence of the empirical validity of the relationship between excessive monetary growth and high rates of inflation. Look back at Figure 16-1 on page 341. There you see the loose correspondence between money supply growth and the rate of inflation in the United States from 1960 to the present.

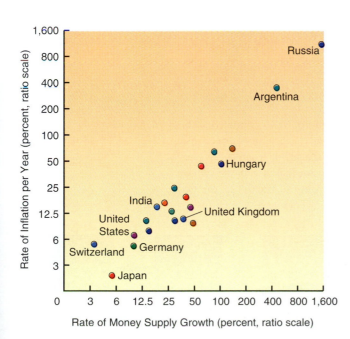

FIGURE 17-6

International Relationship Between Money Supply Growth Rates and Rates of Inflation

If we plot rates of inflation and rates of monetary growth for different countries, we come up with a scatter diagram that shows an obvious direct relationship. If you were to draw a line through the "average" of the points in this figure, it would be upward-sloping, showing that an increase in the rate of growth of the money supply leads to an increase in the rate of inflation.

Source: International Monetary Fund. Data are for latest available periods.

CONCEPTS IN BRIEF

- The equation of exchange states that the expenditures by some people will equal income receipts by others, or $M_sV \equiv PQ$ (money supply times velocity equals nominal national income).

- Viewed as an accounting identity, the equation of exchange is always correct, because the amount of money spent on final output must equal the total amount of money received for final output.

- The crude quantity theory of money and prices states that a change in the money supply will bring about an equiproportional change in the price level.

MONETARY POLICY IN ACTION: THE TRANSMISSION MECHANISM

At the start of this chapter, we talked about the direct and indirect effects of monetary policy. The direct effect is simply that an increase in the money supply causes people to have excess money balances. To get rid of these excess money balances, they increase their expenditures. The indirect effect occurs because some people have decided to purchase interest-bearing assets with their excess money balances. This causes the price of such assets—bonds—to go up. Because of the inverse relationship between the price of existing bonds and the interest rate, the interest rate in the economy falls. This lower interest rate induces people and businesses to spend more than they otherwise would have spent.

The Keynesian Transmission Mechanism

One school of economists believes that the indirect effect of monetary policy is the more important. This group, typically called Keynesian because of its belief in Keynes's work, asserts that the main effect of monetary policy occurs through changes in the interest rate. The Keynesian money transmission mechanism is shown in Figure 17-7. There you see that the money supply changes the interest rate, which in turn changes the desired rate of investment. This transmission mechanism can be seen explicitly in Figure 17-8. In panel (a), you see that an increase in the money supply reduces the interest rate. This reduction in the interest rate causes desired investment expenditures to increase from I_1 to I_2 in panel (b). This increase in investment shifts aggregate demand outward from AD_1 to AD_2 in panel (c).

The Monetarists' View of Money Supply Changes. **Monetarists,** economists who believe in a modern quantity theory of money and prices, contend that monetary policy works its way more directly into the economy. They believe that changes in the money supply lead to changes in nominal GDP in the same direction. An increase in the money supply because of expansionary open market operations (purchases of bonds) by the Fed leads the public to have larger money holdings than desired. This excess quantity of

Monetarists
Macroeconomists who believe that inflation is always caused by excessive monetary growth and that changes in the money supply affect aggregate demand both directly and indirectly.

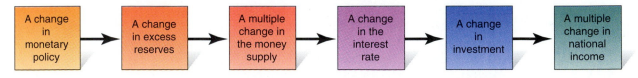

FIGURE 17-7
The Keynesian Money Transmission Mechanism

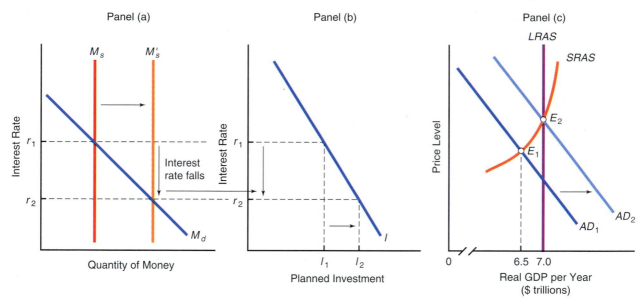

Panel (a)

Panel (b)

Panel (c)

FIGURE 17-8

Adding Monetary Policy to the Keynesian Model

In panel (a), we show a demand for money function, M_d. It slopes downward to show that at lower rates of interest, a larger quantity of money will be demanded. The money supply is given initially as M_s, so the equilibrium rate of interest will be r_1. At this rate of interest, we see from the planned investment schedule given in panel (b) that the quantity of planned investment demanded per year will be I_1. After the shift in the money supply to M'_s, the resulting increase in investment from I_1 to I_2 shifts the aggregate demand curve in panel (c) outward from AD_1 to AD_2. Equilibrium moves from E_1 to E_2, at $7 trillion real GDP per year.

money demanded induces the public to buy more of everything, especially more durable goods such as cars, stereos, and houses. If the economy is starting out at its long-run equilibrium rate of output, there can only be a short-run increase in real GDP. Ultimately, though, the public cannot buy more of everything; it simply bids up prices so that the price level rises.

Monetarists' Criticism of Monetary Policy. The monetarists' belief that monetary policy works through changes in desired spending does not mean that they consider such policy an appropriate government stabilization tool. According to the monetarists, although monetary policy can affect real GDP (and employment) in the short run, the length of time required before money supply changes take effect is so long and variable that such policy is difficult to conduct. For example, an expansionary monetary policy to counteract a contractionary gap may not take effect for a year and a half, by which time inflation may be a problem. At that point, the expansionary monetary policy will end up making the then current inflation worse. Monetarists therefore see monetary policy as a *destabilizing* force in the economy.

Monetary rule

A monetary policy that incorporates a rule specifying the annual rate of growth of some monetary aggregate.

According to the monetarists, therefore, policymakers should follow a **monetary rule:** Increase the money supply *smoothly* at a rate consistent with the economy's long-run average growth rate. *Smoothly* is an important word here. Increasing the money supply at 20 percent per year half the time and decreasing it at 17 percent per year the other half of the time would average out to about a 3 percent increase, but the results would be disastrous, say the monetarists. Instead of permitting the Fed to use its discretion in setting monetary policy, monetarists would force it to follow a rule such as "Increase the money supply smoothly at 3.5 percent per year" or "Abolish the Fed and replace it with a computer program allowing for a steady rise in the money supply."

FED TARGET CHOICE: INTEREST RATES OR MONEY SUPPLY?

Money supply and interest rate targets cannot be pursued simultaneously. Interest rate targets force the Fed to abandon control over the money supply; money stock growth targets force the Fed to allow interest rates to fluctuate.

Figure 17-9 shows the relationship between the total demand for money and the supply of money. Note that in the short run (in the sense that nominal national income is fixed), the demand for money is constant; short-run money supply changes leave the demand for money curve unaltered. In the short run, the Fed can choose either a particular interest rate (r_e or r_1) or a particular money supply (M_s or M'_s).

If the Fed wants interest rate r_e, it must select money supply M_s; if it desires a lower interest rate in the short run, it must increase the money supply. Thus by targeting an interest rate, the Fed must relinquish control of the money supply. Conversely, if the Fed wants to target the money supply at, say, M'_s, it must allow the interest rate to fall to r_1.

Consider now the case in which the Fed wants to maintain the present level of interest rates. If actual market interest rates in the future rise persistently above the present (desired) rates, the Fed will be continuously forced to increase the money supply. The initial increase in the money supply will only temporarily lower interest rates. The increased money stock eventually will induce inflation, and inflationary premiums will be included in nominal interest rates. To pursue its low-interest-rate policy, the Fed must *again* increase the money stock because interest rates are still rising. Note that to attempt to maintain an interest rate target (stable interest rates), the Fed must abandon an independent money stock target. Symmetrical reasoning indicates that by setting growth rate targets at M_s or M'_s, the Fed must allow short-run fluctuations in interest rates when the economy experiences a contraction or an expansion.

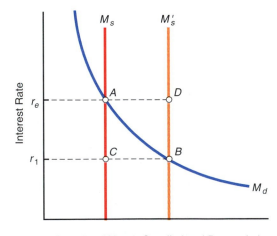

Quantity of Money Supplied and Demanded

FIGURE 17-9

Choosing a Monetary Policy Target
The Fed, in the short run, can select an interest rate or a money supply target but not both. It cannot, for example, choose r_e and M'_s; if it selects r_e, it must accept M_s; if it selects M'_s, it must allow the interest rate to fall to r_1. The Fed can obtain point *A* or *B*. It cannot get to point *C* or *D*. It must therefore choose one target or the other.

But which should the Fed target, interest rates or monetary aggregates? (And which interest rate or which money stock?) It is generally agreed that the answer depends on the source of instability in the economy. If the source of instability is variations in private or public spending, monetary aggregate (money supply) targets should be set and pursued. However, if the source of instability is an unstable demand for (or perhaps supply of) money, interest rate targets are preferred.

One perennial critic of the Federal Reserve, Milton Friedman, argues that no matter what, "I believe that the idea that a central bank can target interest rates is utterly false. Interest rates are partly a real magnitude, partly a nominal magnitude. The Federal Reserve cannot target real interest rates and has done great damage by trying to do so." Here Friedman is referring to the concept of the nominal rate of interest being comprised of the real interest rate plus the future expected inflation rate.

POLICY EXAMPLE
The Second Great Stock Market Crash and Fed Targeting

The chair of the Federal Reserve, Alan Greenspan, faced a target choice—the interest rate or the money supply—in a dramatic way during the week of Monday, October 19, 1987. The Dow Jones Industrial Average (the most widely followed stock price index) fell 508 points in one day. Over a one-week period, the value of the Dow Jones dropped by one-third. Would this lead to a general economic panic? Many loans are taken out, for which shares of stock are pledged as collateral. Depository institutions might want to call in those loans because the underlying collateral value had dropped by so much. Greenspan decided to "step up to bat." He said, "The Fed is willing to provide whatever amount of liquidity is necessary to avert this crisis." The Fed provided additional funds to the market, thereby lowering short-term interest rates. Greenspan said that the Fed would keep providing additional funds as long as needed. The next day, stock prices went up, and GDP did not fall in that quarter. A crisis was averted.

FOR CRITICAL ANALYSIS: *How did the Fed's providing increased liquidity avert the crisis?* •

CONCEPTS IN BRIEF

• In the Keynesian model, monetary transmission operates through a change in the interest rates, which changes investment, causing a multiple change in the equilibrium level of national income.

• Monetarists believe that changes in the money supply lead to changes in nominal GDP in the same direction. The effect is both direct and indirect, however, as individuals spend their excess money balances on cars, stereos, houses, and a variety of many other things.

• Monetarists, among others, argue in favor of a monetary rule—increasing the money supply smoothly at a rate consistent with the economy's long-run average growth rate. Monetarists do not believe in discretionary monetary (or fiscal) policy.

• The Fed can choose to stabilize interest rates or to change the money supply but not both.

Is the Fed Independent, and If Not, Does It Matter?

Concepts Applied: *Monetary policy, inflation, money supply, central banking*

Although, in principle, the Federal Reserve System is an independent agency, Fed bashing by Congress or the president may cause either an easing or tightening of monetary policy. A central bank's degree of independence may influence the nation's long-term rate of inflation.

In principle, the Federal Reserve System is not "owned" by the government; it is an independent agency. Nonetheless, the president of the United States appoints its governors to 14-year terms. The president also appoints the Fed chair, who, if not reappointed at the end of a term, resigns that position. Clearly, the board members and particularly the chair of the Fed are beholden to the president. The all-powerful Federal Open Market Committee (FOMC) is chaired by the Fed chair, and its members, in addition to the governors, are 5 of the 12 presidents of the Federal Reserve district banks. These members of the FOMC are *not* appointed by the president. So, is the Fed an independent policymaking body or not?

What Does the Evidence Show?

Recent research by economists Thomas Havrilesky of Duke University and John Gildea of Wheaton College shed some light on this subject. They argue that the evidence shows that the administration and Congress systematically signal their desires for changes in monetary policy to the leaders of the Fed. Under certain circumstances, these leaders respond accordingly.

Because the Fed was not created by the U.S. Constitution, Congress could dismantle the Fed if it wanted to.

The Fed officials are aware of this. Thus the Fed must pay some attention to statements by Congress and the president that are critical of its behavior. These criticisms are typically called "Fed bashing," which signals a desire by Congress or the president for an easing or tightening of monetary policy. Economist Havrilesky found that the Fed seems to be more sensitive to Fed bashing by the president and the executive branch than to that done by Congress.

Does Fed Independence Matter?

Whether the Fed is more or less independent of the administration is not just an academic issue. Rather, there is now evidence to show that a central bank's degree of independence over time influences a country's long-term rate of inflation. The evidence indicates that at least since the 1950s, greater central bank independence tends to lessen a nation's inflation rate during periods of high worldwide inflation.

A Case in Point: New Zealand

The government in New Zealand decided to give its central bank one job: keeping the price level stable. It passed the Reserve Bank Act of 1989, setting desired price stability at inflation rates of zero to 2 percent. Only if New Zealand's central bank fails to achieve these goals can its governor be fired. Consequently, New Zealand's central bank no longer has to concern itself with short-term ups and downs in GDP growth rates. So far, its new independence and explicit mission have seemed to work: In 1989, the CPI increased by 5.7 percent; today, that increase is running at less than 1.5 percent per year.

FOR CRITICAL ANALYSIS

1. Some members of the governing body of the Federal Reserve claim that because the system is owned by its member banks, it is not part of the government. Analyze this statement.
2. Who would oppose an act of the U.S. Congress similar to New Zealand's Reserve Bank Act?

CHAPTER SUMMARY

1. The determinants of the demand for money balances are the transactions demand, the precautionary demand, and the asset demand.
2. Because holding money carries an opportunity cost—the interest income forgone—the demand for money curve showing the relationship between money balances and the interest rate slopes downward.
3. The direct effect of an increase in the money supply occurs through people desiring to spend more on real goods and services when they have excess money balances. The indirect effect of an increase in the money supply works through a lowering of the interest rate, thereby encouraging businesses to make new investments with the money loaned to them. Individuals will also engage in more consumption because of lower interest rates.
4. When the Fed sells bonds, it must offer them at a lower price. When the Fed buys bonds, it must pay a higher price. There is an inverse relationship between the prevailing rate of interest in the economy and the market price of existing bonds.
5. If we start out in long-run and short-run equilibrium, contractionary monetary policy initially leads to a decrease in aggregate demand, resulting in a reduction in real GDP and in the price level. Eventually, though, the short-run aggregate supply curve shifts downward, and the new equilibrium is at *LRAS* but at an even lower price level. Expansionary monetary policy works the opposite way if we are starting out in both long-run and short-run equilibrium. The end result is simply a higher price level rather than a change in the equilibrium level of real GDP per year.
6. If expansionary monetary policy reduces U.S. interest rates, there is a positive net export effect because

foreigners will demand fewer U.S. financial instruments, thereby demanding fewer dollars, causing the international price of the dollar to fall. This makes our exports cheaper for the rest of the world.
7. Expansionary monetary policy during periods of underutilized resources can cause the equilibrium level of real GDP to increase up to that rate of real output consistent with the vertical long-run aggregate supply curve.
8. The equation of exchange states that the expenditures by some people will equal income receipts by others: $M_sV \equiv PQ$ (money supply times velocity equals nominal national income). Viewed as an accounting identity, the equation of exchange is always correct because the amount of money spent on final output must equal the total amount of money received for final output.
9. The crude quantity theory of money and prices states that a change in the money supply will bring about a proportional change in the price level.
10. In the Keynesian model, monetary transmission operates through a change in the interest rates, which changes investment, causing a multiple change in national income.
11. Monetarists believe that changes in the money supply lead to changes in nominal GDP in the same direction. The effect is direct and indirect because individuals have excess money balances that they spend on cars, stereos, houses, and other things. Monetarists, among others, argue in favor of a monetary rule—increasing the money supply smoothly at a rate consistent with the economy's long-run growth rate. Monetarists do not believe in discretionary monetary (or fiscal) policy.

DISCUSSION OF PREVIEW QUESTIONS

1. **What is the demand for money curve, and how is it related to the interest rate?**
   Three types of demands—transactions, precautionary, and asset—motivate people to hold money, and each type provides benefits to money holders. Because people get paid at discrete intervals but want to make expenditures more or less continuously, they find it convenient to hold a stock of money (transactions

demand); the benefit they receive is *convenience*. People also desire a pool of readily available purchasing power in order to meet emergencies (precautionary demand); the benefit is a measure of *security*. Finally, money is an asset; it is a means of storing value or wealth. At certain times money becomes a superior form of wealth—superior to other asset forms (bonds, stocks, real estate, and the like) that are risky. Asset demand money holders receive the benefit of *liquidity*. There is an opportunity cost to holding money (especially the narrow form of money, M1). The opportunity cost is forgone interest. The demand for money curve shows an inverse relationship between the interest rate and desired money holdings. As the interest rate falls, the opportunity cost of holding money falls concomitantly; people are more and more disposed to avail themselves of the benefits of holding money as the cost of doing so falls.

2. Why is the price of existing bonds inversely related to the interest rate?

Suppose that you know nothing about some faraway planet except that a bond (or an investment project) there yields $100 per year forever. Can you determine whether that bond or investment project will have a high price; that is, will it be "valuable"? No, you can't; you would have to know what the interest rate was on that planet. If interest rates are very, very low, say, one-thousandth of 1 percent, that bond or investment would be very valuable indeed. This is because the interest rate summarizes the opportunity cost for investment projects or bonds; if interest rates are very low, a given amount of money can earn very little annually, but if interest rates are very high, a given amount of money can earn a great deal annually. Thus $100 per year looks good (high) or bad (low) depending on whether prevailing interest rates are low or high, respectively. The nature of a bond is such that it yields a given and known stream of revenues (nominal dollar amounts) over time. This given revenue stream will be priced relatively high if interest rates are relatively low and will command a low price if interest rates are high. In short, an inverse relationship exists between the price (market value) of an existing bond and the prevailing economywide interest rate.

3. How do the supply of and demand for money determine the interest rate?

The accompanying graph depicts the total supply and demand for money in an economy. To demonstrate that given these supply and demand schedules for money, the equilibrium interest rate will eventually be established at i_e, we must rule out all other possible interest rates. Thus let i_2 represent any interest rates below i_e. At i_2, the group wants to hold more money than is actually available ($M_d = 300 > M_s = 200$), and a shortage of liquidity exists. People

become more liquid (hold more cash) by selling bonds (converting bonds, which are nonmoney, into money). As many people try to become more liquid, they attempt to sell many bonds. This forces bond prices down and interest rates up. These same conditions exist at all interest rates below i_e. Similarly, at all interest rates above i_e (i_1 in particular), $M_s > M_d$, and the group will be holding more money than it wants to hold to meet the three money-holding motives demands. Hence many people will buy bonds (to rid themselves of the opportunity cost of holding money), forcing bond prices up—and interest rates down toward i_e. At i_e, $M_d = M_s = 200$, and the group is voluntarily holding the available money supply.

4. What is a monetarist?

Monetarists are economists who maintain that changes in the money supply are the *primary* influence on the levels of employment, output, and prices. They maintain that there is little theoretical or empirical evidence to indicate the effectiveness of fiscal policy. Moreover, they maintain that monetary policy is not desirable either. This is because the time lag between changes in the money supply and changes in these macroeconomic variables is too long and imprecise and that control of the money supply is not independent of politics. Consequently, present-day monetarists suggest that the government get out of the stabilization business; governments should use neither fiscal nor monetary policy. Instead, monetarists say governments should raise taxes and make expenditures only for pressing social matters (national defense, welfare, and so on), and monetary authorities should be commanded to increase the money supply at some constant and predetermined rate.

PROBLEMS

(Answers to the odd-numbered problems appear at the back of the book.)

17-1. Briefly outline the Keynesian monetary transmission mechanism.

17-2. The equation that indicates the value (price) right now of a nonmaturing bond (called a consol) is $V = R/i$, where V is the present value, R is the annual net income generated from the bond, and i is the going interest rate.

    a. Assume that a bond promises the holder $1,000 per year forever. If the interest rate is 10 percent, what is the bond worth now (V)?

    b. Continuing part (a), what happens to the value of the bond (V) if interest rates rise to 20 percent? What if they fall to 5 percent?

    c. Suppose that there were an indestructible machine that was expected to generate $2,000 per year in revenues but costs $1,000 per year to maintain—forever. How would that machine be priced relative to the bond described in part (a)?

17-3. Show in the form of a chart the processes by which the Fed can reduce inflationary pressures by raising the discount rate.

17-4. Assume that $M = \$300$ billion, $P = \$1.72$, and $Q = 900$ billion units per year. What is the income velocity of money?

17-5. Briefly outline expansionary monetary policy according to a monetarist.

COMPUTER-ASSISTED INSTRUCTION

The basic comparative statics implications of changes in monetary policy are demonstrated with extensive use of graphics. An additional series of questions illustrates the operation of the basic tools of the Federal Reserve System.

Complete problem and answer appear on disk.

APPENDIX D

MONETARY POLICY: A KEYNESIAN PERSPECTIVE

According to the traditional Keynesian approach to monetary policy, changes in the money supply can affect the level of aggregate demand only through their effect on interest rates. Moreover, interest rate changes act on aggregate demand solely by changing the level of investment spending. Finally, the traditional Keynesian approach argues that there exist plausible circumstances under which monetary policy may have little or no effect on aggregate demand.

Figure D-1 measures real national income along the horizontal axis and total planned expenditures (aggregate demand) along the vertical axis. The components of aggregate demand are consumption (C), investment (I), government spending (G), and net exports (X). The height of the schedule labeled $C + I + G + X$ shows total planned expenditures (aggregate demand) as a function of income. This schedule slopes upward because consumption depends positively on income. Everywhere along the line labeled $Y = C + I + G + X$, planned spending equals income. At point Y^*, where the $C + I + G + X$ line intersects this 45-degree reference line, planned spending is consistent with income. At any income less than Y^*, spending exceeds income, so income and thus spending will tend to rise. At any level of income greater than Y^*, planned spending is less than income, so income and thus spending will tend to decline. Given the determinants of C, I, G, and X, total spending (aggregate demand) will be Y^*.

INCREASING THE MONEY SUPPLY

According to the Keynesian approach, an increase in the money supply pushes interest rates down. This reduces the cost of borrowing and thus induces firms to increase the level of investment spending from I to I'. As a result, the $C + I + G + X$ line shifts upward in Figure D-1 by the full amount of the rise in investment spending, thus yielding the line $C + I' + G + X$. The rise in investment spending causes income to rise, which in turn

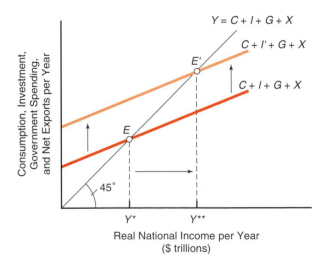

FIGURE D-1

An Increase in the Money Supply
An increase in the money supply increases income by lowering interest rates and thus increasing investment from I to I'.

causes consumption spending to rise, which further increases income. Ultimately, aggregate demand rises to Y^{**}, where spending again equals income. A key conclusion of the Keynesian analysis is that total spending rises by *more* than the original rise in investment spending because consumption spending depends positively on income.

DECREASING THE MONEY SUPPLY

Not surprisingly, contractionary monetary policy works in exactly the reverse manner. A reduction in the money supply pushes interest rates up, which increases the cost of borrowing. Firms respond by reducing their investment spending, and this starts income downward. Consumers react to the lower income by scaling back on their consumption spending, which further depresses income. Thus the ultimate decline in income is larger than the initial drop in investment spending. Indeed, because the change in income is a multiple of the change in investment, Keynesians note that changes in investment spending (similar to changes in government spending) have a *multiplier* effect on the economy.

ARGUMENTS AGAINST MONETARY POLICY

It might be thought that this multiplier effect would make monetary policy a potent tool in the Keynesian arsenal, particularly when it comes to getting the economy out of a recession. In fact, however, many traditional Keynesians argue that monetary policy is likely to be relatively ineffective as a recession fighter. According to their line of reasoning, although monetary policy has the potential to reduce interest rates, changes in the money supply have little actual impact on interest rates. Instead, during recessions, people try to build up as much as they can in liquid assets to protect themselves from risks of unemployment and other losses of income. When the monetary authorities increase the money supply, individuals are willing to allow most of it to accumulate in their bank accounts. This desire for increased liquidity thus prevents interest rates from falling very much, which in turn means that there will be virtually no change in investment spending and thus little change in aggregate demand.

PROBLEMS

D-1. Assume that the following conditions exist:

a. All banks are fully loaned up—there are no excess reserves, and desired excess reserves are always zero.

b. The money multiplier is 3.

c. The planned investment schedule is such that at a 10 percent rate of interest, investment is $200 billion; at 9 percent, investment is $225 billion.

d. The investment multiplier is 3.

e. The initial equilibrium level of national income is $2 trillion.

f. The equilibrium rate of interest is 10 percent.

Now the Fed engages in expansionary monetary policy. It buys $1 billion worth of bonds, which increases the money supply, which in turn lowers the market rate of interest by 1 percent. Indicate by how much the money supply increased, and then trace out the numerical consequences of the associated reduction in interest rates on all the other variables mentioned.

ISSUES IN STABILIZATION POLICY

Presidential elections involve debates, millions of dollars of paid-for political announcements on television and radio, and countless hours of candidates flying around the country trying to convince voters to elect them. The burning issues in public opinion polls may be crime and violence, the decline in our school system, or balancing the federal budget, but two other important variables appear to carry great weight regarding who the president will be every four years. These variables are the rate of economic growth and the unemployment rate. The relationship between these economic variables and presidential election outcomes has been labeled the *political business cycle*. Some economists argue that because of this relationship, the Federal Reserve has a built-in bias toward creating more inflation. Is this true? To answer this question, you need to know more about certain issues pertaining to stabilization policies.

PREVIEW QUESTIONS

1. What does the ration expectations hypothesis say about people's forecasting errors?

2. How do the new classical economists view economic policy?

3. What does the real business cycle theory say about the causes of recession?

4. How does the new Keynesian economics explain the stickiness of wages and prices?

**Active (discretionary)
policymaking**

All actions on the part of monetary and fiscal policymakers that are undertaken in response to or in anticipation of some change in the overall economy.

**Passive (nondiscretionary)
policymaking**

Policymaking that is carried out in response to a rule. It is therefore not in response to an actual or potential change in overall economic activity.

Did You Know That . . . since the recession that started in November 1948 until today, Congress, usually at the behest of the president, has passed at least a dozen bills aimed at fighting recession with fiscal policy? In the mid-1990s, in one 17-month period, the Fed increased short-term interest rates seven times and cut them once. And over a longer period, the Fed has even changed its basic operating targets.

ACTIVE VERSUS PASSIVE POLICYMAKING

All of these actions constitute part of what is called **active (discretionary) policymaking.** At the other extreme is **passive (nondiscretionary) policymaking,** in which there is no deliberate stabilization policy at all. You have already been introduced to one nondiscretionary policymaking idea in Chapter 17—the *monetary rule,* by which the money supply is allowed to increase at a fixed rate per year. In the fiscal arena, passive (nondiscretionary) policy might be simply to balance the federal budget over the business cycle. Recall from Chapter 13 that there are numerous time lags between when the national economy enters into a recession or a boom and when that event becomes known, acted on, and sensed by the economy. Proponents of passive policy argue strongly that such time lags often render short-term stabilization policy ineffective, or worse, procyclical.

To take a stand on this debate concerning active versus passive policymaking, you first need to know what the potential trade-offs are that policymakers believe they face. Then you need to see what the data actually show. The most important policy trade-off appears to be between price stability and unemployment. Before exploring that trade-off, we need first to look at the economy's natural, or long-run, rate of unemployment.

THE NATURAL RATE OF UNEMPLOYMENT

Recall from Chapter 7 that there are different types of unemployment: frictional, cyclical, seasonal, and structural. Frictional unemployment arises because individuals take the time to search for the best job opportunities. Except when the economy is in a recession or a depression, much unemployment is of this type.

Note that we did not say that frictional unemployment was the *sole* form of unemployment during normal times. There is also *wait unemployment,* caused by a variety of "rigidities" throughout the economy. Wait unemployment results from factors such as these:

1. Union activity that sets wages above the equilibrium level and also restricts the mobility of labor
2. Government-imposed licensing arrangements that restrict entry into specific occupations or professions
3. Government-imposed minimum wage laws and other laws that require all workers to be paid union wage rates on government contract jobs
4. Welfare and unemployment insurance benefits that reduce incentives to work

In each case, these factors reduce individuals' abilities or incentives to choose employment rather than unemployment.

As an example, consider the effect of unemployment insurance benefits on the probability of an unemployed person's finding a job. When unemployment benefits run out, according to economists Lawrence Katz and Bruce Meyer, the probability of an unemployed person's finding a job doubles. The conclusion is that unemployed workers are more serious about finding a job when they are no longer receiving such benefits.

Frictional and wait unemployment both exist even when the economy is in long-run equilibrium—they are a natural consequence of costly information (the need to conduct a job search) and the existence of rigidities such as those noted. Because these two types of unemployment are a natural consequence of imperfect information and rigidities, they are related to what economists call the **natural rate of unemployment.** It is defined as the rate of unemployment that would exist in the long run after everyone in the economy fully adjusted to any changes that have occurred. Recall that national output tends to return to the level implied by the long-run aggregate supply curve *(LRAS)*. Thus whatever rate of unemployment the economy tends to return to can be called the natural rate of unemployment.

Natural rate of unemployment

The rate of unemployment that is estimated to prevail in long-run macroeconomic equilibrium, when all workers and employers have fully adjusted to any changes in the economy.

EXAMPLE
The U.S. Natural Rate of Unemployment

At the end of World War II, the unemployment rate was below 4 percent. By the early 1990s, it was above 6 percent. These two endpoints for half a cycle of unemployment rates prove nothing by themselves. But look at Figure 18-1. There you see not only what has happened to the unemployment rate over that same time period but an esti-

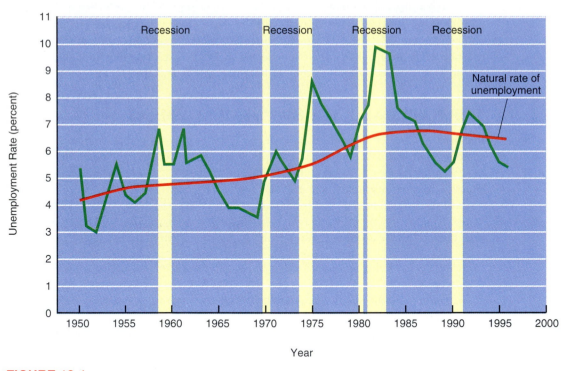

FIGURE 18-1

Estimated U.S. Natural Rate of Unemployment

As you can see in this figure, the actual rate of unemployment has varied widely in the United States in the second half of the twentieth century. If we estimate the natural rate of unemployment by averaging unemployment rates from five years earlier to five years later at each point in time, we get the heavy solid line so labeled. It rose from the 1950s until the mid-1980s and seems to be gradually descending since then. (Post-1991 natural rate is approximated.)

Sources: Economic Report of the President; Economic Indicators, various issues.

mate of the natural rate of unemployment. The solid line labeled "Natural rate of unemployment" is estimated by averaging unemployment rates from five years earlier to five years later at each point in time. This computation reveals that until about 1983, the natural rate of unemployment was rising. But since then, a downward trend appears to have taken hold.

FOR CRITICAL ANALYSIS: Of the four factors listed on page 389 that create wait unemployment, which do you think may explain the gradual trend upward in the natural rate of unemployment since World War II in the United States? ●

Departures from the Natural Rate of Unemployment

Even though the unemployment rate has a strong tendency to stay at and return to the natural rate, it is possible for fiscal and monetary policy to move the actual unemployment rate away from the natural rate, at least in the short run. Deviations of the actual unemployment rate from the natural rate are called *cyclical unemployment* because they are observed over the course of nationwide business fluctuations. During recessions, the overall unemployment rate exceeds the natural rate; cyclical unemployment is positive. During periods of economic booms, the overall unemployment rate can go below the natural rate; at such times, cyclical unemployment is in essence negative.

To see how departures from the natural rate of unemployment can occur, let's consider two examples. Referring to Figure 18-2, we begin in equilibrium at point E, with the associated price level P_1 and real GDP per year of level Q_1.

The Impact of Expansionary Policy. Now imagine that the government decides to use fiscal or monetary policy to stimulate the economy. Further suppose, for reasons that will soon become clear, that this policy surprises decision makers throughout the economy in the sense that they did not anticipate that the policy would occur. The aggregate demand curve shifts from AD_1 to AD_2 in Figure 18-2, so both the price level and real GDP rise to P_2 and Q_2, respectively. In the labor market, individuals would find that conditions had

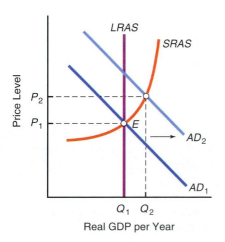

FIGURE 18-2

Impact of an Increase in Aggregate Demand on Output and Unemployment

If the economy is operating at *E*, it is in both short-run and long-run equilibrium. Here the actual rate of unemployment is equal to the natural rate of unemployment. Subsequent to expansionary monetary or fiscal policy, the aggregate demand curve shifts outward to AD_2. The price level rises to P_2; real GDP per year increases to Q_2. The unemployment rate will fall to below the natural rate of unemployment.

FIGURE 18-3

Impact of a Decline in Aggregate Demand on Output and Unemployment

Starting from equilibrium at E, a decline in aggregate demand to AD_2 leads to a lower price level, P_2, and real GDP declines to Q_2. The unemployment rate will rise above the natural rate of unemployment.

improved markedly relative to what they expected. Firms seeking to expand output will want to hire more workers. To accomplish this, they will recruit more actively and possibly ask workers to work overtime, so that individuals in the labor market will find more job openings and more possible hours they can work. Consequently, as you learned in Chapter 7, the average duration of unemployment will fall so that the unemployment rate falls. This unexpected increase in aggregate demand simultaneously causes the price level to rise to P_2 and the unemployment rate to fall.

The Consequences of Contractionary Policy. Instead of expansionary policy, the government could have decided to engage in contractionary (or deflationary) policy. As shown in Figure 18-3, the sequence of events would have been in the opposite direction of those in Figure 18-2. Again, beginning from an initial equilibrium E, an unanticipated reduction in aggregate demand puts downward pressure on both prices and real GDP; the price level falls to P_2, and real GDP declines to Q_2. Fewer firms will be hiring, and those that are hiring will offer fewer overtime possibilities. Individuals looking for jobs will find that it takes longer than predicted. As a result, unemployed individuals will remain unemployed longer. The average duration of unemployment will rise, and so, too, will the rate of unemployment. The unexpected decrease in aggregate demand simultaneously causes the price level to fall to P_2 and the unemployment rate to rise.

The Phillips Curve: The Trade-Off?

Let's recap what we have just observed. An *unexpected* increase in aggregate demand causes the price level to rise and the unemployment rate to fall. Conversely, an *unexpected* decrease in aggregate demand causes the price level to fall and the unemployment rate to rise. Moreover, although not shown explicitly in either diagram, two additional points are true:

1. The greater the unexpected increase in aggregate demand, the greater the amount of inflation that results, and the lower the unemployment rate.

2. The greater the unexpected decrease in aggregate demand, the greater the deflation that results, and the higher the unemployment rate.

The Negative Relationship Between Inflation and Unemployment. Figure 18-4 summarizes these findings. The inflation rate (*not* the price level) is measured along the vertical axis, and the unemployment rate is measured along the horizontal axis. Point *A* shows an initial starting point, with the unemployment rate at the natural rate, U^*. Note that as a matter of convenience, we are starting from an equilibrium in which the price level is stable (the inflation rate is zero). Unexpected increases in aggregate demand cause the price level to rise—the inflation rate becomes positive—and cause the unemployment rate to fall. Thus the economy moves up to the left from *A* to *B*. Conversely, unexpected decreases in aggregate demand cause the price level to fall and the unemployment rate to rise above the natural rate—the economy moves from point *A* to point *C*. If we look at both increases and decreases in aggregate demand, we see that high inflation rates tend to be associated with low unemployment rates (as at *B*) and that low (or negative) inflation rates tend to be accompanied by high unemployment rates (as at *C*).

Is There a Trade-Off? The apparent negative relationship between the inflation rate and the unemployment rate shown in Figure 18-4 has come to be called the **Phillips curve,** after A. W. Phillips, who discovered that a similar relationship existed historically in Great Britain. Although Phillips presented his findings only as an empirical regularity, economists quickly came to view the relationship as representing a *trade-off* between inflation and unemployment. In particular, policymakers believed they could *choose* alternative combinations of unemployment and inflation (or worse, that the trade-off was inevitable because you could not get more of one without giving up the other). Thus it seemed that a government that disliked unemployment could select a point like *B* in Figure 18-4, with a positive inflation rate but a relatively low unemployment rate. Conversely, a government that feared inflation could choose a stable price level at *A,* but only at the expense of a higher associated unemployment rate. Indeed, the Phillips curve seemed to suggest that it was possible for policymakers to fine-tune the economy by selecting the policies that would produce the exact mix of unemployment and inflation that suited current government objectives. As it turned out, matters are not so simple.

Phillips curve
A curve showing the relationship between unemployment and changes in wages or prices. It was long thought to reflect a trade-off between unemployment and inflation.

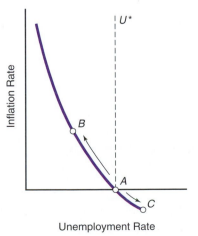

FIGURE 18-4

The Phillips Curve
Unanticipated changes in aggregate demand produce a negative relationship between the inflation rate and unemployment. U^* is the natural rate of unemployment.

The NAIRU. If we accept that a trade-off exists between the rate of inflation and the rate of unemployment, then the notion of "noninflationary" rates of unemployment seems appropriate. In fact, some economists have proposed what they call the **nonaccelerating inflation rate of unemployment (NAIRU).** If the Phillips curve trade-off exists and if the NAIRU can be estimated, that estimate will define the short-run trade-off between the rate of unemployment and the rate of inflation. Economists who have estimated the NAIRU for the world's 24 richest industrial countries claim that it has been steadily rising since the 1960s. Critics of the NAIRU concept argue that inflationary expectations must be taken into account.

Nonaccelerating inflation rate of unemployment (NAIRU)
The rate of unemployment below which the rate of inflation tends to rise and above which the rate of inflation tends to fall.

The Importance of Expectations

The reduction in unemployment that takes place as the economy moves from A to B in Figure 18-4 occurs because the wage offers encountered by unemployed workers are unexpectedly high. As far as the workers are concerned, these higher *nominal* wages appear, at least initially, to be increases in *real* wages; it is this fact that induces them to reduce their duration of search. This is a sensible way for the workers to view the world if aggregate demand fluctuates up and down at random, with no systematic or predictable variation one way or another. But if policymakers attempt to exploit the apparent trade-off in the Phillips curve, according to some macroeconomists, aggregate demand will no longer move up and down in an *unpredictable* way.

The Effects of an Unanticipated Policy. Consider Figure 18-5, for example. If the Federal Reserve attempts to reduce the unemployment rate to U_1, it must increase the money supply enough to produce an inflation rate of π_1. If this is a one-shot affair in which the money supply is first increased and then held constant, the inflation rate will temporarily rise to π_1 and the unemployment rate will temporarily fall to U_1; but as soon as the money supply stops growing, the inflation rate will return to zero and unemploy-

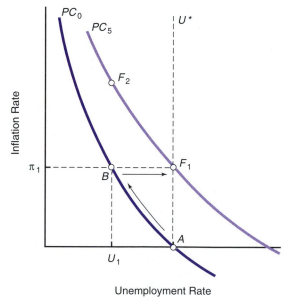

FIGURE 18-5

A Shift in the Phillips Curve
When there is a change in the expected inflation rate, the Phillips curve *(PC)* shifts to incorporate the new expectations. PC_0 shows expectations of zero inflation; PC_5 reflects an expected inflation rate of 5 percent.

ment will return to U^*, its natural rate. Thus a one-shot increase in the money supply will move the economy from point A to point B, and the economy will move of its own accord back to A.

If the authorities wish to prevent the unemployment rate from returning to U^*, some macroeconomists argue that the Federal Reserve must keep the money supply growing fast enough to keep the inflation rate up at π_1. But if the Fed does this, all of the economic participants in the economy—workers and job seekers included—will come to *expect* that inflation rate to continue. This, in turn, will change their expectations about wages. For example, suppose that π_1 equals 5 percent per year. When the expected inflation rate was zero, a 5 percent rise in nominal wages meant a 5 percent expected rise in real wages, and this was sufficient to induce some individuals to take jobs rather than remain unemployed. It was this perception of a rise in real wages that reduced search duration and caused the unemployment rate to drop from U^* to U_1. But if the expected inflation rate becomes 5 percent, a 5 percent rise in nominal wages means *no* rise in *real* wages. Once workers come to expect the higher inflation rate, rising nominal wages will no longer be sufficient to entice them out of unemployment. As a result, as the *expected* inflation rate moves up from 0 percent to 5 percent, the unemployment rate will move up also.

The Role of Expected Inflation. In terms of Figure 18-5, as authorities initially increase aggregate demand, the economy moves from point A to point B. If the authorities continue the stimulus in an effort to keep the unemployment rate down, workers' expectations will adjust, causing the unemployment rate to rise. In this second stage, the economy moves from B to point F_1: The unemployment rate returns to the natural rate, U^*, but the inflation rate is now π_1 instead of zero. Once the adjustment of expectations has taken place, any further changes in policy will have to take place along a curve such as PC_5, say, a movement from F_1 to F_2. This new schedule is also a Phillips curve, differing from the first, PC_0, in that the actual inflation rate consistent with any given unemployment rate is higher because the expected inflation rate is higher.

Not surprisingly, when economic policymakers found that economic participants engaged in such adjustment behavior, they were both surprised and dismayed. If decision makers can adjust their expectations to conform with fiscal and monetary policies, then policymakers cannot choose a permanently lower unemployment rate of U_1, even if they are willing to tolerate an inflation rate of π_1. Instead, the policymakers would end up with an unchanged unemployment rate in the long run, at the expense of a permanently higher inflation rate.

Initially, however, there did seem to be a small consolation, for it appeared that in the short run—before expectations adjusted—the unemployment rate could be *temporarily* reduced from U^* to U_1, even though eventually it would return to the natural rate. If an important national election were approaching, it might be possible to stimulate the economy long enough to get the unemployment rate low enough to assure reelection. However, policymakers came to learn that not even this was likely to be a sure thing.

The U.S. Experience with the Phillips Curve

In separate articles in 1968, Milton Friedman and E. S. Phelps published pioneering studies suggesting that the apparent trade-off suggested by the Phillips curve could not be exploited by policymakers. Friedman and Phelps both argued that any attempt to reduce unemployment by inflating the economy would soon be thwarted by economic participants'

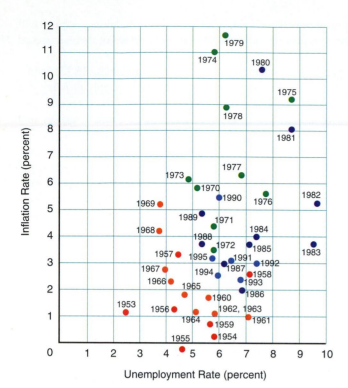

FIGURE 18-6

The Phillips Curve: Theory Versus Data

If you plot points representing the rate of inflation and the rate of unemployment for the United States from 1953 to the present, there does not appear to be any Phillips curve trade-off between the two variables.

Sources: Economic Report of the President; Economic Indicators, various issues.

incorporating the new higher inflation rate into their expectations. The Friedman-Phelps research thus implies that for any given unemployment rate, *any* inflation rate is possible, depending on the actions of policymakers. As reflected in Figure 18-6, the propositions of Friedman and Phelps were to prove remarkably accurate.

When we examine the data for unemployment and inflation in the United States over the past half century, we see virtually no clear relationship between them. Although there seemed to have been a Phillips curve trade-off between unemployment and inflation from the mid-1950s to the mid-1960s, apparently once people in the economy realized what was happening, they started revising their forecasts accordingly. So, once policymakers attempted to exploit the Phillips curve, the apparent trade-off between unemployment and inflation disappeared.

INTERNATIONAL POLICY EXAMPLE
Can European Policymakers Exploit the Phillips Curve?

Although the data for the United States seem clear—policymakers cannot exploit the Phillips curve trade-off—what about Europe? It appears that European policymakers cannot exploit the trade-off either. As Figure 18-7 shows, the unemployment rate in Europe remained almost constant from 1967 to 1974 in spite of a skyrocketing inflation rate.

If one believes in the Phillips curve analysis, there seems to be little hope today for European policymakers to reduce their double-digit unemployment rates. More complete research was conducted by two British economists, David Blanchslower and Andrew Oswald, who spent five years analyzing numerous data points across 12 countries. Their conclusion was that there is no relationship between inflation and unemployment.

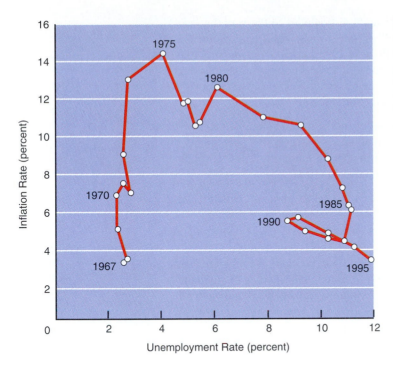

FIGURE 18-7

Relationship Between Inflation and Unemployment in Europe

If we examine the so-called Philips curve trade-off in Europe since 1967, there does not appear to be any long-run stable relationship between the rate of inflation and the rate of unemployment.

Source: David Blanchslower and Andrew Oswald.

FOR CRITICAL ANALYSIS: *How do the data in Figure 18-6 and Figure 18-7 support the proponents of a monetary rule?* ●

CONCEPTS IN BRIEF

- The natural rate of unemployment is the rate that exists in long-run equilibrium, when workers' expectations are consistent with actual conditions.

- Departures from the natural rate of unemployment can occur when individuals encounter unanticipated changes in fiscal or monetary policy; an unexpected rise in aggregate demand will reduce unemployment below the natural rate, whereas an unanticipated decrease in aggregate demand will push unemployment above the natural rate.

- The Phillips curve exhibits a negative relationship between the inflation rate and the unemployment rate that can be observed when there are *unanticipated* changes in aggregate demand.

- It was originally believed that the Phillips curve represented a trade-off between inflation and unemployment. In fact, no trade-off exists because workers' expectations adjust to any systematic attempts to reduce unemployment below the natural rate.

RATIONAL EXPECTATIONS AND THE NEW CLASSICAL MODEL

You already know that economists assume that economic participants act *as though* they were rational and calculating. We think of firms that rationally maximize profits when they choose today's rate of output and consumers who rationally maximize utility when they choose how much of what goods to consume today. One of the pivotal features of current macro policy research is the assumption that rationality also applies to the way that economic participants think about the future as well as the present. This relationship was developed by Robert Lucas, who won the Nobel Prize in 1995 for his work. In particular, there is widespread agreement among a growing group of macroeconomics researchers that the **rational expectations hypothesis** extends our understanding of the behavior of the macroeconomy. There are two key elements to this hypothesis:

1. Individuals base their forecasts (or expectations) about the future values of economic variables on all available past and current information.
2. These expectations incorporate individuals' understanding about how the economy operates, including the operation of monetary and fiscal policy.

In essence, the rational expectations hypothesis assumes that Abraham Lincoln was correct when he stated, "It is true that you may fool all the people some of the time; you can even fool some of the people all of the time; but you can't fool *all* of the people *all* of the time."

If we further assume that there is pure competition in all markets and that all prices and wages are flexible, we obtain the **new classical model** (referred to in Chapter 13 when discussing the Ricardian equivalence theorem). To see how rational expectations operate within the context of this model, let's take a simple example of the economy's response to a change in monetary policy.

The New Classical Model

Consider Figure 18-8, which shows the long-run aggregate supply curve ($LRAS$) for the economy, as well as the initial aggregate demand curve (AD_1) and the short-run aggregate supply curve ($SRAS_1$). The money supply is initially given by $M = M_1$, and the price level and real GDP are shown by P_1 and Q_1, respectively. Thus point A represents the initial equilibrium.

Suppose now that the money supply is unexpectedly increased to M_2, thereby causing the aggregate demand curve to shift outward to AD_2. Given the location of the short-run aggregate supply curve, this increase in aggregate demand will cause output and the price

Rational expectations hypothesis
A theory stating that people combine the effects of past policy changes on important economic variables with their own judgment about the future effects of current and future policy changes.

New classical model
A modern version of the classical model in which wages and prices are flexible, there is pure competition in all markets, and the rational expectations hypothesis is assumed to be working.

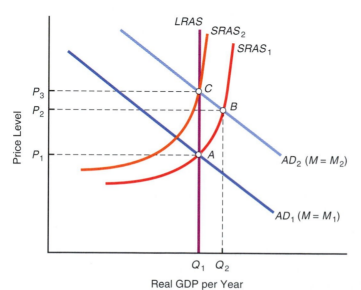

FIGURE 18-8

Response to an Unanticipated Rise in Aggregate Demand
Unanticipated changes in aggregate demand have real effects. In this case, the rise in demand causes real output to rise from Q_1 to Q_2.

level to rise to Q_2 and P_2, respectively. The new short-run equilibrium is at B. Because output is *above* the long-run equilibrium level of Q_1, unemployment must be below long-run levels (the natural rate), and so workers will soon respond to the higher price level by demanding higher nominal wages. This will cause the short-run aggregate supply curve to shift upward vertically, moving the economy to the new long-run equilibrium at C. The price level thus continues its rise to P_3, even as real GDP declines back down to Q_1 (and unemployment returns to the natural rate). So as we have seen before, even though an increase in the money supply can raise output and lower unemployment in the short run, it has no effect on either variable in the long run.

The Response to Anticipated Policy. Now let's look at this disturbance with the perspective given by the rational expectations hypothesis, as it is embedded in the new classical model. Suppose that workers (and other input owners) know ahead of time that this increase in the money supply is about to take place. Assume also that they know when it is going to occur and understand that its ultimate effect will be to push the price level from P_1 to P_3. Will workers wait until after the price level has increased to insist that their nominal wages go up? The rational expectations hypothesis says that they will not. Instead, they will go to employers and insist on nominal wages that move upward in step with the higher prices. From the workers' perspective, this is the only way to protect their real wages from declining due to the anticipated increase in the money supply.

The Policy Irrelevance Proposition. As long as economic participants behave in this manner, when we draw the *SRAS* curve, we must be explicit about the nature of their expectations. This we have done in Figure 18-9. In the initial equilibrium, the short-run aggregate supply curve is labeled to show that the expected money supply (M_e) and the actual money supply (M_1) are equal ($M_e = M_1$). Similarly, when the money supply changes in a way that is anticipated by economic participants, the aggregate supply curve shifts to reflect this expected change in the money supply. The new short-run aggregate supply

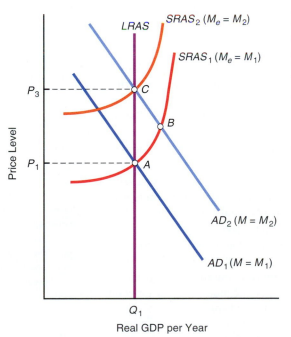

FIGURE 18-9

Effects of an Anticipated Rise in Aggregate Demand
When policy is fully anticipated, a rise in the money supply causes a rise in the price level from P_1 to P_3, with no change in real output.

curve is labeled ($M_e = M_2$) to reveal this. According to the rational expectations hypothesis, the short-run aggregate supply will shift upward *simultaneously* with the rise in aggregate demand. As a result, the economy will move directly from point A to point C in Figure 18-9 without passing through B: The *only* response to the rise in the money supply is a rise in the price level from P_1 to P_3; neither output nor unemployment changes at all. This conclusion—that fully anticipated monetary policy is irrelevant in determining the levels of real variables—is called the **policy irrelevance proposition:**

> **Under the assumption of rational expectations on the part of decision makers in the economy, anticipated monetary policy cannot alter either the rate of unemployment or the level of real GDP. Regardless of the nature of the anticipated policy, the unemployment rate will equal the natural rate, and real GDP will be determined solely by the economy's long-run aggregate supply curve.**

What Must People Know? There are two important matters to keep in mind when considering this proposition. First, our discussion has assumed that economic participants know in advance exactly what the change in monetary policy is going to be and precisely when it is going to occur. In fact, the Federal Reserve does not announce exactly what the future course of monetary policy (down to the last dollar) is going to be. Instead, the Fed tries to keep most of its plans secret, announcing only in general terms what policy actions are intended for the future. It is tempting to conclude that because the Fed's intended policies are not freely available, they are not available at all. But such a conclusion would be wrong. Economic participants have great incentives to learn how to predict the future behavior of the monetary authorities, just as businesses try to forecast consumer behavior and college students do their best to forecast what their next economics exam will look like. Even if the economic participants are not perfect at forecasting the course of policy, they are likely to come a lot closer than they would in total ignorance. The policy irrelevance proposition really assumes only that *people don't persistently make the same mistakes in forecasting the future*.

What Happens If People Don't Know Everything? This brings us to our second point. Once we accept the fact that people are not perfect in their ability to predict the future, the possibility emerges that some policy actions will have systematic effects that look much like the movements A to B to C in Figure 18-8. For example, just as other economic participants sometimes make mistakes, it is likely that the Federal Reserve sometimes make mistakes—meaning that the money supply may change in ways that even the Fed does not predict. And even if the Fed always accomplished every policy action it intended, there is no guarantee that other economic participants would fully forecast those actions. What happens if the Fed makes a mistake or if firms and workers misjudge the future course of policy? Matters will look much as they do in panel (a) of Figure 18-10, which shows the effects of an unanticipated increase in the money supply. Economic participants expect the money supply to be M_0, but the actual money supply turns out to be M_1. Because $M_1 > M_0$, aggregate demand shifts relative to aggre-

Policy irrelevance proposition
The new classical and rational expectations conclusion that policy actions have no real effects in the short run if the policy actions are anticipated and none in the long run even if the policy actions are unanticipated.

THINKING CRITICALLY ABOUT THE MEDIA

High Interest Rates and "Tight" Monetary Policy

The media often report changes in interest rates to indicate changes in monetary policy, whether they are referring to the United States or any other country. The problem with such analyses is that they fail to distinguish between real and nominal interest rates. Normally, a high interest rate is evidence that a country's central bank has been pursuing *loose* monetary policy in the past rather than tight monetary policy now. Why? Because in the long run, consistent increases in the rate of growth of the money supply lead to a higher rate of inflation. A higher rate of inflation normally leads to expectations of inflation and therefore higher *nominal* interest rates. After all, the nominal interest rate is equal to the real rate of interest plus the expected rate of inflation. In the long run, evidence shows that monetary authorities have little effect on an economy's real rate of interest.

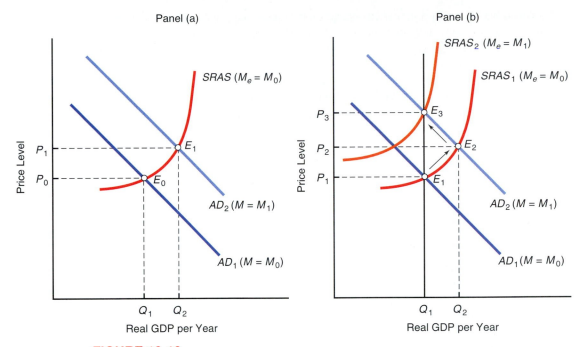

FIGURE 18-10

Effects of an Unanticipated Rise in Aggregate Demand

Even with rational expectations, an unanticipated change in demand can affect output in the short run.

gate supply. The result is a rise in real output (real GDP) in the short run from Q_1 to Q_2; corresponding to this rise in real output will be an increase in employment and hence a fall in the unemployment rate. So even under the rational expectations hypothesis, monetary policy *can* have an effect on real variables in the short run, but only if the policy is unsystematic and therefore unanticipated.

In the long run, this effect on real variables will disappear because people will figure out that the Fed either accidentally increased the money supply or intentionally increased it in a way that somehow fooled individuals. Either way, people's expectations will soon be revised so that the short-run aggregate supply curve will shift upward. As shown in panel (b) of Figure 18-10, real GDP will return to long-run levels, meaning that so will the employment and unemployment rates.

The Policy Dilemma

Perhaps the most striking and disturbing feature of the new classical model is that it seems to suggest that only mistakes can have real effects. If the Federal Reserve always does what it intends to do and if other economic participants always correctly anticipate the Fed's actions, monetary policy will affect only the price level and nominal input prices. It appears that only if the Fed makes a mistake in executing monetary policy or people err in anticipating that policy will changes in the money supply cause fluctuations in real output and employment. If this reasoning is correct, the Fed is effectively precluded from using monetary policy in any rational way to lower the unemployment rate or to raise the level of real

GDP. This is because fully anticipated changes in the money supply will lead to exactly off-setting changes in prices and hence no real effects. Many economists were disturbed at the prospect that if the economy happened to enter a recessionary period, policymakers would be powerless to push real GDP and unemployment back to long-run levels. As a result, they asked the question, In light of the rational expectations hypothesis, is it *ever* possible for systematic policy to have predictable real effects on the economy? The answer has led to even more developments in the way we think about macroeconomics.

CONCEPTS IN BRIEF

- The rational expectations hypothesis assumes that individuals' forecasts incorporate all available information, including an understanding of government policy and its effects on the economy.

- The new classical economics assumes that the rational expectations hypothesis is valid and also that there is pure competition and that all prices and wages are flexible.

- The policy irrelevance proposition says that under the assumptions of the new classical model, fully anticipated monetary policy cannot alter either the rate of unemployment or the level of real GDP.

- The new classical model implies that policies can alter real economic variables only if the policies are unsystematic and therefore unanticipated, otherwise people learn and defeat the desired policy goals.

REAL BUSINESS CYCLE THEORY

The modern extension of new classical theory involves reexamining the first principles that assume fully flexible prices.

The Distinction Between Real and Monetary Shocks

The research of the new business cycle theorists differs importantly from that of new classical theorists in that business cycle theorists seek to determine whether real, as opposed to purely monetary, forces might help explain aggregate economic fluctuations. An important stimulus for the development of **real business cycle theory,** as it has come to be known, was the economic turmoil of the 1970s. During that decade, world economies were staggered by two major disruptions to the supply of oil. The first occurred in 1973, the second in 1979. In both episodes, members of the Organization of Petroleum Exporting Countries (OPEC) reduced the amount of oil they were willing to supply and raised the price at which they offered it for sale. Each time, the price level rose sharply in the United States, and real GDP declined. Thus each episode produced a period of "stagflation"—real economic stagnation combined with high inflation. Figure 18-11 illustrates the pattern of events.

We begin at point E_1 with the economy in both short- and long-run equilibrium, with the associated supply curves, $SRAS_1$ and $LRAS_1$. Initially, the level of real GDP is Q_1, and the price level is P_1. Because the economy is in long-run equilibrium, the unemployment rate must be at the natural rate.

A reduction in the supply of oil, as occurred in 1973 and 1979, causes the $SRAS$ curve to shift to the left to $SRAS_2$ because fewer goods will be available for sale due to the reduced supplies. If the reduction in oil supplies is (or is believed to be) permanent, the

Real business cycle theory
An extension and modification of the theories of the new classical economists of the 1970s and 1980s, in which money is neutral and only real, supply-side factors matter in influencing labor employment and real output.

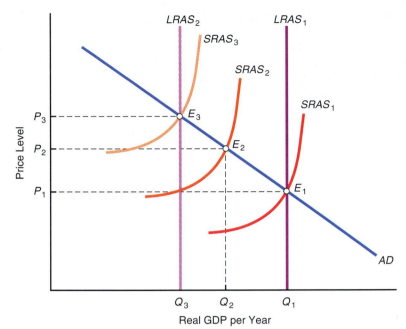

FIGURE 18-11

Effects of a Reduction in the Supply of Resources
The position of the *LRAS* depends on our endowments of all types of resources. Hence a reduction in the supply of one of those resources, such as oil, causes a reduction—an inward shift—in the aggregate supply curve. In addition, there is a rise in the equilibrium price level and a fall in the equilibrium rate of real GDP per year (output).

LRAS shifts to the left also. This assumption is reflected in Figure 18-11, where $LRAS_2$ shows the new long-run aggregate supply curve associated with the lowered output of oil.

In the short run, two adjustments begin to occur simultaneously. First, the prices of oil and petroleum-based products begin to rise, so that the overall price level rises to P_2. Second, the higher costs of production occasioned by the rise in oil prices induce firms to cut back production, so total output falls to Q_2 in the short run. The new temporary short-run equilibrium occurs at E_2, with a higher price level (P_2) and a lower level of real GDP (Q_2).

Impact on the Labor Market

If we were to focus on the labor market while this adjustment from E_1 to E_2 was taking place, we would find two developments occurring. The rise in the price level pushes the real wage rate downward, even as the scaled-back production plans of firms induce them to reduce the amount of labor inputs they are using. So not only does the real wage rate fall, but the level of employment declines as well. On both counts, workers are made worse off due to the reduction in the supply of oil.

Now this is not the full story, because owners of nonoil inputs (such as labor) who are willing to put up with reduced real payments in the short run simply will not tolerate them in the long run. Thus, for example, some workers who were willing to continue working at lower wages in the short run will eventually decide to retire, switch from full-time work to part-time employment, or drop out of the labor force altogether. In effect, there is a reduction in the supply of nonoil inputs, reflected in an upward shift in the $SRAS$ from $SRAS_2$ to $SRAS_3$. This puts additional upward pressure on the price level and exerts a downward force on real GDP. The final long-run equilibrium thus occurs at point E_3, with the price level at P_3 and real GDP at Q_3. (In principle, because the oil supply shock has had no long-term effect on labor markets, the natural rate of unemployment does not change when equilibrium moves from E_1 to E_3.)

Generalizing the Theory

Naturally, the focus of real business cycle theory goes well beyond the simple "oil shock" that we have discussed here, for it encompasses all types of real disturbances, including technological changes and shifts in the composition of the labor force. Moreover, a complete treatment of real shocks to the economy is typically much more complex than we have allowed for in our discussion. For example, an oil shock such as is shown in Figure 18-11 would likely also have effects on the real wealth of Americans, causing a reduction in aggregate demand as well as aggregate supply. Nevertheless, our simple example still manages to capture the flavor of the theory.

It is clear that real business cycle theory has improved our understanding of the economy's behavior, but there is also agreement among economists that it alone is incapable of explaining all of the facets of business cycles that we observe. For example, it is difficult to imagine a real disturbance that could possibly account for the Great Depression in this country, when real income fell more than 30 percent and the unemployment rate rose to 25 percent. Moreover, real business cycle theory continues to assume that prices are perfectly flexible and so fails to explain a great deal of the apparent rigidity of prices throughout the economy.

NEW KEYNESIAN ECONOMICS

Although the new classical and real business cycle theories both embody pure competition and flexible prices, a body of research called the **new Keynesian economics** drops both of these assumptions. The new Keynesian economists do not believe that market-clearing models of the economy can explain business cycles. Consequently, they argue that macroeconomics models must contain the "sticky" wages and prices assumption that Keynes outlined in his major work. Thus the new Keynesian research has as its goal a refinement of the theory of aggregate supply that explains how wages and prices behave in the short run. There are several such theories. The first one relates to the cost of changing prices.

New Keynesian economics
Economic models based on the idea that demand creates its own supply as a result of various possible government fiscal and monetary coordination failures.

Small-Menu Cost Theory

If prices do not respond to demand changes, two conditions must be true: Someone must be consciously deciding not to change prices, and that decision must be in the decision maker's self-interest. One combination of facts that is consistent with this scenario is the **small-menu cost theory,** which supposes that much of the economy is characterized by imperfect competition and that it is costly for firms to change their prices in response to changes in demand. The costs associated with changing prices are called *menu costs,* and they include the costs of renegotiating contracts, printing price lists (such as menus), and informing customers of price changes.

Small-menu cost theory
A hypothesis that it is costly for firms to change prices in response to demand changes because of the cost of renegotiating contracts, printing price lists, and so on.

Many such costs may not be very large in magnitude; that is why they are called *small-menu costs.* Some of the costs of changing prices, however, such as those incurred in bringing together business managers from points around the nation or the world for meetings on price changes or renegotiating deals with customers, may be significant.

Firms in different industries have different cost structures. Such differences explain diverse small-menu costs. Therefore, the extent to which firms hold their prices constant in the face of changes in demand for their products will vary across industries. Not all prices will be rigid. Nonetheless, new Keynesian theorists argue that many—even most—firms' prices are sticky for relatively long time intervals. As a result, the aggregate level of prices could be very nearly rigid because of small-menu costs.

Although most economists agree that such costs exist, there is considerably less agreement on whether they are sufficient to explain the extent of price rigidity that is observed.

Efficiency Wage Theory

Efficiency wage theory
The hypothesis that the productivity of workers depends on the level of the real wage rate.

An alternative approach within the new Keynesian framework is called the **efficiency wage theory.** It proposes that worker productivity actually *depends on* the wages that workers are paid, rather than being independent of wages, as is assumed in other theories. According to this theory, higher real wages encourage workers to work harder, improve their efficiency, increase morale, and raise their loyalty to the firm. Across the board, then, higher wages tend to increase workers' productivity, which in turn discourages firms from cutting real wages because of the damaging effect that such an action would have on productivity and profitability. Under highly competitive conditions, there will generally be an optimal wage—called the *efficiency wage*—that the firm should continue paying, even in the face of large fluctuations in the demand for its output.

The efficiency wage theory model is a rather simple idea, but it is somewhat revolutionary. All of the models of the labor market adopted by traditional classical, traditional Keynesian, monetarist, new classical, and new Keynesian theorists alike do not consider such real-wage effects on worker productivity.

There are significant, valid elements in the efficiency wage theory, but its importance in understanding national business fluctuations remains uncertain. For example, although the theory explains rigid real wages, it does not explain rigid prices. Moreover, the theory ignores the fact that firms can (and apparently do) rely on a host of incentives other than wages to encourage their workers to be loyal, efficient, and productive.

EXAMPLE
Henry Ford and the Efficiency Wage Model

One of the most clear-cut examples of the efficiency wage model involved the Ford Motor Company. When nominal wage rates were about $2 to $3 a day in 1914 (about $30 in today's dollars and with no benefits such as health insurance), Henry Ford ordered his managers to start paying workers $5 a day. Ford later argued that the increase in wages was a "cost-cutting" move. The evidence bears him out. Absenteeism dropped by over 70 percent. Moreover, labor turnover virtually disappeared. Consequently, Ford's managers had to spend less time training new workers.

FOR CRITICAL ANALYSIS: What alternative ways do managers have to provide incentives to their workers to become more efficient? ●

Effect of Aggregate Demand Changes on Output and Employment in the Long Run

Some new Keynesian economists argue that a reduction in aggregate demand that causes a recession may affect output and employment even in the long run. They point out that workers who are fired or laid off may lose job skills during their period of unemployment. Consequently, they will have a more difficult time finding new employment later.

Furthermore, those who remain unemployed over long periods of time may change their attitudes toward work. They may even have a reduced desire to find employment later on. For these reasons and others, a recession could permanently raise the amount of frictional unemployment.

As yet, little research has been done to quantify this theory.

MACROECONOMIC MODELS AND THEIR IMPLICATIONS FOR STABILIZATION POLICY

Although it is impossible to compare accurately and completely every single detail of the various macroeconomic approaches we have examined, it is useful to summarize and contrast some of their key aspects. Table 18-1 presents features of our five key models: tradi-

TABLE 18-1

A Comparison of Macroeconomic Models

	Macroeconomic Model				
Issue	Traditional Classical	Traditional Keynesian	New Classical	New Keynesian	Modern Monetarist
Stability of capitalism	Yes	No	Yes	Yes, but can be enhanced by policy	Yes
Price-wage flexibility	Yes	No	Yes	Yes, but imperfect	Yes, but some restraints
Belief in natural rate of employment hypothesis	Yes	No	Yes	Yes	Yes
Factors sensitive to interest rate	Saving, consumption, investment	Demand for money	Saving, consumption, investment	Saving, consumption, investment	Saving, consumption, investment
View of the velocity of money	Stable	Unstable	No consensus	No consensus	Stable
Effect of changes in money supply on economy	Changes aggregate demand	Changes interest rates, which change investment and real output	No effect on real variables if anticipated	Changes aggregate demand	Directly changes aggregate demand
Effects of fiscal policy on the economy	Not applicable	Multiplier changes in aggregate demand and output	Generally ineffective*	Changes aggregate demand	Ineffective unless money supply changes also
Causes of inflation	Excess money growth	Excess real aggregate demand	Excess money growth	Excess money growth	Excess money growth
Stabilization policy	Unnecessary	Fiscal policy necessary and effective; monetary policy ineffective	Too difficult to conduct	Both fiscal and monetary policy may be useful	Too difficult to conduct

*Some fiscal policies affect relative prices (interest rates) and so many have real effects on economy.

tional classical, traditional Keynesian, new (modern) classical, new (modern) Keynesian, and modern monetarist. Realize when examining the table that we are painting with a broad brush.

STABILIZATION POLICY AND THE NEW GROWTH THEORISTS

Recall from Chapter 9 that there is a group of economists who support what is now called new growth theory. In this theory, real wealth creation comes from innovation, which is part of new technology. Such new growth theorists as Paul Romer of the University of California at Berkeley and Robert Barro of Harvard repeatedly point out that small differences in annual rates of growth over a few decades make a tremendous difference in the standard of living of each individual. Indeed, they argue that short-run monetary and fiscal stabilization policies are in fact beside the point. To them, the Keynesian emphasis on the business cycle appears to be a strange fixation.

If what really matters is the underlying growth rate rather than the business cycle around it, then any efforts to fine-tune the economy are perhaps misguided. Actually, according to the new growth theorists, one of the processes underlying the business cycle is that of discovery and innovation. This process generates long-run improvements in the standard of living. It determines in large part how steep the slope is over a long-run upward trend. The little wiggles—business cycles—take on less importance. The federal government should not be concerned with them.

Does that mean that government policy has no place in our economy? The answer from the new growth theorists is that the government does have a place, but it has little to do with discretionary changes in taxes or spending or monetary growth rates. Rather, it has to do with speeding up the pace of innovation. It also has to do with government's devising policies that promote new technology. One of these policies might be to strengthen patent protection. In any event, the new growth theorists would probably agree with economists who argue in favor of passive nondiscretionary stabilization policy.

In sum, stabilization policy analysis is really about the costs and benefits of getting the economy to where it *eventually* will go anyway—to its long-run aggregate supply curve (*LRAS*). According to the new growth theorists, the costs outweigh the benefits so that short-run stabilization policy should not be the main macroeconomic activity of the federal government. It is economic growth that shifts *LRAS* rightward. Government macroeconomic policy should focus, according to the new growth theorists, solely on this issue.

CONCEPTS IN BRIEF

- Real business cycle theory holds that even if all prices and wages are perfectly flexible, real shocks to the economy (such as technological change and changes in the supplies of factors of production) can cause national business fluctuations.

- The new Keynesian economics explains why various features of the economy, such as small-menu costs and wage rates that affect productivity, make it possible for monetary shocks to cause real effects.

- Although there remain significant differences between the classical and Keynesian branches of macroeconomics, the rivalry between them is an important source of innovation that helps improve our understanding of the economy.

- New growth theorists in general reject the efficacy of short-run discretionary stabilization policies and argue, in contrast, that the federal government should focus its policy efforts on fostering a climate that will generate higher economic growth rates.

Does the Political Business Cycle Cause a Fed Bias Toward Inflation?

Concepts Applied: Monetary policy, time lags, policy irrelevance theorem, inflation, money supply

The rate of economic growth and the unemployment rate are key variables in determining who will be elected to the presidential office. Some economists argue that this relationship is responsible for creating more inflation.

On Election Day, in the best of all possible worlds, there will be low unemployment and stable prices. How often does this actually happen?

The Data

The evidence about a political business cycle does not guarantee its validity. Nonetheless, the presidential elections of 1956, 1964, 1972, and 1984 all had the basic pattern of unemployment and inflation predicted by the political business cycle, and the incumbents—Eisenhower, Johnson, Nixon, and Reagan, respectively—won by landslides. The elections of 1960, 1968, 1976, and 1980 did not have the political business cycle pattern, and as predicted, the White House changed hands. The election of 1988 resulted in a major victory by Republican candidate George Bush, who benefited from low unemployment, slowing but still healthy economic growth, and moderate inflation inherited from the Reagan years. Bush's loss in the 1992 election appears to contradict the political business cycle. Although the economy had been in a recession that started in 1990, the rate of growth of real GDP had been rising for several quarters and the unemployment level had been falling slightly for four months prior to the election. It was only *after* the election, however, that government statistics were released showing improvement in the rate of growth of real GDP, so that Bill Clinton was nonetheless effectively able to campaign on Bush's "dismal" economic record.

The Political Business Cycle, the Fed, and a Bias Toward Inflation

If our theory is correct, the Fed has to be part of the picture by increasing the rate of growth of the money supply about a year and a half before each presidential election. There is in fact some evidence that certain Fed chairmen, such as Arthur Burns under Richard Nixon, actually pursued such politically motivated policies. To the extent that Fed policymaking is motivated by political considerations, there is a built-in bias toward more inflation rather than less. The reason is that there is the political incentive to increase the rate of growth of the money supply for short-run economic gains, but there is no political payoff to reducing the rate of growth in the money supply *after* presidential elections. Presidents and heads of the Fed simply permit the economy to revert to its natural level of employment and rate of economic growth. Thus we see changing rates of inflation but almost never *deflation* in the United States (or Europe).

FOR CRITICAL ANALYSIS

1. How could Congress legislate against the political business cycle?

2. If the public had perfect information about the political business cycle, could expansionary monetary and fiscal policy have any short-run effect on real output and employment? Explain your answer.

CHAPTER SUMMARY

1. The natural rate of unemployment is the rate that exists in long-run equilibrium, when workers' expectations are consistent with actual conditions. Departures from the natural rate of unemployment can occur when individuals are surprised by unanticipated changes in fiscal or monetary policy.

2. The Phillips curve shows a negative relationship between the inflation rate and the unemployment rate that can be observed when there are unanticipated changes in aggregate demand. It was originally believed that the Phillips curve represented a trade-off between inflation and unemployment. In fact, no trade-off exists because workers' expectations adjust to systematic attempts to reduce unemployment below its natural rate.

3. The rational expectations hypothesis assumes that individuals' forecasts incorporate all available information, including an understanding of government policy and its effects on the economy. The new classical economics assumes that the rational expectations

hypothesis is valid and also that there is pure competition and that all prices and wages are flexible.

4. The policy irrelevance proposition says that under the assumptions of the new classical model, anticipated monetary policy cannot alter either the rate of unemployment or the level of real GDP. Thus according to the new classical model, policies can alter real economic variables only if the policies are unsystematic and therefore unanticipated; such policies cannot affect output and employment systematically.

5. Real business cycle theory holds that even if all prices and wages are perfectly flexible, real shocks to the economy (such as technological change and changes in the supplies of factors of production) can cause national business fluctuations.

6. The new Keynesian economics explains why various features of the economy, such as small-menu costs and wage rates that affect productivity, make it possible for monetary shocks to cause real effects.

DISCUSSION OF PREVIEW QUESTIONS

1. **What does the rational expectations hypothesis say about people's forecasting errors?**
   The simplest version of the rational expectations hypothesis simply says that people do not persistently make the same mistakes in forecasting the future. More generally, the hypothesis says that individuals base their forecasts about the future values of economic variables on the basis of all available past and current information and that these forecasts incorporate individuals' understanding about how the economy operates, including the operation of monetary and fiscal policy. As a result, people's forecasting errors are completely unpredictable over time and thus cannot be used by policymakers in formulating policy.

2. **How do the new classical economists view economic policy?**
   The new classical economists assume that the rational expectations hypothesis is valid and also that

there is pure competition and that all prices and wages are flexible. As a result, they say, anticipated monetary policy cannot alter either the rate of unemployment or the level of real GDP. Regardless of the nature of the anticipated policy, the unemployment rate will equal the natural rate, and real GDP will be determined solely by the economy's long-run aggregate supply curve. This conclusion is called the policy irrelevance theorem.

3. **What does the real business cycle theory say about the causes of recession?**
   Real business cycle theory shows that even if all prices and wages are perfectly flexible, real shocks to the economy (such as technological change and changes in the supplies of factors of production) can cause national business fluctuations. One example of such real shocks is the type of oil shock that hit the United States economy during the 1970s.

4. How does the new Keynesian economics explain the stickiness of wages and prices?
Generally, a combination of factors is cited, including the existence of contracts, small-menu costs, and efficiency wages. The key point is that there are a variety of rational reasons that economic participants have for entering into agreements that fix either nominal or real relative prices (including wages). Given the existence of such agreements, as well as the existence of costs of changing prices of all types, monetary policy can have real effects on the economy by changing aggregate demand.

PROBLEMS

(Answers to the odd-numbered problems appear at the back of the book.)

18-1. Answer the following questions based on the accompanying graph.

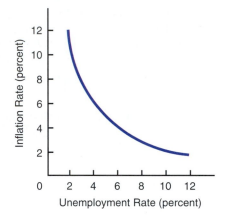

a. If we regard this curve as showing a trade-off between inflation and unemployment, how much unemployment will it "cost" to reduce inflation to 2 percent per year?
b. What might cause this curve to shift upward?
c. Why do economists argue that there is generally no useable trade-off between unemployment and inflation?

18-2. The natural rate of unemployment is a function of a variety of factors, including wage and price rigidities and interferences with labor mobility. Give some examples of such rigidities and interferences.

18-3. How does the existence of contracts, small-menu costs, and efficiency wages affect the amount of discretion available to policymakers?

18-4. Explain how the average duration of unemployment may be different for a given rate of unemployment.

18-5. What effect does the average duration of unemployment have on the rate of unemployment if we hold constant the variables you used to explain Problem 18-4?

18-6. What is meant by an optimal duration of unemployment? What may affect such an optimal duration of unemployment?

18-7. If both employers and workers incorrectly perceive the rate of inflation to the same extent, would the Phillips curve still be expected to be negatively sloped?

18-8. Unemployment is arbitrarily defined. What differences do different definitions have with respect to policy?

COMPUTER-ASSISTED INSTRUCTION

This session focuses on changes in the unemployment rate to illustrate the views of the new classical economists, the real business cycle theorists, and the new Keynesian economists.

Complete problem and answer appear on disk.

PART 9

GLOBAL ECONOMICS

Chapter 33

Comparative Advantage and the Open Economy

Chapter 34

Exchange Rates and the Balance of Payments

Chapter 35

Development: Economic Growth Around the World

The chapters in this book were extracted from the hardbound one-volume edition of *Economics Today*. In previous editions, the hardbound text and the macroeconomics and microeconomics paperbound texts were all numbered individually. Instructors and students who were using different versions of the book (or the software or other supplements) were forced to consult a conversion chart to find their place. Instead, the chapters in all three volumes of this edition are numbered the same—even if there are lapses in sequence—in order to avoid confusion and make the books as easy to use as possible.

CHAPTER 33

COMPARATIVE ADVANTAGE AND THE OPEN ECONOMY

If you use a VCR, camcorder, camera, or pocket calculator, chances are it was made in Japan. In the 1950s, "made in Japan" was synonymous with low quality; today, the opposite is true. The Japanese dominate consumer electronics. And their cars are often favored over American counterparts. It is indeed due to the rising share of Japanese car imports that the United States has on several occasions been willing to threaten a trade war with Japan. To understand why, you need to know about international trade, comparative advantage, and protectionism.

PREVIEW QUESTIONS

1. Is international trade important to the United States?

2. What is the relationship between imports and exports?

3. What is the ultimate effect of a restriction on imports?

4. What are some arguments against free trade?

Did **You Know That...** Boeing's latest airplane and the world's largest twin-engine jetliner, the 777, is made in Everett, Washington, but its parts come from 13 other countries, including Australia (rudder and elevators), Brazil (wingtips and dorsal fins), France (landing gears), Ireland (landing gear doors), Italy (wing outboard flaps), and Great Britain (flight computers and engines)? Japan provides 20 percent of the structure, including most of the fuselage.

The story of the Boeing 777 is repeated in the automobile industry. Parts from literally all over the world end up in cars "made in America." The running shoes you buy, the sheets you sleep on, and the clothes you put on your back are often wholly or partly produced outside the United States. Clearly, international trade today affects you whether you are aware of it or not. We are entering an age of a truly global economy. Learning about international trade is simply learning about everyday life.

THE WORLDWIDE IMPORTANCE OF INTERNATIONAL TRADE

Look at panel (a) of Figure 33-1. Since the end of World War II, world output of goods and services (world gross domestic product, or GDP) has increased almost every year until the present, when it is almost six times what it was. Look at the top line in panel (a). World trade has increased to almost 13 times what it was in 1950.

The United States figured prominently in this expansion of world trade. In panel (b) of Figure 33-1, you see imports and exports expressed as a percentage of total annual yearly

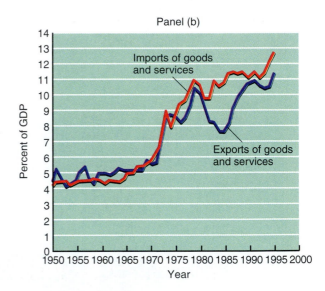

FIGURE 33-1

The Growth of World Trade

In panel (a), you can see the growth in world trade in relative terms because we use an index of 100 to represent real world trade in 1950. By the mid-1990s, that index had increased to over 1,300. At the same time, the index of world GDP (annual world income) had gone up to only around 600. World trade is clearly on the rise: Both imports and exports, expressed as a percentage of annual national income (GDP) in panel (b), have been rising.

Sources: Steven Husted and Michael Melvin, *International Economics,* 3d ed. (New York: HarperCollins, 1995), p. 11, used with permission; *International Trade;* Federal Reserve System; and U.S. Department of Commerce.

income (GDP). Whereas imports added up to barely 4 percent of annual national income in 1950, today they account for over 12 percent. International trade has definitely become more important to the economy of the United States.

INTERNATIONAL EXAMPLE
The Importance of International Trade in Various Countries

Whereas both imports and exports in the United States each account for more than 10 percent of total annual national income, in some countries the figure is much greater (see Table 33-1).

Another way to understand the worldwide importance of international trade is to look at trade flows on the world map in Figure 33-2 on page 736

TABLE 33-1

Importance of Imports in Selected Countries

Country	Imports as a Percentage of Annual National Income
Luxembourg	95.0
Netherlands	58.0
Norway	30.0
Canada	23.5
Germany	23.0
United Kingdom	21.0
China	19.0
France	18.4
Japan	6.8

Source: International Monetary Fund.

FOR CRITICAL ANALYSIS: *The yearly volume of imports in Hong Kong exceeds Hong Kong's total national income by several times. How is that possible? (Hint: Is there another reason to import a good besides wanting to consume it?)* ●

WHY WE TRADE: COMPARATIVE ADVANTAGE AND EXHAUSTING MUTUAL GAINS FROM EXCHANGE

You have already been introduced to the concept of specialization and mutual gains from trade in Chapter 2. These concepts are worth repeating because they are essential to understanding why the world is better off because of more international trade. The best way to understand the gains from trade among nations is first to understand the output gains from specialization between individuals.

The Output Gains from Specialization

Suppose that a creative advertising specialist can come up with two pages of ad copy (written words) an hour or generate one computerized art rendering per hour. At the same time, a computer artist can write one page of ad copy per hour or complete one computerized art

FIGURE 33-2

World Trade Flows

International merchandise trade amounts to over $3 trillion worldwide. The percentage figures show the proportion of trade flowing in the various directions.

Source: World Trade Organization (data are for 1995).

rendering per hour. Here the ad specialist can come up with more pages of ad copy per hour than the computer specialist and seemingly is just as good as the computer specialist at doing computerized art renderings. Is there any reason for the creative specialist and the computer specialist to "trade"? The answer is yes, because such trading will lead to higher output.

Consider the scenario of no trading. Assume that during each eight-hour day, the ad specialist and the computer whiz devote half of their day to writing ad copy and half to computerized art rendering. The ad specialist would create eight pages of ad copy (4 hours × 2) and four computerized art renderings (4 × 1). During that same period, the computer specialist would create four pages of ad copy (4 × 1) and four computerized art renderings (4 × 1). Each day, the combined output for the ad specialist and the computer specialist would be 12 pages of ad copy and eight computerized art renderings.

If the ad specialist specialized only in writing ad copy and the computer whiz specialized only in creating computerized art renderings, their combined output would rise to 16 pages of ad copy (8 × 2) and eight computerized art renderings (8 × 1). Overall, production would increase by four pages of ad copy per day.

The creative advertising employee has a comparative advantage in writing ad copy, and the computer specialist has a comparative advantage in doing computerized art renderings. **Comparative advantage** involves the ability to produce something at a lower opportunity cost compared to other producers, as we pointed out in Chapter 2.

Comparative advantage
The ability to produce a good or service at a lower opportunity cost compared to other producers.

TABLE 33-2

Comparative Costs of Production

Product	United States (worker-days)	France (worker-days)
Wine (1 liter)	1	1
Beer (1 liter)	1	2

Specialization Among Nations

To demonstrate the concept of comparative advantage for nations, let's take the example of France and the United States. In Table 33-2, we show the comparative costs of production of wine and beer in terms of worker-days. This is a simple two-country, two-commodity world in which we assume that labor is the only factor of production. As you can see from the table, in the United States, it takes one worker-day to produce 1 liter of wine, and the same is true for 1 liter of beer. In France, it takes one worker-day to produce 1 liter of wine but two worker-days for 1 liter of beer. In this sense, Americans appear to be just as good at producing wine as the French and actually have an **absolute advantage** in producing beer.

Absolute advantage
The ability to produce more output from given inputs of resources than other producers can.

Trade will still take place, however, which may seem paradoxical. How can trade take place if we can produce both goods at least as cheaply as the French can? Why don't we just produce both ourselves? To understand why, let's assume first that there is no trade and no specialization and that the workforce in each country consists of 200 workers. These 200 workers are divided equally in the production of wine and beer. We see in Table 33-3 that 100 liters of wine and 100 liters of beer are produced per day in the United States. In France, 100 liters of wine and 50 liters of beer are produced per day. The total daily world production in our two-country world is 200 liters of wine and 150 liters of beer.

Now the countries specialize. What can France produce more cheaply? Look at the comparative costs of production expressed in worker-days in Table 33-2. What is the cost of producing 1 liter more of wine? One worker-day. What is the cost of producing 1 liter more of beer? Two worker-days. We can say, then, that in France the opportunity cost of producing wine is less than that of producing beer. France will specialize in the activity that has the lower opportunity cost. In other words, France will specialize in its comparative advantage, which is the production of wine.

According to Table 33-4 on page 738, after specialization, the United States produces 200 liters of beer and France produces 200 liters of wine. Notice that the total world production per day has gone up from 200 liters of wine and 150 liters of beer to 200 liters of wine and 200 liters of beer per day. This was done without any increased use of resources. The gain, 50 "free" liters of beer, results from a more efficient allocation of resources worldwide. World output is greater when countries specialize in producing the goods in

TABLE 33-3

Daily World Output Before Specialization
It is assumed that 200 workers are available in each country.

Product	United States Workers	Output (liters)	France Workers	Output (liters)	World Output (liters)
Wine	100	100	100	100	200
Beer	100	100	100	50	150

| Product | United States | | France | | World Output (liters) |
	Workers	Output (liters)	Workers	Output (liters)	
Wine	—	—	200	200	200
Beer	200	200	—	—	200

TABLE 33-4
Daily World Output After Specialization
It is assumed that 200 workers are available in each country.

which they have a comparative advantage and then engage in foreign trade. Another way of looking at this is to consider the choice between two ways of producing a good. Obviously, each country would choose the less costly production process. One way of "producing" a good is to import it, so if in fact the imported good is cheaper than the domestically produced good, we will "produce" it by importing it. Not everybody, of course, is better off when free trade occurs. In our example, U.S. wine makers and French beer makers are worse off because those two *domestic* industries have disappeared.

Some people are worried that the United States (or any country, for that matter) might someday "run out of exports" because of overaggressive foreign competition. The analysis of comparative advantage tells us the contrary. No matter how much other countries compete for our business, the United States (or any other country) will always have a comparative advantage in something that it can export. In 10 or 20 years, that something may not be what we export today, but it will be exportable nonetheless because we will have a comparative advantage in producing it.

Other Benefits from International Trade: The Transmission of Ideas

Beyond the fact that comparative advantage generally results in an overall increase in the output of goods produced and consumed, there is another benefit to international trade. International trade bestows benefits on countries through the international transmission of ideas. According to economic historians, international trade has been the principal means by which new goods, services, and processes have spread around the world. For example, coffee was initially grown in Arabia near the Red Sea. Around A.D. 675, it began to be roasted and consumed as a beverage. Eventually, it was exported to other parts of the world, and the Dutch started cultivating it in their colonies during the seventeenth century and the French in the eighteenth century. The lowly potato is native to the Peruvian Andes. In the sixteenth century, it was brought to Europe by Spanish explorers. Thereafter, its cultivation and consumption spread rapidly. It became part of the American agricultural scene in the early eighteenth century.

All of the *intellectual property* that has been introduced throughout the world is a result of international trade. This includes new music, such as rock and roll in the 1950s and hip-hop and grunge in the 1990s. It includes the software applications that are common for computer users everywhere.

New processes have been transmitted through international trade. One of those involves the Japanese manufacturing innovation which emphasized redesigning the system rather than running the existing system in the best possible way. Inventories were reduced to just-in-time levels by reengineering machine setup methods. Just-in-time inventory control is now common in American factories.

INTERNATIONAL EXAMPLE
International Trade and the Alphabet

Even the alphabetic system of writing that appears to be the source of most alphabets in the world today was spread through international trade. According to some scholars, the Phoenicians, who lived on the long, narrow strip of Mediterranean coast north of Israel from the ninth century B.C. to around 300 B.C., created the first true alphabet. Presumably, they developed the alphabet to keep international trading records on their ships rather than having to take along highly trained scribes.

FOR CRITICAL ANALYSIS: Before alphabets were used, how might have people communicated in written form? ●

THE RELATIONSHIP BETWEEN IMPORTS AND EXPORTS

The basic proposition in understanding all of international trade is this:

In the long run, imports are paid for by exports.[1]

The reason that imports are ultimately paid for by exports is that foreigners want something in exchange for the goods that are shipped to the United States. For the most part, they want goods made in the United States. From this truism comes a remarkable corollary:

Any restriction of imports ultimately reduces exports.

This is a shocking revelation to many people who want to restrict foreign competition to protect domestic jobs. Although it is possible to protect certain U.S. jobs by restricting foreign competition, it is impossible to make *everyone* better off by imposing import restrictions. Why? Because ultimately such restrictions lead to a reduction in employment in the export industries of the nation.

Think of exports as simply another way of producing goods. International trade is merely an economic activity like all others; it is a production process that transforms exports into imports.

INTERNATIONAL EXAMPLE
The Importation of Priests into Spain

Imports affect not only goods but also services and the movement of labor. In Spain, some 3,000 priests retire each year, but barely 250 young men are ordained to replace them. Over 70 percent of the priests in Spain are now over the age of 50. The Spanish church estimates that by 2005, the number of priests will have fallen to half the 20,441 who were active in Spain in 1990. The Spanish church has had to seek young seminarians from Latin America under what it calls Operation Moses. It is currently subsidizing the travel and training of an increasing number of young Latin Americans to take over where native Spaniards have been before.

FOR CRITICAL ANALYSIS: How might the Spanish Catholic church induce more native Spaniards to become priests? ●

---

[1] We have to modify this rule by adding that in the short run, imports can also be paid for by the sale (or export) of real and financial assets, such as land, stocks, and bonds, or through an extension of credit from other countries.

INTERNATIONAL COMPETITIVENESS

"The United States is falling behind." "We need to stay competitive internationally." These and similar statements are often heard in government circles when the subject of international trade comes up. There are two problems with this issue. The first has to do with a simple definition. What does "global competitiveness" really mean? When one company competes against another, it is in competition. Is the United States like one big corporation, in competition with other countries? Certainly not. The standard of living in each country is almost solely a function of how well the economy functions *within that country,* not relative to other countries.

Another problem arises with respect to the real world. According to the Institute for Management Development in Lausanne, Switzerland, the United States continues to lead the pack in world competitiveness, ahead of Japan, Hong Kong, Germany, and the rest of the European Union. According to the report, America's top-class ranking is due to the rapid U.S. economic recovery from its 1990–1991 recession, widespread entrepreneurship, and a decade of economic restructuring. Other factors include America's sophisticated financial system and large investments in scientific research.

CONCEPTS IN BRIEF

- Countries can be better off materially if they specialize in producing goods for which they have a comparative advantage.
- It is important to distinguish between absolute and comparative advantage; the former refers to the ability to produce a unit of output with fewer physical units of input; the latter refers to producing output that has the lowest opportunity cost for a nation.
- Different nations will always have different comparative advantages because of differing opportunity costs due to different resource mixes.

ARGUMENTS AGAINST FREE TRADE

Numerous arguments are raised against free trade. They mainly point out the costs of trade; they do not consider the benefits or the possible alternatives for reducing the costs of free trade while still reaping benefits.

The Infant Industry Argument

A nation may feel that if a particular industry were allowed to develop domestically, it could eventually become efficient enough to compete effectively in the world market. Therefore, if some restrictions were placed on imports, domestic producers would be given the time needed to develop their efficiency to the point where they would be able to compete in the domestic market without any restrictions on imports. In graphic terminology, we would expect that if the protected industry truly does experience improvements in production techniques or technological breakthroughs toward greater efficiency in the future, the supply

Infant industry argument
The contention that tariffs should be imposed to protect from import competition an industry that is trying to get started. Presumably, after the industry becomes technologically efficient, the tariff can be lifted.

curve will shift outward to the right so that the domestic industry can produce larger quantities of each and every price. This **infant industry argument** has some merit in the short run and has been used to protect a number of industries in their infancy around the world. Such a policy can be abused, however. Often the protective import-restricting arrangements remain even after the infant has matured. If other countries can still produce more cheaply, the people who benefit from this type of situation are obviously the stockholders (and specialized factors of production that will earn economic rents) in the industry that is still being protected from world competition. The people who lose out are the consumers, who must pay a price higher than the world price for the product in question. In any event, it is very difficult to know beforehand which industries will eventually survive. In other words, we cannot predict very well the specific infant industries that should be protected. Note that when we talk about which industry "should be" protected, we are in the realm of normative economics. We are making a value judgment, a subjective statement of what *ought to be*.

EXAMPLE
An Infant Industry Blossoms Due to Protection from Foreign Imports: The Case of Marijuana

Marijuana was made illegal in the United States in the 1930s, but just as for many other outlawed drugs, a market for it remained. Until about 25 years ago, virtually all the marijuana consumed in the United States was imported. Today, earnings from the burgeoning and increasingly high-tech "pot" industry are estimated at $35 billion a year, making it the nation's biggest cash crop (compared to corn at $15 billion). Starting with President Richard Nixon in the 1970s, the federal government has in effect ended up protecting the domestic marijuana industry from imports by declaring a war on drugs. Given virtually no foreign competition, the American marijuana industry expanded and invested millions in developing both more productive and more potent seeds as well as more efficient growing technologies. Domestic marijuana growers now dominate the high end of a market in which consumers pay $300 to $500 an ounce for a reengineered home-grown product. New growing technologies allow domestic producers, using high-intensity sodium lights, carbon dioxide, and advances in genetics, to produce a kilogram of the potent sinsemilla variety every two months in a space no bigger than a phone booth.

FOR CRITICAL ANALYSIS: What has spurred domestic producers to develop highly productive indoor growing methods? ●

Countering Foreign Subsidies and Dumping

Another strong argument against unrestricted foreign trade has to do with countering other nations' subsidies to their own producers. When a foreign government subsidizes its producers, our producers claim that they cannot compete fairly with these subsidized foreigners. To the extent that such subsidies fluctuate, it can be argued that unrestricted free trade will seriously disrupt domestic producers. They will not know when foreign governments are going to subsidize their producers and when they are not. Our competing industries will be expanding and contracting too frequently.

Dumping
Selling a good or a service abroad at a price below its cost of production or below the price charged in the home market.

The phenomenon called *dumping* is also used as an argument against unrestricted trade. **Dumping** occurs when a producer sells its products abroad at a price below its cost of production or below the price that is charged in the home market. Although cries of dumping against foreign producers are often heard, they typically occur only when the foreign nation is in the throes of a serious recession. The foreign producer does not want to slow down its production at home. Because it anticipates an end to the recession and doesn't want to hold large inventories, it dumps its products abroad at prices below its costs. This does, in fact, disrupt international trade. It also creates instability in domestic production and therefore may impair commercial well-being at home.

POLICY EXAMPLE
How Should Antidumping Laws Be Administered?

It is one thing to pass a law against dumping but quite another to administer it. Current antidumping laws are the bailiwick of the Import Administration, in the U.S. Commerce Department. With its $30 million annual budget and 300 employees, it routinely decides which products should be targeted for antidumping duties, whether they be Chinese garlic or Colombian flowers. Once a decision has been made by the Import Administration, there is virtually no way to reverse it. The manner in which this government agency operates is patently unfair to our trading partners. When a U.S. company or industry files a dumping case against a foreign company, the Import Administration requires that the foreign company answer impossibly long questionnaires in a relatively short period of time. Most foreigners cannot respond by the deadline, at which point the Import Administration slaps on the highest possible duties.

FOR CRITICAL ANALYSIS: The Institute for International Economics estimates that the Import Administration's actions cost American consumers at least $2.6 billion per year. How do consumers suffer? ●

Protecting American Jobs

Perhaps the argument used most often against free trade is that unrestrained competition from other countries will eliminate American jobs because other countries have lower-cost labor than we do. (Less restrictive environmental standards in other countries might also lower their costs relative to ours.) This is a compelling argument, particularly for politicians from areas that might be threatened by foreign competition. For example, a representative from an area with shoe factories would certainly be upset about the possibility of constituents' losing their jobs because of competition from lower-priced shoe manufacturers in Brazil and Italy. But of course this argument against free trade is equally applicable to trade between the states.

Economists David Gould, G. L. Woodbridge, and Roy Ruffin examined the data on the relationship between increases in imports and the rate of unemployment. Their conclusion was that there is no causal link between the two. Indeed, in half the cases they studied, when imports increased, unemployment fell.

Another issue has to do with the cost of protecting American jobs by restricting international trade. The Institute for International Economics examined just the restrictions on foreign textiles and apparel goods. U.S. consumers pay $9 billion a year more to protect jobs in those industries. That comes out to $50,000 a year for each job saved in an industry in which the average job pays only $20,000 a year. Similar studies have yielded similar results: Restrictions on the imports of Japanese cars have cost $160,000 *per year* for every job saved in the auto industry. Every

THINKING CRITICALLY ABOUT THE MEDIA

Unfair Competition from Low-Wage Countries

Protectionists are able to get the media to carry stories about how low-wage countries are stealing American jobs. The facts are exactly the opposite. The highest-labor-cost country in the world is Germany, and it is also the largest exporter in the world. The United States, Japan, France, and the United Kingdom also have relatively high labor costs, and they, too, are some of the world's biggest exporters. If the low-wage myth were true, the United States would never be able to compete with, say, Mexican labor. Yet the reality is that the United States exports much more to Mexico than it imports. Finally, both the World Bank and the Organization for Economic Cooperation and Development have done exhaustive studies on the issue. Their conclusion is that there is no evidence that trade with low-wage countries results in large-scale job losses to industrial countries. The real competition for American manufacturing comes from high-wage countries, such as Germany and Japan.

job preserved in the glass industry has cost $200,000 each and every year. Every job preserved in the U.S. steel industry has cost an astounding $750,000 per year.

In the long run, the industries that have had the most protection—textiles, clothing, and iron and steel—have seen the most dramatic reductions in employment in the United States.

CONCEPTS IN BRIEF

- The infant industry argument against free trade contends that new industries should be protected against world competition so that they can become technologically efficient in the long run.

- Unrestricted foreign trade may allow foreign governments to subsidize exports or foreign producers to engage in dumping—selling products in other countries below their cost of production. To the extent that foreign export subsidies and dumping create more instability in domestic production, they may impair our well-being.

WAYS TO RESTRICT FOREIGN TRADE

There are many ways in which international trade can be stopped or at least stifled. These include quotas and taxes (the latter are usually called *tariffs* when applied to internationally traded items). Let's talk first about quotas.

Quotas

Quota system
A government-imposed restriction on the quantity of a specific good that another country is allowed to sell in the United States. In other words, quotas are restrictions on imports. These restrictions are usually applied to one or several specific countries.

Under the **quota system,** individual countries or groups of foreign producers are restricted to a certain amount of trade. An import quota specifies the maximum amount of a commodity that may be imported during a specified period of time. For example, the government might not allow more than 50 million barrels of foreign crude oil to enter the United States in a particular year.

Consider the example of quotas on textiles. Figure 33-3 presents the demand and the supply curves for imported textiles. In an unrestricted import market, the equilibrium quantity

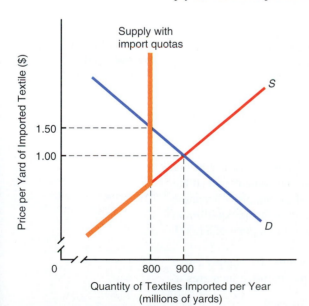

FIGURE 33-3

The Effect of Quotas on Textile Imports
Without restrictions, 900 million yards of textiles would be imported each year into the United States at the world price of $1.00 per yard. If the federal government imposes a quota of only 800 million yards, the effective supply curve becomes vertical at that quantity. It intersects the demand curve at the new equilibrium price of $1.50 per yard.

imported is 900 million yards at a price of $1 per yard (expressed in constant-quality units). When an import quota is imposed, the supply curve is no longer *S*. Rather, the supply curve becomes vertical at some amount less than the equilibrium quantity—here, 800 million yards per year. The price to the American consumer increases from $1.00 to $1.50. The domestic suppliers of textiles obviously benefit by an increase in revenues because they can now charge a higher price.

POLICY EXAMPLE
Is America Being "Fair" in Its Textile Trade Wars?

Textiles provide a real-world example of quotas in action. On the one hand, the federal government claims to be in favor of freer trade; on the other hand, it routinely imposes stricter quotas on textile imports. Take Kenya, a country to which the United States has given over $1 billion in foreign aid since 1980. The goal was to help Kenya develop its private sector. Kenya's textile industry did develop, and it started exporting pillowcases and shirts. Then the U.S. Commerce Department turned around and determined that the United States should reduce imports of Kenyan pillowcases by 1,565,616 in 1995.

A similar example involves Egyptian shirts. The United States has given Egypt over $30 billion in foreign aid since 1980, partly in the hope that it would develop its private sector. In the mid-1990s, the Commerce Department announced plans to impose import quotas on shirts manufactured in Egypt. The list continues: import quotas on men's shirts from El Salvador, on silk-blend men's and boys' coats and jackets from Hong Kong, on shirts made in Kuwait, on men's and women's coats produced in Oman, and on cotton shirts made in Pakistan.

FOR CRITICAL ANALYSIS: *Who benefits from quotas on foreign-made textiles?* ●

Voluntary Quotas. Quotas do not have to be explicit and defined by law. They can be "voluntary." Such a quota is called a **voluntary restraint agreement (VRA)**. In the early 1980s, the United States asked Japan voluntarily to restrain its exports to the United States. The Japanese government did so, limiting itself to exporting 2.8 million Japanese automobiles. Today, there are VRAs on machine tools and textiles.

The opposite of a VRA is a **voluntary import expansion (VIE)**. Under a VIE, a foreign government agrees to have its companies import more foreign goods from another country. The United States almost started a major international trade war with Japan in 1995 over just such an issue. The U.S. government wanted Japanese automobile manufacturers voluntarily to increase their imports of U.S.-made automobile parts.

Voluntary restraint agreement (VRA)
An official agreement with another country that "voluntarily" restricts the quantity of its exports to the United States.

Voluntary import expansion (VIE)
An official agreement with another country in which it agrees to import more from the United States.

Tariffs

We can analyze tariffs by using standard supply and demand diagrams. Let's use as our commodity laptop computers, some of which are made in Japan and some of which are made domestically. In panel (a) of Figure 33-4, you see the demand and supply of Japanese laptops. The equilibrium price is $1,000 per constant-quality unit, and the equilibrium quantity is 10 million per year. In panel (b), you see the same equilibrium price of $1,000, and the *domestic* equilibrium quantity is 5 million units per year.

Now a tariff of $500 is imposed on all imported Japanese laptops. The supply curve shifts upward by $500 to S_2. For purchasers of Japanese laptops, the price increases to

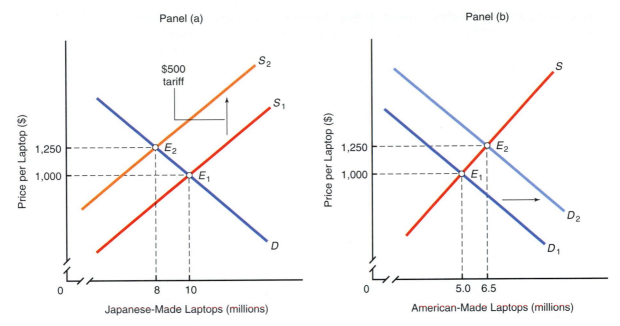

FIGURE 33-4

The Effect of a Tariff on Japanese-Made Laptop Computers

Without a tariff, the United States buys 10 million Japanese laptops per year at an average price of $1,000, as shown in panel (a). American producers sell 5 million domestically made laptops, also at $1,000 each, as shown in panel (b). A $500-per-laptop tariff will shift the Japanese import supply curve to S_2 in panel (a), so that the new equilibrium is at E_2, with price $1,250 and quantity sold reduced to 8 million per year. The demand curve for American-made laptops (for which there is no tariff) shifts to D_2 in panel (b). Sales increase to 6.5 million per year.

$1,250. The quantity demanded falls to 8 million per year. In panel (b), you see that at the higher price of imported Japanese laptops, the demand curve for American-made laptops shifts outward to the right to D_2. The equilibrium price increases to $1,250, but the equilibrium quantity increases to 6.5 million units per year. So the tariff benefits domestic laptop producers because it increases the demand for their products due to the higher price of a close substitute, Japanese laptops. This causes a redistribution of income from American consumers of laptops to American producers of laptops.

Tariffs in the United States. In Figure 33-5 on page 746, we see that tariffs on all imported goods have varied widely. The highest rates in the twentieth century occurred with the passage of the Smoot-Hawley Tariff in 1930.

POLICY EXAMPLE
Did the Smoot-Hawley Tariff Worsen the Great Depression?

By 1930, the unemployment rate had almost doubled in a year. Congress and President Hoover wanted to do something that would help stimulate U.S. production and reduce unemployment. The result was the Smoot-Hawley Tariff, which set tariff schedules for over 20,000 products, raising duties on imports by an average of 52 percent. This attempt to improve the domestic economy at the expense of foreign economies backfired. Each trading partner of the United States in turn imposed its own high tariffs, including the United Kingdom, the Netherlands, France, and Switzerland. The result was a massive reduction in international trade by an incredible 64 percent in three years. Some believe that the ensuing world Great Depression was partially caused by such tariffs.

FOR CRITICAL ANALYSIS: *The Smoot-Hawley Tariff has been labeled a "beggar thy neighbor" policy. Explain why.* ●

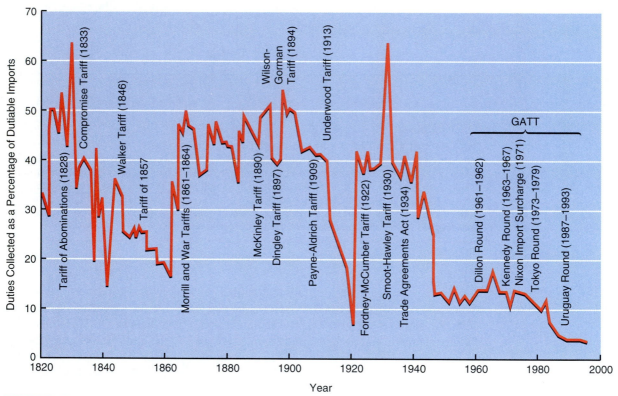

FIGURE 33-5

Tariff Rates in the United States Since 1820

Tariff rates in the United States have bounced around like a football; indeed, in Congress, tariffs are a political football. Import-competing industries prefer high tariffs. In the twentieth century, the highest tariff we have had was the Smoot-Hawley Tariff of 1930, which was almost as high as the "tariff of abominations" in 1828.

Source: U.S. Department of Commerce.

Current Tariff Laws. The Trade Expansion Act of 1962 gave the president the authority to reduce tariffs by up to 50 percent. Subsequently, tariffs were reduced by about 35 percent. In 1974, the Trade Reform Act allowed the president to reduce tariffs further. In 1984, the Trade and Tariff Act resulted in the lowest tariff rates ever. All such trade agreement obligations of the United States are carried out under the auspices of the **General Agreement on Tariffs and Trade (GATT),** which was signed in 1947. Member nations of GATT account for more than 85 percent of world trade. As you can see in Figure 33-5, there have been a number of rounds of negotiations to reduce tariffs since the early 1960s. The latest round was called the Uruguay Round because that is where the meetings were held.

General Agreement on Tariffs and Trade (GATT)
An international agreement established in 1947 to further world trade by reducing barriers and tariffs.

The World Trade Organization (WTO)

The Uruguay Round of the General Agreement on Tariffs and Trade (GATT) was ratified by 117 nations at the end of 1993. A year later, in a special session of Congress, the entire treaty was ratified. As of January 1, 1995, the new **World Trade Organization (WTO)** replaced GATT.

World Trade Organization (WTO)
The successor organization to GATT, it handles all trade disputes among its 117 member nations.

The ratification of GATT by the United States will result in a roughly 40 percent cut in tariffs worldwide. Agricultural subsidies will be reduced and perhaps eventually eliminated. Protection for patents will be extended worldwide. The WTO will have arbitration boards to settle international disputes over trade issues. No country has a veto. A country that loses a WTO ruling has to comply or face trade sanction by the country that wins arbitration.

In short, the passage of GATT and the creation of the WTO constitute the furthest-reaching global trade agreement in history. Advanced technologies in particular will benefit from the worldwide extension of the protection of patents. Copyrights on books and recordings will be protected from piracy better than ever before. Protectionist rules, such as "local content" requirements that force foreign firms to use locally produced inputs, will be eliminated. Also, other countries will have to treat American service suppliers no less favorably than they treat their own service suppliers.

CONCEPTS IN BRIEF

- One means of restricting foreign trade is a quota system. Beneficiaries of quotas are the importers who get the quota rights and the domestic producers of the restricted good.

- Another means of restricting imports is a tariff, which is a tax on imports only. An import tariff benefits import-competing industries and harms consumers by raising prices.

- The main international institution created to improve trade among nations is the General Agreement on Tariffs and Trade (GATT). The latest round of trade talks under GATT, the Uruguay Round, led to the creation of the World Trade Organization.

Waging the Second War on Japan

Concepts Applied: *Comparative advantage, specialization, competitiveness, protectionism, benefits from trade*

American cars may not be selling well in Japan, but that probably has little to do with Japanese import restrictions. German car manufacturers have thrived in Japan by heavily investing in car dealerships and new models.

The facts seem simple enough. For many years, the value of goods imported from Japan has exceeded the value of goods exported to Japan. "Japan bashers" use this information to argue that Japan does not provide a "level" playing field with respect to international trade.

Japanese Restrictions on Imports

As proof that the Japanese are unfair when it comes to international trade, proponents of getting tough with Japan point out that (1) many Japanese markets are completely closed to foreign competition, (2) Japanese government officials routinely take months to examine American imports for safety and quality (in particular, American automobiles), and (3) Japan's business system is not conducive to American suppliers "breaking in."

The *Keiretsu*

It is true that the Japanese have a corporate system that is different from that in the United States. One major difference is the existence in Japan of the *keiretsu,* a grouping arrangement that links companies together. Even in the absence of tariffs on auto parts, American auto part manufacturers cannot crack the tight links that automakers, such as Nissan and Toyota, maintain with their *keiretsu*

suppliers. Many of these links go back decades and today are reinforced by cross-ownership of shares. It is not atypical for Nissan to send its own managers to a supplier to get operations in order.

The Problem with Focusing on Automobiles

The United States' focus on the success of the Japanese automobile industry is inconsistent with our ideas of a market economy that rewards performance. Economist William Kline uses the following analogy: It would be the same as convicting Michael Jordan of being unfairly compensated in basketball but not in baseball. Why? Because when Michael Jordan plays basketball, he earns many times more than when he plays baseball. The reason, of course, is that Michael Jordan is relatively much better at playing basketball.

The same is true for Japanese automobile producers. The reason there is such a large difference between the sales of Japanese cars in Japan and competing U.S. imports there is that Japanese automobile producers make a better product. According to Kline, there is virtually no evidence that Japanese consumers buy Japanese cars because of trade barriers that keep out U.S. imports. German automakers are doing quite well in Japan because they have invested in their own dealer networks and started producing right-hand-drive cars years ago, something U.S. automakers started doing only recently.

What About "Fairness"?

Even if we assume that the Japanese restrict American imports, that still does not mean we should engage in a trade war with Japan by setting up a system of impediments to Japanese imports. Americans do not lose because of imports and gain from exports. As long as Americans continue to obtain Japanese goods on cheaper terms than by producing them ourselves, Americans will gain. It does not matter why we are getting Japanese goods on cheaper terms.

"We Don't Need Trading Partners like That"

On occasion, American politicians declare that "we don't need that kind of trade" whenever they look at the fact that Americans import more from Japan than Americans export to Japan. This assumption is equivalent to saying that you should not continue trading with your hairstylist, accountant, lawyer, or butcher. After all, you are buying more from all of them than they are buying from you.

FOR CRITICAL ANALYSIS

1. Recently, U.S. mail-order companies, such as L. L. Bean, have started sending thousands of catalogs to consumers in Japan and obtaining orders from them. What do you think accounts, at least in part, for the new success of American mail-order companies in that country?

2. For the world as a whole during any one-year period, what has to be true about the value of total world imports relative to the value of total world exports?

CHAPTER SUMMARY

1. It is important to distinguish between absolute and comparative advantage. A person or country that can do everything "better" (with higher labor productivity) than every other person or country has an absolute advantage in everything. Nevertheless, trade will still be advantageous if people will specialize in the things that they do *relatively* best, exploiting their respective comparative advantage.

2. Along with the gains, there are costs from trade. Certain industries and their employees may be hurt if trade is opened up.

3. An import quota restricts the quantity of imports coming into the country. It therefore raises the price. Consumers always lose.

4. When governments impose "voluntary" quotas, they are called voluntary restraint agreements (VRAs).

5. An import tariff raises the domestic price of foreign produced goods. It therefore allows domestic producers to raise their own prices. The result is a higher price to consumers, a lower quantity of imports, and a lower volume of international trade.

6. The main international institution created to improve trade among nations was the General Agreement on Tariffs and Trade (GATT), replaced in 1993 by the World Trade Organization (WTO).

DISCUSSION OF PREVIEW QUESTIONS

1. **Is international trade important to the United States?**
   The direct impact of international trade on the United States, as measured by the ratio of exports to GDP, is relatively small compared with many other nations. Yet it is hard to imagine what life would be like without international trade. Initially, many prices would rise rapidly, but eventually domestic production would begin on many goods we presently import. However, consider life without imports of coffee, tea, bananas, and foreign wines, motorcycles, automobiles, televisions, VCRs, and hundreds of other goods from food and clothing to electronics—not to mention vital imports such as bauxite, chromium, cobalt, nickel, platinum, and tin.

2. **What is the relationship between imports and exports?**
   Because foreigners eventually want real goods and services as payment for the real goods and services they export to other countries, ultimately each country pays for its imports with its exports. Hence on a worldwide basis, the value of imports must equal the value of exports.

3. **What is the ultimate effect of a restriction on imports?**

   Because each country must pay for its imports with its exports, any restriction on imports must ultimately lead to a reduction in exports. So even though restrictions on imports because of tariffs or quotas may benefit workers and business owners in the protected domestic industry, such protection will harm workers and business owners in the export sector in general.

4. **What are some arguments against free trade?**

   The infant industry argument maintains that new industries developing domestically need protection from foreign competitors until they are mature enough themselves to compete with foreigners, at which time protection will be removed. One problem with this argument is that it is difficult to tell when maturity has been reached, and domestic industries will fight against weaning. Moreover, this argument is hardly relevant to most U.S. industries. It is also alleged (and is true to a large extent) that free trade leads to instability for specific domestic industries as comparative advantage changes in a dynamic world. Nations that have traditionally held a comparative advantage in the production of some goods occasionally lose that advantage (while gaining others). Regional hardships are a result, and protection of domestic jobs is demanded.

PROBLEMS

(Answers to the odd-numbered problems appear at the back of the book.)

33-1. Examine the hypothetical table of worker-hours required to produce caviar and wheat in the United States and in Russia.

Product	United States	Russia
Caviar (ounce)	6 worker-hours	9 worker-hours
Wheat (bushel)	3 worker-hours	6 worker-hours

   a. What is the opportunity cost to the United States of producing one ounce of caviar per time period? What is the opportunity cost to the United States of producing one bushel of wheat?
   b. What is the opportunity cost to Russia of producing one ounce of caviar per time period? What is the opportunity cost to Russia of producing one bushel of wheat?
   c. The United States has a comparative advantage in what? Russia has a comparative advantage in what?

33-2. Study the hypothetical table of worker-hours required to produce coffee and beans in Colombia and Turkey.

Product	Colombia	Turkey
Coffee (pound)	2 worker-hours	1 worker-hour
Beans (pound)	6 worker-hours	2 worker-hours

   a. What is the opportunity cost to Colombia of producing one pound of coffee? One pound of beans?
   b. What is the opportunity cost to Turkey of producing one pound of coffee? One pound of beans?
   c. Colombia has a comparative advantage in what? Turkey has a comparative advantage in what?

33-3. Assume that the United States can produce *everything* with fewer labor-hours than any other country on earth. Even under this extreme assumption, why would the United States still trade with other countries?

33-4. Examine the hypothetical table of worker-hours required to produce cheese and cloth in two countries, A and B.

Product	Country A	Country B
Cheese (pound)	$\frac{2}{3}$ worker-hours	2 worker-hours
Cloth (yard)	$\frac{1}{2}$ worker-hours	1 worker-hour

a. What is the opportunity cost to country A of producing one pound of cheese? One yard of cloth?
b. What is the opportunity cost to country B of producing one pound of cheese? One yard of cloth?
c. Country A has a comparative advantage in what?
d. Country B has a comparative advantage in what?

33-5. The use of tariffs and quotas to restrict imports results in higher prices and is successful in reducing imports. In what way is using a tariff different from using a quota?

33-6. Two countries, Austral Land and Boreal Land, have the following production opportunities shown in the graphs.

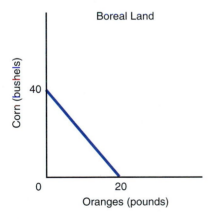

a. Who has an absolute advantage in corn? In oranges?
b. Who has a comparative advantage in corn? In oranges?
c. Should Boreal Land export at all? If so, which good should it export?

d. What is Austral Land's opportunity cost of oranges in terms of corn? What is Boreal Land's opportunity cost of corn in terms of oranges?

33-7. The accompanying graph gives the supply and demand for grapes. S and D are the United States' supply and demand curves, respectively. Assume that the world price of grapes is 50 cents per pound.

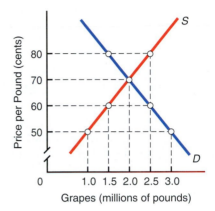

a. How many pounds are produced domestically? How many pounds are imported?
b. Suppose that the United States imposes a 10-cent-per-pound tariff. How many pounds would now be produced domestically? How many pounds would be imported? What are the U.S. government's revenues?
c. Suppose now that the government imposes a 20-cent-per-pound tariff. What price can domestic growers now receive for their grapes? How many pounds will domestic growers produce? How many pounds will be imported? What are government revenues?

33-8. If free trade is so obviously beneficial, why are there so many restrictions on international trade? (Hint: Review the theory presented in Chapter 32.)

33-9. Explain why an increase in taxes on imports (tariffs) will reduce exports.

33-10. Assume that a country with whom the United States is trading imposes restrictions on U.S.-made imports into that country. Will the United States be better off by simultaneously imposing restrictions on the other country's imports into the United States? Why or why not?

COMPUTER-ASSISTED INSTRUCTION

We show that the combination of specialization and exchange is the next best thing to a free lunch.

Complete problem and answer appear on disk.

INTERACTING WITH THE INTERNET

The text of the GATT agreement can be found at
http://ananse.irv.uit.no/trade_law/gatt/nav/toc.html
and the text of NAFTA at
gopher://cyfer.esusda.gov/11/ace/policy/nafta
and
gopher://wiretap.spies.com/11/Gov/NAFTA
Find links to sites with pro and con material on NAFTA at
http://www.yahoo.com/Business_and_Economy/Trade/North_American_Free_Trade_Agreement__NAFTA/
A very good source for general information on the nations of the world is the CIA's *World Factbook* at
http://www.odci.gov/cia/publications/95fact/index.html
Information on different countries' economic and trade policies can be found at
gopher://UMSLVMA.UMSL.EDU:70/11/LIBRARY/GOVDOCS/CRPT

CHAPTER 34

EXCHANGE RATES AND THE BALANCE OF PAYMENTS

If you talk to Americans who traveled to Europe in the mid-1980s, they will probably regale you with stories of how cheap their trip was. If you go to Europe today, the stories will be quite different— more like cries of outrage at having been gouged by shopkeepers and restaurateurs. What difference does a decade make? Well, when you are talking about the dollar, a lot. Today, in some countries, such as Germany and Japan, the dollar buys barely half what it did in 1985. Should we be worrying about a weaker dollar? To answer this question, you need to know about international financial transactions and the determinants of foreign exchange rates.

PREVIEW QUESTIONS

1. What is the difference between the balance of trade and the balance of payments?

2. What is a foreign exchange rate?

3. What is a flexible exchange rate system?

4. What is the gold standard?

Did You Know That . . . every day, around the clock, over $1 trillion of foreign currencies are traded? Along with that trading come news headlines, such as "The dollar weakened today," "The dollar is clearly overvalued," "The dollar is under attack," and "Members of the Group of Seven agreed to prevent the dollar from rising." If you are confused by such newspaper headlines, join the crowd. Surprisingly, though, if you regard the dollar, the pound, the deutsche mark, the yen, and the franc as assets that are subject to the laws of supply and demand, the world of international finance can be quickly demystified. Perhaps the first step is to examine the meaning of the terms used with respect to America's international financial transactions during any one-year period.

THE BALANCE OF PAYMENTS AND INTERNATIONAL CAPITAL MOVEMENTS

Governments typically keep track of each year's economic activities by calculating the gross domestic product—the total of expenditures on all newly produced final domestic goods and services—and its components. In the world of international trade also, a summary information system has been developed. It relates to the balance of trade and the balance of payments. The **balance of trade** refers specifically to exports and imports of *goods and services* as discussed in Chapter 33. When international trade is in balance, the value of exports equals the value of imports.

The **balance of payments** is a more general concept that expresses the total of all economic transactions between two nations, usually for a period of one year. Each country's balance of payments summarizes information about that country's exports, imports, earnings by domestic residents on assets located abroad, earnings on domestic assets owned by foreign residents, international capital movements, and official transactions by central banks and governments. In essence, then, the balance of payments is a record of all the transactions between households, firms, and government of one country and the rest of the world. Any transaction that leads to a *payment* by a country's residents (or government) is a deficit item, identified by a negative sign (−) when we examine the actual numbers that might be in Table 34-1. Any transaction that leads to a *receipt* by a country's residents (or government) is a surplus item and is identified by a plus sign (+) when actual numbers are considered. Table 34-1 gives a listing of the surplus and deficit items on international accounts.

Balance of trade
The value of goods and services bought and sold in the world market.

Balance of payments
A summary record of a country's economic transactions with foreign residents and governments over a year.

TABLE 34-1

Surplus (+) and Deficit (−) Items on the International Accounts

Surplus Items (+)	Deficit Items (−)
Exports of merchandise	Imports of merchandise
Private and governmental gifts from foreigners	Private and governmental gifts to foreigners
Foreign use of domestically owned transportation	Use of foreign-owned transportation
Foreign tourists' expenditures in this country	Tourism expenditures abroad
Foreign military spending in this country	Military spending abroad
Interest and dividend receipts from foreigners	Interest and dividends paid to foreigners
Sales of domestic assets to foreigners	Purchases of foreign assets
Funds deposited in this country by foreigners	Funds placed in foreign depository institutions
Sales of gold to foreigners	Purchases of gold from foreigners
Sales of domestic currency to foreigners	Purchases of foreign currency

Accounting Identities

Accounting identities—definitions of equivalent values—exist for financial institutions and other businesses. We begin with simple accounting identities that must hold for families and then go on to describe international accounting identities.

If a family unit is spending more than its current income, such a situation necessarily implies that the family unit must be doing one of the following:

1. Drawing down its wealth. The family must reduce its money holdings, or it must sell stocks, bonds, or other assets.
2. Borrowing.
3. Receiving gifts from friends or relatives.
4. Receiving public transfers from a government, which obtained the funds by taxing others. (A transfer is a payment, in money or in goods or services, made without receiving goods or services in return.)

In effect, we can use this information to derive an identity: If a family unit is currently spending more than it is earning, it must draw on previously acquired wealth, borrow, or receive either private or public aid. Similarly, an identity exists for a family unit that is currently spending less than it is earning: It must increase its wealth by increasing its money holdings or by lending and acquiring other financial assets, or it must pay taxes or bestow gifts on others. When we consider businesses and governments, each unit in each group faces its own identities or constraints; thus, net lending by households must equal net borrowing by businesses and governments.

Even though our individual family unit's accounts must balance, in the sense that the identity discussed previously must hold, sometimes the item that brings about the balance cannot continue indefinitely. *If family expenditures exceed family income and this situation is financed by borrowing, the household may be considered to be in disequilibrium because such a situation cannot continue indefinitely.* If such a deficit is financed by drawing on previously accumulated assets, the family may also be in disequilibrium because it cannot continue indefinitely to draw on its wealth; eventually, it will become impossible for that family to continue such a lifestyle. (Of course, if the family members are retired, they may well be in equilibrium by drawing on previously acquired assets to finance current deficits; this example illustrates that it is necessary to understand circumstances fully before pronouncing an economic unit in disequilibrium.)

Individual households, businesses, and governments, as well as the entire group of households, businesses, and governments, must eventually reach equilibrium. Certain economic adjustment mechanisms have evolved to ensure equilibrium. Deficit households must eventually increase their incomes or decrease their expenditures. They will find that they have to pay higher interest rates if they wish to borrow to finance their deficits. Eventually their credit sources will dry up, and they will be forced into equilibrium. Businesses, on occasion, must lower costs and/or prices—or go bankrupt—to reach equilibrium.

When nations trade or interact, certain identities or constraints must also hold. Nations buy goods from people in other nations; they also lend to and present gifts to people in other nations. If a nation interacts with others, an accounting identity ensures a balance (but not an equilibrium, as will soon become clear). Let's look at the three categories of balance of payments transactions: current account transactions, capital account transactions, and official reserve account transactions.

Current Account Transactions

During any designated period, all payments and gifts that are related to the purchase or sale of both goods and services constitute the current account in international trade. The three major types of current account transactions are the exchange of merchandise goods, the exchange of services, and unilateral transfers.

Merchandise Trade Transactions. The largest portion of any nation's balance of payments current account is typically the importing and exporting of merchandise goods. During 1996, for example, as can be seen in lines 1 and 2 of Table 34-2, the United States exported $609.6 billion of merchandise and imported $770.8 billion. The balance of merchandise trade is defined as the difference between the value of merchandise exports and the value of merchandise imports. For 1996, the United States had a balance of merchandise trade deficit because the value of its merchandise imports exceeded the value of its merchandise exports. This deficit amounted to $161.2 billion (line 3).

Service Exports and Imports. The balance of (merchandise) trade has to do with tangible items—you can feel them, touch them, and see them. Service exports and imports have to do with invisible or intangible items that are bought and sold, such as shipping, insurance, tourist expenditures, and banking services. Also, income earned by foreigners on U.S. investments and income earned by Americans on foreign investments are part of service imports and exports. As can be seen in lines 4 and 5 of Table 34-2, in 1996, service exports were $220.4 bil-

---

THINKING CRITICALLY ABOUT THE MEDIA

Perhaps the Trade Situation Isn't So Bad After All

Virtually every month, there appears a spate of articles and TV sound bites about America's trade deficit. The official numbers may be in error, however, for they ignore the multinational nature of modern firms. American international trade figures exclude sales in other countries for subsidiaries of American-owned companies. Because of a host of other problems, some government economists believe that they are underestimating the value of U.S. exports by as much as 10 percent. Economist Paul Krugman of Stanford University agrees. When he added up the value of world exports and compared it with the value of world imports, he found that the planet Earth had a trade deficit of $100 billion! Perhaps we are trading with aliens and don't know it.

TABLE 34-2

U.S. Balance of Payments Account, 1996 (in Billions of Dollars)

Current Account		
(1) Exports of goods	+609.6	
(2) Imports of goods	−770.8	
(3) Balance of trade		−161.2
(4) Exports of services	+220.4	
(5) Imports of services	−151.6	
(6) Balance of services		+68.8
(7) Balance on goods and services [(3) + (6)]		−92.4
(8) Net unilateral transfers	−30.7	
(9) Balance on current account		−123.1
Capital Account		
(10) U.S. capital going abroad	−314.8	
(11) Foreign capital coming into the United States	+431.5[a]	
(12) Balance on capital account [(10) + (11)]		+116.7
(13) Balance on current account plus balance on capital account [(9) + (12)]		−6.4
(14) Official transactions		+6.4
(15) Total (balance)		$00.0

Sources: U.S. Department of Commerce, Bureau of Economic Analysis; U.S. Department of the Treasury.

[a]Includes a $24 billion statistical discrepancy, probably unaccounted capital inflows, many of which relate to the illegal drug trade.

lion and service imports were $151.6 billion. Thus the balance of services was about $68.8 billion in 1996 (line 6). Exports constitute receipts or inflows into the United States and are positive; imports constitute payments abroad or outflows of money and are negative.

When we combine the balance of merchandise trade with the balance of services, we obtain a balance on goods and services equal to −$92.4 billion in 1996 (line 7).

Unilateral Transfers. Americans give gifts to relatives and others abroad. The federal government grants gifts to foreign nations. Foreigners give gifts to Americans, and some foreign governments have granted money to the U.S. government. In the current account, we see that net unilateral transfers—the total amount of gifts given by Americans minus the total amount received by Americans from abroad—came to −$30.7 billion in 1996 (line 8). The fact that there is a minus sign before the number for unilateral transfers means that Americans gave more to foreigners than foreigners gave to Americans.

Balancing the Current Account. The balance on current account tracks the value of a country's exports of goods and services (including military receipts plus income on investments abroad) and transfer payments (private and government) relative to the value of that country's import of goods and services (including military payments) and transfer payments (private and government). In 1996, it was a *negative* $123.1 billion.

If exports exceed imports, a current account surplus is said to exist; if imports exceed exports, a current account deficit is said to exist. A current account deficit means that we are importing more than we are exporting. Such a deficit must be paid for by the export of money or money equivalent, which means a capital account surplus.

Capital Account Transactions

In world markets, it is possible to buy and sell not only goods and services but also real and financial assets. This is what the capital accounts are concerned with in international transactions. Capital account transactions occur because of foreign investments—either foreigners investing in the United States or Americans investing in other countries. The purchase of shares of stock on the London stock market by an American causes an outflow of funds. The building of a Japanese automobile factory in the United States causes an inflow of funds. Any time foreigners buy U.S. government securities, that is an inflow of funds. Any time Americans buy foreign government securities, there is an outflow of funds. Loans to and from foreigners cause outflows and inflows.

Line 10 of Table 34-2 indicates that in 1996, the value of private and government capital going out of the United States was −$314.8 billion, and line 11 shows that the value of private and government capital coming into the United States (including a statistical discrepancy) was $431.5 billion. U.S. capital going abroad constitutes payments or outflows and is therefore negative. Foreign capital coming into the United States constitutes receipts or inflows and is therefore positive. Thus there was a positive net capital movement of $116.7 billion into the United States (line 12). This is also called the balance on capital account.

There is a relationship between the current account and the capital account, assuming no interventions by the central banks of nations. *The current account and the capital account must sum to zero. Stated differently, the current account deficit equals the capital account surplus. Any nation experiencing a current account deficit, such as the United States, must also be running a capital account surplus.*

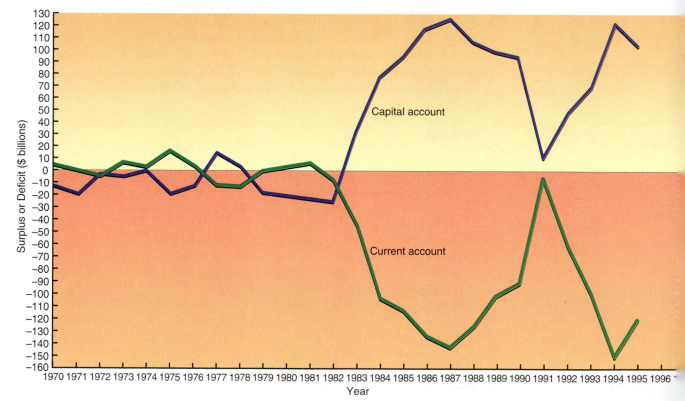

EXAMPLE
Does America's Continuing Trade Deficit Mean It Has a Weak Economy?

The current account in the United States has been in deficit continuously since the early 1980s. This is not something new. During the 1880s, the United States had many years of current account deficits. They were equally matched by capital account surpluses, as the rest of the world sent capital to the United States to finance the building of the railroads and the development of the trans-Mississippi West. By the early 1900s, the United States accumulated a long string of current account surpluses. By World War I, Americans had repaid all their external debt and had become a net creditor. In 1980, the United States was in fact the world's largest creditor. By 1986, it was the world's largest debtor nation. This can be seen in Figure 34-1. Whenever America is in deficit in its current account, it is in surplus in its capital account.

Contrary to popular belief, the United States does not necessarily have a trade deficit because it is a weak economy and cannot compete in world markets. Rather, the United States appears to be a good place to invest capital because there are strong prospects for growth and investment opportunities. So long as foreigners wish to invest more in the United

FIGURE 34-1
The Relationship Between the Current Account and the Capital Account
To some extent, the capital account is the mirror image of the current account. We can see this in the years since 1970. When the current account was in surplus, the capital account was in deficit. When the current account was in deficit, the capital account was in surplus. Indeed, virtually the only time foreigners can invest in America is when the current account is in deficit.

Sources: International Monetary Fund;: *Economic Indicators.*

States than Americans wish to invest abroad, there will always be a deficit in our current account balance. Americans are the beneficiaries of international capital flows.

FOR CRITICAL ANALYSIS: Why are politicians, nonetheless, so worried about the international trade deficit? ●

Official Reserve Account Transactions

The third type of balance of payments transaction concerns official reserve assets, which consist of the following:

1. Foreign currencies
2. Gold
3. **Special drawing rights (SDRs),** which are reserve assets that the International Monetary Fund created to be used by countries to settle international payment obligations
4. The reserve position in the International Monetary Fund
5. Financial assets held by an official agency, such as the U.S. Treasury Department

Special drawing rights (SDRs)
Reserve assets created by the International Monetary Fund that countries can use to settle international payments.

To consider how official reserve account transactions occur, look again at Table 34-2. The surplus in our capital account was +$116.7 billion. But the deficit in our current account was −$123.1 billion, so we had a net deficit on the combined accounts (line 13) of −$6.4 billion. In other words, the United States obtained less in foreign money in all its international transactions than it used. How is this deficiency made up? By our central bank drawing down its existing balances of foreign monies, or the +$6.4 billion in official transactions shown on line 14 in Table 34-2. You might ask why there is a plus sign on line 14. The answer is because this represents a *supply* (an inflow) of foreign exchange into our international transactions.

The balance (line 15) in Table 34-2 is zero, as it must be with double-entry bookkeeping. Our balance of payments deficit is measured by the official transactions figure on line 14. (This does not mean we are in equilibrium, though.)

What Affects the Balance of Payments?

A major factor affecting our balance of payments is our rate of inflation relative to that of our trading partners. Assume that the rate of inflation in the United States and in France is equal. All of a sudden, our inflation rate increases. The French will find that American products are becoming more expensive, and we will export fewer of them to France. Americans will find French products relatively cheaper, and we will import more. The converse will occur if our rate of inflation suddenly falls relative to that of France. All other things held constant, whenever our rate of inflation exceeds that of our trading partners, we expect to see a "worsening" of our balance of trade and payments. Conversely, when our rate of inflation is less than that of our trading partners, other things being constant, we expect to see an "improvement" in our balance of trade and payments.

Another important factor that sometimes influences our balance of payments is our relative political stability. Political instability causes *capital flight:* Owners of capital in countries anticipating or experiencing political instability will often move assets to countries that are politically stable, such as the United States. Hence our balance of payments is likely to improve whenever political instability looms in other nations in the world.

THINKING CRITICALLY ABOUT THE MEDIA

Developing Countries Are Getting All the Capital

Many developing countries are growing more rapidly than the developed countries. Several reports have been commented on by the media in recent years in which it is argued that developing economies are "sucking up" all the world's capital. Let's put the numbers in context. About $60 billion a year of capital moves from advanced to developing countries. All of the countries in the world, in contrast, invest over $4 trillion a year. So such capital flows represent only 1.5 percent of total world investment. What's to worry?

CONCEPTS IN BRIEF

- The balance of payments reflects the value of all transactions in international trade, including goods, services, financial assets, and gifts.

- The merchandise trade balance gives us the difference between exports and imports of tangible items. Merchandise trade transactions are represented by exports and imports of tangible items.

- Service exports and imports relate to the trade of intangible items, such as shipping, insurance, and tourist expenditures. They include income earned by foreigners on U.S. investments and income earned by Americans on foreign investments.

- Unilateral transfers involve international private gifts and federal government grants or gifts to foreign nations.

- When we add the balance of merchandise trade plus the balance of services and take account of net unilateral transfers, we come up with the balance on current account, which is a summary statistic taking into account the three transactions that form the current account transactions.

- There are also capital account transactions that relate to the buying and selling of financial and real assets. Foreign capital is always entering the United States, and American capital is always flowing abroad. The difference is called the balance on capital account.

- Another type of balance of payments transaction concerns the official reserve assets of individual countries, or what is often simply called official transactions. By standard accounting convention, official transactions are exactly equal to but opposite in sign to the balance of payments of the United States.

- Our balance of trade can be affected by our relative rate of inflation and by political instability elsewhere compared to the stability that exists in the United States.

DETERMINING FOREIGN EXCHANGE RATES

When you buy foreign products, such as French wine, you have dollars with which to pay the French winemaker. The French winemaker, however, cannot pay workers in dollars. The workers are French, they live in France, and they must have francs to buy goods and services in that country. There must therefore be some way of exchanging dollars for the francs that the winemaker will accept. That exchange occurs in a **foreign exchange market,** which in this case specializes in exchanging francs and dollars. (When you obtain foreign currencies at a bank or an airport currency exchange, you are participating in the foreign exchange market.)

Foreign exchange market
The market for buying and selling foreign currencies.

The particular exchange rate between francs and dollars that would prevail depends on the current demand for and supply of francs and dollars. In a sense, then, our analysis of the exchange rate between dollars and francs will be familiar, for we have used supply and demand throughout this book. If it costs you 20 cents to buy one franc, that is the **foreign exchange rate** determined by the current demand for and supply of francs in the foreign exchange market. The French person going to the foreign exchange market would need five francs to buy one dollar. (Our numbers are, of course, hypothetical.)

Foreign exchange rate
The price of one currency in terms of another.

We will continue our example in which the only two countries in the world are France and the United States. Now let's consider what determines the demand for and supply of foreign currency in the foreign exchange market.

Demand for and Supply of Foreign Currency

You wish to buy some French Bordeaux wine. To do so, you must have French francs. You go to the foreign exchange market (or your American bank). Your desire to buy the French wine therefore causes you to offer (supply) dollars to the foreign exchange market. Your demand for French francs is equivalent to your supply of American dollars to the foreign exchange market. Indeed:

> **Every U.S. transaction concerning the importation of foreign goods constitutes a supply of dollars and a demand for some foreign currency, and the opposite is true for export transactions.**

In this case, this import transaction constitutes a demand for French francs.

In our example, we will assume that only two goods are being traded, French wine and American jeans. The American demand for French wine creates a supply of dollars and a demand for francs in the foreign exchange market. Similarly, the French demand for American jeans creates a supply of francs and a demand for dollars in the foreign exchange market. In the situation of **flexible exchange rates,** the supply of and demand for dollars and francs in the foreign exchange market will determine the equilibrium foreign exchange rate. The equilibrium exchange rate will tell us how many francs a dollar can be exchanged for—that is, the dollar price of francs—or how many dollars (or fractions of a dollar) a franc can be exchanged for—the franc price of dollars.

Flexible exchange rates
Exchange rates that are allowed to fluctuate in the open market in response to changes in supply and demand. Sometimes called *floating exchange rates.*

The Equilibrium Foreign Exchange Rate

To determine the equilibrium foreign exchange rate, we have to find out what determines the demand for and supply of foreign exchange. We will ignore for the moment any speculative aspect of buying foreign exchange; that is, we assume that there are no individuals who wish to buy francs simply because they think that their price will go up in the future.

The idea of an exchange rate is no different from the idea of paying a certain price for something you want to buy. If you like coffee, you know you have to pay about 75 cents a cup. If the price went up to $2.50, you would probably buy fewer cups. If the price went down to 5 cents, you might buy more. In other words, the demand curve for cups of coffee, expressed in terms of dollars, slopes downward following the law of demand. The demand curve for francs slopes downward also, and we will see why.

"WELL, THAT COMPLETES YOUR PHYSICAL...AND YOU'RE AS SOUND AS A YEN!..."

Demand Schedule for French Francs. Let's think more closely about the demand schedule for francs. Let's say that it costs you 20 cents to purchase one franc; that is the exchange rate between dollars and francs. If tomorrow you had to pay 25 cents for the same franc, the exchange rate would have changed. Looking at such an increase with respect to the franc, we would say that there has been an **appreciation** in the value of the franc in the foreign exchange market. But this increase in the value of the franc means that there has been a **depreciation** in the value of the dollar in the foreign exchange market. The dollar used to buy five francs; tomorrow, the dollar will be able to buy only four francs at a price of 25 cents per franc. If the dollar price of francs rises, you will probably demand fewer francs. Why? The answer lies in looking at the reason you demand francs in the first place.

You demand francs in order to buy French wine. Your demand curve for French wine, we will assume, follows the law of demand and therefore slopes downward. If it costs you more American dollars to buy the same quantity of French wine, presumably you will not buy the same quantity; your quantity demanded will be less. We say that your demand for French francs is *derived from* your demand for French wine. In panel (a) of Figure 34-2, we present the hypothetical demand schedule for French wine in the United States by a representative wine drinker. In panel (b), we show graphically the American demand curve for French wine in terms of American dollars taken from panel (a).

Let us assume that the price per liter of French wine in France is 20 francs. Given that price, we can find the number of francs required to purchase up to 4 liters of French wine. That information is given in panel (c) of Figure 34-2. If one liter requires 20 francs, 4 liters require 80 francs. Now we have enough information to determine the derived demand curve for French francs. If one franc costs 20 cents, a bottle of wine would cost \$4 (20 francs per bottle × 20 cents per franc = \$4 per bottle). At \$4 per bottle, the typical representative American wine drinker would, we see from panel (a) of Figure 34-2, demand 4 liters. From panel (c) we see that 80 francs would be demanded to buy the 4 liters of wine. We show this quantity demanded in panel (d). In panel (e), we draw the derived demand curve for francs. Now consider what happens if the price of francs goes up to 30 cents. A bottle of French wine costing 20 francs in France would now cost \$6. From panel (a) we see that at \$6 per liter, 3 liters will be imported from France into the United States by our representative domestic wine drinker. From panel (c) we see that 3 liters would require 60 francs to be purchased; thus in panels (d) and (e) we see that at a price of one franc per 30 cents, the quantity demanded will be 60 francs. We continue similar calculations all the way up to a price of 50 cents per franc. At that price a bottle of French wine costing 20 francs in France would cost \$10, and our representative wine drinker would import only one bottle.

Downward-Sloping Derived Demand. As can be expected, as the price of francs falls, the quantity demanded will rise. The only difference here from the standard demand analysis developed in Chapter 3 and used throughout this text is that the demand for francs is derived from the demand for a final product—French wine in our example.

Supply of French Francs. The supply of French francs is a derived supply in that it is derived from a French person's demand for American jeans. We could go through an example similar to the one for wine to come up with a supply schedule of French francs in France. It slopes upward. Obviously, the French want dollars in order to purchase American goods. In principle, the French will be willing to supply more francs when the dollar price of francs goes up because they can then buy more American goods with the same quantity of francs; that is, the franc would be worth more in exchange for American goods than when the dollar price for francs was lower. Let's take an example. Suppose a pair of jeans in the United States costs \$10. If the exchange rate is 25 cents for one franc, the French have to come up with 40 francs (= \$10 at 25 cents per franc) to buy one pair of

Appreciation
An increase in the value of a currency in terms of other currencies.

Depreciation
A decrease in the value of a currency in terms of other currencies.

Panel (a)
Demand Schedule for French Wine in the United States per Week

Price per Liter	Quantity Demanded (liters)
$10	1
8	2
6	3
4	4

Panel (b)
American Demand Curve for French Wine

Panel (c)
Francs Required to Purchase Quantity Demanded (at P = 20 francs per liter)

Quantity Demanded (liters)	Francs Required
1	20
2	40
3	60
4	80

Panel (d)
Derived Demand Schedule for Francs in the United States with Which to Pay for Imports of Wine

Dollar Price of One Franc	Dollar Price of Wine	Quantity of Wine Demanded (liters)	Quantity of Francs Demanded per Week
$ .50	$10	1	20
.40	8	2	40
.30	6	3	60
.20	4	4	80

FIGURE 34-2

Deriving the Demand for French Francs

In panel (a), we show the demand schedule for French wine in the United States, expressed in terms of dollars per liter. In panel (b), we show the demand curve, *D,* which slopes downward. In panel (c), we show the number of francs required to purchase up to 4 liters of wine. If the price per liter of wine in France is 20 francs, we can now find the quantity of francs needed to pay for the various quantities demanded. In panel (d), we see the derived demand for francs in the United States in order to purchase the various quantities of wine given in panel (a). The resultant demand curve, D_1, is shown in panel (e). It is the American derived demand for francs.

Panel (e)
American Derived Demand for Francs

FIGURE 34-3

The Equilibrium Exchange Rate for Two Individuals
The derived demand curve for French francs is taken from panel (e) of Figure 34-2. The derived supply curve, S, results from the representative French purchaser of American jeans, who supplies francs to the foreign exchange market when demanding U.S. dollars in order to buy American jeans. D_1 and S intersect at E. The equilibrium exchange rate is 20 cents per franc.

jeans. If, however, the exchange rate goes up to 50 cents for one franc, the French must come up with only 20 francs (= $10 at 50 cents per franc) to buy a pair of American jeans. At a lower price (in francs) of American jeans, the French will demand a larger quantity. In other words, as the price of French francs goes up in terms of dollars, the quantity of American jeans demanded will go up, and hence the quantity of French francs supplied will go up. Therefore, the supply schedule of foreign currency (francs) will slope upward.[1]

We could easily work through a detailed numerical example to show that the supply curve of French francs slopes upward. Rather than do that, we will simply draw it as upward-sloping in Figure 34-3. In our hypothetical example, assuming that there is only one wine drinker in America and one demander of jeans in France, the equilibrium exchange rate will be set at 20 cents per franc, or 5 francs to one dollar. Let us now look at the aggregate demand for and supply of French francs. We take all demanders of French wine and all demanders of American jeans and put their demands for and supplies of francs together into one diagram. Thus we are showing an aggregate version of the demand for and supply of French francs. The horizontal axis in Figure 34-4 represents a quantity of foreign exchange—the number of francs per year. The vertical axis represents the exchange rate—the price of foreign currency (francs) expressed in dollars (per franc). Thus at the foreign currency price of 25 cents per franc, you know that it will cost you 25 cents to buy one franc. At the foreign currency price of 20 cents per franc, you know that it will cost you 20 cents to buy one franc. The equilibrium is again established at 20 cents for one franc. This equilibrium is not established because Americans like to buy francs or because the French like to buy dollars. Rather, the equilibrium exchange rate depends on how many pairs of jeans the French want and how much French wine the Americans want (given their respective incomes, their tastes, and the relative price of wine and jeans).[2]

A Shift in Demand. Assume that a successful advertising campaign by American wine importers has caused the American demand (curve) for French wine to double. Americans

---

[1]Actually, the supply schedule of foreign currency will be upward-sloping if we assume that the demand for American imported jeans on the part of the French is price-elastic. If the demand schedule for jeans is price-inelastic, the supply schedule will be negatively sloped. In the case of unit elasticity of demand, the supply schedule for francs will be a vertical line. Throughout the rest of this chapter, we will assume that demand is price-elastic. Remember that the price elasticity of demand tells us whether or not total expenditures by jeans purchasers in France will rise or fall when the French franc drops in value. In the long run, it is quite realistic to think that the price elasticity of demand for imports is numerically greater than 1 anyway.

[2]Remember that we are dealing with a two-country world in which we are considering only the exchange of American jeans and French wine. In the real world, more than just goods and services are exchanged among countries. Some Americans buy French financial assets; some French buy American financial assets. We are ignoring such transactions for the moment.

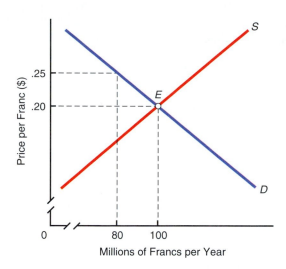

FIGURE 34-4

Aggregate Demand for and Supply of French Francs
The aggregate supply curve for French francs results from the total French demand for American jeans. The demand curve, D, slopes downward like most demand curves, and the supply curve, S, slopes upward. The foreign exchange price, or the U.S. dollar price of francs, is given on the vertical axis. The number of francs, in millions, is represented on the horizontal axis. If the foreign exchange rate is 25 cents—that is, if it takes 25 cents to buy one franc—Americans will demand 80 million francs. The equilibrium exchange rate is at the intersection of D and S. The equilibrium exchange rate is 20 cents. At this point, 100 million French francs are both demanded and supplied each year.

demand twice as much wine at all prices. Their demand curve for French wine has shifted outward to the right.

The increased demand for French wine can be translated into an increased demand for francs. All Americans clamoring for bottles of French wine will supply more dollars to the foreign exchange market while demanding more French francs to pay for the wine. Figure 34-5 presents a new demand schedule, D_2, for French francs; this demand schedule is to the right of and outward from the original demand schedule. If the French do not change their desire for American jeans, the supply schedule for French francs will remain stable. A new equilibrium will be established at a higher exchange rate. In our particular example, the new equilibrium is established at an exchange rate of 30 cents per franc. It now takes 30 cents to buy one French franc, whereas it took 20 cents before. This is translated as an increase in the price of French wine to Americans and as a decrease in the price of American jeans to the French. (Otherwise stated, there has been a decline in the foreign exchange value of the dollar.)

A Shift in Supply. We just assumed that Americans' preference for French wine had shifted. Because the demand for French francs is a derived demand by Americans for

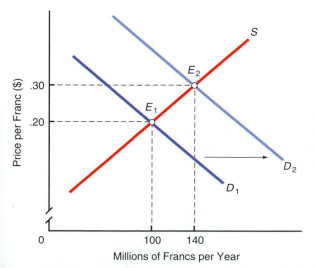

FIGURE 34-5

A Shift in the Demand Schedule
The demand schedule for French wine shifts to the right, causing the derived demand schedule for francs to shift to the right also. We have shown this as a shift from D_1 to D_2. We have assumed that the French supply schedule for francs has remained stable—that is, French demand for American jeans has remained constant. The old equilibrium foreign exchange rate was 20 cents. The new equilibrium exchange rate will be E_2; it will now cost 30 cents to buy one franc. The higher price of francs will be translated into a higher U.S. dollar price for French wine and a lower French franc price for American jeans.

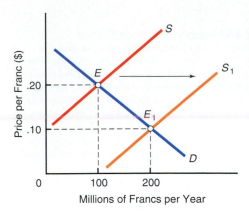

FIGURE 34-6

A Shift in the Supply of French Francs
There has been a shift in the supply curve for French francs. The new equilibrium will occur at E_1, meaning that 10 cents, rather than 20 cents, will now buy one franc. After the exchange rate adjustment, the amount of francs demanded and supplied will increase to 200 million per year.

French wine, it has caused a shift in the demand curve for francs. Alternatively, assume that the supply curve of French francs shifts outward to the right. This may occur for many reasons, the most probable one being a relative rise in the French price level. For example, if the price of all French-made clothes went up 100 percent in francs, American jeans would become relatively cheaper. That would mean that French people would want to buy more American jeans. But remember that when they want to buy more American jeans, they supply more francs to the foreign exchange market. Thus we see in Figure 34-6 that the supply curve of French francs moves from S to S_1. In the absence of restrictions—that is, in a system of flexible exchange rates—the new equilibrium exchange rate will be one franc equals 10 cents, or $1 equals 10 francs. The quantity of francs demanded and supplied will increase from 100 million per year to 200 million per year. We say, then, that in a flexible international exchange rate system, shifts in the demand for and supply of foreign currencies will cause changes in the equilibrium foreign exchange rates. Those rates will remain in effect until supply or demand shifts.

Market Determinants of Exchange Rates

The foreign exchange market is affected by many other changes in market variables in addition to changes in relative price levels, including these:

1. *Changes in real interest rates.* If the United States interest rate, corrected for people's expectations of inflation, abruptly increases relative to the rest of the world, international investors elsewhere will increase their demand for dollar-denominated assets, thereby increasing the demand for dollars in foreign exchange markets. An increased demand for dollars in foreign exchange markets, other things held constant, will cause the dollar to appreciate and other currencies to depreciate.
2. *Changes in productivity.* Whenever one country's productivity increases relative to another's, the former country will become more price competitive in world markets. The demand for its exports will increase, and so, too, will the demand for its currency.
3. *Changes in product preferences.* If Germany's citizens suddenly develop a taste for American-made automobiles, this will increase the derived demand for American dollars in foreign exchange markets.
4. *Perceptions of economic stability.* As already mentioned, if the United States looks economically and politically more stable relative to other countries, more foreigners will want to put their savings into U.S. assets than in their own domestic assets. This will increase the demand for dollars.

CONCEPTS IN BRIEF

- The foreign exchange rate is the rate at which one country's currency can be exchanged for another's.

- The demand for foreign exchange is a derived demand; it is derived from the demand for foreign goods and services (and financial assets). The supply of foreign exchange is derived from foreigners' demands for our goods and services.

- In general, the demand curve of foreign exchange slopes downward and the supply curve of foreign exchange slopes upward. The equilibrium foreign exchange rate occurs at the intersection of the demand and supply curves for a currency.

- A shift in the demand for foreign goods will result in a shift in the demand for foreign exchange. The equilibrium foreign exchange rate will change. A shift in the supply of foreign currency will also cause a change in the equilibrium exchange rate.

THE GOLD STANDARD AND THE INTERNATIONAL MONETARY FUND

The current system of more or less freely floating exchange rates is a recent development. We have had, in the past, periods of a gold standard, fixed exchange rates under the International Monetary Fund, and variants of these two.

The Gold Standard

Gold standard

An international monetary system in which nations fix their exchange rates in terms of gold. All currencies are fixed in terms of all others, and any balance of payments deficits or surpluses can be made up by shipments of gold.

Until the 1930s, many nations were on a **gold standard.** The values of their currencies were tied directly to gold.[3] Nations operating under this gold standard agreed to redeem their currencies for a fixed amount of gold at the request of any holder of that currency. Although gold was not necessarily the means of exchange for world trade, it was the unit to which all currencies under the gold standard were pegged. And because all currencies in the system were linked to gold, exchange rates between those currencies were fixed. Indeed, the gold standard has been offered as the prototype of a fixed exchange rate system. The heyday of the gold standard was from about 1870 to 1914. England had been on such a standard as far back as the 1820s.

There turns out to be a relationship between the balance of payments and changes in domestic money supplies throughout the world. Under a gold standard, the international financial market reached equilibrium through the effect of gold flows on each country's money supply. When a nation suffered a deficit in its balance of payments, more gold would flow out than in. Because the domestic money supply was based on gold, an outflow of gold to foreigners caused an automatic reduction in the domestic money supply. This caused several things to happen. Interest rates rose, thereby attracting foreign capital and improving the balance of payments. At the same time, the reduction in the money supply was equivalent to a restrictive monetary policy, which caused national output and prices to fall. Imports were discouraged and exports were encouraged, thereby again improving the balance of payments.

---

[3]This is a simplification. Most nations were on a *specie metal standard* using gold, silver, copper, and other precious metals as money. Nations operating under this standard agreed to redeem their currencies for a fixed exchange rate.

Two problems that plagued the gold standard were that no nation had control of its domestic monetary policy and that the world's commerce was at the mercy of gold discoveries.

POLICY EXAMPLE
Should We Go Back to the Gold Standard?

In the past several decades, the United States has consistently run a current account deficit. The dollar has become weaker. We have had inflation. We have had recessions. Some economists and politicians argue that we should return to the gold standard. The United States actually operated under two gold standards. From 1879 to 1933, the dollar was defined as 32.22 grains of gold, yielding a gold price of $20.671835 an ounce. During that time period, general prices more than doubled during World War I, there was a major depression in 1920–1921, and the Great Depression occurred. The second gold standard prevailed from 1933 to 1971, when the price of gold was pegged at $35 an ounce. A dollar was defined as 13.714286 grains of gold. During that time period, general prices quadrupled.

Clearly, a gold standard guarantees neither stable prices nor economic stability.

FOR CRITICAL ANALYSIS: *Why does no country today operate on a gold standard?* ●

Bretton Woods and the International Monetary Fund

In 1944, as World War II was ending, representatives from the world's capitalist countries met in Bretton Woods, New Hampshire, to create a new international payment system to replace the gold standard, which had collapsed during the 1930s. The Bretton Woods Agreement Act was signed on July 31, 1945, by President Harry Truman. It created a new permanent institution, the **International Monetary Fund (IMF),** to administer the agreement and to lend to member countries in balance of payments deficit. The arrangements thus provided are now called the old IMF system or the Bretton Woods system.

Each member nation was assigned an IMF contribution quota determined by its international trade volume and national income. Twenty-five percent of the quota was contributed in gold or U.S. dollars and 75 percent in its own currency. At the time, the IMF therefore consisted of a pool of gold, dollars, and other major currencies.

Member governments were then obligated to intervene to maintain the values of their currencies in foreign exchange markets within 1 percent of the declared **par value**—the officially determined value. The United States, which owned most of the world's gold stock, was similarly obligated to maintain gold prices within a 1 percent margin of the official rate of $35 an ounce. Except for a transitional arrangement permitting a one-time adjustment of up to 10 percent in par value, members could alter exchange rates thereafter only with the approval of the IMF. The agreement stated that such approval would be given only if the country's balance of payments was in *fundamental disequilibrium,* a term that has never been officially defined.

Special Drawing Rights. In 1967, the IMF created a new type of international money, *special drawing rights (SDRs)*. SDRs are exchanged only between monetary authorities (central banks). Their existence temporarily changed the IMF into a world central bank. The IMF creates SDRs the same way that the Federal Reserve can create dollars. The IMF allocates SDRs to member nations in accordance with their quotas. Currently, the SDR's

International Monetary Fund (IMF)
An institution set up to manage the international monetary system, established in 1945 under the Bretton Woods Agreement Act, which established fixed exchange rates for the world's currencies.

Par value
The legally established value of the monetary unit of one country in terms of that of another.

value is determined by making one SDR equal to a bundle of currencies. In reality, the SDR rises or falls in terms of the dollar.

End of the Old IMF. On August 15, 1971, President Richard Nixon suspended the convertibility of the dollar into gold. On December 18, 1971, we officially devalued the dollar against the currencies of 14 major industrial nations. Finally, on March 16, 1973, the finance ministers of the European Economic Community (now the EU) announced that they would let their currencies float against the dollar, something Japan had already begun doing with its yen. Since 1973, the United States and most other trading countries have had either freely floating exchange rates or managed ("dirty") floating exchange rates.

THE DIRTY FLOAT AND MANAGED EXCHANGE RATES

Dirty float
A system between flexible and fixed exchange rates in which central banks occasionally enter foreign exchange markets to influence rates.

The United States went off the Bretton Woods system in 1973, but it has nonetheless tried to keep certain elements of that system in play. We have occasionally engaged in what is called a **dirty float,** or management of flexible exchange rates. The management of flexible exchange rates has usually come about through international policy cooperation. For example, the Group of Five (G-5) nations—France, Germany, Japan, the United Kingdom, and the United States—and the Group of Seven (G-7) nations—the G-5 nations plus Italy and Canada—have for some time shared information on their policy objectives and procedures. They do this through regular meetings between economic policy secretaries, ministers, and staff members. One of their principal objectives has been to "smooth out" foreign exchange rates. Initially, the G-5 attempted to push the value of the dollar downward to help correct U.S. trade deficits and reduce Japanese foreign trade surpluses. What the five nations agreed to do was supply dollars in foreign exchange markets. This increased supply would reduce the dollar's value.

Is it possible for these groups to "manage" foreign exchange rates? Some economists do not think so. For example, economists Michael Bordo and Anna Schwartz studied the foreign exchange intervention actions coordinated by the Federal Reserve and the U.S. Treasury for the second half of the 1980s. Besides showing that such interventions were sporadic and variable, Bordo and Schwartz came to an even more compelling conclusion: Exchange rate interventions were trivial relative to the total trading of foreign exchange on a daily basis. For example, in April 1989, total foreign exchange trading amounted to $129 billion per day, yet the American central bank purchased only $100 million in deutsche marks and yen during that entire month (and did so on a single day). For all of 1989, Fed purchases of marks and yen were only $17.7 billion, or the equivalent of less than 14 percent of the amount of an average *day's* trading in April of that year. Their conclusion is that neither the American central bank nor the central banks of the other G-7 nations can influence exchange rates in the long run.

CONCEPTS IN BRIEF

- The International Monetary Fund was developed after World War II as an institution to maintain fixed exchange rates in the world. Since 1973, however, fixed exchange rates have disappeared in most major trading countries.

- A dirty float occurs in a flexible exchange rate system whenever central banks intervene to influence exchange rates.

Should We Worry About the Weak Dollar?

Concepts Applied: *Flexible exchange rates, current account deficit, depreciation*

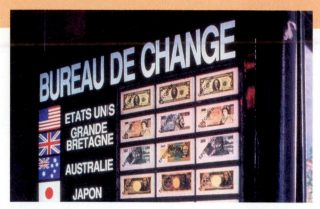

The dollar became relatively weaker against the yen and deutsche mark in 1985. However, the dollar has held its value when weighted against the currencies of all U.S. trading partners.

Rome's currency was the world's strongest for a period of 400 years, but then it lost its attractiveness in world trade. The United Kingdom saw its currency, the pound sterling, lose its world dominance over a period of 50 years. Now the United States' currency is on top. But need we worry that its days of dominance are numbered?

At first blush, the dollar appears strong. It accounts for over 60 percent of foreign exchange reserves and over 50 percent of global private financial wealth. In addition, almost 70 percent of world trade is invoiced in dollars, as is 75 percent of international bank lending. Not bad for a country that accounts for only 24 percent of world output and 14 percent of world exports.

The Dwindling Value of the Dollar

But the dollar definitely does not seem to buy as much as it used to. Figure 34-7 shows what has happened to dollar exchange rates with respect to the yen and the deutsche mark. The value of the dollar with respect to those two currencies has been falling steadily since 1985. There are several reasons why the yen and the mark have become so strong and the dollar so weak. Both Japan and Germany have had lower rates of inflation than the United States. Also, at least in Germany, investors have earned higher rates of return.

Who Is Hurt by the Falling Dollar?

Besides the outraged American tourist in Germany, France, Switzerland, and Japan, who else is hurt by the weak dollar? The weaker dollar translates into higher prices for imported goods, such as BMWs, Mercedes, Toyotas, NEC computers, and Nintendo videogames. So

FIGURE 34-7

The Dollar Relative to the Mark and the Yen
Since the mid-1980s, the value of the U.S. dollar in terms of the German (Deutsche) mark and the Japanese yen has tended to decline.
Source: International Monetary Fund.

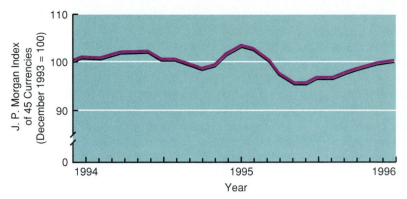

FIGURE 34-8

The Dollar Relative to an Index of 45 Currencies

If we look at the dollar relative to a basket of 45 of the world's currencies, it has held rather firm since the end of 1993.

Sources: J. P. Morgan Company; Federal Reserve Board.

Americans who purchase imported goods from countries whose currencies are stronger relative to the dollar must now pay more than they did before. But there is a flip side to this equation. Foreigners now find our products cheaper, so employees and shareholders in American companies that export find themselves better off.

Is the Dollar Really So Weak?

The dollar is indisputably changing relative to the yen, the deutsche mark, the Swiss franc, the French franc, and a few other currencies. But as you can see in Figure 34-8, the dollar has actually been getting stronger since mid-1995. Weighted against the currencies of *all* of the United States' trading partners, the dollar has been relatively stable since 1988, and in the past few years, it has strengthened considerably against the other North American currencies (those of Canada and Mexico).

The Dollar Is Still in Demand

Almost $400 billion in U.S. currency is held overseas. Much of it is used by Russians, Mexicans, and others because they do not trust their own currencies. To obtain these dollar bills, foreigners have had to give up something of value, such as oil, fur hats, and tomatoes. In return, we were kind enough to give them pieces of paper money that cost us virtually nothing to produce. As long as they hold on to those pieces of paper, we are obtaining an interest-free loan. According to economist Richard Cooper of Harvard University, that saves the United States roughly $15 billion a year in interest.

FOR CRITICAL ANALYSIS

1. Why would a lower rate of inflation in Japan lead to a weaker dollar?
2. Why would foreigners agree to hold dollar bills instead of their own currencies?

CHAPTER SUMMARY

1. The balance of merchandise trade is defined as the value of goods bought and sold in the world market, usually during the period of one year. The balance of payments is a more inclusive concept that includes the value of all transactions in the world market.

2. Americans purchase financial assets in other countries, and foreigners purchase American financial assets, such as stocks or bonds. The buying and selling of foreign financial assets has the same effect on the balance of payments as the buying and selling of goods and services.

3. Our balance of trade and payments can be affected by our relative rate of inflation and by political instability elsewhere compared to the stability that exists in the United States.

4. Market determinants of exchange rates are changes in real interest rates (interest rates corrected for inflation), changes in productivity, changes in product preferences, and perceptions of economic stability.

5. To transact business internationally, it is necessary to convert domestic currencies into other currencies. This is done via the foreign exchange market. If we were trading with France only, French producers would want to be paid in francs because they must pay their workers in francs. American producers would want to be paid in dollars because American workers are paid in dollars.

6. An American's desire for French wine is expressed in terms of a supply of dollars, which is in turn a demand for French francs in the foreign exchange market. The opposite situation arises when the

French wish to buy American jeans. Their demand for jeans creates a demand for American dollars and a supply of French francs. We put the demand and supply schedules together to find the equilibrium foreign exchange rate. The demand schedule for foreign exchange is a derived demand—it is derived from Americans' demand for foreign products.

7. With no government intervention, a market clearing equilibrium foreign exchange rate will emerge. After a shift in demand or supply, the exchange rate will change so that it will again clear the market.

8. If Americans increase their demand for French wine, the demand curve for French wine shifts to the right. The derived demand for francs also shifts to the right. The supply schedule of francs, however, remains stable because the French demand for American jeans

has remained constant. The shifted demand schedule intersects the stable supply schedule at a higher price (the foreign exchange rate increases). This is an appreciation of the value of French francs (a depreciation of the value of the dollar against the franc).

9. In a managed exchange rate system (a "dirty float"), central banks occasionally intervene in foreign exchange markets to influence exchange rates.

10. Under a gold standard, movement of gold across countries changes domestic money supplies, causing price levels to change and to correct balance of payments imbalances.

11. In 1945, the International Monetary Fund (IMF) was created to maintain fixed exchange rates throughout the world. This system was abandoned in 1973.

DISCUSSION OF PREVIEW QUESTIONS

1. What is the difference between the balance of trade and the balance of payments?

The balance of trade is defined as the difference between the value of exports and the value of imports. If the value of exports exceeds the value of imports, a trade surplus exists; if the value of exports is less than the value of imports, a trade deficit exists; if export and import values are equal, we refer to this situation as a trade balance. The balance of payments is more general and takes into account the value of *all* international transactions. Thus the balance of payments identifies not only goods and services transactions among nations but also investments (financial and nonfinancial) and gifts (private and public). When the value of all these transactions is such that one nation is sending more to other nations than it is receiving in return, a balance of payments deficit exists. A payments surplus and payments balance are self-explanatory.

2. What is a foreign exchange rate?

We know that nations trade with one another; they buy and sell goods, make and receive financial and nonfinancial investments, and give and receive gifts. However, nations have different currencies. People who sell to, invest in, or receive gifts from the United States ultimately want their own currency so that they can use the money domestically. Similarly, U.S. residents who sell in, invest in, or receive gifts from people in other countries ultimately want U.S. dollars to spend in the United States. Because most people ultimately want to end up with their own currencies, for-

eign exchange markets have evolved to enable people to sell one currency for other currencies. A foreign exchange rate, then, is the rate at which one country's currency can be exchanged for another's. For example, the exchange rate between the United Kingdom (U.K.) and the United States might dictate that one pound sterling is equivalent to $1.50; alternately stated, the U.S. dollar is worth .667 pound sterling.

3. What is a flexible exchange rate system?

A flexible exchange rate system is an international monetary system in which foreign exchange rates are allowed to fluctuate to reflect changes in the supply of and demand for international currencies. Say that the United States and the U.K. are in payments balance at the exchange rate of one pound sterling to U.S. $1.50. The U.S. demand for sterling is derived from private and government desires to buy British goods, to invest in the U.K., or to send gifts to the British people and is *inversely* related to the number of dollars it takes to buy one pound. Conversely, the supply of sterling is derived from the U.K.'s private and governmental desires to buy U.S. goods and services, to invest in the United States, and to send gifts to U.S. residents. The supply of sterling is *directly* related to the number of dollars one pound is worth. The intersection of the supply and demand curves for sterling determines the market foreign exchange rate of dollars per pound. In a system of flexible exchange rates, shifts in the supply or demand curves will lead to changes in the foreign exchange rates between nations.

4. What is the gold standard?

The gold standard is an international monetary system in which each nation values its currency unit at a specific quantity of gold. Under such a standard, exchange rates are fixed in terms of each other. For example, the U.S. dollar was originally backed by one-twentieth of an ounce of gold, and the British valued their coins (or paper backed by gold) at one-quarter of an ounce of gold; the British monetary unit was therefore worth five times the U.S. monetary unit. The resulting exchange rate was that one pound sterling was worth $5. The gold standard was, in matters of exchange rates, similar to the fixed exchange rate system. However, payment imbalances were automatically corrected by gold flows. For instance, if the United States had a payment deficit with the U.K. (which therefore had a payment surplus with the United States), gold would flow from the United States to the U.K. The result of these gold flows (which, in effect, are equivalent to money movements) would be to raise the price level in the U.K. and lower it in the United States. This would lead to an increase in U.S. exports and a decrease in U.S. imports and a corresponding increase in British imports and decrease in British exports. Thus, in the past, the gold standard brought nations into payment balance by altering price *levels* in each country. The current system of flexible exchange rates corrects payment imbalances leaving price levels unaltered; it changes *one* price—the exchange rate.

PROBLEMS

(Answers to the odd-numbered problems appear at the back of the book.)

34-1. In the graph, what can be said about the shift from D to D_1?

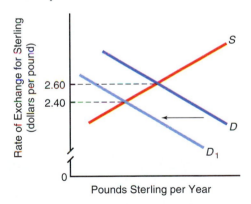

Rate of Exchange for Sterling (dollars per pound)

Pounds Sterling per Year

a. It could be caused by Britons demanding fewer U.S. products.

b. It is a result of increased U.S. demand for British goods.

c. It causes an appreciation of the dollar relative to the pound.

d. It causes an appreciation of the pound relative to the dollar.

34-2. If the rate of exchange between the pound and the dollar is $1.45 for one pound, and the United States then experiences severe inflation, we would expect the exchange rate (under a flexible rate system) to shift. What would be the new rate?

a. More than $1.45 for one pound

b. Less than $1.45 for one pound

c. More than one pound for $1.45

d. None of the above

34-3. The dollar, the pound sterling, and the deutsche mark are the currency units of the United States, the United Kingdom, and Germany, respectively. Suppose that these nations decide to go on a gold standard and define the value of their currencies in terms of gold as follows: $35 = 1 ounce of gold; 10 pounds sterling = 1 ounce of gold; and 100 marks = 1 ounce of gold. What would the exchange rate be between the dollar and the pound? Between the dollar and the mark? Between the mark and the pound?

34-4. Examine the following hypothetical data for U.S. international transactions, in billions of dollars.

Exports: goods, 165.8; services, 130.5
Imports: goods, −250.7; services, −99.3
Net unilateral transfers: −20.0

a. What is the balance of trade?

b. What is the balance on goods and services?

c. What is the balance on current account?

34-5. Maintenance of a fixed exchange rate system requires government intervention to keep exchange rates stable. What is the policy implication of this fact? (Hint: Think in terms of the money supply.)

34-6. Suppose that we have the following demand schedule for German beer in the United States per week:

Price per Case	Quantity Demanded (cases)
$40	2
32	4
24	6
16	8
8	10

a. If the price is 30 deutsche marks per case, how many marks are required to purchase each quantity demanded?

b. Now derive the demand schedule for marks per week in the United States to pay for German beer.

c. At a price of 80 cents per mark, how many cases of beer would be imported from Germany per week?

34-7. The accompanying graph shows the supply of and demand for pounds sterling.

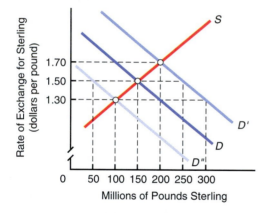

a. Assuming that the demand for sterling is represented by *D*, what is the dollar price of pounds? What is the equilibrium quantity?

b. Suppose that there is general inflation in the United States. Starting at *D*, which demand curve could represent this situation? If exchange rates are allowed to float freely, what would be the new dollar price of one pound sterling? What would be the equilibrium quantity?

c. Suppose that the inflation in part (b) occurs and the United States has the dollar price of one pound sterling fixed at $1.50. How would the Federal Reserve be able to accomplish this?

d. Now suppose that instead of inflation, there was general deflation in the United States. Which demand curve could represent this situation? How could the United States maintain a fixed price of $1.50 per pound sterling in this situation?

34-8. Which of the following will cause the yen to appreciate? Explain.

a. U.S. real incomes increase relative to Japanese real incomes.

b. It is expected that in the future the yen will depreciate relative to the dollar.

c. The U.S. inflation rate rises relative to the Japanese inflation rate.

d. The after-tax, risk-adjusted real interest rate in the United States rises relative to that in Japan.

e. U.S. tastes change in favor of Japanese-made goods.

COMPUTER-ASSISTED INSTRUCTION

Suppose that the United States and France have formed a two-country gold standard, and a balance of payments equilibrium exists. What happens if tastes change so that U.S. residents now prefer French goods more than they did previously, other things being constant? This problem shows how balance of payments equilibrium is restored under a gold standard, a specific fixed exchange rate system.

Complete problem and answer appear on disk.

INTERACTING WITH THE INTERNET

Current exchange rates for a number of countries can be found at
http://bin.gnn.com/cgi-bin/gnn/currency
These rates are updated twice a week. More current rates on a just a few countries can be found at
gopher://una.hh.lib.umich.edu/00/ebb/monetary/tenfx.frb
(however, sometimes delays occur with this site).

CHAPTER 35

DEVELOPMENT: ECONOMIC GROWTH AROUND THE WORLD

If you are like many Americans, you do not yet use a home-banking program on your computer in order to make transactions with your local bank. But if you live in Brazil, one of the world's developing countries, you can use a system developed by União de Bancos Brasileiros. How is it possible that such a technological advancement can take place more rapidly in a less developed country than in one of the most developed countries in the world? The answer lies in understanding what causes economic development and why there may be a bright future for the world's developing economies.

PREVIEW QUESTIONS

1. What is a developing country?

2. Must developing countries develop by industrializing?

3. Can developing countries create their own capital stock?

4. Does a lack of protected property rights hinder a developing country's development?

Did You Know That . . . a business best-seller in 1967 called *The American Challenge* predicted that by 1985, the world's economies would be owned and run by a dozen huge American multinationals, producing over 90 percent of the world's manufactured goods? Of course, nothing could be further from the truth today. American companies remain important in the world economy, but they do not dominate. Since that prediction was made, Germany, Japan, South Korea, Hong Kong, Singapore, and Taiwan have grown to become economic powerhouses. Today, there are indeed many "rich" countries, including, of course, the United States. But this nation was not always rich. In fact, it was quite poor 200 years ago. If you go back far enough, every country was poor and undeveloped. Why do some countries develop faster than others? In other words, what causes economic development? Although there are no easy answers to this important question, economists now have enough data to know what conditions favor economic development in the developing world.

PUTTING WORLD POVERTY IN PERSPECTIVE

Most Americans cannot even begin to understand the reality of poverty in the world today. At least one-half, if not two-thirds, of the world's population lives at subsistence level, with just enough to eat for survival. The official poverty level in the United States exceeds the average income in at least half the world. That is not to say that we should ignore problems at home with the poor and homeless simply because they are living better than many people elsewhere in the world. Rather, it is necessary for Americans to keep their perspective on what are considered problems for this country relative to what are considered problems elsewhere.

WHAT IS DEVELOPMENT ECONOMICS?

How did developed countries travel the path out of extreme poverty to relative riches? That is the essential issue of development economics. It is the study of why some countries develop and others do not. Further, it is the study of changes in policies that might help developing countries get richer. It is not good enough simply to say that people in different countries are different and therefore that is why some countries are rich and some countries are poor. Economists do not deny that different cultures create different work ethics, but they are unwilling to accept such a pat and fatalistic answer.

Look at any world map. About four-fifths of the countries you will see on that map are considered relatively poor. The goal of students of development economics is to help the more than 4 billion people today with low living standards join the billion or so who have relatively high living standards.

INDUSTRIALLY ADVANCED ECONOMIES

Any system of defining poor countries and rich countries, developing countries and developed countries, is, of course, arbitrary. Nonetheless, it is instructive to examine some figures on the difference between **industrially advanced countries (IACs)** and so-called developing countries. There are 19 IACs. (Excluded from this classification are countries whose economies are based on a single resource, such as oil, but whose industrial development in other fields is minimal.) The latest data available on the IACs (1995) show an estimated per capita income of $16,341, an annual growth rate of about 2.2 percent, and a population

Industrially advanced countries (IACs)
Canada, Japan, the United States, and the countries of Western Europe, all of which have market economies based on a large skilled labor force and a large technically advanced stock of capital goods.

The Gap Between the Rich and the Poor

Contrary to what we are often told by the media, government statisticians, and politicians, the rich countries are not leaving the poor countries in the dust. The International Monetary Fund revised its estimates of relative size of economies a few years ago and came up with this startling conclusion: The share of world output produced by the rich industrial economies is only 54 percent rather than the 75 percent formerly reported. Because the majority of countries in the developing world are growing faster than those in the developed world, the world's rich countries will dominate the world economy less and less in the future.

growth of about .6 percent. At the other end of the scale, the more than 100 developing countries have a per capita income of $980, an annual growth rate of almost 3 percent, and a population growth rate of 2 percent per year, more than three times that of the IACs.

To be sure, we must be careful about accepting such data at face value. There is a tremendous disparity in incomes among the developing countries, and the data are notoriously inaccurate. Nonetheless, it is certain that a tremendous gap exists between average incomes in the IACs and in the developing countries.

Newly Industrialized Economies

Not all developing countries are stuck in abject poverty. The developing countries vary greatly in their ability to experience economic growth, but one group of recently industrialized economies has achieved annual growth rates two and three times that of the United States. These newly industrialized economies are the so-called Four Tigers—Singapore, Hong Kong, Taiwan, and South Korea—all on the Pacific Rim. From 1960 to 1995, per capita income in these economies grew sixfold. One of the reasons the newly industrialized countries have grown so rapidly is that a huge increase in world trade and in international communications has allowed technology to be disseminated much more quickly today than in the past. Indeed, these countries have advanced so quickly that three of the four now have a higher per capita income than Spain, the United Kingdom, and Italy. Yet during the same 35-year period, a number of sub-Saharan African nations experienced a *fall* in real per capita income.

CONCEPTS IN BRIEF

- Any definition of developing countries or industrially advanced countries (IACs) is arbitrary. Nonetheless, we have identified 19 IACs and over 100 developing countries.

- The IACs have per capita incomes that are roughly 17 times the per capita incomes in the developing nations. Population in developing nations is growing more than three times as fast as in the IACs.

- Four newly industrialized nations on the Pacific Rim—Singapore, Taiwan, South Korea, and Hong Kong—have increased their real per capita incomes sixfold since 1960.

ECONOMIC DEVELOPMENT: INDUSTRY VERSUS AGRICULTURE

One of the most widely discussed theories of development concerns the need for balanced growth, with industry and agriculture given equal importance. One characteristic of many developed countries is their high degree of industrialization, although there are clearly exceptions—Hong Kong, for example. In general, nations with relatively high standards of living are more industrialized than countries with low standards of living. The policy prescription then seems obvious: Less developed nations in which a large percentage of the total resources are devoted to agricultural pursuits should attempt to obtain more balanced growth by industrializing.

Although the theory is fairly acceptable at first glance, it leads to some absurd results. We find in many developing countries with steel factories and automobile plants that the people are actually worse off because of this attempted industrialization. Most developing countries currently cannot profitably produce steel or automobiles because they lack the necessary domestic human and physical capital. They can engage in such industrial activities only with heavy government subsidization of the industry itself. Import restrictions abound, preventing the purchase of foreign, mostly cheaper substitutes for the industrial products that the country itself produces. Also, in general, the existence of subsidies leads to a misallocation of resources and a lower economic welfare for the country as a whole.

INTERNATIONAL EXAMPLE
Industrialized Poverty

Amazingly, some of the poorest countries in the world today have some of the highest rates of industrialization. Industry's share of gross output is greater in sub-Saharan Africa than in Denmark, is greater in Zimbabwe, Botswana, and Trinidad and Tobago than in Japan, and is greater in Argentina than in every country in the European Union!

Agriculture represents a relatively low share of gross output in some of the world's poorest countries. For example, agriculture represents a greater share of national output in Denmark than it does in Trinidad and Tobago. The same is true in Spain relative to Botswana and in Portugal relative to Gabon. It is clear that industrialization does not necessarily lead to high standards of living.

FOR CRITICAL ANALYSIS: *If industry represents a large share of gross output in extremely poor countries, what does this tell you about the rate of return on investment in industry in those countries?* ●

The Stages of Development: Agriculture to Industry to Services

If we analyze the development of modern rich nations, we find that they went through three stages. First is the agricultural stage, when most of the population is involved in agriculture. Then comes the manufacturing stage, when much of the population becomes involved in the industrialized sector of the economy. And finally there is a shift toward services. That is exactly what happened in the United States: The so-called tertiary, or service, sector of the economy continues to grow, whereas the manufacturing sector (and its share of employment) is declining in relative importance.

However, it is important to understand the need for early specialization in a nation's comparative advantage. We have repeatedly referred to the doctrine of comparative advantage, and it is even more appropriate for the developing countries of the world. If trading is allowed among nations, a nation is normally best off if it produces what it has a comparative advantage at producing and imports the rest (see Chapter 33). This means that many developing countries should continue to specialize in agricultural production or in labor-intensive manufactured goods.

How Subsidized Agriculture Affects Developing Nations

Modern Western countries have continually subsidized their own agricultural sectors to allow them to compete more easily with the developing countries in this area. If we lived in a world of no subsidization, we would probably see less food being produced in the highly developed Western world (except for the United States, Canada, and Australia) and much more being produced in the developing countries of the rest of the world. They would trade food for manufactured goods. It would seem, then, that one of the most detrimental aspects of our economic policy for the developing countries has been the continued subsidization of the American farmer. The United States, of course, is not alone; virtually the entire European Union does exactly the same thing.

Even with this situation, however, a policy of using higher taxes on imported goods or domestic manufacturing subsidies in order to increase industrialization in the developing countries may do more harm than good. Industrialization is generally beneficial only if it comes about naturally, when the market conditions are such that the countries' entrepreneurs freely decide to build factories instead of increasing farm output because it is profitable to do so.

CONCEPTS IN BRIEF

- A balanced-growth theory predicts that industry and agriculture must grow together in order for a nation to experience growth.

- For many developing countries, balanced growth requires subsidization of manufacturing firms.

- Historically, there are three stages of economic development: the agricultural stage, the manufacturing stage, and the service-sector stage, when a large part of the workforce is employed in providing services.

NATURAL RESOURCES AND ECONOMIC DEVELOPMENT

One theory of development states that for a country to develop, it must have a large natural resource base. The theory continues to assert that much of the world is running out of natural resources, thereby limiting economic growth and development. We must point out that only the narrowest definition of a natural resource could lead to such an opinion. In broader terms, a natural resource is something scarce occurring in nature that we can use for our own purposes. Natural resources therefore include knowledge of the use of something. The natural resources that we could define several hundred years ago did not, for example, include hydroelectric power—no one knew that such a natural resource existed or, indeed, how to make it exist.

In any event, it is difficult to find a strong correlation between the natural resources of a nation and its stage of development. Japan has virtually no crude oil and must import most of the natural resources that it uses as inputs for its industrial production. Brazil has huge amounts of natural resources, including fertile soil and abundant minerals, yet Brazil has a much lower per capita income than Japan. Only when we include the human element of natural resources can we say that natural resources determine economic development.

Natural resources by themselves are not particularly useful for economic development. They must be transformed into something usable for either investment or consumption. This leads us to another aspect of development, the trade-off between investment and consumption. The normal way this subject is analyzed is by dealing with investment simply as capital accumulation.

CAPITAL ACCUMULATION

It is often asserted that a necessary prerequisite for economic development is a large capital stock—machines and other durable goods that can be used to aid in the production of consumption goods and more capital goods in the future. It is true that industrially advanced countries indeed have larger capital stocks per capita than developing countries.

It is also true that the larger the capital stock for any given population, the higher the possible rate of economic growth (assuming that the population makes good use of the capital goods). This is basically one of the foundations for many of the foreign aid programs in which the United States and other countries have engaged. We and other nations have attempted to give developing countries capital so that they, too, might grow. However, the amount of capital that we have actually given to other nations is quite small: a steel mill here, a factory there.

Domestic Capital Formation

How does a developing nation accumulate capital? The answer is that it must save and invest those accumulated savings profitably. Saving, of course, means not consuming. Resources must be released from consumer goods production in order to be used for investment.

Saving and the Poor. It is often stated that people in developing countries cannot save because they are barely subsisting. This is not actually true. Many anthropological studies—of villages in India, for example—have revealed that saving is in fact going on, but it takes forms that we don't recognize in our money economy; for example, saving may involve storing dried onions that can later be traded for other goods. Some researchers speculate that much saving in developing countries takes the form of rearing children who then feel a moral obligation to support their parents during the latter's retirement. In any event, saving does take place even in the most poverty-stricken areas. In general, there is no pronounced relationship between the *percentage* of income saved and the level of income (over the long run).

Basically, then, saving is a method by which individuals can realize an optimal consumption stream throughout their expected lifetimes. The word *optimal* here does not mean adequate or necessary or decent; it means most desirable from the *individual's* point of view (given that individual's resources).

Evidence of Saving in Developing Countries. Savings in developing countries do not necessarily flow into what we might consider productive capital formation projects. We do see the results of literally centuries of saving in the form of religious monuments, such as cathedrals and government buildings. Indeed, one major problem in developing nations is that much of the saving that occurs does not get channeled into productive capital formation. This is also true of much of the foreign aid that has been sent to developing nations. These nations could productively use more factories and a better infrastructure—roads and communications—rather than more government buildings and fancy stadiums built exclusively for merrymaking and sports.

Property Rights and Economic Development

If you were in a country in which bank accounts and businesses were periodically expropriated by the government, how willing would you be to leave your money in a savings account or to invest in a business? Certainly, you would be less willing than if such things never occurred. Periodic expropriation of private property rarely occurs in developed countries. It *has* occurred in numerous developing countries, however. For example, private property was once nationalized in Chile and still is in Cuba. In some cases, former owners are compensated, but rarely for the full value of the property taken over by the state.

THINKING CRITICALLY ABOUT THE MEDIA

The Dark Side of the PC Revolution

According to more than a handful of articles, the "PC revolution" will increase the gap between the rich and the poor. According to one "expert," technology can only be afforded by the rich, and furthermore, computers displace "hordes of workers." Nothing could be further from the truth. The country that has the most computers in place per capita is the United States, and its unemployment rate has not varied much in the past two decades. Moreover, even if computers are essential to the success of a business, their prices are dropping every month. And what is to prevent several businesses in less developed countries from sharing a PC if the price is too high?

Empirically, we have seen that, other things being equal, the more certain private property rights are, the more private capital accumulation there will be. People are more willing to invest their savings in endeavors that will increase their wealth in future years. They have property rights in their wealth that are sanctioned and enforced by the government. In fact, some economic historians have attempted to show that it was the development of well-defined private property rights that allowed Western Europe to increase its growth rate after many centuries of stagnation. The degree of certainty with which one can reap the gains from investing also determines the extent to which businesspeople in *other* countries will invest capital in developing countries. The threat of nationalization in some countries may scare away foreign investment that would allow these nations to become more developed.

In a sentence, economic development depends more on individuals who are able to perceive opportunities and then take advantage of those opportunities than it does on capital or natural resources.[1] Risks will not be taken, though, if the risk takers cannot expect a reward. The political institutions must be such that risk takers are rewarded. That requires well-established property rights, lack of the threat of expropriation of profits, and no fear of government nationalization of businesses.

CONCEPTS IN BRIEF

- Some policymakers believe that a large capital stock is a prerequisite for economic growth and development. They therefore suggest that developing countries need more capital.

- The human element, however, is vital; the labor force must be capable of using any capital that the developing country acquires. This requires training and education.

- Saving is a prerequisite for capital formation.

- Saving goes on even in poor developing countries, although not necessarily in the same form as in rich developed countries.

- Saving and individual capital accumulation will be greater the more certain individuals are about the safety of their wealth.

THE IMPORTANCE OF AN OPEN ECONOMY

The data are conclusive: Open economies experience faster economic development than economies closed to international trade. That is to say, the less government protects the domestic economy by imposing trade barriers, the faster that economy will experience economic development. According to a study by economists Nouriel Roubini and Xavier Sala-i-Martin, when a country goes from being relatively open to relatively closed via government-enacted trade barriers, it will have a 2.5 percentage point decrease in its growth rate.

Open economies accomplish several things. For one, individuals and businesses end up specializing in those endeavors in which they have a comparative advantage. International trade encourages individuals and businesses to discover ways to specialize so that they can become more productive and earn higher incomes. Increased productivity and the subsequent increase in the rate of economic development are the results. Open economies also allow the importation of already developed technology. For instance, no developing country today needs to spend years to figure out how to make computers or how to use them; that has already been done elsewhere.

---

[1]The member nations of OPEC might be considered exceptions to this generalization.

The True Cost of Protectionism

A statistical study of the cost of trade barriers might give the impression that taxes on imported goods simply raise their price to domestic consumers. But there is another cost that is normally hidden. Statisticians call it a *Type II error*—the cost of omission. It is the cost of what would have been had there not been tariff barriers. The best example of a Type II error is the cost of overregulating the pharmaceutical industry. If it causes fewer lifesaving drugs to be introduced, it is a Type II error. When trade is restricted in a developing country, that country's people are deprived of a potential larger range of new goods and production processes. Such new foreign products could spur local support businesses, which in turn would cause other businesses to be created. Developing countries that have restricted the entry of computer products have clearly slowed down the development of their own software industry. Trade barriers sometimes guarantee that new goods and services never appear in protected countries. According to economist Paul Romer of the University of California at Berkeley, because of protectionism, many developing countries do not simply cut back on their consumption of the entire range of goods available to rich countries; rather, they use a smaller quantity of a much smaller range of goods. He calculates that the cumulative forgone benefits from new economic activity blocked by an across-the-board 10 percent tariff in a developing country might be as high as 20 percent of annual national income.

THE IMPORTANCE OF AN EDUCATED POPULATION

Both theoretically and empirically, we know that a more educated workforce aids economic development because it allows individuals to build on the ideas of others. According to economists David Gould and Roy Ruffin, increasing the rate of enrollment in secondary schools by only 2 percentage points, from 8 to 10 percent, raises the average rate of economic growth by half a percent per year. Thus we must conclude that developing countries can advance more rapidly if they invest more heavily in secondary education. Or stated in the negative, economic development cannot be sustained if a nation allows a sizable portion of its population to avoid education. After all, education allows young people who grew up poor to acquire skills that enable them to avoid poverty as adults.

Some of the fastest-growing countries in the world, including the Four Tigers, virtually eliminated illiteracy very early on.

INTERNATIONAL POLICY EXAMPLE
Should School Tuition Vouchers Be Used in Developing Countries?

Nobel Prize–winning economist Gary Becker has argued in favor of a school voucher system in developing countries. According to his scheme, low-income parents would receive the vouchers, which could then be used at any approved school in their country. The participating schools would also have to provide meals for their students. According to Becker, such vouchers would stimulate competition among private and public schools in developing countries. There is a problem for very poor families, however. They want their children to work to provide income. Becker suggests that such families be given a bonus that offsets the income loss while their children are going to school.

FOR CRITICAL ANALYSIS: Do parents in developed countries have to be compensated for sending their children to school? Explain. •

LETTING COMPANIES DISAPPEAR: CREATIVE DESTRUCTION

Harvard economist Joseph Schumpeter (1883–1950) championed the concept of *creative destruction*. He pointed out that new technologies and successful new businesses end up destroying old jobs, old companies, and old industries. Change is painful and costly, but it is necessary for economic advancement. Nowhere is this more important than in developing countries, where the principle is often ignored.

Developing countries have had a history of supporting current companies and industries by preventing new technologies and new companies from entering the marketplace. The process of creative destruction has not been allowed to work its magic.

One key element in providing the most favorable condition for economic development is allowing businesses to fail. A corollary to this principle is that governments should not consistently use their taxpayers' money to subsidize or even own businesses. It does little good (and normally lots of harm) for governments in developing countries to own banks, phone companies, electric companies, car companies, or airlines. There are few historical examples of state-owned companies doing other than one thing—draining the public coffers.

Do not get the impression that government-owned and -operated businesses are run by individuals who are somehow less competent than those in the private sector. Rather, the incentive structure for managers in private businesses is different from that for managers in state-owned businesses.

THE RELATIONSHIP BETWEEN POPULATION GROWTH AND ECONOMIC DEVELOPMENT

World population is growing at the rate of 2.8 people each and every second. That turns out to be 242,000 a day, or 88.3 million a year. Today, there are about 5.8 billion people on earth. By the year 2030, according to the United Nations, there will be 8.5 billion. Look at Figure 35-1 on page 784 to see which countries are growing the most.

Just to make sure the message is clear, look at Figure 35-2 on page 784. There you see that virtually all of the growth in population comes from developing nations. Some countries, such as Germany, are expected to lose population over the next several decades.

The Conventional Wisdom

Ever since the Reverend Thomas Robert Malthus wrote his essay *The Principle of Population* in 1798, excessive population growth has been a concern. Modern-day Malthusians are able to generate just as much enthusiasm for the concept that population growth is bad. We are told that rapid population growth threatens economic development and the quality of life. This message was made loud and clear by numerous participants in the United Nations' International Conference on Population and Development held in Cairo, Egypt, in the fall of 1994.

What the Data Show. First of all, Malthus's prediction that population would outstrip food supplies has never held true for the entire world according to economist Nicholas Eberstadt of the Harvard Center for Population Development Studies. Figure 35-3 on page 785 shows how population has grown over the past 35 years. At the same time, the food supply, measured by calories per person, has also increased somewhat steadily.

Also, as you learned in Chapter 32, the price of food, corrected for inflation, has been falling steadily for over a century. That means that the supply of food is expanding faster than the demand caused by increased population.

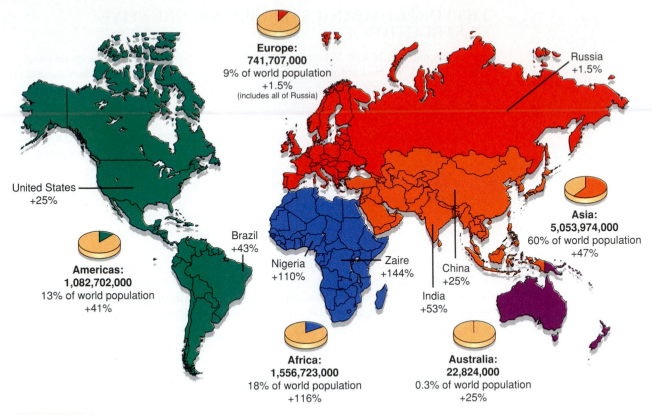

FIGURE 35-1

Expected Growth in World Population by 2030

Asia and Africa are expected to gain the most in population by the year 2030.

Source: United Nations.

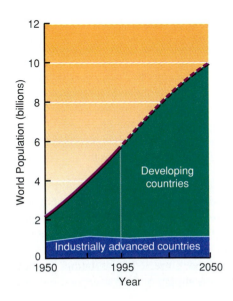

FIGURE 35-2

Population Growth by 2050

Population will increase dramatically in the developing countries. The industrially advanced countries will grow very little in population over the next half century.

Source: Population Reference Bureau.

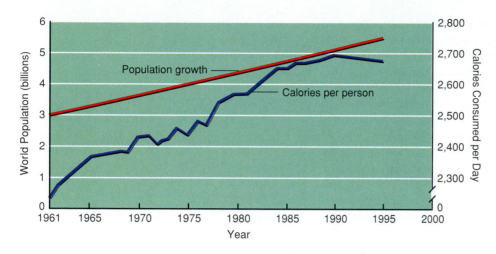

FIGURE 35-3
Population and Food Supplies
Malthus has been proved wrong: Population has not outstripped the world's food supply. In fact, for at least the past half century, calories consumed per person have been increasing at a rate even faster than the increase in population.
Source: U.S. Department of Agriculture.

Population Density and Economic Development. There is no consistent relationship between population density and economic development. Ethiopia has the same number of people per square mile as the United States, but per capita income is only about one-tenth that in the United States. Japan has a higher per capita income than many Western European nations, yet it has more people per square mile than India, one of the poorest nations. Hong Kong is the most densely populated country. Fifty years ago it was one of the poorest, but today its per capita income exceeds that in France and Great Britain. (Hong Kong has almost no natural resources either—it has to import even its drinking water.) As a general proposition, some of the richest countries in the world today are the most densely populated—South Korea, Taiwan, Belgium, the Netherlands, England, Germany, and Japan.

The Relationship Between Population Growth Rates and Economic Development. Again there seems to be little relationship between economic development and rapid population growth. Consider Malaysia, which grew from a sparsely populated country of villages in the 1890s to a nation of cities in the 1930s. During this period, its population increased from 1.5 million to 6 million, but its standard of living also increased, by about 140 percent. Historically, the largest increases in Western living standards took place during the period when the Western population was growing faster than it is in today's developing countries. Also, in spite of relatively high population growth rates, per capita incomes in many, if not most, developing countries are much higher today than they were four decades ago. Much of the population growth in developing countries has occurred because both adults and children live longer than they used to, not necessarily because families are having more children. There are just fewer deaths caused by malnutrition and contagious diseases than there used to be.

The Relationship Between Average Family Income and Size

One thing that economists know for sure is that over the past century, as nations became richer, the average family size fell. Otherwise stated, the more economic development occurs, the slower the population growth rate. Predictions of birthrates in developing countries have often turned out to be overstated if those countries experience rapid economic growth. This was the case in Hong Kong, Mexico, Taiwan, and Colombia.

Recent research on population and economic development has revealed that social and economic modernization has been accompanied by what might be called a fertility revolution—the spread of deliberate family size limitation within marriage and a decline in childbearing. Modernization reduces infant mortality, which in turn reduces the incentive for couples to have many children to make sure that enough will survive to satisfy each couple's demand. Also, modernization lowers the demand for children for a variety of reasons, not the least being that couples in more developed countries do not need to rely on their children to take care of them in old age.

Population and Productivity

Recall the discussion of comparative advantage and specialization in Chapter 33. Specialization turns out to be a function of the size of the market, which is, of course, a function of population. Thus a growing population can help improve the quality of life because it allows individuals to devote their talents to what they are best suited to do—whatever their comparative advantage is. Individuals don't "exhaust" the earth's resources. People create wealth through imagination and innovation. It was not long ago that oil was considered useless. So was sand; today, it is used to make silicone and glass from which computer chips and fiber optics are manufactured.

Three hundred years ago, there were one-tenth the number of humans who now live. Yet the world is incredibly more wealthy than it was three centuries ago. Today, there are four times as many Americans as there were 100 years ago. Yet today we live longer and are about six times richer per capita.

POLICY EXAMPLE
Are the Antinatalists Right?

Paul Ehrlich, the author of several books on the population explosion, argues that the earth can sustain only about 2 billion people. To him and others, the future of the earth looks grim unless the world sustains *negative* population growth—hence the term *antinatalists,* meaning "against births." The nonprofit organization Negative Population Growth (NPG) has produced ads telling us that the optimum U.S. population is about where it was in the 1940s, with 125 to 150 million people. NPG tells us that we should reduce annual immigration to about 200,000 and lower our fertility rate. Pentti Linkola, an amateur biologist in the remote village of Saaksmaki, Finland, wants to go several steps further. He argues that the United States symbolizes the worst ideologies in the world: growth and freedom. He argues that "everything we have developed over the last 100 years should be destroyed." He argues for an end to aid to developing countries, no more asylum for refugees, and other draconian measures to reduce the world's population. His goal is to "save humanity."

FOR CRITICAL ANALYSIS: *Would the United States be better off with 100 million fewer Americans?* ●

FOREIGN AID

Many nations, including the United States, extend assistance to developing countries. A number of reasons are given to justify this assistance, which can be in the form of grants, low-interest loans, food, military supplies, or technical expertise. Although the humanitarian argument in support of foreign aid is often given, security and economics also enter into the discussion. During the Cold War, the United States gave foreign aid to developing countries in order to support noncommunist regimes or to prevent communist takeovers. The United States also extends foreign aid to help develop foreign markets for the output of U.S. firms. This is particularly true when foreign aid is tied to the purchase of American products. Tied foreign aid requires that the recipient spend all or part of the sum extended as foreign aid on U.S.-produced goods.

The major landmark in the history of foreign aid from the United States was the Marshall Plan. Proposed by Secretary of State George Marshall in an address at Harvard University in June 1948, the plan established the European Recovery Program, which granted over $10 billion ($64 billion in 1996 dollars) in foreign assistance to Europe following World War II. Many observers contend that the Marshall Plan was instrumental in allowing Europe's productive capacity to grow dramatically during the late 1940s and early 1950s.

The United States gives relatively little aid to developing countries on a per capita basis today, and this amount is shrinking in inflation-corrected terms because of the U.S. federal government deficit. Most foreign aid goes to two countries, Israel and Egypt. Japan now gives a greater absolute amount of foreign aid than does the United States.

The Situation in the Developing Countries

The developing countries in the world today cannot be compared to those war-torn European countries at the end of World War II. The modernization of developing countries is a much more complicated task than the restoration of postwar Europe. In many cases, foreign aid to Europe simply helped those countries rebuild an existing and well-functioning capital base. It is one thing merely to replace locomotives and repair tracks in an existing railroad system and quite another to build a railroad system in a country that has none. Perhaps more important is potentially misdirected aid to developing countries. Remember that post–World War II Europe had the human capital of an experienced industrial workforce. Today's developing countries do not, so we cannot expect that foreign aid given to them will have the same result as the aid given to Europe for its restoration after the war. There are many barriers to economic growth in developing countries, including a lack of technical skills and capacities, poorly organized markets, political and social elites unreceptive to change, and non-growth-oriented foreign trade policies.

The Results of Foreign Aid

Since the end of World War II, the developed world has transferred about $2.4 trillion (in today's dollars) to developing countries. The results have been mixed. According to one study by economist Peter Bauer at the London School of Economics, there is little correlation between the level of foreign aid received and changes in living standards. He also found that foreign aid did not necessarily reduce infant mortality rates. His conclusion was that foreign aid simply raised the standard of living of the recipient countries' richest people.

Consider Tanzania. Between 1970 and 1988, this African country received $8.6 billion in aid, four times that country's 1988 gross domestic product. This is the equivalent of someone giving the United States around $20 trillion. During the same period, Sudan was given $9.6 billion, an amount equal to one year's output. Zaire, Togo, Zambia, Mozambique, and Niger each received around $6 billion during the same period. What happened to these billions of dollars? In all of these countries, gross output actually fell. Critics of foreign aid point out that much of the money went into new government centers, showy airports, and grand conference halls. Some of it also went into government officials' Swiss bank accounts. According to economist George Ayittey, Zaire president Mobutu Sese Seko is now worth $10 billion, and Zambia's Kenneth Kaunda is worth $6 billion.

INTERNATIONAL EXAMPLE
The World Bank and the Development of Poor Nations (or Lack Thereof)

The International Bank for Reconstruction and Development, known as the World Bank, was established in 1944. To date it has lent over $300 billion, mostly to poor nations. However, its accomplishments have recently been questioned. For example, since 1951, India has received $55 billion—more foreign aid than any other country on earth—yet over 40 percent of India's population still lives in poverty. In sub-Saharan Africa, massive amounts of money have gone into development planning, yet that region has a lower per capita income than it did before it received aid.

Another criticism of the World Bank is that its lending policies during the 1970s encouraged large-scale, capital-intensive technology, which helped governments in less developed nations to plunder their natural resources. These large-scale projects displaced millions of poor and tribal peoples. In India, World Bank development projects uprooted over 20 million people. Throughout the world, dam projects have altered natural ecologies. Indeed, a mid-1990's internal review of the bank's lending portfolio found that almost 40 percent of recently evaluated projects did not adhere to established environmental and social policies.

The major problem with the World Bank's lending activities is that they help government bureaucracies flourish with funds that could be used to help individuals in the host countries.

FOR CRITICAL ANALYSIS: *How does lending to governments in less developed countries hinder market reforms?* ●

CONCEPTS IN BRIEF

- The openness of an economy can determine it rate, or lack thereof, of economic development. Open economies allow, among other things, the importation of technology from the rest of the world.

- The more educated the workforce, the greater the chance of successful economic development, so enrollment in secondary schools is a key determinant of economic growth.

- While many believe population growth hinders economic development, there is little historic relationship between either population density or growth rates and economic growth rates.

- Critics of foreign aid point out that foreign aid will not increase the rate of economic growth unless a well-functioning capital base and infrastructure are in place.

Can PCs Bridge the Gap Between Less Advanced and More Advanced Economies?

Concepts Applied: *International trade, technology, open economies*

The PC revolution allows less advanced economies to benefit from new technology at a low investment cost and at a faster rate than in already developed countries.

The PC revolution is showing up in the world's developing countries, sometimes at a faster pace than in the United States. In its wake is a quickly narrowing competitive gap between the more advanced and the less advanced economies. There are several reasons why the PC may be at the heart of improved economies in developing countries.

Low-Price Accessibility

Even in the developed countries, the PC revolution would never have happened without dramatic improvements in microprocessors, memory chips, and software, all occurring while prices continue to drop. Computer technology is now economically viable for most businesses except in the extremely poor countries, according to Eduardo Talero, information technology specialist at the World Bank.

Necessity: The Mother of Invention

Another reason why PC technology has taken off in some countries is simply because of necessity. The advanced home-banking system in Brazil referred to at the beginning of this chapter did depend on cheap technology and software. Also, high inflation rates in Brazil have meant that people who did not deposit their earnings immediately would see the real value of their wealth drop through inflation. Home banking allows for instantaneous transfers of earnings. Necessity is the mother of invention.

The Benefit of Being a Latecomer

Perhaps just as important for developing countries, the fact that they are latecomers has helped them tremendously. Developing countries by definition have had low levels of technology in their business infrastructure. Consequently, they have not invested large amounts in old systems, such as IBM mainframe computers. When the PC revolution came along, they were able to take advantage of it without waiting for their old equipment to wear out. Economic theory predicts that late starters—developing nations—can benefit from new technology at a much faster rate than the already developed countries. And that is what has been happening.

Bringing Down the Trade Barriers

The developing countries that have reduced their trade barriers fastest have seen technology circulate the most freely and have experienced the greatest benefits. Many Latin American countries are leading the way by allowing unfettered imports of computer equipment and software. The PC market in Latin America is growing at a rate of almost 25 percent a year. Sales in Eastern Europe are growing at 15 percent a year. Software sales are growing even faster.

FOR CRITICAL ANALYSIS
1. Why do latecomers adopt technology faster than already established economies?
2. Why is an open economy necessary for technological innovation to spread rapidly?

CHAPTER SUMMARY

1. The 19 industrially advanced countries (IACs)—the United States, Japan, Canada, and the countries of Western Europe—have market economies based on a large skilled labor force and a large technically advanced stock of capital goods.

2. One of the major characteristics of developing countries is a high rate of population growth. However, high population growth does not necessarily prevent or retard economic development.

3. Some authorities contend that balanced development of industry and agriculture is necessary for growth in the developing countries. There are, however, exceptions to this rule; Hong Kong is one.

4. Industrialization in many developing countries has involved subsidization of manufacturing. Such subsidization leads to a misallocation of resources and to a lower per capita standard of living for the population even though the country may become more highly industrialized.

5. Capital accumulation is an important determinant of economic development. However, massive transfers of capital to developing countries do not guarantee economic development. Appropriately trained personnel must be available to use the capital given to these countries.

6. Domestic capital formation requires saving—nonconsumption of current income. Even the poorest countries' citizens do some saving. In fact, there is no pronounced relationship between percentage of income saved and level of income.

7. Saving in the developing countries may take on different forms than in more developed countries. For example, having children is a form of saving if those children feel an obligation to support their parents during retirement.

8. The more certain private property rights are, the more private capital accumulation there will be, other things being equal.

DISCUSSION OF PREVIEW QUESTIONS

1. What is a developing country?

Developing countries are arbitrarily defined as those with very low per capita incomes. Relative to developed countries, people in developing countries have lower incomes, life expectancies, literacy rates, and daily caloric intake and higher infant mortality rates.

2. Must developing countries develop by industrializing?

Proponents of the balanced-growth theory point out that the industrially advanced countries (IACs) are highly industrialized and the developing countries are mostly agrarian. They feel that balanced growth requires that the developing countries expand the manufacturing sector; laborers and other resources should be reallocated to promote industrialization. It is often suggested that the developing countries restrict imports of nonagricultural goods to help industrialization. It is alleged that these nations must

industrialize even if their comparative advantage lies in the production of agricultural goods because they can't compete with the subsidized agricultural sectors of the IACs. Yet it is easy to oversell the pro-industrialization balanced-growth approach. Numerous examples of gross inefficiency can be cited when the developing countries attempted to develop steel and automobile industries. Moreover, when the developing countries restrict the imports of manufactured goods, they lower living standards and promote inefficiency. It would seem that the time to develop the industrial sector would be when it is profitable for businesses to do so.

3. Can developing countries create their own capital stock?

It is often asserted that a large capital stock is necessary for economic development, the developing countries are too poor to save sufficient amounts to develop domestic capital formation, and the IACs should therefore give capital to the developing countries. Experts disagree about the validity of each contention. The question under discussion here deals with the second proposition. A good deal of evidence exists to support the notion that the developing countries do save—although in forms that are not easily observed or cannot be readily converted into capital. Even people with extremely low incomes are forced by economic circumstances to provide for future consumption; they often store dried or cured food. On a nationwide scale, much evidence of capital formation exists: cathedrals, pyramids, great walls, fortresses, government buildings, and so on. Of course, the problem is to get savings into forms that can be used to produce goods or services.

4. Does a lack of protected property rights hinder a developing country's development?

Yes. When individuals fear that their property rights will not be protected, they invest in ways that reflect this risk. Thus people in politically and economically unstable countries prefer to accumulate diamonds, gold, silver, and currency in foreign banks rather than invest in factories, equipment, and savings in domestic bank accounts. Similarly, a nation that expropriates property or nationalizes industry discourages investment by foreign businesses. Many developing countries could be aided to a great extent by attracting foreign investment—but foreign investors will require property right guarantees.

PROBLEMS

(Answers to the odd-numbered problems appear at the back of the book.)

35-1. List five developing countries and five industrially advanced countries.

35-2. What problems are associated with advancements in medicine and health that are made available to developing countries?

35-3. Outline a typical pattern of economic development.

35-4. Suppose that you are shown the following data for two countries, known only as country X and country Z:

Country	GDP	Population
X	$ 81 billion	9 million
Z	135 billion	90 million

a. From this information, which country would you expect to be classified as a developing country? Why?

b. Now suppose that you were also given the following data:

Country	Life Expectancy at Birth (years)	Infant Mortality per 1,000 Live Births	Literacy (%)
X	70	15	60
Z	58	50	70

Are these figures consistent with your answer to part (a)?

c. Should we expect the developing country identified in part (a) to have a much greater population density than the other country?

35-5. Would unrestricted labor immigration end up helping or hurting developing countries? Explain.

35-6. Many countries in Africa have extremely large potential stocks of natural resources. Nonetheless, those natural resources often remain unexploited. Give reasons why this situation continues to exist.

35-7. Sketch a scenario in which population growth causes an increase in income per capita.

COMPUTER-ASSISTED INSTRUCTION

This chapter brings the tutorial full circle; it applies the principles of scientific thinking to questions of economic development, illustrating once again such concepts as observational equivalence, the fallacy of composition, tautologies, and correlation versus causation.

Complete problem and answer appear on disk.

INTERACTING WITH THE INTERNET

Summary macroeconomic data on most countries of the world, including developing ones, can be found in the Penn World Tables at

http://nber.harvard.edu/pwt56.html

If the release number of the data changes, it might be necessary to search from

http://nber.harvard.edu

and at

http://cansim.epas.utoronto.ca:5680/pwt/pwt.html

The latter site allows you to plot the data on-line.

The World Bank maintains two sites with valuable information on economic development. Perhaps the more important is "Social Indicators of Development," which covers a wide variety of health, demographic, and economic information. It is found at

http://www.ciesin.org/IC/wbank/sid-home.html

Brief reports on countries that borrow from the World Bank are contained in "Trends in Developing Economies," which is located at

http://www.ciesin.org/IC/wbank/tde-home.html

ANSWERS TO ODD-NUMBERED PROBLEMS

CHAPTER 1

1-1. A large number of possible factors might affect the probability of death, including age, occupation, diet, and current health. Thus one model would show that the older someone is, the greater is the probability of dying within the next five years; another would show that the riskier the occupation, other things being equal, the greater the probability of dying within five years; and so forth.

1-3. a. We should observe younger drivers to be more frequently involved in traffic accidents than older persons.
  b. Slower monetary expansion should be associated with less inflation.
  c. Professional basketball players receiving smaller salaries should be observed to have done less well in their high school studies.
  d. Employees being promoted rapidly should have lower rates of absenteeism than those being promoted more slowly.

1-5. The decreasing relative attractiveness of mail communication has no doubt decreased students' demand for writing skills. Whether or not the influence has been a significant one is a subject for empirical research. As for the direction of causation, it may well be running both ways. Cheaper nonwritten forms of communication may decrease the demand for writing skills. Lower levels of writing skills probably further increase the demand for audio and video communications media.

1-7. a. Normative, involving a value judgment about what should be
  b. Positive, for it is a statement of what has actually occurred
  c. Positive, for it is a statement of what actually is
  d. Normative, involving a value judgment about what should be

CHAPTER 2

2-1. The law of increasing relative cost does seem to hold because of the principle that some resources may be more suited to one productive use than to another. In moving from butter to guns, the economy will first transfer those resources most easily sacrificed by the butter sector, holding on to the very specialized (to butter) factors until the last. Thus different factor intensities will lead to increasing relative costs.

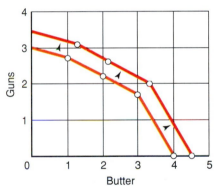

Production Possibilities Curve
for Guns and Butter
(before and after 10 percent growth)

2-3. a. Neither, because each can produce the same total number of jackets per time period (2 jackets per hour)
  b. Neither, because each has the same cost of producing ties ($\frac{2}{3}$ jacket per tie)
  c. No, because with equal costs of production, there are no gains from specialization
  d. Output will be the same as if they did not specialize (16 jackets per day and 24 ties per day)

2-5. a. Only the extra expense of lunch in a restaurant, above what lunch at home would have cost, is part of the cost of going to the game.

b. This is part of the cost of going to the game because you would not have incurred it if you had watched the game on TV at home.

c. This is part of the cost of going to the game because you would not have incurred it if you had watched the game on TV at home.

2-7. For most people, air is probably not an economic good because most of us would not pay simply to have a larger volume of the air we are currently breathing. But for almost everyone, *clean* air is an economic good because most of us would be willing to give something up to have cleaner air.

APPENDIX A

A-1.

y	x
12	4
9	3
6	2
3	1
0	0
−3	−1
−6	−2
−9	−3
−12	−4

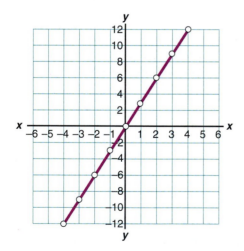

CHAPTER 3

3-1. The equilibrium price is $30. The quantity supplied and demanded is about 10.5 million skateboards per year.

3-3. a. The demand curve for vitamin C will shift outward to the right because the product has taken on a desirable new quality.

b. The demand curve for teachers will shift inward to the left because the substitute good, the interactive educational CD-ROM, is now a lower-cost alternative. (Change in the price of a substitute)

c. The demand curve for beer will shift outward to the right because the price of a complementary good—pretzels—has decreased. Is it any wonder that tavern owners often give pretzels away? (Change in the price of a complement)

3-5. As the graph indicates, demand doesn't change, supply decreases, the equilibrium price of oranges rises, and the equilibrium quantity falls.

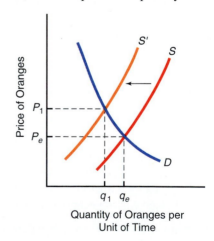

3-7. The speaker has learned well the definition of a surplus but has overlooked one point. The "surpluses" that result from the above-equilibrium minimum prices don't go begging; the excess quantities supplied are in effect purchased by the

Department of Agriculture. In that sense, they are not surpluses at all. When one includes the quantity that is demanded by the Department of Agriculture, along with the quantities being purchased by private purchasers at the support price, the quantity demanded will equal the quantity supplied, and there will be an equilibrium of sorts.

3-9. As the graph illustrates, rain consumers are not willing to pay a positive price to have nature's bounty increased. Thus the equilibrium quantity is 200 centimeters per year (the amount supplied freely by nature), and the equilibrium price is zero (the amount that consumers will pay for an additional unit, given that nature is already producing 200 centimeters per year).

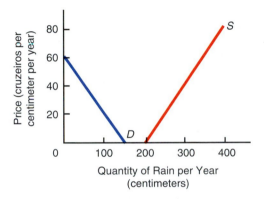

CHAPTER 4

4-1. a. The demand curve will shift to the right (increase).
   b. The supply curve will shift to the right (increase).
   c. Because the price floor, or minimum price, is below the equilibrium price of 50 cents, there will be no effect on price or quantity.
   d. Because the price floor is now greater than the equilibrium price, there will be a surplus at the new price of 75 cents.
   e. Assuming that grapefruits are a substitute for oranges, the demand curve for oranges will shift to the right (increase).
   f. Assuming that oranges are a normal good, the demand curve will shift to the left (decrease).

4-3. The "equilibrium" price is $40 per calculator, and the equilibrium quantity is zero calculators per year. This is so because at a price of $40, the quantity demanded—zero—is equal to the quantity supplied—also zero. None will be produced or bought because the highest price that any consumer is willing to pay for even a single calculator ($30) is below the lowest price at which any producer is willing to produce even one calculator ($50).

4-5. The equilibrium price is $4 per crate, and the equilibrium quantity is 50 million crates per year. At $2 per crate, the quantity demanded is 90 million crates per year and the quantity supplied is 10. This is called a shortage, or excess quantity demanded. The excess quantity demanded is 80 million crates per year. At $5 per crate, the quantity demanded is 20 million crates per year and the quantity supplied is 80 million crates. This is called a surplus, or excess quantity supplied. The excess quantity supplied is 60 million crates per year.

4-7. As shown in the graph, if the equilibrium price of oranges is 10 cents, a price floor of 15 cents will result in a surplus equal to $Q_s - Q_d$. A price floor of 5 cents per orange will have no effect, however, because it is below the equilibrium price and thus does not prevent suppliers and demanders from doing what they want to do—produce and consume Q_e oranges at 10 cents each.

CHAPTER 5

5-1. The marginal tax rate on the first $3,000 of taxable income is 0 percent because no taxes are imposed until $5,000 is earned. The marginal rate on $10,000 is 20 percent, as it is on $100,000 and all other amounts above the $5,000 level, because for each additional dollar earned after $5,000, 20 cents will be taxed away. The average tax rate, which is the tax amount divided by the pretax income, is 0 for $3,000, 10 percent for $10,000,

A-4 ANSWERS TO ODD-NUMBERED PROBLEMS

and 19 percent for $100,000. The average tax rate will *approach* a maximum of 20 percent as income increases. It cannot reach *exactly* 20 percent because of the untaxed $5,000 at the beginning. Such is the nature of a *degressive* tax system.

5-3. Mr. Smith pays nothing on his first $1,500 of income, 14 percent ($70) on the $500 of earnings between $1,500 and $2,000, and 20 percent ($100) on the $500 that he earns above $2,000. Thus Mr. Smith has a total tax bill of $170 on an income of $2,500; his average tax rate is 6.8 percent, and his marginal tax rate is 20 percent.

5-5. Among the ideas that have been proposed is that a good tax system should meet the requirements of equity, efficiency, and ease of administration. Equity means that each person should pay a "fair share." The efficiency requirement is that the tax system should minimize interferences with economic decisions. Ease of administration means that the tax system should not be excessively costly to administer and that it should be understandable to the taxpayer. Even though the U.S. tax system was not designed through a master plan, these ideas have had their influence on the American system.

5-7. There are both public good and private good aspects to police protection. When an officer patrols the neighborhood in a police car, criminals are deterred from burglarizing every home in the neighborhood; this is a public good aspect of police protection because the protection afforded one person is simultaneously afforded all of the neighbors. But when an officer spends time arresting the person who broke into Mr. Smith's home, that is time the officer cannot spend arresting the person who broke into Ms. Jones's home; this is the private good aspect of police protection, for when these services are provided Mr. Smith, Ms. Jones is excluded from simultaneously using those services.

5-9. a. If you give and everyone else does also, you account for 1 percent. If you are the only one who gives, you account for 100 percent. If you give nothing, you account for 0 percent, regardless of what others give.
b. In principle, your contribution matters whatever the level of participation. But as a practical matter, if participation is near 100 percent, the absence of your contribution may have little practical effect.
c. There is no free ride. If you do not make your contribution, total contributions will be lower,

and the quality of the services provided will be lower.

5-11. Strictly speaking, probably all the items except national defense should go into the column labeled "Private Goods," either because residents *could* be excluded from consuming them or because one person's consumption reduces the amount available for other individuals. As a practical matter, however, there are several goods on the list (public television, elementary education, and the museum) for which full exclusion generally does not take place and/or consumption by one person reduces the amount that other persons can consume by only a small amount.

CHAPTER 6

6-1. On the supply side, all of the industries responsible for automobile inputs would have to be considered. This would include steel (and coke and coal), glass, tires (and rubber), plastics, railroads (and thus steel again), aluminum (and electricity), and manufacturers of stereos, hubcaps, and air conditioners, to name a few. On the demand side, you would have to take into account industries involving complements (such as oil, gasoline, concrete, and asphalt) and substitutes (including bicycles, motorcycles, buses, and walking shoes). Moreover, resource allocation decisions regarding labor and the other inputs, complements, and substitutes for these goods must also be made.

6-3. a. Profit equals total revenue minus total cost. Because revenue is fixed (at $172), if the firm wishes to maximize profit, this is equivalent to minimizing costs. To find total costs, simply multiply the price of each input by the amount of the input that must be used for each technique.

Costs of A = ($10)(7) + ($2)(6) + ($15)(2) + ($8)(1) = $120
Costs of B = ($10)(4) + ($2)(7) + ($15)(6) + ($8)(3) = $168
Costs of C = ($10)(1) + ($2)(18) + ($15)(3) + ($8)(2) = $107

Because C has the lowest costs, it yields the highest profits, and thus it will be used.
b. Profit equals $172 − $107 = $65.
c. Each technique's costs rise by the increase in the price of labor multiplied by the amount of

labor used by that technique. Because technique A uses the least amount of labor, its costs rise the least, and it thus becomes the lowest-cost technique at $132. (The new cost of B is $182, and the new cost of C is $143.) Hence technique A will be used, resulting in profits of $172 − $132 = $40.

6-5. a. In the market system, the techniques that yield the highest (positive) profits will be used.

b. Profit equals total revenue minus total cost. Because revenue from 100 units is fixed (at $100), if the firm wishes to maximize profit, this is equivalent to minimizing costs. To find total costs, simply multiply the price of each input by the amount of the input that must be used for each technique.

Costs of A = ($10)(6) + ($8)(5) = $100
Costs of B = ($10)(5) + ($8)(6) = $98
Costs of C = ($10)(4) + ($8)(7) = $96

Because technique C has the lowest costs, it also yields the highest profits ($100 − $96 = $4).

c. Following the same methods yields these costs: A = $98, B = $100, and C = $102. Technique A will be used because it is the most profitable.

d. The profits from using technique A to produce 100 units of X are $100 − $98 = $2.

CHAPTER 7

7-1. Although your boss gave you a raise of $1,200 ($30,000 × .04), you are not $1,200 better off after taxes. You are now in the 28 percent marginal tax bracket. You must pay .28 × $1,200 in additional taxes, or $336. That leaves you with an additional $864 in take-home pay. That is how much better off you are because of the raise.

7-3. a. 5 percent
b. One month
c. 5 percent
d. 10 percent
e. In this example, the unemployment rate doubled, but it is not obvious that the economy has gotten sicker or that workers are worse off.

7-5. a. The nominal rate of interest is composed of the real rate of interest plus the anticipated rate of inflation. If the current rate of inflation is zero and people anticipate that there will continue to be no inflation, the real rate of interest equals the nominal rate of interest—in this example, 12 percent.

b. If the nominal rate of interest stays at 12 percent while the rate of inflation goes to 13 percent, and if that rate is anticipated to last, the real rate of interest drops to a *negative* 1 percent! Lending money at 12 percent would not normally be advisable in such a situation.

7-7. a. 10, 9, 8, 7, 6, 5, 4, 3
b. 8.0, 8.3, 9.4, 10.9, 12.0, 13.8, 16.0

CHAPTER 8

8-1. a. GDP = $950; NDP = $900; NI = $875
b. GDP = $825
c. The value of depreciation exceeding gross private investment implies that the total capital stock of the country is declining. This would likely decrease future productivity because capital is a productive resource.

8-3. a. Coal; $2
b. $3. Auto manufacturers took something worth $5 and transformed it into an auto that they sold for $8.
c. $9 because intermediate goods are *not* counted.
d. $9, resulting from adding the value added at each stage. Note that in this economy, which produces only autos, the earnings and the income approaches both yield a GDP estimate of $9.

8-5. a. It falls.
b. It is unchanged because illegal transactions are not measured anyway.
c. It rises.

8-7. a. Nominal GDP for 1992 = ($4)(10) + ($12)(20) + ($6)(5) + ($25)(10) = $560. Nominal GDP for 1997 = ($8)(12) + ($36)(15) + ($10)(15) + ($30)(12) = $1,146.
b. Real GDP for 1992 = $560. Real GDP for 1997 = ($4)(12) + ($12)(15) + ($6)(15) + ($25)(12) = $618.

CHAPTER 9

9-1. Point *B* is associated with the highest feasible growth rate. Capital goods implicitly represent future consumption, and point *B* has the highest feasible ratio of capital goods to current consumption (and thus the highest ratio of future consumption to current consumption).

9-3. a. *M*
b. *K*

CHAPTER 10

10-1. At P_1, the quantity of *AS* exceeds the quantity of *AD;* therefore, a surplus of real national income (output) exists. At that price level, suppliers are willing to produce more than buyers want to purchase; in this surplus situation, producers find their inventories rising involuntarily, and they find it profitable to reduce prices and output. At P_2, the quantity of *AD* exceeds the quantity of *AS,* and a shortage exists. At that price level, buyers want more than producers are willing to produce, and buyers, competing for goods and services, will bid the price level upward. A higher price level induces an increase in the quantity of *AS* and a decrease in the quantity of *AD*. Only at P_e does the quantity of *AS* equal the quantity of *AD;* at P_e, equilibrium exists.

10-3. The long-run aggregate supply curve is vertical at the point representing the maximum potential output possible. Prices can vary, but output cannot. In the short run, some increase in the level of output is possible with prices rising. This is possible because of the existence of some excess capacity, as well as flexibility in the nature and intensity of work. Therefore, the positively sloped portion of the aggregate supply curve constitutes the short-run aggregate supply curve.

10-5. a. The price level increases.
b. National output decreases.

CHAPTER 11

11-1. If the interest rate is higher than equilibrium, desired saving exceeds desired investment. Those who desire investment funds from savers will offer to pay lower rates of interest. Savers, in competition with each other, will be willing to accept lower rates of interest. The interest rate will be bid down, which will simultaneously decrease the quantity of saving desired and increase the quantity of investment desired.

11-3. Equilibrium starts out at E_1 with the price level at 100 and equilibrium real GDP at Q_0. When AD_1 shifts to AD_2, the end result is that the equilibrium

is at E_1 with the same equilibrium level of real GDP per year but a price level of only 90. The equilibrium level of real GDP is supply-determined.

CHAPTER 12

12-1.

Disposable Income	Consumption	Saving
$ 500	$510	$−10
600	600	0
700	690	10
800	780	20
900	870	30
1,000	960	40

a.

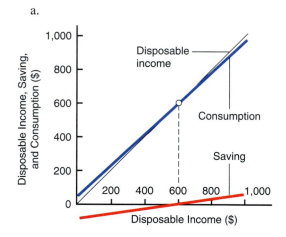

b. The marginal propensity to consume is .9; the marginal propensity to save is .1.

c.

Disposable Income	Average Propensity to Consume	Average Propensity to Save
$ 500	1.0200	−.0200
600	1.0000	0
700	.9857	.0142
800	.9750	.0250
900	.9667	.0333
1,000	.9600	.0400

12-3. Stock: a, c; Flow: b, d, e, f, g

12-5.

Real National Income	Consumption Expenditures	Saving	Investment	APC	APS	MPC	MPS
$1,000	$1,100	$−100	$100	1.1	−.1	.9	.1
2,000	2,000	0	100	1.0	.0	.9	.1
3,000	2,900	100	100	.967	.033	.9	.1
4,000	3,800	200	100	.950	.050	.9	.1
5,000	4,700	300	100	.940	.060	.9	.1
6,000	5,600	400	100	.933	.067	.9	.1

a.

b.

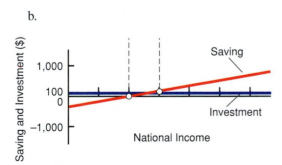

c. The multiplier effect from the inclusion of investment is to raise equilibrium national income by $1,000 over the equilibrium level it would otherwise have reached.
d. The value of the multiplier is 10.
e. The equilibrium level of national income without investment is $2,000; with investment, it is $3,000.

f. Equilibrium income will rise by $1,000.
g. Equilibrium income will again rise by $1,000 to $4,000.

12-7. a. Multiplier = 10
        b. Multiplier = 3.33
        c. Multiplier = 6.67
        d. Multiplier = 2.86

CHAPTER 13

13-1. Discretionary fiscal policy is policy in which the levels of government spending and taxes change as a result of a deliberate decision by the government. *Example:* A change in the structure of tax rates, a change in government expenditures not associated with a change in government revenues.

Automatic stabilizers cause the level of government spending or taxes to change as a result of endogenous changes in a variable such as income, other than changes due to deliberate decisions of the government. *Example:* Government revenues increasing from taxes during an economic expansion.

13-3. Consumers must not regard current budget deficits as equivalent to higher future taxes and current budget surpluses as equivalent to lower future taxes. For example, if consumers regard a $1 million deficit as imposing an equivalent amount of new taxes on them in the future, they will increase current saving so as to be in a position to pay the higher future taxes. As a result, current consumption will decline, and at least some and possibly all of the stabilizing effect of the deficit will be wiped out.

APPENDIX B

B-1. a. The marginal propensity to consume is equal to $1 - MPS$, or $\frac{6}{7}$.

b. Investment or government spending must increase by $50 billion.

c. The government would have to cut taxes by $58.33 billion.

B-3. a. Aggregate demand will shift downward by $500; therefore, national income will fall by $5,000.

b. Aggregate demand will shift upward by $.9(\$500) = \$450$; therefore, national income will rise by $4,500.

CHAPTER 14

14-1. The federal budget deficit is the difference between federal spending and federal taxes—in this case, $300 billion.

14-3. Ultimately, all government debt must be repaid by means of taxation. (The government cannot forever "repay" its debt by issuing more debt because ultimately the public debt would exceed the wealth of the entire nation!) Thus when the government adds to the debt, it is simultaneously adding to future taxes that must be equivalent in present value to the added debt.

14-5. Some observers say that the true burden of government is the real value of the resources it uses. Changing the way the books are kept leaves this burden unchanged. Moreover, neither current nor future taxes would be affected by this accounting change, so no one's tax liability would be altered. In brief, the change will have no real consequences. The net public debt equals the gross public debt *minus* the portion held by government agencies (what the government owes to itself).

CHAPTER 15

15-1. a. The painting by Renoir would have the greatest advantage as a store of value, for works of art have generally appreciated over time. As a medium of exchange or a unit of accounting, it would be deficient because of its high and sometimes variable value and the limited market for its exchange.

b. A 90-day U.S. Treasury bill also has a good store of value; it is guaranteed by the government and it will pay some interest. Of course, to the extent that the money to be returned for the matured bill is an imperfect store of value, so will be the bill. A 90-day bill will not vary much in value over its life because the redemption date is not far off and there is a ready market for its exchange; thus it is a serviceable medium of exchange and unit of accounting. But the large denominations in which these bills are issued detract from the latter functions.

c. It is important to distinguish between the balances in a time deposit account and the account itself. The account is a relationship between depositor and bank. The money in the account will have the attributes of money, qualified by the increased return that interest pays, the "notice" risk of withdrawal, and the solvency of the savings and loan association in Reno.

d. There are significant transactions costs in exchanging one share of IBM stock, and its value can be volatile in the short run, making it an imperfect medium of exchange and unit of accounting. Its qualities as a store of value depend on the health of the company and the economy in which it operates.

e. A $50 Federal Reserve note is cash, and its qualities will correspond accordingly. Of course, its denomination is a multiple of the common unit of our account, which is $1.

f. A MasterCard, like the savings account, indicates the existence of a relationship. Its transferability is severely limited, and its value depends on the terms of the credit agreement. (There is probably an illegal market for MasterCards, in which they assume an independent value for exchange, although they probably lack most of the advantages of a store of value or unit of accounting.)

g. Because it is negotiable, a checkable account could be a useful medium of exchange, as long as its size does not restrict the available market too strongly. The only limits on its qualities as a store of value are the reliability of the bank and the value of the money into which it can be converted. Because the value is determined by the size of an anticipated transaction, there is no real independent unit of accounting to be measured by the checkable account.

h. Assuming that the pass is for the lifetime of the Dodgers and not for an owner who could not trade the pass, the ticket would be like many other nonmoney goods. Its money qualities would depend on the market available for its exchange and the value taken on by the good in the market. The fortunes of the Dodgers, the Los Angeles consumers' taste for baseball, and other demand determinants would affect the three monetary qualities of a lifetime pass.

15-3. M2 consists of the values of M1 plus overnight repurchase agreements (REPOs), overnight Euro-dollars, money market mutual funds, savings de-posits, and small-denomination time deposits.

15-5. a. V
b. A
c. P
d. E

15-7. If there are *n* goods, the number of exchange rates will be $n(n - 1)/2$. In this case, $n = 10$, so the number of exchange rates will be $10(10 - 1)/2 = 90/2 = 45$.

15-9. The *number* of payments and the *value* of the payments are two different concepts. Specifically, the value of the payments must equal the average size of the payments, multiplied by the number of payments. Consider this example: A family of four buys a secondhand Rolls-Royce for $99,900, using a wire transfer to pay for it. To celebrate the pur-chase, the family goes out and has lunch, each family member using cash to pay for his or her own lunch. Each person's lunch costs $25, for a total of $100. There are five transactions (one car plus four lunches), so cash accounts for $4/5 = 80$ percent of the *number* of transactions. Yet there is $100,000 worth of transactions, so the wire trans-fer accounts for $99,000/$100,000 = 99.9$ percent of the *value* of the transactions.

CHAPTER 16

16-1. a. Multiple Deposit Creation

Bank	Deposits	Reserves	Loans
Bank 1	$1,000,000	$ 250,000	$ 750,000
Bank 2	750,000	187,500	562,500
Bank 3	562,500	140,625	421,875
Bank 4	421,875	105,469	316,406
Bank 5	316,406	79,102	237,304
All other banks	949,219	237,304	711,915
Totals	4,000,000	1,000,000	3,000,000

The money multiplier is 4.

b. Multiple Deposit Creation

Bank	Deposits	Reserves	Loans
Bank 1	$ 1,000,000	$ 50,000	$ 950,000
Bank 2	950,000	47,500	902,500
Bank 3	902,500	45,125	857,375
Bank 4	857,375	42,869	814,506
Bank 5	814,506	40,725	773,781
All other banks	15,475,619	773,781	14,701,838
Totals	20,000,000	1,000,000	19,000,000

The money multiplier is 20.

16-3. a. No change.
b. The money supply decreases by $50,000.
c. The money supply rises by $100,000.
d. This is a little tricky. If the Fed had been "keep-ing track" of currency, the $1,000 currency buried in Smith's backyard is accounted for; therefore, the money supply will rise by $9,000 because the Fed did not have to "create" the $1,000 already in existence.
e. The money supply will decrease by $9,000; see (d).

16-5. a.

ASSETS		LIABILITIES	
Total reserves	+$1,000,000	Demand deposits	+$1,000,000
Required reserves ($50,000) + excess reserves ($950,000)			
Total	+$1,000,000	Total	+$1,000,000

b. Bank 1 can increase its lending by $950,000.

16-7. a. The bank's excess reserves have decreased by $2,550,000.
b. The money supply has decreased by $3 million.
c. The money supply can decrease by as much as $20 million.

16-9. a. The maximum money multiplier will be $1/r$ where r = reserve ratio. In this case, $r = .05$, so the multiplier is $1/.05 = 20$.
b. Deposits will rise by an amount equal to the multiplier times the initial change in reserves. In this case, the rise will be equal to $1 million $\times$ 20 = $20 million.

CHAPTER 17

17-1. A change in monetary policy leads to a change in interest rates, which leads to a change in investment. This, then, through the multiplier process, leads to a change in income.

17-3.

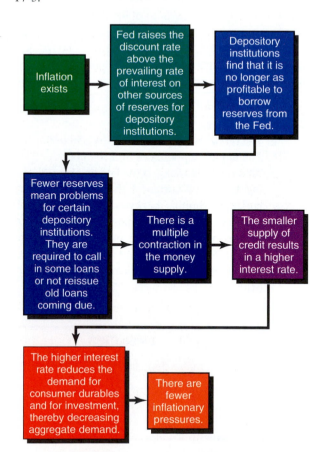

APPENDIX D

D-1. By its purchase of $1 billion in bonds, the Fed increased excess reserves by $1 billion. This ultimately caused a $3 billion increase in the money supply after full multiple expansion. The 1 percent drop in the interest rate, from 10 to 9 percent, caused investment to rise by $25 billion, from $200 billion to $225 billion. An investment multiplier of 3 indicates that equilibrium national income rose by $75 billion to $2,075 trillion.

CHAPTER 18

18-1. a. 10 percent
b. A rise in the expected rate of inflation will cause the curve to shift upward by the amount of the rise.
c. Because the systematic policies that attempt to exploit the seeming trade-off will be incorporated into workers' and firms' expectations. As a result, the expected inflation rate will move in lockstep with the actual rate (excepting random errors), so that the unemployment rate will not change when the inflation rate changes.

18-3. The existence of contracts, small-menu costs, and efficiency wages will increase the amount of discretion available to policymakers because all of these will tend to slow the adjustment of wages to changes in expectations.

18-5. A rise in the duration of unemployment will tend to raise the average unemployment rate because each unemployed person will be counted as unemployed more times over any given time period.

18-7. Yes. It is precisely the fact both employers and workers incorrectly perceive a change in nominal demand as a change in real demand that generates the negatively sloping Phillips curve.

CHAPTER 33

33-1. a. The opportunity cost to the United States of producing one ounce of caviar is two bushels of wheat. The six hours that were needed to make the caviar could have been used to grow two bushels. The opportunity cost of producing one bushel of wheat is $\frac{1}{2}$ ounce of caviar.
   b. The opportunity cost to Russia of producing one ounce of caviar is $1\frac{1}{2}$ bushels of wheat. The opportunity cost of producing a bushel of wheat in Russia is $\frac{2}{3}$ ounce of caviar.
   c. The United States has a comparative advantage in wheat because it has a lower opportunity cost in terms of caviar. Russia has a comparative advantage in caviar. Less wheat is forgone to produce an ounce of caviar in Russia.

33-3. The assumption given in the question is equivalent to the United States' having an absolute advantage in the production of all goods and services. But the basis of world trade lies in differences in *comparative* advantage. As long as other countries have a lower opportunity cost in producing some goods and services, the United States will benefit from international trade.

33-5. Tariffs yield government revenues; quotas do not.

33-7. a. One million pounds are produced and 2 million pounds are imported.
   b. With a 10-cent tariff, 1.5 million pounds would be produced and 1 million pounds would be imported. Government revenues would amount to ($2.5 million − $1.5 million) × $.10 = $100,000.
   c. With a 20-cent tariff, domestic growers can receive 70 cents per pound. They will produce 2 million pounds, and no grapes will be imported, in which case government revenues are zero.

33-9. Consider trade between the United States and Canada. The United States purchases timber from Canada, and Canada purchases computers from the United States. Ultimately, the Canadians pay for U.S.-made computers with the timber that they sell here. If the United States imposes a tax on Canadian timber and thus reduces the amount of timber that the Canadians are able to sell to the United States, the necessary result is that the Canadians will be able to buy fewer American computers. American exports of computers will decline as a result of the reduction in American imports of timber.

CHAPTER 34

34-1. The answer is (c). A declining dollar price of the pound implies an increasing pound price of the dollar—appreciation of the dollar. (a) is incorrect because an increase in demand for U.S. products would affect the supply of pounds and the demand for dollars, whereas here we are dealing with the demand for pounds. (b) explains a phenomenon that would have just the opposite result as that shown in the graph: An increased U.S. demand for British goods would lead to an increase in the demand for the pound, not a decrease as shown. (d) is incorrect because the pound depreciates.

34-3. One pound equals $3.50; $1 equals .2857 pound. One mark equals 35 cents; $1 equals 2.857 marks. One mark equals .1 pound; one pound equals 10 marks.

34-5. To maintain the exchange rate, domestic policy variables such as the money supply are also affected. Suppose that the government plans an expansive monetary policy to encourage output growth. A balance of payments deficit leads the government to buy up dollars, which in turn leads to a contraction in the domestic money supply. Therefore, in order to maintain the expansionary monetary policy, the government would have to expand the money supply in larger magnitudes than it would without the balance of payments deficits with a fixed exchange rate system.

34-7. a. The dollar price of pounds is $1.50. The equilibrium quantity is 150 million.
   b. Curve D' describes this situation. The new dollar price of pounds would be $1.70, and the equilibrium quantity would be 200 million.
   c. At a price of $1.50 per pound, 250 million pounds sterling would be demanded and only 150 million would be supplied, so the Fed would have to supply an extra 100 million to

American buyers of British goods or British exporters.

d. Curve D'' describes this situation. 150 million pounds sterling would be supplied at a price of $1.50, but only 50 million pounds would be demanded. Therefore, the Fed would have to buy up 100 million pounds sterling.

CHAPTER 35

35-1. The following countries may be considered developing countries: Burkina Faso, Bangladesh, Afghanistan, India, and China; there are many others. The following are considered IACs: the United States, Canada, Australia, Germany, and France; there are many others.

35-3. Initially, there is an agricultural stage where most of the population is involved in agriculture. Many developing countries are still in this stage. Then comes the manufacturing stage. Industry dominates the economy, and gains from the division of labor lead to rapid increases in output. In the final stage, the service sector becomes prominent in the economy. The United States and other advanced countries are in this stage.

35-5. Economic development depends greatly on individuals who are able to perceive and take advantage of opportunities. Immigrants who possessed attributes such as these started America on the road to greatness. In general, voluntary exchange is mutually beneficial. If the potential immigrants are willing and able to offer their services at prices (wages) that existing residents are willing to pay and to purchase the goods and services offered for sale by existing residents, their arrival is likely to benefit existing residents as well as themselves.

35-7. It is important to remember that all resources are owned by human beings and that in general there is an optimal (wealth-maximizing) mix of land, labor, and capital. So even though population growth (relative to growth in capital or land) would be expected to lower wages, it would also be expected to raise the earnings of capital and land. On balance, if the population growth moved the country closer to the optimal mix of land, labor, and capital, the added income accruing to the owners of land and capital would more than offset the reduced earnings of labor, producing an overall rise in per capita income.

GLOSSARY

Absolute advantage The ability to produce a good or service at an "absolutely" lower cost, usually measured in units of labor or resource input required to produce one unit of the good or service. *Can also be viewed as* the ability to produce more output from given inputs of resources than other producers can.

Accounting identities Statements that certain numerical measurements are equal by accepted definition (for example, "assets equal liabilities plus stockholders' equity").

Accounting profit Total revenues minus total explicit costs.

Action time lag The time required between recognizing an economic problem and putting policy into effect. The action time lag is short for monetary policy but quite long for fiscal policy, which requires congressional approval.

Active (discretionary) policymaking All actions on the part of monetary and fiscal policymakers that are undertaken in response to or in anticipation of some change in the overall economy.

Adverse selection A problem created by asymmetric information prior to a transaction. Individuals who are the most undesirable from the other party's point of view end up being the ones who are most likely to want to engage in a particular financial transaction, such as borrowing. *Can also be viewed as* the circumstance that arises in financial markets when borrowers

who are the worst credit risks are the ones most likely to seek loans.

Age-earnings cycle The regular earnings profile of an individual throughout his or her lifetime. The age-earnings cycle usually starts with a low income, builds gradually to a peak at around age 50, and then gradually curves down until it approaches zero at retirement.

Aggregate demand The total of all planned expenditures for the entire economy.

Aggregate demand curve A curve showing planned purchase rates for all goods and services in the economy at various price levels, all other things held constant.

Aggregate demand shock

Any shock that causes the aggregate demand curve to shift inward or outward.

Aggregates Total amounts or quantities; aggregate demand, for example, is total planned expenditures throughout a nation.

Aggregate supply The total of all planned production for the entire economy.

Aggregate supply shock Any shock that causes the aggregate supply curve to shift inward or outward.

Anticipated inflation The inflation rate that we believe will occur; when it does, we are in a situation of fully anticipated inflation.

Antitrust legislation Laws that restrict the formation of monopolies and regulate certain anticompetitive business practices.

Appreciation An increase in the value of a currency in terms of other currencies.

Asset demand Holding money as a store of value instead of other assets such as certificates of deposit, corporate bonds, and stocks.

Assets Amounts owned; all items to which a business or household holds legal claim.

Asymmetric information Information possessed by one side of a transaction but not the other. The side with more information will be at an advantage.

Automatic, or **built-in, stabilizers** Special provisions of the tax law that cause changes in the economy without the action of Congress and the president. Examples are the progressive income tax system and unemployment compensation.

Autonomous consumption The part of consumption that is independent of (does not depend on) the level of disposable income. Changes in autonomous consumption shift the consumption function.

Average fixed costs Total fixed costs divided by the number of units produced.

Average physical product Total product divided by the variable input.

Average propensity to consume (APC) Consumption divided by disposable income; for any given level of income, the proportion of total disposable income that is consumed.

Average propensity to save (APS) Saving divided by disposable income; for any given level of income, the proportion of total disposable income that is saved.

Average tax rate The total tax payment divided by total income. It is the proportion of total income paid in taxes.

Average total costs Total costs divided by the number of units produced; sometimes called *average per-unit total costs*.

Average variable costs Total variable costs divided by the number of units produced.

Balance of payments A summary record of a country's economic transactions with foreign residents and governments over a year.

Balance of trade The value of goods and services bought and sold in the world market.

Balance sheet A statement of the assets and liabilities of any business entity, including financial institutions and the Federal Reserve System. Assets are what is owned; liabilities are what is owed.

Bank runs Attempts by many of a bank's depositors to convert checkable and time deposits into currency out of fear for the bank's solvency.

Barter The direct exchange of goods and services for other goods and services without the use of money.

Base year The year that is chosen as the point of reference for comparison of prices in other years.

Bilateral monopoly A market structure consisting of a monopolist and a monopsonist.

Black market A market in which goods are traded at prices above their legal maximum prices or in which illegal goods are sold.

Bond A legal claim against a firm, usually entitling the owner of the bond to receive a fixed annual coupon payment, plus a lump-sum payment at the bond's maturity date. Bonds are issued in return for funds lent to the firm.

Budget constraint All of the possible combinations of goods that can be purchased (at fixed prices) with a specific budget.

Bureaucrats Nonelected government officials who are responsible for the day-to-day operation of government and the observance of its regulations and laws.

Business fluctuations The ups and downs in overall business activity, as evidenced by changes in national income, employment, and the price level.

Capital consumption allowance Another name for depreciation, the amount that businesses would have to save in order to take care of the deterioration of machines and other equipment.

Capital gain The positive difference between the purchase price and the sale price of an asset. If a share of stock is bought for $5 and then sold for $15, the capital gain is $10.

Capital goods Producer durables; nonconsumable goods that firms use to make other goods.

Capitalism An economic system in which individuals own productive resources; these individuals can use the resources in whatever manner they choose, subject to common protective legal restrictions.

Capital loss The negative difference between the purchase price and the sale price of an asset.

Capture hypothesis A theory of regulatory behavior that predicts that the regulators will eventually be captured by the special interests of the industry being regulated.

Cartel An association of producers in an industry that agree to set common prices and output quotas to prevent competition.

Central bank A banker's bank, usually an official institution that also serves as a country's treasury's bank. Central banks normally regulate commercial banks.

Certificate of deposit (CD) A time deposit with a fixed maturity date offered by banks and other financial institutions.

***Ceteris paribus* [KAY-ter-us PEAR-uh-bus] assumption** The assumption that nothing changes except the factor or factors being studied.

Checkable deposits Any deposits in a thrift institution or a commercial bank on which a check may be written.

Closed shop A business enterprise in which employees must belong to the union before they can be hired and must remain in the union after they are hired.

Collateral An asset pledged to guarantee the repayment of a loan.

Collective bargaining Bargaining between the management of a company or of a group of companies and the management of a union or a group of unions for the purpose of setting a mutually agreeable contract on wages, fringe benefits, and working conditions for all employees in all the unions involved.

Collective decision making How voters, politicians, and other interested parties act and how these actions influence nonmarket decisions.

Common property Property that is owned by everyone and therefore by no one. Air and water are examples of common property resources.

Communism In its purest form, an economic system in which the state has disappeared and individuals contribute to the economy according to their productivity and are given income according to their needs.

Comparable-worth doctrine The belief that women should receive the same wages as men if the levels of skill and responsibility in their jobs are equivalent.

Comparative advantage The ability to produce a good or service at a lower opportunity cost compared to other producers.

Complements Two goods are complements if both are used together for consumption or enjoyment—for example, coffee and cream. The more you buy of one, the more you buy of the other. For complements, a change in the price of one causes an opposite shift in the demand for the other.

Concentration ratio The percentage of all sales contributed by the leading four or leading eight firms in an industry; sometimes called the *industry concentration ratio.*

Constant-cost industry An industry whose total output can be increased without an increase in long-run per-unit costs; an industry whose long-run supply curve is horizontal.

Constant dollars Dollars expressed in terms of real purchasing power using a particular year as the base or standard of comparison, in contrast to current dollars.

Constant returns to scale No change in long-run average costs when output increases.

Consumer optimum A choice of a set of goods and services that maximizes the level of satisfaction for each consumer, subject to limited income.

Consumer Price Index (CPI) A statistical measure of a weighted average of prices of a specified set of goods and services purchased by wage earners in urban areas.

Consumption The use of goods and services for personal satisfaction. *Can also be viewed as* spending on new goods and services out of a household's current income. Whatever is not consumed is saved. Consumption includes such things as buying food and going to a concert.

Consumption function The relationship between amount consumed and disposable income. A consumption function tells us how much people plan to consume at various levels of disposable income.

Consumption goods Goods bought by households to use up, such as food, clothing, and movies.

Contraction A business fluctuation during which the pace of national economic activity is slowing down.

Contractionary gap The gap that exists whenever the equilibrium level of real national income per year is less than the full-employment level as shown by the position of the long-run aggregate supply curve.

Cooperative game A game in which the players explicity collude to make themselves better off. As applied to firms, it involves companies colluding in order to make higher than competitive rates of return.

Corporation A legal entity that may conduct business in its own name just as an individual does; the owners of a corporation, called shareholders, own shares of the firm's profits and enjoy the protection of limited liability.

Cost-of-living adjustments (COLAs) Clauses in contracts that allow for increases in specified nominal values to take account of changes in the cost of living.

Cost-of-service regulation Regulation based on allowing prices to reflect only the actual cost of production and no monopoly profits.

Cost-push inflation Inflation caused by a continually decreasing short-run aggregate supply curve.

Craft unions Labor unions composed of workers who engage in a particular trade or skill, such as baking, carpentry, or plumbing.

Creative response Behavior on the part of a firm that allows it to comply with the letter of the law but violate the

spirit, significantly lessening the law's effects.

Cross elasticity of demand (E_{xy}) The percentage change in the demand for one good (holding its price constant) divided by the percentage change in the price of a related good.

Crowding-out effect The tendency of expansionary fiscal policy to cause a decrease in planned investment or planned consumption in the private sector; this decrease normally results from the rise in interest rates.

Crude quantity theory of money and prices The belief that changes in the money supply lead to proportional changes in the price level.

Cyclical unemployment Unemployment resulting from business recessions that occur when aggregate (total) demand is insufficient to create full employment.

Decreasing-cost industry An industry in which an increase in output leads to a reduction in long-run per-unit costs, such that the long-run industry supply curve slopes downward.

Deficiency payment A direct subsidy paid to farmers equal to the amount of a crop they produce multiplied by the difference between the target price for that good and its market price.

Deflation The situation in which the average of all prices of goods and services in an economy is falling.

Demand A schedule of how much of a good or service people will purchase at any price during a specified time period, other things being constant.

Demand curve A graphical representation of the demand schedule; a negatively sloped line showing the inverse relationship between the price and the quantity demanded (other things being equal).

Demand-pull inflation Inflation caused by increases in aggregate demand not matched by increases in aggregate supply.

Demerit good   A good that has been deemed socially undesirable through the political process. Heroin is an example.

Dependent variable   A variable whose value changes according to changes in the value of one or more independent variables.

Depository institutions   Financial institutions that accept deposits from savers and lend those deposits out at interest.

Depreciation   Reduction in the value of capital goods over a one-year period due to physical wear and tear and also to obsolescence; also called *capital consumption allowance. Can also be viewed as a decrease in the value of a currency in terms of other currencies.*

Depression   An extremely severe recession.

Deregulation   The elimination or phasing out of regulations on economic activity.

Derived demand   Input factor demand derived from demand for the final product being produced.

Diminishing marginal utility   The principle that as more of any good or service is consumed, its extra benefit declines. Otherwise stated, increases in total utility from the consumption of a good or service become smaller and smaller as more is consumed during a given time period.

Direct expenditure offsets
Actions on the part of the private sector in spending money that offset government fiscal policy actions. Any increase in government spending in an area that competes with the private sector will have some direct expenditure offset.

Direct relationship   A relationship between two variables that is positive, meaning that an increase in one variable is associated with an increase in the

other and a decrease in one variable is associated with a decrease in the other.

Dirty float   A system between flexible and fixed exchange rates in which central banks occasionally enter foreign exchange markets to influence rates.

Discounting   The method by which the present value of a future sum or a future stream of sums is obtained.

Discount rate   The interest rate that the Federal Reserve charges for reserves that it lends to depository institutions. It is sometimes referred to as the rediscount rate or, in Canada and England, as the bank rate.

Discouraged workers   Individuals who have stopped looking for a job because they are convinced that they will not find a suitable one. Typically, they become convinced after unsuccessfully searching for a job.

Diseconomies of scale   Increases in long-run average costs that occur as output increases.

Disposable personal income (DPI)   Personal income after personal income taxes have been paid.

Dissaving   Negative saving; a situation in which spending exceeds income. Dissaving can occur when a household is able to borrow or use up existing owned assets.

Distributional coalitions   Associations such as cartels, unions, and cooperatives that are formed to gain special government privileges in order to redistribute wealth by taking small amounts from each of many people and giving large amounts to each of only a few.

Distribution of income   The way income is allocated among the population.

Dividends   Portion of a corporation's profits paid to its owners (shareholders).

Division of labor   The segregation of a resource into different specific tasks; for example, one automobile worker puts on bumpers, another doors, and so on.

Dominant strategies   Strategies that always yield the highest benefit. Regardless of what other players do, a dominant strategy will yield the most benefit for the player using it.

Dumping   Selling a good or a service abroad at a price below its cost of production or below the price charged in the home market.

Durable consumer goods   Consumer goods that have a life span of more than three years.

Economic goods   Goods that are scarce.

Economic growth   Increases in per capita real GDP measured by its rate of change per year.

Economic profits   Total revenues minus total opportunity costs of all inputs used, or the total of all implicit and explicit costs. *Can also be viewed as* the difference between total revenues and the opportunity cost of all factors of production.

Economic rent   A payment for the use of any resource over and above its opportunity cost.

Economics   The study of how people allocate their limited resources to satisfy their unlimited wants.

Economic system   The institutional means through which resources are used to satisfy human wants.

Economies of scale   Decreases in long-run average costs resulting from increases in output.

Effect time lag   The time that elapses between the onset of policy and the results of that policy.

Efficiency   The case in which a given level of inputs is used to produce the maximum output possible. Alternatively, the situation in which a given output is produced at minimum cost.

Efficiency wages   Wages set above competitive levels to increase labor productivity and profits by enhancing the efficiency of the firm through lower turnover, ease of attracting higher-quality workers, and better efforts by workers.

Efficiency wage theory   The hypothesis that the productivity of workers depends on the level of the real wage rate.

Effluent fee   A charge to a polluter that gives the right to discharge into the air or water a certain amount of pollution. Also called a *pollution tax*.

Elastic demand   A demand relationship in which a given percentage change in price will result in a larger percentage change in quantity demanded. Total expenditures are invariant to price changes in the unit's elastic portion of the demand curve.

Empirical   Relying on real-world data in evaluating the usefulness of a model.

Endowments   The various resources in an economy, including both physical resources and such human resources as ingenuity and management skills.

Entitlements   Guaranteed benefits under a government program such as Social Security, Medicare, or Medicaid.

Entrepreneurship   The factor of production involving human resources that perform the functions of raising capital, organizing, managing, assembling other factors of production, and making basic business policy decisions. The entrepreneur is a risk taker.

Entry deterrence strategy   Any strategy undertaken by firms in an industry, either individually or together, with the intent or effect of raising the cost of entry into the industry by a new firm.

Equation of exchange   The formula indicating that the number of monetary units times the number of times each unit is spent on final goods and services is identical to the price level times output (or nominal national income).

Equilibrium   The situation when quantity supplied equals quantity demanded at a particular price.

Eurodollar deposits   Deposits denominated in U.S. dollars but held in banks outside the United States, often in overseas branches of U.S. banks.

Excess reserves   The difference between legal reserves and required reserves.

Exclusion principle   The principle that no one can be excluded from the benefits of a public good, even if that person hasn't paid for it.

Expansion   A business fluctuation in which overall business activity is rising at a more rapid rate than previously or at a more rapid rate than the overall historical trend for the nation.

Expansionary gap   The gap that exists whenever the equilibrium level of real national income per year is greater than the full-employment level as shown by the position of the long-run aggregate supply curve.

Expenditure approach   A way of computing national income by adding up the dollar value at current market prices of all final goods and services.

Explicit costs   Costs that business managers must take account of because they must be paid; examples are wages, taxes, and rent.

Externality   A consequence of an economic activity that spills over to affect third parties. Pollution is an externality. *Can also be viewed as* a situation in which a private cost diverges from a social cost; a situation in which the costs of an action are not fully borne by the two parties engaged in exchange or by an individual engaging in a scarce-resource-using activity. (Also applies to benefits.)

Featherbedding   Any practice that forces employers to use more labor than they would otherwise or to use existing labor in an inefficient manner.

The Fed   The Federal Reserve System; the central bank of the United States.

Federal Deposit Insurance Corporation (FDIC)   A government agency that insures the deposits held in member banks; all members of the Fed and other banks that qualify can join.

Federal funds market   A private market (made up mostly of banks) in which banks can borrow reserves from other banks that want to lend them. Federal funds are usually lent for overnight use.

Federal funds rate   The interest rate that depository institutions pay to borrow reserves in the interbank federal funds market.

Fiduciary monetary system   A system in which currency is issued by the government and its value is based uniquely on the public's faith that the currency represents command over goods and services.

Final goods and services   Goods and services that are at their final stage of production and will not be transformed into yet other goods or services. For example, wheat is normally not a final good because usually it is used to make bread, which is a final good.

Financial capital   Money used to purchase capital goods such as buildings and equipment.

Financial intermediaries   Institutions that transfer funds between ultimate lenders (savers) and ultimate borrowers.

Financial intermediation   The process by which financial institutions accept savings from businesses, households, and governments and lend the savings to other businesses, households, and governments.

Firm   A business organization that employs resources to produce goods or services for profit. A firm normally owns and operates at least one plant in order to produce.

Fiscal policy   The discretionary changing of government expenditures and/or taxes in order to achieve national economic goals, such as high employment with price stability.

Fixed costs   Costs that do not vary with output. Fixed costs include such things as rent on a building. These costs are fixed for a certain period of time; in the long run, they are variable.

Fixed investment Purchases by businesses of newly produced producer durables, or capital goods, such as production machinery and office equipment.

Flexible exchange rates Exchange rates that are allowed to fluctuate in the open market in response to changes in supply and demand. Sometimes called *floating exchange rates.*

Flow A quantity measured per unit of time; something that occurs over time, such as the income you make per week or per year or the number of individuals who are fired every month.

Foreign exchange market The market for buying and selling foreign currencies.

Foreign exchange rate The price of one currency in terms of another.

45-degree reference line The line along which planned real expenditures equal real national income per year.

Fractional reserve banking A system in which depository institutions hold reserves that are less than the amount of total deposits.

Free-rider problem A problem that arises when individuals presume that others will pay for public goods so that, individually, they can escape paying for their portion without causing a reduction in production.

Frictional unemployment Unemployment due to the fact that workers must search for appropriate job offers. This takes time, and so they remain temporarily ("frictionally") unemployed.

Full employment As presented by the Council of Economic Advisers, an arbitrary level of unemployment that corresponds to "normal" friction in the labor market. In 1986, the council declared that 6.5 percent unemployment was full employment. Today, it is around 5.5 percent.

Game theory A way of describing the various possible outcomes in any situation involving two or more interacting individuals when those individuals are aware of the interactive nature of their situation and plan accordingly.

The plans made by these individuals are known as *game strategies.*

GDP deflator A price index measuring the changes in prices of all new goods and services produced in the economy.

General Agreement on Tariffs and Trade (GATT) An international agreement established in 1947 to further world trade by reducing barriers and tariffs.

Gold standard An international monetary system in which nations fix their exchange rates in terms of gold. All currencies are fixed in terms of all others, and any balance of payments deficits or surpluses can be made up by shipments of gold.

Goods All things from which individuals derive satisfaction or happiness.

Government, or **political, goods** Goods (and services) provided by the public sector; they can be either private or public goods.

Gross domestic income (GDI) The sum of all income—wages, interest, rent, and profits—paid to the four factors of production.

Gross domestic product (GDP) The total market value of all final goods and services produced by factors of production located within a nation's borders.

Gross private domestic investment The creation of capital goods, such as factories and machines, that can yield production and hence consumption in the future. Also included in this definition are changes in business inventories and repairs made to machines or buildings.

Gross public debt All federal government debt irrespective of who owns it.

Horizontal merger The joining of firms that are producing or selling a similar product.

Human capital The accumulated training and education of workers.

Hyperinflation Extremely rapid rise of the average of all prices in an economy.

Implicit costs Expenses that managers do not have to pay out of pocket and hence do not normally explicitly calculate, such as the opportunity cost of factors of production that are owned; examples are owner-provided capital and owner-provided labor.

Import quota A physical supply restriction on imports of a particular good, such as sugar. Foreign exporters are unable to sell in the United States more than the quantity specified in the import quota.

Incentive-compatible contract A loan contract under which a significant amount of the borrower's assets are at risk, providing an incentive for the borrower to look after the lender's interests.

Incentives Rewards for engaging in a particular activity.

Incentive structure The motivational rewards and costs that individuals face in any given situation. Each economic system has its own incentive structure. The incentive structure is different under a system of private property than under a system of government-owned property, for example. *Can also be viewed as* the system of rewards and punishments individuals face with respect to their own actions.

Income approach A way of measuring national income by adding up all components of national income, including wages, interest, rent, and profits.

Income-consumption curve The set of optimum consumption points that would occur if income were increased, relative prices remaining constant.

Income elasticity of demand (E_i) The percentage change in demand for any good, holding its price constant, divided by the percentage change in income; the responsiveness of the demand to changes in income, holding the good's relative price constant.

Income in kind Income received in the form of goods and services, such as housing or medical care; to be contrasted with money income, which is simply income in dollars, or general purchasing power, that can be used to buy *any* goods and services.

Income velocity of money The number of times per year a dollar is spent on final goods and services; equal to GDP divided by the money supply.

Increasing-cost industry An industry in which an increase in industry output is accompanied by an increase in long-run per-unit costs, such that the long-run industry supply curve slopes upward.

Independent variable A variable whose value is determined independently of, or outside, the equation under study.

Indifference curve A curve composed of a set of consumption alternatives, each of which yields the same total amount of satisfaction.

Indirect business taxes All business taxes except the tax on corporate profits. Indirect business taxes include sales and business property taxes.

Industrially advanced countries (IACs) Canada, Japan, the United States, and the countries of Western Europe, all of which have market economies based on a large skilled labor force and a large technically advanced stock of capital goods.

Industrial unions Labor unions that consist of workers from a particular industry, such as automobile manufacturing or steel manufacturing.

Industry supply curve The locus of points showing the minimum prices at which given quantities will be forthcoming; also called the *market supply curve*.

Inefficient point Any point below the production possibilities curve at which resources are being used inefficiently.

Inelastic demand A demand relationship in which a given percentage change in price will result in a less than proportionate percentage change in the quantity demanded. Total expenditures and price are directly related in the inelastic region of the demand curve.

Infant industry argument The contention that tariffs should be imposed to protect from import competition an industry that is trying to get started. Presumably, after the industry becomes technologically efficient, the tariff can be lifted.

Inferior goods Goods for which demand falls as income rises.

Inflation The situation in which the average of all prices of goods and services in an economy is rising.

Innovation Transforming an invention into something that is useful to humans.

Inside information Information that is not available to the general public about what is happening in a corporation.

Insider-outsider theory A theory of labor markets in which workers who are already employed have an influence on wage bargaining in such a way that outsiders who are willing to work for lower real wages cannot get a job.

Interest The payment for current rather than future command over resources; the cost of obtaining credit. Also, the return paid to owners of capital.

Interest group Any group that seeks to cause government to change spending in a way that will benefit the group's members or to undertake any other action that will improve their lot. Also called a *special-interest group*.

Interest rate effect One of the reasons that the aggregate demand curve slopes down is because higher price levels indirectly increase the interest rate, which in turn causes businesses and consumers to reduce desired spending due to the higher cost of borrowing.

Intermediate goods Goods used up entirely in the production of final goods.

International Monetary Fund (IMF) An institution set up to manage the international monetary system, established in 1945 under the Bretton Woods Agree-

ment Act, which established fixed exchange rates for the world's currencies.

Inventory investment Changes in the stocks of finished goods and goods in process, as well as changes in the raw materials that businesses keep on hand. Whenever inventories are decreasing, inventory investment is negative; whenever they are increasing, inventory investment is positive.

Inverse relationship A relationship between two variables that is negative, meaning that an increase in one variable is associated with a decrease in the other and a decrease in one variable is associated with an increase in the other.

Investment Any use of today's resources to expand tomorrow's production or consumption. *Can also be viewed as* the spending by businesses on things such as machines and buildings, which can be used to produce goods and services in the future. The investment part of total income is the portion that will be used in the process of producing goods in the future.

Job leaver An individual in the labor force who quits voluntarily.

Job loser An individual in the labor force who was employed and whose employment was involuntarily terminated or who was laid off.

Jurisdictional dispute A dispute involving two or more unions over which should have control of a particular jurisdiction, such as a particular craft or skill or a particular firm or industry.

Keynesian short-run aggregate supply curve The horizontal portion of the aggregate supply curve in which there is unemployment and unused capacity in the economy.

Labor Productive contributions of humans who work, involving both mental and physical activities.

Labor force Individuals aged 16 years or older who either have jobs or are looking and available for jobs; the number of employed plus the number of unemployed.

Labor force participation rate
The percentage of noninstitutionalized working-age individuals who are employed or seeking employment.

Labor market signaling The process by which a potential worker's acquisition of credentials, such as a degree, is used by the employer to predict future productivity.

Labor productivity Total real domestic output (real GDP) divided by the number of workers (output per worker).

Labor unions Worker organizations that seek to secure economic improvements for their members; they also seek to improve the safety, health, and other benefits (such as job security) of their members.

Laissez-faire French for "leave [it] alone"; applied to an economic system in which the government minimizes its interference with economy.

Land The natural resources that are available from nature. Land as a resource includes location, original fertility and mineral deposits, topography, climate, water, and vegetation.

Law of demand The observation that there is a negative, or inverse, relationship between the price of any good or service and the quantity demanded, holding other factors constant.

Law of diminishing (marginal) returns The observation that after some point, successive equal-sized increases in a variable factor of production, such as labor, added to fixed factors of production, will result in smaller increases in output.

Law of increasing relative cost The observation that the opportunity cost of additional units of a good generally increases as society attempts to produce more of that good. This accounts for the bowed-out shape of the production possibilities curve.

Law of supply The observation that the higher the price of a good, the more of that good sellers will make

available over a specified time period, other things being equal.

Least-cost combination The level of input use that produces a given level of output at minimum cost.

Legal reserves Reserves that depository institutions are allowed by law to claim as reserves—for example, deposits held at Federal Reserve district banks and vault cash.

Lemons problem The situation in which consumers, who do not know details about the quality of a product, are willing to pay no more than the price of a low-quality product, even if a higher-quality product at a higher price exists.

Liabilities Amounts owed; the legal claims against a business or household by nonowners.

Limited liability A legal concept whereby the responsibility, or liability, of the owners of a corporation is limited to the value of the shares in the firm that they own.

Limit-pricing model A model that hypothesizes that a group of colluding sellers will set the highest common price that they believe they can charge without new firms seeking to enter that industry in search of relatively high profits.

Liquidity The degree to which an asset can be acquired or disposed of without much danger of any intervening loss in *nominal* value and with small transaction costs. Money is the most liquid asset.

Liquidity approach A method of measuring the money supply by looking at money as a temporary store of value.

Logrolling The practice of exchanging political favors by elected representatives. Typically, one elected official agrees to vote for the policy of another official in exchange for the vote of the latter in favor of the former's desired policy.

Long run The time period in which all factors of production can be varied.

Long-run aggregate supply curve A vertical line representing real output of goods and services based on full information and after full adjustment has occurred. *Can also be viewed as* representing the real output of the economy under conditions of full employment—the full-employment level of real GDP.

Long-run average cost curve The locus of points representing the minimum unit cost of producing any given rate of output, given current technology and resource prices.

Long-run industry supply curve A market supply curve showing the relationship between price and quantities forthcoming after firms have been allowed the time to enter into or exit from an industry, depending on whether there have been positive or negative economic profits.

Lorenz curve A geometric representation of the distribution of income. A Lorenz curve that is perfectly straight represents perfect income equality. The more bowed a Lorenz curve, the more unequally income is distributed.

Lump-sum tax A tax that does not depend on income or the circumstances of the taxpayer. An example is a $1,000 tax that every family must pay, irrespective of its economic situation.

M1 The money supply, taken as the total value of currency plus checkable deposits plus traveler's checks not issued by banks.

M2 M1 plus (1) savings and small-denomination time deposits at all depository institutions, (2) overnight repurchase agreements at commercial banks, (3) overnight Eurodollars held by U.S. residents other than banks at Caribbean branches of member banks, (4) balances in retail money market mutual funds, and (5) money market deposit accounts (MMDAs).

Macroeconomics The study of the behavior of the economy as a whole, including such economywide phenomena as changes in unemployment, the general price level, and national income.

Majority rule A collective decision-making system in which group decisions are made on the basis of 50.1 percent of the vote. In other words, whatever more than half of the electorate votes for, the entire electorate has to accept.

Marginal cost pricing A system of pricing in which the price charged is equal to the opportunity cost to society of producing one more unit of the good or service in question. The opportunity cost is the marginal cost to society.

Marginal costs The change in total costs due to a one-unit change in production rate.

Marginal factor cost (MFC) The cost of using an additional unit of an input. For example, if a firm can hire all the workers it wants at the going wage rate, the marginal factor cost of labor is the wage rate.

Marginal physical product The physical output that is due to the addition of one more unit of a variable factor of production; the change in total product occurring when a variable input is increased and all other inputs are held constant; also called *marginal productivity* or *marginal return*.

Marginal physical product (MPP) of labor The change in output resulting from the addition of one more worker. The MPP of the worker equals the change in total output accounted for by hiring the worker, holding all other factors of production constant.

Marginal propensity to consume (MPC) The ratio of the change in consumption to the change in disposable income. A marginal propensity to consume of .8 tells us that an additional $100 in take-home pay will lead to an additional $80 consumed.

Marginal propensity to save (MPS) The ratio of the change in saving to the change in disposable income. A marginal propensity to save of .2 indicates that out of an additional $100 in take-home pay, $20 will be saved. Whatever is not saved is consumed. The marginal propensity to save plus the marginal propensity

to consume must always equal 1, by definition.

Marginal revenue The change in total revenues resulting from a change in output (and sale) of one unit of the product in question.

Marginal revenue product (MRP) The marginal physical product (MPP) times marginal revenue. The MRP gives the additional revenue obtained from a one-unit change in labor input.

Marginal tax rate The change in the tax payment divided by the change in income, or the percentage of additional dollars that must be paid in taxes. The marginal tax rate is applied to the highest tax bracket of taxable income reached.

Marginal utility The change in total utility due to a one-unit change in the quantity of a good or service consumed.

Market All of the arrangements that individuals have for exchanging with one another. Thus we can speak of the labor market, the automobile market, and the credit market.

Market clearing, or **equilibrium, price** The price that clears the market, at which quantity demanded equals quantity supplied; the price where the demand curve intersects the supply curve.

Market demand The demand of all consumers in the marketplace for a particular good or service. The summing at each price of the quantity demanded by each individual.

Market failure A situation in which an unrestrained market economy leads to too few or too many resources going to a specific economic activity.

Market share test The percentage of a market that a particular firm controls, used as the primary measure of monopoly power.

Medical savings accounts (MSAs) A tax-exempt health care account to which individuals would pay into on a regular basis and from which medical care expenses could be paid.

Medium of exchange Any asset that sellers will accept as payment.

Merit good A good that has been deemed socially desirable through the political process. Museums are an example.

Microeconomics The study of decision making undertaken by individuals (or households) and by firms.

Minimum efficient scale (MES) The lowest rate of output per unit time at which long-run average costs for a particular firm are at a minimum.

Minimum wage A wage floor, legislated by government, setting the lowest hourly rate that firms may legally pay workers.

Mixed economy An economic system in which decisions about how resources should be used are made partly by the private sector and partly by the government, or the public sector.

Models, or **theories** Simplified representations of the real world used as the basis for predictions or explanations.

Monetarists Macroeconomists who believe that inflation is always caused by excessive monetary growth and that changes in the money supply directly affect aggregate demand both directly and indirectly.

Monetary rule A monetary policy that incorporates a rule specifying the annual rate of growth of some monetary aggregate.

Money Any medium that is universally accepted in an economy both by sellers of goods and services as payment for those goods and services and by creditors as payment for debts.

Money illusion Reacting to changes in money prices rather than relative prices. If a worker whose wages double when the price level also doubles thinks he or she is better off, the worker is suffering from money illusion.

Money market deposit accounts (MMDAs) Accounts issued by banks yielding a market rate of interest with a minimum balance requirement and a limit on transactions. They have no minimum maturity.

Money market mutual funds   Funds of investment companies that obtain funds from the public that are held in common and used to acquire short-maturity credit instruments, such as certificates of deposit and securities sold by the U.S. government.

Money multiplier   The reciprocal of the required reserve ratio, assuming no leakages into currency and no excess reserves. It is equal to 1 divided by the required reserve ratio.

Money multiplier process   The process by which an injection of new money into the banking system leads to a multiple expansion in the total money supply.

Money price   The price that we observe today, expressed in today's dollars. Also called the *absolute, nominal,* or *current price.*

Money supply   The amount of money in circulation.

Monopolist   A single supplier that comprises its entire industry for a good or service for which there is no close substitute.

Monopolistic competition   A market situation in which a large number of firms produce similar but not identical products. Entry into the industry is relatively easy.

Monopolization   The possession of monopoly power in the relevant market and the willful acquisition or maintenance of that power, as distinguished from growth or development as a consequence of a superior product, business acumen, or historical accident.

Monopoly   A firm that has great control over the price of a good. In the extreme case, a monopoly is the only seller of a good or service.

Monopsonist   A single buyer.

Monopsonistic exploitation   Exploitation due to monopsony power. It

leads to a price for the variable input that is less than its marginal revenue product. Monopsonistic exploitation is the difference between marginal revenue product and the wage rate.

Moral hazard   A situation in which, after a transaction has taken place, one of the parties to the transaction has an incentive to engage in behavior that will be undesirable from the other party's point of view. *Can also be viewed as* a problem that occurs because of asymmetric information *after* a transaction occurs. In financial markets, a person to whom money has been lent may indulge in more risky behavior, thereby increasing the probability of default on the debt.

Multiplier   The ratio of the change in the equilibrium level of real national income to the change in autonomous expenditures; the number by which a change in autonomous investment or autonomous consumption, for example, is multiplied to get the change in the equilibrium level of real national income.

National income accounting   A measurement system used to estimate national income and its components; one approach to measuring an economy's aggregate performance.

National income (NI)   The total of all factor payments to resource owners. It can be obtained by subtracting indirect business taxes from NDP.

Natural monopoly   A monopoly that arises from the peculiar production characteristics in an industry. It usually arises when there are large economies of scale relative to the industry's demand such that one firm can produce at a lower average cost than can be achieved by multiple firms.

Natural rate of unemployment   The rate of unemployment that is estimated to prevail in long-run macroeconomic equilibrium, when all workers and employers have fully adjusted to any changes in the economy.

Near monies   Assets that are almost money. They have a high degree of liq-

uidity; they can be easily converted into money without loss in value. Time deposits and short-term U.S. government securities are examples.

Negative-sum game   A game in which all players are worse off at the end of the game.

Net domestic product (NDP)   GDP minus depreciation.

Net investment   Gross private domestic investment minus an estimate of the wear and tear on the existing capital stock. Net investment therefore measures the change in capital stock over a one-year period.

Net public debt   Gross public debt minus all government interagency borrowing.

Net worth   The difference between assets and liabilities.

New classical model   A modern version of the classical model in which wages and prices are flexible, there is pure competition in all markets, and the rational expectations hypothesis is assumed to be working.

New entrant   An individual who has never held a full-time job lasting two weeks or longer but is now in the labor force.

New growth theory   A relatively modern theory of economic growth that examines the factors that determine why technology, research, innovation, and the like are undertaken and how they interact.

New Keynesian economics   Economic models based on the idea that demand creates its own supply as a result of various possible government fiscal and monetary coordination failures.

Nominal rate of interest   The market rate of interest expressed in today's dollars.

Nominal values   The values of variables such as GDP and investment expressed in current dollars, also called *money values;* measurement in terms of the actual market prices at which goods are sold.

Nonaccelerating inflation rate of unemployment (NAIRU)   The rate of unemployment below which the rate of inflation tends to rise and above which the rate of inflation tends to fall.

Noncooperative game   A game in which the players neither negotiate nor collude in any way. As applied to firms in an industry, this is the common situation in which there are relatively few firms and each has some ability to change price.

Nondurable consumer goods   Consumer goods that are used up within three years.

Nonincome expense items   The total of indirect business taxes and depreciation.

Nonprice rationing devices   All methods used to ration scarce goods that are price controlled. Whenever the price system is not allowed to work, nonprice rationing devices will evolve to ration the affected goods and services.

Normal goods   Goods for which demand rises as income rises. Most goods are considered normal.

Normal rate of return   The amount that must be paid to an investor to induce investment in a business; also known as the *opportunity cost of capital.*

Normative economics   Analysis involving value judgments about economic policies; relates to whether things are good or bad. A statement of *what ought to be.*

Number line   A line that can be divided into segments of equal length, each associated with a number.

Oligopoly   A market situation in which there are very few sellers. Each seller knows that the other sellers will react to its changes in prices and quantities.

Open economy effect   One of the reasons that the aggregate demand curve slopes downward is because higher price levels result in foreigners' desiring to buy fewer American-made goods while Americans now desire more foreign-made goods, thereby reducing net exports, which is equivalent to a reduction in the amount of real goods and services purchased in the United States.

Open market operations   The purchase and sale of existing U.S. government securities (such as bonds) in the open private market by the Federal Reserve System.

Opportunistic behavior   Actions that ignore the possible long-run benefits of cooperation and focus solely on short-run gains.

Opportunity cost   The highest-valued, next-best alternative that must be sacrificed to attain something or to satisfy a want.

Opportunity cost of capital   The normal rate of return, or the available return on the next-best alternative investment. Economists consider this a cost of production, and it is included in our cost examples.

Optimal quantity of pollution   The level of pollution for which the marginal benefit of one additional unit of clean air just equals the marginal cost of that additional unit of clean air.

Origin   The intersection of the *y* axis and the *x* axis in a graph.

Partnership   A business owned by two or more co-owners, or partners, who share the responsibilities and the profits of the firm and are individually liable for all of the debts of the partnership.

Par value   The legally established value of the monetary unit of one country in terms of that of another.

Passive (nondiscretionary) policymaking   Policymaking that is carried out in response to a rule. It is therefore not in response to an actual or potential change in overall economic activity.

Patent   A government protection that gives an inventor the exclusive right to make, use, or sell an invention for a limited period of time (currently, 17 years).

Payoff matrix   A matrix of outcomes, or consequences, of the strategies available to the players in a game.

Perfect competition   A market structure in which the decisions of individual buyers and sellers have no effect on market price.

Perfectly competitive firm   A firm that is such a small part of the total industry that it cannot affect the price of the product it sells.

Perfectly elastic demand   A demand that has the characteristic that even the slightest increase in price will lead to zero quantity demanded.

Perfectly elastic supply   A supply characterized by a reduction in quantity supplied to zero when there is the slightest decrease in price.

Perfectly inelastic demand   A demand that exhibits zero responsiveness to price changes; no matter what the price is, the quantity demanded remains the same.

Perfectly inelastic supply   A supply for which quantity supplied remains constant, no matter what happens to price.

Personal income (PI)   The amount of income that households actually receive before they pay personal income taxes.

Phillips curve   A curve showing the relationship between unemployment and changes in wages or prices. It was long thought to reflect a trade-off between unemployment and inflation.

Physical capital   All manufactured resources, including buildings, equipment, machines, and improvements to land that is used for production.

Planning curve   The long-run average cost curve.

Planning horizon   The long run, during which all inputs are variable.

Plant size   The physical size of the factories that a firm owns and operates to produce its output. Plant size can be defined by square footage, maximum physical capacity, and other physical measures.

Policy irrelevance proposition The new classical and rational expectations conclusion that policy actions have no real effects in the short run if the policy actions are anticipated and none in the long run even if the policy actions are unanticipated.

Positive economics Analysis that is strictly limited to making either purely descriptive statements or scientific predictions; for example, "If A, then B." A statement of *what is*.

Positive-sum game A game in which players as a group are better off at the end of the game.

Precautionary demand Holding money to meet unplanned expenditures and emergencies.

Present value The value of a future amount expressed in today's dollars; the most that someone would pay today to receive a certain sum at some point in the future.

Price ceiling A legal maximum price that may be charged for a particular good or service.

Price-consumption curve The set of consumer optimum combinations of two goods that the consumer would choose as the price of one good changes, while money income and the price of the other good remain constant.

Price controls Government-mandated minimum or maximum prices that may be charged for goods and services.

Price differentiation Establishing different prices for similar products to reflect differences in marginal cost in providing those commodities to different groups of buyers.

Price discrimination Selling a given product at more than one price, with the price difference being unrelated to differences in cost.

Price elasticity of demand (E_p) The responsiveness of the quantity de-

manded of a commodity to changes in its price; defined as the percentage change in quantity demanded divided by the percentage change in price.

Price elasticity of supply (E_s) The responsiveness of the quantity supplied of a commodity to a change in its price; the percentage change in quantity supplied divided by the percentage change in price.

Price floor A legal minimum price below which a good or service may not be sold. Legal minimum wages are an example.

Price index The cost of today's market basket of goods expressed as a percentage of the cost of the same market basket during a base year.

Price leadership A practice in many oligopolistic industries in which the largest firm publishes its price list ahead of its competitors, who then match those announced prices. Also called *parallel pricing*.

Price searcher A firm that must determine the price-output combination that maximizes profit because it faces a downward-sloping demand curve.

Price system An economic system in which relative prices are constantly changing to reflect changes in supply and demand for different commodities. The prices of those commodities are signals to everyone within the system as to what is relatively scarce and what is relatively abundant.

Price taker A competitive firm that must take the price of its product as given because the firm cannot influence its price.

Price war A pricing campaign designed to drive competing firms out of a market by repeatedly cutting prices.

Primary market A financial market in which newly issued securities are bought and sold.

Principal-agent problem The conflict of interest that occurs when agents—managers of firms—pursue

their own objectives to the detriment of the goals of the firms' principals, or owners.

Principle of rival consumption The recognition that individuals are rivals in consuming private goods because one person's consumption reduces the amount available for others to consume.

Principle of substitution The principle that consumers and producers shift away from goods and resources that become relatively higher priced in favor of goods and resources that are now relatively lower priced.

Prisoners' dilemma A famous strategic game in which two prisoners have a choice between confessing and not confessing to a crime. If neither confesses, they serve a minimum sentence. If both confess, they serve a maximum sentence. If one confesses and the other doesn't, the one who confesses goes free. The dominant strategy is always to confess.

Private costs Costs borne solely by the individuals who incur them. Also called *internal costs*.

Private goods Goods that can be consumed by only one individual at a time. Private goods are subject to the principle of rival consumption.

Private property rights Exclusive rights of ownership that allow the use, transfer, and exchange of property.

Privatization The sale or transfer of state-owned property and businesses to the private sector, in part or in whole. Also refers to *contracting out*—letting private business take over government-provided services such as trash collection.

Producer durables, or **capital goods** Durable goods having an expected service life of more than three years that are used by businesses to produce other goods and services.

Producer Price Index (PPI) A statistical measure of a weighted average of prices of commodities that firms purchase from other firms.

Product differentiation The distinguishing of products by brand name, color, and other minor attributes. Product differentiation occurs in other than perfectly competitive markets in which products are, in theory, homogeneous, such as wheat or corn.

Production Any activity that results in the conversion of resources into products that can be used in consumption.

Production function The relationship between inputs and output. A production function is a technological, not an economic, relationship.

Production possibilities curve (PPC) A curve representing all possible combinations of total output that could be produced assuming (1) a fixed amount of productive resources of a given quality and (2) the efficient use of those resources.

Profit-maximizing rate of production The rate of production that maximizes total profits, or the difference between total revenues and total costs; also, the rate of production at which marginal revenue equals marginal cost.

Progressive taxation A tax system in which as income increases, a higher percentage of the additional income is taxed. The marginal tax rate exceeds the average tax rate as income rises.

Property rights The rights of an owner to use and to exchange property.

Proportional rule A decision-making system in which actions are based on the proportion of the "votes" cast and are in proportion to them. In a market system, if 10 percent of the "dollar votes" are cast for blue cars, 10 percent of the output will be blue cars.

Proportional taxation A tax system in which regardless of an individual's income, the tax bill comprises exactly the same proportion. Also called a *flat-rate tax.*

Proprietorship A business owned by one individual who makes the business decisions, receives all the profits, and is legally responsible for all the debts of the firm.

Public debt The total value of all outstanding federal government securities.

Public goods Goods to which the principle of rival consumption does not apply; they can be jointly consumed by many individuals simultaneously at no additional cost and with no reduction in quality or quantity.

Purchasing power The value of money for buying goods and services. If your money income stays the same but the price of one good that you are buying goes up, your effective purchasing power falls, and vice versa.

Purchasing power parity Adjustment in exchange rate conversions that takes into account differences in the true cost of living across countries.

Quota system A government-imposed restriction on the quantity of a specific good that another country is allowed to sell in the United States. In other words, quotas are restrictions on imports. These restrictions are usually applied to one or several specific countries.

Random walk theory The theory there are no predictable trends in security prices that can be used to "get rich quick."

Rate of discount The rate of interest used to discount future sums back to present value.

Rate-of-return regulation Regulation that seeks to keep the rate of return in the industry at a competitive level by not allowing excessive prices to be charged.

Rational expectations hypothesis A theory stating that people combine the effects of past policy changes on important economic variables with their own judgment about the future effects of current and future policy changes.

Rationality assumption The assumption that people do not intentionally make decisions that would leave them worse off.

Reaction function The manner in which one oligopolist reacts to a change in price, output, or quality made by another oligopolist in the industry.

Real-balance effect The change in the real value of money balances when the price level changes, all other things held constant. Also called the *wealth effect.*

Real business cycle theory An extension and modification of the theories of the new classical economists of the 1970s and 1980s, in which money is neutral and only real, supply-side factors matter in influencing labor employment and real output.

Real-income effect The change in people's purchasing power that occurs when, other things being constant, the price of one good that they purchase changes. When that price goes up, real income, or purchasing power, falls, and when that price goes down, real income increases.

Real rate of interest The nominal rate of interest minus the anticipated rate of inflation.

Real values Measurement of economic values after adjustments have been made for changes in the average of prices between years.

Recession A period of time during which the rate of growth of business activity is consistently less than its long-term trend or is negative.

Recognition time lag The time required to gather information about the current state of the economy.

Recycling The reuse of raw materials derived from manufactured products.

Reentrant An individual who used to work full time but left the labor force and has now reentered it looking for a job.

Regressive taxation A tax system in which as more dollars are earned, the percentage of tax paid on them falls. The marginal tax rate is less than the average tax rate as income rises.

Reinvestment Profits (or depreciation reserves) used to purchase new capital equipment.

Relative price The price of a commodity expressed in terms of another commodity.

Rent control The placement of price ceilings on rents in particular cities.

Rent seeking The use of resources in an attempt to get government to bestow a benefit on an interest group.

Repricing, or menu, cost of inflation The cost associated with recalculating prices and printing new price lists when there is inflation.

Repurchase agreement (REPO, or RP) An agreement made by a bank to sell Treasury or federal agency securities to its customers, coupled with an agreement to repurchase them at a price that includes accumulated interest.

Required reserve ratio The percentage of total deposits that the Fed requires depository institutions to hold in the form of vault cash or deposits with the Fed.

Required reserves The value of reserves that a depository institution must hold in the form of vault cash or deposits with the Fed.

Reserves In the U.S. Federal Reserve System, deposits held by Federal Reserve district banks for depository institutions, plus depository institutions' vault cash.

Resource allocation The assignment of resources to specific uses by determining what will be produced, how it will be produced, and for whom it will be produced.

Resources Things used to produce other things to satisfy people's wants.

Retained earnings Earnings that a corporation saves, or retains, for investment in other productive activities;

earnings that are not distributed to stockholders.

Ricardian equivalence theorem The proposition that an increase in the government budget deficit has no effect on aggregate demand.

Right-to-work laws Laws that make it illegal to require union membership as a condition of continuing employment in a particular firm.

Saving The act of not consuming all of one's current income. Whatever is not consumed out of spendable income is, by definition, saved. *Saving* is an action measured over time (a flow), whereas *savings* are a stock, an accumulation resulting from the act of saving in the past.

Savings deposits Interest-earning funds that can be withdrawn at any time without payment of a penalty.

Say's law A dictum of economist J. B. Say that supply creates its own demand; producing goods and services generates the means and the willingness to purchase other goods and services.

Scarcity A situation in which the ingredients for producing the things that people desire are insufficient to satisfy all wants.

Seasonal unemployment Unemployment resulting from the seasonal pattern of work in specific industries. It is usually due to seasonal fluctuations in demand or to changing weather conditions, rendering work difficult, if not impossible, as in the agriculture, construction, and tourist industries.

Secondary boycott A boycott of companies or products sold by companies that are dealing with a company being struck.

Secondary market A financial market in which previously issued securities are bought and sold.

Separation of ownership and control The situation that exists in corporations in which the owners (shareholders) are not the people who control the operation of the corpora-

tion (managers). The goals of these two groups are often different.

Services Mental or physical labor or help purchased by consumers. Examples are the assistance of doctors, lawyers, dentists, repair personnel, housecleaners, educators, retailers, and wholesalers; things purchased or used by consumers that do not have physical characteristics.

Share of stock A legal claim to a share of a corporation's future profits; if it is *common stock,* it incorporates certain voting rights regarding major policy decisions of the corporation; if it is *preferred stock,* its owners are accorded preferential treatment in the payment of dividends.

Share-the-gains, share-the-pains theory A theory of regulatory behavior in which the regulators must take account of the demands of three groups: legislators, who established and who oversee the regulatory agency; members of the regulated industry; and consumers of the regulated industry's products or services.

Shortage A situation in which quantity demanded is greater than quantity supplied at a price below the market clearing price.

Short run The time period when at least one input, such as plant size, cannot be changed.

Short-run aggregate supply curve The relationship between aggregate supply and the price level in the short run, all other things held constant; the curve is normally positively sloped.

Short-run break-even price The price at which a firm's total revenues equal its total costs. At the break-even price, the firm is just making a normal rate of return on its capital investment. (It is covering its explicit and implicit costs.)

Short-run shutdown price The price that just covers average variable costs. It occurs just below the intersection of the marginal cost curve and the average variable cost curve.

Signals Compact ways of conveying to economic decision makers information needed to make decisions. A true signal not only conveys information but also provides the incentive to react appropriately. Economic profits and economic losses are such signals.

Slope The change in the *y* value divided by the corresponding change in the *x* value of a curve; the "incline" of the curve.

Small-menu cost theory A hypothesis that it is costly for firms to change prices in response to demand changes because of the cost of renegotiating contracts, printing price lists, and so on.

Social costs The full costs borne by society whenever a resource use occurs. Social costs can be measured by adding private, or internal, costs to external costs.

Socialism An economic system in which the state owns the major share of productive resources except labor. Socialism also usually involves the redistribution of income.

Special drawing rights (SDRs) Reserve assets created by the International Monetary Fund that countries can use to settle international payments.

Specialization The division of productive activities among persons and regions so that no one individual or one area is totally self-sufficient. An individual may specialize, for example, in law or medicine. A nation may specialize in the production of coffee, computers, or cameras.

Standard of deferred payment A property of an asset that makes it desirable for use as a means of settling debts maturing in the future; an essential property of money.

Stock The quantity of something, measured at a given point in time—for example, an inventory of goods or a bank account. Stocks are defined independently of time, although they are assessed at a point in time.

Store of value The ability to hold value over time; a necessary property of money.

Strategic dependence A situation in which one firm's actions with respect to price, quality, advertising, and related changes may be strategically countered by the reactions of one or more other firms in the industry. Such dependence can exist only when there are a limited number of major firms in an industry.

Strategy Any rule that is used to make a choice, such as "Always pick heads"; any potential choice that can be made by players in a game.

Strikebreakers Temporary or permanent workers hired by a company to replace union members who are striking.

Structural unemployment Unemployment resulting from fundamental changes in the structure of the economy. It occurs, for example, when the demand for a product falls drastically so that workers specializing in the production of that product find themselves out of work.

Subsidy A negative tax; a payment to a producer from the government, usually in the form of a cash grant.

Substitutes Two goods are substitutes when either one can be used for consumption to satisfy a similar want—for example, coffee and tea. The more you buy of one, the less you buy of the other. For substitutes, the change in the price of one causes a shift in demand for the other in the same direction as the price change.

Substitution effect The tendency of people to substitute cheaper commodities for more expensive commodities.

Supply A schedule showing the relationship between price and quantity supplied for a specified period of time, other things being equal.

Supply curve The graphical representation of the supply schedule; a line

(curve) showing the supply schedule, which generally slopes upward (has a positive slope), other things being equal.

Supply-side economics The notion that creating incentives for individuals and firms to increase productivity will cause the aggregate supply curve to shift outward.

Surplus A situation in which quantity supplied is greater than quantity demanded at a price above the market clearing price.

Sympathy strike A strike by a union in sympathy with another union's strike or cause.

Target price A price set by the government for specific agricultural products. If the market clearing price is below the target price, a *deficiency payment,* equal to the difference between the market price and the target price, is given to farmers for each unit of the good they produce.

Tariffs Taxes on imported goods.

Tax bracket A specified interval of income to which a specific and unique marginal tax rate is applied.

Tax incidence The distribution of tax burdens among various groups in society.

Technology Society's pool of applied knowledge concerning how goods and services can be produced.

Terms of exchange The terms under which trading takes place. Usually the terms of exchange are equal to the price at which a good is traded.

Theory of contestable markets A hypothesis concerning pricing behavior that holds that even though there are only a few firms in an industry, they are forced to price their products more or less competitively because of the ease of entry by outsiders. The key aspect of a contestable market is relatively costless entry into and exit from the industry.

Theory of public choice The study of collective decision making.

Third parties Parties who are not directly involved in a given activity or transaction. For example, in the relationship between caregivers and patients, fees may be paid by third parties (insurance companies, government).

Thrift institutions Financial institutions that receive most of their funds from the savings of the public; they include mutual savings banks, savings and loan associations, and credit unions

Time deposit A deposit in a financial institution that requires notice of intent to withdraw or must be left for an agreed period. Withdrawal of funds prior to the end of the agreed period may result in a penalty.

Tit-for-tat strategic behavior In game theory, cooperation that continues so long as the other players continue to cooperate.

Total costs The sum of total fixed costs and total variable costs.

Total income The yearly amount earned by the nation's resources (factors of production). Total income therefore includes wages, rent, interest payments, and profits that are received, respectively, by workers, landowners, capital owners, and entrepreneurs.

Total revenues The price per unit times the total quantity sold.

Transaction costs All of the costs associated with exchanging, including the informational costs of finding out price and quality, service record, and durability of a product, plus the cost of contracting and enforcing that contract.

Transactions accounts Checking account balances in commercial banks and other types of financial institutions, such as credit unions and mutual savings banks; any accounts in financial institutions on which you can easily write checks without many restrictions.

Transactions approach A method of measuring the money supply by looking at money as a medium of exchange.

Transactions demand Holding money as a medium of exchange to make payments. The level varies directly with nominal national income.

Transfer payments Money payments made by governments to individuals for which in return no services or goods are concurrently rendered. Examples are welfare, Social Security, and unemployment insurance benefits.

Transfers in kind Payments that are in the form of actual goods and services, such as food stamps, low-cost public housing, and medical care, and for which in return no goods or services are rendered concurrently.

Traveler's checks Financial instruments purchased from a bank or a nonbanking organization and signed during purchase that can be used as cash upon a second signature by the purchaser.

Unanticipated inflation Inflation at a rate that comes as a surprise, either higher or lower than the rate anticipated.

Unemployment The total number of adults (aged 16 years or older) who are willing and able to work and who are actively looking for work but have not found a job.

Union shop A business enterprise that allows the hiring of nonunion members, conditional on their joining the union by some specified date after employment begins.

Unit elasticity of demand A demand relationship in which the quantity demanded changes exactly in proportion to the change in price. Total expenditures are invariant to price changes in the unit-elastic portion of the demand curve.

Unit of accounting A measure by which prices are expressed; the common denominator of the price system; a central property of money.

Unlimited liability A legal concept whereby the personal assets of the owner of a firm can be seized to pay off the firm's debts.

Util A representative unit by which utility is measured.

Utility The want-satisfying power of a good or service.

Utility analysis The analysis of consumer decision making based on utility maximization.

Value added The dollar value of an industry's sales minus the value of intermediate goods (for example, raw materials and parts) used in production.

Variable costs Costs that vary with the rate of production. They include wages paid to workers and purchases of materials.

Vertical merger The joining of a firm with another to which it sells an output or from which it buys an input.

Voluntary exchange An act of trading, done on a voluntary basis, in which both parties to the trade are subjectively better off after the exchange.

Voluntary import expansion (VIE) An official agreement with another country in which it agrees to import more from the United States.

Voluntary restraint agreement (VRA) An official agreement with another country that "voluntarily" restricts the quantity of its exports to the United States.

Wait unemployment Unemployment that is caused by wage rigidities resulting from minimum wages, unions, and other factors.

Wants What people would buy if their incomes were unlimited.

Wealth The stock of assets owned by a person, household, firm, or nation. For a household, wealth can consist of a house, cars, personal belongings, bank accounts, and cash.

World Trade Organization (WTO) The successor organization to GATT, it handles all trade disputes among its 117 member nations.

x axis The horizontal axis in a graph.

y axis The vertical axis in a graph.

Zero-sum game A game in which any gains within the group are exactly offset by equal losses by the end of the game.

INDEX

consumption, 247
demerit, 102
economic, 19
final, 164–166
inferior, 53
intermediate, 166–167
merit, 102
normal, 53
private, 100
public, 100–101
related, 53–54
secondhand, 168
Gould, David, 742, 782
Government. *See also* Taxes
assurance of economywide
stability, 101
changes in spending, 276–277,
294
changes in taxes, 278–279, 295
correction of negative
externalities, 97
correction of positive
externalities, 97–98
cutbacks, 304, 310–311
economic factors, 95–101
expenditures, 170
Federal Reserve as fiscal agent
of, 332
finance, 298–301
income redistribution, 102
as macroeconomic factor,
258–260
merit/demerit goods, 102
political functions, 102–103
price controls imposed by,
80–82
promotion of competition, 99
provision of legal system, 98–99
provision of public goods,
100–101
regulation, 97–98, 354, 359
spending, 108–110, 276–277,
289
transfer payments, 168
Graduate schools, 30–31
Graphs
direct/inverse relationships, 38
external benefits, 96–97
external costs, 96

independent/dependent variables,
38
linear/nonlinear curves, 41–44
number lines, 39–40
numbers on, 40–41
PPC analysis, 22
Great Depression, 101, 109,
142–143, 157–158, 172,
234–238, 253, 263–264, 279,
288,
354–355, 745–746
Greece, ancient, fractional reserve
banking in, 340–341
Greenspan, Alan, 381
Gross domestic income (GDI),
173–174
Gross domestic product (GDP),
186
correcting for price changes,
177–178
deficit expressed as percentage
of, 298–299
defined, 166–167
deriving components of, 176
and economic growth, 188–190
exclusions, 168–169
expenditure approach, 169–173
income approach, 169, 173–175
international comparisons,
180–183
nominal, 177–179, 208, 340
per capita, 178–179
real, 177–179, 224–225,
231–232, 235–236, 246, 267
Gross domestic product deflator,
151–152, 178
Gross private domestic investment,
170–171
Gross public debt, 301
Growth. *See* Economic growth
G-7 (Group of Seven) nations, 769

Handelman, Stephen, 127
Harvard School of Public Health,
34
Hausman, Jerry, 151–152
Havrilesky, Thomas, 382
Health care, 102

Helpman, Elhanan, 198
Holding money, 365
Hong Kong, economic growth, 130,
188, 776–777
Hoover, Herbert, 745
Horizontal number lines, 39–40
Household production, 168–169
Household responsibility system,
128
Housekeepers, 164, 168
Houses, 47
Housing, 82–84, 102, 170
Human capital, 19, 200,
Human life, value of, 33–34
Hungary, transition to capitalism,
126
Hyperinflation, 152, 377

IBM, 4
Iceland, salmon farming in, 61
Ideas, 199–200, 738–739
IMF. *See* International Monetary
Fund
Immigration, 200–201
Import Administration, 742
Imports, 31, 171, 739
quotas, 87
service, 756–757
Incentive structure, 129
Incentive to work/not work, 242
Incentives, 7–8, 120–121, 182
Income
circular flow of, 164–166
as demand determinant, 53
determined with flexible prices,
236–237
disposable personal, 175
family, 785–786
flow of, 170
money, 118–119,
national, 175
personal, 175
real national, 255–260
redistribution of, 102
security of, 29, 107–109
total, 164–166
Income approach to measuring
GDP, 169, 173–175

MACROECONOMIC PRINCIPLES

Nominal Versus Real Interest Rate

$$i_n = i_r + \text{expected rate of inflation}$$

where i_n = nominal rate

i_r = real rate of interest

Average and Marginal Propensities

$$APC = \frac{\text{consumption}}{\text{real disposable income}}$$

$$APS = \frac{\text{saving}}{\text{real disposable income}}$$

$$MPC = \frac{\text{change in consumption}}{\text{change in real disposable income}}$$

$$MPS = \frac{\text{change in saving}}{\text{change in real disposable income}}$$

Marginal Versus Average Tax Rates

$$\text{Marginal tax rate} = \frac{\text{change in taxes due}}{\text{change in taxable income}}$$

$$\text{Average tax rate} = \frac{\text{total taxes due}}{\text{total taxable income}}$$

GDP—The Expenditure and Income Approaches

$$GDP = C + I + G + X$$

where C = consumption expenditures

I = investment expenditures

G = government expenditures

X = net exports

GDP = wages + rent + interest + profits

The Multiplier Formula

$$\text{Multiplier} = \frac{1}{MPS} = \frac{1}{1 - MPC}$$

$$\text{Multiplier} \times \begin{array}{c}\text{change in} \\ \text{autonomous} \\ \text{spending}\end{array} = \begin{array}{c}\text{change in} \\ \text{equilibrium level} \\ \text{of national income}\end{array}$$

Relationship Between Bond Prices and Interest Rates

The market price of existing (old) bonds is inversely related to "the" rate of interest prevailing in the economy.

Say's Law

Supply creates its own demand, or *desired* aggregate expenditures will equal *actual* aggregate expenditures.

Government Spending and Taxation Multipliers

$$M_g = \frac{1}{MPS}$$

$$M_t = -MPC \times \frac{1}{MPS}$$

Saving, Consumption, and Investment

Consumption + saving = disposable income

Saving = disposable income − consumption

Actual saving = actual investment

Gresham's Law

Bad money drives good money out of circulation.